I0529895

The Mindful Way to Wellness Workbook

Healing Through Guided Imagery & Expressive Art

Mari A. Lee, LMFT & **Wendy Quinton**, LCSW

Illustrations by **John Dubin**

SANO PRESS, LLC
CLAREMONT, CA

Copyright © 2025 by Mari. A. Lee and Wendy Quinton. All rights reserved. No part of this publication may be used or reproduced, stored or entered into a retrieval system, transmitted, photocopied, recorded, or otherwise reproduced in any form by any mechanical or electronic means, without the prior written permission of the authors, with the exception of brief quotations for the purposes of review articles.

Illustrated by John Dubin.

1st Edition

DISCLAIMER

The information provided in this book is for educational purposes only and should not be considered a substitute for professional medical, health, or legal advice. It is not intended to replace professional diagnosis treatment or guidance. The content is based on general knowledge, the authors' personal and professional experiences, and the authors' research, but may not be applicable to individual circumstances. The authors and publisher are not liable for any actions taken based on the information presented. Consult a qualified healthcare professional for personalized medical advice and treatment. Consult a qualified attorney for legal advice.

ISBN: 978-1-956620-09-2

Disclaimer

The stories and examples in this workbook are entirely fictional and intended solely as tools to illustrate key concepts. Any resemblance to real individuals or situations is purely coincidental.

Please note that the mindfulness scripts, breathwork exercises, somatic practices, guided imagery, and art activities within this workbook are not designed as forms of hypnotherapy, hypnosis, psychotherapy, or clinical interventions. They are meant for educational and personal enrichment purposes only and are not substitutes for professional therapeutic counseling or medical care. These tools are not designed to diagnose, treat, or replace psychotherapy, mental health support, or any form of licensed medical or clinical treatment.

For safe and effective engagement, it is strongly recommended to practice these exercises under the guidance of a qualified mental health professional, particularly if you have a history of trauma or mental health challenges. If you choose to explore these practices independently, please prioritize self-care and self-awareness, ensure a secure environment, and be mindful of any emotional discomfort that may arise.

If you experience significant emotional, psychological, or physical distress, seek immediate support from a licensed mental health professional or healthcare provider. In the event of a life-threatening crisis, please contact emergency services without delay. The practices in this workbook may not be suitable for everyone; by choosing to engage with them, you accept full responsibility for your participation. Prioritizing your well-being is strongly encouraged, and professional guidance is recommended while working through the materials and information provided.

Praise for **The Mindful Way to Wellness Workbook:**
Healing Through Guided Imagery & Expressive Art

We are truly grateful for the thoughtful endorsements from our esteemed colleagues and respected clinical experts. Their insights and reflections on this book's value are deeply meaningful to us, affirming its potential to support healing and growth. Their generous words serve as both encouragement and a reminder of the shared commitment to helping others on their journey toward mindful well-being.

• • • • •

"Therapists Mari Lee and Wendy Quinton have created an incredibly powerful workbook to support healing trauma. Each chapter is well constructed starting with an engaging case study that is supplemented with educational sections that thoroughly describe therapeutic concepts. This is followed by mindfulness-based tools such as guided imagery, breath and body work, and creative art exercises. The effect is a carefully crafted map through challenging emotional territory—all with an expert guide not only to help us feel secure but to help us understand accurately what is getting activated along the way. We cannot wait to begin using this workbook with our clients to help them to harness the power of mindfulness to overcome long standing trauma-based patterns. Well done!"

~ **Drs. Bill & Ginger Bercaw.** Authors of *The Couple's Guide to Intimacy*

"*The Mindful Way to Wellness Workbook* contains gentle, insightful guided imagery scripts and workbook exercises to assist both clients and therapists to apply the tools of mindfulness in a straightforward, practical way. With its focus on self-compassion and self-care, therapists Mari A. Lee and Wendy Quinton have created a valuable resource for people struggling with a variety of issues including addictions, betrayal, and trauma."

~ **Stefanie Carnes,** PhD. Author of *Courageous Love: A Couples Guide to Conquering Betrayal*

"In this topsy-turvey world, *The Mindful Way to Wellness Workbook* offers a safe harbor for finding peace and locating your inner strength and wisdom. Deftly crafted by two wise women, therapists Lee and Quinton take the reader by the hand and lead them through the painful challenges life brings with compassion and grace so that you never feel alone. If you're considering this book, you've been called to explore the tender places in your heart that need attention toward healing. This highly intentional book is a mindful invitation to meet your authentic self—accept the invitation!"

~ **Alexandra Katehakis,** PhD, MFT. Author of *Mirror of Intimacy: Daily Reflections on Emotional and Erotic Intelligence*

"While many resources exist for healing and recovery, this workbook by therapists Mari A. Lee and Wendy Quinton uniquely stands out for its meaningful use of mindfulness. The guided exercises, paired with relatable stories, offer a clear and compassionate roadmap for individuals and couples navigating their healing journey."

~ **Dr. Kevin Skinner**, LMFT, CSAT-S. Author of *Rebuild Your Relationship After Sexual Betrayal: A Couple's Guide to Healing*

"This is a game-changer for anyone seeking healing from addiction, betrayal, grief, or painful relationship patterns. Created by experienced therapists Mari A. Lee and Wendy Quinton, this mindfulness-centered workbook blends engrossing stories, guided imagery, art, somatic practices, cognitive tools, and reflection exercises to support lasting change. Grounded in research, clinical expertise, and compassionate wisdom, it offers a clear path toward emotional safety, self-trust, and renewal. Whether you're a therapist or an individual on your own healing journey, this workbook is a powerful resource for creating meaningful transformation."

~ **Carol Juergensen Sheets**, LCSW, CSAT-S. Author of *Help.Her.Heal*, *Help.Them.Heal*, *Unleashing Your Power*, *Transformations*, and *Helping Couples Heal*

"Mari A. Lee and Wendy Quinton have created something truly special—an integrative, research-based workbook that is as clinically sound as it is soulfully written. With mindfulness-based scripts, guided imagery practices, and creative art invitations, this book gently supports both clinicians and clients as they navigate the difficult terrain of addiction, complex trauma, grief, betrayal, maternal and paternal trauma, anger, and relationship challenges. It is generous, wise, and timely for anyone doing the courageous work of recovery and restoration."

~ **Darrin Ford**, LMFT, CSAT-S, MBATT-CS. Author of *Awakening from the Sexually Addicted Mind* and Co-Author of *Transforming the Addictive Mind* and *The Recovery Coaching Client Handbook*

"*The Mindful Way to Wellness Workbook: Healing Through Guided Imagery & Expressive Art* is nothing short of a gift to anyone healing from toxic relationships, sex and love addiction, mother or father wounds, or relational trauma. Grounded in science and the transformative power of mindfulness, it offers both education and easy to follow exercises needed to support deep, lasting change. Readers are guided to reconnect with the present, rediscover self-worth, and rebuild a life rooted in authenticity and emotional freedom. Whether you're just beginning your healing process, deepening the work you've already started, or you are a mental health professional seeking to expand your practice, this workbook meets you with grace exactly where you are. It's not just a workbook—it's a deeply supportive roadmap for the path ahead. I wholeheartedly recommend it to anyone ready to step into a life of intention, connection, and peace."

~ **Kim Litton**, LCSW, CSAT. Author of *I Do It for Her: A Memoir of Recovery and Redemption from Sex, Love, and Substances*

"In *The Mindful Way to Wellness Workbook: Healing Through Guided Imagery & Expressive Art*, Mari Lee and Wendy Quinton take the reader on a compassionate and thoughtful healing journey across a minefield of some of the most troublesome issues that we face today. Well researched and thoroughly handled, this book provides a fresh look at issues like narcissism, trauma bonding, addiction, and so much more. Most importantly, the reader will feel the careful and loving presence the authors provide as they take you on the road to a mindful way to wellness!"

~ **Kenneth M. Adams**, PhD. Author or Co-Author of *Silently Seduced, When He's Married to Mom, A Light in the Dark,* and *Clinical Management of Sex Addiction*

"Based on their combined decades of clinical experience and mindfulness training, Mari Lee and Wendy Quinton beautifully weave the two healing approaches into a practical, yet exquisite book. This workbook provides significant information/education about key concepts related to healing, and ties them into specific, guided mindfulness and art exercises related to the topics. Even better, the material is presented in a gentle, compassionate, authentic tone that is soothing and welcoming. *The Mindful Way to Wellness Workbook* is a gem—a thoughtful, inspiring book that will benefit every healing soul."

~ **Marnie C. Ferree**, LMFT, CSAT. Author of *No Stones—Women Redeemed from Sexual Addiction* and *Out of the Doghouse for Christian Men—A Redemptive Guide for Men Caught Cheating*

"*The Mindful Way to Wellness Workbook* is a compassionate, skillful, and deeply human guide to healing that integrates mindfulness, guided imagery, and expressive art in a way that speaks directly to the heart of many relational struggles. Mari Lee, LMFT and Wendy Quinton, LCSW have created a profoundly accessible resource that honors both the clinical complexity, and the inner strength of the individuals who seek to recover. As someone who advocates for secure-functioning relationships, I appreciate how this workbook helps readers recognize harmful patterns, restore self-trust, and foster meaningful, healthy connections. Therapists and clients alike will find this a valuable companion on the journey toward lasting transformation and relational integrity."

~ **Stan Tatkin**, PsyD, MFT. Author of *Wired for Love* and *In Each Other's Care*

"It's rare to find a book equally suited for therapists supporting clients and for individuals walking their own path to wellness, and this workbook delivers both beautifully. *The Mindful Way to Wellness Workbook* is a supportive guide for anyone navigating the aftermath of trauma or seeking to reclaim a grounded sense of self. Blending well-researched, evidence-based practices with insightful reflection, it invites readers to slow down, reconnect, and begin the work of true healing. With gentle pacing, clinical insights, and expressive art-based tools, this workbook offers a clear structure alongside space for personal reflection, providing both direction and the freedom to explore one's own pace and process. Therapists Mari Lee and Wendy Quinton have created the kind of resource therapists hope to find and trauma survivors deserve—clear, compassionate, and deeply effective."

~ **Dr. Sharon Martin**, LCSW. Author of *The CBT Workbook for Perfectionism, The Better Boundaries Workbook,* and *Cutting Ties with Your Parents*

"Therapists Mari Lee and Wendy Quinton have come together to create a beautiful resource for both clinicians and clients. Through their stories, clinical expertise, and thoughtful exercises, *The Mindful Way to Wellness Workbook: Healing Through Guided Imagery & Expressive Art* offers a comprehensive, meaningful tool for individuals, couples, and the therapists who support them."

~ **Dr. Michael J. Salas**, PsyD. Author of *Bridging the Sex Addiction Divide: Mindful Considerations for Vulnerable Clients*

"Created by seasoned therapists Mari Lee, LMFT, and Wendy Quinton, LCSW, *The Mindful Way to Wellness Workbook* is a true gift for therapists and clients alike. This phenomenal workbook offers mindfully based, somatically-grounded, and accessible interventions that help people connect with core emotions and move toward deeper healing. After just the first few chapters, I found myself thinking, *I absolutely love this!* Through honest, relatable stories that speak to real-life struggles—addiction, betrayal, grief, family of origin trauma, and relationship pain—Mari and Wendy show how trauma lives in the body and the therapy room...and, more importantly, how to begin healing. This is a must-have for every trauma-informed clinician's toolbox."

~ **Dr. Christy Cosper**, PhD. Co-Author of *Transforming the Addictive Mind*

"*The Mindful Way to Wellness Workbook* is an exceptional resource for both therapists and clients. As I read through its pages, I found myself thinking, 'I can't wait to train my team with this workbook!' I wholeheartedly recommend this to any clinician seeking to bring deeper healing, creative insight, and mindfulness-based practices into their work."

~ **Jill A. Johnson-Young**, LCSW. Author of *Your Own Path Through Grief: Someone I Love Just Died, What Happens Now?*

"Therapists Mari Lee and Wendy Quinton have crafted a wise and effective guidebook to healing that offers relatable narratives, sound interventions, and creative exercises designed specifically for mindful healing. *The Mindfulness Way to Wellness Workbook* is a gift for anyone wanting a clearly outlined path towards healing that is beautifully written and articulated by esteemed experts in the field."

~ **Whitney Boole**, LMFT. Author of *You Got This: Healing Through Divorce*

"As a therapist who has not previously integrated guided imagery into my clinical practice, I found *The Mindful Way to Wellness Workbook* to be a thoughtful and approachable introduction to this powerful modality. The workbook offers a clear, structured framework for incorporating mindfulness and guided imagery—whether you're a clinician supporting clients or an individual seeking personal healing and self-compassion. I appreciate the trauma-informed lens and the depth of clinical insight woven throughout. I'm excited to begin integrating these practices into my therapeutic work, and I value how this resource makes learning and applying them both accessible and meaningful."

~ **Zara Arshad**, MSc, RP, PMH-c. Author of *Stronger Together: A Couple's Guide to Navigating Your Relationship After Baby*

Dedicated to all those who courageously embark on the journey of transformation— seeking healing, growth, and deeper connection through mindfulness, creativity, and self-compassion.

In a world that can often be harsh, choosing to keep your heart open is an act of true strength. Your bravery and commitment is inspiring.

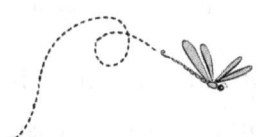

Acknowledgments

My deepest appreciation for my wonderful partner John, and to my sister and best friend Mary: Your unwavering support has been the cornerstone of this endeavor, and I am my most authentic and mindfully present self with you both. To my dear friends, your encouragement has illuminated my path over the years of this writing process. Thank you for the cherished moments of laughter, cupcake deliveries, beach hikes, prayers and late-night calls; I am profoundly grateful for each of you. To our Cambria neighbors Michelle, Ryan, Eden and Lilly, thank you for your warm hearts, plant care, and homemade art, we are so lucky! Deep appreciation to Jennafer Grace and Ian, who draped my ink-stained hours in style and brought a little glam to this writer's midnight grind. To my sweet kitty companions—Stanley, Oliver, Jeremiah, and Sammy—thank you for your cuddles, and precious energy in my world.

To my therapy clients and the couples who have entrusted me with their vulnerabilities, your courage inspires the very essence of this workbook. Your commitment to healing and growth has profoundly impacted me and I am honored by your trust.

To my wonderful co-author Wendy, thank you for your unwavering patience with this healing perfectionist and for bringing such joy and laughter to this project—we truly made magic together, and I adore your gentle heart and kind soul.

John Dubin, your incredible illustrations brought our workbook to life, and we are immensely grateful for your support and artistic talents. It would not be what it is without your creative genius, and we are forever grateful. May the world discover your talent!

To my fellow colleagues and friends who have contributed their valuable time by providing a listening ear, chapter reading, sharing feedback, or simply being present on this journey—I express my heartfelt thanks. This workbook is not merely a reflection of my efforts but a collective achievement shaped by the support and love of an extraordinary community. Special thanks to Darrin Ford and Chris Bordey.

To my fellow therapists and mental health professionals, may this workbook offer valuable tools to support the beautiful healing work you do. Thank you for being a guiding light in a world that deeply needs compassion.

To each reader, may these pages serve as a source of guidance and empowerment on your own path to mindful healing and self-discovery. You are a person of great worth and value.

With gratitude,

Mari

To my courageous therapy clients who have allowed me to walk alongside you on your path to healing, this book is dedicated to you. Your capacity for change and growth never ceases to amaze me, and I am honored to know each of you.

To my co-author, Mari, words cannot do justice to the impact you have had on my life. You have not only guided my journey deeper into mindfulness, but you have also led me step-by-step through the process of writing a book over the last few years. You have been my inspiration, my cheerleader, my coach, and a wonderful friend. Also, to Darrin Ford, thank you for opening my eyes to the concept of mindfulness and for your superb training, which has been invaluable.

To my wonderful husband, Larry, you are my steady rock in the chaos of life and the one who makes me think deeper about the issues I confront. You have always believed in me, and you continue to challenge me to conquer more than I could have imagined. I love you!

To my amazing children, Jesika and Jonathan, who bring me joy every day. It is my greatest honor to be your mother and the recipient of your unwavering faith in me. Watching you confront your challenges has shown me what true courage is, and I hope this book inspires you to keep chasing your dreams. I love you both dearly.

To my bestie, Steph, who has walked with me in heartache and joy and who believes in me more than I believe in myself. Your loving presence and gentle spirit have been a source of strength, and I count our friendship as one of my greatest treasures.

To my colleagues, Gennelle and Donna, whose influence on my life cannot be measured, thank you for everything that you have invested in my life and career. I so appreciate your guidance, assistance, encouragement, and, most of all, your friendship.

To my readers, may this book be a connection from my heart to yours, and may the words on each page further your journey toward living a mindful, joyful, and peaceful life.

And finally, to my late mother, Bernice, who always knew that I would write a book, thank you for cheering me on along every step of my adult journey. Although you are no longer an earthly encouragement to me, your words still echo in my heart. This book is for you.

With hope,

Wendy

Table of Contents

Introduction 01

How to Use This Workbook 08

CHAPTER ONE
Breaking Free: Escaping the Cycle of Trauma Bonding 12
Mari A. Lee

CHAPTER TWO
Mind States: From Resisting and Guarding to Releasing and Growing 66
Wendy Quinton

CHAPTER THREE
The Road to Renewal: Repairing the Betrayal Rupture 94
Mari A. Lee

CHAPTER FOUR
Grief: From Pain and Heartache to Peace and Hope 135
Wendy Quinton

CHAPTER FIVE
Navigating the Maze of Problematic Porn Use 160
Mari A. Lee

CHAPTER SIX
Betrayal Trauma: From Denial and Deception to Courage and Connection 197
Wendy Quinton

CHAPTER SEVEN
Out of the Minefield: Overcoming Maternal Trauma Mindfully 225
Mari A. Lee

CHAPTER EIGHT
Counterweight Bonding: From Guilt and Exhaustion to Growth and Empowerment 267
Wendy Quinton

CHAPTER NINE
A Compassionate Path to Inner Peace: Healing from Love Addiction 301
Mari A. Lee

CHAPTER TEN
Showing Up: From Scared and Suppressed to Safe and Seen 334
Wendy Quinton

CHAPTER ELEVEN
The Storm of Anger: Reclaiming your Calm 359
Mari A. Lee

CHAPTER TWELVE
Spiritual Bypassing: From Silence and Shame to Self-Compassion and Serenity................ 387
Wendy Quinton

Final Message from the Authors.. 415

Author's Bios 416

Glossary 418

Bibliography 425

Resources 439

Foreword

In the journey of healing, the paths we choose often reflect the depth of our experiences, the wisdom of our teachers, and the tools we gather along the way. It is with great honor and respect that I introduce this transformative workbook, *The Mindful Way to Wellness Workbook: Healing Through Guided Imagery & Expressive Art*, crafted by two extraordinary therapists, Mari A. Lee, LMFT and Wendy Quinton, LCSW.

This workbook, which integrates compelling and diverse stories, mindfulness-based information, clinical research, therapeutic information, guided imagery exercises, and art activities, offers a unique and powerful approach to healing. It invites both the therapist and the client alike into a space of creativity, reflection, and profound inner work. The combination of these modalities serves as a bridge between the conscious and unconscious, allowing for deeper exploration and healing for the reader.

To truly grasp the profound impact of this workbook, one must first recognize the exceptional expertise and unwavering dedication of the therapists who brought it to life. Their deep commitment to the healing process, combined with years of clinical experience, has resulted in a resource that is both powerful and transformative. It is through their thoughtful and compassionate dedication that this workbook becomes not just a tool but a meaningful guide on the journey to recovery and personal growth.

Mari A. Lee has been an extraordinary light in my professional journey. She is also a beacon of wisdom and support for nearly two decades for countless other mental health professionals. Her influence extends far beyond her role as a therapist; she is a mentor, teacher, supervisor, and leader whose impact is felt deeply by all who have had the privilege of working with her. Mari possesses a rare and remarkable ability to seamlessly integrate profound compassion with incisive clinical insight. Her expert approach to therapy is both deeply human and rigorously informed, allowing her to connect with individuals on a level that fosters genuine healing and transformation.

Mari's contributions to the field through her numerous books, materials, articles, and presentations allow her to generously share her knowledge and expertise with a broad audience, always with the goal of advancing the field and improving the lives of those who are struggling. She has an innate talent for being deeply present with people while distilling complex concepts into accessible, practical tools that therapists and clients alike can use to navigate the challenges of trauma and addiction. Mari's work is not just about addressing symptoms or managing crises; it's about fostering true, lasting transformation. Her legacy is one of hope, resilience, and profound healing, and it is an honor to recognize her exceptional contributions to our field.

Wendy Quinton, with over a decade of clinical expertise in the fields of addiction and complex trauma, brings a wealth of knowledge and an exceptional level of skill to this work. Her dedication to the field, her clinical clients, and her unwavering passion for her craft are evident in every aspect of her work and in each chapter she has written. Wendy's contributions to this workbook are more than just professional insights; they are a reflection of her heartfelt commitment to guiding others through the often daunting paths of recovery and personal growth. She understands the profound challenges that individuals face in overcoming trauma and addiction, and her compassionate and mindfulness-based approach and methods ensures that each person she works with feels deeply supported and empowered every step of the way.

This workbook, enriched by Mari and Wendy's keen insights, serves not merely as a tool but as a trusted companion on the therapeutic journey. It offers therapists and clients alike a thoughtful, well-crafted guide to navigating the complexities of healing and recovery with empathy, wisdom, and care, ensuring that the process is both deeply meaningful and profoundly effective. As a fellow therapist specializing in complex trauma and addictions, I have witnessed firsthand the profound impact that mindfulness-based therapy, guided imagery, and creative expression can have on the healing process. This workbook is not just a resource—it is an invitation to engage in a healing journey that honors the whole person: mind, body, and spirit.

Mari and Wendy have created something truly special here. What sets each of these therapists apart is their unwavering commitment to mindful, compassionate, and effective therapeutic practices. Both of these remarkable women approach their work with a deep sense of purpose and a genuine desire to help those who are hurting, traumatized, betrayed, and addicted. Their passion as healers is intricately woven into the fabric of this workbook, reflecting their dedication to empowering individuals to heal and create lives and relationships that they can be proud of.

It is a privilege to stand alongside them in their shared mission of fostering healing and transformation. I am honored to have been asked to write this foreword, and it brings me great joy to know this workbook will become an invaluable tool for therapists, clients, and non-therapist readers, guiding them toward greater understanding, healing, and growth.

With deep respect and admiration,
Darrin Ford, LMFT, CSAT-S, CPTT-S, MBATT-CS
Author of *Awakening to the Sexually Addicted Mind* and co-Author of *Transforming the Addictive Mind* and *The Recovery Coaching Client Handbook.*
Founder and President of *The Mindfulness Academy of Addiction and Trauma Training* and *Mindful Centers for Addiction & Trauma Therapy.*

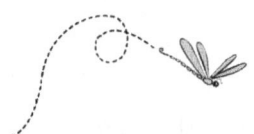

Introduction

Mindfulness is like that; it is the miracle which can call back in a flash our dispersed mind and restore it to wholeness so that we can live each minute of life.

~ Thich Nhat Hanh

Mindfulness offers a pathway to cultivating presence and compassion with self and others, and presence and compassion are the key components in creating a healthy relationship with yourself and with others. Within these pages, we invite you to embark on a shared exploration of self-discovery, insight, and increased awareness and resilience as you get to know the benefits of mindfulness-based practices and their potential for growth and healing. Our sincerest hope is that this workbook becomes a sanctuary for both therapists and non-therapist readers alike, helping you foster a deeper connection with yourself and the transformative power of the present moment.

This workbook has been thoughtfully crafted over many years with heartfelt dedication, and we are honored by the trust you place in us as you explore the pages ahead. As licensed therapists trained and certified in mindfulness-based therapy, we draw from our combined decades of experience helping hurting individuals heal. In our respective practices of treating complex trauma, addiction, betrayal, and grief, we've been privileged to witness firsthand the transformative power of incorporating mindfulness practices into treatment.

However, we also understand that not everyone has access to therapy due to barriers such as location, financial limitations, or cultural factors. Our passion as healers is to make educational materials more affordable and accessible for everyone, regardless of their circumstances. With this in mind, we are committed to offering easy-to-follow resources within these chapters to help individuals and couples, regardless of their circumstances. Our hope in creating this book is to contribute to the broader mission of offering healing and connection in a world that so deeply needs both.

Before you dive into the chapters ahead, let's take a brief walk through the history of mindfulness practices. In the journey of integrating mindfulness into modern therapy, we stand on the shoulders of remarkable pioneers who bridged Eastern wisdom and Western psychological practices.

· · · · ·

While the roots of mindfulness in therapeutic practice trace back to ancient contemplative traditions, its integration into Western psychology gained momentum in the late 20th century. In the 1950s and '60s, visionaries like Thich Nhat Hanh and Shunryu Suzuki began sharing Zen Buddhism and mindfulness with Western audiences, teaching the importance of being fully present in each moment. Alan Watts, with his ability to translate complex Eastern philosophies, played a pivotal role in introducing mindfulness to those seeking deeper meaning in the West.

Then, in the late 1970s, Jon Kabat-Zinn pioneered Mindfulness-Based Stress Reduction (MBSR), introducing mindfulness practices into a structured program. This marked a significant milestone, showcasing the potential benefits of mindfulness in managing various human challenges, mental health issues, addiction recovery, complex trauma, anxiety, grief, depression, and stress while promoting overall wellness. Around the same time, Jack Kornfield and Tara Brach began integrating mindfulness and compassion practices into psychotherapy, offering profound tools for self-acceptance and emotional healing. Marsha Linehan followed with Dialectical Behavior Therapy (DBT), weaving mindfulness into cognitive therapy for some of the most challenging mental health conditions.

In the early 2000s, Zindel Segal introduced Mindfulness-Based Cognitive Therapy (MBCT), using mindfulness to break the cycle of depression, while Richard Davidson's groundbreaking neuroscience research provided scientific backing for the effects of mindfulness on the brain. Dr. Daniel Siegel, with his extraordinary work on interpersonal neurobiology, showed how mindfulness promotes brain health and emotional regulation. Then, Peter A. Levine, Ph.D., a pioneering figure in the field of trauma therapy and somatic psychology, focused on understanding how trauma is stored in the body and how physiological responses can either perpetuate or resolve traumatic experiences. Dr. Gabor Maté, a renowned physician and author who we greatly respect, specializes in trauma, addiction, stress, and childhood development. His work emphasizes the deep connection between emotional suffering and physical illness and the benefits of self-compassion and mindfulness. Their collective wisdom, along with so many other respected mindfulness-based clinicians, have contributed to countless people healing from addiction, trauma, grief, and other conditions.

As you can see, over the past few decades, research-based mindfulness has evolved into an important cornerstone of clinical therapy, demonstrating profound benefits for mental health and well-being. Numerous studies have linked mindfulness to reduced symptoms of anxiety, trauma, depression, and chronic pain, emphasizing its positive impact on psychological and physical well-being. Research has consistently highlighted mindfulness's role in enhancing emotional regulation, attentional focus, and overall resilience. We have listed some of these studies in the bibliography section of this workbook for those who would like to learn more.

Guided imagery (GI) is a compassionate and effective technique that we have used for many years with clients in our clinical therapy practices. When introducing GI to our clients, we start by explaining that guided imagery is a therapeutic technique that uses visualization to help individuals engage their imagination in a purposeful way to promote relaxation, reduce anxiety and depression, decrease trauma and post-traumatic stress disorder (PTSD), promote healing, and increase self-awareness and compassion.

In guided imagery, clients are led through a series of mental images that evoke sensory experiences, such as sights, sounds, and feelings, to achieve specific emotional or psychological outcomes. This practice taps into the mind-body connection, helping individuals harness their inner resources for healing and growth. We have seen incredible and beneficial results with our clients using guided imagery in their therapy sessions. If guided imagery is new to you, it may be interesting to learn more about GI and its history.

The roots of guided imagery can be traced back to ancient practices, but it was not formally introduced into Western therapy until the mid-20th century. One of the early founders of modern guided imagery was Hanscarl Leuner, a German psychiatrist who developed Katathym Imaginative Psychotherapy in the 1950s, blending imagination with psychotherapeutic work. Around the same time, Carl Jung also explored active imagination as a means of accessing deeper parts of the psyche, which influenced many later therapeutic approaches.

In the 1970s, Dr. Helen Bonny, a music therapist, further advanced guided imagery through her development of the Bonny Method of Guided Imagery and Music (GIM), which used music to deepen the imagery experience. This method was particularly influential in integrating guided imagery into counseling and therapeutic practices in the West. Gerald Epstein, M.D., also played a key role in the expansion of guided imagery into mainstream therapy with his focus on the healing potential of mental imagery.

Today, Belleruth Naparstek is considered one of the leading pioneers of guided imagery. She has created numerous guided imagery programs for health, healing, and emotional well-being, which have been widely used in clinical settings. Other modern researchers and therapists, such as David Bresler and Martin Rossman, have contributed significantly to understanding the therapeutic benefits of guided imagery for stress reduction, pain management, and trauma recovery.

One question that we frequently hear from clients is, "Is guided imagery the same as being hypnotized?" While guided imagery and hypnosis may seem similar, they are quite different. Hypnosis typically involves an altered state of consciousness where the person is in a "trance-like" state, often with the goal of accessing the subconscious mind for behavioral changes. In contrast, guided imagery encourages participants to stay fully conscious and aware while using visualization to engage their imagination and tap into their body's natural healing processes. GI does not aim to "suggest" or "reprogram" the mind; instead, it empowers individuals to explore their inner landscape and draw on their own insights for healing.

It is important to note that guided imagery may not be appropriate for everyone. It may be contraindicated for individuals with severe mental health conditions like psychosis, schizophrenia, or dissociative disorders, or acute complex trauma, as it might exacerbate symptoms or trigger emotional instability. In such cases, the vivid mental imagery could lead to increased anxiety or difficulty distinguishing between imagination and reality. It's important for these individuals to engage in guided imagery only under the supervision of a trained therapist who can ensure safety and appropriate boundaries.

Research consistently supports the benefits of guided imagery for various mental and physical health conditions. Studies show its effectiveness in reducing stress, improving sleep, and alleviating symptoms of PTSD and chronic pain (Bresler & Rossman, 2003; Naparstek, 1994). This technique offers a gentle yet powerful way to enhance emotional resilience and promote healing through the power of the mind-body connection.

Individuals seeking therapy or mental health support are increasingly discerning about the value of finding mental health professionals who are well-versed and trained in the benefits of mindfulness-based therapy and guided imagery. Simultaneously, there is a growing demand among therapists and mental health professionals for advanced training in mindfulness-based approaches. Contemporary research continues to explore the neural mechanisms underlying mindfulness, providing valuable insights into its effects on brain structure and function. The dynamic interplay between ancient wisdom and modern scientific inquiry has positioned research-based mindfulness as a transformative force in clinical therapy, offering individuals practical tools for cultivating mental and emotional well-being. You are welcome to explore the bibliography to learn more about these studies.

As we journeyed with our clients, helping them navigate their healing and assisting individuals and couples toward their goals, it became clear that each client's process was greatly enhanced by incorporating mindfulness-based practices into the treatment plan. This included breath work, guided imagery, art exercises, journaling, meditation, body scans, and somatic practices. As licensed therapists specializing in addiction and complex trauma and as Certified Mindfulness-Based Addiction and Trauma Therapists (MBATT), we began to see transformation and deep recovery that went far beyond talk therapy or cognitive task-oriented therapy. While both of these modalities are important to clinical work, along with other modalities such as Eye Movement Desensitization and Reprocessing (EMDR) and Internal Family Systems (IFS), weaving in mindfulness-based interventions, exercises, and guided imagery was a game changer—for us as therapists and for the clients we support.

•　•　•　•　•

As you journey through this workbook, remember there's no need to follow the chapters in a strict sequence. Instead, feel free to browse the table of contents and choose the sections that resonate most with you or your client. Let your intuition guide you to what feels right in the moment.

Additionally, as you explore the workbook, you might notice that some topics reappear in different chapters. This is intentional and important, as each recurrence offers a fresh perspective tailored to the specific focus of that chapter. Even if the theme feels familiar, you'll discover a new gem or insight each time, adding depth to your understanding.

In our individual therapy practices, where we draw from various certifications, modalities, and treatment models, a consistent truth has emerged: incorporating mindfulness-based therapeutic interventions has proven to be essential in delivering the most beneficial outcomes for our clients. This recognition stems not from a rigid adherence to a singular approach but from the profound impact we've witnessed when including mindfulness in the therapeutic process with whatever modality we are drawing from.

Irrespective of the client's background or the nature of their unique challenges, we have discovered that approaching each person and couple with a genuine sense of compassion, curiosity, and respect lays the groundwork for fostering trust and connection. We have immense appreciation and awe for the shared moments of growth, healing, and resilience that have unfolded within the therapeutic space as a result. This humble acknowledgment underscores our belief in the transformative power of mindfulness, self-compassion, empathy, and human connection—values that guide us not only in our commitment to providing supportive and meaningful therapeutic experiences but also in the creation of this workbook.

Whether you are a licensed therapist, certified coach, or mental health professional trained in mindfulness and guided imagery, or a client or couple wanting to explore and heal, this workbook is designed to be your companion. Each story and exercise is written to support self-compassion, self-discovery, healing, and empowerment. Woven within each chapter is evidence-based educational information located in the "Message from Mari" and "Word from Wendy" sections of each chapter. Our aim was to merge the powerful modalities of guided imagery, mindfulness scripts and exercises, and expressive arts to create a holistic approach to well-being. Every chapter unfolds with a narrative, and while the diverse individuals and couples within these stories are fictional, their experiences vividly portray genuine struggles that resonate with the shared human experience.

Amidst the hectic pace of our everyday existence, our clients share that they frequently discover themselves maneuvering through myriad challenges, bearing the weight of those difficulties. As you'll read in the following chapters, people often try to soothe their pain in unhealthy ways—turning to substances like alcohol and drugs, engaging in compulsive or out-of-control sexual behaviors, or struggling with problematic pornography use. Others may lose themselves in video games for hours, work exhausting schedules, suppress grief, battle anger issues, overspend online, numb with food, or face financial crises due to gambling addiction.

No human being is exempt from the highs and lows of life, including healing professionals. As a society, we have become so accustomed to carrying these burdens alone and in silence, much like a sack of heavy stones strapped to one's back, that it has become our "normal." These experiences that we carry pile on year after year, decade after decade, and often encompass heartbreaking situations, losses, traumas, betrayals, anger, addictions, shame, sadness, confusion, and various other challenges. This workbook extends an invitation for you to seek support to gently unpack those stones and embark on a compassionate journey into your inner landscape—an expedition where you will heal while you unearth the treasures of self-awareness, resilience, self-compassion, deeper insight, and connection to yourself and to the ones you love.

The core essence of this workbook is the belief in the profound impact of mindful presence on the healing process, a quality that is sadly lacking in our world today. Mindful presence serves as the guiding force that gently leads us toward understanding, acceptance, and, ultimately, transformation. As you engage with the guided imagery activities, mindfulness exercises, and expressive arts within these pages, you are encouraged to approach yourself with kindness, acknowledging the uniqueness of your own story.

Guided Imagery: Painting With the Mind's Eye

Each chapter includes guided imagery, a process that transcends the boundaries of the physical world and invites you, with guided support if you choose to work with a therapist or healing professional, to gently explore the vast landscapes of your imagination. Through carefully crafted visualizations and scripts, you will embark on inner voyages, discovering hidden reservoirs of strength, resilience, and hope. Guided imagery is a powerful tool that allows you to connect with your subconscious, offering insights and revelations that may have remained concealed in the routine of everyday life. Again, if possible, working with a mental health professional to support your journey through this workbook is advised.

Mindfulness Exercises: Cultivating Presence

Mindfulness is the art of being fully present in the moment, with presence being the key to well-being. We live in a world with constant distractions—bells ringing, alarms going off, chimes and chirps, tweets and texts—a literal cacophony of sound and stress. This workbook introduces a variety of mindfulness exercises to cultivate a calm state of present awareness and offer a space of stillness and presence with self, even if only for a few minutes. From mindful breathing practices to body scans, you will learn to anchor yourself in the present, fostering a profound connection with your thoughts, emotions, and physical sensations. Mindfulness becomes a compass guiding you through the landscapes of your inner world, promoting clarity, tranquility, and a connection to self. This, in turn, enhances the relationships you have with your loved ones.

Expressive Arts: Crafting Your Narrative

Our clients sometimes say, "I am not an artist. I cannot draw!" and that is OK. Truth be told, we can barely draw a stick figure between the two of us, yet the exercises are not about the quality of your artwork. Rather, they are designed to increase insight into your process. Creativity is a powerful vehicle for self-expression and understanding. Each chapter includes a specific expressive arts section that encourages you to engage in artistic endeavors, whether through drawing, writing, or other forms of creative expression. Think about it this way: the activities and exercises serve as a medium for translating the insights gained from guided imagery and mindfulness into tangible, personalized artifacts. As you craft your narrative through art, you become both the artist and the masterpiece, actively shaping your journey toward healing and self-discovery.

A Personalized Exploration

As you are likely understanding, this workbook is not a one-size-fits-all solution; rather, it is a canvas for your unique exploration. Feel free to adapt the exercises to suit your preferences, pace, and comfort levels. Whether you are a mental health professional guiding clients through these practices or an individual or couple on a personal journey, our sincere hope is that the flexibility of these exercises allows for a tailored and meaningful experience.

Inclusivity and Supporting Diversity

In creating this mindfulness workbook, we honor the unique backgrounds, identities, and experiences of all individuals. Mindfulness is for everyone, and this workbook is designed with inclusivity in mind, recognizing that each person's journey with growth, healing, and self-awareness is deeply personal. Regardless of age, culture, ethnicity, gender, orientation, or ability, this resource invites you to approach its practices with respect for your unique path. We aim to foster a safe, compassionate space where various perspectives are not only acknowledged but celebrated, encouraging everyone to engage with these tools in ways that resonate with their lived experiences.

Embark on the Journey

As you step into the following pages, remember that this is more than just a workbook— it is an invitation. May each story, informative exercise, visualization, and creative endeavor bring you closer to the core of your being, illuminating the path to compassionate healing. We stand alongside you in spirit as you pursue a deeper connection with yourself.

A final gentle reminder is to consider collaborating with a therapist, trained coach, or supportive person while engaging in the guided imagery activities and exercises presented in this workbook. The topics and experiences may be triggering for some individuals, and your well-being is important to us. If you are currently experiencing crisis—such as acute trauma symptoms, depression, or other severe mental health conditions—or if you find that you are becoming overwhelmed, uncomfortably activated, or experiencing dissociation when working through this workbook, we highly recommend seeking the support of a therapist and attending to your mental health before continuing in the workbook. Your safety is our number one concern.

If you're a therapist or mental health professional, it's essential to work within your scope of practice. Understanding addiction, dissociation, and complex trauma, obtaining informed consent, and creating a safe, supportive space are key to ethically integrating mindfulness-based strategies and ensuring client well-being.

As you move through the chapters, may the information and exercises serve as a source of hope, encouragement, and meaningful growth. We hope this journey brings you greater self-awareness and healing, and that each step forward is met with warmth and self-compassion. Wishing you a mindful and transformative experience ahead!

With care and compassion,
Mari & Wendy

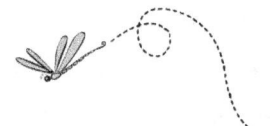

How to Use This Workbook

We warmly welcome you to this transformative journey. Whether you are a therapist looking to enhance your clinical practice, a mental health professional seeking materials to support clients, or an individual or couple on a personal healing journey, this material is designed to be a valuable companion.

This workbook is thoughtfully written to guide you or the clients you work with through a process that includes connected stories, clinical insights, assessments, guided imagery, and creative expression. It does not replace therapy; rather, it provides stories, educational research-based information, and supportive exercises designed to help with personal growth and insight. Whether you are working with a mental health professional or exploring this material on your own, the following information will help you explore this material with care and intention. Think of this as your roadmap to navigate the chapters ahead.

As mentioned in the introduction, you are not required to read the chapters in consecutive order. Instead, feel free to browse the table of contents and choose the sections that resonate most with you or your client. Let your intuition guide you to what feels right in the moment. Additionally, as you explore the workbook, you might notice some topics reappearing in different chapters. This is important and intentional, as each recurrence offers a fresh perspective tailored to the specific focus of that chapter. Even if the theme seems familiar, each encounter offers fresh insights that deepen your understanding.

We have also included guided imagery scripts that include preparation, safety reminders, assessments, and prompts in each chapter so that the reader or the mental health professional can easily navigate that particular chapter topic and guided imagery exercise. A helpful tip: If you are a therapist or mental health professional assisting the client through a guided imagery where you take notes, you will want to consider taking the notes in the least intrusive way possible. Keyboards can be noisy at times, so perhaps consider a quieter way of note-taking, such as a journal or notepad.

Step 1: Start with a Story

Each chapter begins with a story—a narrative that invites you into the experience of fictional characters. Each story is meant to create a safe space for you to connect with the themes and emotions that may resonate with your own journey. Though the people you will meet in the following chapters are not real, their stories are incredibly relatable.

Step 2: Clinical Information and Psychotherapy Education

After the story, you'll find educational content in the sections titled either "A Message from Mari" or "A Word from Wendy." The educational sections in each chapter provide valuable insights into the therapeutic concepts and psychological theories that align with the topic of that particular chapter. Understanding the clinical background can deepen your engagement with the material and enhance your personal growth. Our goal is to provide you with many "aha!" moments.

Step 3: Guided Imagery Preparation

Before diving into the guided imagery, you'll be guided through safety reminders, preparation exercises and assessments. These instructions are tailored for both mental health professionals and the solo reader. These include setting intentions, creating a comfortable environment without distractions, and becoming aware of any emotional or physical sensations or a potential crisis that could emerge. Preparation is key to maximizing the benefits of guided imagery.

If you are a facilitator or mental health professional, feel free to adjust the timing of the guided imagery, silently counting a little less or a little longer than the suggested 20 seconds to best support the person's experience. If you are working through this on your own and using a recording device for the guided imagery scripts, feel free to adjust the pauses between prompts—extending them beyond 20 seconds if that feels more supportive for you.

Additionally, you may find that you need more or less time with the guided imagery exercises. These times are approximate and may vary by a few minutes depending upon your pace and/or facilitation style.

Please keep in mind that if dissociation has been one of your client's primary survival strategies, as is often the case for individuals who have experienced trauma, mindfulness exercises may initially feel unfamiliar, overwhelming, or even provoke anxiety. Take care to introduce these practices slowly, offering extra grounding and support as needed.

Step 4: Breath and Body Work

Next, you'll engage in breath and body work. These exercises are designed to help you ground yourself in the present moment, relax your nervous system, and become more attuned to your inner experience. This section will help you or the client you are supporting focus on breath and gently guide the body into a state of calm.

Important Note: If you (or your client) are physically able, taking 1 to 5 minutes for gentle movement—such as stretching, walking, rhythmic swaying, yoga poses, or even dancing to music—after completing guided imagery is highly recommended. This somatic engagement helps release stored tension, supports emotional processing, and reconnects the body and mind, making the healing experience more complete and embodied.

Step 5: Pre-Guided Imagery Assessment

Before starting the guided imagery, take a pre-guided imagery assessment. This involves reflecting on your current emotional state, physical sensations, and any thoughts or concerns you may have. This step helps you become more aware of your baseline before the guided imagery.

Step 6: The Guided Imagery

The heart of each chapter is the guided imagery. Each chapter will provide the reader with a specific guided visualization exercise designed to take you or the client you are supporting on a journey within to explore your inner world in a safe and structured way. Follow the prompts and allow your imagination to guide you. As always, if you feel activated or overwhelmed, please pause, practice self-care, and come back to the exercise later. If you are doing this work solo, proceed with caution. You may wish to record the guided imagery script on a device and then play it back if you choose not to work with a mental health professional or a trusted facilitator.

Step 7: Post-Guided Imagery Assessment

After completing the guided imagery, take the post-assessment provided in each chapter. Reflect on any changes in your emotional state, thoughts, or physical sensations. Compare these observations with your pre-assessment to notice any shifts or insights gained during the guided imagery exercise.

Step 8: Assessment Comparison and Reflection

This will give the reader or facilitator a chance to reflect on any changes they may notice between the pre and post-assessments.

Step 9: Creative Art Exercises

Following the post-assessment, you'll have the opportunity to express yourself through artwork. We provide illustrations and instructions in each chapter based on the theme of that particular chapter. Use this space to creatively express yourself and support your healing. While we provide helpful instruction, there are no rules with expressive art—let your intuition guide you.

Feel free to use whatever medium feels right for you; however, please note that heavier inks or markers may bleed through the pages. Using colored pencils or gel pens is recommended if you wish to minimize bleed-through.

Step 10: A Mindful Reflection Moment and Questions

We have provided space after the art section so you can take time for reflection after your creative expression. Write down your thoughts, feelings, and any insights you gained from the experience. We include questions to support this process. This reflective practice is an essential part of integrating the work you've done.

Step 11: Affirmation Space

We conclude each chapter with a prompt to list out affirmations. Practicing affirmations reinforces your healing journey and encourages a compassionate, nurturing mind state.

Step 12: Working With a Mental Health Professional

If you are using this workbook under the guidance of a licensed or certified mental health professional, they will facilitate this process and track your progress, offering personalized support and feedback. They can help you process challenging emotions, provide deeper insights, and tailor the exercises to your unique needs.

Important Reminder if Using This Workbook On Your Own

If you are working through this workbook on your own, please approach each exercise with kindness and patience toward yourself. Healing is a deeply personal process, and it's normal to need breaks, move slowly, or seek extra support along the way. If you find yourself in an emotional crisis, please reach out to a local emergency service or crisis line for immediate help.

If dissociation has been one of your primary survival strategies, as it often is for those who have experienced trauma, you may find that mindfulness exercises feel unfamiliar, overwhelming, or even stir anxiety at first. This is a natural and understandable response. A helpful suggestion for solo readers is to record the guided imagery scripts in your own voice, so you can listen back at a pace that feels safe, familiar, and supportive. Throughout the workbook, we have taken special care to include gentle suggestions and preparation steps to help guide and steady you as you move through the material. Trust your instincts, honor your own rhythm, and remember: healing is not a race—it's a return to yourself.

Helpful Note for Telehealth Therapists

Healing can travel across any distance with care and intention. This workbook can be a powerful support for your Telehealth clients. Guided imagery, mindfulness, breathwork, and creative exercises can be shared meaningfully through the screen when approached with patience and flexibility. As therapists, we have successfully used these practices with Telehealth clients for many years, and Mari has been a full Telehealth therapist for nearly eight years. You may find it helpful to slow the rhythm, add more frequent check-ins, pause for additional grounding when needed, and gently adapt to each client's space and needs. Always be sure you are practicing within your licensing board's Telehealth guidelines and licensed where your client is physically located. Begin by confirming your client is in a safe, private space and that you have a clear emergency plan in place. If emotional distress arises, follow your crisis procedures. With steady presence, ethical procedures, good instruction, clear communication, and a compassionate heart, deep work can unfold even across the miles.

Important Note: To Mental Health Professionals

As colleagues, we are honored by your trust in using this workbook. If you are applying this information to support your clients, we have added helpful directions and guidance in the preparation sections of the chapters prior to the guided imagery. As always, please operate within your scope of practice and expertise. If you need assistance in better understanding mindfulness-based modalities, Mari A. Lee is a Certified Mindfulness-Based Therapist and Consulting Supervisor, and Wendy Quinton is a Certified Mindfulness-Based Therapist. You are welcome to reach out to schedule a consultation if that will support your professional growth. You can reach Mari by emailing mari@thecounselorscoach.com or Wendy via wendyquintonlcsw.com.

Note: If you are living with a disability that affects mobility, please adapt the guided imagery exercises in the following chapters in whatever way feels most supportive for you—whether that's moving with a wheelchair, cane, service animal, or even floating or flying in your imagination. Your experience and creativity are fully welcomed and honored.

Gentle Reminder

This workbook is not a substitute for professional therapy. If you experience distress, encounter difficult emotions, are activated to the point of distress, or are dealing with an acute mental health condition or diagnosis, please practice self-care and reach out to a mental health professional or a trusted support system. In cases of crisis, immediately contact your local emergency services or your local crisis hotline.

CHAPTER ONE

Breaking Free: Escaping the Cycle of Trauma Bonding

Mari A. Lee

A bad relationship can make you doubt everything good you ever felt about yourself.

~ Dionne Warwick

As I concluded my conference presentation on betrayal trauma and trauma bonding, I noticed a petite, professionally dressed woman lingering in the second row. Her brown eyes were filled with questions as she approached the stage at the end of my talk. She introduced herself as Keisha, a California-based therapist specializing in working with adolescents and families. I invited her to sit with me, and she tentatively shared, "Mari, I learned so much today. I believe I am dealing with trauma bonding in my own relationship but have been procrastinating starting therapy. I'd like to begin meeting with you if your therapy schedule has room."

We exchanged information, and two weeks later, Keisha and I met via telehealth. In all my first sessions, I ask the client to share what brought them to therapy and what they hope to accomplish, "Keisha, I am glad to have this time with you. This is a safe and confidential space for you to share your challenges and what you'd like to work on." With a nervous but determined smile, she began sharing about her ten-and-a-half-year relationship, a romantic partnership filled with emotional abuse and neglect.

"Jamal and I have known one another since we were in our early twenties," Keisha began with a sigh. "We had mutual church friends, and all the girls were fascinated by Jamal. He was so handsome and reserved, sort of a mystery man. Sometimes, he would attend the services and social gatherings, and other times, he vanished. He was the guy sitting off in a corner reading a book of poetry or gazing at the sky. If I believed in love at first sight, then Jamal was it for me," Keisha said quietly, a wistful look crossing her lovely face.

Keisha continued, "I had a crush on Jamal for three years before we even began dating. Our paths would cross about half a dozen times a year, and though I was attracted to him, I was always in a relationship or Jamal was with his latest girlfriend. Yet, he was not far from my thoughts. I've never been one to flirt, and he seemed shy. During those years, we probably exchanged no more than a handful of words and glances."

One December, while attending the same holiday party, Keisha discovered that they were both single after non-serious breakups, "As I stood on the wide front porch, enjoying the music and Christmas lights, Jamal stepped out into the crisp evening air, sidled up next to me, and whispered in my ear, "This is our time, Keisha. Will you finally go out with me?" It felt like a dream come true as I stood there smiling into his incredible green eyes. We were both in our early thirties by then, and I had enough past relationship experience to know what I wanted and what I didn't. Or so I thought.

"I left the party walking on air and was not able to sleep a wink. When Jamal called me the following Monday and asked me to meet him for a brownie sundae and coffee, I thought I had died and gone to heaven! I remember trying on three different outfits before running out the door in a red mini skirt, black tights, a turtleneck, suede boots, and a black beret. I can still remember how fast my heart was beating as I walked into the café and how his beautiful smile lit up the room as his strong arms embraced me. We talked for hours, quietly sharing stories. He had an introverted, intense energy and magnetic gaze. Truth be told, part of me fell head over heels in love that night. Our first date felt like a dream—I was finally with the man I had thought about for so long!"

"The first few months were bliss, as if I was in a movie—he brought me flowers, wrote me cards, opened doors, pulled out chairs, made delicious meals, said all the right things, kissed me in all the right ways, and called to wish me good morning and good night. He was a perfect gentleman. I wrote him love letters, bought special gifts I knew he would love, and listened for hours on end to the different topics he was interested in. Jamal made me feel like the most special woman on earth. He encouraged me to announce to my friends and family that we were a couple while introducing me to his family members, all of whom were warm and welcoming."

Jamal declared his love to Keisha on Valentine's Day, "He sent me a dozen red roses, took me to a special Thai food dinner, read a romantic poem by candlelight, gave me a pair of silver swan earrings, and told me he loved me with all his heart and that I was 'the one.' I fell into his arms, sharing that I was also in love with him. It was as if we were in our own little love cloud, floating together, untouched by the world around us. We made love for the first time that night, and as we drifted off to sleep wrapped in each other's arms, the sheets tangled around us, he murmured into my neck, 'I think next December is the perfect time for a wedding; you'll be my beautiful winter swan bride.' My heart burst with joy at finally finding my person, my mate, my truest love."

However, by late spring, Keisha shared that the fantasy began to fade: "While I was on a business trip, I called Jamal for our pre-bedtime chat at 8:00 PM, and there was no answer. I left a message—no response. I called again at 9:00 PM—no answer. I texted at 10:00 PM— no response. As the hours ticked by, I was increasingly worried. He sometimes had to work late, but never this late, and when he did, he always let me know. At that time, he drove an older, unreliable vehicle, and I was concerned that maybe he had been in an accident or was stranded on the side of the road somewhere. Maybe his phone had died?"

Keisha shared that she tossed and turned all night, fearful thoughts keeping her awake, "The next morning, exhausted and stressed, before boarding an early flight, I tried calling two more times to no avail, 'Jamal, if I don't hear from you, I am going to start calling the hospitals and police departments when I land. I am sick with worry, and I am praying you are safe.' That flight was a nightmare, to say the least; my mind kept leaping between all our beautiful moments and then imagining him in a coma, his car a twisted heap of metal. I kept reciting the same prayers repeatedly, 'God, please let him be safe, please don't take him from me.' Once the plane landed, I immediately checked my voicemail and felt a rush of relief to see he had called. Relief, until I heard his tense, flat tone: 'Hey, I was working late. Sorry I missed your calls. I have another late night, so let's talk in a few days.' No, I love you. No, I miss you. No, sorry I worried you. Just a loud click."

As Keisha crept along in Los Angeles traffic, her sleep-deprived head was understandably buzzing with questions, "Part of me wanted to drive to his place to see him, part of me wanted to call him and demand to know what had happened, part of me was deeply confused, and another part of me was angry and hurt. The Jamal I had fallen in love with over the last few months was the opposite of the man who had left that ice-cold voicemail message."

Three days passed, and Keisha still had not heard from him: "My stomach was in knots trying to make sense of what was happening. Later that week, as I was catching up on paperwork at my office, I suddenly found myself dialing his number. He answered, sounding distant and cautious, 'Hey Keisha, what's up?' On the verge of tears, I asked, 'I don't know Jamal, what *is* up? I haven't heard from you for a few days, and I am confused. You sounded so different in your message. Are you upset with me? Has something changed?'

"A long silence ensued, and I was about to check if he was still there when he flatly stated, 'Yeah, well...Kathleen contacted me a month ago and started prowling around.'

'Kathleen? Do you mean the girl that you dated before me?'

'Yeah, her.'

'Ok, but what does that have to do with us, Jamal?' I asked, trying to keep the tears out of my shaking voice.

'Well, *uh*, it's all really confusing...' his voice trailed off.

'What do you mean? When did she contact you?'

'She called me a few days before Valentine's Day to return a book I had loaned her a while back. I went by to pick up my book, and you know, we started talking and, well, it just seemed like it made sense.'

'What made sense? Did you take her out on Valentine's Day, too?'

'Well, not exactly, but the day before, yeah. I took her to see a movie, dinner, that kind of thing.'

'Did you give her gifts and stay with her?' By now, I was quietly sobbing, my heart shattering into my belly.

'Just flowers and candy, not jewelry,' he replied defensively, 'She begged me to spend the night, but we did not have sex. She just wanted me to hold her. What was I supposed to do? She was crying!'

'Jamal, was Valentine's Day with me just an act? Why did you tell me you loved me, that I was the one, that you wanted to marry me, and then make love to me when you had already started seeing her again? Are you in love with her?'"

Keisha gazed at me with intense sadness edging her expression, "Mari, questions were flooding my mind. I honestly felt like I was falling off a cliff!" As Keisha recounted this to me,

I noticed her entire body was trembling. We paused as I checked in, had her breathe, and engaged her in mindful grounding. Then, she continued with Jamal's impatient response.

"'Keisha, I do love you, but I think I am still in love with Kathleen as well. Like I said, it's confusing. This kind of thing happens all the time all over the world with people. Love isn't always a straight line! Stop making me feel so guilty, and quit crying! I can't choose between the two of you! I need time.'"

With a deep breath, Keisha sat up straighter, stating, "Mari, I recall feeling like I was going to faint. I realized I was holding my breath, and it burst out in a long wail. I said something like, 'Then I will choose for you, Jamal. Go be with Kathleen! You only dated her for a few weeks before you and I got together. I had no idea that it was that serious between the two of you and that you still had feelings for her! I guess I was just the rebound woman. You've clearly made your choice; I was the dummy who did not realize you were seeing her again while professing your love for me.'"

Keisha shook her head in frustration, "Do you know what his response was, Mari? 'As you wish, Keisha. Just don't forget that you broke it off. I hope you know that rebound women are like medicine, and you were my medicine woman who made me feel loved and wanted after Kathleen broke my heart by cheating on a dating site. Take care, I wish you all the best.'"

Keisha shared that she hung up and balled like a child. "I had no idea until that night that his time with Kathleen had been anything more than a casual dating relationship that ran its course. I drove home from my office in a blur and fell into bed, worn out, heartbroken, and numb."

Keisha called in sick to work the following day, "I turned my phone off and basically hid under the covers crying. I did not eat a bite of food that day or night. The following morning, I arrived late to work, plopped down behind my desk, tired with puffy eyes, defeated, and feeling like the biggest fool. I was so despondent and unfocused that my assistant and coworkers were worried about me. I was also ashamed because I had ignored my loved ones' concerns about how quickly things had developed with Jamal. I refused to listen to their worries, ignoring what was right in front of my face."

She shared that she passed that day at work in a robotic haze, "When I finally checked my office voicemail messages, despondently jotting reminders for the next day, 'Your Song' by Elton John started playing on a voicemail, followed by a message from Jamal who pleaded for forgiveness in a mournful tone, 'I screwed up Keisha. Big time. I now realize that I love you, not Kathleen. I know I don't deserve a second chance, but what we have is special. It is magical—we both know it. I got scared, and I messed up. Please call me back. I derailed us, but I promise I will take care of your heart. I am meeting with Kathleen on Friday to break it off, and I want you to come over this weekend so I can get us back on track. I am so sorry I hurt you this way; I love you, Keisha. Please forgive me for being such a cad. Everyone deserves a second chance.'"

Keisha shook her head at this point, a look of disgust crossing her face, "Mari, I am embarrassed to admit that despite the red flags and the warnings from friends, when the weekend arrived, I raced back into his arms, relieved and desperate for us to get back to what I thought we had created. I wanted so much to be the woman Jamal wanted me to be, to have the fairytale I thought we were experiencing. The happily ever after. I told myself that he was right—everyone deserves a second chance, and I convinced myself that we could heal. How wrong I was, and I wish I could go back in time and tell myself to run in the opposite direction, far from this man!"

As the relationship progressed and weeks turned into months, and months into years, the dark shadows of Jamal's personality continued to arise. She explained that there were days, even weeks, when he was a great partner—attentive, nurturing, loving, and kind. But, as his mood swings happened more and more frequently, Keisha learned that he could easily go from sunny to stormy within a couple of days or even hours. "Jamal would drift away emotionally, become easily frustrated, smoke a lot of marijuana, and disappear into himself. Sometimes he would binge on online porn for weeks on end; some of it was extremely hardcore, like rape scenes. Or he would seek porn with men having sex with men, which I did not understand, and he refused to discuss this. I would find hidden stories about sibling incest or bestiality or discover dildos that he was using on himself. It was confusing because he seemed checked out when we had sex, as if he was not entirely there or would lose his erection."

"When I tried to discuss this with him to see if there was something we could enjoy exploring together, no matter how kind or open I was, he was often dismissive or defensive. This was the pattern that I became accustomed to. He had been diagnosed with an acute anxiety disorder but refused to see a therapist or take medication, often stating, 'Weed is my medication—it always mellows me out. I'll be fine. Just give me space and patience.'"

As I listened with compassion, I encouraged Keisha to continue, "Underneath his remote and mysterious exterior, Jamal was an extremely angry and deceptive guy, like Dr. Jekyll and Mr. Hyde. When he was in a bad mood, frustrated, hungry, or tired, he had a hair-trigger temper. He frightened me with his frequent fits of rage that would seemingly come out of nowhere and would sometimes last for days. He would also lie about the smallest things. He lied about flirting with women at his workplace. He lied about places he would go. He lied about the amount of porn he watched. He lied about having an adult bookstore account. He lied constantly."

"Once, he had to go to an anger management class and invented an entire story about attending a conference. I could always sense when his tension was building, and I would find myself watching my words and walking on eggshells to avoid setting him off. Inevitably, something would trigger him, and he would transform—bulging eyes, veins on his neck popping out, yelling with spittle inches from my face, and punching a wall, kicking, or breaking something."

From what Keisha shared, the items Jamal broke during arguments were always things she had purchased as gifts for him, "It might be a special mug, a ceramic bowl, a mirror, a piece of furniture—the list goes on and on. He never broke anything he bought with his own money when he was enraged. There were always at least two holes in a wall or a door in the places he rented. This is now a red flag that I warn women about: If you see holes in the walls of your man's place, run! During the first year of our relationship, like an idiot, I would repair the holes so his landlord wouldn't see the damage he was causing. At one point, he was renting a historic Craftsman bungalow in Los Angeles, and I knew he would be evicted if this was discovered. I didn't want him to blame me if he got kicked out, and I knew I would be the scapegoat if that happened."

Keisha continued unfolding the timeline of their relationship, "By this time, we had been together a little over three years. I lived for the weeks when all was blissful and beautiful, and I dreaded the explosive times. What was most disturbing is that he seemed to escalate around my birthdays or the holidays. I remember most of my birthdays, Valentine's Days, or Christmas holidays being alone, in tears, or being yelled at by him. I sometimes wondered if it was because he put pressure on himself to spend money, something he never had much of. When I tried to assure him that I would be happy with a home-cooked meal and a day at the beach, he would stare at me with a sneer and sarcastic remark.

"Jamal never hit me, but his contempt toward me grew as the years went by, often with him yelling for me to 'eff' off and, one time, screaming that he could snap my neck like a twig if he wanted to. After that threat, I left him for two months. I refused to interact with him. Eventually, he wore me down with apologies, promises, sweet talk, and tears, sharing that his life was falling apart and vowing to do better. Like Charlie Brown and Lucy with the football, I'd once again step back into the relationship. I have a kind heart and a compassionate spirit, and he would rely on me feeling sorry for him as if I was obligated to tolerate his moods and rages or deal with the endless series of crises in his life." Keisha paused to dry the tears running down her cheeks. As I engaged her in a few deep breaths and helped her stay present in the moment with me, I invited her to stand, stretch, and then continue.

"Let me tell you, there was always a crisis with him!" Keisha stated, her mouth now set in anger. "Jamal rarely stayed on top of his bills; he did not have a budget, a savings account, or even a credit card. I was his safety net when he overextended himself, as if I was made of money. He hardly ever paid me back or paid for anything when it came to social activities. At one point in time, I went into debt trying to help him when he was fired from another job due to his anger issues. His credit score was terrible. His car was constantly in need of repair because he did not take it in for regular service, and he had a hard time staying at a job for more than a year or two because of his anxiety, anger, and refusal to seek help. He moved four times during our relationship, and each time, I would locate the place, pay the first and last, help him get the utilities turned on, help him pack and move, decorate, and buy the furniture. Within a year, he would let his place fall to pieces.

"On top of his anxiety disorder, he had been diagnosed with attention deficit hyperactivity disorder (ADHD) and brain trauma due to his time in the military, yet he would not investigate assistance through the VA. He would fight with neighbors, family members, friends, people in a martial arts group, or even strangers in public, and his paranoia was off the charts. Jamal split constantly, moving quickly into a defensive stance where he would see people or situations as entirely good or entirely bad. His friends were either in the penthouse or the doghouse with him, and everything was always black and white. Despite all of this, he refused to see a therapist or work with a psychiatrist until I broke up with him a second time after he had yet another raging fit where he threatened to harm me."

At this point, Keisha dropped her head into her hands as if in pain. I checked in with her and helped her define what she was feeling and where this feeling was in her body. After taking a few mindful moments, she continued with quiet sadness in her voice, "Mari, as a mental health professional, I knew this man I loved needed help and that I needed help as well, but I kept hanging on to the sweet times, hoping somehow that Jamal would grow or that I could show him he was worth loving. Eventually, after a horrible weekend where he was yelling, threatening, and storming, I held my ground and refused to get back together unless he sought help. He reluctantly agreed, and I said a prayer of relief. Once he started on medication and attended regular therapy and a Twelve-Step group, I finally started experiencing the best parts of Jamal, and I was deeply thankful that the trauma and pain that he'd been bottling up were being addressed. He was wonderful to be with during this chapter of our relationship, and life finally felt 'normal' and peaceful for almost two years."

Keisha's gentle smile faded from her face as she shared that the last straw for her occurred in early 2020 with the pandemic and lockdown. Along with a significant change in the management at Jamal's workplace, followed by his landlord selling his rental and him having to relocate again, Jamal's father, with whom he had a difficult relationship, unexpectedly passed away from COVID-19 and alcohol addiction. It was the perfect storm of events, and due to Jamal's addictions and erratic behaviors, his formerly supportive sister refused to speak with him any longer. He began isolating, and his drinking greatly increased during this time.

According to Keisha, Jamal was born to teenage parents and had endured numerous traumas, neglect, and sexual abuse as a child. As a result, he struggled with various addictions in his life—pornography, marijuana, nicotine, and, eventually, alcohol. Unbeknownst to Keisha, his drinking increased dangerously during the first year of the pandemic, where he was consuming large quantities of vodka daily. Jamal, like many addicts, had hidden this well. Keisha shared that the combination of liquor and his anxiety medication was destructive. Not only was he angry and moody, but he was also intoxicated most days of the week: "He was either yelling, acting bizarre, threatening me and others, being highly paranoid, or feeling ashamed and begging for my forgiveness. There were days where I felt like I was losing my mind, all the while trying to keep him together and myself safe and sane through a worldwide pandemic."

Keisha began to quietly rock back and forth at this point, staring off into space, her trauma clearly surfacing. I asked her to stay connected and breathe with me and introduced her to a technique called butterfly hug. The butterfly hug is performed by crossing your arms over your chest so each hand rests lightly on the opposite upper arm or shoulder. Then, gently move your hands in a fluttering motion, tapping your arms or shoulders alternately, mimicking the wings of a butterfly.

We practiced this together for a few minutes, followed by deep breaths, and after a drink of cool water, she proceeded: "He was so out of control that I finally had to block him for a few days on my phone and email. During this time, I contacted his mother despite his threats to harm me if I shared his struggles and addiction with his family. It was only when his mother got involved and when I told Jamal I would cut him off for good that he finally agreed to go to rehab. I promised to take care of his place, and with a great deal of encouragement from me and his family, he admitted that his life had completely fallen apart.

"The morning that I arrived to help him get ready for rehab, I was shocked. I had not seen him in months, and he looked as if he had aged 25 years. He had lost so much weight that he looked shrunken and skeletal. His skin and hair were a mess, his eyes and skin were tinged with yellow, and he was bent over and shuffling like an old man. He had been renting a condo that belonged to my sister after his last rental place was sold out from under him, and my sister graciously reduced the rent by half and paid all the utilities to help him get on his feet. In spite of her generosity, he had let it fall into disrepair, and it was absolutely filthy. There were dirty dishes and pans piled in the sink and on the stove, mold growing in the shower, unopened mail, and bills scattered around everywhere.

"On top of that, his clothing was lying all over the floor, along with cat hair, cat food, and cat vomit and feces all over the place. There was even dried food on the floor, trash spilling out of the trashcan, litter on the stairway, dried vomit in the bathroom sink, roaches crawling in the corners, and empty vodka bottles rolling around. The toilets were either broken or disgustingly dirty, the smell was overwhelming, and the air was thick with cigarette and marijuana smoke, with cigarette butts filling a container. I was stunned—it was heartbreaking and frightening to witness his decline. His mental health issues, along with the nicotine, weed, alcohol, and prescription drug abuse, had taken its toll on him and all of us."

Keisha shared that the minute Jamal was admitted to rehab, she pulled together a team of people: "This included his aunt, my best friend, and my housecleaner—we all got to work. It took us hours every day for three weeks and thousands of dollars to finally get his life in order and my sister's condo back in shape. I hired a person to fix the broken doors and toilets, repair the locks, patch the rage holes in the walls and doors, hang curtains for privacy, fix the sink, dump endless bags of trash, clean up the animal urine and feces, clean and sanitize everything, clean out the spoiled food in the cupboards, and spray for roaches. I hired a vet and pet groomer to attend to his cats, who were in bad shape. We cleaned out the refrigerator of rotting food, replaced damaged things, and added plants to the little patio. His friend replaced the light bulbs, and we purchased new trash cans, sheets, towels, litter boxes, dishes, lamps, silverware, and you name it.

"I paid his overdue bills and taxes, took his car in for maintenance and registration, organized everything into a filing system, and basically got his life completely back in order. His mother and stepfather, both retired and on a budget, footed the bill for some of this and did the best they could to help while living out of state. This was in the middle of an incredibly hot September during a pandemic, with me racing around with a mask on and dealing with his family members who were anxious, overwhelmed, and upset, all the while working full time with therapy clients who were going through their own grief, depression, and anxiety due to COVID-19. The stress was overwhelming, and I cannot believe I made it through!" At this point, Keisha was again rocking back and forth, soothing herself while we practiced mindful breathing techniques.

Sadly, during Jamal's time in rehab, he was diagnosed with psoriasis of the liver: "This is a disease I knew nothing about, and one I would not wish on a worst enemy. On top of everything else, we then had to arrange medical visits every week for stomach drains and blood testing due to his condition and take turns driving him as he was in such a weakened condition and close to death. He could not drive. He could not eat. He could not walk very far or stand for very long. During the first few months after rehab, I would come and stay with him during the day several times a week, praying with him, giving him light foot and leg massages to ease his discomfort, cleaning, bringing supplies, running errands, and helping the best I could.

"The diagnosis was a wake-up call for Jamal. He is now sober from alcohol, and due to his dedication to his recovery, his health has improved but will forever be impacted. Unfortunately, after rehab, he lost his job, a job that my sister had helped secure for him, and he could no longer pay his rent. But my sister, God bless her, allowed him to live in her rental condo for free for the next two years. She also paid all the utilities on top of the rent so he could focus on regaining his health. Despite all of this, he still smokes weed and cigarettes, is still not in therapy, deals with mood issues, blames everyone for his problems, including me, and is hanging on by a thread emotionally."

After three years of unwavering support from Keisha when others had given up on him, Jamal gradually regained his health. In spite of this, their lives faced new and significant challenges. A troubling incident with his neighbor jeopardized Jamal's safety, his financial state was grave, and a serious health scare due to the immense stress she had endured for years forced Keisha to finally prioritize her own well-being. During this medical crisis, Keisha was unable to focus her care on anyone but herself. Within a few short weeks into her own health issues, Jamal realized that she was unable to assist him at the level he had grown accustomed to and decided to move to another state to live with his mother and stepfather, who could provide him and his two cats with a room and bathroom.

"While I am grateful that he has a safe place to stay and is surrounded by loving people, it was my sister and I who once again stepped in to assist when he reached out," Keisha shared. "We helped pack his belongings, cleaned and organized his things, hired people to assist, and gave him money. All of this happened while I was dealing with my own medical struggles. Despite maintaining a brave and encouraging façade throughout the moving process, the emotional pain of watching special gifts that I had given him or things that we had collected during our years together go into the junk man's truck or get tossed into the trash dumpster was extremely difficult. I never had a chance to say goodbye to the kitties that I had come to love either.

"Our last hour together before he began the long drive to his new state was very hard. I was trying to keep it together, put on a brave face, and be supportive, yet he collapsed at my feet, throwing his arms around me with his head in my lap, sobbing, with me comforting *him* once again. The emotions I felt while I watched him drive away with a scared look on his face, his car filled to the brim with his clothing and the bare necessities, is a feeling I will never forget. I walked back inside my home feeling hollow, alone, and deeply sad in ways that I will never have words for."

Keisha paused, staring out her window, tears coursing down her neck. I gently suggested that we pause, check in with her body through breath work, and then refocus on the session. "I wept the entire weekend after he left. I cried for the broken dreams, the years filled with anguish, everything I had invested in him, all the lies and unkept promises, the dignity that was trampled, the accusations and threats I endured, and the hope and prayers I had held onto for so long. I had purchased a wedding dress that I never showed him, and it still hangs in the back of my closet to this day." Keisha shared that the first song she heard after Jamal left was "Landslide" by Stevie Nicks. "I had to pull my car over in tears while I listened to the song.

"I guess it took a worldwide pandemic for me to finally see the disease in my former relationship and how far I had fallen. I am no longer that carefree, confident young woman with stars in her eyes from all those years ago. I built my life around this man, and now...I *am* older, and I am tired. I am alone, I do not have a child, and I am sad and lonely. These days, I have been able to hold better boundaries and maintain a distant friendship with Jamal, who contacts me every few weeks so I can lend a listening ear, ask for advice, or when he requests financial support. However, now that he has a job and no longer needs money, I rarely hear from him, only if he needs something—I can barely remember the sound of his voice as it has been months since we have spoken."

With a shake of her head, Keisha continued, "On top of this, his family seems to have forgotten that I ever existed, and I have never once received a heartfelt thank you for all that my sister and I provided during those years. That was equally heartbreaking for me as his family meant a lot to me, especially his mother. I am finally on my own, and I have no idea who I am as a middle-aged woman. Despite all that I endured during the years of that relationship, I do have compassion for Jamal. At the same time, I also feel resentful of the time, love, trust, heart, soul, support, and money I invested into trying to create a life and future together. I feel broken—afraid for him and for myself. If I had to guess, it will only be a matter of time where he paints me as the enemy who never showed up for him, or gave enough, or abandoned him in his hour of need while I tended to my own health emergency. Though I tried hard not to step into my therapist role with Jamal, I watched him split over and over again—painting people as all good or all bad, depending upon his ruminations and the stories he would create. One day, I will likely receive a call or text that he no longer wants to be friends due to something he is projecting on to me."

As Keisha ended her story, her shoulders dropped as she wrapped her arms around herself. She shared softly, "Mari, I feel so much shame that as a smart woman and as a therapist, I tolerated this for so long. I did not realize how bad it had gotten until I was out of the relationship. My heart hurts, my mind hurts, and my spirit aches. I don't know how to start untangling all of this. It seems like a cage of pain that I am trapped in. Over the last month, I have started to feel so depressed. I have stomach issues and acid reflux, and I grind my teeth at night. I've never had migraines in my life, but every few weeks, I can barely get out of bed—either because I feel unmotivated, my head is splitting open, or my stomach is a mess. I hope you can help me," Keisha concluded with a deep sigh, tears once again filling her exhausted eyes.

With compassionate support, I assured Keisha that she was not alone in this, and together, we would help her heal and move forward, one step, one breath, and one courageous decision at a time.

A message from Mari

The term "trauma bonding" was introduced by Dr. Patrick Carnes in 1997. It describes the deep emotional connection that forms between two people who have gone through traumatic experiences together, often in situations where one person is an abuser. This bond is usually marked by strong feelings of loyalty, attachment, dependence, and non-integrated trauma. Trauma bonds can develop in various kinds of relationships, whether it's romantic, with friendships, or even within a family. Trauma bonding differs significantly from healthy intimacy or love because it is rooted in ongoing traumatic experiences rather than in mutual trust, respect, and affection. It can be thought of as a maladaptive "survival mode" response, where the bond is formed as a means to cope with the ongoing trauma.

When Keisha and I first started working together, it was clear that she was in a state of crisis. As we progressed and explored the layers of her relationship experience, it became increasingly apparent just how complex her situation was. Through a careful and thorough examination of the timeline of her relationship with Jamal, we uncovered several key elements that shed light on the challenges she was facing. Each session revealed new insights, helping us to understand the dynamics at play and guiding us toward meaningful solutions. Let's explore the dynamics that lead to her trauma bonding.

Dynamic I: Love Bombing

Jamal's love bombing didn't just occur in the initial courtship phase. Rather, it persisted throughout a significant portion of their relationship, notably intensifying during the first three years. Despite episodes of rage and deceit, Jamal consistently countered with gestures of affection like sending flowers, making promises for the future, or offering romantic gestures. He would state commitments to his own healing, even amid deception and turmoil.

Love bombing is a manipulation tactic where someone overwhelms another person with excessive attention, flattery, gifts, or affection in order to gain control or create a sense of dependency early in a relationship. This pattern is sometimes repeated over the first several months. A sentiment frequently echoed by women who've undergone similar experiences to Keisha's is: "How did I allow myself to endure such treatment, and why did I remain for so long?" Love bombing operates insidiously, much like a spider's web—extremely difficult to recognize at first. Once ensnared in this intricate trap—a cocoon of crazy-making—individuals become susceptible to a cycle of devaluation and manipulation. Let's further deconstruct this by exploring the next dynamic in trauma bonding, devaluing.

Dynamic II: Devaluing

Devaluing includes the following elements. Feel free to check the boxes below if any of the items resonate with you:

- ☐ Your partner withdraws emotionally, only to change back, then change again.

- ☐ Your partner has a habit of rewriting history, making you doubt your experiences.

- ☐ Your partner frequently criticizes you—everything is your fault.

- ☐ Your partner can easily become frustrated and enraged.

- ☐ Your partner punishes you with silence.

- ☐ Your partner blames you for the challenges in your relationship.

- ☐ Your partner shames you, mocks you, or puts you down in front of others.

- ☐ Your partner projects their abusive, unhealthy traits onto you.

- ☐ Your partner minimizes your concerns and fears.

- ☐ Your partner frequently gaslights you, making you question your sanity.

- ☐ Your partner frequently issues threats of abandonment.

□   Your partner abandons the relationship regularly.

□   Your partner minimizes your concerns about their addictions.

□   Your partner ignores your requests for connection.

□   Your partner undermines your efforts in creating a secure relationship and future.

As this cycle spiraled out of control, Jamal's manipulation and abuse continued while the romance eventually faded into the background. Love bombing and devaluation can be a very effective way of ensnaring a love interest, as the person who has been love-bombed and devalued often seeks to recapture what once was, and the cycle continues as the traumatic bonding grows tighter. Keisha, like many abused women, began to believe that if she could just be more, do more, improve herself more, and love Jamal more, that somehow, she could prove her worth, and Jamal would behave differently. I call it the teeter-totter effect.

A teeter-totter, as you may know, is sometimes present on children's playgrounds. It is a long wooden plank with handles on either end that balances in the middle. The teeter-totter relies on both people to trust one another. Each person must take a turn at helping their partner up, balance while in mid-air, and then make sure their partner is safely grounded—repeatedly. If one of the participants steps off their side of the teeter totter once they've raised their partner up into the air, the trusting partner will come crashing down, frightened, emotionally shattered, and sometimes, physically injured.

A healthy and safe relationship requires that both people trust each other to do the work of lifting one another up and balancing while helping the other stay safely grounded. When a person has been love-bombed to the point of traumatic bonding, then quickly devalued, love-bombed again, abandoned, love-bombed, abused, love-bombed, abandoned, love-bombed, then threatened, love-bombed once more, this consistent pattern sends the nervous system into a state of chaos. A survivor of this type of complex trauma may not know they are being abused and traumatized because there wasn't a single earth-shattering event but rather a regular pattern of ongoing big and small trust ruptures, which are often explained away by the abuser and eventually by the victim of the abuse. This slow and steady drip of pain eventually becomes normal.

Dynamic III: Weaponizing Empathy

In an abusive relationship, empathy can become a powerful tool for manipulation and control, transforming a caring trait into a weapon of emotional harm and another strong bind in trauma bonding.

This subtle form of emotional abuse unfolds as the abuser reframes their own harmful actions as consequences of personal hardships like childhood abuse, trauma, mental health struggles, medical issues, or difficult life circumstances, placing the responsibility for their well-being onto their compassionate partner. Through this tactic, the abusive partner subtly pressures the other to prioritize supporting and "fixing" them over recognizing or addressing the abuse itself. They may reinforce this manipulation by citing financial struggles, religious beliefs, or marital obligations, creating a sense of duty, fear, or shame that discourages the partner from stepping back. The abuser is rarely at fault and does not take ownership of their struggles and choices. Instead, it is everyone and everything around them that has created their unhappiness.

Driven by a deep sense of duty, the empathetic partner may begin to rationalize the abuser's behavior, hoping that their understanding, love, and patience will bring change. Over time, years or even decades are invested, and this dynamic entrenches the empathetic partner in a self-sacrificing cycle of providing emotional support at great personal cost, often suppressing their own needs and boundaries in the process. The abuser's control strengthens as they exploit this generosity and compassion, leaving the partner emotionally drained, conflicted, and further bound to the relationship, as their caring nature becomes the very tie that holds them captive.

Dynamic IV: Control Dramas

Control drama is a term that describes a set of unconscious behaviors people use to feel a sense of power or influence in relationships. These behaviors often arise from unresolved insecurities or unmet needs and manifest as strategies for gaining attention, sympathy, or dominance in social interactions or romantic relationships.

When someone engages in a control drama, they typically evoke predictable responses in others, creating a cycle where each person's actions reinforce the other's behavior. For instance, a person who relies on intimidation might provoke fear or compliance in others, while someone who adopts a victim role might elicit sympathy and support. Understanding these patterns is crucial in therapeutic settings, where individuals and couples can begin to see how these dramas play out and explore healthier, more direct ways of expressing their needs.

Examining control dramas can help people break down recurring relationship struggles and understand the underlying emotional triggers that drive their behavior. Therapists guide clients toward recognizing the impact of these patterns on their well-being and their relationships, helping them to see how control dramas may limit genuine connection.

Dynamic V: Trauma Bonding and Domestic Violence

Various forms of domestic violence are often a part of trauma bonding. When Keisha and I started our work together, it was clear she was not only traumatically bonded to Jamal, but she was also a survivor of domestic violence (DV) and intimate partner abuse. When I first proposed that she was a DV survivor, though Keisha is also a mental health professional, she seemed genuinely taken aback, and her initial reaction was to defend Jamal and protect him. Keisha adamantly stated that even though Jamal had shoved her a couple of times, left her in public when he was upset, shouldered past her and knocked her off balance, or called her names, she did not feel this was abuse. It took her some time to understand that when he kicked her purse out of her hands, shoved a car door into her back, broke special gifts she had given him, or screamed profanities in her face, this was, in fact, abusive.

During one session, Keisha described an incident that had happened one weekend: "We were at the farmer's market, something we did almost every week. Nearly every time, Jamal would go to great lengths to get out of people's paths, open doors, or help, especially with attractive young women, elderly people, or mothers with small children or strollers. Normally, this would be something I would love in a partner, but with Jamal, even though he appeared to be a gentleman, it was all for show. He left me in the dust, let me pay for everything, and barely acknowledged me. Whenever he jumped out of someone's way in this exaggerated manner, tipping his hat, he banged into me, ran me off the sidewalk, tripped me, stepped on my foot, or stepped on the heel of my shoe. Every time. After a few months of this, I tried to carefully point this out, and he blew up at me on the drive home, accusing me of not appreciating him, and then gave me the silent treatment until I apologized. Even simple pleasures, like a weekend morning at the farmers market, turned into a giant issue with Jamal. He just wore me out."

As she advanced in her healing, other incidents where Jamal had been violent or abusive surfaced. Keisha shared memories of him smashing a pillow in her face, punching holes into walls and doors, driving recklessly while screaming profanities at her, pushing her, grabbing her wrist, and threatening her. She also shared that he had once slammed her to the ground so hard she injured her elbow, and another time, he chased her into his bathroom and pinned her against the wall with his fist in her face.

When friends shared their concerns, Keisha defended Jamal, stating that he had never hit her with his fist or slapped her. This type of justification is not unusual for abused individuals who have endured this level of ongoing relational trauma. Feeling compassion for Jamal and making sure he was safe had been her role for the better part of a decade. During these years, Keisha had forgotten that she could feel empathy for his struggles and still place her own well-being above the abuse, unhealed trauma, and unpredictable moods, drama, and demands of Jamal.

At the start, Keisha would often criticize herself in our therapy sessions, sharing that after weeks of his unpredictable moods and violent words, she would sometimes raise her voice in self-defense or curse at Jamal and had even called him names such as "a-hole," "bastard," "jerk," and "tyrant." Once, she admitted throwing a glass of water against her living room wall after Jamal had taunted her for several hours. While name-calling and throwing items is not an appropriate way of expressing one's pain, it was important for Keisha to understand that what she was describing was "reactive anger abuse" due to the relationship dynamics. As she moved forward in our work, Keisha began to identify these patterns of abuse and was eager to learn more about the consequences of intimate partner violence. We discussed many of the ways that Keisha's mental and physical health had been harmed in her relationship with Jamal.

Dynamic VI: Reactive Abuse in Victims of Domestic Violence

Keisha and I worked through several sessions to help her understand that reactive anger abuse in individuals who have experienced domestic violence, love bombing, ongoing relational trauma, gaslighting, and chronic devaluation are elements of trauma bonding and are quite common. Reactive anger abuse is not a spontaneous outburst but rather a culmination of long-suppressed emotions, feelings of betrayal, manipulation, and the persistent burden of mistreatment. This type of anger emerges from ongoing psychological and emotional abuse. When it surfaces, the abuser, in this case Jamal, often exploits the victim's reaction to shift blame onto the victim (Keisha), projecting their own abusive behavior onto the person they have been mistreating. As a result, the victim may be unfairly labeled as the abusive partner.

It is important to understand that reactive anger abuse happens when a person like Keisha, after enduring ongoing emotional, psychological, or physical abuse, responds in a way that appears, or is, aggressive or intense. This reaction might involve yelling, profanity, striking back, or heated words, often because the person feels pushed beyond their human limit. Abusers may intentionally provoke this kind of response for weeks, months, or years and then use it to paint the victim as the aggressor, flipping roles to appear as if they are the ones being harmed.

Let's explore the characteristics and implications of reactive anger abuse dynamic more deeply.

- **Accumulated Resentment**: Victims who have endured domestic violence or love bombing often internalize their feelings of frustration, anger, humiliation, confusion, and pain. Over time, these suppressed emotions accumulate, creating a reservoir of pent-up anger and resentment. When pushed to their limits, victims may finally reach a breaking point where they can no longer contain their emotions, leading to a powerful and often unexpected explosion of anger. An extreme example of this is a movie called The Burning Bed, which is based on the true story of Francine Hughes, who was mercilessly victimized and relentlessly physically and emotionally threatened and abused by her husband. She set fire to his bed in 1977, killing him and destroying their home. Francine was tried for murder but found not guilty. It was one of the first cases to use battered woman syndrome.

- **Sense of Betrayal**: Victims of love bombing often experience a profound sense of betrayal. Initially showered with affection and promises of love, devotion, and attention, they are manipulated into believing in a false reality. As the illusion shatters and the true nature of the love bomber is revealed, feelings of horror and betrayal intensify. This sense of betrayal, along with the stages of love bombing and devaluation, fuels reactive anger as victims grapple with the realization that their trust and vulnerability were exploited.

- **Loss of Control**: One of the most distressing aspects of domestic violence, emotional abuse, and love bombing is the loss of control victims experience. Manipulated and dominated by their abuser, victims often feel powerless and trapped. When the victim's reactive anger eventually surfaces, it can be a desperate attempt to reclaim a sense of control over their lives and emotions. This explosion of anger sometimes serves as a manifestation of their desire to break free from the chains of manipulation and mistreatment. Again, this is not an excuse for harmful words or behavior but rather an explanation and exploration of reactive anger abuse.

- **Cathartic Release**: While reactive anger can be overwhelming, it can also serve as a cathartic release for victims. By expressing their pent-up emotions and confronting their abuser, victims may experience a temporary sense of relief and empowerment. This act of standing up for themselves often feels like a crucial step towards reclaiming their autonomy. It can also serve as a catalyst for seeking help. It is important to note that this can trigger homicidal tendencies in extremely violent abusers. If you are in a domestically violent situation, please see the resource section of this book and seek help and support.

It is essential for victims of any type of abuse—whether physical, emotional, verbal, sexual, financial, spiritual, or otherwise—to understand that reactive anger is a complex emotional response rooted in prolonged abuse, mistreatment, betrayal, and a deep need for respect, safety, and autonomy. While this anger is a natural reaction to ongoing abuse, it's crucial to repeat that responding with anger or aggression is not safe or constructive, as abusers often escalate their abuse or use these incidents against the victim, framing them as the aggressor. This cycle reflects the profound effects of manipulation and highlights the longing of victims striving to reclaim their lives and self-respect.

During this stage of our work together, Keisha's insight illustrates this dynamic well. She shared in one session, "Mari, Jamal had a conflict-seeking brain. He actually enjoyed pushing, poking, debating, arguing, lying, and provoking me over and over, escalating his abusive words and actions or threats to hurt me or leave me until I finally snapped. If I attempted to leave or ask him to leave, he would block my path or lock himself in my bathroom. Then he played the victim, calmly accusing me of being out of control and abusive. This dynamic nearly broke my spirit, and I could not continue in a relationship like this. Sadly, even if I tried to share what I am learning about reactive anger abuse and what our cycle was, he would just negate what I am sharing and use the information against me." Recognizing this pattern can be empowering, allowing abused individuals to take steps toward safer ways of reclaiming their sense of self and freedom, moving from victim to survivor.

The Impact of Emotional Abuse

As Keisha learned, the way you view and relate to yourself can change in the wake of chronic emotional abuse, manipulation, and neglect. For example, Keisha felt a great deal of shame and disgust with herself after incidents of reactive anger. Her shame and self-loathing were further exacerbated by Jamal telling Keisha that she was the abusive one, calling her a "sinner", citing her cursing and name-calling, often reducing her to apologies and tears for her words. Support, understanding, and intervention are essential to help victims channel their emotions constructively and break free from the cycle of abuse. Without insight and healing, DV victims will continue to spiral downward, and the impact can result in serious consequences. Let's examine some of the ways that emotional abuse can impact partners:

- **Epigenetics, Domestic Violence, and Depression**: A 2019 research study (Park, C.) connected domestic abuse to depression and found that ongoing emotional abuse creates changes to certain genes in the hypothalamic-pituitary-adrenal (HPA) axis, which is an area of the brain that's involved in the stress response. Another study (Ferrari, G. 2016) found that:

  Women DVA (domestic violence abuse) survivors who seek support from DVA services have recently experienced high levels of abuse, depression, anxiety, and especially PTSD. Clinicians need to be aware that patients presenting with mental health conditions or symptoms of depression or anxiety may be experiencing or have experienced DVA. The high psychological morbidity in this population means that trauma-informed psychological support is needed for survivors who seek support from DVA services.

  Chronic emotional abuse can affect how you see yourself in relationships and your increased tolerance toward certain behaviors. For women whose mothers and grandmothers were exposed to domestic violence, as was Keisha's experience, epigenetics can play an important role as well. Epigenetics refers to how your environment and the behavior of people in your environment impact you and affect your genes. A 2011 study (Radtke, K. M.) concluded:

  Stress during pregnancy, particularly from intimate partner violence (IPV), can change gene activity related to stress regulation in unborn children. Specifically, it increases the methylation of the GR gene, which can impact the child's mental health later in life. This highlights the importance of addressing IPV not only for the mother's health but also to protect the well-being of the child and opens new research paths into how stress affects future generations.

- **Trauma Bonding**: When a person has experienced long-term emotional abuse (or other types of abuse), eventually, they come to believe that their needs are not as important as others. When this mind state and mind story is set, trauma bonding can happen. As you have learned, trauma bonding is a condition where a negative bond occurs in an unhealthy relationship when a person develops a powerful attachment to a person who is destructive to them. When this unhealthy bond intensifies, the person begins to ignore their own needs and boundaries, makes excuses for their unhealthy partner, and often overcompensates while the abusive spouse or neglectful partner undercompensates. This pattern can exist for months, years, and even decades while the betrayed, abused, and traumatically bonded partner does all they can to sustain the relationship at any cost.

Many people who are in emotionally abusive relationships walk on eggshells, engage in people-pleasing, and have a very difficult time saying no, which further reinforces the trauma bond. The moment they begin to break free of the trauma bond—either by their own healing, due to an emergency such as the pandemic that Keisha and all of us went through, or because they must finally attend to themselves due to a life-threatening illness—the abuser will often vanish the moment they realize that they can no longer manipulate, shame, guilt, or abuse the victim. When the abuser's needs, demands, and dramas are not front and center, when the person being abused begins to set boundaries and limits, and when the abuser's tactics no longer work, they will abandon the relationship.

- **Traumatic Independence**: Ongoing emotional abuse and neglect make it very hard to trust other people in one's life. When you have been continuously yanked around and emotionally harmed, chronically blamed, physically assaulted, or historically let down by a significant other or loved ones—and if you've been victimized by abusive words, behaviors, and neglect—it is not surprising that you may feel uncertain about trusting yourself or others. Survivors often develop traumatic independence where they do not allow themselves to be vulnerable or rely on other people in any part of their lives. Traumatic independence is very different from resiliency as it leaves a traumatized person isolated and feeling as if they cannot trust another person or depend on anyone else to help them meet a need. The roots of traumatic independence are fear, sadness, resentment, indifference, wariness, detachment, and loneliness.

- **Low Self-Worth**: When a person has been verbally abused or emotionally neglected, this can eat away at one's self-worth. This eventually leads to feelings of hopelessness or worthlessness. Victims of emotional abuse, neglect, love bombing, gaslighting, trauma bonding, and the complex trauma resulting from intimate partner betrayal often share that they feel less deserving of love and respect than other people. They feel that somehow, they must prove their value in every relationship they have, even with friends and family members. Eventually, a person may withdraw from relationships to the point of isolation and loneliness, finally believing that they are destined to be alone, they cannot have a healthy relationship, the walls of protection must stay up, and they will never be loved in a healthy and respectful way. An internal question is often, *What is wrong with me?*

- **Transactional Relationships**: Survivors of abuse and toxic relationships sometimes share that the only people they feel will be friends with them are those they pay—such as hair stylists, housekeepers, yoga instructors, pet sitters, massage therapists, personal assistants—or friends who rely on them to borrow money, provide advice, encouragement, and support. These friends may also expect them to cover their extracurricular activities together, such as dinners, lunches, or vacations. It isn't that abuse survivors want to pay for friendships or love relationships; rather, it is a result of the trauma they have experienced. It is difficult for abuse survivors to believe that people will show up for them without something being given in return because, historically, those closest to them have taken advantage of their generosity and vulnerability without reciprocation and disappeared when they are in need. This dynamic is sometimes referred to as "fair-weather friendships." When the survivor begins to share their needs in a one-sided love relationship or friendship, they often find that if the connection is not based on mutual loving respect and the person they care about is not healthy, their needs go unmet. Their texts go unanswered, their invitations are not returned, and the nurturance, inclusion, love and support they freely give is taken for granted or not returned.

- **Self-Doubt**: Gaslighting is a hot topic on social media and in our world at large. It is also a topic and term that is often misunderstood. Gaslighting is not just about lying; rather, it is a deliberate, orchestrated, pre-mediated form of manipulative abuse. It can leave the person on the receiving end of this abuse questioning their own perception of reality or doubting their own thoughts and abilities. During our work together, Kiesha shared numerous experiences of being gaslit by Jamal, sometimes stating, "I felt as if I was going crazy! I would see or hear something with my own eyes and ears, and he'd deny it and spin a convincing story that left me believing I was the one to blame, or I was the paranoid or controlling one in our relationship."

Many victims of gaslighting struggle with identifying their feelings and trusting their instincts. They often question or blame themselves for not doing enough or not doing things just "right." Trusting our intuition and self-perception is crucial for survival, especially for women. While both men and women can be perpetrators of gaslighting, the men I work with in my practice who have been gaslighters are often shocked to realize that gaslighting is a severe form of abuse. When working with gaslighters, particularly those whose victims are women, I emphasize that one of the tragedies of this persistent abuse is that it leaves their female partners extremely vulnerable in a world that isn't always safe for women. This abuse erodes their female partners' ability to trust their instincts, making them more susceptible to harm by others.

- **Projected Shame Identification**: Emotional abusers are masters at projecting their own self loathing, shame, and insecurities onto their partner. This often results in the abused person feeling shame about parts of who they are. This includes their likes and dislikes, their goals and plans, their friends and family, the music they listen to, the books they read, the shows they watch, and the hobbies they enjoy. Many people who have survived intimate partner abuse share that they began to stifle or "deaden" parts of themselves, or they put off dreams or gave up activities they enjoyed to avoid feeling the shame they began to associate with people, places, and things they formerly enjoyed. This results in feeling as if they no longer know who they are or what or who they like. Keisha shared that she was previously passionate about practicing yoga and different forms of dance but stopped when Jamal ridiculed her activities and coaches and expressed jealousy over her dance instructor.

Not surprisingly, the unaddressed traumatic effects of emotional trauma can lead to mental health issues over time. These may include:

- Depression

- Anxiety

- Chronic shame

- Complex post-traumatic stress disorder (C-PTSD)

- Social anxiety

- Eating disorders

- Addictions (gambling, drugs, alcohol, shopping, media)

- Suicidal ideation or attempts at suicide

- Homicidal ideation

Working with a therapist can be an important first step toward healing; however, it is important to remember that therapy may not be easily available to everyone. This is especially true if a person is being financially abused and on a limited budget, comes from a background or culture that does not embrace therapy, belongs to a faith community that minimizes its benefits, or is a mental health professional who feels vulnerable and fearful of being judged. All these issues can impact a person's motivation to seek treatment and support. If you are struggling to find support, please refer to the resource section at the end of this book for free and low-cost options.

In addition to affecting mental health, prolonged emotional and intimate partner abuse can seriously impact physical health. Studies by Black (2011) and Barrios (2015) indicate that ongoing abuse can either trigger or worsen various health conditions. These include cardiovascular issues, chronic pain, gastrointestinal disorders, and other stress-related ailments, underscoring the widespread effects of sustained abuse on overall health.

During Keisha's sessions, she learned that domestic violence is not only physical abuse like slapping, shoving, punching, pinching, or yanking hair. DV is also categorized as emotional abuse, verbal abuse, sexual abuse, spiritual abuse, and financial abuse. For example, Keisha shared that she had always wanted to be married and have children but was afraid to marry or have children with Jamal due to his anger and lack of responsibility. In retaliation, Jamal would cruelly tell Keisha she was an "old dried-up spinster" and blame her for their lack of marrying or having children, all the while denying his culpability.

When Keisha would attempt to defend herself, and once again outline what needed to change for her to safely step into marriage and parenthood with Jamal, or tearfully ask that he not speak to her in that way, Keisha shared that Jamal would often smirk, shrug his shoulders, mimic her tears, yell, or taunt her by saying, "The truth hurts old lady. Better get pregnant with me before your eggs dry up and you end up alone because no one else will want you when you are past your prime!"

During our early work, it was difficult for Keisha to understand the devastating impact of the emotional abuse she had endured. A breakthrough happened when she recalled several incidents of physical abuse that she had not previously identified as domestic violence, and we targeted these in a series of Eye Movement Desensitization and

Reprocessing (EMDR) sessions. EMDR is a therapeutic approach designed to help individuals process and heal from traumatic memories. On one occasion, Jamal had kicked her purse out of her hand, injuring her finger for "talking back" to him. Another time, he shoved her into her car in a fit of rage for dancing with a male friend at a wedding they were attending and then drove recklessly while drunk.

She shared an argument where Jamal was intoxicated and started following her around, pushing his chest into her back as she was cleaning and taunting her. When she brushed him aside with the broom she was using and attempted to lock herself in the bedroom, he banged open the door and slammed her to the ground, injuring her elbow, "Jamal was like a crazy man, screaming that I had hit him with the broom, furious that I had called him out of his name, and he became more enraged when I told him to leave me alone."

Another incident occurred where Jamal shouted in her face while waving a burning cigarette an inch from her eyes, singeing her eyelashes when she disagreed with him, and yet another time where he chased her into the bathroom, punched the door open, pushed her into a wall, held her neck, and screamed in her face. Several other incidents surfaced in her memory that included countless acts of throwing objects, destroying items, and kicking or punching holes in walls, as well as threatening her safety. Keisha quietly stated, "I never wanted to think of myself as an abused woman. I pride myself on being a woman of intelligence, strength, and dignity, an honest person who makes good choices in life. My mother did not raise me like this.

"Mama and my aunts lived with an abusive father who beat my grandmother, and my mom vowed that she would never allow herself to go through what her mother had endured. Mama bravely left my own father when he hit her early in their relationship. She always told me to walk away if a man was a user or abuser. I know she had her concerns about Jamal over the years, but I hid the worst parts from her and from everyone. I guess I buried his abuse so deeply because it was too difficult to face reality—a reality that felt like I was too old or too damaged to find someone who would treat me right. I just can't believe I allowed this to happen."

To her credit, Keisha courageously dedicated herself to understanding this cycle. As she continued to peel back the layers of what had contributed to the trauma bond and took the difficult but necessary steps to heal, it was a joy to see the wind come back under her wings little by little. Each week, she excitedly pointed out various passages in the books, mindfulness-based activities, clinical exercises, and the articles and videos I assigned as part of her counseling. When doing so, she often shared, "This was another 'aha' moment for me, Mari!"

About eight months into our work, during an especially vulnerable session, Keisha bravely explained that though she had not personally struggled with addiction, she had come to realize: "Jamal was my addiction, plain and simple. I was trauma-bonded to him, and I am a classic love addict, an abuse survivor, with features of codependency steeped in complex trauma. However, I refuse to be that forever. I know some women hate the term 'codependent,' but as I continue to heal, I see it as a trauma response that I learned early in my life—a coping mechanism that kept me stuck in gear and trauma bonded in this unsafe relationship that almost killed me. I did nothing to deserve this type of treatment, but now that I know better, I will do better for myself. I am outgrowing and healing those labels that were placed on me and that I placed on myself for too long, even before Jamal came into my life."

Trauma Bonding and the Hijacked Brain

Keisha was correct: Trauma bonding does indeed feel like an addiction, and for some individuals, there may be elements of codependency present. While complex trauma, love addiction, and codependent traits can create the "perfect" recipe for trauma bonding, it is vitally important to note that codependency is not always present. Equally important to clarify is that even if codependency and love addiction are present, it does not mean the person who is being wounded is a "co-addict" or that they are responsible in any way for their partner or spouse's abusive words, behaviors, destructive actions, or their addictions. Let me underscore once again that no partner or spouse is ever responsible, in any way, for the addict's or abuser's actions. Ever.

I hope we can agree that "co-addict" is a revolting and dangerous label that is intended to blame and shame the person who has been abused, deceived, and traumatized. People who struggle with love addiction, trauma bonding, and codependency traits are *not* co-addicts. They are traumatized individuals who deserve compassion, support, information, and tools to help integrate and heal their trauma so they can move forward. As a therapist who has dedicated my career to helping people heal from complex trauma, my hope is that we can strike the term "co-addict" from our clinical vocabulary once and for all.

Additionally, codependency is vastly different from being interdependent. In healthy relationships, human beings practice interdependency. This is a process where both people in the relationship give and take, encourage, and support one another with empathy and boundaries, where both people are committed to reciprocity and the health of the relationship. Interdependency makes space for each person to lean into the support of the other when need be, depending upon who is requiring the support at any given time. The heavy lifting is not on the shoulders of one or the other in a healthy, interdependent relationship. If we go back to the example of the teeter-totter, interdependency is when both people are willingly working together to safely support each other and the relationship.

Conversely, one of the key features of codependency in romantic relationships is feeling an overwhelming sense of responsibility for the significant other's issues—often to the point of caretaking. Infants, children, the elderly, injured individuals, the infirmed, or the vulnerable require caretaking to some degree. However, capable adults should not require this level of care. Care*giving*—the practice of extending loving support with boundaries—is not the same as codependent caretaking. When caretaking exists as a regular part of an adult love relationship, people who are prone to codependency eventually lose a sense of themselves as their identity becomes more deeply entwined with the person whom they are in a relationship with. In the worst-case scenarios, this enmeshment increases to the point of losing other important relationships in their life.

In the case of Keisha and Jamal, Keisha lost touch with her own value and worth. Her dreams and goals slipped away or were put on the back burner, and friendships faded away as she attended to Jamal's relentless needs and mood swings, week after week, month after month, year after year, for a decade. Her life was organized around his schedule and needs. Like many women and people who have experienced intimate partner abuse, love bombing, betrayal bonding, and gaslighting, over time, Keisha felt resentment, confusion, shame, hopelessness, and despair when her efforts did not help Jamal grow, change, or improve their relationship.

As her light dimmed, Jamal became more abusive, criticizing Keisha for being too controlling, too nagging, too serious, or not being "enough" for him. As she strived to show Jamal that he could learn to live a more productive and responsible life and that she and their relationship were worth the effort, he undermined her attempts in big and small ways, sometimes by self-sabotage and sometimes by sabotaging Keisha. This is called "leveling" the person down rather than leveling up. It was clear that Jamal had his own unresolved trauma at the root of his behaviors, and life likely felt too overwhelming and frightening for Jamal to step into adulthood. Additionally, as you will learn in the chapters ahead, Jamal likely had a disorganized attachment style, which resulted in Keisha believing that she had to do all the "adulting" in their relationship, as well as all of the emotional, relational, and financial heavy lifting. This does not excuse Jamal; rather, it provides insight into his specific challenges.

As the years slipped by, Keisha discovered that Jamal did not experience gratitude for her support. Instead, he experienced increased fear, guilt, resentment, and shame. Fear because he did not feel adequate as a man or a partner and was fearful about being abandoned by his primary support person. Guilt because he understood that he was relying too heavily on Keisha. Shame due to his verbal and emotional abuse and his uncertainty about how to manage his own life and responsibilities. Resentment in being reliant on Keisha's support.

Keisha shared in one of our later sessions: "Mari, I felt as if I was taking on a mother role. I recall the very moment when I no longer felt sexually attracted to Jamal. I had just paid off his car repair bill the week prior, and a few days later, he needed help with his rent. When I sighed in frustration, letting him know that I could not keep bailing him out as I had my own bills to pay and was hemorrhaging money helping him, he went into a sulk, reminding me that I had just received a promotion and raise. When I reminded him that I had put in many years of professional effort for this career advancement and increase in income, this led to a tantrum where he began lecturing me on my 'extravagant' spending because I get my hair and nails done regularly and attend a workout class twice a week. He felt as if that money was owed to him.

"I explained that I worked hard and that these were normal self-care expenses. I even went as far as to say that if he stopped spending all his time and money on video games, smoking weed, vaping, junk food, and looking at porn, then maybe he could get his life in order—something a mother would say. Naturally, he blew up at my daring to speak the truth. When his rage did not work initially, he resorted to guilt tactics, saying, "I hope you are ready for me to move in with you when they kick me out of here because that's what will happen."

By this time, he'd been trying to pick a fight for hours, and I was exhausted and worn down. I had an early meeting, my head was throbbing, and my stomach was in knots, so once again, I succumbed to his pressure and wrote a check for his rent. Later that night, he wanted sex, but for the first time, I found myself repulsed by him. At one point, he was suckling my nipple with his head cradled on my chest like a baby, and I pushed him off me in total disgust. During that time, I stopped being sexual with Jamal and my feelings for him began to decrease. Even so, I wasn't able to completely walk away due to these overwhelming feelings of responsibility for him, especially during the pandemic, his health crisis, and his father's death."

Though there were many setbacks along the way as he pulled out all his usual manipulations, Keisha, now a year into therapy and armed with information and insight, made steady progress. Inch by inch, step by step, with a one-day-at-a-time approach, she eventually found her way back to herself, back to safety, and back to sanity. Part of her work was to decide that this was not the relationship she wanted to be in and that she was unwilling to be manipulated by a person who was supposed to be her partner.

Understanding Narcissistic Sadistic Supply

In the aftermath of emotional abuse, survivors often struggle to make sense of behaviors that seem intentionally cruel, manipulative, or destabilizing. One concept that may bring clarity is "narcissistic sadistic supply"—a term used to describe the emotional and psychological "fuel" that some individuals with narcissistic and sadistic traits extract from the harm they cause others.

Let's break this down. Narcissistic supply refers to the attention, validation, or admiration that individuals with narcissistic tendencies rely on to sustain their self-worth. Narcissists rely on others to provide a sense of self-worth, and this can lead to exploitative, controlling, and emotionally abusive behaviors in close relationships (Campbell & Miller, 2011). This supply can come from praise and admiration—but also from control, fear, or even chaos. However, when sadism is layered in, the supply doesn't just come from being seen or admired—it comes from watching others suffer, feel confused, or lose confidence. For these individuals, the pain or distress of others affirms their dominance, and that sense of power becomes addictive.

In Keisha and Jamal's relationship, this dynamic is painfully clear. Jamal consistently lies, belittles Keisha, gaslights her, and has been physically and verbally abusive. He avoids accountability and shifts all financial and emotional responsibility onto Keisha. When she tries to speak up, he turns the conversation around to make her doubt herself. When she struggles with mental health challenges because of his abuse, and eventual physical issues and illness, he discards her and blames her, making himself the victim. This isn't just manipulation—it's emotional sadism. Jamal seems to draw energy and control from Keisha's confusion and pain. The more depleted she becomes, the more powerful he feels.

It's important to note that terms like "narcissism" can be overused or misapplied in casual conversation. Not every person who is self-absorbed or difficult is narcissistic, and not every narcissist is abusive. True narcissistic personality disorder (NPD) is complex, and there are many variations and traits that exist on a spectrum. However, when narcissistic behaviors are consistently coupled with emotional cruelty or abusive control—especially in an intimate relationship—the resulting harm can be deep and long-lasting.

When survivors like Keisha begin to name and understand these patterns, it can help untangle the trauma bond that often keeps them feeling stuck, confused, or even responsible for their abuser's behavior. Gaining language and understanding around dynamics like narcissistic sadistic supply is one step in reclaiming clarity, power, and self-worth.

It took the better part of a year for Keisha to break the toxic bonds that once felt impossible to free herself from. An important part of the work was giving herself permission to truly and deeply not only care for herself but to practice that self-care daily. In addition to regular process work in our counseling sessions, Keisha responded well to EMDR therapy and mindfulness-based exercises, especially those that focused on moving back to caring for herself.

Keisha also enjoyed practicing mindfulness-based strategies and exercises that assisted her trauma bond healing. Journaling, breath work, prayer, yoga, meditative walks in nature, music meditations, dance, sound baths, and guided imagery were the main tools that she often drew from. These tools are especially helpful for people who are trying to heal a trauma bond and end an abusive relationship.

· · · · ·

Recognizing and healing from trauma bonding can be a difficult and complex process, but it's essential to approach the work with compassion, patience, and self-care. Understanding the dynamics of trauma bonding allows you to differentiate between healthy attachment and harmful patterns that may be holding you back.

Before moving on to the assessments, the mindfulness guided imagery, and the art exercise on the following pages, here are some potential indicators of trauma bonding within a relationship, along with supportive antidotes to help you on your healing journey. It's important to remember that all relationships have their ups and downs, and experiencing deep and abiding love for your partner during difficult times is not inherently negative. The goal is to identify when these feelings are intertwined with unhealthy behaviors and patterns that keep you chained in an abusive marriage or partnership. As you read through, feel free to check any that resonate with your experience.

Trauma Bond Indicators

☐ **Intense Emotional Attachment**: If you have been love bombed, you might experience an immediate and overwhelming connection to the other person, perhaps even believing that you've known them in a past life or are living out a timeless fairytale romance. This bond can intensify rapidly, especially if your love interest engages in grooming behaviors—like noticing your tastes and preferences, not as a way of building a healthy bond but rather to manipulate your emotions. They may begin to scan your environment to see what books you read or pay special attention to the offhand comments you make, which they then use to their advantage. For example, let's say you are someone who loves astronomy and often wears jewelry symbolic of your interest, and suddenly, they discuss a degree that they have in this field that cannot be verified. Or you may have a special animal that means a lot to you, such as a tiger or elephant, and they share that they lived in Africa as a missionary, yet there is no physical evidence to support this, or the details don't align. Perhaps your faith is a top priority, and you have books that reflect this, or you mention your interest in Italy. Suddenly, your new love interest shares that they believe that you were together in a past life or that God has told them you are the one. Or they reveal that they are a special attaché to the Italian government, but this must be held as a secret for your safety. Healthy relationships express interests in the other without using the information to manipulate or deceive. When a new partner is attempting to groom you, this can lead you to "fall" deeply in love, even if the intensity feels disproportionate to the actual pace of the relationship. While it's important to respect those who believe in mystical connections, and not every story is to be doubted, it's equally vital to stay aware of when emotions might be clouding your judgment.

☐ **Overvaluing**: You might refer to this person as "your one and only true love," "your twin flame you cannot live without," or "your long-lost soulmate who has saved you." While valuing and loving your partner is healthy and positive, overvaluing to the point of idealizing them can distort your sense of reality. I call this the Romeo and Juliet syndrome—where you believe life wouldn't be worth living without this person by your side. We explore this in depth in the love addiction chapter of this workbook.

☐ **Ignoring Red Flags**: Ignoring red flags in a spouse or dating partner—such as improbable or outlandish stories that are difficult to verify (like claims of being an undercover government spy), inconsistencies in their schedule, reluctance to introduce you to friends or family, or avoidance of meeting your own circle—can lead to significant isolation and emotional harm. Other red flags include a partner requiring you to keep special secrets for them—such as hiding their identity, warning you not to tell others that they have children, are unemployed, have been to prison, or are in a gang—or threatening that revealing their secret may have harmful or dangerous consequences for you or your loved ones. Additional red flags include asking you to hold money, weapons, or drugs, engage in illegal activities, or conceal their addiction. These warning signs often indicate deception, manipulative plans, a hidden agenda, or a lack of genuine commitment, and overlooking them can result in deepening involvement in a relationship built on dishonesty and manipulation.

☐ **Cognitive Dissonance**: Cognitive dissonance in intimate relationships happens when a person's beliefs and actions don't match, causing internal conflict. To reduce this discomfort, they may try to justify their negative behaviors instead of changing them. For example, a partner who believes they are always right might constantly dismiss their partner's feelings or concerns, reinforcing their belief and causing ongoing conflict. This pattern is especially common in unhealthy or emotionally abusive relationships, where conflicting values or behaviors create tension and discomfort, particularly in relationships with narcissists, who may manipulate or dismiss their partner's reality.

Imagine a person, we will call Dennis, who sees themselves as a supportive partner. However, they often criticize and belittle their significant other, Ann, when she expresses emotions or sets boundaries. Deep down, Dennis feels uneasy about Ann's behavior because it doesn't align with Dennis's self-image.

To reduce this discomfort, instead of acknowledging the harm he is causing and making changes, Dennis justifies his actions by telling himself:

- "Ann is impatient and controlling."

- "I'm just being honest—it's for her own good."

- "If she really loved me, she would just accept me for who I am and wouldn't get upset so easily."

By rationalizing his behavior instead of taking responsibility, Dennis avoids the discomfort of admitting his actions don't match his values. Over time, this pattern creates emotional distance and conflict, leaving Ann feeling unheard and invalidated. This is especially common in toxic or emotionally abusive relationships, where one partner manipulates the other's reality to maintain control.

☐ **Not Vetting**: It's essential to vet your new love interest with trusted friends and family and be open to their feedback, even if it's not what you want to hear. Just as we carefully choose doctors, lawyers, therapists, hair stylists, and mechanics, we should also seek the guidance of those who know us best when it comes to relationships. While vetting can be difficult for those who do not have family members, such as former foster care adults or only children who are orphaned, it is still vitally important. Cutting off important friendships or relationships because you don't like the feedback can lead to isolation and poor decision-making. After all, the people who care about you most often see things you might miss.

☐ **Confirmation Bias**: Confirmation bias in a love-addicted, trauma-bonded, or unhealthy relationship can be particularly dangerous, as it reinforces destructive patterns and blinds you to red flags. When you're emotionally invested in someone, you may unconsciously seek out information or behaviors that confirm your idealized view of the relationship while ignoring or rationalizing warning signs. This bias can lead you to overlook issues like manipulation, dishonesty, loneliness, or emotional unavailability, convincing yourself that the relationship is perfect or destined, even when it's harmful. Over time, this distorted perception can trap you in a cycle of dependency and denial, making it increasingly difficult to recognize the relationship's toxic nature and break free.

☐ **Heavy Lifting**: You carry the weight of keeping the relationship going. That may be financially, socially, intimately, or in other ways, such as household chores, child rearing, managing family gatherings, vacation planning, finances, and so forth. You do most of what it takes to keep the relationship afloat, your requests for support are ignored, or empty promises are repeatedly broken.

☐ **Overlooking Negatives**: In the throes of intense emotions or infatuation, it can be incredibly challenging to recognize or admit to the harmful aspects of the person or the relationship. You might find yourself downplaying or ignoring a pattern of behaviors that would normally raise concern, convincing yourself that they are minor flaws or things you can "fix" over time. Perhaps you accept "crumbs," such as very little time together or inconsistent communication. This tendency to overlook negatives often stems from a desire to preserve the idealized image you've built around the relationship, leading you to make excuses for actions that, in reality, are damaging. As a result, you may miss critical warning signs, such as emotional manipulation, dishonesty, or even abusive behavior, ultimately trapping yourself in an unhealthy dynamic that erodes your well-being and self-worth.

☐ **Defending Harmful Behavior**: When deeply emotionally attached or invested in a relationship, you might find yourself justifying or defending the other person's actions, even when those actions are clearly hurtful. This often occurs because you're trying to maintain the relationship at all costs, convincing yourself that their behavior is understandable or that they didn't mean to cause harm. You might tell yourself that their outbursts of anger are just a result of stress or mental illness or that their controlling tendencies stem from love and concern. You may excuse words and actions that do not align, or accept stories that seem improbable or deceptive. This defense mechanism can also manifest as taking the blame for their harmful actions, believing that if you were different or acted a certain way, they wouldn't behave this way. Over time, this pattern of rationalizing or excusing harmful behavior can erode your self-esteem and cloud your judgment, making it difficult to see the relationship for what it truly is and further entrenching you in a cycle of emotional dependency and abuse.

☐ **Going Into Debt**: This occurs when you start spending beyond your own budget to support or rescue your romantic partner from the consequences of their financial decisions or irresponsibility. You may feel compelled to cover their expenses, pay off their debts, or fund their lifestyle, even at the expense of your own financial stability. You may also feel pressured to spend money out of your budget on makeup, skincare, and clothing in order to look and dress exactly how your partner or spouse prefers. These patterns can quickly spiral out of control, leaving you in significant debt and deepening your emotional and financial entanglement in an unhealthy relationship. Conversely, if your abusive love interest helps you financially or in other ways, leaving can feel frightening if you have come to rely on this type of support.

- [ ] **Push/Pull**: Your feelings may conflict at times, where one moment you feel angry and ready to leave, then suddenly feel compassion for your abuser, followed by shame, fear, and guilt. This back-and-forth tug of war can cloud your judgment and keep you tethered to an unhealthy relationship. When considering leaving your spouse or partner, you may find yourself cycling through these feelings—fear of being alone, worry that you're too old or have too many children to make it on your own, concern that you have too much "baggage" to find someone new, or a sense of obligation to stay out of duty or commitment. Guilt might also weigh heavily on you, especially if you feel responsible for your partner's well-being or worry about how your departure will affect them. These powerful emotions can create an internal struggle that distorts your perspective, making it difficult to make decisions that are in your best interest.

- [ ] **Feeling Trapped**: Even when faced with negative consequences, you may feel stuck or unable to leave the relationship. This sense of entrapment can stem from a variety of factors, such as emotional dependency, fear of the unknown, or a belief that you have no better options. You might convince yourself that things will improve or that you're somehow obligated to stay despite the harm being done. This feeling of being trapped can be paralyzing, leading you to endure a relationship that continually undermines your happiness and well-being rather than seeking a healthier and more fulfilling path forward. This is especially true if your abusive or avoidant significant other is dealing with a mental health issue, an addiction, or an illness.

- [ ] **Enduring Harm**: You might find yourself tolerating harmful behavior simply to keep the relationship intact, even when it's detrimental to your well-being. This can stem from a desire to prove to yourself that you made the right choice in your partner or show your friends and family that their concerns are unfounded. You may also endure the harm to avoid appearing foolish, particularly if you've experienced failed or unhealthy relationships in the past. The fear of admitting that the relationship isn't what you hoped it would be can drive you to stay, even when the cost to your emotional, mental, or physical health is high. This pattern of enduring harm can lead to a cycle of self-denial and further entrenchment in a toxic relationship, making it increasingly difficult to break free and seek a healthier future.

- [ ] **Fear of Consequences**: In many cases, individuals remain in abusive relationships because the abuser wields a multifaceted arsenal of threats that deeply undermine their sense of safety and autonomy. Abusers often use the fear of retaliatory actions—such as threatening to take away their children, inflicting harm on cherished pets, committing physical violence, ending their life by suicide, or spreading harmful rumors—to maintain control and discourage any attempt to leave. This calculated intimidation creates an environment where the victim perceives that escaping the relationship could lead to even more devastating consequences, not only for themselves but also for those they love. Over time, this persistent fear can erode self-confidence and foster a feeling of entrapment, making the idea of leaving seem not only frightening but nearly impossible.

☐ **Faith-Based Pressure**: Your faith or spiritual beliefs might compel you to stay in a relationship, even when it's unhealthy, because you believe that divorce is a sin or that leaving would bring judgment from your faith community. You may fear disappointing your family who share your religious values or worry that you would let down God or your higher power by ending the relationship. This pressure can create an overwhelming sense of obligation, making it difficult to prioritize your well-being and recognize that staying in a harmful situation may not align with the deeper principles of love, respect, and self-care that many faiths also espouse.

☐ **Reliance Based on Specific Needs**: You may find yourself heavily relying on your trauma-bonded spouse or partner due to specific circumstances, such as financial security, isolation from friends or family, a physical disability, chronic illness, age, loneliness, or a mental health challenge. This dependency can deepen the trauma bond, making it even harder to recognize or break free from the unhealthy dynamics at play. When your support system is limited, the relationship can become your primary, or even sole, source of emotional and practical support, which can further entrench you in the cycle of trauma bonding.

☐ **Trauma Blocking**: Keisha was caught in a trauma-bonded relationship with Jamal. Part of the trauma bond was her unconscious use of trauma blocking to avoid the pain, doubt, and fear her relationship stirred up. She often immersed herself in work, staying late at the office or taking on extra projects to occupy her mind. Outside of work, she shared that she would scroll endlessly through social media or shop online and run errands for hours at a time, seeking a temporary escape in the rush of new purchases. Additionally, she ignored the red flags in her relationship, focusing on the rare moments of connection with Jamal to dismiss the more painful realities. Trauma blocking like this, whether through busyness, digital distraction, denial, or substance abuse, is common for people in traumatic situations, as it temporarily eases emotional pain without directly addressing it.

Did you notice yourself checking several, or even all, of the boxes above? Or perhaps you found yourself resisting, making excuses, feeling overwhelmed, or tuning out while reading through them? Be gentle with yourself—untangling the complexities of trauma bonding is not an easy process. Take a few moments to practice rigorous yet compassionate honesty with yourself. In the space provided, I invite you to reflect on what is working in your relationship, what isn't, and what resonated with you as you went through the previous list above.

> ## Self-Honesty and Reflection Exercise

_____

_____

_____

_____

_____

_____

Supportive Countermeasures

Now that we have outlined some of the indicators of trauma bonding and you've taken some mindful time to reflect, you are gaining awareness that addressing these challenging dynamics in a relationship requires substantial effort. You've likely spent so much of your life holding things together, carrying responsibilities that often weren't yours alone. You've been the pillar others lean on and the rock in your relationship, yet rarely have you had someone to lean on in return. You've been so strong, even when you craved the freedom to rest, let go, and feel safe enough to be vulnerable. Imagine finding that—someone whose loyalty, compassion, and energy meet yours, who's as committed and steady as you've been for that person and others. Imagine meeting that person in yourself!

You've walked long paths alone, bearing the weight of broken promises and disappointments, yet here you are, moving forward with resilience. Know that your needs, the care and respect you give so openly, deserve to be reciprocated. You don't have to keep excusing or diminishing what you expect in return. It's time to allow yourself to expect the same love, dedication, and honesty you offer. You *are* worthy of genuine connection, of a bond that meets you where you are.

By focusing on supportive countermeasures, you can begin to break free from harmful patterns, regain your sense of self, and cultivate healthier, more balanced relationships. These strategies involve setting boundaries, increasing self-care, seeking outside perspectives, expanding your support network, reconnecting with supportive loved ones, and practicing self-compassion, all of which are crucial steps toward mindfulness-based healing and personal growth.

It is important to note that these countermeasures are designed for individuals in destructive relationships who feel uncertain about how to heal or find a way forward. Let's explore some supportive strategies that can help if you're navigating challenging or abusive relationship dynamics. These practices aim to build your strength, clarify your boundaries, and empower you to prioritize your well-being, whether you're working toward healing within the relationship or preparing to break free.

Intense Emotional Attachment

Supportive Countermeasure: Slow down and take a step back to evaluate the relationship with a clear mind. No matter if you've been in the relationship for weeks, months, or even years, can you pull the lens back to gain perspective? Engage in mindfulness practices to ground yourself and keep emotions in check. Consult with trusted friends or a therapist to gain an outside perspective. Remind yourself that true love takes time to build and that a healthy relationship grows at a natural pace without the need for immediate intensity.

Overvaluing

Supportive Countermeasure: Practice self-reflection and challenge the pedestal you've placed your partner on. Acknowledge that no one is perfect and allow space for imperfections. Consider journaling about the relationship's positives and negatives to maintain a balanced perspective. Remember that a healthy partnership is built on mutual respect, not on idealization or dependency.

Ignoring Red Flags

Supportive Countermeasure: Trust your intuition and listen to the concerns of those you trust. Make a list of any red flags, unlikely stories, illegal activities, requests to keep secrets, or concerns you may be dismissing or excusing. Take the time to discuss them with a therapist, close family member, or trusted friend. Don't dismiss inconsistencies or behaviors that make you uncomfortable—these can be early signs of deeper issues. Equally important is to take into consideration the concerns of trusted loved ones. It's crucial to face these concerns head-on rather than sweeping them under the rug, blaming those closest to you, or cutting people off to protect your relationship at all costs.

Cognitive Dissonance

Supportive Countermeasure: Acknowledge the discomfort that comes with conflicting beliefs or values and confront it directly. Practice cognitive-behavioral techniques to challenge and reframe distorted thinking, such as identifying negative self-talk and replacing it with affirmations or recognizing when you're catastrophizing and instead focusing on more balanced, realistic outcomes. For example, if you find yourself thinking, "I can't live without this person," you might reframe it as "I am capable of building a fulfilling life on my own." Or, if you believe, "I'm not good enough for anyone else," try replacing that thought with, "I have inherent worth and deserve a healthy, loving relationship." Seek out supportive resources, groups, and information to help realign your beliefs with healthy relationship behaviors. It's important to address the underlying issues causing dissonance rather than allowing them to perpetuate unhealthy thought patterns.

Not Vetting

Supportive Countermeasure: Make a conscious effort to include your trusted friends and family at the start of and throughout your relationship. This does not mean that they must be a part of every decision or included in every social gathering, as that is not healthy either. For those who deal with social anxiety or anxiety in general or those who are introverts, this can be challenging. However, as stated earlier, it is a very important antidote. Please be open to the feedback of a trusted friend or family member, even if it's not what you want to hear. Recognize that others who love you may see red flags you miss due to your emotional involvement. Use their helpful insights, which are different from hurtful opinions, as a valuable tool to ensure your relationship is healthy and grounded in reality.

Confirmation Bias

Supportive Countermeasure: Actively seek out information and perspectives that challenge your idealized view of the relationship. Reflect on the reality of your partner's behavior rather than just what you want to believe. Consider journaling to track instances where you may have overlooked warning signs. This does not mean that you must stand in a place of suspicion or paranoia; rather, practice grounded awareness with yourself and trust your gut. Staying aware of your bias can help you make more informed decisions about your relationship.

Heavy Lifting

Supportive Countermeasure: Assess the balance of responsibilities in your relationship. Communicate openly with your partner about the need for shared effort and mutual support. Set boundaries and agree to share tasks to ensure you're not shouldering the entire burden. A healthy relationship is a partnership, not a one-person effort. If your partner or spouse refuses to support you in this way, ask yourself if this is something that can be addressed with a therapist or an objective third party. If your partner requires you to do all the heavy lifting in most areas of your relationship, seek out individual support to address why you feel you must overcompensate to be loved by a person who is chronically undercompensating.

Overlooking Negatives

Supportive Countermeasure: Practice self-awareness and honesty about the relationship's challenges. Engage in regular self-reflection and seek outside perspectives to avoid making excuses for harmful, manipulative, controlling, inconsistent, or deceptive behavior. Consider writing down specific instances where you've overlooked issues and discuss them with a trusted friend or therapist. Be honest about what you have lost in this relationship such as money, self respect, peace of mind, friends, hobbies and other things. Confronting these negatives is crucial to maintaining your self honesty, self-worth and well-being.

Defending Harmful Behavior

Supportive Countermeasure: Recognize the tendency to justify or excuse harmful behavior and take a step back to evaluate the situation objectively. Seek support from a therapist or trusted friends who can help you see the relationship more clearly. Practice assertiveness and set boundaries to protect yourself from further harm. Remember that defending hurtful actions only perpetuates the cycle of abuse and emotional dependency. If you are experiencing violence of any kind in your relationship or feel that your life is in danger, call an emergency team, leave immediately, and reach out for support. Remember, you are not to blame for their abusive words and actions. We have provided helpful information in the resource section of this book.

Going Into Debt

Supportive Countermeasure: Set clear financial boundaries and communicate them openly with your partner. Prioritize your own financial stability and avoid taking on your partner's financial burdens. If you feel pressured to spend beyond your means, seek advice from a financial advisor or mentor. A healthy relationship should support, not compromise, your financial well-being.

Push/Pull Syndrome

Supportive Countermeasure: Acknowledge the emotional pressures you're facing and give yourself permission to prioritize your needs and well-being. Seek therapy or a support group to explore these feelings and develop strategies to overcome them. Practice self-compassion and remind yourself it's okay to make decisions that are best for you, even if they're difficult. Breaking free from the back-and-forth agonizing cycle allows you to make choices that align with your true desires and values.

Feeling Trapped

Supportive Countermeasure: Explore your options and regain a sense of control over your life. Recognize that feeling trapped is often a result of emotional or psychological manipulation, where your partner may undermine your confidence, isolate you from support systems, or make you feel dependent on them for your well-being. This manipulation can distort your sense of reality, making it difficult to see a way out or to believe that you deserve better. A solution begins with acknowledging that these feelings are not a reflection of your actual situation but rather a result of the control exerted by the abuser. Start by reaching out to a trusted friend, therapist, or support group to regain perspective and build a plan for regaining your independence. Taking small, deliberate steps to reconnect with your support network and rebuild your self-esteem can help you break free from the cycle of manipulation and move toward a healthier life.

Enduring Harm

Supportive Countermeasure: Reflect on the reasons you're enduring harm and challenge the beliefs that keep you stuck. Remind yourself you are not to blame, and you can gain the help you need to leave. Practice self-compassion and give yourself permission to prioritize your well-being over the relationship. It's essential to remember that enduring harm is not a testament to your strength but a signal that it's time to seek a healthier path. Consider developing a safety plan or exit strategy if you feel unable to leave or you are in danger. A safety plan often includes identifying a trusted friend or family member or a church or shelter that can provide support and a safe place to go. Keep important documents, medication, a phone charger, spare keys, glasses, cash, a packed bag, and emergency contacts in an easily accessible and out-of-sight location. When the time is right, leave quickly and reach out for professional help to ensure your ongoing safety. Empower yourself by focusing on small steps you can take to regain independence and move toward a healthier, more fulfilling future.

Faith-Based Pressure

Supportive Countermeasure: Reflect on your faith or spiritual beliefs and consider how they align with your current relationship. Seek counsel from a spiritual advisor or therapist who can help you explore these pressures without judgment. Remember that many faiths also emphasize love, respect, and self-care, and staying in a harmful situation may not align with these deeper principles. It's important to find a balance that honors both your spiritual beliefs and well-being. Set boundaries with people, even those who mean well, when they offer advice that feels shaming or judgmental.

Reliance Based on Specific Needs

Supportive Countermeasure: Acknowledge that your reliance on your partner, who may also act as your caretaker, may be amplified by your specific needs, such as isolation, physical disability, chronic illness, or mental health challenges. While it's natural to seek support from your partner, it's important to ensure that this reliance doesn't deepen unhealthy dynamics. Start by expanding your support network—reach out to local community groups, online support communities, or a therapist or doctor who can help you build connections and reduce isolation or over-dependence. Explore resources and services that cater to your specific needs, enabling you to regain a sense of independence. Empower yourself by gradually increasing your self-sufficiency in manageable ways, and remember that a healthy relationship should enhance your well-being, not exacerbate your vulnerabilities.

Trauma Blocking

Supportive Countermeasure: A supportive countermeasure for those who are dealing with trauma blocking includes gradually creating space to acknowledge and process emotions in safe, manageable ways. Instead of blocking or avoiding feelings, you might start with small moments of mindful reflection, perhaps setting aside a few minutes daily to journal your thoughts or feelings, even if they're difficult. Engaging in supportive therapy or life coaching can also help you explore challenging feelings and identify healthy coping strategies, fostering self-awareness without judgment. Additionally, reconnecting with compassionate friends or family members who understand your situation and help you feel supported without judgment can provide grounding and reinforce your capacity to confront and process your lived experiences. These small steps can help one replace trauma blocking with healthier ways to navigate the emotional landscape, making you less reliant on avoidance mechanisms.

Art Exercise—Spider Web

The following web captures the concepts we have just walked through, the indicators of trauma bonding and abuse, and countermeasures.

Now, take a few minutes to complete the exercise by adding your own words that best represent your current challenges. A visual representation can be helpful in highlighting indicators specific to your situation:

Before continuing to the next sections of this chapter, I invite you to take a few moments to journal about your thoughts and feelings. This information may feel like a lot to process, so approach it with kindness toward yourself. Pay attention to what resonates with you and what feels difficult—each emotion holds a meaningful message worth exploring.

Additionally, consider any small steps you're ready to take in the coming week to support the countermeasure that spoke to you. This could be finding a therapist, reaching out to a trusted friend, sharing a concern with a loved one, setting a boundary, or creating a safety plan. Use the space below to note any steps or realizations that have surfaced. Can you think of supportive actions that will help you move forward in your healing?

_____

_____

_____

_____

_____

_____

_____

Mindfulness Healing Part I:
Preparation, Assessment, and Script
for Guided Imagery Exercise

Important Safety Tips for Therapists, Facilitators, and Healing Individuals

Environment Consideration and Tips: It can be helpful to "set the stage" prior to a guided imagery exercise. For example, consider the lighting—is it too bright or too low? Another helpful step is putting phones on silent. Also, think about outside distractions, such as barking dogs, traffic, and other interruptions. If possible, minimize outside noises the best that you can. Finally, some individuals like having a blanket or pillow to hold, or you may enjoy diffusing essential oils to support deeper relaxation if there are no allergy concerns. While mindfulness-based guided imagery is not hypnosis, it can be helpful to prepare your environment prior to beginning the guided imagery exercise.

Voice Prosody: An additional gentle reminder is to be aware of your voice prosody. Prosody refers to the rhythm and melody of the voice, including intonation, stress, and pauses. Speaking in a softer tone and slower cadence than your normal speaking voice is useful in supporting the guided imagery practice. If you typically speak more rapidly or loudly, it will take some practice to slow down and modulate your voice.

Diversity Considerations: Consider the client's culture, age, race, physical differences (such as hearing loss), gender and orientation, and other unique experiences that may invite a softer or different speaking tone or pace or require that the client keep their eyes open if they prefer. If you are bilingual and you and your client speak the same languages, ask your client what language they prefer. If your client prefers to go by a nickname, a title such as Dr., Mr., or Mrs., or a specific pronoun, honor their request.

Pace Yourself: Remind yourself to take your time as you walk through this process. There is no need to rush. If you are the person facilitating this exercise, slow down for a relaxed, calming pace. Additionally, it is wise for the facilitator to first practice the exercise with themselves prior to practicing with another person.

Safety Reminder: Safety is the number one consideration with any therapeutic approach or healing intervention. As you lead your clients through the following guided imagery exercise, please instruct your clients to alert you if they are experiencing any of the following trauma responses. If you are an individual doing this work solo, you will also want to consider the following:

- Traumatic memories that are creating a high level of distress

- Feelings of intense fear or panic

- Disturbing or intrusive thoughts

- Suicidal or homicidal thoughts

- Dissociation (if there is an awareness of the dissociative states)

- Other crisis concerns (list on the line): _____

_____

It is also important to ask the client to alert you if they experience any of the following symptoms. Likewise, if someone is doing this work solo, they should pay compassionate and close attention to their process and monitor for distressing or physical symptoms such as:

- A racing heart

- Tightness in the chest

- Shortness of breath

- Nausea or intestinal distress

- Feeling faint or dizzy

- Body pain

- Feeling as if you are floating outside of your body

- Other somatic concerns (list on the line): _____

_____

Note for Therapist or Facilitator: Before moving into the guided imagery, please have your client begin with the assessment below. If you are not a trained mental health professional and your client is in crisis and exhibiting or discussing symptoms that are out of your scope of practice or experience, please refer to an appropriate mental health or medical professional. *If your client is experiencing an immediate life-threatening emergency, please call 911 or the appropriate emergency number if located outside of the United States.*

Note to Solo Reader: *If you are doing this work on your own and believe you are in crisis or may be at risk to yourself, please stop and seek emergency support immediately by calling 911 or your local emergency number.*

Pre-Guided Imagery Assessment Scale

On a scale from 1 to 10 (with 1 = very low, and 10 = very high), please take a mindful moment to assess the following. Circle the number that most accurately applies to you:

Feeling	Assessment (1-10)									
▫ Anxiety	1	2	3	4	5	6	7	8	9	10
▫ Anger	1	2	3	4	5	6	7	8	9	10
▫ Shame	1	2	3	4	5	6	7	8	9	10
▫ Sadness	1	2	3	4	5	6	7	8	9	10
▫ Fear	1	2	3	4	5	6	7	8	9	10
▫ Numbness	1	2	3	4	5	6	7	8	9	10
▫ Confusion	1	2	3	4	5	6	7	8	9	10
▫ Curiosity	1	2	3	4	5	6	7	8	9	10
▫ Hopefulness	1	2	3	4	5	6	7	8	9	10
▫ Calm	1	2	3	4	5	6	7	8	9	10
▫ Joyful	1	2	3	4	5	6	7	8	9	10
▫ Other:	1	2	3	4	5	6	7	8	9	10

Assessment Notes: _____

_____

_____

Mindfulness Healing Part II:
Breath and Somatic Preparation & Prompts

This exercise involves tuning into your breath and body and is followed by the guided imagery exercise. It's important to note that this may not be suitable for everyone. It's recommended that the following be adapted to the specific needs and comfort levels of the individual(s) involved.

Physical Space and Comfort: Have your client settle into a comfortable sitting or lying down position, with their feet on the floor or cross-legged if that is the preference. If your client—or you if you are doing this solo—has a yoga mat or a couch and prefers to lie down, that is fine. Whatever position will help the client feel comfortable is perfectly acceptable.

Prompt 1: Let's pause while you take a few moments to get comfortable.

Prompt 2: When you are ready, you are welcome to close your eyes if that feels comfortable for you. Or, if you prefer to leave your eyes open, that is just fine. Whatever allows you to feel most secure is more than acceptable. If your eyes remain open, feel free to rest your gaze on a calming point—near the floor if you're sitting or on the ceiling if you're lying down.

Prompt 3: We will now move forward into the grounded breathing exercise. This will take approximately two to three minutes.

Grounded Breath Exercise

Now that you are in a comfortable position, before we begin the guided imagery, let's move through the grounded breath work.

1. We will start with the 4-2-7 breath. Start by breathing in deeply through the nose to the count of four, hold for two, and then exhale slowly and intentionally through the mouth to the count of seven. Let's do this three times at your own pace. **Note to Facilitator: Count to 20 silently.**

2. Now, let's return to easy, relaxed, deep breathing. Take a long breath in through the nose and let out a long exhale out through the mouth. Continue with this breath. **Note to Facilitator: Count to 20 silently.**

3. As you are noticing the gentle rhythm of deep breathing, I would like you to imagine extending compassion to yourself with each intake breath. **Note to Facilitator: Count to 20 silently.**

Somatic Relaxation Exercise

Now that we have finished with our grounded breaths, please feel free to breathe normally with relaxed, regular breaths. Let's now move into relaxing the body in preparation for guided imagery:

1. Notice that your feet are feeling heavier and more relaxed.

2. Notice that your hands are gently resting at your sides, on your belly, or on your thighs.

3. Feel your jaw relax and your tongue move away from the roof of your mouth.

4. Allow your shoulders to relax down from your ear lobes and your elbows to gently relax down from your shoulders.

5. Bit by bit, the tension moves out of your body as you breathe in and relax and breathe out and relax. Breathe in compassion, hope, and healing, and breathe out stress, judgment, and anger. **Note to Facilitator: Count to 20 silently.**

As we complete our breath work, we will now move on to the guided imagery preparation and exercise section. You can return to your breath work exercises at any point during the guided imagery. The guided imagery exercise will take approximately 10 minutes. You may continue to stay in your comfortable position or shift to a different comfortable position. You may also continue with your eyes closed if that is your preference. At any point, you are welcome to ask for a time-out if needed.

Let's move forward.

Mindfulness Healing Part III:

Guided Imagery Exercise

Free to be Me: Unlinking the Trauma Bond Chains

Note to Therapist or Facilitator: If you notice that the client is highly activated during the guided imagery, perhaps demonstrating rapid or shallow breathing, sobbing, or shaking, please have the client pause as you attend to the individual. This can be done by gently stating that you would like to pause the exercise for a moment, then quietly asking the person by name if they would like a break, support with deep breath work, or to step out of the guided imagery entirely if it has become too overwhelming.

Note to the Reader(s): If you are doing this solo without the support of a mental health professional, again, please be gentle with yourself. If you have a trusted person to lead you through this, you may want to consider this option, or perhaps you can read this into a recording device and then play it back and follow the prompts. If you become overwhelmed or feel as if you are in a crisis state, please stop and reach out for help if need be. Safety comes first, always.

Purpose of the "Free to Be Me" Guided Imagery: The purpose of this guided imagery exercise is to help you move from overcompensating in an abusive relationship and assist you to skillfully and gently break free from the "chains" of trauma bonding. Its aim is to help you envision a path forward toward a life characterized by joy, peace, safety, freedom, and fulfillment. This exercise serves as a tool for reclaiming agency over yourself, your thoughts, feelings, dreams, and plans—empowering you to cultivate a life that feels authentic and fulfilling with safe and supportive people.

Instructions: This guided imagery exercise will take approximately 10 minutes. You will be guided through each step of the exercise slowly. Though questions may be asked of you or you may be given prompts, there is no expectation of a verbal response. You may respond if you would like to do so, or you may quietly respond inside of yourself, which many people prefer. Through this visualization journey, you will be guided to explore the various triggers while simultaneously cultivating the inner strength and clarity needed to transcend their influence.

Let's begin.

First Prompt Step: Take a deep breath in, slowly and deeply, filling your lungs with fresh air. As you exhale, let go of any tension you're holding in your body. Feel yourself settling into this moment, knowing that you are safe and supported. If it feels right, allow your eyes to close, or soften your gaze toward the ground. Let your breath become a steady rhythm, anchoring you in the present. **Note to Facilitator: Count to 20 silently.**

Next Prompt Step: Now, imagine yourself in a peaceful, quiet space—a place that feels safe and comforting. It could be a sunlit meadow, a quiet forest, a cozy room, or somewhere entirely your own. You are standing here, strong and grounded, surrounded by warmth and calm. Take a moment to notice the details around you—the colors, the scents, the feeling of the air against your skin. **Note to Facilitator: Count to 20 silently.**

Next Prompt Step: As you stand here, bring your attention to your hands and wrists. You notice that they are bound—not by heavy steel, but by a chain made of paper links. This chain represents the connection that has kept you tied to a relationship that has caused pain, confusion, betrayal, and exhaustion. At times, it may have felt impossible to break, as if it had control over you. But as you observe it now, you realize that it is only paper—thin, delicate, and unable to truly hold you. You are safe. **Note to Facilitator: Count to 20 silently.**

Next Prompt Step: Take a deep breath in, and as you exhale, gently run your fingers along the paper links. Notice if there are words, images, or emotions imprinted on them. Perhaps they carry old messages, fears, or false beliefs—things that once kept you tied to this relationship. Maybe you see words like *"not enough," "stay," "love should hurt,"* or *"you can't do this alone."* Or perhaps you sense the weight of unspoken feelings. Whatever is there, simply acknowledge it without judgment. These are just remnants of the past. They do not define you. **Note to Facilitator: Count to 20 silently.**

Next Prompt Step: Now, take another deep breath, filling yourself with clarity, strength, and self-trust. As you exhale, reach out and begin to tear the links, one by one. Feel the paper rip effortlessly in your hands. Each breath in and out is a torn link releasing old fears, outdated beliefs, and the hold this relationship once had over you. As the pieces fall to the ground and drift away in the breeze, notice the feeling in your body—perhaps a sense of lightness, relief, or even empowerment beginning to rise within you. **Note to Facilitator: Count to 20 silently.**

Next Prompt Step: As you notice the paper links that have fallen away, if any hesitation or fear arises, remind yourself: You are safe. You are in control. You are allowed to release what no longer serves you. Keep breathing, steady and strong, as you tear each remaining link. With every breath, you are reclaiming your power. **Note to Facilitator: Count to 20 silently.**

Next Prompt Step: As the final link falls away, take a moment to stand in this new sense of freedom. Notice how your body feels without the chain. Look ahead and see a serene, safe, clear path in front of you—one that is yours to walk, free from anything that once held you back. This is your path to healing, to self-trust, to peace. You can take this path one step at a time, no one will rush you or hurt you. **Note to Facilitator: Count to 20 silently.**

Next Prompt Step: I would like you to imagine that you are taking just one small step onto this new path. This is your first step to healing, to self-trust, to peace. Place your hand over your heart and feel its steady rhythm. Whisper to yourself: "I am free. I choose myself. I am worthy of love and peace." **Note to Facilitator: Count to 20 silently.**

Next Prompt Step: Take one final deep breath, anchoring this feeling of release, freedom, courage, and self-compassion. When you're ready, gently bring your awareness back to the present moment. Wiggle your fingers and toes, if you are able to do so, slowly stretching if that feels good. And when it feels right, open your eyes, carrying this strength and freedom forward with you. You have taken a powerful step.

· · · · ·

Note to Facilitator: This is Part II of the guided imagery, what we refer to as an "add on." Some clients may not yet be ready for this next section, so please use your clinical judgment in determining its appropriateness.

If you are reading this on your own, consider recording the script and listening to it when you feel ready. Take your time and check in with yourself to see if this next step aligns with where you are in your healing journey.

Next Prompt Step: Now, I'd like you to imagine a large clear cup or glass in front of you. Imagine that the clear cup or glass contains comfortably warm liquid with fragrant steam rising from the top. The liquid is safe and nourishing. Just take a moment to observe this and notice what you are sensing and smelling. You are safe; you are connected and calm. What does the cup or glass look like, what does the liquid smell like? **Note to Facilitator: Count to 20 silently.**

Next Prompt Step: Now, visualize that you have placed a frozen ice cube in the clear cup of warm liquid. Imagine this ice cube represents all the goals, hopes, and dreams you once had for yourself and your life that have been frozen in time. As you see the ice melting into the warm, nourishing liquid, bringing your beautiful dreams back to life, imagine that this warm mug of hope and healing is just for you, a healing and healthy delicious drink of hope. If you would like to take a sip of this hopefulness now, you are welcome to do so, or you can save this for another time if you prefer, knowing that this is waiting for you anytime you like. Either is fine; you can do what feels best for you at this moment. **Note to Facilitator: Count to 20 silently.**

Next Prompt Step: Breathing normally and deeply as we come back to our time together today, please remind yourself that you have given yourself a gift of self-advocacy and another step to agency and awareness. As you hold this gentle space of reassurance—that you are enough, what you bring to each person in your life is enough, and you deserve relationships that allow you to feel loved, safe, respected, and nurtured—notice a sense of safety or self-acceptance warmly moving from the tip of your head...down through your shoulders...across your back and chest...warming up your stomach...warming your legs...and then gently cradling your feet.

This sense of safety and security will help walk you through this stage of healing in your life, one small step at a time, one freed-up link at a time, moving you lovingly back to yourself, back to your own dreams and desires, and back to your own heart and well-being.

Transitioning to Awareness

Next Step: As we move back into our time together, let's practice another round of the 4-2-7 breaths, breathing in deeply through the nose to the count of four, holding for two, and then exhaling through the mouth for seven. Let's do those three times at your own pace.

Final Prompt Step: When you're ready, if your eyes are closed, notice the light in front of your eyelids. Gently blink, open your eyes, and bring your awareness back to the present moment.

Mindfulness Healing Part IV:
Processing of Guided Imagery
Sharing Your Experience

Purpose for Processing: After the conclusion of the guided imagery, the therapist or facilitator will lead an open and compassionate discussion about what you experienced during the guided imagery. The aim is to allow you to highlight important aspects of the guided imagery exercise and what the experience was like.

Note: If you are doing this solo without a therapist or facilitator, please pace yourself and notice your energy. You may journal your responses to the questions below if you are doing this work on your own.

Important Considerations for the Facilitator: It is not the role of the therapist or facilitator to interpret, minimize, or re-direct as the client shares their experiences. Rather, it is important for the facilitator to skillfully hold a safe space for the client to discuss their guided imagery, including the more difficult aspects. This is a time for the facilitator to honor the pain, as well as highlight and affirm the positive insights the client may have had. Remind the client that participating in a mindfulness-based exercise like this is a signal of hope and aids in the possibility of recovery and healing.

Processing Questions

1. What did you notice in the guided imagery?

2. What challenges did you experience?

3.   What joys did you experience?

4.   Did you have a breakthrough you'd like to share?

5.   Do you have any concerns that you'd like to share?

6.   What are you feeling in your body currently?

7.   Did you notice any self-growth with insight and compassion toward yourself?

8.   Did you notice any triggers or areas of concern?

Post-Guided Imagery Assessment Scale

Now that you have completed the breathwork and somatic exercises, the guided imagery exercise, and the process work, on a scale from 1 to 10 (with 1 = very low, and 10 = very high), let's take a mindful moment to assess the following:

Feeling	Assessment (1-10)									
□ Anxiety	1	2	3	4	5	6	7	8	9	10
□ Anger	1	2	3	4	5	6	7	8	9	10
□ Shame	1	2	3	4	5	6	7	8	9	10
□ Sadness	1	2	3	4	5	6	7	8	9	10
□ Fear	1	2	3	4	5	6	7	8	9	10
□ Numbness	1	2	3	4	5	6	7	8	9	10
□ Confusion	1	2	3	4	5	6	7	8	9	10
□ Curiosity	1	2	3	4	5	6	7	8	9	10
□ Hopefulness	1	2	3	4	5	6	7	8	9	10
□ Calm	1	2	3	4	5	6	7	8	9	10
□ Joyful	1	2	3	4	5	6	7	8	9	10
□ Other:	1	2	3	4	5	6	7	8	9	10

Important Reminder: If you, as the facilitator, are not a licensed therapist or trained mental health professional and your client is in crisis and exhibiting or discussing symptoms that are out of your scope of practice or experience, please refer to an appropriate mental health or medical professional. ***If your client is experiencing an***

immediate life-threatening emergency, please call 911 or the appropriate emergency number if located outside of the United States. If you are doing this solo without support and are in a state of emergency, reach out to 911 immediately.

Mindfulness Healing Part V:
Self-Care

> ### *Art Exercise—Pizza Wheel*

Purpose Statement: The Self-Care Pizza Wheel exercise invites you to have some playful fun and explore which areas of your self-care may be neglected and where you can start making improvements. By dividing your life into focused "slices," this exercise helps you to visually organize self-care into manageable parts, making it feel less overwhelming than trying to tackle everything at once.

Art Exercise Instructions: It is normal to place your own dreams, desires, and self-care on the back burner due to overcompensating in an abusive or trauma-bonded relationship. At the start of recovery, it can be very challenging to begin to shift the focus back to yourself and your own life and goals. Staying gently present with yourself, complete the exercise with colored pencils, a pen or whatever instrument you prefer by identifying the following:

Slice #1 Is Physical Self-Care: What toppings would you like to add to your physical self-care slice of life? Here are some ideas to help guide you:

- Stretching
- Sleep
- Exercising
- Yoga
- Making and keeping an overdue doctor's appointment
- Getting your teeth cleaned
- Wearing sunscreen
- Taking a shower
- Weights
- Dancing
- Bubble bath
- Hike in nature
- A massage

Slice #1 Toppings: Write or draw your physical self-care activities within that slice. Outside of the slice, make a note of the days that you are willing and able to do at least one of these activities.

• • • • •

Slice #2 Emotional Self-Care: What toppings would you like to add to your emotional self-care slice of life? Here are some ideas as a support to you:

- Therapy
- Twelve-Step
- Reiki (see glossary)
- EMDR (see glossary)
- Tapping (see glossary)
- Brain spotting (see glossary)
- Journaling
- Reading
- Faith-based activities or spiritual groups
- Mindfulness breathing
- Guided imagery
- Petting an animal that you love
- Spending time with a child you love

Slice #2 Toppings: Write or draw your emotional self-care ideas within that slice. Outside of the slice, make a note of the days that you are willing and able to do at least one of these activities.

· · · · ·

Slice #3 Relational Self-Care: What toppings would you like to add to your relational self-care slice of life? Here are some ideas that may resonate:

- Practicing and supporting your boundaries

- Setting up a lunch date with a safe friend

- Honoring your voice, and making your requests known

- Buying yourself something loving like a candle, a book, or a special meal

- Attending a concert with someone you love

- Talking with a trusted family member

- Connecting with a healing person, such as a therapist, coach, sponsor, mentor, or spiritual leader

- Taking a class

- Connecting with a new friend

- Sharing your needs with your significant other (if it is safe to do so)

Slice #3 Toppings: Write or draw your relational self-care ideas within that slice. Outside of the slice, make a note of the days that you are willing and able to do at least one of these activities.

· · · · ·

Slice #4 Spiritual Self-Care: What toppings would you like to add to your spiritual self-care slice of life? Here are some ideas as a support:

- Reading

- Journaling

- Meditation

- Prayer

- Yoga

- Attending a retreat

- Attending a faith-based service

- Guided imagery

- Singing

- Playing an instrument

- Volunteering

- Supporting a charity

- Visiting the ocean (or another large body of water)

- Connecting with a healing person or spiritual leader

Slice #4 Toppings: Write or draw your spiritual self-care ideas within that slice. Outside of the slice, make a note of the days that you are willing and able to do at least one of these activities.

• • • • •

Slice #5 Financial Self-Care: What toppings would you like to add to your financial self-care slice of life? Here are some ideas:

- Totaling up your outstanding debts

- Asking a friend to help you get organized

- Contacting a credit card company to lower your interest rate

- Setting up a budget

- Buying something you've been wanting that is within your budget

- Paying back a debt

- Saying no to a toxic borrower

- Asking for a borrower to pay back their debt to you

- Paying an overdue bill

- Filing your taxes

- Outlining questions for an accountant

- Put money in savings

- Opening a retirement account

- Paying off a credit card

Slice #5 Toppings: Write or draw your financial self-care ideas within that slice. Outside of the slice, make a note of the days that you are willing and able to do at least one of these activities.

It is important to note that many people struggle with finances, especially if they have experienced poverty, were not taught skills, or have been financially abused. Please understand that you do not need to be ashamed or afraid of taking control of your financial health. If you experience challenges in this area of your life or feel unsure of where to begin, there are Twelve-Step groups, financial advisors, online support groups, and even books and videos to help you navigate this. Perhaps you are acquainted with a trustworthy person who seems to excel in this area; if so, think about enlisting their help to support you.

• • • • •

Slice #6 Chores and Errands: What toppings would you like to add to your chores and errands self-care slice of life? Here are some ideas that may help motivate you:

- *Making Your Bed*: The act of making your bed each day can help reduce anxiety and depression by creating a sense of accomplishment and control over your environment. This simple routine can help boost your mood, promote feelings of calm and organization, and set a more positive tone for the rest of your day, contributing to improved mental well-being. If that is all you can accomplish due to grief, anxiety, depression, or other challenges, start with this and be proud of yourself. Every step counts!

- *Washing and Putting Dishes Away*: Do your best to wash dishes after each meal or rinse and place your dishes and utensils in the dishwasher. Again, small tasks that you accomplish can help you regain a sense of clarity and agency.

- *Returning Texts*: This can be challenging for those who deal with mental health issues; however, a heart or thumbs-up is a good effort. If you truly cannot return texts or emails, let people know: "I am [struggling, overwhelmed, exhausted, going through some challenges] at this time. My intention is not to ignore your messages or friendship, and I will circle back when I am feeling [better, less overwhelmed, healthier]. Thank you for understanding."

- *Ask for Help*: I understand that this is not always easy, and in all transparency, I struggle from time to time with this as well. It can also be incredibly difficult to reach out for those struggling with mental health issues or severe depression or for those who have been let down time and again by others. You deserve to share your needs with trusted people who can step in and be of support when needed.

- *Taking Care of Your Transportation (Such as a Car, Bike, Motorcycle, etc.)*: This is another challenging chore for many but one that will help you feel in control of your life. Staying up to date on maintenance and registration will promote a sense of self-confidence while you heal from an abusive relationship.

- *Taking a Daily Bath or Shower*: During the depths of my depression in my late twenties, I found even basic self-care overwhelming. I will always be grateful to a platonic female friend who truly understood my pain. She stayed with me for a week, gently untangled my hair, helped me shower, encouraged me to tackle laundry and chores, and assisted with errands and cleaning my small apartment. Believe me, even a quick three-minute rinse, brushing your teeth and hair, and putting on clean clothes can make a huge difference in lifting your spirits, even if that's all you can manage for the day.

- *Drink Water and Stay Hydrated*: This is more important than most people understand. While most human beings, depending on their age and unique health circumstances, can handle about a 3 to 4% reduction in total body water without any noticeable health effects, as little as a 5 to 8% hydration loss can lead to fatigue and dizziness. Losing more than 10% can cause significant physical and mental decline, which impacts organ function, focus, and mood regulation.

- *Limiting Time on Social Media:* Lady Gaga said it best: "Social media is the toilet of the internet" (Jimmy Kimmel Live, 2019). If you find yourself endlessly scrolling and losing hours to social media each week, arguing with strangers, being pulled into frightening world articles, or comparing your circumstances, marriage, friendships, or lifestyle to others, perhaps it is time to delete the app from your phone and set an intention to engage less on these platforms. Set a timer to gauge how much time you are giving over to this activity each day.

- *Make Time for Exercise*: There are endless articles and books on the benefits of adding exercise to one's life. If this is a challenge, start with keeping a set of comfortable clothing that is easy to slip on and a pair of walking shoes by your bed. Then, first thing in the morning, put on your clothes and shoes, and walk 10 minutes in one direction, then turn around and walk 10 minutes back. Add a minute each day and see if you can increase to 45 minutes most days of the week. If you are unable to walk, find a video online that will help support movement if possible. If it is challenging to start this, buddy up with a friend or find a walking group in your area.

- *Take Time for Mindfulness*: Research studies (see Bibliography) indicate that even a minute or two of mindfulness each day is beneficial for mental clarity, emotional wellness, and physical health. Start with 30 seconds, close your eyes if you wish, and bring your breath to your belly slowly and deeply while relaxing various parts of your body: the shoulders, neck, belly, back, arms, legs, and feet. Practice increasing this just a bit each day. Aim for a time and routine that works for you. Everyone's practice is unique—honor your pace.

- *Eat Healthy Meals*: Nutrition plays a key role in overall wellness. Depending upon your individual health needs, increasing leafy greens, fruits and vegetables, and healthy protein and fat sources are key for a healthy gut and microbiome. A healthy microbiome supports mental health by promoting the production of neurotransmitters like serotonin, reducing inflammation, and influencing the gut-brain connection, which can help regulate mood, stress, and cognitive function. Imbalances in the gut microbiome have been linked to conditions like anxiety and depression. An excellent documentary on this topic is Hack Your Gut, which streams on Netflix as of 2024.

Slice #6 Toppings: Write or draw your daily self-care ideas within that slice. Outside of the slice, make a note of the days that you are willing and able to do at least one of these activities.

· · · · ·

When you reflect on the various ideas you've written or drawn on your self-care pizza slices, what thoughts, feelings, or ideas are surfacing for you? Write them here:

_____

_____

_____

_____

_____

_____

Mindful Reflection Moment

Now that you have completed your breath work, guided imagery, and art and journal exercises, please take some mindful time to reflect before we bring this chapter to a close. You are welcome to answer the following questions in the space below, or write in a journal or notebook of your choice. You may do this with your therapist, or if you are working through this book solo, you can do this on your own.

1. What are you noticing after this chapter?

2. What awareness and insight have surfaced?

3. What is the information you have learned?

Write or share your reflections here or in your own journal or notebook if you would like to continue processing. As always, please be gentle with yourself:

_____

_____

_____

_____

_____

_____

Final Step: Self-Affirmation Exercise

Instructions: Before moving on to another chapter in the workbook, can you give yourself the gift of self-affirmation? It can be difficult for people who are experiencing trauma bonding, intimate partner abuse, betrayal trauma, or struggling with anxiety or depression to affirm themselves.

As a support to this step of your healing, affirmation ideas might include statements such as: "I am committed to my safety and sanity," "I am a person who deserves to be treated with respect," and "I will learn how to know, name, and maintain my healthy boundaries." Please use the winged heart to list your own self-affirmation(s). If you can only come up with one affirmation at this time, that is more than acceptable. Perhaps you can return later in your healing process and add more:

In this chapter, we took a deep dive into the complex nature of trauma bonding, focusing on how abusive dynamics can create powerful—and what sometimes feels like impossible, unbreakable attachments—between individuals. We discussed the characteristics of domestic violence and abuse, identifying patterns that can trap people in cycles of dependency and psychological manipulation. Through Keisha's story and similar examples, we illustrated the subtle yet profound ways individuals might unconsciously suppress their pain and block trauma through behaviors like excessive work, social media scrolling, various addictions, or ignoring red flags.

Alongside these insights, we examined a range of supportive countermeasures. These included mindfulness techniques, guided imagery, meditation, and breathing exercises designed to help individuals reconnect with their inner experiences safely and gradually. We explored therapeutic approaches, especially trauma-informed modalities, that empower individuals to recognize and dismantle unhealthy bonds. Additionally, we provided practical, compassionate strategies for replacing avoidance behaviors with self-care practices that foster healing and resilience. By addressing both the underlying trauma and these bonding patterns, individuals can begin to break free from cycles of harm and move toward authentic healing and self-compassion.

As we conclude this chapter and before you continue forward, I want to leave you with an affirmation shared from my heart to yours: You are worthy of love that is safe, kind, and nurturing. The pain of your past does not define you, and every step you take toward healing is a powerful reclaiming of your strength and freedom. You possess the courage to break free, to heal, and to create a life where you are valued and respected. Trust that your journey toward wholeness is already unfolding and that you are truly capable of continuing forward.

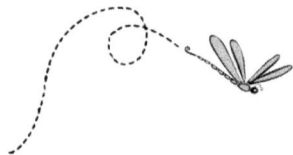

CHAPTER TWO

Mind States: From Resisting and Guarding to Releasing and Growing

Wendy Quinton

When we give ourselves compassion, the tight knot of negative self-judgment starts to dissolve, replaced by a feeling of peaceful, connected acceptance—a sparkling diamond that emerges from the coal.

~ Kristin Neff

Meeting Brady for the first time made me realize why the term "lights up the room with a smile" was invented! While some clients present as uncertain and withdrawn when they attend therapy for the first time, Brady showed no signs of shyness and greeted me with an open demeanor and firm handshake. I was taken aback as I was usually the one making an effort to help people feel welcomed, but with Brady, it almost felt like he was welcoming me! He even jumped ahead to hold my office door open so I could enter. He scanned the room quickly and laughed as he said, "Well, your therapist cardigan is in that chair, so I'll take the other one." He settled into the seat opposite mine, complimented the coziness of my office, and pointed at my bookshelf while remarking, "Nice selection." I smiled while wondering to myself what life experiences had shaped him into such a pleasant, seemingly confident young man.

I was just about to speak when Brady offered, "Well, I'm guessing that we get started with me telling you everything about myself, right? At least that's what happens on TV shows!" I grinned and shook my head slightly and told him that there were some important elements to discuss first, adding, "But it's what we will get into next!"

After explaining the sacred space of the therapy room and going over the only reasons that I would need to break the confidentiality that it offers, Brady let me know that he both understood and agreed with the policy. I also shared with him that I usually take brief notes during the session so that I keep on track and that he is always free to ask me any questions he may have. Once those important points were addressed, I took a breath and said with a smile, "Okay—tell me everything!" That was all the encouragement Brady needed, and he launched into his life story as I listened carefully and made an effort to take it all in.

"Well," he said with a grin, "I'm a military brat—emphasis on the brat! My dad was an officer in the Army, and we moved around a lot. I was born here in the States, but have lived all over the world...Germany, Hawaii, Japan, South Korea...I think that's all...I tend to lose track," he chuckled. He continued, "When I tell my story, people usually ask me which country I enjoyed living in the most, and I tell them that I loved all of them. They were all different but equally special, and I can't name a preference any more than someone could choose their favorite child."

Brady went on, not seeming to need any encouragement from me to continue. "I learned so much from each place I lived: an appreciation of natural beauty, a true enjoyment of various cuisines, and the value of cultural traditions. I learned to ski in Japan and surf in Hawaii." He then added with his now familiar chuckle, "And I also learned how to get into trouble everywhere we went. But that was back in the day, and we don't need to talk about that! Besides, I also learned to be an expert at getting out of trouble."

Brady flashed his picture-perfect smile, and I found myself beaming right back at him almost involuntarily. I had so many questions about his experience of growing up in several different cultures and what a fascinating life he must have had so far, but I restrained myself, knowing already that he could most likely fill the rest of the hour with stories about all the people and places he had experienced. Instead, I simply inserted a suggestion of my own, asking if he could tell me a bit about his family. Brady shrugged and explained, "Oh, you know, typical military family. Stern dad, anxious mom, perfect older sister...and then there was me," he added with a smirk.

Seeing a possible opening to dive into a deeper level of conversation, I took a calm breath and queried, "And who, exactly, is this 'me' you are referring to?" For a moment, his ready smile faded, and his twinkling eyes clouded over. But, he quickly reverted back to his cheerful demeanor. "Let's see, my friends would describe me as interesting, flexible, charming, and spontaneous."

"Okay," I replied and attempted again to get underneath the surface of pleasantries by asking, "And what about you—would you describe yourself that way?"

"Yes, I would," he answered, "and I'd probably add hardworking. Did I mention that I am one of the top realtors in the area? Also open-minded and clever."

My eyes widened as I responded, "Well, that is quite a list! But I guess I'm a little confused. So far, it seems that you are a well-adjusted, affluent young man with a global perspective and admiring friends. So, why are you here?"

Without missing a beat, he stated, "My doctor has been prescribing me Xanax for several years now, but when I asked him for an increase in my dosage this time, he said that I needed to attend therapy first. So, even though everything's fine, here I am."

As I processed Brady's answer, I was curious to ask what first prompted the doctor to prescribe the medication, but my years of practicing Motivational Interviewing, as explained below, allowed me to pause and then summarize Brady's statement. "Okay," I replied, "let me see if I understand what you are telling me. Your doctor is unduly concerned, and you are here only to appease him so that he'll prescribe the higher dose of Xanax that you need."

I think my answer must have caught Brady off guard, probably because he was expecting me to object. He paused uncharacteristically and said, "Well, *um*, when you put it like that...I...I don't really know..."

I knew by this point in our conversation that I only had a fleeting moment before he reapplied his charming mask, so I forged ahead and suggested, "How about we start by looking at why you needed Xanax in the first place? Is that something you'd be willing to discuss?"

I became worried when his grin reappeared, but his reply quelled my fears that he would be unwilling to delve deeper. "Well," Brady stated, "I don't usually talk about this part of my life, but I guess since I'm here, I might as well give it a shot. I don't want you to think that I'm not a hard worker—especially in therapy!" I smiled in reply, noting that perhaps people-pleasing was a part of Brady's persona that we may need to explore in the future.

Brady continued, "I guess I've always been an anxious person, and it escalated as I grew older. Once I started making a name for myself in the real estate market, more and more clients were reaching out to me, and my days became longer and more hectic. I started to have trouble sleeping as I could not turn off my thoughts. My heart would race, and I felt this constant, restless energy in my body, like I should be doing something but didn't know what. Even when I tried to calm down, my brain did not get the message. Everything started to feel overwhelming, and I'd get this nagging fear in the back of my mind that I was missing something, but I didn't know what it was. It felt like I no longer recognized myself. On the outside, I kept up the façade of success, but on the inside..." Brady seemed at a loss for words as the room grew unexpectedly quiet, "I'm not sure what to say next?"

I spoke gently, thanked Brady for his openness and honesty, and asked if he would be willing to try an exercise that would help him delve deeper into his inner world. He agreed, and I continued by prompting him to start by taking a deep breath, as that would help to settle his anxiety. After his breath, I continued, "Now, picture yourself alone in the bathroom and look into the mirror. Take a moment and really observe the person looking back at you. Who do you see?" For the first time, I saw real fear in Brady's eyes, and though he squirmed in his chair, he followed my suggestion, took another deep breath, and extended the silence.

When he began to speak, his voice shook slightly with unreleased tears, "I see the same thing that I often see when looking at a house I may want to have in my inventory. A home with a beautiful exterior and fully remodeled on the inside, but when the inspector comes and really investigates, there's water damage in the walls and termites eating away at the foundation. That's me. Everything looks great but only if you don't look too closely."

After Brady's confession, silence again filled the room, and compassion filled my heart. I said quietly, "I can see that it took a lot of courage for you to really look at yourself in that mirror and honestly report what you see. I'm honored that you trusted me with your truth."

Brady looked up with a surprised expression and shared that he didn't think I would respond that way: "I thought for sure you would berate me for being deceptive." I answered by sharing with him that we often expect people to react to us in the same way that others in our lives have reacted in the past, and I encouraged Brady to tell me who in his life had criticized him for not being transparent.

"Oh," he said with certainty, "that would be my dad, for sure!" I let him know that I would like to hear more about that, and Brady glanced at his watch and gave a slight smile. "Sure, I have time to answer that—it doesn't take long. Dad always wanted me to follow in his footsteps and join the Army, and right up until I graduated high school, I pretended that I was going along with his plans. I played all the sports, hung out with the popular kids, went on dates—you know, all the normal things. But the truth is, I'm gay and love the retail industry, and I knew that there was no way I was cut out for the military. So, when I told my dad I wasn't going to the Academy, he interrogated me so rigorously that I broke down and told him why. The look of shock and disappointment on his face is something I will never forget," Brady admitted painfully.

"And when his lecture started, I realized that he had no idea how hard it had been to hide my sexual identity all these years. He just kept telling me how embarrassed he would be in front of the other officers when he told them why I wasn't going to West Point and how it would affect his reputation. His response drove home the truth I always knew—that only by looking good on the outside and doing what was expected of me could I gain approval and love. And that's what I've continued doing all of my life."

When Brady finished, I let out a long exhale, put my hand on my heart, and told him that I could sense his pain and could see how much it must cost him to keep up the façade of being fine, even when he was feeling anything but fine. As our time together was almost up, I reminded Brady that my office was a safe space where he could be his authentic self and know that he would be accepted for exactly the amazing person that he is. Brady replied, "I appreciate that," and after making a return appointment, his charming smile returned to his face as he left the office.

· · · · ·

During the next two sessions, I began by having Brady complete various screening tools so that I could get to know him better. We started with the Adverse Childhood Experience (ACE) Questionnaire. This is a set of inquiries that targets areas of abuse, neglect, and household dysfunction, and high numbers of affirmative answers indicate high levels of exposure to traumatic events. After we finished the test, Brady commented that perhaps growing up with a harsh father may have affected him in ways he had not yet fully realized.

The next tool we used is the Lee CATI Instrument (Compassionate Attachment Therapy Interview). This is a tool developed by Mari A. Lee that focuses on attachment trauma using questions about childhood caregivers, with special attention given to the emotions that arise in the body when the questions are pondered. This interview helped Brady express his thoughts about his parents and the feelings that he had attached to his relationship with them. It was an important first step in the journey of mindfulness, as Brady was able to slow down long enough to discern the bodily sensations that correspond with his emotions. I introduced Brady to several techniques for processing and moving these feelings and sensations through his body, allowing him to function without constantly carrying them. He was relieved that he no longer had to continue to stifle and ignore these emotions.

One of the strong reactions Brady felt during the Lee CATI exercise, as he had reported feeling often in his life, is anxiety. Given this, the next tool we used was the GAD-7 (Generalized Anxiety Disorder). This is a short screening tool used to gauge the severity of generalized anxiety disorder, using questions about worrying, restlessness, fear, and irritability.

Brady's score gave me a greater understanding of his level of anxiety and how it affected his everyday life. Using his answers as a springboard, we began to explore the roots of his anxiety, which he attributed mostly to work stress. He shared that as a real estate agent, he is always on call, always looking for the next sale, and at any moment, a deal could fall through, costing him thousands of dollars in commission.

During one session, using the tools he learned from the Lee CATI Interview, I invited Brady to relax for a moment, be compassionately present with himself, and find out what was under all the anxiety and where he felt it in his body. He was able to do this and identified fear as the primary emotion, and that it felt like a rock weighing down on his chest. I asked him to continue to breathe and tell me what fears he could identify. At first, Brady named the fears of financial failure and of disappointing his clients. I asked him to ground himself by regulating his breathing and staying with the sensation and feelings, holding space for them in his body. I gently encouraged him to see if he could recall other times in his life when these same sensations were present.

There was silence for a moment, and then tears started to roll down his cheeks. He described having a conversation with his dad, telling him that he did not want to follow in his footsteps and join the military. Brady continued, "When I told my dad that I wanted to pursue a career in real estate, he huffed and told me that the Armed Forces was the only truly honorable career and that people in this country would not even have houses to buy if it weren't for the men and women in the military protecting our freedoms. From that day on, I vowed to be so successful in my career that my dad would have to admit that he was proud of me, even though I didn't pursue a military career. Brady's voice was full of pain as he added, "I'm still striving for success, and I'm still waiting to hear those words."

I allowed my own eyes to fill with tears for Brady, and as I reached for a tissue, I offered him one as well. I let him know that his pain touched me deeply and that when I am feeling discomfort, I find that deep breathing can help, and I asked if he would join me. He agreed, and we sat in silence together. Only the noise of our inhalation and exhalation was audible. After a few breaths, I could see his shoulders relax and his eyes dry up, so we continued. I sensed that my authentic expression of empathy touched Brady and helped build deeper trust and rapport.

As the session ended, I asked Brady to use the time until we would meet again to think about what goals he would like to set for his time in therapy. He shared that the screening tools we had used had already helped him see the areas he needed to focus on and that he would bring his goals to discuss at our next session.

When Brady returned to my office the next week, we used the goals he had written and developed a treatment plan with specific, measurable targets that he identified. Over the next several weeks, Brady worked on challenging his anxious thoughts, practicing healthy coping skills, setting boundaries around his work hours, and practicing self-acceptance.

Brady was committed to his therapy, consistently showing up on time for his appointments. He always had something he wanted to work on and asked to review his treatment goals frequently. However, I sensed that I wasn't yet completely connected to the real Brady and that he may be holding something back. During one session, I noticed that he became extremely uncomfortable when I asked him to share how he was coping with managing his anxiety, given the new mindfulness tools he had acquired. I thought that he might be willing to have a discussion with his doctor about the possibility of lowering his Xanax dosage and suggested it to him. In response, his eyes fell, and he mumbled that he would think about it. I did not pursue the subject further, knowing that our next step in treatment would be to delve further into mindfulness and discuss mind states and mind stories and that the topic would come up again soon.

Since Brady was already introduced to the concept of mindfulness during the Lee CATI Interview, we briefly reviewed its core concepts, such as being present with what the body is feeling and accepting all feelings just as they are, without judgment. We then moved on to discuss the ideas of mind states and mind stories. I explained to Brady that mind states have been studied in numerous spiritual and philosophical practices, and in their most fundamental form, they can be described as people's worldviews. It is a programmed way of thinking that has become deeply rooted over time and includes various mindsets, such as judgmental, reactive, focused, calm, and aversive.

I further explained that there are mind stories connected to these various mind states. Mind stories are internal dialogues created by our core beliefs about what happened to us and influence how we perceive reality. If our mind stories are based on anxieties, unhealthy attachment styles, and distorted thinking, they can be misleading, limiting, and harmful for us. By becoming aware that our mind stories are merely interpretations of our experiences and not absolute truths, we can lessen their impact on our behavior. As we pay attention to our inner dialogue, we can release these unhelpful mind states and stories and embrace a rational view of ourselves and the world around us (Sharma et al., 2023).

While going over examples of various mind states and stories, Brady caught on quickly and would often tell an entertaining tale about a client who perfectly illustrated each one. While I was encouraged that he understood the concepts, I was concerned as he was still very reticent to share examples from his own life and usually managed to shift the conversation away from himself. It was not until we got to the "delusional mind state" that it seemed to click personally for him.

The delusional mind state describes a person who holds strong beliefs that are not grounded in reality, even though there is conflicting evidence. I gave Brady several examples of common delusional mind states that those addicted to substances or behaviors often hold, including the belief that they are in control of the addiction and can stop whenever they want, despite repeated failures to do so. They also believe that there are minimal consequences to the addiction despite evidence of harm, such as legal consequences, relationship problems, and negative effects on their health. I ended the description by explaining that a delusional mind state involves lying to ourselves and others.

I anticipated that Brady would reply with an anecdotal story about one of his clients, but instead, he sat in unaccustomed silence for a few minutes, and when he finally spoke, he revealed the secret he had been hiding—even from me.

Brady disclosed that in the past, he was addicted to cocaine and used Xanax to come down off his high. He shared that, at first, it started as a "harmless" way to be able to stay awake and get more work done. However, he soon found himself having to work harder to pay for his habit, and his addiction took on a life of its own. His dependence on cocaine cost him numerous relationships, as he would not let anyone get close enough to see the extent of his compulsion.

He divulged that one day, his father called to tell him that his mother was in the hospital with a possible heart attack, but he missed his call as he was sleeping off his high, aided by Xanax. When he listened to the voicemail and realized that his mom might have died without him being present, Brady decided that he was done with cocaine. He did well for a while, but lately, when work was exceptionally stressful, he sometimes felt overwhelmed and would spend Saturday night using cocaine and Sunday sleeping it off, aided by Xanax. He continued by summarizing his disclosure by saying, "And that is why I understand the delusional mind state we've been talking about. I've been lying to myself that I can continue living this and that nobody—even you—had to know."

As Brady finished sharing, he sat silently with his head hung, looking at the floor. I could almost see the cloud of shame that enveloped him. I spoke softly to him, letting him know that I could see the courage it took for him to be honest with me and asking him to take a moment to look inward and report what he was feeling and where in his body he felt it. He described his feeling of shame as all-encompassing, filling his body. He was motionless for a moment and then added, "But I also feel a bit lighter now that I don't have anything to hide from you anymore."

Building on Brady's new understanding of mindfulness and his openness to discussing his addiction, we examined the mind stories that related to his mind states. We started with the delusional mind state since it was the one he most identified with, and I asked him to talk about the internal dialogue that revolved around this faulty cognition. He thought for a moment and answered that the delusion he held was that if he didn't tell anyone about his addiction, then it wouldn't affect him and that it was okay to use an illegal substance if it led to financial gain. Brady then chuckled wryly as he acknowledged that when saying these thoughts out loud, he was acutely aware of how delusional they sounded.

Once Brady's secret was revealed in our therapy, he became more engaged and present in our sessions, asking that we add recovery from his cocaine use to his treatment plan. I gave him Darrin Ford's workbook *Transforming the Addicted Mind* to read and complete for homework (Ford, Cosper, & Bordey, 2017).

Since being truthful with himself and others was an important part of Brady's recovery, he also began to attend a Twelve-Step meeting, Narcotics Anonymous, and reported that it was freeing to be around others who had similar experiences and that it helped him to be more accepting of himself.

At first, Brady relapsed several times, typically when he was overwhelmed by his financial worries and forgetting to use his support resources, such as Twelve-Step group members, higher power, and acceptance. Instead, he would rely on himself, using cocaine to aid him to work harder than other real estate agents. The difference now was that he was no longer lying to himself, sharing honestly at meetings, and able to acknowledge the consequences of his addiction. Over time, he learned to manage his anxiety using mindful practices and his other relapse prevention resources. He often said that although his recovery is hard work and he has had setbacks, he wouldn't trade the things that he has learned about life and himself for anything.

During this time, while Brady was learning to live mindfully and practice sobriety, he became grounded in his acceptance of himself and his choices, regardless of how his dad treated him. He realized that he no longer needed to strive for financial success and perfection to be acceptable to others. He came to accept each part of his life as a necessary learning experience and embrace his humanity, not being afraid to share all of himself with others—even the painful parts.

It has been just over a year since Brady and I wrapped up our work together, but he keeps in touch occasionally through email to update me on his recovery journey. Most recently, he shared that he is looking into ways he could use his knowledge of the real estate market to help others, perhaps by volunteering at an organization that provides housing and other services to LGBTQ+ youth in need. As he wrote, "Now that my life isn't a constant struggle for acceptance from others, I have more time and energy to invest in making society a more accepting space for all."

A word from Wendy

Recovery is not a journey that has to be taken alone. There are many supportive resources available to help individuals like Brady who are struggling with trauma, addiction, compulsive behaviors, shame, and related challenges. Let's explore some of these resources now.

Twelve-Step Groups

Twelve-Step groups are free organizations led by peers that support recovery from addiction, compulsive behaviors, or other challenges. They adhere to a structured program based on twelve guiding principles (steps) that promote personal growth, accountability, and spiritual development. The Twelve Steps involve acknowledging struggles, seeking help from a higher power, taking personal inventory, making amends, and committing to personal and spiritual growth while helping others in their recovery journey. An important part of the program involves obtaining a "sponsor," which is a senior member of the group with at least one year of sobriety. A Twelve-Step sponsor provides guidance, support, and encouragement to those new to recovery. These supportive environments place special emphasis on anonymity, self-improvement, and community support (Laudet, Savage, & Mahmood, 2023).

A common misconception about Twelve-Step programs is that a higher power must be defined as God in a religious sense. However, the concept is intentionally broad and personal. A higher power can be anything greater than oneself that provides strength, guidance, and hope—whether it be nature, the universe, a sense of inner wisdom, community, sobriety, or even the support found within the recovery group itself. The flexibility of this concept allows individuals of all backgrounds and beliefs to engage in the program in a way that feels authentic to them.

Participation in Twelve-Step groups like Alcoholics Anonymous (AA), Narcotics Anonymous (NA), and others is linked to reduced substance abuse, higher rates of abstinence, better overall health—covering physical, emotional, and spiritual aspects— improved social interactions, greater engagement with community organizations, and lower healthcare costs. These benefits increase with the level of involvement in Twelve-Step group activities beyond just attending meetings, such as reading literature, having an active sponsor, working through the steps, and helping others. The positive impact of Twelve-Step groups extends to all who make use of its services (White, Galanter, Humphreys, & Kelly, 2020).

I can personally attest to the benefits of Twelve-Step groups as I, myself, have attended Al-Anon, Codependency Anonymous, and the Christian alternative, Celebrate Recovery in the past. Each of these support groups played a significant role in my recovery, offering a safe space for me to learn, grow, and work on my character flaws.

Mindfulness

Mindfulness has been defined by American professor, mindfulness teacher, and author John Kabat-Zinn as referring to the quality of being aware of the present moment with a curious, open-minded, non-judgmental, accepting attitude (Kabat-Zinn, 1982). As the creator of the Mindfulness-Based Stress Reduction (MBSR), Kabat-Zinn's work combines mindfulness with modern medicine and helps people deal with stress, anxiety, pain, and illness through meditation. Although his teachings are based on Buddhist ideas, Kabat-Zinn presents them in a scientific way, making them easily understandable. He is highly respected for making mindfulness a widely used tool in healthcare and therapy and instructed that living mindfully includes focusing one's attention on what is happening in the moment and accepting it without being preoccupied with thoughts of the future or the past (Kabat-Zinn, 2013).

Mindfulness practices can restore clients to a place of equanimity, which is a state of mental serenity and composure, even amid life's hardships. Equanimity allows an individual to observe and examine their thoughts, feelings, and bodily sensations without overidentifying with them or responding rashly to them. Developing equanimity was especially helpful in my work with Brady, and helped him learn to take a step back and observe what's happening without judgment. Creating a space between stimulus and response is a powerful practice that affords the luxury of responding with thoughtful intention rather than reacting from a place of fear. Equanimity involves acceptance as the present moment is observed as it is, without resistance. It differs from apathy and resignation because, instead of stifling engagement, it inspires thoughtful and compassionate action (Weber, 2021).

Mindfulness practices involve several techniques, including breathing exercises, body scans, mindful eating, and mindful walking, among other practices. Deep breathing, as you will learn and practice throughout this workbook, is the practice of taking long, slow breaths while paying attention to the rhythm and sensations of the inhalation and exhalation. This type of breathing helps calm the nervous system and promotes relaxation as it quiets the mind and reduces the impact of distractions. Other benefits include lowering blood pressure and increasing heart rate variability (Shahoud et al., 2023).

Body Scan: A body scan includes bringing focused attention to different parts of the body gradually and intentionally. The most common practice starts with focusing on the head, then moving down through the body and ending with the feet. It can also be used to decipher where an emotion is being held and experienced in the body by concentrating attention on specific areas of sensations, discomfort, or tension. During my therapy sessions with Brady, he often shared how much he appreciated tuning into his body and developing a deeper awareness of himself. Research has found that this practice can reduce stress and lead to improved sleep and emotional well-being (Luberto, Hall, Park, Haramati, & Cotton, 2019).

Mindful Eating: Mindful eating is the practice of bringing focus and intention to the experience of eating. Rather than unconsciously consuming food, it involves tuning into your body, becoming aware of the sensations of hunger and fullness, and savoring the taste of food. Special attention is paid to the smell, look, textures, and flavors of the food, as well as the emotions experienced before, during, and after eating. Mindful eating can help people make deliberate choices, develop a healthier relationship with food, and reduce binge eating (O'Reilly, Cook, Spruijt-Metz, & Black, 2014).

Mindful Walking: Mindful walking, like mindful eating, is walking while bringing focus and attention to the movement. Rather than the mind being on autopilot and just thinking about getting from Point A to Point B, awareness is brought to the feeling of the ground under the feet, the way that the legs move, and the sound of the breath. About 4 months into our work together, Brady began participating in a Sunday morning hiking group twice a month, and started a daily mindful walking practice which he reported as a "game changer" for his recovery. Walk Talk therapy is also a widely accepted therapy practice helping clients move forward mindfully with the support of a therapist or mental health professional. Practicing mindful walking can reduce feelings of anxiety and promote a sense of calm (Gotink et al., 2018).

Window of Tolerance: Practicing mindfulness can also enable people to better tolerate feelings of discomfort and distress. This is a concept that closely follows the teaching by Dr. Dan Siegel on the "Window of Tolerance," which is a term used to describe the range of emotions and stress levels a person can handle while still functioning well. When you're within this window, you can think clearly, manage your emotions, and respond to challenges calmly. If you go outside the window, you might either feel overwhelmed (anxiety, panic) or shut down (numbness, disconnection). This concept is further explored in Chapter 5.

Mindful practices help clients like Brady stay within their window of tolerance as they will gain the ability to be aware of their emotional state and notice when they are getting off balance and moving into a state of panic (hyperarousal) or numbness (hypoarousal). Using mindfulness techniques such as deep breathing, meditation, and body scan will allow clients to return to a level of equanimity. Clients can learn to be more comfortable experiencing a wider range of emotion levels, thus becoming more tolerant and less dysregulated by stressful experiences. This allows individuals to accept difficult situations while remaining serene and centered (Lomas, Edginton, Cartwright, & Ridge, 2015).

Ego States: One of the key concepts of mindfulness is learning not to over-identify with our ego states. The concept of ego states was developed by psychiatrist Eric Berne, the founder of Transactional Analysis (TA), in the 1950s. Berne proposed that a person's personality is made up of three distinct ego states: Parent, Adult, and Child. The Parent includes the values and rules we've been taught, the Adult identifies our objective, logical part, and the Child reflects our instincts and emotions (Rahman & Kodikal, 2020). These ego states interact dynamically in everyday life, shaping how we communicate and relate to others.

Teachers like Eckhart Tolle and Thich Nhat Hanh stressed that clinging to our egos, thoughts, and emotions causes us to suffer (Tolle, 1997; Nhat Hanh, 1998). Rather than saying, "I am anxious," we can realize that worry is an emotion that can come and go, and we can instead say, "I notice my pulse racing and my heart beating quickly, and I feel fear." That way, anxiousness does not become our identity, and we are not defined by it. Rather, we recognize it, experience it, and allow it to pass through us. Brady found this to be especially helpful in reducing his shame based thinking and anxiety states. Mindfulness practice allows us to detach from negative cognitions and an overinflated sense of self, making it possible to look at situations from other people's perspectives and leading to graciousness.

Benefits: The benefits of mindfulness are numerous, and clinical studies have shown that it can improve emotional, physical, and cognitive health (Goyal et al., 2014). Practicing mindfulness helps our emotional health by reducing the symptoms of depression, stress, and anxiety (Strauss et al., 2023). Mindfulness practices enhance our physical health by reducing stress-related inflammation and improving the immune system (Creswell, Pacilio, Lindsay, & Brown, 2016). Cognitive functioning, such as learning and memory, is improved by mindfulness as it facilitates structural brain changes and increases gray matter concentration significantly (Hölzel et al., 2011).

Mind States: Mind states are a programmed pattern of thinking that has become deeply rooted over time. These states describe the way a person perceives the world, which involves an awareness that the mind can be fixed in conditions such as focused, scattered, calm, agitated, judgmental, reactive, aversive, and others.

During my mindfulness certification training, when I was first introduced to the concept of mind states, I quickly recognized the connection between this idea and the concept of "worldview". You see, previous to becoming a therapist, my first career was that of a cross-cultural missionary. While training for this career, I explored the area of worldview extensively, and learned that understanding a person's core beliefs is essential to comprehending their society and individuality, and this insight is gained through careful observation and thoughtful questions. Grasping a person's worldview is crucial when learning their language, as language and culture are deeply intertwined, each shaping the other.

After completing missionary training, my family and I moved to the Island of Papua New Guinea and lived in a village where the people spoke a language called 'Duma'. As I slowly gained fluency in their language and took on the role of teaching literacy and proofreading translations of lessons, I found that understanding the cultural context behind words was of utmost importance. This knowledge proved highly transferable to my work as a clinical therapist. Although my clients all reside in the same State as I do, our experiences and life stories are unique and different. My background helps me carefully explore their mind states and uncover automatic belief patterns rooted in their life experiences.

Mind Stories: Mind stories are the internal dialogues and narratives we create about our experiences, and they play a powerful role in shaping our perceptions of reality. These stories influence what we believe to be true about ourselves, others, and the world around us. In my work with Brady, we uncovered many distressing narratives he carried—stories that shaped his pain and perception of himself. Together, we explored these deep-seated beliefs and gradually worked toward healing. Often, a person's mind stories are rooted in past experiences, trauma, conditioning, and emotional responses, and they can either empower us or reinforce limiting beliefs. The way we interpret events, our sense of self-worth, and how we relate to others are all influenced by these stories. Over time, these internal narratives can become so ingrained that they shape our identity and worldview, often without us even realizing it.

The following are examples of mind states and their corresponding mind stories:

Judgmental

- *Mind State*: An innate belief that I am inadequate and that any personal failures are devastating.

- *Mind Story*: I must be perfect so others will love me, so I must work hard to hide any mistakes I make.

Denial

- *Mind State*: Characterized by a refusal to acknowledge the truth, even though there is evidence to support it.

- *Mind Story*: My alcohol dependence is not an issue because I can stop anytime I want, even though I have never successfully stopped drinking.

Contempt

- *Mind State*: A conviction that I am superior to others who are different from me (i.e., different race, socioeconomic standing, religion, gender, orientation, etc.).

- *Mind Story*: I have a right to be disrespectful to others since they are inferior.

Self-Criticism

- *Mind State*: An outlook that I am a failure and inferior to others.

- *Mind Story*: I can't try anything new because I will fail, and others will judge me.

Locus of Control

Another important part of practicing mindfulness is investigating the concept of locus of control. This refers to a person's conviction about the extent to which they can control the things that affect them. An individual's locus of control can be internal or external. Those with an internal locus of control believe that by their choices and actions, they have control over the outcome of the situations they encounter in life. Those with an external locus of control believe that they are at the mercy of things outside themselves, such as luck or the actions of others, and they are convinced that they have limited influence over what happens to them.

For example, imagine that there are two students who are facing the same difficult exam. The first student takes meticulous notes, studies hard, gets a good night's sleep before the exam, and does well. The second student goes out with friends the night before the exam, gets up an hour early to look over his notes, skips breakfast, barely makes it to class on time, and does poorly. The first student understands that he took responsibility and earned his grade. The second student blames the test for being too hard and believes the teacher has it out for him. The first student has an internal locus of control, whereas the second student has an external locus of control.

When we seek to understand what is impacting the second student, perhaps family of origin trauma, bullying, addiction, mental health issues, learning challenges, or something else, we can help that person better understand themselves in order to make healthier choices and reduce their suffering. Learning mindfulness would be valuable for the second student as it helps increase self compassion, personal responsibility and self-awareness. It would be beneficial for this student to understand the roots to self destructive choices, perhaps unresolved trauma or early abuse if that is part of their story. When the second student begins to heal what is hurting them, or better understand their mental health challenges, and learns to recognize that their thoughts and behaviors contributed to the outcome of their exam and that in the future, they can take steps to increase their chances of success rather than blaming the outcome on something outside of themselves, this can feel empowering! Learning to be mindful will increase this student's awareness that even though they do not have control over outward events, such as difficult exams, their response to these events, such as healing, insight building, seeking support, preparation, self compassion, and self-care, is within their control (Lefcourt, 2014).

Motivational Interviewing

Motivational Interviewing (MI) was developed in the early 1980s by William R. Miller and Stephen Rollnick who are both clinical psychologists. This approach to counseling and healthcare intervention is an effective way to help clients understand and resolve their ambivalence to change and help them access the motivation for behavioral modification, especially as it relates to addiction.

Rather than the therapist expounding on all the reasons the client should want to change, MI relies on a collaborative approach where the therapist uses open-ended questions, reflective listening, and strategies to enhance the client's own inherent motivation. In my own experience, this approach has been very helpful in allowing the client to explore their values and increasing a desire to align their behavior with their goals (Miller & Rollnick, 2013).

Screening Tools

ACE (Adverse Childhood Experiences)

The ACE questionnaire was designed by the Centers for Disease Control and Prevention (CDC) and Kaiser Permanente and administered to over 17,000 people between 1995 and 1997. The questions were designed to investigate the correlation between traumatic childhood events that occurred before the age of 18 and long-term negative health effects (Felitti et al., 1998).

Research has proven that the higher a person's ACE score is, the greater the likelihood of health problems in later life, such as substance abuse, mental health disorders, chronic disease, and early death. It also shows that numerous traumatic experiences have cumulative negative effects on social functioning (Petruccelli, Davis, & Berman, 2019). I find this tool helpful as a supportive way to identify traumatic events that the client may have experienced without them having to describe or relive them.

Often, when a new client is asked the open-ended question, "How would you describe your childhood?" they may be reluctant to reveal painful experiences before trust in the therapist has been developed. Also, they may not identify traumatic childhood experiences as such because they were a normal part of their lives. Over the years, I've noticed that clients are often surprised by the high scores they receive after completing the questions, and hearing that high number is often the first step to acknowledging their trauma and beginning to heal from it. Some clients express audible relief when they realize that perhaps there is an underlying reason for their unhealthy life choices and behaviors.

The Lee CATI (Compassionate Attachment Theory Interview)

This instrument, created by therapist Mari A. Lee, is a tool that is used in the beginning stages of mindfulness-based addiction and trauma therapy. It assists the client in processing and integrating non-integrated attachment trauma. It helps both client and therapist practice being present with whatever thoughts and feelings arise without judgment or resistance. During the interview, the therapist will gain insight into the client's emotional activation level and pace and then aid the client in reducing anxiety and trauma responses. It will also help the client increase their emotional insight and ability to experience equanimity and the calm composure that it brings. Additionally, it is a helpful way for the client and the therapist to explore and understand the client's mind states and mind stories related to their attachment styles.

GAD-7 (Generalized Anxiety Disorder 7-Item Scale)

This self-report test was developed by Dr. Robert L. Spitzer, Dr. Janet B. W. Williams, Dr. Kurt Kroenke, and others (Löwe et al., 2008) and is used extensively in clinical and research settings. It consists of seven questions, and the individual rates the frequency and severity of the symptoms over the past two weeks (minimal, mild, moderate, or severe). This screening tool is especially useful as it can be readministered frequently to monitor how symptoms change over time (Jordan, Shedden-Mora, & Löwe, 2017).

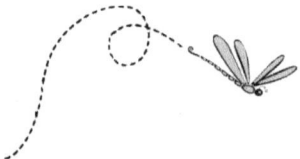

Mindfulness Healing Part I:

Preparation, Assessment, and Script

for Guided Imagery Exercise

Important Safety Tips for Therapists, Facilitators, and Healing Individuals

Environment Consideration and Tips: It can be helpful to "set the stage" prior to a guided imagery exercise. For example, consider the lighting—is it too bright or too low? Another helpful step is putting phones on silent. Also, think about outside distractions, such as barking dogs, traffic, and other interruptions. If possible, minimize outside noises the best you can. Some individuals like having a blanket or pillow to hold, or you may enjoy diffusing essential oils to support deeper relaxation if there are no allergy concerns. While mindfulness-based guided imagery is not hypnosis, it can be helpful to prepare your environment prior to beginning the guided imagery exercise.

Voice Prosody: An additional gentle reminder is to be aware of your voice prosody. Prosody refers to the rhythm and melody of the voice, including intonation, stress, and pauses. Speaking in a softer tone and slower cadence than your normal speaking voice is useful in supporting the guided imagery practice. If you typically speak more rapidly or loudly, it will take some practice to slow down and modulate your voice.

Diversity Considerations: Consider the client's culture, age, race, physical differences (such as hearing loss), gender and orientation, and other unique experiences that may invite a softer or different speaking tone or pace or require that the client keep their eyes open if they prefer. If you are bilingual and you and your client speak the same languages, ask your client what language they prefer. If your client prefers to go by a nickname, a title such as Dr., Mr., or Mrs., or a specific pronoun, honor their request.

Pace Yourself: Remind yourself to take your time as you walk through this process. There is no need to rush. If you are the person facilitating this exercise, slow down for a relaxed, calming pace. Additionally, it is wise for the facilitator to first practice the exercise with themselves prior to practicing with another person or client.

Safety Reminder: Safety is the number one consideration with any therapeutic approach or healing intervention. As you lead your clients through the following guided imagery exercise, please instruct your clients to alert you if they are experiencing any of the following responses.

Note: If you are an individual doing this work solo, you will also want to consider the following:

- Traumatic memories that are creating a high level of distress

- Feelings of intense fear or panic

- Disturbing or intrusive thoughts

- Suicidal or homicidal thoughts

- Dissociation (if there is an awareness of the dissociative states)

- Other crisis concerns (list on the line): _____

_____

It is also important to ask the client to alert you if they experience any of the following symptoms. Likewise, if someone is doing this work solo, they should pay compassionate and close attention to their process and monitor for distressing or physical symptoms such as:

- A racing heart

- Tightness in the chest

- Shortness of breath

- Nausea or intestinal distress

- Feeling faint or dizzy

- Body pain

- Feeling as if you are floating outside of your body

- Other somatic concerns (list on the line): _____

_____

Note for Therapist or Facilitator: Before moving into the guided imagery, please have your client begin with the assessment below. If you are not a trained mental health professional and your client is in crisis and exhibiting or discussing symptoms that are out of your scope of practice or experience, please refer your client to an appropriate mental health or medical professional. *If your client is experiencing an immediate life-threatening emergency, please call 911 or the appropriate emergency number if located outside of the United States.*

Note to Solo Reader: *If you are doing this work on your own and believe you are in crisis or may be at risk to yourself, please stop and seek emergency support immediately by calling 911 or your local emergency number.*

> *Pre-Guided Imagery Assessment Scale*

On a scale from 1 to 10 (with 1 = very low, and 10 = very high), please take a mindful moment on the next page to assess the following. Circle the number that most accurately applies to you:

Feeling	Assessment (1-10)									
▫ Anxiety	1	2	3	4	5	6	7	8	9	10
▫ Anger	1	2	3	4	5	6	7	8	9	10
▫ Shame	1	2	3	4	5	6	7	8	9	10
▫ Sadness	1	2	3	4	5	6	7	8	9	10
▫ Fear	1	2	3	4	5	6	7	8	9	10
▫ Numbness	1	2	3	4	5	6	7	8	9	10
▫ Confusion	1	2	3	4	5	6	7	8	9	10
▫ Curiosity	1	2	3	4	5	6	7	8	9	10
▫ Hopefulness	1	2	3	4	5	6	7	8	9	10
▫ Calm	1	2	3	4	5	6	7	8	9	10
▫ Joyful	1	2	3	4	5	6	7	8	9	10
▫ Other:	1	2	3	4	5	6	7	8	9	10

Assessment Notes: _____

_____

_____

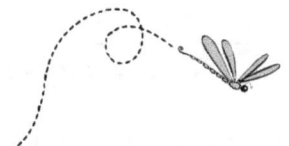

Mindfulness Healing Part II:
Breath and Somatic Preparation & Prompts

This exercise involves tuning into your breath and body and is followed by the guided imagery exercise. It's important to note that this may not be suitable for everyone. It's recommended that the following be adapted to the specific needs and comfort levels of the individual(s) involved.

Physical Space and Comfort: Have your client settle into a comfortable sitting or lying down position, with their feet on the floor or cross-legged if that is the preference. If your client—or you if you are doing this solo—has a yoga mat or a couch and prefers to lie down, that is fine. Whatever position will help the client feel comfortable is perfectly acceptable.

Prompt 1: Let's pause while you take a few moments to get comfortable.

Prompt 2: When you are ready, you are welcome to close your eyes if that feels comfortable for you. Or, if you prefer to leave your eyes open, that is just fine. Whatever allows you to feel most secure is more than acceptable. If your eyes remain open, feel free to rest your gaze on a calming point—near the floor if you're sitting or on the ceiling if you're lying down.

Prompt 3: We will now move forward into the grounded breathing exercise. This will take approximately two to three minutes.

Grounded Breath Exercise

Now that you are in a comfortable position, before we begin the guided imagery, let's move through the grounded breath work.

1. We will start with the 4-2-7 breath. Start by breathing in deeply through the nose to the count of four, hold for two, and then exhale slowly and intentionally through the mouth to the count of seven. Let's do this three times at your own pace. **Note to Facilitator: Count to 20 silently.**

2. Now, let's return to easy, relaxed, deep breathing. Take a long breath in through the nose and let out a long exhale out through the mouth. Continue with this breath. **Note to Facilitator: Count to 20 silently.**

3. As you are noticing the gentle rhythm of deep breathing, I would like you to imagine extending compassion to yourself with each intake breath. **Note to Facilitator: Count to 20 silently.**

Somatic Relaxation Exercise

Now that we have finished with our grounded breaths, please feel free to breathe normally with relaxed, regular breaths. Let's now move into relaxing the body in preparation for guided imagery:

1. Notice that your feet are feeling heavier and more relaxed.

2. Notice that your hands are gently resting at your sides, on your belly, or on your thighs.

3. Feel your jaw relax and your tongue move away from the roof of your mouth.

4. Allow your shoulders to relax down from your ear lobes and your elbows to gently relax down from your shoulders.

5. Bit by bit, the tension moves out of your body as you breathe in and relax and breathe out and relax. Breathe in compassion, hope, and healing, and breathe out stress, judgment, and anger. **Note to Facilitator: Count to 20 silently.**

As we complete our breath work, we will now move on to the guided imagery preparation and exercise section. You can return to your breath work exercises at any point during the guided imagery. The guided imagery exercise will take approximately 10 minutes. You may continue to stay in your comfortable position or shift to a different comfortable position. You may also continue with your eyes closed if that is your preference. At any point, you are welcome to ask for a time out if needed.

Let's move forward.

Mindfulness Healing Part III:
Guided Imagery Exercise
The Garden

Note to Therapist or Facilitator: If you notice that the client is highly activated during the guided imagery, perhaps demonstrating rapid or shallow breathing, sobbing, or shaking, please have the client pause as you attend to the individual. This can be done by gently stating that you would like to pause the exercise for a moment, then quietly asking the person by name if they would like a break, support with deep breath work, or to step out of the guided imagery entirely if it has become too overwhelming.

Note to the Reader: If you are doing this solo without the support of a mental health professional, again, please be gentle with yourself. If you have a trusted person to lead you through this, you may want to consider this option, or perhaps you can read this into a recording device and then play back and follow the prompts. If you become overwhelmed or feel as if you are in a crisis state, please stop and reach out for help if need be. Safety first, always.

Purpose of "The Garden": The purpose of this guided imagery exercise is to help you explore and fully embrace your authentic self by guiding you through a deep and reflective journey. It encourages you to connect with all aspects of your personality, including those that you may have suppressed or overlooked, fostering greater self-awareness and acceptance.

Instructions: This guided imagery exercise will take approximately 10 minutes. You will be guided by your mental health professional or trusted facilitator, or you may guide yourself if you prefer, through each step of the exercise slowly. Though questions may be asked of you or you may be given prompts, there is no expectation of a verbal response. You may respond if you would like to do so, or you may quietly respond inside of yourself, which many people prefer. Through this visualization journey, you will be guided to explore an imagined garden, ground yourself, and then observe what the garden contains. Each item will represent a part of the self, and you will accept each part as necessary.

First Step Prompt: Close your eyes, take a deep breath, and allow yourself to sink into a comfortable position. When you are ready, picture yourself in a serene garden. It may be one that you've visited or one that lives in your imagination. **Note to Facilitator: Count to 20 silently.**

Next Prompt Step: As you stand at the outer edge of the garden, take a moment to just observe and answer the following questions in your mind. What do you see in the garden? **Note to Facilitator: Count to ten silently.**

What can you smell? **Note to Facilitator: Count to ten silently.**

Listen carefully and identify the sounds you hear. **Note to Facilitator: Count to ten silently.**

Now, concentrate on your feet. If you are able to stand, what does the ground feel like underneath them? **Note to Facilitator: Count to ten silently.**

Next Prompt Step: Now, imagine that you move further into the garden. Continue looking around and observing the garden. There may be beautiful flowers or ripe vegetables ready for picking. Notice the colors and textures of everything around you. **Note to Facilitator: Count to 20 silently.**

Next Prompt Step: Now, take a moment and look even closer. You may notice that there are weeds growing in between plants or flowers. Look down at the ground and notice what you see there. There might be rocks and stones in the dirt. There may also be tiny bugs crawling around. You are safe, you are in charge of where you place your feet. Listen closely, and you might hear bees buzzing from plant to plant. These insects are not here to harm you in any way, you are safe. If you prefer to visualize a different type of insect, you are welcome to do so. You are not alone; you are supported. **Note to Facilitator: Count to 20 silently.**

Next Prompt Step: As you continue to listen, you hear a different sound—the gentle pitter-patter of rain falling on the outstretched leaves of the plants. Take a moment with these new sounds. Soon, the rain begins to fall steadily, and you can feel it soak into your clothing. You are not overwhelmed by the feeling of the rain, yet you experience a slight chill and realize the garden you're in is not simply made up of sunshine and flowers. It is a complex ecosystem containing various insects, rocks, and dirt that is now turning into mud due to the rain. As you continue to stand in the rain, you shudder gently from the feeling of wet clothing on your skin and notice some discomfort, and also notice that you are safe and secure despite the discomfort. **Note to Facilitator: Count to 20 silently.**

Next Prompt Step: As the rain continues to soak your skin, take a moment to observe your initial response to this discomfort. You may feel angry at the cold rain that ruined your visit to the garden. You may feel like crying as your hair or clothing is now soaked. You may only be thinking of running as fast as you can to the safe dryness of a shelter, deciding that you never want to return to this garden. Or you may feel something entirely different. What thoughts come to your mind? **Note to Facilitator: Count to 10 silently.**

What emotions are you feeling? **Note to Facilitator: Count to 10 silently.**

What sensations are in your body? **Note to Facilitator: Count to 10 silently.**

Next Prompt Step: Now, I want you to take a deep breath and let it out slowly, and as you do, you decide to just stay where you are in the garden. As the rain continues, a new thought washes over your mind. Observing the garden around you, you realize that it is not just made up of beautiful flowers, ripening vegetables, sunshine, and butterflies. This is a real garden that also contains bugs, bees, weeds, dirt, and rain. You take another deep breath and relax your body, accepting the truth that all parts of the garden are necessary and magnificent in their own way. Each plant, each insect, and every clump of dirt is important to their garden home—even the weeds have a purpose. **Note to Facilitator: Count to 20 silently.**

Next Prompt Step: As you prepare to leave the garden, you look around one last time, thanking it for the lesson you learned today—that all parts of nature are needed and beautiful. You notice that even though you are damp from the rain, you get to decide how to feel and respond to this unexpected experience. You realize that you are safe, and with this new knowledge, you slowly walk back down the garden path, even taking some time to enjoy the mud puddles if you'd like to do so. **Note to Facilitator: Count to 20 silently.**

Next Prompt Step: As you exit the garden, remind yourself that, just like nature, all parts of you are unique and acceptable. And just like the garden contains flowers and bugs, butterflies, and dirt, you, too, are made up of many different emotions, thoughts, physical characteristics, and talents woven together into a wonderful and valuable human being. **Note to Facilitator: Count to 20 silently.**

Next Prompt Step: Know that you have the strength and resilience to learn to mindfully accept all parts of yourself and increase your mindful presence when the unexpected occurs. Please remember that you are not alone in this journey of healing; you are supported. No matter the challenges that come your way, remember that you are worthy of a life filled with love, authenticity, respect, joy, and fulfillment. Take a moment now to give yourself an affirmation. Self-affirmations may take you out of your comfort zone, but do your best to stay present with yourself, even in the discomfort. **Note to Facilitator: Count to 20 silently.**

Transitioning to Awareness

Final Prompt Step: When you're ready, if your eyes are closed, notice the light in front of your eyelids. Gently blink, open your eyes, and bring your awareness back to the present moment.

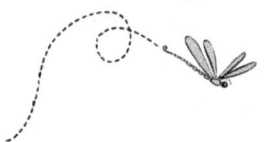

Mindfulness Healing Part IV:
Processing of Guided Imagery
Sharing Your Experience

Purpose for Processing: After the conclusion of the guided imagery, the therapist or facilitator will lead an open and respectful discussion about what the client experienced during the guided imagery. The aim is to allow for a compassionate and honest conversation to highlight important aspects of the guided imagery exercise and what the experience was like.

Note: If you are doing this solo without a therapist or facilitator, pace yourself and notice your energy. You may journal your responses to the questions if you are doing this work on your own.

Important Considerations for the Facilitator: It is not the role of the therapist or facilitator to interpret, minimize, or re-direct. Rather, it is important for the facilitator to skillfully hold a safe space for the client to share their experience, including the more difficult aspects. This is a time for the facilitator to honor the pain, as well as highlight and affirm the positive insights the client may have had. Remind the client that participating in a therapy exercise like this is a signal of hope and aids in the possibility of recovery and healing.

Processing Questions

1. What did you notice in the guided imagery?

2. What challenges did you experience?

3. What joys did you experience?

4. Did you have a breakthrough you'd like to share?

5. Do you have any concerns that you'd like to share?

6. What are you feeling in your body currently?

7. Did you notice any self-growth with insight and compassion toward yourself?

8. Did you notice any triggers or areas of concern?

Now that you have completed the breath work and somatic exercises, the guided imagery exercise, and the process work, on a scale from 1 to 10 (with 1 = very low, and 10 = very high), let's take a mindful moment to assess the following:

Feeling	Assessment (1-10)									
▫ Anxiety	1	2	3	4	5	6	7	8	9	10
▫ Anger	1	2	3	4	5	6	7	8	9	10
▫ Shame	1	2	3	4	5	6	7	8	9	10
▫ Sadness	1	2	3	4	5	6	7	8	9	10
▫ Fear	1	2	3	4	5	6	7	8	9	10
▫ Numbness	1	2	3	4	5	6	7	8	9	10
▫ Confusion	1	2	3	4	5	6	7	8	9	10
▫ Curiosity	1	2	3	4	5	6	7	8	9	10
▫ Hopefulness	1	2	3	4	5	6	7	8	9	10
▫ Calm	1	2	3	4	5	6	7	8	9	10
▫ Joyful	1	2	3	4	5	6	7	8	9	10
▫ Other:	1	2	3	4	5	6	7	8	9	10

Important Reminder: If you, as the facilitator, are not a licensed therapist or trained mental health professional and your client is in crisis and exhibiting or discussing symptoms that are out of your scope of practice or experience, please refer to an appropriate mental health or medical professional. *If your client is experiencing an immediate life-threatening emergency, please call 911 or the appropriate emergency number if located outside of the United States. If you are doing this solo without support and are in a state of emergency, reach out to 911 immediately.*

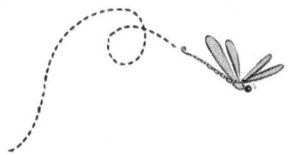

Mindfulness Healing Part V:

Purpose Statement: The following garden artwork will give you an opportunity to identify parts of yourself and begin to practice compassionate acceptance of each part.

Art Exercise Instructions: Gather art supplies such as paper, colored pencils, stickers, or other dry materials. Please be mindful if you choose to use supplies like markers or paints, as these can sometimes bleed through to the next page. You may want to place a blank sheet of paper underneath your work to protect the following pages.

A) Begin by finding a quiet and comfortable space where you can focus without distractions.

B) Take a few moments to center yourself through deep breathing, visualization, or grounding exercises. Allow yourself to become present in the moment, acknowledging without self judgment, any thoughts or emotions that arise.

C) Once you feel grounded, take a moment to look at the picture of the garden provided on the next page, noticing all parts of it. Then, using your art supplies, color the picture to match the garden you imagined during your guided imagery meditation. If you prefer to draw your own garden on a separate piece of paper, you are welcome to do so.

D) Next, think about what the various elements in the garden might represent in your life. For example, the butterfly might be the part of you that is outgoing and friendly. The snail might be the part of you that procrastinates. The bee might be a coworker with whom you disagree. The weeds may be your childhood trauma. The veggies may remind you of nurturing people, places, or things. The clouds may be situations or people who feel oppressive. Feel free to add raindrops, as there may be parts of your life that feel chilling and uncomfortable. The roses may be those in your life who are supportive and kind. These are examples, but I invite you to label the various parts of the garden in a way that feels best for you and what they represent in your life.

E) As you work on your art, pay attention to any emotions or sensations that arise. Allow yourself to explore them openly without negative self-talk Remember there are no right or wrong ways to express yourself through art.

Once you have completed your art exercise, take a step back and observe your creation. Reflect on the journey it represents, recognizing the challenges you have faced and the progress you have made. Think about strategies that will support your path toward healing.

Take a moment to appreciate yourself for engaging in this healing art exercise and for the courage you have shown. Allow yourself to feel a sense of pride and accomplishment as you continue your journey of recovery.

Mindfulness Healing Part V:

Art Exercise II—My Life Story

Purpose Statement: The purpose of the "My Life Story" healing art exercise is to reflect on your life story and how your self-concept developed, accepting all parts of yourself lovingly and without judgment.

Art Exercise Instructions: Gather needed art supplies: poster board, scissors glue, and magazines. If you do not have access to magazines, you can use any of the following: printed images (find images online, print them, and cut them out) old photos (photographs that you no longer need or want), text and handwriting (print out meaningful words or quotes), or found objects (small objects like buttons, string, or fabric). Whatever you prefer is more than acceptable.

A)   Begin by finding a quiet and comfortable space where you can focus without distractions.

B)   Take a few moments to center yourself through deep breathing, visualization, or grounding exercises. Allow yourself to become present in the moment, acknowledging without judgement, any thoughts or emotions that arise.

C)   Once you feel grounded, begin to gather the pictures, words, phrases, or items that accurately represent various parts of your life story. These pictures may represent people, places, or things in your life that have had an impact on you. Perhaps you'll see a picture of the sun and think, *I have a sunny personality*. Perhaps you'll find a picture of a dog that reminds you of a special animal in your life. You may find a picture or object that represents a painful childhood memory that influenced who you are today. Also, if there is a word that is important to you, you might cut out the letters and assemble the word yourself.

D)   After you have collected as many pictures or words as you desire, glue them onto the poster board, creating a collage.

E)   As you add each piece to your page, pay attention to any emotions or sensations that arise. Allow yourself to explore them openly and without negative self-talk. What are the mind states and mind stories you are observing as you engage in this project? Remember there are no right or wrong ways to express yourself through art.

Once you have completed your art exercise, take a step back and observe your creation. Reflect on the journey it represents, recognizing the challenges you have faced and the progress you have made. Think about strategies that will support your path toward healing.

Take a moment to appreciate yourself for engaging in this healing art exercise and for the courage you have shown. Allow yourself to feel a sense of pride and accomplishment as you continue your journey of recovery.

Mindful Reflection Moment

Now that you have completed your breath work, guided imagery, and art and journal exercises, please take some mindful time to reflect before we bring this chapter to a close. You are welcome to answer the following questions in the space below, or write in a journal or notebook of your choice. You may do this with your therapist, or if you are working through this book solo, you can do this on your own.

1. What are you noticing after this chapter?

2. What awareness and insight have surfaced?

3. What is the information you have learned?

Write or share your reflections here or in your own journal or notebook if you would like to continue processing. As always, please be gentle with yourself:

_____

_____

_____

_____

_____

_____

Final Step: Self-Affirmation Exercise

Instructions: Before moving on to the next chapter, can you give yourself the gift of self-affirmation? Affirming oneself can be difficult for those who have experienced trauma, are grieving, coping with addiction, healing from complex trauma, or struggling with anxiety, depression, or other challenges.

As a support to this step of your healing, affirmation ideas might include statements such as: "I accept all parts of myself," "Being truthful with myself protects me from risky behavior," or "Just as the garden needs all its parts to flourish, I can learn to accept all parts of myself as necessary to flourish." On the next page, you are invited to use the winged heart to honor your own self-affirmation(s). If you can only come up with one affirmation at this time, that is more than acceptable. Perhaps you can return later in your healing process and add more:

In this chapter, my aim was to more deeply explore the concept of mindful self-acceptance, and how it relates to mind states and mind stories while providing practical ways to incorporate mindfulness into your daily routine. Additionally, my hope is that you are encouraged to shift toward an internal locus of control, empowering you to take ownership of your thoughts and actions. Through the practice of guided imagery, you can learn to embrace all parts of yourself, cultivating a sense of equanimity, inner peace, and self-compassion.

As you complete this chapter, I would like to offer an encouraging affirmation to you before moving on: You are a courageous human being deserving of support. My hope is that you feel supported in accepting every part of yourself with kindness and understanding. Embrace all that you are without shame or self-judgment, allowing space for growth and self-acceptance as you continue on your journey.

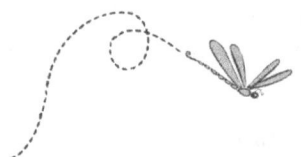

CHAPTER THREE

The Road to Renewal:
Repairing the Betrayal Rupture

Mari A. Lee

Betrayal is, fundamentally, any act or life choice that doesn't prioritize the relationship commitment or put the partner before all others.

~ John Gottman

Maria and Paul, a married couple in their early forties and devoted parents of two young children, reached out to me through my website, hoping to find support during a deeply painful season in their relationship—one where the distance and resentment between them had grown so wide that divorce felt like a very real possibility.

The marital strain stemmed from Paul's involvement in two affairs and his secretive use of pornography and sex websites. Compounding the issue was Maria's recent discovery of Paul exchanging nude photos with a dancer he encountered at a strip club during a business trip. Describing their tumultuous 17-year journey in an email, Maria expressed, "It's been almost two decades of periodic betrayal and deception, and unless we start couple's therapy, I cannot deal with this any longer."

· · · · ·

In their initial couple's session, Paul and Maria acknowledged their love for each other, yet the session revealed that they were in an undeniable crisis. Maria, an intelligent and straightforward woman, articulately conveyed the enduring pain she had carried for many years. She shared, "I grew up in Puerto Rico, witnessing my mother's heart shatter repeatedly due to my father's constant infidelity. I heard my dad's promises, witnessed their frequent arguments, saw my mom's tears, and listened to her threats, but nothing ever changed. This cycle continued until I saw the light fade from her, and she passed away prematurely. Paul and I have created a solid life together—with our two children, my legal career, and his accounting practice, we've exceeded our expectations, enjoying our family and a close-knit circle of friends who cherish us. However, I refuse to replicate my parents' destructive pattern in my own marriage for another day. I have stayed for the kids, but I am worn down by Paul's continual lies and apologies. Enough is enough!"

Despite being a man in his mid-life, Paul's red hair and freckles lent him an innocent boy-next-door appearance. Anxiously adjusting in his seat, Paul hesitatingly shared in a subdued voice, "I love my wife, and the last thing I want is to continue hurting her. Maria is the best thing that ever happened to me, and she is the mother of my children. But I keep hurting her and wrecking our relationship. I've been out of control for years. I don't want to attribute it to an addiction, but every time I try to stop, I find myself right back in it. I don't know what to do at this point, and I'm finally ready to admit that this feels bigger than me."

Over the next three sessions, I assessed their history, what they had been through in their marriage—both as a couple and individually—and their goals for therapy. Our next step was to cover a treatment plan. I shared that while I would be happy to support them with couples counseling, they would greatly benefit from working with their own individual therapists in addition to our work. Paul agreed to begin seeing a therapist who specialized in out-of-control sexual behaviors, sometimes referred to as sex addiction. I referred Maria to a colleague who specializes in partner's betrayal trauma. I explained that until Paul was ready to formally disclose, take ownership, and gain insight into himself and his choices that had left Maria emotionally traumatized, trying to rebuild trust and respect at this early juncture in couples therapy would be like building a house on shifting sand. Before deep healing can take place, establishing a foundation of transparency through a therapy-assisted formal disclosure—along with ownership, insight, and a genuine commitment to healing—is essential.

With compassion, I conveyed to Paul, "Maria deserves the right to make an informed decision about whether to stay in the marriage or to choose a different path once all the cards are laid out. Rebuilding the shattered trust from the outset is an incredibly challenging task and nearly impossible without delving into deeper healing. Part of healing will be increasing self-compassion, building empathy toward Maria who has been profoundly impacted, gaining insight into yourself, and taking full ownership. One of the early pivotal aspects of the couple's healing journey involves engaging in the therapeutic process of clinical formal disclosure." Paul responded that while he was nervous about formal disclosure, he was willing. He said, "Whatever I need to do to finally make this right, I will do it."

Though Maria was on board with formal disclosure and supported Paul seeing a therapist specializing in sexual compulsivity and addiction, she was hesitant to begin her own therapy process, "I did not ask for any of this. I've done nothing wrong! Why do I need to see my own therapist? I'm not the one with the problem here." I validated this understandable reaction, "Maria, you are right. You did not ask for this, and you do not deserve any part of these betrayals. Given that you have suffered through many years of trauma, it will be important for you to have your own dedicated support to help you heal the wounds you have suffered. Your therapist will also help you prepare for the formal disclosure process."

As she pondered this feedback, Maria's eyes filled with tears, "Mari, I've never thought of this as trauma until right this moment, but that is exactly what it feels like. However, I want to be clear that I am not a victim! My whole life, I've prided myself on being able to pull myself up by my bootstraps and put on a brave face. Yet, I see your point. I have been suffering emotionally, and there are also some days I feel so depressed that it is hard to get out of bed. My physical health has been impacted as well. Some weeks, I feel pain in my body, my stomach is a mess, or my sleep is nonexistent. I have less joy as a mother, and I love my children more than anything in this world. I have always been a detail-oriented and organized person, but lately, I find myself making small mistakes within my law practice. I suppose learning a few tools that can help me would be wise. I'm not happy about it, but I'm willing to give it a try."

We scheduled bi-monthly couple's sessions to support communication and boundaries, and Paul and Maria moved courageously forward, settling into their individual therapy processes. Part of their individual therapy treatment plans, as outlined by their primary therapists, included trauma reduction through EMDR for both (see glossary for definition of EMDR), insight, empathy and skills building, an understanding of their individual attachment styles, addiction recovery for Paul, therapy tasks and homework, adjunct support through group therapy and Twelve Step, formal disclosure preparation, as well as inner child work and mindfulness-based work for both. Step-by-step, week-by-week, and month-by-month, this couple began to build a roadmap toward recovery.

In the initial stages of our couples therapy, Maria and Paul came to understand the intricate and complex nature of betrayal trauma. In one of our sessions, I explained that betrayal trauma is complex due to various factors. One crucial aspect is that the person who inflicts the trauma is the trusted significant other. Moreover, this specific form of intimate partner betrayal trauma emerges only after the relational betrayal(s) occur. What sets betrayal trauma apart is its inherent damage, which is often marked by deliberate grooming, premeditation, and intentional, secretive orchestration. It is also characterized by exploitation and manipulation, often involving staggered disclosures and gaslighting. The acute complexity of this trauma is evident in its impact across multiple facets of the partner's life—marital or relational, academic, parenting, career, emotional, spiritual, and, of course, the partner's physical and mental health (Corley, M. D. 2012; Schneider, J. P. 2012; Hudson, R. 2021).

The Formal Disclosure Process: A Transparent Path Toward Healing

An essential aspect of the initial phase in recovering from betrayal trauma was readying Paul and Maria for formal disclosure. This crucial stage in sex addiction and betrayal trauma therapy plays a vital role in facilitating the healing of the betrayed partner and is an important recovery milestone for the betraying partner as well. Individual therapeutic support also helps reduce feelings of isolation, fear, and self-loathing for the recovering person who has done the betraying. Formal disclosure empowers the individual in sex addiction recovery to assume complete and transparent responsibility for the betraying behaviors and deceptions that have inflicted substantial wounds on their significant other, the relationship, and, of course, on themselves.

It is important to share that though formal disclosure is a process to aid in healing and trust rebuilding, it is a multifaceted process that is often anxiety-provoking for both individuals. This process is most successful when it is facilitated by healing professionals who have been trained in this specialization, who are experienced in addiction and complex trauma, and who are sensitive to intimate partner betrayal. When a formal disclosure is led by a therapeutic team in a non-judgmental, compassionate, collaborative, and focused manner, it can help reduce the understandable pain that may occur for each of the partners, most especially the betrayed partner.

If you are new to this concept, let me explain it further. Formal disclosure is a multi-stage process that involves the individual and couple's therapists preparing each person in the relationship for the formal disclosure meeting. Therapists monitor their progress with each member of the treatment team, ensuring confidentiality is maintained when collaborating on treatment goals and when discussing details. Once the couple is adequately prepared, the subsequent step involves scheduling the formal disclosure meeting, during which both individual therapists attend to support the couple.

The primary objective of this meeting is for the person grappling with addiction or compulsive behaviors to unequivocally assume responsibility for their sexual deception, as well as other deceptive behaviors, in the relationship. This includes disclosing a comprehensive and partner-sensitive timeline outlining each instance of sexual betrayal, the accompanying lies, money spent, legal incidents, and any other detrimental actions or addictions that have inflicted harm upon their spouse or partner. The formal disclosure meeting is sometimes followed by a clarification meeting if more questions arise that the partner wants answered.

After the initial formal disclosure meeting and clarification meeting, the betrayed partner works with their individual therapist to prepare their emotional impact letter. This preparation is followed by the emotional impact meeting where the partner, in the presence of their significant other and both therapists, is supported as they share how they have been impacted by their spouse's or partner's betrayal in all areas of their life—as a spouse or partner, a parent, a daughter or son, a sibling, in their professional or academic roles, their mental and physical health, their spirituality, their finances, their sexuality, and other areas where the partner has been struggling due to the betrayal trauma. The emotional impact meeting concludes with the partner reviewing their boundaries and safety requests moving forward.

The final phase of the formal disclosure process is the emotional restitution meeting, where the individual dealing with addiction has conscientiously collaborated with their therapist to compose an amends letter. This letter goes far beyond mere apology, incorporating profound insight, complete ownership, and genuine empathy and outlining a detailed plan toward an ongoing commitment to healing and change.

As I share with the clients and couples I work with, growth and insight do not happen overnight, nor are they achieved within a handful of therapy sessions. Rather, it is the result of focused support over time and a commitment on the part of the therapy client toward dedicated recovery. This includes a sincere willingness to heal, grow, gain insight, change behaviors, increase empathy toward their betrayed significant other, develop self-compassion, and make healthy changes for themselves and their relationship. Bringing attention to early wounded areas that have been left unattended and unresolved is often necessary. Therapy may also include support for a previously undiagnosed mental illness, such as bipolar disorder, or help in increasing the client's understanding of neurodiversity if that is part of the treatment plan. For example, it may incorporate education and tools for attention deficit disorder, address anxiety disorders such as obsessive-compulsive disorder, or provide insight into personality disorders, anger issues, and communication problems. Therapy can also help individuals develop healthy boundaries, gain insight into their attachment style, and address multiple addictions, including marijuana, nicotine, alcohol, drugs, gambling, or gaming.

Additionally, just as trauma is complex, human beings are complex as well, composed of events and memories that pre-exist the relationship. For clients who balk at understanding how their past impacts the present, I often share, "We do not live in the past, but the past lives in us and informs our mind states and stories, as well as our words and actions. Every person deserves to have a season of mindful healing and awareness to integrate those hurting parts, and to better understand themselves."

Formal disclosure is a multi-stage, challenging chapter of healing and requires specialized, focused guidance, as well as a collaborative effort among all therapists involved in assisting the couple. Like many couples, Paul and Maria encountered difficulties along the way; however, by working closely with their respective therapists, along with couples therapy and the treatment team working together, they navigated the formal disclosure path, including the inevitable road bumps, successfully. As they engaged in their therapy sessions, this couple addressed their anxiety and discussed their fears as the first disclosure meeting approached, leaning into their therapy team to help them through the hurdles.

• • • • •

The Highs and Lows of Healing

As Paul and Maria embarked on the next steps after the formal disclosure process, they began to rediscover and revitalize aspects of themselves that had long been frozen in trauma by the abuse and neglect in their personal family backgrounds. Progress was slow but steady as they worked toward healing themselves and their relationship.

Paul was able to attend to long-standing grief and anger because of an estranged relationship with his father, who had left when Paul was 12 years old. In one session, Paul shared, "I was the oldest of my siblings, and two days before my dad walked out for good, I yelled at him and called him a loser and a drunk and told him I hated him. My dad was always drinking and fighting with my mom, hiding porn magazines all over the house, or flirting with the neighbor ladies, and then it would be up to me to comfort my mother. After my dad left, I felt like it was my fault that they split up. I kept hoping he would call or come back, but I did not see him again until I was sixteen—and then only briefly.

"During this time, my mom expected me to be the man of the house, and it felt like everything was on my shoulders. I never felt like I had a real childhood or responsible parents. I just wanted a normal life like my friends, and I hated having to constantly babysit my little sisters, cook and clean, work odd jobs, and be my mom's confidant when she talked poorly about my dad. When I started dating, my mother would find ways to try and sabotage my relationships or guilt me into canceling plans with a girl I was interested in. Sometimes, she would blame me for the divorce, telling me that I was the reason my dad left us. She called me names like 'jerk' or 'idiot' and told me I was a selfish loser like my dad if I did not do as I was told every minute of the day. She was so controlling and smothering, and I could not wait to leave home."

As Paul moved through the process of healing, his commitment to his recovery increased tremendously. A quote that I share with clients is from Dr. Gabor Maté, a preeminent doctor specializing in addiction: "Knowing oneself comes from attending with compassionate curiosity to what is happening within." As Paul learned about his early wounds, it wasn't an immediate transformation, but he was steadfast in his commitment to making the necessary changes to reclaim his authentic self while minimizing harsh self-judgment.

Part of this process involved healing the resentment and pain from his childhood, integrating the parts of himself that had been abused, abandoned, and ignored, and working on the understandable resentment he held toward his mother and father. As his progress continued, Paul was able to hold compassion for his younger self and the trauma he had endured while fully assuming responsibility for his betrayal actions rather than blaming others or Maria.

An important goal for Paul was to rebuild Maria's trust and respect not just through words but, more importantly, through transparent and consistent actions. Along the way, he also acquired skills to aid Maria in healing the profound hurt he had caused. The journey wasn't swift, but Paul's dedication shone through as he worked toward both personal recovery and the restoration of their relationship.

During this vulnerable period, Maria practiced valuable skills in advocating for herself with a focus on maintaining a grounded presence that respected both her and Paul. This involved expressing important boundaries and safety needs in a way that she could be heard rather than resorting to threats or verbal abuse. A courageous breakthrough surfaced in a couple's session when Maria was going over a family of origin timeline exercise and noticed similarities in the way her mother and father had spoken to her during her early development. Verbal abuse, threats of punishment or abandonment, and physical abuse were the ways that Maria and her brother were disciplined.

Maria somberly shared, "It is hard to talk about this because I loved my mother, and I miss her. I think I put her on a pedestal and vilified my father as the abusive cheater. However, I can see that the beatings we endured from Mom and the way my mother screamed at us were child abuse. I was terrified to make a mistake, and because my mother was so unhappy in her marriage, as a little girl and then a teen, I did not want to cause her more stress or grief. I also wanted to protect my little brother from being hit with the belt or yelled at. I recall a time when my brother accidentally broke a holy figurine in our home, and I took the blame. I can still see the spittle flying from my mother's mouth as she screamed at me and slapped me again and again until my mouth and nose were bloody. When I ran to my father for protection and comfort, he just shrugged, laughed at my tears, and said, 'Be more careful, *torpe*,' which means clumsy in Spanish."

Over time, both Paul and Maria gained a deeper understanding of the distinctions between ultimatums, threats, and healthy boundaries. Maria courageously developed the ability to recognize, articulate, and uphold her boundaries, allowing for consequences without attempting to control outcomes as she had done in the past through insults, threats of divorce, parental alienation, verbal abuse, or ultimatums. Embracing these new compassionate communication strategies not only aligned with her therapy goals but also liberated her from the role of constantly caretaking and managing Paul's progress.

As we moved through this part of the work, I explained, "No healthy person wants to be a parent to their partner. As you are both learning, there are early parts within each of you that were wounded in your family of origins and are stuck in gear. These early parts have not fully developed due to non-integrated trauma. Additionally, those hurting parts may be frozen in time at eight years old, twelve years old, eighteen years old, and so forth. For betrayed partners who were parentified or abused in childhood and have learned to assume most of the responsibility and do the heavy lifting in their relationships, they often overcompensate by taking on too much. At their core, most people want healthy partners, not projects to fix or control."

A Breakthrough: Primary and Secondary Gains

As Paul gained more traction in his healing work, he not only increased insight into his behaviors but demonstrated that insight as well. Eventually, Paul was able to discuss his communication boundary needs with Maria in a way that demonstrated empathy for her trauma and pain while honoring his need for healthy and respectful communication within the marriage. Due to Maria's early family of origin abuse and the parentified role that she had been thrust into, perfectionism and control had been maladaptive coping mechanisms that helped her feel safe as a young person and as an adult. Maria learned in our work that as she matured into adulthood, these coping mechanisms were not helping her grow and felt stifling to others in her life, including her siblings, friendships, employees, and especially her spouse.

A breakthrough session occurred when Paul experienced a slip in early recovery. After returning from a three-day conference, without prompting or probing from Maria, he revealed that he had briefly flirted with a server at a restaurant during a business dinner. Understandably, this created a great deal of hurt and confusion for Maria, as well as shame and fear for Paul. Paul sighed in defeat and said, "I have no idea why I did something so stupid; I feel like I have destroyed all of our hard work and set us back to ground zero.

In response, Maria slipped back into old communication patterns, and her trauma was triggered as she began to angrily lecture and threaten Paul, "You are so stupid! How could you do this to me and to us? If you want to be with other women, then fine; be with them. I can go find another man to screw around with this weekend. How about that? How about I divorce you and take you for every penny? How about I tell everyone we know what a cheater you are? How about I tell our kids what a loser you are so they never want to see you again? How about I slap some sense into your idiotic head? When are you going to finally figure this out? How many more years do you think I am going to put up with your cheating foolishness?"

In response, Paul stared at his feet, muttering, "Sorry you ended up with such a loser." Maria's nervous system was flooded, and her reaction was to roll her eyes, ball up her fists, sneer, and shake her head in disgust.

As I assisted Maria and Paul with communication boundaries and mindfulness grounding techniques, we explored the pattern of Paul's self-sabotage and Maria's understandable pain that sometimes escalated into destructive rage and verbal abuse. Part of this exploration was deepening their understanding of post-traumatic stress and sympathetic nervous system responses. The amygdala is the part of the brain responsible for this type of reactivity. For example, when a person feels stressed or afraid, the amygdala releases stress hormones that prepare the body to fight the threat or flee from the danger. Common emotions that trigger this response include fear, anger, disgust, and anxiety.

When Maria's trauma was triggered, she reacted with a limbic fight response—yelling, name-calling, and threatening. Paul's nervous system was wired toward the freeze or fawn response, either silently staring at the ground, freezing in shame, or quickly attempting to appease Maria with empty promises and apologies. Helping them both understand the difference between the sympathetic nervous system that drives certain emotions in stressful situations—fight, flight, freeze, or fawn—versus the parasympathetic nervous system responsible for the "rest and digest" condition was eye-opening for this couple.

As we carefully unpeeled years of this toxic communication pattern, we revealed an important dynamic the couple was not aware of with respect to secondary gains. When I asked Paul what the secondary gains were in damaging the progress in rebuilding Maria's trust, his predictable response was, "Nothing. I gain nothing by relapsing." I explained that a primary gain is one that we are conscious of, and a secondary gain is one that is generally unconscious.

For example, the primary gain of going to a therapist for addiction recovery is that you receive the support and help needed to create a life and relationships you are proud of. In addition, you might have other primary gains by healing old wounds, growing as a person, and restoring marital trust over time. There is a focused plan, and the person clearly understands the primary gains.

However, with secondary gains, there is an unconscious agenda at play. In therapy, when we talk about a "secondary gain," we're referring to the unintentional benefit or reward that a person might unknowingly get from a symptom, behavior, or condition they're experiencing. Therapists explore this to figure out why someone might stick to certain habits even if it seems like there are negative consequences.

For example, let's consider a person who consistently avoids social situations due to anxiety. The primary issue is the anxiety itself, but a secondary gain might be the sense of safety and control the individual feels by avoiding interactions or gatherings that may trigger discomfort. In this case, the avoidance of social situations becomes an unskilled coping mechanism that provides a perceived benefit of comfort and security, even though it restricts the person's social life and doesn't allow for insight or growth to occur. Understanding these underlying secondary gains is crucial in therapy, as addressing them helps therapists work with clients to find healthier alternatives and motivations, ultimately promoting positive change.

Specific to Maria and Paul's marriage, Paul and I explored the roles of resentment and entitlement that supported his unconscious secondary gains: "Paul, some individuals who struggle with addictive behaviors discover that one of the emotional roots that feeds slips and relapses is resentment, and resentment is often the doorway to entitlement. Thus, the more resentment that is festering, the more entitlement some people experience."

My next question was directed to both, "Was there something that occurred prior to your business trip that may have triggered your resentment toward Maria?" Paul and Maria began to nod together, and Maria exclaimed, "Yes! I was upset with Paul for once again leaving wet clothes in the washer for two days. I remember scolding him and seeing that old expression of shame, like a hurt little kid. I was irritated and tired and yelled at him to 'quit acting like a stupid little boy and grow up!' We went to bed, and Paul left early for his flight without saying goodbye and without us talking it through."

A dawning realization now lit up Paul's face, "Wow. I think I am having what Maria calls a 'No shit, Sherlock' moment! I remember feeling angry and hurt all through the night. I was ruminating on Maria's words on the plane and recalled thinking, *Why bother? I'll never do anything right!* Then, after my meeting, while getting ready to connect with my colleagues for dinner, I experienced a feeling of deep resentment toward Maria. I remember thinking, *I hate when she talks to me like I am a stupid kid!*

"I started to text her that I did not want to be spoken to this way but stopped because I often feel intimidated. I was triggered but also felt helpless, and instead of using my tools, my resentment took over. I blamed Maria and then felt entitled to do what I wanted. I had a couple of martinis at dinner, felt drunk, and then flirted with the server. It felt empowering, at least in that moment, almost like I was giving Maria a middle finger.

"I tried to justify it to myself at the time, but on the flight home the following day, I felt guilty and was disappointed with myself. I have learned in therapy that blaming Maria for my choices is not healthy. Despite what would happen, I decided to be transparent with Maria, and I was grateful we had a couple's session today because I knew she was going to be very upset with me, and I don't blame her for being furious and hurt."

Paul further pondered, "I wonder if some of my choices, things I absolutely know get under Maria's skin, like leaving wet laundry for two days, is a way to get back at her when she is controlling and critical, or maybe a way of keeping my resentment tank filled so I have an excuse to act out. She works hard as an attorney and is exhausted at the end of the day, and it is not fair to her to have to deal with everything. When Maria belittles, threatens, insults, or tries to control me, I am starting to understand that this is a big resentment trigger for me that quickly escalates into entitlement. I know it is not her fault for my choices that have betrayed and traumatized her, and I am not blaming Maria for my sexual deception. I need to learn better ways of communicating and following through on my side of things."

With that, Paul dropped his defensive posture, his body softened, and true remorse and insight were apparent. As I turned toward Maria, I saw a ray of hope light up her eyes, and as they gazed at each other, Maria leaned into Paul, saying, "I think we just had a breakthrough."

• • • • •

Through each stage of the couple's healing process, it was important to validate that Maria was not responsible for Paul's choices. It was Paul's responsibility not to soothe his marital challenges through sexual betrayal or subsequent gaslighting and deception. Paul agreed that he could have made other choices in dealing with the issues he was experiencing in the marriage. For example, Paul could have begun individual therapy, taken the lead in initiating the couple's therapy, sought support through a trusted friend, learned ways of expressing his boundaries, or learned tools to advocate for healthier communication in the marriage. As they progressed, Paul began to understand that any of those choices would have been healthier than infidelity and lying.

At the end of one particularly emotional session, Paul stated quietly, "It seems so obvious now. Instead of coming up with solutions for how I was feeling, I snuck around behind Maria's back, creating more damage. Sneaking around is what I learned as a young kid and teen. I often felt like I was impotent in all areas of my life after an argument with my mom, like I was a complete failure who did not deserve a voice. This pattern continued in my marriage without Maria having any understanding of this. However, I could have made different choices; I could have even asked for a separation or divorce if therapy did not work for us versus cheating on Maria."

Maria turned to her husband, placing her hand kindly on his arm, "I had no idea how small you felt in our marriage, and I honestly did not see how my anger was harming you and us. When I hear you share your experience and take full ownership that you chose to sexualize your pain and frustration instead of coming to me with other options for improving our marriage, I feel a little more hopeful about our future. I know I am not responsible for your choices, Paul, choices that devastated me, but as I learn more about your childhood and experience your current growth, I feel less defensive and more willing to look at ways I can grow and communicate better." Paul took his wife's hand, and a genuine moment of tenderness and understanding began to blossom between them.

Healing Old Patterns

During the weeks ahead, we explored their unique communication patterns that had unknowingly supported the cycle of the secondary gains. Together, they discovered that their specific pattern consistently played out in the following way:

↓ An activating event occurred, typically with Paul not following through on a task or a promise to Maria.

↓ This activating event often triggered a frustrated and perfectionistic part of Maria, who shared feeling disrespected and abandoned. A sympathetic nervous system rage response was expressed through yelling, insults, and threats toward Paul.

↓ Paul's limbic response was to freeze with silence or move into a fawn response with excuses and apologies while internalizing his own rage, hopelessness, humiliation, shame, and emotional impotence.

↓ Paul's unspoken boundaries remained buried while Maria's hypervigilant control kicked into high gear. This pattern fueled rising resentment from Paul toward Maria and increased entitlement in Paul, which often led to an acting out sexual incident by Paul, sometimes referred to as "eroticized rage."

↓ Prior to therapy, Paul would sometimes disclose the betrayal incident, or Maria would discover the betrayal incident. This betrayal, disclosure, or discovery triggered understandable trauma responses in Maria, which were typically rage, despair, hopelessness, and grief that manifested as yelling, threats, insults, and verbal abuse.

↓ Paul's sympathetic nervous system response to Maria's trauma response was often shame, fear, hopelessness, freezing, appeasing, or fawning. Rejection and further internalized rage followed, which led to freezing or fawning, buried emotions, and unspoken boundaries.

↓ This was usually followed by Maria threatening to harm Paul parentally, financially, physically, professionally, or socially. Maria would sometimes stonewall Paul by giving him the "silent treatment" for several days.

↓ This communication pattern further fueled Paul's internalized fear, abandonment, silent rage, and resentment and Maria's sense of being alone in the marriage and feeling forced into a punitive parental role. Resentment fuels Paul's entitlement and triggers Maria's hypervigilance and control.

↻ The cycle starts all over again.

It was heartening to see Paul and Maria develop insight into this pattern and uncover the roots that kept them entwined in this destructive cycle. At my prompting, he underwent an assessment for attention deficit hyperactivity disorder (ADHD), specifically for the inattentive type. The inattentive type of ADHD often involves difficulties with sustained attention, follow-through on tasks, and frequent forgetfulness, such as leaving chores incomplete or misplacing items.

After completing a thorough evaluation, Paul was diagnosed with ADHD inattentive type, a realization that brought both frustration and relief. He shared, "Now so much makes sense. I wasn't lazy or ignoring responsibilities; my brain just functions differently than others in my family. If I'd understood this sooner in my life, I might not have been so hard on myself." Maria, nodding, added, "I feel like the pieces are finally falling into place. Knowing this helps me understand that Paul isn't intentionally neglecting things at home. It's simply how his brain processes tasks."

Paul and Maria began to connect the dots between their dynamic and Paul's ADHD inattentive type, especially regarding the cycle of secondary gains. Paul shared his realization with excitement in a subsequent session: "We uncovered another pattern of how I kept my resentment and entitlement alive! For example, Maria likes the dishes in the dishwasher rather than piling up in the sink—it's a simple, reasonable request. But I would only do it if, after reminding me several times, she finally lost her temper and yelled at me. That gave me an excuse to feel justified in acting out by looking at porn or going to a strip club while on business trips.

"It was my way of pushing back without addressing the deeper issues. When my resentment was high, I felt entitled to hurt her as a way of balancing the scales and dealing with my anger and humiliation in passive-aggressive and destructive ways. I understand that my ADHD played a part, but there were also times when I deliberately ignored her requests. I am seeing that this cycle added fuel for my resentment, and I used that as an excuse for my harmful behavior."

Maria smiled in agreement, adding, "When Paul wouldn't follow through, I'd scold him, make threats, or shut down. I felt angry on the outside but hopeless and scared on the inside, like I had to parent him. It's been a huge relief to learn more about his type of ADHD and how it plays a role in all of this. We're also teaming up on practical solutions like reminders and strategies to help Paul follow through on tasks, which is helping us break the cycle."

As they moved forward with these insights and practiced strategies of managing household tasks that were more balanced, we worked on ways to help them express hurts or disappointments. Communicating with respect, calmly negotiating a division of labor in their home, and allowing each person to have their individual way of completing chores was key.

Maria shared a powerful personal insight in one particular session: "Instead of criticizing and trying to control everything Paul thinks, says, or does, I am learning that control is really a mask for my fear, and Paul greatly contributed to that fear by breaking my trust. When I attempt to control Paul, it is because I am trying to lessen any potential future hurt. When I previously blew up at Paul with profanity, name-calling, angry threats, and attempts to control, I guess I thought that Paul would be too scared of me to betray me.

"While I know that his choices to betray me are not my fault, I now understand that my rage and threats over what he did or did not do around the house, how he did the laundry, how he drove, or how he left dishes in the sink had the opposite effect. It's taken me some time and healing to see that while I am not responsible for his betrayals, I am responsible for my own words and behaviors. We both experienced trauma in our families before we even met one another, and we have both contributed to trauma in our marriage on different levels and in different ways. I handled my frustrations and fears with insults and rage. Paul handled his pain by swallowing his hurt and shame and betraying me. Even though I understand that sexual betrayal is a form of emotional abuse, I now also understand that every addiction is rooted in trauma. I am grateful that we are healing these damaging patterns and finally giving ourselves a chance to do things differently."

Maria also shared that not every day was a bed of roses, and that she sometimes struggled with moving forward. She had been terribly hurt and betrayed, and regardless of her own choices in managing her emotions, she did not deserve to be deceived. As Paul supported his recovery consistently and helped Maria heal with his commitment to her well-being, her walls softened over time. With his support, Maria was then able to move into grief work.

Grief, at its core, is the emotional response to loss. It allows the heart to process the absence of something or someone, creating space for reflection, pain, and eventual healing that is unique to each grieving person. Betrayal grief, however, is a deeper, more complex form of grief. It is not just about losing someone; it's about losing trust, security, and sometimes even your sense of self within a relationship. Betrayal grief is often tangled with emotions like anger, shock, fear, shame, and profound sadness that stems from a rupture in the foundation of the relationship. During this stage of her healing, trauma work with her individual therapist, EMDR, and group therapy were important adjunct supports for Maria as she grappled with these challenging road bumps, or what I call the healing crossroads part of therapy. Let's explore this concept more fully in the following exercise:

The Healing Crossroads

When someone is healing from betrayal, they often come to a point where they must choose between two different paths in their journey: Release or Reclaim. Each path has its own unique challenges and rewards, and there is no right or wrong choice. One might go back and forth between the paths. It's about what resonates most deeply with each individual's personal process.

The Release Path

Definition: Honoring your pace as you heal and release the pain and emotional burden tied to specific memories, places, or experiences.

Goal: To free oneself from the weight of the past without necessarily forgetting it.

Key Rewards:

- Release is about finding peace with what has been lost.

- It involves choosing to heal memories, or triggers that cause ongoing pain.

- It opens the door to creating new experiences, memories, or a new direction.

The Reclaiming Path

Definition: Actively taking back control over memories, spaces, or experiences that were tainted by betrayal.

Goal: To empower oneself by confronting and transforming painful triggers into something meaningful.

Key Rewards:

- Reclaiming involves facing the places or experiences connected to betrayal.

- It's about infusing new meaning into those experiences, transforming them into something positive or neutral.

- Reclaiming is often a way to regain a sense of control over your life after the disruption of betrayal.

Choosing the Right Path for You

- *Personal Choice*: Each betrayed spouse or partner must decide which path aligns with their needs. Release may feel freeing to some while reclaiming feels empowering to others.

- *No Right or Wrong*: Both choices and paths are valid, and what matters most is what helps the person move forward in their healing at this particular stage. Some people may find that they choose to reclaim during one part of the healing process, then later choose the release path.

- *Support Is Key*: Whether someone chooses release or reclaiming, or both, having support—be it from a therapist, friends, family members, or community—can make a significant difference.

- *Recovery for the Betrayer*: When the betrayed partner chooses to remain in the relationship, it is crucial for the betrayer to actively engage in their own therapeutic work with a clear and committed recovery plan. This involves aligning their words with their actions to rebuild trust and address the harm they've caused. Key elements of this recovery include consistent personal growth, transparency, self-reflection, insight building, empathy, and accountability. By developing genuine insight and taking ownership of past actions, the betrayer creates a foundation for the betrayed partner to feel the initial sense of safety needed for further healing.

Exercise—Exploring Your Path

This exercise will help you explore whether release or reclaiming resonates more deeply with where you are currently in your healing journey. You may find that your path choice changes over time, I encourage you to honor where you are right now. Take a few mindful minutes to sit with yourself and reflect on what feels right for you at this moment.

Step 1: Reflection

- Close your eyes, take a few deep breaths, and bring to mind a place, memory, or experience tied to the betrayal you've experienced. If you find that this is too activating, stop, breathe, check in with yourself, and return to this at another time.

- How does it feel in your body when you think of this? Are you tense, anxious, angry, fearful, or some other feeling? Hold space for this. Notice where it is in your body.

Step 2: Exploration

- Ask yourself: Do I feel the need to let go of this memory or place (release)?

- Or do I feel drawn to reclaim it and make it my own again?

Step 3: Journaling

- Spend 5 to 10 minutes journaling about what came up for you during this reflection.

- Explore why you feel the way you do and what the next steps might look like in your healing journey—whether it's releasing or reclaiming.

Step 4: Action

Based on your reflections, think of one small step you can take toward either releasing or reclaiming. This could be avoiding a triggering place for a while or revisiting it with the intention of creating a new experience. Here are some additional examples of small steps that can aid in the healing process through either releasing or reclaiming:

1. *Releasing an Emotionally Charged Item*: Choose one item that represents painful memories tied to the betrayal, and consider discarding, donating, or repurposing it in a meaningful way. This can symbolize letting go of the hurt associated with the past.

2. *Reclaiming Personal Space*: If a particular area in your home has become a trigger, consider rearranging or redecorating it to make it feel fresh and personalized. This process can help you reclaim the space with positive intentions and create a new emotional atmosphere.

3. *Setting Boundaries as an Act of Reclaiming*: Identify one boundary that you feel would support your healing. Reclaiming agency in setting boundaries is a step toward regaining control and respect in your life.

4. *Releasing Through Writing*: Many betrayed partners find that writing their emotional impact letter during the formal disclosure process (how they were impacted by the betrayal) is a powerful release. Journaling is another way of releasing the pain of betrayal.

5. *Reclaiming an Activity You've Avoided*: If there's an activity or place that once brought joy but has become associated with the betrayal, consider revisiting it with a trusted friend or family member to create a new, positive memory. This can help you reclaim that experience for yourself, free from the past hurt. If the person who has betrayed you is doing their recovery work, some couples have reclaimed places or activities together as part of their healing work. Be gentle with yourself and honor what feels best for you.

6. *Releasing Expectations of Immediate Healing*: Remind yourself that healing is not a linear process and allow room for setbacks. This step involves releasing the pressure to feel "better" by a certain time and embracing each day's progress without judgment.

7. *Reclaiming Your Self-Worth*: Engage in one activity that boosts your confidence and sense of self-worth. This could be taking a class in something you enjoy, working on a project you're passionate about, taking a nature walk, or spending time with people who genuinely value you. Reclaiming self-worth helps shift focus toward your intrinsic strengths and value.

This crossroads exercise is an opportunity to truly listen to yourself and honor where you are in your healing. Whatever path you choose at this moment, remember that your feelings are valid, and your choices matter and should be respected. Each action you take is a gentle step toward processing, releasing, and reclaiming your personal agency, helping you move forward with greater healing and empowerment.

• • • • •

As we moved toward the end of our therapy work, Maria continued to move forward in releasing, grieving, healing trauma, and reclaiming areas of her life and relationship. Validating their courage, reminding Maria that she was not—and would never be—responsible for Paul's sexually deceptive choices, affirming Paul's commitment to healing and growth, and emphasizing that trauma is at the root of addiction all helped them stay focused on their decision to heal and remain in the marriage. Their progress was rocky at times, but at the end of our nearly two years together, Maria and Paul confirmed that for the first time in their many years together, they not only loved and trusted one another, they truly understood and liked each other as well.

In our last session together, as Paul and Maria discussed the milestones they had achieved, I shared that this is what I call a "confetti" moment. As a therapist, I sometimes wish I had a little lever that opens a panel on the ceiling to allow balloons and confetti to float down on the clients and couples I work with. These pivotal moments deserve to be celebrated, and it brings me such joy to witness this type of progress.

While Maria and Paul chose to work through the challenges in their marriage, not every couple will or should make this same decision. For some, ending the relationship is the healthiest path forward, and it's important to recognize that this choice is not a failure—far from it, in fact! Choosing to leave a relationship that no longer serves your well-being or is destructive can be an act of courage, self-respect, and personal progress.

Healing from betrayal is a deeply personal journey, and there's no single "right" path. Whether you decide to stay and work on rebuilding trust or to move forward independently, both choices reflect your strength and resilience. What matters is that you honor your needs, set boundaries that protect your peace, and allow yourself the freedom to heal fully. Every step you take—whether toward rebuilding together or creating a new beginning—is an opportunity for growth, empowerment, and a future that aligns with your authentic self.

A message from Mari

As a therapist trained in the Gottman Method for couples, part of my work is helping couples identify destructive patterns and learn new ways of communicating and problem solving. For couples with children who choose to end the relationship, this information is also important in supporting a successful co-parenting relationship.

In their decades-long research on couples (Gottman, J., & Gottman, J. 2017), Drs. John and Julie Gottman identified four critical factors that determine whether a relationship will succeed or fail. They labeled these identifiers "The Four Horsemen of the Apocalypse," which is a metaphor to describe destructive communication styles. According to their research, the following four patterns can predict the end of a relationship.

Criticism: The first destructive "horseman" is criticism. Toxic criticism is received by your partner as an attack that leaves them feeling shamed, humiliated, and sometimes enraged. It is important to note that offering a suggestion or sharing a complaint is very different from destructive criticism. For example:

A)   **Complaint**: "When I find your laundry in the washer after two days, I feel unheard, disrespected, and overwhelmed. We have discussed this in the past, yet it continues. Can we come up with a plan together on how to change this pattern, please?"

B)   **Criticism**: "You always expect everyone else to do your chores! You never care about how your irresponsible actions impact me! I'm sick of you making excuses; you are lazy and selfish. You never think of my needs, and the next time, I will throw your smelly wet clothes away!"

While couples may occasionally fall into the pit of criticism and people in love relationships have human moments, these occasional hurtful events do not necessarily indicate that a breakup is looming on the horizon. However, when toxic criticism is a consistent part of the couple's communication style, this pervasive way of sharing one's frustrations or worries is much like a stream of water eroding the relational foundation. Left unchecked, eventually this opens a floodgate for other more caustic horsemen to gallop in.

Contempt: The second destructive relationship "horseman" is contempt. At the core of contempt is deep resentment that translates into abusive disrespect. The ingredients of this communication style are ridicule, sarcasm, name-calling, door-slamming, mocking, bullying, making fun of, shrugging, eye-rolling, sneering, and giving your partner the middle finger, among other things.

The person on the receiving end feels as if they are worthless and of little value to their significant other. Contempt cuts deeper than criticism in that it communicates that you believe your partner is less than you and not worthy of respect. Let's look at this in action:

Example of a Contemptuous Statement: "I don't care how hard your day was or how exhausted you are! I work hard, too. You come home late and then make weak excuses about why you forgot to pick up groceries, like some dumb teenager who needs to be reminded all the time! I can't listen to your stupid, whiny voice or lame excuses for one more second. You are pathetic, and I can't stand you. Get out of my sight!"

For both people to feel safe and respected, this type of communication style must change. Gottman's research indicates that contempt is the single greatest predictor of divorce. Their research also shows that contemptuous couples are more at risk for illness due to weaker immune systems.

A 2015 research study "Conflict Resolution Styles and Health Outcomes in Married Couples, a Systematic Literature Review" (McDowell-Burns Jordan & Patton, n.d.; Moland & Patrick, n.d.; Birditt, Brown, Orbuch, & Mcilvane, 2010; Hysi, 2015) underscores contempt as a defense mechanism rooted in entitlement and superiority, sometimes due to a betrayal or series of betrayals in the relationship.

Another way contempt is fed is when one person in the relationship feels as if they are better than the other, smarter than the other, more responsible or capable, or have a higher morality or worth than their spouse or partner. They may feel that they have a right to even the score with abusive words or behaviors to keep their partner in line or pay their partner back for the hurt they have endured. Some partners will mock the other, saying things like, "*Oh boo hoo*, save your tears for someone else." Or they may mimic the hurting partner's voice in an unkind manner. Other partners use guilt or fear tactics such as telling their partner they will "go to hell for their sins" or "everyone will leave you because you are not worth loving." Contempt had clearly taken root in Maria and Paul's marriage, and if not for their hard work and commitment to healing, it likely would have destroyed the relationship.

Defensiveness: The third "horseman" is defensiveness. When people feel attacked or criticized, it is not unusual to respond defensively. In my work with couples, when the first two horsemen, criticism and contempt, are a frequent part of the communication style, defensiveness is often large and in charge. Many human beings are hypervigilant in defending against real or perceived verbal arrows. With couples, one person attacks (criticism), the other defends (defensiveness), and the first partner may then name-call (contempt) or use silence as violence (stonewalling). The other person then defends and slings another arrow, and the four horsemen gallop around and around in a circle without resolution.

This type of communication is unsuccessful as the person defending feels attacked, and the person hearing the defense response feels unheard and often blamed. By responding defensively, the person who feels attacked hopes their partner will accept the excuses and leave them alone so they don't have to take responsibility for their words and actions. Here is an example of a defensive response:

> *Question*: "I have the gift bag and card for your mom, and you agreed to pick up a gift this week. Did you get around to that?"

> *Defensive Response*: "I had a million other things to do this week, and you should have reminded me! You forget stuff, too. You're not perfect. Plus, you are better at doing this kind of stuff!"

Let's say the person responding defensively in this scenario forgot to purchase the gift. Their response is a projection of their shame onto their partner to minimize their own feelings of shame. This will likely elicit an angry and defensive response from the partner asking the question. A healthier way of responding is to take a moment, take a breath, notice what emotions are surfacing in response to the question, and, if need be, accept responsibility, take ownership, and validate your partner. Here is a healthier response:

Non-Defensive Response: "I appreciate the reminder. My week was busier than expected, but that is no excuse. I will head to the store now and select a gift for my mom. Thank you for picking up the wrapping and card. That was very helpful. I appreciate your patience, and I'm sorry for not following through without the need for a reminder. I will work on ways to remind myself in the future."

Non-Defensive Reply: "This sounds like a good plan. I also appreciate your ownership. When you respond insightfully and are willing to take steps toward growth, I feel safer, seen, heard, and respected. We feel like a team, and I feel loved. Thank you!"

When a couple can practice more compassionate ways of communicating and learn ways to manage their own stress triggers, their connection and attraction for one another increases, and most importantly, respect and trust improve. Responding defensively and refusing to apologize or take ownership leaves your spouse or partner feeling blamed, hopeless, misunderstood, and unappreciated.

Let's look at the last "horseman" the Gottmans' research identified:

Stonewalling: Picture a stone wall in front of you. It is taller than the sky and wider than your line of vision, and it is placed there to deter you from moving forward. When stonewalling occurs in a relationship, I have found that it is almost always a defense response to a pattern of criticism and contempt. The person who is stonewalling has reached a breaking point. Rather than staying in the conversation and dealing with the relational issues, they withdraw, shut down, walk away, or simply refuse to respond to their significant other. They may intentionally evade by focusing their attention elsewhere, such as working late hours, TV, video games, chores, scrolling through social media, hours at the gym, sleeping, golf, drinking or smoking marijuana, spending excessive time on errands, shopping, scrolling for porn, or reading for hours on end. They may also put on headphones, turn up the stereo, leave the house without an explanation, ignore their partner's bids for connection, or stand up mid-sentence and walk out of the room.

Stonewalling can occur during the early stages of a relationship and most often occurs when the first three horsemen are left to run amok in the relationship. Over time, the negative toxicity of criticism, contempt, and defensiveness ushers in stonewalling. When a person feels attacked or fearful, or when they feel neglected, ignored, or unsupported they become mentally and physiologically flooded and, as a result, often shut down. Stonewalling is a tactic that allows the person to escape the attack or fear-inducing situation. We see this frequently in adults who experienced verbal abuse in childhood.

Another reason people may engage in stonewalling is because they feel that change is hopeless and have given up. Still, others may move into stonewalling behavior when a conversation becomes heated. They may feel attacked, or they may feel as if they are once again repeating themselves or are not being heard. As a result, they eventually shut down. While it is understandable that a person wants to flee a situation where they feel helpless or withdraw from a conversation that feels unsafe or repetitive, it sends a message to their significant other that the relationship is not important enough to work on. Let's explore some more skillful ways of managing difficult conversations.

Taking a Time Out...Mindfully

One antidote to stonewalling that therapists often teach couples is the "Time Out" tool when the heat is turned up in conversations. When the couple feels that they have reached a point in the conversation where the topic or issue cannot be discussed rationally or with respect, it is better to stop the discussion, request a break, and come back to the conversation later at an agreed upon time when both people are calmer and more composed, versus stonewalling or allowing the other "horseman" to race in.

> *Time Out Example*: "I am feeling overwhelmed and upset right now, and I am starting to shut down (or rage up). I need to take a break, calm myself, and then come back to this conversation when I am less activated (or shut down). Can we agree to a time out and return to our conversation with mutual respect and compassion in an hour (or an agreed-upon time), please?"

During the time out, I have couples practice individual self-soothing activities such as breathwork, walking, praying, journaling, tapping, meditation, guided imagery, reviewing the positive aspects of their partner, listening to calming music, gardening, reading a book, dancing, or playing with a pet—basically any activity that will help reduce emotional flooding and help the person self-regulate. Once they and their partner feel ready, they will return to the conversation at the agreed time. If after returning to the conversation they need more time, they can ask their partner for more time with the understanding that the time-out tool is not meant to be used as avoidance. The amount of time needed for the time out may differ for each couple and situation. Some couples may need a 20-minute time out, while other situations and discussions would benefit from a longer time out.

Furthermore, it's crucial to support couples in fostering a compassionate understanding of how conflict resolution was handled in their respective families of origin. The way they observed and absorbed challenges being handled by their caregivers during their upbringing significantly impacts how they approach conflicts in their adult relationships. Whether it was through the demonstration of yelling and intimidation or the practice of silence and stonewalling in their family of origin, these learned behaviors can shape their responses to challenges within their marriage or intimate relationship.

By gaining insight into their individual approaches to managing arguments and understanding how their partners or spouses learned to handle conflicts, couples can experience profound revelations. This process not only opens their eyes to patterns formed in the past but also opens their hearts to the possibility of establishing new, constructive rules for their relationship. Breaking free from destructive generational patterns becomes an empowering and compassionate journey toward building a healthier and more fulfilling connection.

Mindfulness-based therapy is an excellent modality to help couples change long-standing mind states, mind stories, and negative communication patterns. In my clinical work, I have found that couples who are willing to learn and practice mindfulness-based tools consistently, such as breathwork and body movement during a time out, can more quickly heal communication ruptures, develop deeper self-insight and self-compassion, and can more easily extend empathy and understanding to their significant other. It is important to note that they may not agree with their spouse or partner's point of view or position, yet they are able to allow for a different perspective. This, in turn, increases curiosity and connection and reduces judgment, anxiety, fear, and harmful communication patterns. Couples who are equipped this way are prone toward solutions versus moving into an attack, shut down, deflect, or defend stance.

When intimate partner betrayal is a key factor that has harmed the relationship, as outlined earlier in this chapter, that specific trauma must be addressed first. It is difficult to help a couple heal and grow without the person who has perpetrated the betrayal being willing to truthfully disclose and take ownership of their harmful choices, make sincere and insightful amends, and actively work to change their behaviors. This recovery must include trauma reduction, building personal insight into the roots of their addictive or compulsive process, and discovering and recovering their authentic selves while they learn and practice tools and employ mindfulness-based strategies.

For the betrayed partner, their betrayal trauma must be compassionately acknowledged and consistently understood and validated by their partner and their therapist. Along with this acknowledgment and validation, the betrayed partner should be supported with trauma therapy, such as EMDR, brain spotting, tapping, somatic-based strategies, task-oriented tools, mindfulness-based therapies, boundaries work, and skillful communication practices that support healthy interactions.

Message for the Reader: The following sections of this chapter are focused on mindfulness-based exercises, including breath and somatic work, guided imagery, and art exercises. If you, the reader, are working with a therapist, coach, or a healing professional, we find it is helpful to have their support in leading you, or you and your partner, through the next section of the workbook. If you do not have a therapist or coach, we encourage you to take this one step at a time, staying present and taking breaks as needed.

Mindfulness Healing Part I:
Preparation, Assessment, and Script
for Guided Imagery Exercise

Important Safety Tips for Therapists, Facilitators, and Healing Individuals

Environment Consideration and Tips: It can be helpful to "set the stage" prior to a guided imagery exercise. For example, consider the lighting—is it too bright or too low? Another helpful step is putting phones on silent. Also, think about outside distractions, such as barking dogs, traffic, and other interruptions. If possible, minimize outside noises the best you can. Finally, some individuals like having a blanket or pillow to hold, or you may enjoy diffusing essential oils to support deeper relaxation if there are no allergy concerns. While mindfulness-based guided imagery is not hypnosis, it can be helpful to prepare your environment prior to beginning the guided imagery exercise.

Voice Prosody: An additional gentle reminder is to be aware of your voice prosody. Prosody refers to the rhythm and melody of the voice, including intonation, stress, and pauses. Speaking in a softer tone and slower cadence than your normal speaking voice is useful in supporting the guided imagery practice. If you typically speak more rapidly or loudly, it will take some practice to slow down and modulate your voice.

Diversity Considerations: Consider the client's culture, age, race, physical differences (such as hearing loss), gender and orientation, and other unique experiences that may invite a softer or different speaking tone or pace or require that the client keep their eyes open if they prefer. If you are bi-lingual and you and your client speak the same languages, ask your client what language they prefer. If your client prefers to go by a nickname, a title such as Dr., Mr., or Mrs., or a specific pronoun, honor their request.

Pace Yourself: Remind yourself to take your time as you walk through this process. There is no need to rush. If you are the person facilitating this exercise, slow down for a relaxed, calming pace. Additionally, it is wise for the facilitator to first practice the exercise with themselves prior to practicing with another person.

Safety Reminder: Safety is the number one consideration with any therapeutic approach or healing intervention. As you lead your clients through the following guided imagery exercise, please instruct your clients to alert you if they are experiencing any of the following trauma responses. If you are a healing individual doing this work solo, you will also want to consider the following:

- Traumatic memories that are creating a high level of distress
- Feelings of intense fear or panic
- Disturbing or intrusive thoughts
- Suicidal or homicidal thoughts
- Dissociation (if there is an awareness of the dissociative states)
- Other crisis concerns (list on the line): _____

_____

It is also important to ask the client to alert you if they experience any of the following symptoms. Likewise, if someone is doing this work solo, they should pay compassionate and close attention to their process and monitor for distressing or physical symptoms such as:

- A racing heart
- Tightness in the chest
- Shortness of breath
- Nausea or intestinal distress
- Feeling faint or dizziness
- Body pain
- Feeling as if you are floating outside of your body
- Other somatic concerns (list on the line): _____

_____

Note for Therapist or Facilitator: Before moving into the guided imagery, please have your client begin with the assessment on the next page. If you are not a trained mental health professional and your client is in crisis and exhibiting or discussing symptoms that are out of your scope of practice or experience, please refer to an appropriate mental health or medical professional. *If your client is experiencing an immediate life-threatening emergency, please call 911 or the appropriate emergency number if located outside of the United States.*

Note to Solo Reader: *If you are doing this work on your own and believe you are in crisis or may be at risk to yourself, please stop and seek emergency support immediately by calling 911 or your local emergency number.*

Pre-Guided Imagery Assessment Scale

On a scale from 1 to 10 (with 1 = very low, and 10 = very high), please take a mindful moment to assess the following. Circle the number that most accurately applies to you:

Feeling		Assessment (1-10)									
▢ Anxiety	Partner 1	1	2	3	4	5	6	7	8	9	10
	Partner 2	1	2	3	4	5	6	7	8	9	10
▢ Anger	Partner 1	1	2	3	4	5	6	7	8	9	10
	Partner 2	1	2	3	4	5	6	7	8	9	10
▢ Shame	Partner 1	1	2	3	4	5	6	7	8	9	10
	Partner 2	1	2	3	4	5	6	7	8	9	10
▢ Sadness	Partner 1	1	2	3	4	5	6	7	8	9	10
	Partner 2	1	2	3	4	5	6	7	8	9	10
▢ Fear	Partner 1	1	2	3	4	5	6	7	8	9	10
	Partner 2	1	2	3	4	5	6	7	8	9	10
▢ Numbness	Partner 1	1	2	3	4	5	6	7	8	9	10
	Partner 2	1	2	3	4	5	6	7	8	9	10
▢ Confusion	Partner 1	1	2	3	4	5	6	7	8	9	10
	Partner 2	1	2	3	4	5	6	7	8	9	10
▢ Curiosity	Partner 1	1	2	3	4	5	6	7	8	9	10
	Partner 2	1	2	3	4	5	6	7	8	9	10
▢ Hopefulness	Partner 1	1	2	3	4	5	6	7	8	9	10
	Partner 2	1	2	3	4	5	6	7	8	9	10
▢ Calm	Partner 1	1	2	3	4	5	6	7	8	9	10
	Partner 2	1	2	3	4	5	6	7	8	9	10
▢ Joyful	Partner 1	1	2	3	4	5	6	7	8	9	10
	Partner 2	1	2	3	4	5	6	7	8	9	10
▢ Other:	Partner 1	1	2	3	4	5	6	7	8	9	10
	Partner 2	1	2	3	4	5	6	7	8	9	10

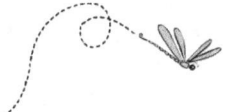

Mindfulness Healing Part II:

Breath and Somatic Preparation & Prompts

This exercise involves tuning into your breath and body and is followed by the couple's guided imagery exercise and then a final art activity. It's important to note that this may not be suitable for everyone. It's recommended that the following be adapted to the specific needs and comfort levels of the individual(s) involved.

Physical Space and Comfort: Both partners should find a comfortable sitting or lying down position, with their feet on the floor or cross-legged if that is the preference. If they have yoga mats or a couch, and one or both prefer to lie down, that is fine. If the couple prefers to sit near each other or touch each other (such as holding hands, back-to-back, or leaning against each other), that is also acceptable. One partner may prefer to sit or lie down apart from their partner, which is also fine. Whatever position will help each partner feel relaxed is best, and each partner's preference should be honored.

Prompt 1: Let's pause while each of you takes a few moments to get comfortable.

Prompt 2: When you are both ready, you are welcome to close your eyes if that feels comfortable for you. Or, if one or both of you prefer to leave your eyes open, that is just fine. Whatever allows each of you to feel most secure is more than acceptable. If your eyes remain open, feel free to rest your gaze on a calming point—near the floor if you're sitting or on the ceiling if you're lying down.

Prompt 3: We will now move forward into the grounded breathing exercise. This will take approximately two to three minutes.

Grounded Breath Exercise

Prompt: Now that you are both in a comfortable position, before we begin the guided imagery, let's move through a minute of ground breathwork.

1. We will start with the 4-2-7 breath. Start by breathing in deeply through the nose to the count of four, hold for two, and then exhale slowly and intentionally through the mouth to the count of seven. Let's do this three times at your own pace.

2. Now, let's return to easy, relaxed, deep breathing. Take in a long breath in through the nose and let out a long exhale out through the mouth. Continue with this breath. **Note to Facilitator: Count to 20 silently.**

3.   As you notice the gentle rhythm of deep breathing, I would like you to imagine extending compassion to yourself with each intake breath. Then, imagine you are extending compassion or support toward your spouse or partner on the release breath. **Note to Facilitator: Count to 20 silently.**

| Somatic Relaxation Exercise |

Now that we have finished with our grounded breaths, please feel free to breathe normally with relaxed, regular breaths. Let's now move into relaxing the body in preparation for guided imagery:

1.   Notice that your feet are feeling heavier and more relaxed.

2.   Notice that your hands are gently resting at your sides, on your belly, or on your thighs.

3.   Feel your jaw relax and your tongue move away from the roof of your mouth.

4.   Allow your shoulders to relax down from your ear lobes and your elbows to gently relax down from your shoulders.

5.   Bit by bit, the tension moves out of your body as you breathe in and relax and breathe out and relax. Breathe in compassion, hope, and healing, and breathe out stress, judgment, and anger. **Note to Facilitator: Count to 20 silently.**

6.   As we complete our breath work, we will now move into guided imagery. You can return to your breath work exercises at any point during the guided imagery. The guided imagery exercise will take approximately 10 minutes. You may continue to stay in your comfortable position or shift to a different comfortable position. You may both also continue with your eyes closed if that is your preference. At any point, either of you can ask for a time out if needed.

Let's move forward.

Mindfulness Healing Part III:

Couples Guided Imagery

Rebuilding the Heart / Repairing the Hurt

PART A

Note to Therapist or Facilitator: If you notice that one or both partners are highly activated during the guided imagery, perhaps demonstrating rapid or shallow breathing, sobbing, or shaking, please have the couple pause as you attend to the individual or couple.

This can be done by gently stating that you would like to pause the exercise for a moment, then quietly asking the person by name if they would like a break, support with deep breath work, or to step out of the guided imagery entirely if it has become too overwhelming for one or both.

Note to the Reader(s): If you and your partner or spouse are doing this solo without the support of a mental health professional, again, please be gentle with yourselves and each other. If you have a trusted person to lead you through this, you may want to consider this, or perhaps you can read this into a recording device and then play it back so both of you can follow the prompts. If you become overwhelmed or feel as if you are in a crisis state, please stop and reach out for help if need be. Safety first, always.

Purpose of the Heart Repair Guided Imagery: The aim of this guided imagery exercise is to support steps in the relationship restoration, to increase insight, to advance healthy communication, to increase trust and respect, to build compassion for self and your significant other, and to support mindful attendance to the relationship ruptures in need of repair.

Instructions for Therapist or Facilitator to Read Aloud: This guided imagery exercise will take approximately 10 minutes. You both will be guided through each step of the exercise slowly. Though questions may be asked of you or you may be given prompts, there is no expectation of a verbal response. You may respond if you would like to do so, or you may quietly respond inside of yourself, which many people prefer.

First Step Prompt: Staying with your intentional, normal, relaxed breathing, I'd like you to both begin by imagining the "heart" of your relationship. With your eyes closed (or open if you prefer), I'd like each of you to visualize a heart that represents your relationship. What does this heart look like? What color is it? What size is it? Is it beating, or is it still? Does it look like a human heart, Valentine's heart, or some other image or shape? What other qualities are you noticing about the image of this heart that represents your relationship? *Note to Facilitator: Count to 20 silently.*

Next Prompt Step: I'd like you both to now imagine that the heart you are visualizing is currently broken into pieces, symbolizing the trust that has been damaged due to betrayal and trauma. Without assigning blame or disappearing in shame, can you hold compassionate space while you observe the broken pieces of the relationship heart? Can you visualize kneeling next to the various pieces of the broken heart, perhaps touching those parts that are scattered and broken? Honor whatever emotions are surfacing without judgement, and return to your breath work as needed. *Note to Facilitator: Count to 20 silently.*

Acknowledging Emotions

Next Prompt Step: As you both visualize yourself moving toward each of the broken pieces, perhaps kneeling and gently touching those pieces or holding various pieces in loving hands or rocking arms, please reflect silently on the emotions associated with the various parts of the relationship broken heart. If you would like to hold your own arms and rock back and forth, sway your body in a way that feels comforting, or place both hands over your heart or stomach, you are welcome to do that now, as somatic movement can be very helpful. If you prefer to be still, that is fine as well. This is about your safety and comfort. *Note to Facilitator: Count to 20 silently.*

Next Prompt Step: What feelings are each of you noticing, and where are those feelings located in your bodies? Can you place a hand there comfortably? Let's take a few seconds to notice. *Note to Facilitator: Count to 20 silently.*

Next Prompt Step: Whatever feelings are rising to the surface, they are there as guides to help you recognize the pain, betrayal, and vulnerability. These guides are not there to cast judgment or punitively lecture or shame either of you. Instead, the emotion guides serve to comfort you and acknowledge your experiences—recognizing both the pain you have endured and the hurt or betrayal you may have caused your loved one. At the same time, your loved one honors their own emotion guides, reflecting on how they may have contributed to the brokenness and recognizing the parts of themselves that have been wounded. *Note to Facilitator: Count to 20 silently.*

If either of you are feeling overwhelmed, activated, or numb, you may use your 4-2-7 breath to help you stay present and grounded. You may also ask for a time-out at any point. We will move on to the second part of our guided imagery next.

· · · · ·

Couples Guided Imagery
Rebuilding the Heart / Repairing the Hurt

PART B

Note to Therapist or Facilitator: Once again, this next part of the guided imagery is quiet, with each partner having their own experience versus speaking those experiences out loud. You will guide the couple to quietly visualize themselves working together to repair the broken heart. The following prompts are for the therapist or facilitator.

Note to Reader: If you are both doing this on your own, as noted earlier, please take special care of yourselves during this process. Step away if either of you are overwhelmed or find yourself dissociating.

First Prompt Step: Let's take a deep breath and again visualize the broken pieces of the relationship heart. Some parts of the broken heart represent both pain and betrayal; other pieces represent hope and the possibility of rebuilding trust and respect. Please imagine yourself gently and lovingly picking up the pieces with your significant other. Imagine that you are both communicating openly and respectfully while doing so, telling the other about how that broken piece has impacted you or sharing how a more hopeful piece of the relationship heart is impacting you. Let's take a few moments for each of you to visualize this. *Note to Facilitator: Count to 20 silently.*

Next Prompt Step: Let's pause for a moment and breathe in and out deeply two times. If either of you needs to adjust your body or stretch, let's do that now.

Next Prompt Step: Now, imagine that you are showing support, acknowledging the pain one or both of you have contributed, and expressing sadness for how your relationship or marriage has been impacted. Remind yourself and your loved one that it is understandable to feel fear, anger, or apathy, as well as hope and the first glimmers of connection. It is also normal to want to blame, project, or give up. This is an important step in acknowledging the broken parts and holding space for repair work. *Note to Facilitator: Count to 20 silently.*

Next Prompt Step: Let's pause for a moment and take two deep breaths in and out.

Next Prompt Step: Now, visualize that you are both placing the heart pieces back together imperfectly, understanding that relationships go through very difficult and sometimes painful seasons. As you imagine working with your partner to place the heart pieces back together, like puzzle pieces, consider what you would like to heal within the heart piece you are holding. Does it feel as if you need to give that piece of the heart to your partner to heal, along with a clear request for what you need? If so, imagine handing the piece to your partner and sharing what you need from your partner to heal that piece of the broken heart. As you are handing this part of the heart to them, imagine your partner accepting this piece, reflecting to you an understanding of the need you've expressed, and then honoring that request. **Note to Facilitator: Count to 20 silently.**

Next Prompt Step: Let's pause for a moment and deeply breathe in and out twice. If you need to adjust your body or stretch, you may do that now.

Next Prompt Step: Imagine that there are parts of the broken heart that you would like to work on for yourself. What would you like to name that part of the heart? Instead of deception, perhaps that piece can now be called honesty. Instead of anger, perhaps that part can be called assertiveness. Instead of brokenness, perhaps that part can be renamed as boundaries. Instead of destruction, perhaps that part can be called possibility. **Note to Facilitator: Count to 20 silently.**

Next Prompt Step: This is our last step in the guided imagery. I want each of you to visualize placing each heart piece carefully next to the other, holding an intention toward healing and growth. Notice that each torn seam is a place where light can come through and infuse the heart of your relationship with empathy, honesty, respect, hopefulness, and strength, one step at a time. To quote Rumi, "The wound is the place where the light enters you." **Note to Facilitator: Count to 20 silently.**

Next Prompt Step: Let's pause for a moment and take two deep breaths in and out.

Transitioning to Awareness

Next Prompt Step: As we bring this guided imagery exercise to a close and move back into our time together, back to the awareness of each other and our session, let's practice one more round of the 4-2-7 breaths, breathing in deeply through the nose to the count of four, holding for two, and then exhaling through the mouth for seven. Breathe in healing compassion for self; exhale healing compassion for your significant other. Breathe in peace; breathe out anger, anxiety, or stress. Let's do this three times at your own pace.

Next Prompt Step: If your eyes are closed, notice the light in front of your eyelids. When you are ready, go ahead and flutter your eyes back open, and we will resume your session.

Final Prompt: This now ends our guided imagery exercise. If either or both of you would like to stand, stretch, move into a different position, or get a glass of water, please do that now.

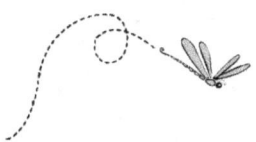

Mindfulness Healing Part IV:
Couple's Processing of Guided Imagery
Sharing Our Experiences

Purpose for Couple's Processing: After the conclusion of the guided imagery, the therapist or facilitator will lead an open and respectful discussion about what each partner experienced during the guided imagery. The aim is to allow a guided and honest conversation between the partners as they highlight important aspects of the guided imagery exercise and what their experience was like. Neither partner should interrupt, try to interpret, judge, or correct; instead, extending curiosity and compassion is the goal and the gift.

Note: If you are both doing this solo without a therapist or facilitator, pace yourselves and notice your energy while respecting the energy of your spouse or partner.

Important Considerations for the Couple: For this processing part of the work, it will be vitally important to validate and honor each partner's voice and experience with the guided imagery.

Important Considerations for the Facilitator: It is not the role of the therapist or facilitator to interpret, minimize, or re-direct. Rather, it is important for the facilitator to skillfully hold a safe space for each partner to share their experience and hear the more difficult aspects that their partner may have experienced. This is a time for the facilitator to honor the pain, as well as highlight and emphasize the positive aspects each partner may have experienced, such as collaboration, communication, and commitment to healing. Affirm the painful aspects such as betrayal, anger, and fears as well. Remind them that participating in a mindfulness-based exercise like this is a signal of hope and aids in the possibility of restoration.

Note: If you and your partner are doing this without a therapist or a facilitator, this is the time to practice respectful communication without interruption or assumption.

Processing Questions for the Couple

Each partner will take a turn and answer each question before moving on to the next question:

1. What did you notice in the guided imagery?

2. What challenges did you experience?

3. What joys did you experience?

4. Did you have a breakthrough you'd like to share?

5. Do you have any concerns that you'd like to share?

6. What are you feeling in your body currently?

7. Are there any specific thoughts you'd like to share about your experience?

8. Would you like to affirm, thank, or share anything specific with your partner?

9. Did you notice any self-growth with insight and compassion toward yourself?

10. Did you notice any growth in insight and compassion toward your partner?

Post-Guided Imagery Assessment Scale

Now that you have completed the breathwork and somatic exercises, the guided imagery exercise, and couples process work, on a scale from 1 to 10 (with 1 = very low, and 10 = very high), let's take a mindful moment to assess the following feelings listed below and on the next page:

Feeling		Assessment (1-10)									
□ Anxiety	Partner 1	1	2	3	4	5	6	7	8	9	10
	Partner 2	1	2	3	4	5	6	7	8	9	10
□ Anger	Partner 1	1	2	3	4	5	6	7	8	9	10
	Partner 2	1	2	3	4	5	6	7	8	9	10
□ Shame	Partner 1	1	2	3	4	5	6	7	8	9	10
	Partner 2	1	2	3	4	5	6	7	8	9	10
□ Sadness	Partner 1	1	2	3	4	5	6	7	8	9	10
	Partner 2	1	2	3	4	5	6	7	8	9	10
□ Fear	Partner 1	1	2	3	4	5	6	7	8	9	10
	Partner 2	1	2	3	4	5	6	7	8	9	10
□ Numbness	Partner 1	1	2	3	4	5	6	7	8	9	10
	Partner 2	1	2	3	4	5	6	7	8	9	10

Feeling		Assessment (1-10)									
▢ Confusion	Partner 1	1	2	3	4	5	6	7	8	9	10
	Partner 2	1	2	3	4	5	6	7	8	9	10
▢ Curiosity	Partner 1	1	2	3	4	5	6	7	8	9	10
	Partner 2	1	2	3	4	5	6	7	8	9	10
▢ Hopefulness	Partner 1	1	2	3	4	5	6	7	8	9	10
	Partner 2	1	2	3	4	5	6	7	8	9	10
▢ Calm	Partner 1	1	2	3	4	5	6	7	8	9	10
	Partner 2	1	2	3	4	5	6	7	8	9	10
▢ Joyful	Partner 1	1	2	3	4	5	6	7	8	9	10
	Partner 2	1	2	3	4	5	6	7	8	9	10
▢ Other:	Partner 1	1	2	3	4	5	6	7	8	9	10
	Partner 2	1	2	3	4	5	6	7	8	9	10

Important Reminder: If you, as the facilitator, are not a licensed therapist or trained mental health professional and your client is in crisis and exhibiting or discussing symptoms that are out of your scope of practice or experience, please refer to an appropriate mental health or medical professional. *If your client is experiencing an immediate life-threatening emergency, please call 911 or the appropriate emergency number if located outside of the United States. If you are doing this solo without support and are in a state of emergency, reach out to 911 immediately.*

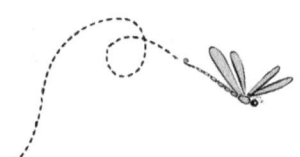

Mindfulness Healing Part V:
Couple's Mindful Reflection Moment

Purpose Statement: Taking time to mindfully reflect on your experience and what you learned about your significant other's experience can enhance insight, connection, awareness, and empathy. This also allows each partner to stay grounded in the moment, deepening the experience.

Instructions: Each partner is invited to take a moment to answer the following questions on a sheet of paper. This can be accomplished by the facilitator asking the question or writing or typing the question on two separate pieces of paper for the couple. The authors also give permission for the facilitator to copy this specific page to give to the couple as handouts if that is helpful. Please note that copyright will apply to the other parts of this book.

Partner 1: What are you noticing with respect to your emotions and body after the guided meditation and breathwork? Take two to three minutes to notice and write down your reflections here:

_____

_____

_____

_____

_____

_____

_____

_____

Partner 2: What are you noticing with respect to your emotions and body after the guided meditation and breathwork? Take two to three minutes to notice and write down your reflections here:

_____

_____

_____

_____

_____

_____

_____

_____

Facilitator: Please instruct the couple to share their reflections with one another. Again, this is a time to increase insight, compassion, and understanding versus correcting, controlling, or judging your significant other.

Note: If you are a couple doing this work on your own, walk through this gently with one another, use your tools, take a time out, and incorporate deep breathing or movement if either of you or both of you become overwhelmed.

Mindfulness Healing Part VI:
Couple's Communication Exercise
Nine-Step Reflective Listening Practice Tool

Purpose Statement: I developed this exercise to help couples learn a tool they could practice daily. This exercise supports couples in moving out of the "Four Horsemen of the Apocalypse" stage (Criticism, Contempt, Defensiveness, Stonewalling) while being present with themselves, their emotions, and one another to build healthier communication patterns.

Instructions: Reflective listening is a communication skill that involves being present and focused, actively listening to your partner, being attuned to your own emotions, and then summarizing or reflecting back what your partner expressed. It's like a mental mirror that helps the speaker feel heard and understood. Set aside 10 minutes a day, three to four times a week, to practice this tool together. First, choose a short time frame that works for both of you. Then, each partner selects a minimally triggering topic, and you take turns discussing your respective topics for three to five minutes each.

Important Note for Couples: If you tend to speak at length, do your best to summarize your point within a minute or less when it is your turn to speak. That may feel like a short amount of time, but if you count to 60 right now—one-one thousand, two-one thousand, three-one thousand, and so on—you'll see that it is a long time for some people to sit and listen, especially for neurodiverse individuals, such as people with ADHD.

Reflective Listening—Nine-Step Couple's Tool

The following steps will help guide you through the above exercise:

Step 1: Be Present—Reflective listening starts with giving your partner your full attention. Put away distractions and focus on what they're saying.

Step 2: Do Not Interrupt—Let your partner finish their thought. If they tend to speak for a long period of time, after you are both done practicing this tool, respectfully ask if they can speak for a shorter period at the next practice. For example, "I am glad we are practicing better communication. Thank you for doing this—it means a lot to me, and I appreciate you. I notice I have a difficult time staying present and absorbing what you are sharing if the share goes longer than a minute. Can we agree to keep our shares to a minute or less? How should we practice this—would a timer for each of us be helpful?" Observe that this request begins with an affirmation, the use of "I statements" throughout this request, and an invitation to find a solution.

Step 3: Repeat in Your Own Words—After your spouse or partner shares, try repeating it back in your own words. For example, if they say, "I had a tough day at work, my boss doesn't seem to appreciate my efforts, and I wonder if they even notice all I am doing." You might respond with, "It sounds like your day was tough. You work so hard, and I can understand how challenging it is that your boss doesn't seem to appreciate all of your contributions."

Step 4: Show You're Listening—Use body language and facial expressions to show you're engaged. Nodding your head, reflecting an appropriate expression, or maintaining eye contact lets them know you're actively listening.

Step 5: Validate Their Feelings—Acknowledge their emotions. If they express frustration, you could say, "It sounds like you're really frustrated. I can understand why you'd feel this way." If they express sadness, you could say, "I can see how sad you are, and I want you to know I care and am here for you."

Step 6: Ask Clarifying Questions—After they have finished sharing, if you're unsure about something, ask questions for clarification. This shows you're genuinely interested in understanding their perspective. A clarifying question is not intended to engage in a debate or try and "catch" them in something. For example, "Thank you for sharing about feeling neglected during our dinner out with my family. I was unclear about what I said or did that left you feeling neglected, and I want to better understand. Would you mind clarifying that part for me so I do not repeat this in the future?"

Step 7: Avoid Jumping to Solutions—Reflective listening is about understanding, not fixing. Hold off on offering solutions right away. Let your loved one express themselves fully. Ask if they would like your help in coming up with a solution; they may or may not. For example, "I am glad you shared this about your sister with me, and I can see how this is impacting you. Is there something I can do to help? Would you like a suggestion or to discuss a solution, or do you need me to just listen and be supportive?"

Step 8: Express Empathy—Put yourself in their shoes. If they're excited, share in their excitement. You might say, "I am so happy to hear about your promotion and raise! You have earned this, and you deserve it. I am really excited for you!" If they're sad, convey empathy by acknowledging their feelings. You might say, "I see how sad you are due to this situation. I care about your feelings, and I am here to help if you'd like me to. What do you need from me currently? How can I help?"

Step 9: Summarize Main Points—Periodically summarize what they've shared without interruption. It demonstrates that you're following the conversation and helps them see that you're trying to understand the bigger picture. You could say, "I appreciate you sharing how your friend hurt your feelings. It makes sense that this bothers you because your boundaries were crossed when they shared your private information. That would bother me as well."

Reflective listening is a powerful tool for building strong connections. It fosters open communication, builds trust, and allows the other person to feel valued. For some couples, it can feel a bit awkward and scripted at the start, but over time, most couples notice that this practice eventually flows much more organically.

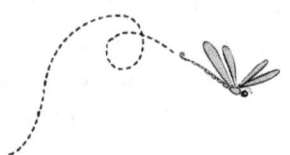

Mindfulness Healing Part VII:

Restoring the Relationship

Art Exercise for Couples—Broken Heart

Purpose Statement: The purpose of this couple's healing art exercise is to visually identify the various pieces of your relationship's broken heart that need repair and how each of you will help your relationship heart heal. Even if only one person in the relationship is responsible for the wounding, doing the exercise together can support the first steps toward healing and repair.

Art Exercise Instructions:

A)   Each partner chooses and completes one heart on the following pages, Heart 1 or Heart 2, taking time to write a descriptive word inside each piece of the broken heart based on their own experience (i.e., deception, verbal abuse, neglect, contempt, betrayal, etc.).

B)   Next, once you have completed your heart, you will list out ways you will help heal the wounds on the lines above the heart you completed, and your significant other will then list out ways they will help heal the wounds on lines provided at the bottom of the heart you have completed. You will both do the same for each other's hearts.

C)   Healing statement examples for the betrayed partner might include attending couple's therapy, using I statements, maintaining boundaries, and practicing self-care, prayer, or meditation.

D)   Healing statement examples for the betraying spouse might include a commitment to ongoing therapy and sobriety, making passwords transparent, listening with empathy, respecting boundaries, practicing rigorous honesty, and expressing insight.

_____

_____

_____

_____

_____

_____

_____

_____

_____

_____

_____

_____

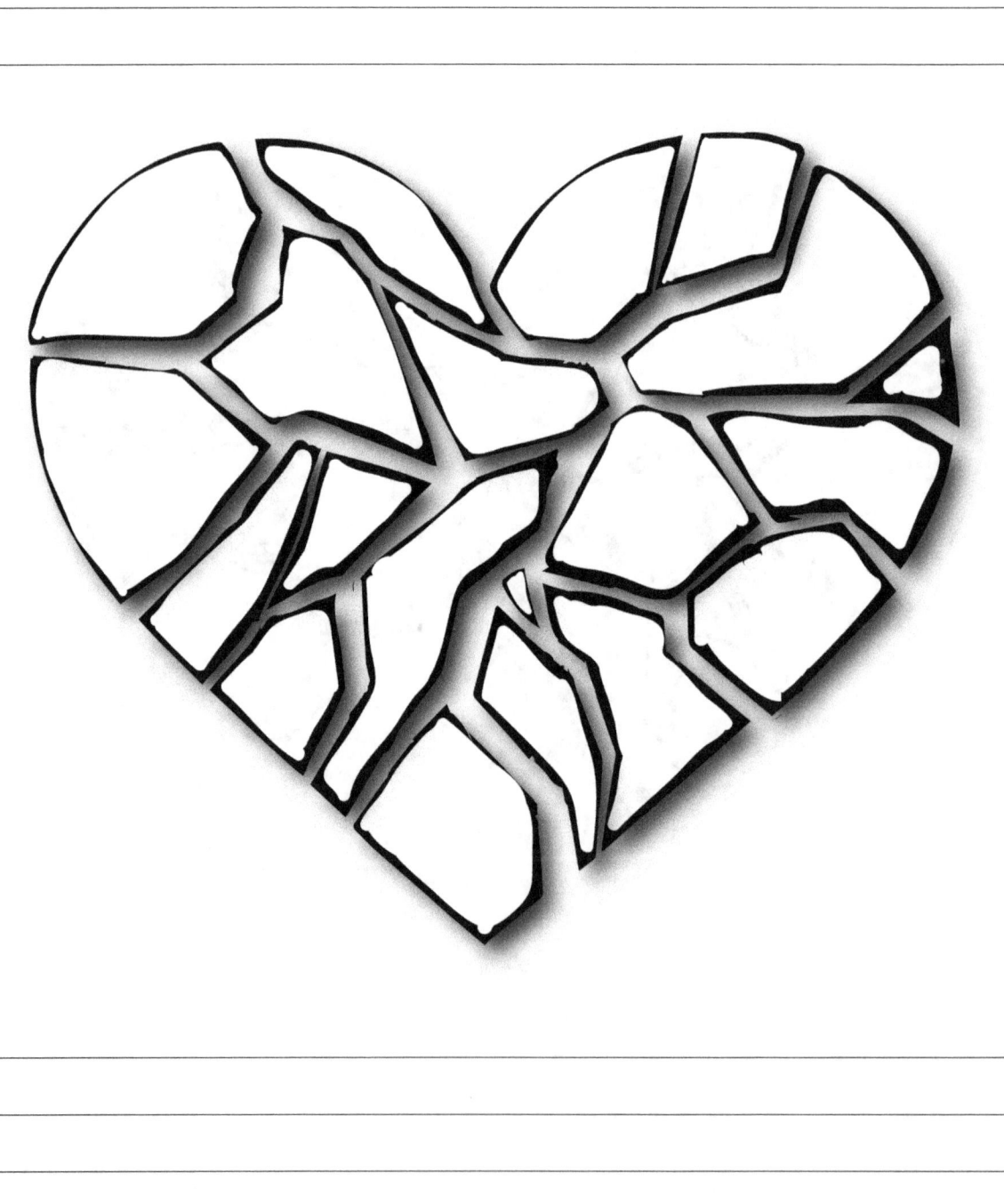

_____

_____

_____

_____

Cornerstones of Rebuilding Trust with a Betrayed Partner

As we have outlined in this chapter, when betrayal enters a relationship through infidelity, addiction, secrecy, or deception—trust is fractured. The hurt partner may feel disoriented, emotionally raw, and unsure of what's real. As you have learned, rebuilding trust isn't a quick fix or a single apology—it is a *process* rooted in daily, embodied actions, including consistent attunement and transparency.

It's common for people in recovery from sexual betrayal or addiction to confuse secrecy with privacy—but the two are not the same. Privacy is a healthy part of any relationship. It allows each partner to have personal thoughts, interests, and space while still operating in honesty and trust. Secrecy, on the other hand, is the intentional withholding of information or behaviors that, if revealed, would damage trust or hurt the relationship.

In the aftermath of sexual infidelity, rebuilding trust requires moving away from secrecy and toward transparency. This doesn't mean giving up all personal boundaries or living with no privacy—it means practicing openness that encourages safety and repair. Privacy protects the relationship. Secrecy protects the deception. Learning the difference between the two is a vital step in restoring relational integrity and rebuilding connection. (*Carnes, P., & Laaser, M. R. (2004).*

The PAACTS Method

To support couples navigating the painful aftermath of betrayal, I developed the **PAACTS Method**—a trauma-informed, relational framework for rebuilding trust. PAACTS stands for *Predictable, Accountable, Attuned, Consistent, Transparent, and Safe.* It invites the person who caused harm to make a daily commitment—a *pact* not only with their partner, but also with themselves—to live in alignment with these principles.

The PAACTS Method helps shift the focus from promises and apologies to embodied, trustworthy actions over time. It's not only what the hurt partner needs—it's what the person who caused harm must commit to practicing. Let's look at each of the PAACT cornerstone principals:

1. **Predictable**—Reliability brings stability. This means showing up on time, following through with commitments, attending to your recovery, and reducing emotional or behavioral surprises. Predictability restores a sense of structure in a world that felt shaken, and a relationship that feels shattered.

2. **Accountable**—Taking full, non-defensive ownership of past and present actions. Accountability says, "I caused harm, I take responsibility, I understand how I hurt you, and I understand what triggered my action. I am willing to face the discomfort of repair." It requires humility, not justification.

3. **Attuned**—This is about emotional presence. Attunement means tuning in, noticing your partner's distress, and responding with care—not logic or defensiveness. It's practicing emotional empathy and connection, even when it's uncomfortable.

4. **Consistent**—Healing doesn't come from a good day or week—it comes from sustained, repeated care. Consistency says, "You don't have to wonder who

I'll be tomorrow." No one is perfect or expected to be a robot, but showing up with steady effort over time helps rebuild the safety that betrayal took away.

5. **Transparent**—Transparency is the opposite of secrecy. It means living with integrity and sharing information before being asked, allowing access to important areas of your life, and building a life of openness rather than control.

6. **Safe**—Trust cannot grow without safety. Safety means creating an environment free of emotional volatility, dishonesty, manipulation, or coercion. It also means respecting boundaries and protecting your partner's emotional and physical well-being.

Together, these six cornerstone principals form PAACTS—a daily promise you offer not just in words, but in how you live, speak, and show up. Over time, these relational principals begin to reweave a sense of security and hope.

Reflective Exercise: Practicing PAACTS

For the person committed to rebuilding trust:

1. **Daily Inventory Prompt:**

    Choose one behavior you practiced today (or will commit to tomorrow) for each of the six principles and write that next to each principle:

    -   Predictable: _____
    -   Accountable: _____
    -   Attuned: _____
    -   Consistent: _____
    -   Transparent: _____
    -   Safe: _____

2. **Weekly Reflection Prompt:**

    -   Which of the six was the most difficult for you to embody this week, and why?
    -   Which was the most natural for you?
    -   What support, skill-building, or insight might help you grow in the area you're struggling with?

3. **Partner Practice** (*if shared in a therapeutic setting, or a safe space*):
    If your partner is open, you can ask:

    -   "Which of these six areas helped you feel most supported this week?"
    -   "Which area needed improvement?"

Note to person healing the betrayal: Gentle reminder to listen without defense. The goal is to understand, not correct. Use the communication tools outlined in this chapter to support healing.

Note to the betrayed partner: Gentle reminder to use the communication tools you've learned in this chapter to share your feedback clearly, concisely and respectfully.

4. **Affirmation for the person rebuilding trust**:
    I rebuild trust not through promises, but through my actions. I choose to be predictable, accountable, attuned, consistent, transparent, and safe. I honor the healing journey we are on with integrity and care.

    If you would like to write your own affirmation, you may do that here:

    _____

    _____

    _____

5. **Affirmation for the betrayed partner**:
    I am allowed to hurt and to take the time I need to heal. I did not cause this pain, and I am worthy of honesty, safety, and care. As I watch my partner do their work, I give myself permission to move at the pace that feels right for me. I honor my heart and the hope that trust can be rebuilt over time, one step at a time.

    If you would like to write your own affirmation, you may do that here:

    _____

    _____

    _____

6. **Affirmation for Us as a Couple**:
    Together, we choose to stand in this moment and face the hard work of healing. I (the one who caused the betrayal) take responsibility for the pain I have caused and commit to rebuilding trust through consistent, honest, and caring actions. I (the one who was betrayed) give myself permission to move at my own pace and honor what I need to heal. We are choosing, for now, to walk this path side by side—and if that ever needs to change, we will continue to honor our own and each other's healing with honesty and respect.

    If you would like to write your own affirmation, you may do that here:

    _____

    _____

    _____

Mindful Reflection Moment

Now that you have completed your guided imagery and art journal exercises, take some mindful time to reflect on what you have learned. What awareness and insight have surfaced? What are you noticing after this chapter and the information you have learned? You may do this together, or each of you may take a moment to reflect separately. Write or share your reflections here. Be gentle with yourself and your significant other.

Partner 1 Reflection:

_____

_____

_____

_____

_____

_____

_____

_____

Partner 2 Reflection:

_____

_____

_____

_____

_____

_____

_____

_____

Self-Affirmation and Awareness Exercise

Instructions: Can you each give yourself the gift of self-affirmation? It can be difficult for people who have experienced complex trauma, addiction, betrayal, and other painful experiences to create affirmations. As a support to this step of your healing, affirmation ideas might include statements such as: "I am working on my communication skills and doing better," "I am holding a little more hope for the future," "I am healing myself and helping my partner heal", and "I am learning that honesty and respect are the cornerstones of a healthy relationship." Each of you is invited to add your own affirmations in the winged heart below:

This chapter provided mindfulness-based exercises, tools, and insights to help you better understand and navigate addiction recovery, deepen empathy around betrayal trauma, and foster self-awareness and mutual understanding. The guided imagery and journaling practices are designed to promote healing, enhance insight, support healthy communication, and cultivate a deeper connection. Healing from betrayal and sex addiction takes time, but the work you've done here marks a significant step toward rebuilding trust and respect.

As we close this chapter, I want to leave you both with an affirmation: Healing from betrayal, addiction, and complex trauma is a profoundly challenging journey that demands immense courage. By moving through this chapter, each of you has shown a strong commitment to your individual healing and a deep understanding of what it takes to move forward in healing your relationship if that is what you choose to do.

While the future may still be uncertain, a hopeful outcome will depend on your ongoing commitment to sobriety, your continued honesty, practicing compassion and healthy communication, and rebuilding trust and respect consistently. The work you've accomplished together in this chapter is a significant step forward, and I commend you both for your dedication.

CHAPTER FOUR

Grief: From Pain and Heartache to Peace and Hope

Wendy Quinton

Joy does not simply happen to us. We must choose joy and keep choosing it every day.

~ Henri Nouwen

I knew from the biographical information Joon had filled out before our first session that she was 34 years old. However, when her face appeared on my screen to begin our teletherapy session, I was surprised by how young she looked.

She was wearing a blue top, which I later learned is the traditional color of mourning in South Korea, where Joon was born. I introduced myself, welcomed her to the session, and asked her if she was currently in a safe and confidential place where she felt free to talk. She replied that she was alone in her favorite chair in her bedroom.

To put Joon at ease, I shared that I would be asking several questions during our time together and that it would only be fair if she, too, felt free to ask anything she wanted. I invited questions, and she thought for a moment as her eyes darted from the screen to her lap and back again, before saying, "No, I don't think so...this is my first time in therapy, so I'm not even sure what to ask." I assured her that the offer would continue for the duration of our time together.

To help her ease into our session, I asked Joon if she would like to start with a mindfulness exercise, to which she eagerly nodded. I gently led through a breath exercise, breathing in deeply through her nose and out through her mouth while asking her to relax her shoulders down from her earlobes and her elbows down from her shoulders. Once she was centered, I asked Joon to share from her comfort level what concerns she would like to focus on during our session when she was ready.

Looking more relaxed after her breathwork, Joon began, "I think that in order for you to understand the issues I need help with, it would be best for me to explain a bit about my family." Joon shared the details that she was born in South Korea and had emigrated to the

States with her parents as a 10-year-old. As she continued to talk, I noted that her voice grew stronger, and her eye contact lasted longer as she recalled her childhood.

"My parents opened a small restaurant, and I spent most of my time after school and weekends there. My mom and dad worked long hours and eventually moved the restaurant to a larger space. They hired more staff, and their restaurant became known as the go-to place for the best Korean fried chicken and bibimbap! I have wonderful memories of the times when I would work alongside my parents to prepare my favorite dish, bulgogi. However, those special occasions were not as frequent as I wished since my education was extremely important to my parents, and they insisted that I spend the majority of my time studying so that I could always stay at the top of my class.

"The fondest memory I have is of the rare times when my father would sit with me after school while I enjoyed a snack of kimchi fried rice and listen to me talk about my day. These moments with him were far too brief, and if I tried to sneak back into the kitchen, my father would give me a stern look that sent me scampering back to my little nook to sit alone and do my homework." Joon stopped talking, and her eyes took on a far-away look. A sad expression crossed her face. After a moment, she shook her head a little and appeared to come back to our session mentally. When she again met my eyes, I smiled and told her that I could almost smell the spicy odor of ginger as she spoke, which brought her back into our session.

Joon smiled briefly, and I nodded to let her know I wanted to hear more. She continued, "Deciding what to do after high school was tough, as my mom wanted me to go to a prestigious university and get a 'fancy' degree, as she called it. However, my dad understood that my dream was to work together with them in the restaurant business and perhaps someday open a location of my own. Being an only child, I instinctively felt that I didn't want to venture too far away from home. Much to my mother's disappointment, Dad and I won the argument. I attended a local community college and earned my business degree. After graduation and a few more years of hard work alongside my parents in their restaurant, I put my education to good use and facilitated the expansion of our family business by opening a second location. I was so proud to realize my dream and contribute to our family revenue in this way.

"The restaurant required long hours of hard work, but occasionally, I took time out and dated a few men casually over the years. Most of the men I met worked nine-to-five jobs, and wanted to live it up on the weekends, but my schedule at the restaurant didn't allow for many days off. However, last year, as I was thinking ahead to my upcoming thirty-third birthday, I decided that it was time to get serious about starting a family of my own." Joon's voice broke, and tears glistened in her eyes as she continued, "But then my father passed away suddenly." She was silent for several moments as she struggled to regain her composure. I said softly, "Joon, I am so sorry for your loss. It's okay to cry." We sat in silence for a few moments, and then I offered, "I can see that your tears are a sign of deep emotion. Would you be willing to share more about what you are feeling whenever you feel ready?"

Joon wiped her eyes and said, "I have shed so many tears over the past few months. I struggled with so many things: trying hard to honor my father by mourning in the traditional way, fulfilling all the required ceremonies that follow the death of a family member, coming to terms with the responsibility I have for my mother now that my father is gone, and trying to keep both restaurants going. It's all been overwhelming! And I feel so guilty admitting it, but I have also felt some anger toward my father that he died when he did—just as I was finally ready to start a family of my own. My mother now relies on me for everything at home and at the restaurant. I have considered shutting down one of them, but that would feel so disrespectful, given the enormous amount of work we put into it. I guess I always imagined my mom passing away before my father because I couldn't bear to think of her living without him, and yet, that is now reality. I'm not sure how much of my grief is for myself or for my mom. She's just so heartbroken and lost."

Joon continued, "I understand that my mom is sad because she lost her best friend of many years. It feels incredibly selfish to admit, but I feel like I have lost my future. Even if the time came when I could think about dating again and possibly meeting someone that I want to spend the rest of my life with, it hurts so much to know that I will never be able to introduce them to my father or ask for his advice and blessing. How would I have time to think about having children of my own when I must care for my mother and keep the restaurants going as well? And if somehow children were a part of my future, it breaks my heart to picture raising them without their *Harabeoji*, their grandfather, around. It's all too much!"

Joon's shoulders seemed to slouch even further, as if the weight of the entire world was pressing down on her. She sat slumped with her eyes downcast, an air of hopelessness filling the space around her. Noticing that Joon's attention had drifted off, I gently suggested that it could be helpful to practice a few techniques that would help ground her to the present moment. I suggested that she take a few deep breaths and guided her to focus on the feeling of her feet on the ground. I invited her to place her hands on her lap and feel the texture of her clothing, helping her reconnect with her physical surroundings. Once Joon had completed the grounding exercises and was ready to re-engage with the session, I prompted her to continue her story.

"Even though all of this is weighing on me, I know that my father would want me to move on and make space for myself and my dreams. He knew that once I had a restaurant of my own, the next step for me would be starting a family, and he was excited for that dream to come true. But I have no idea how to pursue that dream now while still managing the responsibilities I have to my mother and the restaurants. I want to be mentally prepared to date again, but I just feel hopeless. How can I leave my mother alone to go out and have fun? Do I even remember how to have fun? What if I start to cry on a date? Who would want to date someone with so many responsibilities and a broken heart? I want to be able to find joy again, but I don't remember how."

I assured Joon that everything she was feeling was completely normal for someone who had experienced such a great loss, and if she was willing, we could work together to find and reclaim her joy. Joon's expression seemed doubtful, and her eyes held many unanswered questions, but she nodded slightly. "Okay, Wendy," she murmured, "it feels impossible, but there is a part of me that wants to accomplish my dream for my father's sake."

Over the next year, Joon and I worked together towards that goal. The first thing we did was discuss grief since that is what she indicated as her hardest struggle. I began by sharing with her that in the past, there was a school of thought that presented grief as a process of traveling chronologically through stages, starting with denial and ending with acceptance. However, it has since become evident through additional research that grief is not a straightforward, linear process, and it often involves moving back and forth between stages or even skipping certain stages altogether.

Joon shared with me that she had not yet experienced significant grief in her life but expressed an interest in learning about the stages of grief. She wanted to become familiar with the possible ways grief might manifest so she could better understand the emotional process she may experience.

The first stage we discussed was anger, as this is often the hardest for people to acknowledge. I explained to Joon that as people come to terms with the loss they have experienced, they may have felt anger. This anger may be directed at themselves, other people, or even at the person they lost. I asked her to take a moment and contemplate whether or not she had felt anger since her father passed away. She was still for a moment and then answered, "Yes, it is really hard to acknowledge this to myself, never mind say it out loud, but I have felt angry."

After assuring her again that anger is a normal reaction to a loss, I asked her if she would like to share more about the anger she experienced. She explained that for a time, she was angry at her father for abandoning her and necessitating the major changes she had to make to accommodate his absence. She also admitted that she was often angry with her mother for her open displays of grief and wished that she would mourn in private, as Joon forced herself to do. I reassured Joon that it's common to try to suppress anger, deny its existence, or criticize herself for feeling it. However, I encouraged her to acknowledge and allow herself to experience the anger fully. By offering herself compassion during these moments, she could prevent the anger from being trapped in her body and instead allow it to move through her, eventually dissipating on its own.

We discussed another stage of grief, which is denial. Joon was able to relate to this aspect of grief as she remembered thinking that her father could not possibly be dead because he was still so young. At first, she refused to call any of her relatives back in Korea to tell them about the news for several days because that would mean admitting that he was really gone. She was able to see that this stage served as a defense mechanism that allowed her the time she needed to gradually begin to process her emotions.

Joon did not immediately relate to the bargaining stage, and I explained that some people who are facing a loss sometimes promise things to their higher power as a way to manipulate circumstances to prevent the loss from happening. I shared that it can happen after a loss as well, and as Joon continued to self-reflect, she could see that focusing all her energy on running the restaurant was a form of bargaining that she used to cope with her loss. She reasoned with herself that if she worked hard enough, the pain of her father's absence would not be as unbearable.

Before looking in depth at the next stage, I reiterated to Joon that these emotional stages are rarely felt in order and that even though the bereaved person may find a place of acceptance one day, they may experience anger again the next day and that this is perfectly normal. She reported that she could definitely relate to this rollercoaster-like experience, and then we moved on to the acceptance stage.

Joon told me that she felt that long-term acceptance was an elusive goal and that she lives in fear that if she accepts her father's death completely and begins to move on with her life, others would think that she was coldhearted and unaffected by his passing. She believed that if she stopped grieving, others would judge her as a daughter who dishonors her father and that it would diminish his importance in her life. We worked on her ability to focus on her own thoughts and feelings rather than trying to manage others' thoughts. She was open to the idea that she could eventually come to the point in her life when she could honor her father's memory by caring for herself and creating a life that she could be proud of—knowing that he would also be proud.

As I prepared to discuss the next stage with Joon, she anticipated that it might be sadness and depression, and she was correct. She shared that this is where she felt stuck in her grieving process at the moment. I explained that, unlike temporary feelings of sadness, depression in grief can involve a prolonged loss of interest in daily activities, feelings of hopelessness, and intense emotional pain. While sadness is a natural part of grieving, depression can sometimes make it difficult for individuals to move forward. I assured her that as we continued working together, she would be learning about mindfulness and how it can alleviate symptoms of depression and help to get her unstuck. We also discussed a referral to a psychiatrist if medication was needed in the future.

Before moving into another area of treatment, I explained two additional theories of grieving to Joon, which are explained below in the "Word from Wendy" section. I made sure Joon truly understood that the concept of grief moving through distinct stages is a common idea, but in reality, grief is far from a linear process. It doesn't unfold in neat, predictable phases. Instead, grief is a deeply personal and fluid experience, with emotions that ebb and flow unpredictably. Joon attested to the fact that she could feel sadness, anger, acceptance, and denial all at once or in different combinations on any given day and was glad to know that there is no set timeline or path that grief follows. She learned that instead of trying to figure out the right way to grieve, she could accept all of her emotions and let her mourning process unfold in its own unique way.

· · · · ·

Over the course of our year working together, Joon often shared how her emotions fluctuated—sometimes daily—as she navigated the deep and painful loss of her father. At first, she felt pressure to "move on" or "feel better," as if grief had an expiration date. But through therapy, she began to understand that grief is not linear, nor does it follow a predictable path. It's a deeply personal experience, and there is no single "right" way to mourn.

Joon gradually gave herself permission to slow down, to feel what she was feeling without judgment, and to stop comparing her process to others'. Around the ninth month of our work together, she began to feel a shift—subtle but meaningful. Though she still carried the sadness of her loss, she started to sense moments of lightness. With gentle curiosity and caution, she allowed herself to consider the idea of dating again—not as a replacement for what was lost, but as a sign of healing and openness to life.

Now, Joon is beginning to explore a new relationship. While she doesn't have all the answers—and isn't looking for certainty—she is showing up with honesty, mindfulness, and a growing trust in herself. Grief still walks beside her, but so does the hope for connection and joy. Through mindfulness practices and self-compassion, Joon is learning that healing doesn't mean forgetting; it means making space for both love and loss to coexist.

Grief is a part of the human experience, and the loss of someone close to us can change us in various ways. Although each of us will experience grief in a unique fashion, there are themes common to the experience that we need to be aware of if we seek to support ourselves and others during this process.

Theories of Grief

Stages of Grief: As noted above, part of my work with grieving clients involves normalizing their experiences, and I have found that discussing the stages of grief is a good place to start. When Elisabeth Kübler-Ross first published the stages of grief in her book *On Death and Dying* in 1969, readers were deeply appreciative of having their experiences of loss categorized and standardized. The stages she outlined are denial, anger, bargaining, depression, and acceptance (Kübler-Ross & Kessler, 2005). This stage theory continues to be explored extensively, and in light of the evidence that grief is a nonlinear process, some professionals have chosen to abandon this theory altogether (Stroebe, Schut, & Boerner, 2017). However, Kübler-Ross's contributions remain influential in how we understand the emotional experience of grief and loss.

Grief is an intensely personal experience, and more recently, scholars have expanded the existing stages to include shock, reconstruction, and making meaning (Rando, 2018) (Kessler, 2019). Numerous other models of grief exist, but they hold in common the understanding that grief stages are not chronological and linear. Instead, they are mercurial.

After clients have moved back and forth between the stages of grief, the place where we spend most of our time in sessions is the "acceptance and hope" phase. As explained further in Chapter Two of this workbook, acceptance is an important element of mindfulness. Coming to a place where hope feels real again usually comes once the grieving person can envision their future without the person they have lost, they have identified a purpose for their lives, and are able to formulate a plan to accomplish this goal. Each client is unique, and it takes a deep level of knowledge on the part of the therapist and a deep level of trust on the part of the client to work together to set small goals and plans, which progress step-by-step while the client's pace is honored.

For Joon, her plans for a hopeful future included implementing self-care and being open to the possibility of finding a partner and starting a family. For others, it may be venturing into a new career, moving to a new city, or perhaps volunteering at a local agency that will bring meaning to the next stage of their lives. This process may require some trial and error, and as long as the client is able to look to the future mindfully, they will make progress on their healing journey.

It should be noted that it is not just the death of a loved one that brings the experience of sorrow. Grief can also be the primary emotion felt after a betrayal. In the book *Mending a Shattered Heart: A Guide for Partners of Sex Addicts*, the fourth stage of recovery includes grieving the losses that came as a result of betrayal (Carnes, 2009). The loss of pets can be extremely difficult as well. Additionally, losses such as jobs, friendships, financial stability, possessions, health, mobility, a home, and a sense of safety are all areas of grief. Remember that loss will be processed uniquely, as each person is unique. Our role as therapists is to support the client in mindful grieving and healthy recovery.

The Dual Process Model of Grief: This model suggests that individuals who are grieving may navigate two distinct types of stressors following a loss: loss-oriented and restoration-oriented stressors. Loss-oriented stressors are the challenges directly related to the death of a loved one, such as emotional pain, memories, and grief. Restoration-oriented stressors are additional challenges that arise because of the loss and the readjustment and reorganization that must occur, such as taking on new responsibilities or adjusting to a new reality, as Joon had experienced. Coping with a loss successfully requires shifting attention between both orientations as opposed to getting stuck in either domain.

As therapists, it is imperative that we are aware of when a client may be experiencing a high amount of stressors in both domains. When this occurs, they may become overburdened, creating further difficulty in dealing with the loss (Eisma, de Lang, & Stroebe, 2021). Joon found this distinction in processes to be helpful as it allowed her to understand why she would often feel overwhelmed and to be especially careful to offer herself compassion and rest during these difficult times. As her therapist, I was able to assist Joon in finding additional resources, both internal (through mindfulness) and external (through additional support systems), that aided her on her journey to finding hope after loss.

Worden's Four Tasks of Mourning: This concept describes tasks that the bereaved must actively work on to cope with the loss. These undertakings include accepting the reality of the loss, processing the pain of grief, adjusting to a world without the deceased, and finding an enduring connection with the deceased while moving forward with life. To complete the task of acceptance, one must come to terms with reality—both mentally and emotionally. Completing the task of processing grief involves confronting and experiencing the pain and emotions associated with the loss. Completing the process of adjustment requires the bereaved to adapt to the loss by experiencing external, internal, and spiritual changes so that they learn to function without the deceased.

For Joon, this involved changing her daily routines, including setting aside time to pause, be still, and sit with her emotions. She also had to shift some of her roles, becoming more of a caretaker in her mother's life and embracing her top management position at the restaurants. She also re-examined some of her beliefs in order to complete the task of finding a continued connection with her father. At first, Joon was confused about how she could honor her father's continued influence on her life. As a help, I shared with her a meaningful way I had been able to do this after the death of my mother. Since I lived a distance from my mom, we set aside time each week to catch up with each other, and I sorely missed these weekly phone calls after she passed. It was almost like the events in my life were not complete until I was able to share them with my mother, so I continued to do so, just in a different way.

Each week, I took time to sit quietly, looking back at all that had transpired and imagining myself telling my mom about it. This helped me to feel that she was still close to me, and since I knew her so well, I could hear her voice in my head cautioning or congratulating me, depending on the circumstances. I encouraged Joon to find her own way to continue to integrate her father's memory into her daily life, and she decided to write him a letter each time something happened that she wanted to tell him about.

Through this exercise, she found a way to balance the remembrance of the loss with embracing new opportunities (Worden, 2009).

Dependency: When a relationship with a caretaker remains a dependent one, even into adulthood, the process of grieving their passing is difficult. For Joon, this occurred when she realized how much she and her mother had relied on their patriarch for stability. She learned that her father had sheltered them from much of the day-to-day worry as he cared for the family and the restaurants. At first, she was upset with him for not preparing her more fully to live without him and at herself for leaning on him so much.

At the start, Joon felt averse to taking on these new responsibilities and doubted her ability to do so. This type of ambivalent grieving is difficult as emotions can fluctuate from anger to guilt at being angry, to pain, and back again in rapid succession. Joon was grateful for the safe place that therapy afforded her where she could explore all these emotions and learn to tolerate them so that her energy was freed up to take on new tasks. As she became increasingly proficient at caring for both her mother and the restaurants, she realized how strong she actually was, and her feelings toward her father shifted from resentful to fulfilled, knowing that he would be proud of her accomplishments.

Guilt: Guilt is a common emotion to experience after a loss. It can be activated after a death by thoughts such as, "I could have done something to prevent it," or "I should have done more to care for them while they were alive." We can also feel tremendous guilt if even a twinge of relief is sensed, which is common if caretaker burnout has been experienced or if the deceased suffered greatly. Making peace with ambivalent feelings and knowing it is normal to feel more than one emotion at a time can be helpful. Practicing self-compassion, rather than self-judgment, can aid in healing (Devine, 2017).

Mind States and Stories Relating to Grief: Mind states and stories, which are described extensively in Chapter Two of this workbook, are important to explore with clients as they relate to grief. During our therapy sessions, Joon would often express self-defeating thoughts related to the loss of her father, such as: "I can't survive without my father," "I'll never feel happy again," and "I'm so selfish for being angry that my father passed." When these thoughts were expressed, I would suggest that she take the time to discover what mind state was prompting her to think in that way.

When she expressed her fear of not being able to survive without her father's presence, she was able to take a breath, ground herself by placing her feet firmly on the floor, relax her muscles, and allow her mind to float back to the earliest memories that related to this belief. She remembered being taught as a child that a woman needed to find a man, as life without one would be impossible. She realized that this deeply held belief had caused her to create the story that even though she was not yet married, she was still under the protection of her father and could, therefore, survive.

She was then able to spend time during the next week journaling about the things she had accomplished on her own and realized that she was more than capable of having a successful life even though her father was no longer physically present. She also found a local wellness studio that offered sound baths, and she attended one that specifically targeted grief. Joon found that listening to the soothing vibrations and frequencies allowed her to release her pent-up emotions, helped her relax, and gave her space for self-reflection.

Exploring Secondary Losses: When a loved one passes away, we may judge our grief as out of proportion to the loss and wonder why we cannot "get over it" as quickly as we feel that we should or as quickly as others believe we should be able to move on. Joon questioned this during her process, and it was helpful for her to explore the secondary losses she suffered when her father died. Secondary losses are the experiences that result from the death of a loved one or any significant loss we experience, and they can be just as impactful and challenging as the primary loss. Joon explored these secondary losses by listing all the things that changed when her dad passed away and anything she felt that she lost. Her list included numerous things, including a sense of security, freedom from worry and responsibility, a source of wisdom, her routine, and her independence.

Once she realized the extent of her losses, Joon was able to practice self-compassion and be gentler with herself as she grieved. During our time together, my respect for Joon continued to deepen, and I witnessed the hard work she invested into her process, the presence she cultivated for herself, and the new way she honored her emotions. As Joon continued to process her father's death and the changes it brought, she was eventually able to be receptive to experiencing joy again.

Wendy, learning the Duma language in the Elimbari tribe.
Chimbu Province, Papua New Guinea, 1994.

Cultural Competency: A truth that I learned early on in my first career—one that has continued to be true in my work as a therapist—is that understanding people's mind states and stories is an important key to experiencing a relationship of trust with them. At the time of this book's writing, I have been a therapist for over a decade, but my first occupation was that of an overseas missionary.

My journey to understanding the value of learning and accepting others' worldviews started when I entered training to become a cross-cultural missionary as I studied the process of how to understand a culture vastly different from my own and how to become fluent in an unwritten language. That schooling was put into practice when I lived in Papua New Guinea for thirteen years and studied the culture and language of the Duma people.

One of the clearest examples of the importance of truly understanding another culture occurred when I came across an idiom used by the Duma people, which described a woman as a "bean pole," which refers to the stick that supports string beans as they grow. Initially, I interpreted this as a metaphor for the woman's grounding and supportive role within her family. However, recognizing the importance of avoiding assumptions based on my own cultural perspective, I delved deeper and discovered that the idiom actually reflected the woman's transient role in the family. Because she marries into her husband's clan, she is considered movable, subject to where her husband wishes her to be. What I first thought symbolized the vital role of women within the clan was actually an expression of their transient and subordinate status. This experience reinforced the necessity of staying mindful of my own cultural biases and narratives, particularly when navigating a culture as distinct from my own as that of the Duma people.

For most of us, practicing cultural sensitivity will not require living overseas, but it will require a mindful awareness of our beliefs and assumptions. Even if someone looks like us, lives in the same neighborhood, attends the same schools, eats the same foods, or worships in the same denomination as we do, there are still likely numerous differences between us. Making assumptions about someone's cultural identity based on outward appearances, rather than inquiring about their worldview, can be a costly mistake and create wounding and misunderstandings. (Huey, Park, Galán, & Wang, 2023). Because of this, I am forever grateful for the training and experiences I had living in a culture vastly different from my own, as cultural competence is of vital importance to being an effective therapist. In my experience, being a culturally competent therapist (and human!) requires possessing the following traits.

- **Awareness:** As clinicians, we must be aware that each client is a unique individual. This may be easier to remember when others look or speak differently than we do. However, we must be aware that not everyone we meet has had the same experiences as we have and that even though they may have grown up in the same country, state, city, and even neighborhood as us, they can hold vastly different core values and traditions. This difference includes being mindful of how a person grieves in their own unique way.

- **Desire to learn:** We must also cultivate a genuine curiosity about others. Conducting basic research on the diverse cultures, languages, and orientations of those around you is valuable, but remember that the client is the true expert on their own life. Trust is built when you're willing to acknowledge gaps in your knowledge and take steps to fill them through available resources, never forcing the client to be your teacher. By showing openness to learning about their unique experiences and beliefs, you position yourself as a learner, and this humility fosters a stronger, more authentic connection with the client.

- **Humility:** Always keep in mind that others are the experts in their own lives. Having a sense of humor that gives you the ability to laugh at yourself will go a long way to putting others at ease. Also, it is wise not to compare your own culture, language, and experiences to that of others. Instead, foster an atmosphere of openness and trust so that your client feels comfortable correcting you and challenging you. Be willing to make mistakes and leave your ego at the door so you can receive corrections while you continue to learn. Our personal growth should never be at the expense of another.

Had I not valued cultural competence as an integral part of my work with Joon, I may have made many avoidable mistakes during our time together. I might have encouraged her to find independence by letting her mom figure out her own life, forgo her responsibility to the restaurant, and find her own happiness. I may have tried to comfort her by asking her to picture her father looking down and guiding her along the way, or I could have criticized her father for doing all of the heavy lifting and, without any malicious intent, offended Joon. Instead, I spent time learning more about Korean culture on my own and gently asking Joon questions to confirm that I understood correctly. Additionally, it was important for me to take my cues from Joon so that I could be an effective therapist who could compassionately and respectfully help her manage her grief in a culturally appropriate way.

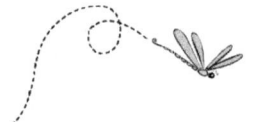

Mindfulness Healing Part I:

Preparation, Assessment, and Script
for Guided Imagery Exercise

Important Safety Tips for Therapists, Facilitators, and Healing Individuals

Environment Consideration and Tips: It can be helpful to "set the stage" prior to a guided imagery exercise. For example, consider the lighting—is it too bright or too low? Another helpful step is putting phones on silent. Also, think about outside distractions, such as barking dogs, traffic, and other interruptions. If possible, minimize outside noises the best that you can. Some individuals like having a blanket or pillow to hold, or you may enjoy diffusing essential oils to support deeper relaxation if there are no allergy concerns. While mindfulness-based guided imagery is not hypnosis, it can be helpful to prepare your environment prior to beginning the guided imagery exercise.

Voice Prosody: An additional gentle reminder is to be aware of your voice prosody. Prosody refers to the rhythm and melody of the voice, including intonation, stress, and pauses. Speaking in a softer tone and slower cadence than your normal speaking voice is useful in supporting the guided imagery practice. If you typically speak more rapidly or loudly, it will take some practice to slow down and modulate your voice.

Diversity Considerations: Consider the client's culture, age, race, physical differences (such as hearing loss), gender and orientation, and other unique experiences, which may invite a softer or different speaking tone or pace or require that the client keep their eyes open if they prefer. If you are bilingual and you and your client speak the same languages, ask your client what language they prefer. If your client prefers to go by a nickname, a title such as Dr., Mr., or Mrs., or a specific pronoun, honor their request.

Pace Yourself: Remind yourself to take your time as you walk through this process. There is no need to rush. If you are the person facilitating this exercise, slow down for a relaxed, calming pace. Additionally, it is wise for the facilitator to first practice the exercise with yourself prior to practicing with another person or client.

Safety Reminder: Safety is the number one consideration with any therapeutic approach or healing intervention. As you lead your clients through the following guided imagery exercise, please instruct your clients to alert you if they are experiencing any of the following responses.

Note: If you are an individual doing this work solo, you will also want to consider the following:

- Traumatic memories that are creating a high level of distress

- Feelings of intense fear or panic

- Disturbing or intrusive thoughts

- Suicidal or homicidal thoughts

- Dissociation (if there is an awareness of the dissociative states)

- Other crisis concerns (list on the line): _____

_____

It is also important to ask the client to alert you to the below symptoms or for the person doing this work solo to pay compassionate and close attention to your process if you are experiencing distressing or physical symptoms such as:

- A racing heart

- Tightness in the chest

- Shortness of breath

- Nausea or intestinal distress

- Feeling faint or dizziness

- Body pain

- Feeling as if you are floating outside of your body

- Other somatic concerns (list on the line): _____

_____

Note for Therapist or Facilitator: Before moving into the guided imagery, please have your client begin with the assessment below. If you are not a trained mental health professional and your client is in crisis and exhibiting or discussing symptoms that are out of your scope of practice or experience, please refer your client to an appropriate mental health or medical professional. *If your client is experiencing an immediate life-threatening emergency, please call 911 or the appropriate emergency number if located outside of the United States.*

Note to Solo Reader: *If you are doing this work on your own and believe you are in crisis or may be at risk to yourself, please stop and seek emergency support immediately by calling 911 or your local emergency number.*

On a scale from 1 to 10 (with 1 = very low, and 10 = very high), please take a mindful moment to assess the following. Circle the number that most accurately applies to you:

Feeling	Assessment (1-10)									
▢ Anxiety	1	2	3	4	5	6	7	8	9	10
▢ Anger	1	2	3	4	5	6	7	8	9	10
▢ Shame	1	2	3	4	5	6	7	8	9	10
▢ Sadness	1	2	3	4	5	6	7	8	9	10
▢ Fear	1	2	3	4	5	6	7	8	9	10
▢ Numbness	1	2	3	4	5	6	7	8	9	10
▢ Confusion	1	2	3	4	5	6	7	8	9	10
▢ Curiosity	1	2	3	4	5	6	7	8	9	10
▢ Hopefulness	1	2	3	4	5	6	7	8	9	10
▢ Calm	1	2	3	4	5	6	7	8	9	10
▢ Joyful	1	2	3	4	5	6	7	8	9	10
▢ Other:	1	2	3	4	5	6	7	8	9	10

Assessment Notes: _____

_____

_____

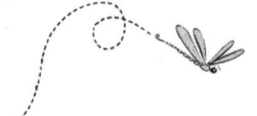

Mindfulness Healing Part II:
Breath and Somatic Preparation & Prompts

This exercise involves tuning into your breath and body and is followed by the guided imagery exercise. It's important to note that this may not be suitable for everyone. It's recommended that the following be adapted to the specific needs and comfort levels of the individual(s) involved.

Physical Space and Comfort: Have your client settle into a comfortable sitting or lying down position, with their feet on the floor or cross-legged if that is the preference. If your client—or you if you are doing this solo—has a yoga mat or a couch and prefers to lie down, that is fine. Whatever position will help the client feel comfortable is perfectly acceptable.

Prompt 1: Let's pause while you take a few moments to get comfortable.

Prompt 2: When you are ready, you are welcome to close your eyes if that feels comfortable for you. Or, if you prefer to leave your eyes open, that is just fine. Whatever allows you to feel most secure is more than acceptable. If your eyes remain open, feel free to rest your gaze on a calming point—near the floor if you're sitting or on the ceiling if you're lying down.

Prompt 3: We will now move forward into the grounded breathing exercise. This will take approximately two to three minutes.

Grounded Breath Exercise

Now that you are in a comfortable position, before we begin the guided imagery, let's move through the grounded breath work.

1. We will start with the 4-2-7 breath. Start by breathing in deeply through the nose to the count of four, hold for two, and then exhale slowly and intentionally through the mouth to the count of seven. Let's do this three times at your own pace. **Note to Facilitator: Count to 20 silently.**

2. Now, let's return to easy, relaxed, deep breathing. Take a long breath in through the nose and let out a long exhale out through the mouth. Continue with this breath. **Note to Facilitator: Count to 20 silently.**

3. As you are noticing the gentle rhythm of deep breathing, I would like you to imagine extending compassion to yourself with each intake breath. **Note to Facilitator: Count to 20 silently.**

Somatic Relaxation Exercise

Now that we have finished with our grounded breaths, please feel free to breathe normally with relaxed, regular breaths. Let's now move into relaxing the body in preparation for guided imagery:

1. Notice that your feet are feeling heavier and more relaxed.

2. Notice that your hands are gently resting at your sides, on your belly, or on your thighs.

3. Feel your jaw relax and your tongue move away from the roof of your mouth.

4. Allow your shoulders to relax down from your ear lobes and your elbows to gently relax down from your shoulders.

5.   Bit by bit, the tension moves out of your body as you breathe in and relax and breathe out and relax. Breathe in compassion, hope, and healing, and breathe out stress, judgment, and anger. **Note to Facilitator: *Count to 20 silently.***

As we complete our breath work, we will now move on to the guided imagery preparation and exercise section. You can return to your breath work exercises at any point during the guided imagery. The guided imagery exercise will take approximately 10 minutes. You may continue to stay in your comfortable position or shift to a different comfortable position. You may also continue with your eyes closed if that is your preference. At any point, you are welcome to ask for a time out if needed.

Let's move forward.

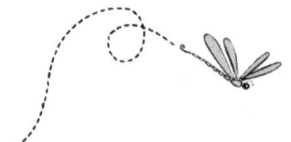

Mindfulness Healing Part III:
Guided Imagery Exercise
The Photograph

Note to Therapist or Facilitator: If you notice that the client is highly activated during the guided imagery, perhaps demonstrating rapid or shallow breathing, sobbing, or shaking, please have the client pause as you attend to the individual. This can be done by gently stating that you would like to pause the exercise for a moment, then quietly asking the person by name if they would like a break, support with deep breath work, or to step out of the guided imagery entirely if it has become too overwhelming.

Note to the Reader: If you are doing this solo without the support of a mental health professional, again, please be gentle with yourself. If you have a trusted person to lead you through this, you may want to consider this option, or perhaps you can read this into a recording device and then play it back and follow the prompts. If you become overwhelmed or feel as if you are in a crisis state, please stop and reach out for help if need be. Safety comes first, always.

Purpose of the Photograph Exercise: This guided imagery exercise is designed to help you reconnect to the emotion of joy, thereby stimulating positive bodily sensations such as increased circulation, lowered heart rate, and decreased stress. By focusing on joy, the mind is drawn away from negative thoughts, thus decreasing depression and anxiety.

Instructions: This guided imagery exercise will take approximately 10 minutes. You will be guided by your mental health professional or trusted facilitator—or you may guide yourself if you prefer—through each step of the exercise slowly. Though questions may be asked of you or you may be given prompts, there is no expectation of a verbal response. You may respond if you would like to do so, or you may quietly respond inside of yourself, which many people prefer. Through this visualization journey, you will be guided to explore a memory of a time you felt joy, allowing you to re-experience that feeling in your body.

Note: Some clients, especially those who are newly grieving, may find it difficult or even impossible to experience joy. We should be mindful of this and create a supportive environment that allows clients to honor whatever emotions come up. It's important to give the client permission to feel and express any emotion that arises in them without the expectation of only feeling joy.

First Step Prompt: Close your eyes if you would like to do so, or you may rest them toward a comfortable spot toward the floor or toward the ceiling if you are lying down. Take a deep breath, and allow yourself to sink into a comfortable position. When you are ready, bring to mind the image of a photo album. What does the album look like? *Note to Facilitator: Count to 20 silently.*

Next Prompt Step: Where is the photo album located—a table, a shelf, somewhere else? Imagine yourself walking over and picking it up. As you do, what does it feel like in your hands? You notice a comfortable chair that is well-suited for you, and you sit down and gaze at the photo album's cover. You notice that it is an old photo album, and you remove a cloth from your pocket and carefully begin to wipe away the layers of dust covering it. *Note to Facilitator: Count to 20 silently.*

Next Prompt Step: As you continue to wipe the accumulated dust from the old album, you notice that there is something written on its cover. As the last of the dust is cleared away, you see that the word "JOY" is written there. Take a moment to imagine this. *Note to Facilitator: Count to 20 silently.*

Next Prompt Step: Now, imagine yourself opening the album. What sound does it make as you open this? Does it have a particular scent? As you begin to slowly and carefully flip through the pages of pictures, a picture catches your eye, and you stop turning to get a closer look. You see that it is a photo of you at a time when you felt joyful, happy, and free. Take a moment and allow that wonderful picture to become clearer in your mind. It is OK to take your time if an image does not immediately come to mind. Just allow yourself to breathe and know that you are safe and supported. *Note to Facilitator: Count to 20 silently.*

Next Prompt Step: As you breathe deeply, you take in all the details of the picture. Notice where you are. Notice how old you are. Notice what you are wearing. Notice what you are doing. *Note to Facilitator: Count to 20 silently.*

Next Prompt Step: Now, just take a moment to allow yourself to feel the joy, happiness, and freedom that this picture inspires. Remember that joy is different for everyone, and you may feel different layers and levels of joy on any given day or moment. Joy might feel like a small flicker, or an embracing warm light, or something else entirely. There is no wrong way to feel joy. *Note to Facilitator: Count to 20 silently.*

Next Prompt Step: As you continue to concentrate on the feeling of joy, allow your attention to focus on the part of your body that holds this feeling of joy. It may be your face as you notice your lips curve into a smile. Your stomach might be feeling like happy butterflies are fluttering around in it. Perhaps you feel a sense of warmth in your chest or a calmness deep in your heart. When you locate the part of your body that feels joy, gently place your hand on it and feel the warmth. *Note to Facilitator: Count to 20 silently.*

Next Prompt Step: Continue to breathe in and out with that wonderful feeling, repeating silently to yourself, "I can feel joy." If this is difficult, then honor what feels best for you. All emotions are honored in this safe space, and your pace and process are respected. **Note to Facilitator: *Count to 20 silently.***

Next Prompt Step: As you continue to gaze at this picture that brings you such joy, you may notice that other feelings are coming up. Perhaps you feel sadness that a loved one who was with you in the picture is no longer here. Perhaps you feel a sense of loss that this joyful memory is in the past and seems so long ago. Allow yourself to feel any emotion that comes up. Keep in mind that there are no "bad" emotions; they are all messengers, though some may feel more difficult to experience than others. **Note to Facilitator: *Count to 20 silently.***

Next Prompt Step: If you are sensing emotions other than joy, take a moment to name each of these emotions within you. Then, take them one by one and mentally place them into separate albums, each labeled with the emotion you are feeling. If you're feeling sadness, place that in the sadness album. If you're feeling grief, place that into the grief album. Perhaps you feel anger; mentally place that in the anger album. **Note to Facilitator: *Count to 20 silently.***

Next Prompt Step: Continue to put each emotion in its own album, and then mentally put those albums back on the shelf. Those albums containing other emotions can be explored another day. Today is your day to remember the feeling of joy. Again, no emotion is bad, but today, in this present moment, you are focusing on the emotion of feeling joy and practicing making just a little room for this in your life once again. **Note to Facilitator: *Count to 20 silently.***

Next Prompt Step: Now that the other emotions are safely secured, gently refocus on your picture and allow yourself to experience joy. Breathe in deeply and repeat in your mind, "I feel joy." And exhale, repeating, "I feel joy." Continue inhaling and exhaling, repeating this phrase. If you need to pause, or if you find that your joy feels fleeting or mercurial, that is OK. Be gentle with yourself; you do not need to force yourself to feel anything, only to observe and experience, even if just for a moment, the feeling of joy. **Note to Facilitator: *Count to 20 silently.***

Next Prompt Step: As we come to the end of this joy meditation, remember that at any time you desire, you can return to this compassionate exercise, opening your "Joy album" and focusing again on the feeling of joy that the picture brings to you. You may even find that when you open the joy album again in your mind, a new picture of joy is waiting there for you to focus on. For now, I invite you to gently close the album in your mind's eye and return it to where you found it, knowing that it is there waiting for you at any time. **Note to Facilitator: *Count to 20 silently.***

Next Prompt Step: Know that you have the strength and resilience to work through your grief and eventually find moments of joy. Can you take a deep breath and hold this understanding? Breathe in deeply through your nose and out through your mouth. Please remember that you are not alone in this journey of healing; you are supported. No matter the challenges that come your way, know that you are worthy of a life filled with love, authenticity, respect, joy, and fulfillment. Take a moment now to give yourself an affirmation. Self-affirmations may take you out of your comfort zone, but do your best to stay present with yourself, even in the discomfort. **Note to Facilitator: *Count to 20 silently.***

Transitioning to Awareness

Final Prompt Step: When you're ready, if your eyes are closed, notice the light in front of your eyelids. Gently blink, open your eyes, and bring your awareness back to the present moment.

Mindfulness Healing Part IV:
Processing of Guided Imagery
Sharing Your Experience

Purpose for Processing: After the conclusion of the guided imagery, the therapist or facilitator will lead an open and respectful discussion about what you experienced during the guided imagery. The aim is to allow for a compassionate and honest conversation as you highlight important aspects of the guided imagery exercise and what the experience was like.

Note: If you are doing this solo without a therapist or facilitator, please pace yourself and notice your energy. You may journal your responses to the questions below if you are doing this work on your own.

Important Considerations for the Facilitator: It is not the role of the therapist or facilitator to interpret, minimize, or re-direct. Rather, it is important for the facilitator to skillfully hold a safe space for the client to share their experience, including the more difficult aspects. This is a time for the facilitator to honor the pain, as well as highlight and affirm the positive insights the client may have had. Remind the client that participating in a therapy exercise like this is a signal of hope and aids in the possibility of recovery and healing.

Processing Questions

1. What did you notice in the guided imagery?

2. What challenges did you experience?

3. Were you able to experience joy?

4. Did you have a breakthrough you'd like to share?

5. Do you have any concerns that you'd like to share?

6. What are you feeling in your body currently?

7. Did you notice any self-growth with insight and compassion toward yourself?

8. Did you notice any triggers or areas of concern?

Post-Guided Imagery Assessment Scale

Now that you have completed the breathwork and somatic exercises, the guided imagery exercise, and the process work, on a scale from 1 to 10 (with 1 = very low, and 10 = very high), let's take a mindful moment to assess the following:

Feeling	Assessment (1-10)									
▫ Anxiety	1	2	3	4	5	6	7	8	9	10
▫ Anger	1	2	3	4	5	6	7	8	9	10
▫ Shame	1	2	3	4	5	6	7	8	9	10
▫ Sadness	1	2	3	4	5	6	7	8	9	10
▫ Fear	1	2	3	4	5	6	7	8	9	10
▫ Numbness	1	2	3	4	5	6	7	8	9	10
▫ Confusion	1	2	3	4	5	6	7	8	9	10
▫ Curiosity	1	2	3	4	5	6	7	8	9	10
▫ Hopefulness	1	2	3	4	5	6	7	8	9	10
▫ Calm	1	2	3	4	5	6	7	8	9	10
▫ Joyful	1	2	3	4	5	6	7	8	9	10
▫ Other:	1	2	3	4	5	6	7	8	9	10

Important Reminder: If you, as the facilitator, are not a licensed therapist or trained mental health professional and your client is in crisis and exhibiting or discussing symptoms that are out of your scope of practice or experience, please refer to an appropriate mental health or medical professional. *If your client is experiencing an immediate life-threatening emergency, please call 911 or the appropriate emergency number if located outside of the United States. If you are doing this solo without support and are in a state of emergency, reach out to 911 immediately.*

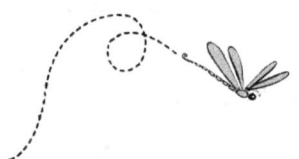

Mindfulness Healing Part V:

Purpose Statement: The purpose of the Photo of Joy art exercise is to draw a physical representation of the photo that brought you a memory of joy during the guided imagery exercise. This will increase creativity, helping you to stay mindful in the present moment and experience a positive somatic state.

Art Exercise Instructions: Gather art supplies such as paper, colored pencils, stickers, or other dry materials. Please be mindful if you choose to use supplies like markers or paints, as these can sometimes bleed through to the next page. You may want to place a blank sheet of paper underneath your work to protect the following pages.

1. Begin by finding a quiet and comfortable space where you can focus without distractions.

2. Take a few moments to center yourself through deep breathing, visualization, or grounding exercises. Allow yourself to become present in the moment, acknowledging any thoughts or emotions that arise.

3. Once you feel grounded, look at the photo album pictured after these instructions and remember the photo you saw in your mind that brought you a feeling of joy during the guided imagery exercise.

4. Using your art supplies, begin to draw or paint a representation of the photo you pictured during the meditation on the left-hand side of the page, paying attention to any emotions or sensations that arise without judgment.

5. Next, on the right-hand side of the page, draw a representation of what joy felt like in your body. It may be a big smile on your face or a throbbing heart that represents where you felt it in your body. Consider what color best represents it and how much of the page your joy fills. If you were not able to feel joy, that is OK. You can take the time you need. In that case, consider drawing the emotions that surfaced during the guided imagery. All emotions are messengers, and are important.

6. As you work on your art, pay attention to any emotions or sensations that arise. Allow yourself to explore them openly and without negative self-talk. Remember that there are no right or wrong ways to express yourself through art.

7. Once you have completed your art exercise, take a step back and observe your creation. Reflect on the journey it represents, recognizing the challenges you have faced and the progress you have made.

8. Finally, think about strategies, activities, or people that will support your path toward healing. You are welcome to list those here:

_____

_____

_____

_____

_____

_____

9. Take a moment to appreciate yourself for engaging in this healing art exercise and for the courage you have shown. Allow yourself to feel a sense of pride and accomplishment as you continue your journey of recovery.

Mindfulness Healing Part V:

Purpose Statement: The purpose of the Mandala of Joy art exercise is to allow your body to experience the feeling of joy while relaxing the mind by coloring a Mandala.

A mandala is a circular design that symbolizes wholeness, balance, and harmony. Using a mandala can aid in healing and self-reflection as the process of coloring can calm your mind, allow you space to explore your inner world, to be present with yourself, and to invite a sense of equanimity.

Again, it is important to remember that joy is not forcing yourself to be happy or positive. That is not healthy or authentic, especially while grieving. However, overtime you may find that you can begin to make room for yourself to experience even small moments of joy during grief, such as petting a beloved pet, cuddling with a child, eating a favorite meal, or gazing at the sunset. Joy can be quiet or consuming, and it is different for each person. Additionally, we can experience joy very differently from day to day and moment to moment. The aim of this exercise is to help you be present with yourself, honor your emotions as they arise, build compassion for yourself, relieve stress, improve mindful focus, enhance creativity, and foster a deeper spiritual connection with yourself.

Art Exercise Instructions: Gather art supplies such as paper, colored pencils, stickers, or other dry materials. Please be mindful if you choose to use supplies like markers or paints, as these can sometimes bleed through to the next page. You may want to place a blank sheet of paper underneath your work to protect the following pages.

1. Begin by finding a quiet and comfortable space where you can focus without distractions.

2. Take a few moments to center yourself through deep breathing, visualization, or grounding exercises. Allow yourself to become present in the moment, acknowledging any thoughts or emotions that arise.

3. Once you feel grounded, focus on the Mandala located at the end of these instructions and the word "JOY" contained in it, and recall the feeling of joy, even if just for a fleeting moment, you felt during the guided imagery, or a different moment of joy. Set the intention of focusing on this joyful feeling as you are able and as you are working on exercise. Remind yourself what brings you joy and that it is OK to feel any level of joy, no matter how large or how small. This can be difficult, so please be gentle with yourself.

4. Using your art supplies, begin to color the Mandala. You can start from the center and move outward or in any way that feels natural to you. There is no exact way of doing this exercise.

5. As you work on your art, pay attention to any emotions or sensations that arise. Allow yourself to explore them openly and without negative self-talk. Remember that there are no right or wrong ways to express yourself through art. If you find your mind wandering or judging your work, gently bring your focus back to the act of coloring and feeling joy in your body.

6. Once you have completed your art exercise, take a step back and observe your creation. Reflect on the journey it represents, recognizing the challenges you have faced and the progress you have made.

7. Finally, think about strategies that will support your path toward healing. This might include setting aside time to rest, engaging in meaningful rituals to honor your loss, journaling, talking with a trusted friend or therapist, or finding comfort in creative expression. The process of grieving takes time—there is no deadline and no "right" way to move through it. Some days may feel heavier than others, and that's okay. Healing is not about forgetting, but about learning how to carry your grief with compassion. Please be gentle with yourself. You are doing the best you can, and that is more than enough.

8. Take a moment to appreciate yourself for engaging in this healing art exercise and for the courage you have shown. Allow yourself to feel a sense of pride and accomplishment as you continue your journey of recovery.

Mindful Reflection Moment

Now that you have completed your breath work, guided imagery, and art and journal exercises, and before we bring this chapter to a close, please take some mindful time to reflect. You are welcome to answer the following questions in the space below, or write in a journal or notebook of your choice. You may do this with your therapist, or if you are working through this book solo, you can do this on your own.

1. What are you noticing after this chapter?

2. What awareness and insight have surfaced?

3. What is the information you have learned?

Write or share your reflections here or in your own journal or notebook if you prefer if you would like to process further. As always, please be gentle with yourself:

_____

_____

_____

_____

_____

_____

_____

_____

_____

_____

Final Step: Self-Affirmation Exercise

Instructions: Before moving on to the next chapter, can you give yourself the gift of self-affirmation? It can be difficult for people who have had traumatic experiences or are experiencing grief, dealing with addiction, healing from complex trauma, or struggling with anxiety, depression, or other challenges to take time to affirm themselves.

As a support to this step of your healing, affirmation ideas might include statements such as: "My grief is valid, and I am learning to be gentle with myself in this process." "It's okay to seek joy or have moments of happiness even as I grieve." "I acknowledge my pain and my resilience." Please use the winged heart on the next page to honor your own self-affirmation(s). If you can only come up with one affirmation at this time, that is more than acceptable. Perhaps you can return later in your healing process and add more:

In this chapter, my hope was to offer you compassionate support and meaningful insights as you deepen your understanding of grief. Every expression of grief is valid, and each person's unique journey deserves empathy and respect. By exploring varied perspectives and theories on grief, honoring cultural contexts, and recognizing the impact of secondary losses, I hope you feel encouraged to approach your experience with patience and self-compassion. May the mindfulness exercises and moments of reflection provide you with opportunities to reconnect with cherished memories and, perhaps, provide you with moments of peace or joy along your own path. You are healing, and so much awaits you on this journey.

As you complete this chapter, I would like to offer an affirmation to you before moving on: You have experienced an important and likely heartbreaking loss, and grieving is a difficult part of living and loving. No one can or should tell you how to grieve or what your timeline should look like. You deserve to heal at your own pace. You can honor the memory of what or who you've lost while finding strength and moments of joy within yourself and around you. Be gentle with yourself.

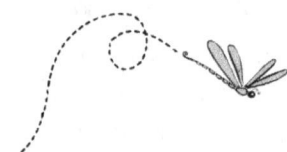

CHAPTER FIVE

Navigating the Maze of Problematic Pornography Use

Mari A. Lee

*"Addiction is not a choice that anybody makes; it's not a moral failure.
Rather, addiction is a response to human suffering."*

~ Dr. Gabor Mate

As I prepared for my clinical day ahead, reviewing my agenda, I saw that Will was scheduled as my first client that morning. Will, an energetic, expressive, and intelligent individual in his early thirties, was affectionately known as "Whirlwind Will" among his loved ones. This title seemed to embody more than just a casual nickname; it was a persona he enthusiastically embraced, and I enjoyed working with him.

During the session, it became evident that the typically lively Will was unusually subdued. Amid furrowed brows and weary sighs, he candidly discussed the setback he had encountered the weekend prior in his recovery from hardcore pornography addiction. With a tone tinged with defeat, Will expressed, "My sobriety has vanished—gone up in smoke! I indulged in hours of porn and marijuana all weekend. Four months of progress lost, and now it feels like I'm starting over from scratch!" His frustration radiated through the room as he angrily tossed the couch pillow aside.

When Will and I first began working together, he shared about his lifelong struggle with pornography starting at an early age. Despite numerous attempts to break free from his compulsive porn use, which had escalated to more explicit content over the years, his journey was marked by repeated slips and relapses. The breaking point came when he faced the consequences of being fired from a job in the tech industry—a coveted position he had diligently worked to secure. Reflecting on this, Will admitted, "I messed up that opportunity big time. The company had a strict rule against employees viewing porn at the office, and, of course, that's exactly what I did. I got two warnings, and then I was shown the door. Once again, my insatiable thirst for porn got me into trouble, ruining something important in my life."

After this event, Will realized that online porn was not a distraction he could easily pick up or put down. Instead, he described his problematic 20-year battle as a mind-numbing "maze," sharing that when he stepped into an online porn session, he would become trapped in what he referred to as a "porn maze" for days and weeks at a time. "I am powerless when it comes to porn. Everything else falls to the side when I am in the porn maze. My bills go unpaid, I don't return calls or texts, and I can't meet any of my work or school deadlines. On top of that, I neglect my relationships. My weed habit goes up, I drink way too much, and basically, I am a total mess. I lie, I cheat, I lie more, I make excuses, and no matter what I do, I cannot stop! I am like a porn zombie once I get hooked into the maze."

After the loss of his dream job, Will's world further crashed around him when he failed out of his graduate program. He shared that he had worked for years to qualify to be accepted into the prestigious program, but his relentless porn use overshadowed his academic goals: "Mari, I didn't even make it through the first year. The program was not that difficult. I found the subjects enjoyable, and the required work was easy. However, instead of showing up for class, I'd end up looking at online porn for hours, sleeping late, and missing class after class. My advisor suggested therapy, and I saw a school counselor who thought I had attention deficit disorder or an anxiety disorder. I hoped I did so I had a reason that made sense, but nope, that wasn't the case. I begged the school to give me a second chance, and they did. However, I continued to minimize my issues and made promises to myself and my teachers that I could not keep. I left with my tail between my legs. Another blown opportunity."

The pivotal moment prompting Will to seek specialized addiction therapy occurred when his fiancée of two years, a survivor of sexual abuse, ended their relationship for good upon discovering pornographic content on his phone depicting rape scenes and adult mother-and-son sexual fantasy scenarios. Will confessed that this wasn't the first instance; it marked the sixth time she had stumbled upon such material, revealing that he had been deceitful throughout their relationship. "She was incredible to me, putting so much effort into our relationship, and I just couldn't stop," he lamented. "I tried, believe me! But no matter how many promises that I made, I kept falling back into the same pattern. Over time, even though I never delved into illegal content, the porn I sought out became increasingly disturbing to me."

During our first few sessions, I learned that extroverted Will had been a lonely kid raised by a young, divorced mother who worked two jobs to make ends meet. He shared that after his father moved out, Will felt an overwhelming sense of loneliness and isolation, "I was on my own a lot of the time, and mom couldn't afford a babysitter. I had to lock myself into our apartment and be very quiet so none of the neighbors caught on. We did not have a TV, so I would occupy myself by reading comics and eating junk food for dinner—chips, candy, and ramen from the dollar store most nights. A family friend gave me their old Nintendo, and I would play games, fantasize, and read. One day, I found a trash bag of porn magazines behind a convenience store and hid those in my closet. Suddenly, masturbation became a regular thing every day after school. Then, after I put myself to bed, I would wake up in the middle of the night and listen to my mom cry. When I would ask her what was wrong the next morning, she'd put on a happy face and tell me everything was fine, which left me feeling confused and untrusting of what was real."

During this time, Will shared that he walked in on his mother stepping out of the shower, "Mom was probably in her late twenties, and I was maybe eleven years old. I remember her surprised laughter while she continued toweling off her wet breasts. I slammed the door and stood there, embarrassed and confused. Part of me wanted to protect her, part of me felt angry with her, and part of me felt aroused seeing my young, pretty mom naked. It was all so confusing and weird." Will went on to share that his mother would often discuss details of her dating and sex life while asking Will to massage her back, legs, feet, and arms, sometimes when she was dressed only in a bra and panties. Other times, Will would be called to sleep in his mother's bed if she was having a nightmare. His nicknames included "my little hubby" or "my handsome, brave little man." Will confided that he felt an increasing weight on his shoulders at that time in his life, feeling an overwhelming responsibility for his mother's emotional and physical well-being. Adding to his distress, he revealed that he started fantasizing about his mother, concocting sexual scenarios that left him deeply unsettled and ashamed.

In our work together, Will came to understand that this kind of unhealthy dynamic between a parent and child is considered emotional incest, a term coined by Dr. Kenneth Adams in his book *Silently Seduced: When Parents Make Children Their Partners*. Will's mother was clearly dealing with her own unresolved trauma, poor parenting skills, boundary issues, financial distress, and lack of support. Though she did not have sexual intercourse with her son, her behaviors crossed appropriate parent/child boundaries. It was difficult for Will to grapple with the idea that his mother had shattered boundaries and trust when relying on him for emotional support, inappropriate physical touch, and instances of nudity. It was clear that Will had blamed himself for their detrimental enmeshment, not understanding that as a child, he was not responsible for the harmful aspects of their relationship, nor was he responsible for the traumatic experiences that his mother had endured.

Many individuals who have experienced abuse often develop maladaptive coping mechanisms such as avoidance, substance abuse, compulsive behaviors, aggression, people-pleasing, perfectionism, eating disorders, lying, vandalism, or other challenges. Over time, these coping strategies can solidify into defense mechanisms, serving to shield the person from further harm. Survivors of abuse commonly grapple with issues such as depression, anxiety disorders, self-loathing, low self-esteem, people pleasing, poor boundaries, anger issues, shame-based thinking, and addictions.

For Will, acknowledging his status as an abuse survivor proved challenging. His love for his mother and sense of obligation to care for her persisted well into his adult years. Reflecting on his situation, he realized, "She loved me, but she was a kid herself in many ways. And the aftermath of the divorce took a toll on her. I always saw my dad as the villain, but now I recognize that my mom was also struggling, and that resulted in some awful choices on her part. Unfortunately, I paid the price."

During his formative years, Will wrestled with the challenging dynamic of being shuttled between his mother's apartment and the home of his abusive biological father. "I'd visit my dad twice a month for what he saw as his 'duty to deal with the kid' or during forced outings my mom arranged, like camping trips, which he clearly had no interest in," Will recalled. With a 15-year age difference between his parents, his father, adhering to old-school beliefs, possessed a volatile temper and often cited the adage, "Spare the rod and spoil the child." His punishments were severe, involving punches to Will's arms and legs or backhands for minor infractions such as burning toast or spilling paint in the garage. Any failure to meet his father's exacting standards resulted in dire consequences. "I dreaded the time I spent with him. He was a mean bully who instilled fear in me, and as those horrible weekends approached, I couldn't sleep or eat much," Will recounted.

Will shared that he first accessed online porn at his father's home: "My dad had a huge stash of online porn. He worked constantly or was out with one of his girlfriends, so I was sometimes alone on my weekends with him. I'd get on to his computer and masturbate to his porn for hours; I think I was around twelve years old when this started. More than a few times, I could hear him having sex with his date, and one time, I walked in on some woman giving him oral sex in our kitchen. He'd laugh and toss out lines like, 'It'll toughen you up and turn you into a man.'

"A part of me craved his approval, wanting to appear mature and cool in his eyes rather than just a bothersome kid. Back then, it all seemed like harmless fun, but reflecting on it now, I feel sadness for that younger version of myself. I remember wanting so much to spend time with my school friends doing typical childhood things like swimming, biking, climbing trees, scouting, and just playing together—simple, innocent fun! My dad's house was on the other side of town, and he was a jerk and refused to let me get to know the other kids in the neighborhood after I got in trouble showing his porn websites to a couple of the other boys. Their parents hit the roof when they found out, and I was banned from their homes. When I was at my dad's house, it was always chores, homework, beating, porn, masturbating, chores, homework, beating, porn, masturbating. I could never get it right with that guy, and masturbating to porn was a soothing escape from him and my only fun outlet. My mind exploded seeing all the crazy porn he was looking at. Online porn, compared to porno magazines, was like moving from weed to heroin in the blink of an eye, and I was hooked!"

As he matured, Will found himself struggling to be present when having sex with a partner, "It was difficult, sometimes impossible, for me to stay erect when having sex with one of my girlfriends. I would have to shift into a fantasy or squeeze my eyes shut and play my favorite porn loops repeatedly in my head. I could have been having sex with a hole in my mattress; that is how checked out I was during most encounters. My girlfriends, all attractive in their own ways, shared how distant I felt, like a light switch went out the moment we started to make out or have sex.

"After all the hundreds of hours I had spent watching porn, regular sex seemed vanilla and boring. I wanted my girlfriends to do all the crazy stuff I'd seen or let me try more extreme sex acts with them—anal, group sex, rape scenes, using sex toys, pretending to be my mom, you name it. My late teens and most of my twenties were focused on finding the perfect sex partner to act out my inner fantasies with. Nothing was off limits, but very few of my girlfriends wanted to do these more extreme things, and even when they tried, it was still hard for me to be present during sex."

As Will delved deeper into his experiences, he revealed that he had been dealing with erectile dysfunction since his early 20s up to the present day. "The only thing that truly arouses me is internet porn," he confessed. "Don't get me wrong, I enjoy sex, but I can only maintain an erection about a third of the time when I am with a partner. It is scary because I am still fairly young! I began to wonder if it was a health issue, so I saw a doctor and went through a physical exam, blood tests, and ultrasound. But after all of that, it turned out I was fine. However, I started noticing that whenever I stopped watching porn during times when I would grit my teeth and try and control my porn use, my erectile issues disappeared." During each therapy session, Will expressed profound frustration and resentment toward the destructive cycle that kept him trapped.

A 2016 research study (Park, B.Y.) concludes that traditional explanations for sexual problems in men under 40 years of age are inadequate to explain the rising rates of sexual dysfunctions and low desire. Park et al. suggest a thorough investigation into the effects of internet pornography, noting that quitting pornography can improve sexual function. Healthcare providers should use validated tools to identify both non-organic sexual issues and those related to pornography use. While mental health problems may play a role in sexual dysfunction, this should not be assumed as the sole cause in younger men. Given all that we are learning and what therapists are hearing from clients like Will, as well as considering the couples who have been impacted, further research in this field is necessary.

Will described a relentless pattern of deleting his porn accounts, discarding magazines and videos, and battling through periods of self-restraint, only to inevitably relapse into his addiction a few weeks later, experiencing all the negative side effects that came with it, including the end of a meaningful love relationship.

"When I first met Diana, my ex-fiancée, I felt like I had hit the jackpot. She was intelligent, confident, beautiful, sexy, well-educated, hardworking, and she wouldn't tolerate my excuses and lies. Within three months of dating her, I was convinced she was 'the one.' However, the grip of my porn addiction resurfaced. I pressured her into uncomfortable sexual acts, reaching a point where I caused her physical harm with a sex toy, leaving her rightfully furious. Instead of respecting her boundaries, I convinced myself that I was entitled to indulge in porn because she seemed 'prudish,' which was far from the truth. I failed to consider her desires or comfort level. When she would not do what I wanted during sex, I felt entitled to check out and then fantasize about pornography, using her body as a vessel for my own sexual gratification," Will admitted, his gaze fixed on his feet.

"The lies, they were constant. I consistently deceived her, initiated fights, gaslit her, and made promises, only to inevitably shatter them. It got to the point where I'd rather shut myself up in my condo lying about having to work and then smoke weed and masturbate to online porn all weekend versus going out with her, seeing friends, or doing the things I used to enjoy, like surfing, hiking and going to movies. During the rare times I was porn free, I'd drown myself in booze and pot and engage in reckless behavior while under the influence.

"One weekend, Diana had to go out of town overnight to visit a relative and asked me to check on her cat and make sure he was OK. Once I got into my porn maze and pot high, I completely forgot about her poor cat until she texted me the following afternoon to check in. There were so many times I let her down. I even went as far as seeking out a prostitute, a transgression that Diana eventually uncovered. That was the breaking point for her. I had unprotected sex with the prostitute and, lost in my usual fog of sexual indulgence, had unprotected sex with Diana the next day. I don't blame her for leaving; I could have exposed both of us to a disease. Thankfully, that didn't happen, but I spent days holding my breath, anxious about the potential consequences. A month after she left me, I pawned her engagement ring for a wild weekend in Las Vegas, convincing myself that I deserved it and that it was great to be single. In truth, it was the lowest and saddest weekend of my life," Will quietly disclosed with a catch in his throat.

Throughout the chapters of their shared journey, Will felt as if he was constantly showcasing his challenges and flaws to his ex-fiancé at every turn, "I found myself in a perpetual cycle of testing the limits, increasing the stakes, and yet, Diana remained by my side, believing my empty promises and graciously offering me another opportunity each time. The resilience of her love both surprised and humbled me. Deep down, I was aware that this game of chance I played with her heart couldn't last forever, and it didn't."

In the backdrop of their time together, Will was, in many ways, a gambler, risking the currency of her devotion without fully comprehending the consequences. Despite his awareness that the odds were against him, he continued to bet on the endurance of her love while doing all he could to sabotage his fiancé's trust. Will realized far too late that the gamble didn't pay off: "Since our breakup, the fear of worsening into someone unrecognizable keeps me up at night. I am haunted by the thought of a life of loneliness or dying from some sort of horrible illness all alone. In my worst moments, I blame her in my head, listing out all the ways I think she wronged me, even though I know I am at fault for the issues in our relationship and the breakup, which I know must have been traumatic for her as well.

"What shames me the most is that when I met Diana, she was so loving, active, physically fit, joyful, and optimistic. By the time I was done with her, she was shut down, deeply depressed, very lonely, overweight, and dealing with some serious physical issues." As Will uttered these words, his shoulders sagging beneath the weight of regret, tears traced down his face, bearing witness to the profound sorrow and shame that enveloped him.

In future sessions, Will and I would explore his attachment style and the impact of his early trauma that his addictions were rooted in. We also discussed the impact of betrayal trauma on Diana, the difference between healthy intimacy and toxic intensity, and the difference between true love and traumatic bonding.

In these moments of deep vulnerability and ownership, Will found the strength within himself to make a courageous choice—to continue his healing and self-discovery through therapy and recovery. The feelings of shame and helplessness that once consumed him began to dissipate over time as he took the pivotal step of showing up for his own well-being.

About 15 months into our sessions, Will eloquently expressed, "I can't believe it's been over a year since I started this process. When I made a conscious decision to stop going through the motions in therapy, my life changed for the better. My commitment to fully engaging in my recovery journey has changed everything. Instead of lying to myself and others and charming my way through the world, I am finally able to live life authentically, not perfectly, but fully accepting all parts of myself."

Will's transformative path wasn't paved with instant results; rather, it unfolded gradually, marked by stumbles, as well as resilience and determination. The road to change and healing proved to be a winding one, with occasional challenges casting shadows along the way. Yet, what sets Will apart was his refusal to surrender to these challenges.

To his credit, he didn't let the hurdles define his journey. With unwavering determination and a commitment to his own growth, Will pressed forward. The support he found wasn't confined to our therapeutic sessions alone—it extended to the camaraderie of a men's recovery support group, as well as a Twelve-Step group. In the safety of these communities and armed with a newfound willingness to prioritize his mental health, Will achieved remarkable progress, including making sincere amends to those he had hurt. Through the twists and turns of his story and recovery, he finally found his way out of the maze. Will's resolve shines as a testament to the transformative power of self-investment and the unwavering spirit it takes to navigate the intricate path of healing.

After therapy concluded with Will, I found myself pondering a recurring sentiment he shared within his men's support group. He would often assert, with profound sincerity, that grappling with his addiction demons was far from a casual stroll through the park; rather, it demanded a persistent commitment to steering clear of the labyrinthine complexities that ensnared him. His words continue to resonate deeply within me, serving as a poignant reminder of the enduring struggle and unwavering dedication required to chart a course toward recovery.

• • • • •

Several years had passed since my sessions with Will concluded when, quite unexpectedly, he reached out to schedule a check-in session. I anticipated learning about the chapters that had unfolded in Will's life since our last meeting, nurturing a hopeful belief that he had continued to embody the healing he had committed to. As he entered the session, a noticeable shift was apparent—Will, once a whirlwind of emotions, now carried a sense of centeredness, a tranquility that echoed in the joy and peace that emanated from him.

In a heartwarming revelation, Will shared, "I scheduled this session to express my gratitude for our work and to share a milestone—I've just celebrated my fifth year of sobriety from porn, weed, and alcohol." Will's grin glowed with the warmth of his achievement. As he delved into the details, he opened his phone and shared photos of a life transformed—pictures from his wedding to his lovely wife Rachel, capturing moments of connection and commitment, a tender image of his baby girl, and holiday photos with his wife's loving family—all gifts of a newfound purpose.

Will reflected on how pivotal it had been to finally name and validate the pain of his childhood in our past work together. He shared with calm clarity the insights he had gained that had stayed with him—particularly about the abuse from his father and the ways it had shaped his identity and relationships. What stood out most was his deepened understanding of the importance of caring for his inner child—that younger part of himself who had once been so vulnerable and unprotected. Will spoke of the ongoing commitment he carried to show up for his inner child with compassion, strength, and the protection he never received growing up. It was a quiet but powerful confirmation to the healing work he had done and continued to do.

He shared deeper insights into his mother as well, recognizing that she, too, was an abuse survivor—one whose unhealed wounds deeply impacted her ability to parent in safe, healthy ways. Her trauma did not excuse her behavior, but it helped Will understand the generational roots of their dysfunction. Will explained that he had recently accepted that accountability and compassion could coexist—that he could grieve the harm, protect himself with healthy boundaries, and still hold space for the complexity of his mother's story.

Will shared, "Now that mom has begun her own therapy, she is slowly confronting the abuse and losses she buried for most of her life. She is taking accountability for the harm that I endured and making amends; we are moving in a better direction." Though the past could not be undone, there was repair. There was softening. And in the spaces where silence and shame once lived, a new kind of connection—one grounded in honesty, safety, and mutual respect—was starting to emerge.

That was my last session with Will, a time filled with gratitude, triumph, and the beauty of redemption. His journey became a living testament to the transformative power of recovery, resilience, self-discovery, and the unwavering commitment to rewrite one's narrative.

It is important to note that while Will made the decision to have a relationship with his mother, one with boundaries and healing, not all survivors of abuse reach a place where they desire, or feel safe maintaining, a relationship with a parent who caused harm. Each survivor's healing journey is personal and unique. For some, distance or estrangement is the healthiest choice. For others, like Will, healing may include finding a new kind of connection—one rooted in clear boundaries, accountability, and self-trust.

A message from Mari

Will's experience is like so many of the individuals I've had the privilege of working with. These are people who, despite their intelligence, creativity, and good intentions, find themselves ensnared in the enticing world of online pornography. It's important to note that the allure of the porn maze is not exclusive to men; women and non-gender conforming individuals grapple with its challenges as well. Pornography addiction, with its far-reaching impact, transcends demographic boundaries. It doesn't discriminate based on ethnicity, age, orientation, education, or socioeconomic status. Anyone, regardless of their background, can find themselves entangled in the complexities of problematic pornography use in the digital age.

Interestingly, in the mental health field, there is a faction of clinicians who adamantly reject the notion of porn addiction or problematic porn use, deeming it an unfounded concept. Some of these clinicians argue that therapists specializing in porn addiction or out of control sexual behaviors are nothing more than moralizing counselors pathologizing their clients. Or they assume that we have failed to grasp the difference between a fetish and a true addiction. There are those who presume that therapists specializing in porn addiction or hypersexual behavior do not thoroughly conduct mental health assessments or that we neglect to consider comorbid diagnoses or conditions such as bipolar disorder, OCD, or other related challenges. All of these are unfounded assumptions.

Multiple research studies, as cited in the appendix of this book and readily accessible online, confirm that problematic porn use, sometimes referred to as "pornography addiction," is recognized as a process addiction. For instance, one study conducted by Brand et al. (2016) found significant neural changes in individuals with internet pornography addiction compared to controls. Another study by Laier et al. (2013) demonstrated that internet pornography addiction shares similarities with substance addiction in terms of brain activity and behavior. Based on the study conducted by Bőthe et al. (2020), the researchers utilized the International Sex Survey and compared different assessment tools to gain insights into this issue. In this study, it can be concluded that problematic pornography use (PPU) is a phenomenon that occurs across various countries, genders, and sexual orientations. Key findings from this study include:

1. **Prevalence of Problematic Pornography Use (PPU)**: The study suggests that PPU is not limited to specific demographics but is observed across different countries, genders, and sexual orientations. This indicates that PPU may be a global concern affecting individuals regardless of their background.

2. **Assessment Tools**: The researchers compared different assessment tools to measure PPU and found variations in prevalence rates depending on the tool used. This highlights the importance of utilizing standardized and validated assessment measures to accurately assess PPU across populations.

3. **Gender and Sexual Orientation Differences**: The study also examined differences in PPU prevalence based on gender and sexual orientation. While specific findings may vary, the overall conclusion suggests that PPU can affect individuals regardless of their gender or sexual orientation.

4. **Implications for Research and Practice**: The findings of this study have implications for both research and clinical practice. It underscores the need for further research to better understand the factors contributing to Problematic Pornography Use (PPU) and to develop effective supportive strategies. Additionally, clinicians should be aware of the prevalence of PPU across diverse populations and utilize appropriate assessment measures to identify and address this issue in their practice. Overall, this study contributes valuable insights into the prevalence and characteristics of problematic pornography use, highlighting its significance as a global phenomenon affecting individuals across different demographics.

Ongoing emerging research continues to underscore the connection between early life trauma and problematic pornography use in men. One recent study (Henry, Bridges, & Shaw, 2025) found that adverse childhood experiences (ACEs)—such as abuse, neglect, or household dysfunction—were significantly associated with both earlier exposure to pornography and higher rates of use in adulthood. In a sample of adult males, those with a greater number of ACEs were more likely to encounter pornography at a younger age and report more frequent or compulsive patterns of consumption later in life. These findings suggest that for many men, pornography may serve as an early form of escape, regulation, or coping in the absence of safety, attunement, and emotional support. Understanding the link between childhood adversity and sexual behavior is crucial for developing trauma-informed approaches to treatment, especially when pornography use feels problematic for the client, out of alignment with a client's values, negatively impacts relationships, interferes with life goals, or is in opposition with what the client deems to be healthy sexuality for their life.

Though it is not my role to convince mental health professionals or others of the legitimacy of problematic porn use, these findings underscore the validity and seriousness of problematic porn use as a distinct phenomenon in our modern society. I encourage each person and therapist to read the available research, evaluate the information they gather, examine personal biases, and make their own informed decisions. Everyone should have the freedom to explore the topic independently and come to their own conclusions based on the evidence and insights they uncover.

Many individuals facing struggles similar to Will, along with their betrayed and traumatized partners, would strongly refute the claim that online porn addiction is a myth. For them, the ordeal is characterized by a profound sense of lost control, feeling trapped in the grip of problematic porn use, experiencing its damaging effects, and enduring the aftermath of trauma. Their pain is tangible, a constant presence in their lives—a reality filled with the genuine challenges of feeling addicted to porn, regardless of the dismissals and skepticism from critics. People who struggle in this way understand firsthand how devastating the consequences can be as they navigate a landscape of genuine suffering. The voices of people dealing with problematic porn use, as well as the betrayed partner's experience, are often drowned out in the clinical debates. Yet these hurting individuals resonate with the stark reality of the impact and relentless pull of porn. Their stories serve as an essential reminder that, beyond theoretical disputes, there exists a lived experience of pain and turmoil that demands acknowledgment, understanding, and support.

For those of us who assist individuals struggling with problematic pornography use, our firsthand experiences as mental health professionals allow us to witness the overwhelming entanglement they face, the dire consequences that often follow, and a palpable sense of hopelessness that often propels them towards seeking help.

It is also important to clarify that therapists specializing in this area don't assume the role of moral arbiters, deny underlying conditions such as bipolar disorder, ADHD, or an anxiety disorder, nor do we pathologize a fetish. Our mission isn't to pass judgment or condemn individuals for their sexual choices; instead, our role is centered on providing ethical therapeutic support. As we delve into the complexities of our clients' experiences, our approach is rooted in research, objectivity, non-judgment, and compassion. We recognize that everyone's journey is unique, and the goal is to foster an environment where each person can openly explore their specific challenges without fear of condemnation. This commitment extends beyond merely addressing the symptoms of problematic pornography use; it encompasses a holistic understanding of the individual, acknowledging the multifaceted factors that contribute to their experiences. By doing so, we strive to empower our clients to create their own narratives, fostering resilience and facilitating positive transformations in their lives. In this way, the therapeutic space becomes a refuge, a place where they can confront their struggles and biases, embrace what feels like healthy sexuality to *the client*, dismantle the barriers to change, and embark on a path towards healing—creating a sex life that feels uniquely beneficial and exciting for that one-of-a-kind human being.

When Porn Feels Like a Maze

When adults derive satisfaction from legal pornography without causing harm to themselves or their loved ones, they are supported in making choices that align with their sexual well-being and internal compass. As I often say to clients, "I am not the penis or vagina police, and your choices in how you express and enjoy your sexuality are respected in this space as long as everyone is a consenting adult." In cases like Will's story, the consumption of porn undergoes a destructive shift, evolving from ego-syntonic—where decisions align with personal choices, values, and self-concepts—to becoming ego-dystonic.

Essentially, ego-dystonic denotes thoughts, impulses, and behaviors that stray from a person's internal compass, beliefs, or self-concepts, creating significant distress, anxiety, depression, or fear. Will, during the process of understanding himself and what influenced his thoughts, ideas, beliefs, and behaviors, defined his online pornography behaviors as causing him distress. For Will, his porn use had become problematic and ego-dystonic in nature. "This is not how I want to express myself sexually any longer," Will stated after exploring the various parts of himself. This becomes a moving example of the internal conflict experienced in such situations. Will shared in one session, "I feel like porn has made me a prisoner. I am like a chained lapdog, going back for more even though I don't want to, no matter how severe the consequences."

Historically, addiction models predominantly focused on substances like drugs or alcohol, neglecting behavioral process addictions. These potentially addictive behaviors span a spectrum, including gambling, video gaming, internet pornography, shopping, and even exercise. Will's experience highlights the necessity of recognizing that addictive patterns can manifest in various forms, underscoring the importance of expanding our understanding beyond traditional substance-centric models.

Exploring the criteria for addiction uncovers a broad framework that applies to both substance and behavioral (or process) addictions. If you, or a client you work with, are grappling with problematic online pornography use and questioning whether it's more than a passing interest, consider whether any of the following points reflect your or your client's experiences. Do any of the following resonate?

☐ **1. Compulsion and Out-of-Control Behavior:** Do you feel an irresistible craving to engage in this behavior, accompanied by a pattern of behavior spiraling out of control?

☐ **2. Consequences:** Have you, or someone you love, faced serious or negative consequences directly tied to your behavior?

☐ **3. Inability to Stop**: Despite adverse consequences, have you found yourself unable to halt this behavior?

☐ **4. Self-Destructive Patterns:** Are you persistently involved in self-destructive or high-risk behavior?

☐ **5. Failed Attempts at Limitation:** Do you continually desire or make efforts to limit this behavior, only to find those efforts repeatedly unsuccessful?

☐ **6. Coping Mechanism:** Is this behavior serving as a coping strategy for you? If so, in what way?

☐ **7. Escalation:** Have you noticed an increase in the frequency or intensity of this behavior because your current level of engagement is no longer satisfying?

☐ **8. Mood Changes:** Are there notable shifts in your mood surrounding this behavior?

> - ☐ **9. Time Consumption:** Do you find yourself dedicating inordinate amounts of time to engage in this behavior?
>
> - ☐ **10. Sacrifices in Activities:** Have important aspects of your life—social, academic, occupational, or recreational—been sacrificed or reduced due to this behavior?
>
> - ☐ **11. Self-Denial:** Is there an element of self-denial present where you might be downplaying the impact of your behavior?
>
> - ☐ **12. Secrecy, Deception, and Gaslighting:** Do you hide this behavior? Do you notice elements of deception or gaslighting in your engagement with this behavior?

By reflecting on these points, one can gain insights into their relationship with online pornography and begin to assess whether it aligns with addictive or problematic patterns. Ruling out or diagnosing comorbid conditions is also vitally important, as stated earlier in this chapter.

The Neurobiology of Sexual Fantasy

Another area Will found himself struggling with was recurring fantasies that didn't feel aligned with his well-being or the health of his relationship. For example, he sometimes sexually fantasized about his former fiancé's roommate, and had a pattern of fantasizing about friend's wives, co-workers, neighbors, or even the sisters or mothers of romantic partners.

Sexual fantasy, especially when repeated or emotionally charged, engages the brain's reward system in powerful ways. Regions like the ventral striatum, nucleus accumbens, and anterior cingulate—areas rich in dopamine—become activated not only during real sexual experiences, but also during *imagined* ones. This means the brain responds to fantasy in ways that are neurologically similar to actual sexual behavior. Over time, these repeated mental patterns can strengthen neural pathways, reinforce the fantasy loop, and make certain images or scenarios feel increasingly automatic and difficult to interrupt.

A recent neuroimaging review by Bittoni and Kiesner (2023) found that both visual and imagined sexual stimuli consistently activate the brain's reward circuitry. While their study also highlights methodological limitations in current research—such as inconsistent definitions and small sample sizes—the takeaway remains clear: fantasy has real influence on how the brain organizes desire and arousal, even if scientists are still refining their understanding of the mechanisms. In short, what we mentally rehearse, we reinforce, and what we reinforce can shape how we show up in our relationships, how we experience connection, and how we access integrity.

It is important to state that fantasy, in itself, is not inherently wrong or unhealthy. In fact, it can serve a variety of important functions: stress relief, play, escape, emotional regulation, or self-soothing. And as Lehmiller and Gormezano (2023) emphasize in their contemporary review, sexual fantasy does not always reflect a person's real-world desires or intentions. Many individuals fantasize about things they would never want to experience outside their imagination. Fantasy can be symbolic, paradoxical, or serve an emotional purpose unrelated to action.

But while fantasy may be private, it doesn't always remain *harmless*—especially when it involves real people within a relational system, such as your partner or spouse's sibling, parent, friend, or a co-worker or neighbor. If a partner discovers the fantasy involves someone from their shared social or emotional world—it can be devastating. Even if no physical act occurred, the fantasy may still feel like an emotional betrayal. Because of this, it's essential to hold both truths:

- Fantasy is not shameful and is not a behavior—and doesn't automatically signal future action.

- However, fantasy can still carry emotional weight, especially in monogamous relationships where mutual safety and exclusivity are part of the agreement.

What we imagine—even in private—still shapes the emotional climate of our relationships. Integrity doesn't mean policing thoughts or fantasies; it means bringing awareness to whether our private inner world reflects the kind of partner we want to be and is aligning with who we want to be.

For the spouse or partner, discovering that their significant other has been sexually fantasizing about someone close to them can trigger deep emotional pain. They may experience feelings of humiliation, confusion, or self-doubt. Trust may erode. Even if the fantasy was never meant to be acted upon, the secrecy or repeated nature of it can feel like a rupture in the emotional contract of the relationship.

When the person being sexualized is someone the couple regularly interacts with—such as a close friend, coworker, or neighbor—it can create a complex emotional strain. Intrusive thoughts may surface during shared time, making it difficult to remain present. The partner who knows or suspects that their significant other has been engaging in sexual fantasy of a mutual friend or family member may begin to feel uncomfortable or hypervigilant. They may even develop resentment toward the person who is being sexualized and pull away. Overtime, this dynamic can erode trust, disrupt community or family connections, and lead to emotional isolation within the relationship.

In committed partnerships, especially those rooted in monogamy, deceptive or hurtful erotic imagination has relational impact. The intent may have been private, but the emotional consequences are often shared. And for the person who has been fantasized about—without consent, agency, or awareness—there is also a deeper issue of objectification and boundary violation.

Bringing mindfulness and choice to fantasy doesn't mean shutting it down or shaming yourself—it means making sure it honors both your internal integrity and your external relational agreements.

The Role of Healthy Fantasy: Privacy vs. Secrecy

Throughout our work, Will began to develop a deeper awareness of the role fantasy played in his emotional life. He wrestled with the tension between private thoughts and relational impact and grew increasingly reflective and curious about the difference between privacy and secrecy. As our conversations unfolded, Will became more attuned to the internal conflict stirred by certain fantasies that objectified and sexualized people he knew, and more mindful of how they aligned—or didn't—with his values and commitments. What emerged for Will was a clearer, more grounded understanding of his inner world and how it shaped his sense of self and connection.

As I often shared with Will, fantasy, in and of itself, is not the enemy. In fact, healthy erotic fantasy can be a natural, creative, and even healing part of sexual expression. It can spark desire, enhance intimacy, and reflect deeper emotional or relational longings. Fantasy allows the imagination to explore, rehearse, play, and create pleasure. For individuals and couples who engage in kink or consensual non-monogamy, fantasy can be an intentional and enriching part of their sexual expression—what matters most is that it's rooted in consent, communication, and mutual agreement. For many individuals and couples, shared or private fantasy becomes part of a vibrant, fun and consensual sexual life. Key word: consensual.

Every person has a right to an internal world—and that includes the right to privacy. Your thoughts, fantasies, and daydreams are personal, and they do not have to be narrated or confessed unless they begin to interfere with your well-being or your relationship. Privacy also includes self-respect and boundaries, and it allows space for introspection, fantasy, and growth.

However, secrecy is different.

Secrecy is when something is hidden *because* it would cause harm or conflict if known. It sometimes carries energy of deceit, fear, shame, and emotional withdrawal. Secrecy can erode intimacy, especially when it becomes a place to indulge compulsions, betrayals, or avoid relational discomfort or connection. For example, when a fantasy about someone outside the relationship becomes a repeated escape, is used compulsively to regulate emotions or replace connection, or violates the sexualized person or the partner's trust, it begins to shift from private to secret—and from healthy to potentially harmful.

The difference lies in intention and impact:

• Privacy honors your autonomy.

• Secrecy shields a behavior that violates trust or boundaries.

In recovery work, the goal isn't to eliminate all fantasy, far from it in fact. Rather, it's to explore whether a fantasy aligns with your values, enhances your connection, enhances you as a sexual person, supports growth, brings joy, or does it protect you from vulnerability and healthy attachment? When a fantasy becomes compulsive, involves betrayal, or creates emotional distance, that's a signal to pause, get curious, extend self-compassion, and consider whether it's serving or sabotaging your integrity.

Healthy fantasy is integrated with mindful awareness and consciousness. It does not hijack your relationship or your peace of mind, but lives in harmony with your choices. You get to decide how you relate to your fantasies—whether they remain private, are shared, or are transformed. You get to be the artist of your internal sexual canvas!

When Fantasy Becomes Harmful

While fantasy can be a natural and healthy part of sexual expression, as you are learning, not all fantasies are benign. This is particularly true when they involve objectification, emotional betrayal, or real-life individuals within close relational proximity who have not given consent. When someone has chosen to be in a committed relationship—where this kind of sexual play or fantasy hasn't been mutually agreed upon—and they repeatedly turn to fantasies for sexual release and abandon the partner's needs, or they continue to fantasize about their partner's sister, best friend, mother, coworker, nanny, or neighbor, it can cross a line into territory that causes both internal and relational harm.

These kinds of fantasies aren't always just private escapes—they are sometimes rooted in power dynamics, boundary violations, or an unconscious desire to create tension, intensity, risk, to punish, or maintain disconnection. They objectify the imagined friend or person, stripping them of personhood and consent, reducing them to a means of personal arousal without regard to their humanity or the emotional fallout. And while these types of fantasies may seem "harmless" because they're not acted on physically, they are far from consequence-free. Here's why:

- **They can create betrayal energy,** even if no physical affair occurs. Fantasizing about someone close to your spouse or partner—without their knowledge or consent—can deeply erode intimacy and trust when discovered, revealed or sensed.

- **They can fracture emotional presence.** The spouse or partner becomes less emotionally and sexually safe when the fantasy world involves people from their inner circle. It brings a third party into the relational space without the partner's knowledge or consent.

- **They can harm the person being fantasized about**, even if that person never knows. It's a violation of their agency. To be mentally undressed or sexualized without consent—especially in the context of friendship, family, or professional boundaries—is dehumanizing.

- **They can increase shame and secrecy in the person fantasizing.** Often, individuals report feeling ashamed after these fantasies, but also compulsively returning to them. That shame fuels secrecy, and secrecy feeds disconnection—from the partner, from the self, and from authentic intimacy.

These aren't fantasies of connection or curiosity. Sometimes these are fantasies of distance, domination, and disembodiment.

Again, there is no intention here to judge or police erotic imagination, nor to impose a single moral framework. "Don't yuck my yum!" is a playful and respectful way of saying, "Just because something isn't for you doesn't mean it's wrong or bad for someone else." This saying is often used in conversations about preferences—especially around food, sex, relationships, and identity—to encourage nonjudgment and openness. Just as a myriad of fantasies exist, unique to each human being, there are also many types of relationships—open, polyamorous, monogamish, fluid—and each person has the right to choose the sexual fantasy structure that aligns with their values, agreements, and needs. However, if you are choosing to be in a committed, monogamous relationship, then erotic imagination must be paired with ethical responsibility, so that you and your partner can have fun while you both feel safe.

We all have the right to our private inner world—but we also have the responsibility to examine whether that world aligns with the values we want to live by, and the commitment we have made, the kind of partner we want to be, and the kind of relationships we want to protect.

The Impact on the Spouse or Partner

As discussed earlier, when fantasies involving someone close to the spouse or monogamous partner are discovered or disclosed, the emotional fallout can be devastating for the betrayed partner. Even if no physical boundary was crossed, the internal world of the person fantasizing begins to feel just as violating. For many committed spouses or partners, the discovery of these fantasies feels like an emotional affair of the mind, a betrayal of both trust and safety.

Here's why:

- **It feels deeply personal.** Fantasies about someone in the partner's inner circle feel targeted, humiliating, and violating. The betrayed partner often begins to question their own worth, asking painful questions like, *"Why her/him/them?"* *"Was I being compared?"* *"Was she/he around me while she/he was thinking about her, him, or them?"*

- **It damages core safety in the relationship.** In healthy intimacy with an agreed upon monogamous relationship, there is a shared sacredness around emotional and sexual exclusivity. When a partner realizes that fantasies were being directed toward someone they love, trust, or see regularly, it creates a rupture not just in the romantic relationship—but in their broader emotional world.

- **It can destroy important external relationships.** The fantasy doesn't just live in the mind anymore. If the fantasized person is someone in the couple's community or family, the betrayed partner may feel they can no longer maintain those relationships, attend events, or feel comfortable in familiar spaces.

- **It creates shame and hypervigilance.** The betrayed partner may begin comparing themselves to the fantasized person, scrutinizing their body, personality, or behavior. They may feel pressure to perform sexually or emotionally in ways that aren't authentic, simply to compete with an imaginary version of another person.

- **It can retraumatize existing attachment wounds.** For partners with a history of abandonment, betrayal, or relational trauma, discovering these fantasies can reinforce deeply painful beliefs: *"I'm not enough." "I can't trust anyone." "Love always hurts."*

- **It can erode erotic and emotional intimacy.** Even if there is no affair, as shared prior, the fantasy has already invited someone else into the relational space. This can lead to a shutdown of sexual desire, increased conflict, or distance that can be difficult to repair without intentional healing work.

And it is worth repeating, most importantly, there was no consent. The betrayed partner did not agree to be in a relationship where their best friend or sister or coworker, or nameless, faceless strangers on the Internet are being sexualized and invited into the relationship through fantasy. They did not sign up to compete with someone they trust and love. They did not agree to be the silent partner in someone else's hidden narrative.

Healing from this kind of betrayal requires more than a simple apology or reassurance. It requires the partner who created the harm to take full ownership, to explore the root of the fantasy pattern, and to rebuild trust through transparency, empathy, consistency, and emotional presence.

• • • • •

The Mindful Fantasy Awareness Technique™

As you have learned, unwanted or harmful fantasy loops don't just happen—they're sometimes rooted in deeper emotional patterns like avoidance, loneliness, attachment issues, unresolved trauma, anger, or unmet needs. I developed *The Mindful Fantasy Awareness Technique*™ to help individuals disrupt compulsive or relationally injurious fantasies, reduce their arousal power, and replace them with healthier, integrity-aligned internal experiences. This is not about shame or repression—it's about conscious choice, mindful self-awareness, relational repair, and internal congruence.

Here are the seven core steps to this technique:

Step 1: Name It

Acknowledge what the fantasy is, without minimizing or rationalizing it. Speak it out loud to yourself without shame, or write it down:

- *I'm fantasizing about someone who has not given consent.*

- *This fantasy objectifies a real person in my partner's life.*

- *If my partner or spouse were aware I am sexualizing this person they love, they would be hurt.*

We cannot heal what is hidden. Naming it helps bring the unconscious to light—and light is where transformation begins.

Step 2: Identify the Emotional Trigger

Ask yourself:

- *What was I feeling just before this fantasy started?*

- *Am I bored, lonely, angry, anxious, or feeling rejected?*

- *Am I unhappy in areas of my life or marriage/relationship that need attention?*

Some compulsive fantasies that objectify are not about sex—they are about regulation. This step invites emotional awareness and curiosity rather than acting from autopilot.

Step 3: Add Reality and Consequence

Interrupt the fantasy by introducing the real-life impact. Ask yourself:

- *What would this do to my partner if she/he/they knew?*

- *How would this affect the person I'm fantasizing about?*

- *How would I feel if the person I am objectifying found out?*

- *Would I still respect myself afterward?*

Visualize your partner's hurt, your colleague's disappointment, the sadness or discomfort of the friend you are sexualizing, or the trust that would be lost. This grounds the fantasy in truth, not illusion.

Step 4: Break the Arousal Pattern

Dr. Patrick Carnes coined the term "fantasy contamination" to describe the intentional act of introducing reality into a fantasy to break its addictive or idealized power. This can be done by adding absurd, boring, or non-sexual elements, such as:

- *Picture the person doing something completely un-arousing (nose picking for example).*

- *Picture the person acting rude to a waiter.*

- *Imagine the person is annoyed with you.*

- *Imagine that they are disengaged.*

This can disrupt the brain's loop of reward and desire. Remember: the goal isn't cruelty, or to shame yourself—it's to stop glamorizing or idealizing what is, in truth, a boundary violation in the making.

Step 5: Speak to the Part of You That Needs Escape

Using a parts-based lens (Internal Family Systems/IFS-informed), ask:

- *Which part of me is turning to this fantasy?*

- *What does this part need—comfort, attention, healing, support, rest, honesty?*

- Instead of judging the part, be curious and compassionate. Offer it healthy alternatives:

    - *"You're lonely. Let's connect instead of escape."*

    - *"You feel rejected. Let's soothe that pain another way."*

    - *"You're feeling anxious. Let's invite peace in a different manner."*

Step 6: Replace with a Relational or Values-Based Fantasy

Choose an internal experience that aligns with your values and relationship goals—one that feels both emotionally honest and erotically satisfying. Each person is unique, and your desires deserve space, curiosity, and care. This isn't about shutting down arousal or restricting fantasy. It's about letting your imagination move in a direction that excites *and* connects, that turns you on without turning you away from your integrity. When fantasy is rooted in presence, consent, and emotional depth, it doesn't just feel good—it feels right. And that kind of arousal has power, staying power, and the potential to deepen intimacy, not just escape it.

If you, like Will, have been struggling with fantasy that doesn't align with your sexual compass, consider redirecting your fantasy arousal by focusing on:

- A memory of intimate connection with your partner—where you felt safe, desired, and fully present.

- A sexual activity that centers mutual pleasure, eye contact, and emotional presence.

- A moment of mindfulness, where you drop into the body—feeling breath, sensation, warmth, and grounding.

- An arousing fantasy with your partner that elevates connection, deepens trust, and builds shared erotic energy.

- A sensual memory that includes laughter, playfulness, or spontaneous touch that made you feel alive.

- A values-aligned fantasy where desire is mutual, and consent is clear.

- A situation where your partner is emotionally and sexually responsive.

- A guided visualization or daydream where you imagine emotional intimacy building slowly, with a growing sense of sexual closeness and anticipation.

- A personal erotic script that allows room for passion *and* presence—where you remain connected to yourself, your values, and your partner.

Redirecting doesn't mean repressing your erotic self—it means choosing what you're feeding. The goal is not perfection, but alignment: turning inward in a way that excites, soothes, and supports the kind of connection you're working toward.

This step can help "retrain" your arousal system—helping it to associate pleasure with real connection instead of escapism, shame, or secrecy.

Step 7: Reconnect and Repair

If you're in a relationship, use the disrupted fantasy moment as a mindful nudge to reconnect with your partner. This may be emotional—sharing a vulnerable truth—or physical, with affection or presence. If you've caused harm or crossed an internal line, take steps to repair. That might include journaling, reaching out to a sponsor or therapist, or committing to transparency. If you've sexually objectified someone in your social circle or your partner or spouses' friend or sibling, this repair will be especially valuable.

Important Note: The Mindful Fantasy Awareness Technique™ is not a one-time fix—it's a daily practice of turning inward with honesty, interrupting fantasy loops that *you* have deemed as harmful, returning to your core values, and reclaiming your authentic self. The more you practice, the less power these old fantasies hold. Over time, what once felt compulsive can become conscious, redirected, and mindfully aligned with your deepest commitments—to yourself, your partner, to your unique sexuality, and your integrity.

Exercise: Practicing The Mindful Fantasy Awareness Technique™

The following exercise invites you to bring mindful awareness to your fantasy life—not to shame, suppress, or eliminate it, but to understand it, examine its emotional roots, and assess whether it aligns with your personal and relational values. The goal is internal integrity, not perfection, and to honor and support your unique and evolving sexuality. Take your time. This can be done privately or in collaboration with a therapist or support person you trust.

Step 1: Identify the Fantasy

- What is the fantasy you are noticing or reflecting on today?
- Is it recurring?
- Does it involve a specific person or situation that feels relationally inappropriate or emotionally charged?

Describe it briefly and honestly:

_____

_____

_____

_____

_____

Step 2: Observe the Emotional Setup

What emotional state, memory, or internal experience preceded the fantasy? Check all that apply or write your own:

- ☐ Loneliness
- ☐ Anxiety or stress
- ☐ Rejection or abandonment
- ☐ Boredom or restlessness
- ☐ Shame
- ☐ Grief or sadness
- ☐ Desire for control or escape
- ☐ Something else: _____

Write a few words about what was happening before the fantasy emerged:

_____

_____

_____

_____

_____

Step 3: Acknowledge Impact

Ask yourself the following questions and answer them honestly:

- If this fantasy were shared with my partner (if I am in an intimate relationship), how might they feel?

- If this fantasy involves sexualizes someone I know, or my partner knows, how might the sexualized person feel if they knew I was objectifying them?

- Does this fantasy align with the agreements and values of my relationship (if in a relationship)?

- Does this fantasy increase or erode connection, trust, or safety?

- Does this fantasy align with my own personal values?

- How do I define consent?

Reflect here:

_____

_____

_____

_____

_____

_____

Step 4: Bring in Mindful Disruption

Without self-judgment, imagine gently interrupting the fantasy. This is not about punishment or shaming yourself—it's about awareness and choice.

Ask yourself:

- Can I pause and breathe for a moment instead of continuing the fantasy?

- What would it feel like to notice this fantasy *without* automatically following it?

- How would I like to feel right now (e.g., peaceful, content, connected, aligned)?

Write a statement of mindful interruption (e.g., "I notice this, but I don't need to follow it"):

_____

_____

_____

_____

_____

_____

Step 5: Explore the Need Beneath the Fantasy

Using compassionate curiosity, ask:

- What part of me needed something just now?

- Was it a part that felt unseen, lonely, rejected, exhausted, angry, or unloved?

- What does this part truly need or want from me?

Write a comforting response to that part of you here:

_____

_____

_____

_____

_____

_____

Step 6: Redirect or Reconnect

Can you gently redirect to a fantasy or experience rooted in connection, mutual desire, and emotional integrity? Or can you return to the present moment with grounding?

For example you might:

- Shift your fantasy to something that better aligns with _your_ sexual integrity

- Take a walk or hike

- Take a few deep breaths, place a hand on your chest

- Perhaps run a warm bath or take a cool shower

- Cuddle with a pet

- Do something fun like gardening or listening to music

- Take a moment for a journal check-in

- Take care of something you've been putting off

- Contact a friend or loved one to meet up

Note what you chose to do instead of continuing the original fantasy:

_____

_____

_____

_____

_____

_____

Step 7: Integration and Insight

What did you learn about yourself through this process?

What surprised you, challenged you, or made you feel empowered?

Reflect here:

_____

_____

_____

_____

_____

_____

Gentle reminder: Becoming more mindful about one's fantasy life is not about being "perfect" or never fantasizing. It is not about self-judgment or shame. It's about becoming aware of what drives your inner sexual fantasy world and making choices that support emotional and relational wholeness. Practice and awareness create space for freedom—and freedom is where integrity lives.

• • • •

Central to the process of long-term porn addiction recovery is the cultivation of insight and self-compassion. I've witnessed the powerful impact of incorporating mindfulness techniques through guided imagery and self-grounding tools in the therapeutic journeys of my clients. In the intricate tapestry of healing so unique to each human being, these tools serve as invaluable companions.

In the upcoming sections, you will find a breathwork exercise designed to foster a deeper connection with your inner self and to provide a grounded presence, followed by a guided imagery exercise that walks you through navigating the trigger maze. Finally, you are invited to explore an art reflection exercise, offering a beneficial channel for expression, insight, and self-compassion. While you are welcome to do this work solo, it is important to emphasize the significance of seeking support during these next transformative steps rather than navigating them alone. Remember that having a supportive presence can make a meaningful difference as you embark on this next part of your exploration toward healing and growth.

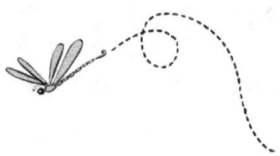

Mindfulness Healing Part I:

Preparation, Assessment, and Script
for Guided Imagery Exercise

Important Safety Tips for Therapists, Facilitators, and Healing Individuals

Environment Consideration and Tips: It can be helpful to "set the stage" prior to a guided imagery exercise. For example, consider the lighting—is it too bright or too low? Another helpful step is putting phones on silent. Also, think about outside distractions, such as barking dogs, traffic, and other interruptions. If possible, minimize outside noises the best that you can. Finally, some individuals like having a blanket or pillow to hold, or you may enjoy diffusing essential oils to support deeper relaxation if there are no allergy concerns. While mindfulness-based guided imagery is not hypnosis, it can be helpful to prepare your environment prior to beginning the guided imagery exercise.

Voice Prosody: An additional gentle reminder is to be aware of your voice prosody. Prosody refers to the rhythm and melody of the voice, including intonation, stress, and pauses. Speaking in a softer tone and slower cadence than your normal speaking voice is useful in supporting the guided imagery practice. If you typically speak more rapidly or loudly, it will take some practice to slow down and modulate your voice.

Diversity Considerations: Consider the client's culture, age, race, physical differences (such as hearing loss), gender and orientation, and other unique experiences that may invite a softer or different speaking tone or pace or require that the client keep their eyes open if they prefer. If you are bilingual and you and your client speak the same languages, ask your client what language they prefer. If your client prefers to go by a nickname, a title such as Dr., Mr., or Mrs., or a specific pronoun, honor their request.

Pace Yourself: Remind yourself to take your time as you walk through this process. There is no need to rush. If you are the person facilitating this exercise, slow down for a relaxed, calming pace. Additionally, it is wise for the facilitator to first practice the exercise with yourself prior to practicing with another person.

Examine Your Biases: As a mental health professional, it's essential to approach the topic of pornography with mindful awareness. Take time to reflect on any personal beliefs, assumptions, former trauma, or emotional reactions you may hold. Being conscious of your own biases, potential judgments, or countertransference allows you to remain present, non-judgmental, and ethically grounded in your work—creating a safe and supportive space for your clients.

Safety Reminder: Safety is the number one consideration with any therapeutic approach or healing intervention. As you lead your clients through the following guided imagery exercise, please instruct your clients to alert you if they are experiencing any of the following trauma responses. If you are an individual doing this work solo, you will also want to consider the following:

- Traumatic memories that are creating a high level of distress

- Feelings of intense fear or panic

- Disturbing or intrusive thoughts

- Suicidal or homicidal thoughts

- Dissociation (if there is an awareness of the dissociative states)

- Other crisis concerns (list on the line): _____

  _____

It is also important to ask the client to alert you if they experience any of the following symptoms. Likewise, if someone is doing this work solo, they should pay compassionate and close attention to their process and monitor for distressing or physical symptoms such as:

- A racing heart

- Tightness in the chest

- Shortness of breath

- Nausea or Intestinal distress

- Feeling faint or dizziness

- Body pain

- Feeling as if you are floating outside of your body

- Other somatic concerns (list on the line): _____

  _____

Note for Therapist or Facilitator: Before moving into the guided imagery, please have your client begin with the assessment below. If you are not a trained mental health professional and your client is in crisis and exhibiting or discussing symptoms that are out of your scope of practice or experience, please refer to an appropriate mental health or medical professional. *If your client is experiencing an immediate life-threatening emergency, please call 911 or the appropriate emergency number if located outside of the United States.*

Note to Solo Reader: *If you are doing this work on your own and believe you are in crisis or may be at risk to yourself, please stop and seek emergency support immediately by calling 911 or your local emergency number.*

> **Pre-Guided Imagery Assessment Scale**

On a scale from 1 to 10 (with 1 = very low, and 10 = very high), please take a mindful moment on the next page to assess the following. Circle the number that most accurately applies to you:

Feeling	Assessment (1-10)									
▫ Anxiety	1	2	3	4	5	6	7	8	9	10
▫ Anger	1	2	3	4	5	6	7	8	9	10
▫ Shame	1	2	3	4	5	6	7	8	9	10
▫ Sadness	1	2	3	4	5	6	7	8	9	10
▫ Fear	1	2	3	4	5	6	7	8	9	10
▫ Numbness	1	2	3	4	5	6	7	8	9	10
▫ Confusion	1	2	3	4	5	6	7	8	9	10
▫ Curiosity	1	2	3	4	5	6	7	8	9	10
▫ Hopefulness	1	2	3	4	5	6	7	8	9	10
▫ Calm	1	2	3	4	5	6	7	8	9	10
▫ Joyful	1	2	3	4	5	6	7	8	9	10
▫ Other:	1	2	3	4	5	6	7	8	9	10

Assessment Notes: _____

_____

_____

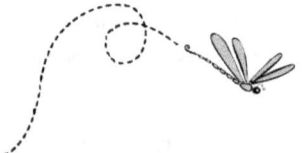

Mindfulness Healing Part II:

Breath and Somatic Preparation & Prompts

This exercise involves tuning into your breath and body and is followed by the guided imagery exercise. It's important to note that this may not be suitable for everyone. It's recommended that the following be adapted to the specific needs and comfort levels of the individual(s) involved.

Physical Space and Comfort: Have your client settle into a comfortable sitting or lying down position, with their feet on the floor or cross-legged if that is the preference. If your client—or you if you are doing this solo—has a yoga mat or a couch and prefers to lie down, that is fine. Whatever position will help the client feel comfortable is perfectly acceptable.

Prompt 1: Let's pause while you take a few moments to get comfortable.

Prompt 2: When you are ready, you are welcome to close your eyes if that feels comfortable for you. Or, if you prefer to leave your eyes open, that is just fine. Whatever allows you to feel most secure is more than acceptable. If your eyes will remain open, feel free to rest your gaze on a calming point near the floor or ceiling if you are laying down.

Prompt 3: We will now move forward into the grounded breathing exercise. This will take approximately two to three minutes.

Grounded Breath Exercise

Prompt: Now that you are in a comfortable position, before we begin the guided imagery, let's move through the grounded breath work.

1. We will start with the 4-2-7 breath. Start by breathing in deeply through the nose to the count of four, hold for two, and then exhale slowly and intentionally through the mouth to the count of seven. Let's do this three times at your own pace. **Note to Facilitator: Count to 20 silently.**

2. Now, let's return to easy, relaxed, deep breathing. Take a long breath in through the nose and let out a long exhale out through the mouth. Continue with this breath. **Note to Facilitator: Count to 20 silently.**

3. As you are noticing the gentle rhythm of deep breathing, I would like you to imagine extending compassion to yourself with each intake breath. **Note to Facilitator: Count to 20 silently.**

Somatic Relaxation Exercise

Now that we have finished with our grounded breaths, please feel free to breathe normally with relaxed, regular breaths. Let's now move into relaxing the body in preparation for guided imagery:

1. Notice that your feet are feeling heavier and more relaxed.

2. Notice that your hands are gently resting at your sides, on your belly, or on your thighs.

3. Feel your jaw relax and your tongue move away from the roof of your mouth.

4. Allow your shoulders to relax down from your ear lobes and your elbows to gently relax down from your shoulders.

5. Bit by bit, the tension moves out of your body as you breathe in and relax and breathe out and relax. Breathe in compassion, hope, and healing, and breathe out stress, judgment, and anger. **Note to Facilitator: Count to 20 silently.**

As we complete our breath work, we will now move into the guided imagery exercise. You can return to your breath work exercises at any point during the guided imagery. The guided imagery exercise will take approximately 10 minutes. You may continue to stay in your comfortable position or shift to a different comfortable position. You may also continue with your eyes closed if that is your preference. At any point, you are welcome to ask for a time out if needed.

Let's move forward.

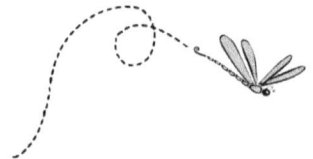

Mindfulness Healing Part III:

Guided Imagery

Navigating the Maze of Problematic Pornography Use

Note to Therapist or Facilitator: If you notice that the client is highly activated during the guided imagery, perhaps demonstrating rapid or shallow breathing, sobbing, or shaking, please have the client pause as you attend to the individual. This can be done by gently stating that you would like to pause the exercise for a moment, then quietly asking the person by name if they would like a break, support with deep breath work, or to step out of the guided imagery entirely if it has become too overwhelming.

Note to the Reader: If you are doing this solo without the support of a mental health professional, again, please be gentle with yourself. If you have a trusted person to lead you through this, you may want to consider this option, or perhaps you can read this into a recording device and then play back and follow the prompts. If you become overwhelmed or feel as if you are in a crisis state, please stop and reach out for help if need be. Safety comes first, always.

Note: If you are a person with a disability and are unable to walk, please imagine yourself moving through this guided imagery in whatever manner feels best for you. That could be in a wheelchair, with a cane, with pet assistance, or even flying or floating if you prefer. Your own imagination will be honored and valued.

Purpose of the Navigating the Maze Guided Imagery: This guided imagery exercise is designed to help you gain mindful insight into your porn use. The aim is to assist you in skillfully navigating the complex maze of triggers, help support sobriety if that is your choice, or develop a healthy relationship with porn if that feels best for you. This GI will assist you in envisioning a path forward toward a life characterized by freedom and fulfillment. This exercise serves as a tool for reclaiming agency over your thoughts and actions, empowering you to cultivate a life that feels authentic and fulfilling.

Instructions: This guided imagery exercise will take approximately 10 minutes. You will be guided through each step of the exercise slowly. Though questions may be asked of you or you may be given prompts, there is no expectation of a verbal response. You may respond if you would like to do so, or you may quietly respond inside of yourself, which many people prefer. Through this visualization journey, you will be guided to explore the various triggers while simultaneously cultivating the inner strength and clarity needed to transcend their influence. You will visualize yourself confidently navigating through the maze, emerging on the other side with a renewed sense of purpose and direction.

First Prompt Step: Close your eyes, take a deep breath, and allow yourself to sink into a comfortable position. When you are ready, picture yourself standing at the entrance of a maze. What does the maze look like in your mind's eye? Picture that now. The maze represents the complex network of triggers and pathways that lead you into the world of problematic pornography use. There is no outside judgment; there is no need to judge yourself. You are safe. You are supported. You are not alone as you move forward. **Note to Facilitator: Count to 20 silently.**

Next Prompt Step: As you step into the maze, envision where the maze is: outdoors, inside, or somewhere else. If outdoors, feel the soft breeze against your skin and hear the rustle of leaves beneath your feet. If inside or in a different environment, take a moment to notice the sound and temperature of the maze. Take a moment to ground yourself in this present moment, knowing that you are completely safe, and that you have the strength and resilience to find your way out. If you are experiencing a challenging or difficult emotion, take a deep breath, acknowledge the emotion, and give yourself permission to notice the emotion without allowing the emotion to overwhelm you. You are safe. You are supported. You are not alone on this journey. **Note to Facilitator: Count to 20 silently.**

Next Prompt Step: Now, imagine yourself walking slowly through the maze. At the start, you are moving through the maze well, but eventually, you encounter a trigger along the way. This trigger may be an image, intrusive thought, fantasy, experience, or emotion that tempts you to engage in pornographic content that you have decided doesn't feel healthy for *you*. What are you noticing about this trigger? What experiences are linked to this trigger? You do not need to be afraid of the trigger; remember, this is a chance to learn from it. Rather than turning away from the trigger, visualize yourself pausing and taking a deep breath, holding space for any feelings that arise. Remind yourself that you are observing and not being absorbed into the trigger. **Note to Facilitator: Count to 20 silently.**

Next Prompt Step: As you breathe deeply, noticing the trigger in front of you, can you find a space of compassion and a sense of resolve within yourself? **Note to Facilitator: Count to 20 silently.**

Next Prompt Step: Take a moment to silently state a compassionate affirmation to yourself. A non-judging compassionate statement may sound like, "I did not have a true understanding of how lonely and isolated I have felt, and even though I no longer want to be in this maze dealing with this trigger, it makes sense that porn would fill that empty space inside of me." Take a few moments to hold space for an affirmation of your choosing. **Note to Facilitator: Count to 20 silently.**

Next Prompt Step: As you continue to reflect on the challenges of this presenting trigger, remind yourself of the healthy reasons you have shared for wanting to break free from your problematic pornography use. Perhaps it's to regain control of your life, improve your relationships, or reclaim your self-worth. Whatever your reasons may be, hold onto them as you compassionately engage with and mindfully learn from this trigger. **Note to Facilitator: Count to 20 silently.**

Next Prompt Step: Imagine the trigger becoming very small or nearly invisible, like a puff of smoke dissipating away on a breeze. Notice that the trigger has less and less pull on you. Breathe in deeply; breathe out deeply. *Note to Facilitator: Count to 20 silently.*

Next Prompt Step: Now that this trigger has loosened its hold on you, it is time to choose a different path out of the maze. These pathways may be filled with activities that bring you joy, such as spending time with loved ones, pursuing hobbies, or engaging in self-care practices. Take a moment now to think of one healthy and fun activity you've missed or would like to explore. Visualize yourself embracing this healthy alternative path with open arms, feeling a sense of fulfillment and satisfaction wash over you. *Note to Facilitator: Count to 20 silently.*

Next Prompt Step: As you move toward this healthy alternative, you notice the exit to the maze—an opening that looks inviting and filled with possibilities. As you move closer to the exit, notice how this trigger is beginning to lose its power over you. With each passing moment and step, you feel more empowered and in control of your choices. You realize more than ever that you can create small but consistent changes, you can break free from the grip of pornography addiction *Note to Facilitator: Count to 20 silently.*

Next Prompt Step: Take a moment now to consider one small but consistent change you can make to support yourself. Some ideas to help you might be adding a filter on your devices, asking someone you trust to be an accountability partner, attending a support group, connecting with a safe friend or loved one, communicating with your higher power, seeking out therapy, or practicing daily mindfulness activities. Is there one small task or change you can commit to over the next week? Whatever feels "doable" for you to try is fine; each step, no matter how small, is a success. *Note to Facilitator: Count to 20 silently.*

Next Prompt Step: Finally, imagine yourself reaching the exit of the maze, holding tight to this commitment. As you step out into the open air, if your maze is outdoors, notice the sun on your relaxed shoulders, feel the breeze on your face, and embrace the growing sensation of peace washing over you. If it is indoors or in another environment, take a moment to appreciate the safety and joy of that environment. Bask in the warmth of this newfound freedom, insight, and self-compassion, knowing that you have successfully navigated through the maze with a better understanding of yourself and the trigger we explored, with steps toward creating a new plan that feels healthier for your life. *Note to Facilitator: Count to 20 silently.*

Next Prompt Step: Know that you have the strength and resilience to work through the trigger you identified. Remember that you are not alone in this journey of healing; you are supported. No matter the challenges that come your way, remember that you are worthy of a life filled with love, authenticity, respect, joy, and fulfillment. Take a moment now to give yourself an affirmation. Self-affirmations may take you out of your comfort zone, but do your best to stay present with yourself, even in the discomfort. *Note to Facilitator: Count to 20 silently.*

Transitioning to Awareness

Final Prompt Step: When you're ready, if your eyes are closed, notice the light in front of your eyelids. Gently blink, open your eyes, and bring your awareness back to the present moment.

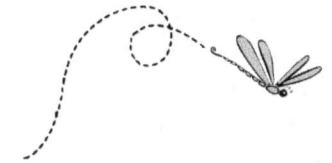

Mindfulness Healing Part IV:

Processing of Guided Imagery

Sharing Your Experience

Purpose for Processing: After the conclusion of the guided imagery, the therapist or facilitator will lead an open and respectful discussion about what you experienced during the guided imagery. The aim is to allow for a compassionate and honest conversation as you highlight important aspects of the guided imagery exercise and what the experience was like.

Note: If you are doing this solo without a therapist or facilitator, please pace yourself and notice your energy. You may journal your responses to the questions below if you are doing this work on your own.

Important Considerations for the Facilitator: It is not the role of the therapist or facilitator to interpret, minimize, or re-direct. Rather, it is important for the facilitator to skillfully hold a safe space for the client to share their experience, including the more difficult aspects. This is a time for the facilitator to honor the pain, as well as highlight and affirm the positive insights the client may have had. Remind the client that participating in a mindfulness-based exercise like this is a signal of hope and aids in the possibility of recovery and healing.

Processing Questions:

1. What did you notice in the guided imagery?

2. What challenges did you experience?

3. What successes or insights did you experience?

4. Did you have a breakthrough you'd like to share?

5. Do you have any concerns that you'd like to share?

6. What are you feeling in your body currently?

7. Did you notice any self-growth with insight and compassion toward yourself?

8. Did you notice any triggers or areas of concern?

Post-Guided Imagery Assessment Scale

Now that you have completed the breath work and somatic exercises, the guided imagery exercise, and the process work, on a scale from 1 to 10 (with 1 = very low, and 10 = very high), let's take a mindful moment to assess the following:

Feeling	Assessment (1-10)									
▢ Anxiety	1	2	3	4	5	6	7	8	9	10
▢ Anger	1	2	3	4	5	6	7	8	9	10
▢ Shame	1	2	3	4	5	6	7	8	9	10
▢ Sadness	1	2	3	4	5	6	7	8	9	10
▢ Fear	1	2	3	4	5	6	7	8	9	10
▢ Numbness	1	2	3	4	5	6	7	8	9	10
▢ Confusion	1	2	3	4	5	6	7	8	9	10
▢ Curiosity	1	2	3	4	5	6	7	8	9	10
▢ Hopefulness	1	2	3	4	5	6	7	8	9	10
▢ Calm	1	2	3	4	5	6	7	8	9	10
▢ Joyful	1	2	3	4	5	6	7	8	9	10
▢ Other:	1	2	3	4	5	6	7	8	9	10

Note to Facilitator or Reader: Engaging in somatic movement, if you are able to do so, such as gentle stretching, walking, rhythmic body movements, or dancing to music, following guided imagery is vital for healing trauma as it allows individuals to release stored tension, process emotions, and reconnect with their bodies, facilitating a holistic approach to healing. Please take 3-5 minutes to move your body in a way that feels good for you. Yoga poses, stretching, dance, bouncing gently, rhythmically swaying, or a short walk are all excellent ways to honor yourself.

Important Reminder: If you, as the facilitator, are not a licensed therapist or trained mental health professional and your client is in crisis and exhibiting or discussing symptoms that are out of your scope of practice or experience, please refer to an appropriate mental health or medical professional. *If your client is experiencing an immediate life-threatening emergency, please call 911 or the appropriate emergency number if located outside of the United States. If you are doing this solo without support and are in a state of emergency, reach out to 911 immediately.*

Mindfulness Healing Part V:

Window of Tolerance

Before you begin the art exercise, let's explore what is called the "Window of Tolerance." This concept was developed by Dr. Daniel J. Siegel, a renowned psychiatrist and author known for his work in the field of interpersonal neurobiology and attachment theory. He introduced the window of tolerance concept to describe the optimal zone of emotional arousal within which individuals can effectively manage stressors and triggers. The window of tolerance has since become a widely used framework in psychology and therapy, particularly in understanding and treating trauma-related conditions and addiction. In the context of addiction, such as dealing with problematic porn use triggers, the window of tolerance represents the range of emotional and physiological states in which a person feels stable and capable of coping with challenges and triggers without resorting to addictive or maladaptive coping behaviors.

In keeping with the theme of the maze, I want you to imagine the window of tolerance as the central path through a maze. When you're on this path, you're able to navigate the twists and turns of life's challenges with relative ease. You may encounter triggers along the way, represented by the maze's walls and dead ends, but you possess the resilience and coping skills needed to stay calmly on course and continue moving forward.

However, when you stray outside of your window of tolerance, either by becoming hyper-aroused or hypo-aroused, it's as if you've wandered off the main path and into the maze's more challenging areas of frustrating and discouraging dead ends. When hyper-aroused, you may feel overwhelmed by intense emotions or cravings, making it difficult to think clearly and make healthy choices. On the other hand, when hypo-aroused, you may feel emotionally numb or disconnected, unable to engage with the world around you or effectively address triggers as they arise.

The goal of therapy and mindfulness-based recovery is to expand your window of tolerance, making it wider and more flexible. Using the metaphor of the maze, it means staying focused on the new healthy path in front of you. This means strengthening your ability to remain within the optimal zone even when faced with challenging triggers. Think of this as mastering the maze, becoming more adept at navigating its twists and turns with insight, practice, support, and resilience. By developing coping strategies, increasing confidence and self-awareness, and fostering emotional regulation skills, you can gradually enlarge your window of tolerance, stay true to your path and empower yourself to face triggers with greater confidence and resilience on your journey toward recovery.

Purpose Statement: The purpose of this healing art exercise is to provide a creative outlet for managing triggers, expanding your window of tolerance, and navigating the complexities of overcoming problematic porn use, sometimes referred to as porn addiction. By engaging in this exercise, you will have the opportunity to explore your triggers in a non-judging way while developing strategies to effectively navigate them. The maze symbolizes the intricate journey of recovery, offering a visual representation of the challenges and triumphs along the way. Through this process, you will have the opportunity to cultivate resilience, practice mindful presence, increase self-awareness, and strengthen your ability to overcome triggers more skillfully.

Art Exercise Instructions: Gather art supplies such as paper, colored pencils, stickers, or other dry materials. Please be mindful if you choose to use supplies like markers or paints, as these can sometimes bleed through to the next page. You may want to place a blank sheet of paper underneath your work to protect the following pages.

1. Begin by finding a quiet and comfortable space where you can focus without distractions.

2. Take a few moments to center yourself through deep breathing, visualization, or grounding exercises. Allow yourself to become present in the moment, acknowledging any thoughts or emotions that arise.

3. Once you feel grounded, envision the maze as a representation of your journey toward recovery from problematic porn use, sometimes referred to as porn addiction. Reflect on the triggers that have challenged you along the way, acknowledging their presence without judgment.

4. Using your art supplies, begin to draw or paint the maze on your paper. *If you prefer not to draw a maze, you are welcome to use the maze art provided.* Please be gentle with yourself; remember that this is about insight and agency and not about the quality of your art or drawing skills. Let your intuition guide you as you create the winding paths and intricate passages. If you are using the maze art here, you are welcome to color the maze as you wish. Consider how each twist and turn represents a different trigger or obstacle you have encountered. You are invited to add a box, arrow, or label to the triggers that are part of your maze.

5. As you work on your maze, pay attention to any emotions or sensations that arise. Allow yourself to explore them openly and without negative self-talk. Remember that there are no right or wrong ways to express yourself through art.

6. Once you have completed your maze, take a step back and observe your creation. Reflect on the journey it represents, recognizing the challenges you have faced and the progress you have made.

7. Finally, consider ways to strengthen your resilience and expand your window of tolerance moving forward. Think about strategies you can implement to navigate triggers more effectively and continue your path toward healing.

8. Take a moment to appreciate yourself for engaging in this healing art exercise and for the courage you have shown. Allow yourself to feel a sense of pride and accomplishment as you continue your journey of recovery.

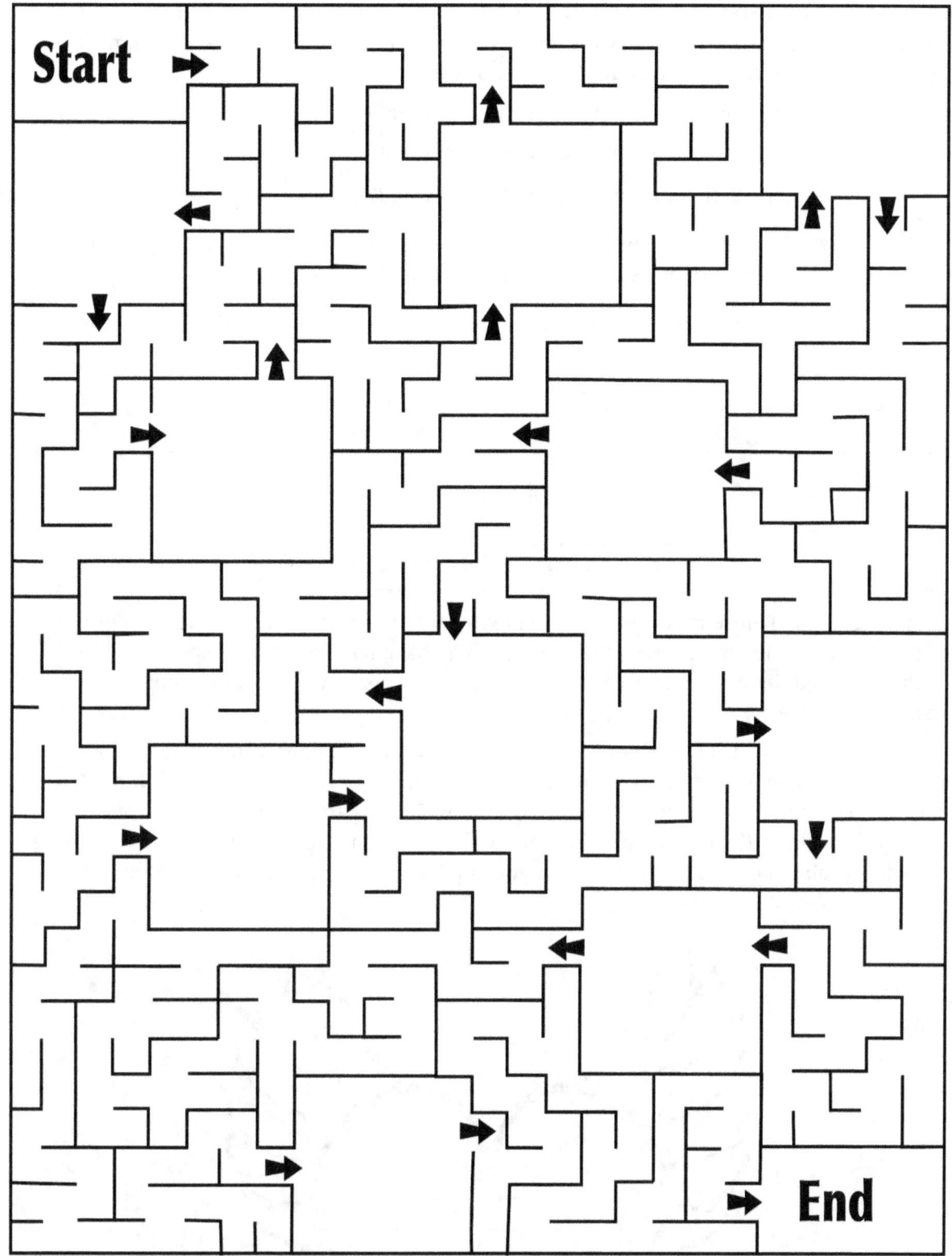

Mindful Reflection Moment

Now that you have completed your breath work, guided imagery, and art journal exercise and we bring this chapter to a close, please take some mindful time to reflect. You are welcome to answer the following questions in the space below, or write in a journal or notebook of your choice. You may do this with your therapist, or if you are working through this book solo, you can do this on your own.

1. What are you noticing after this chapter?

2. What awareness and insight have surfaced?

3. What is the information you have learned?

Write or share your reflections here or in your own journal or notebook if you would like to process them further. As always, please be gentle with yourself:

_____

_____

_____

_____

_____

Final Step: Self-Affirmation Exercise

Instructions: Before moving on to the next chapter, can you give yourself the gift of self-affirmation? It can be difficult for people who have had traumatic experiences, are dealing with addiction, or struggling with anxiety, depression, or other challenges to affirm themselves.

As a support to this step of your healing, affirmation ideas might include statements such as: "I am committed to my recovery," "I am a person of worth and value," and "My past choices do not define my future." Please use the winged heart provided to list your own self-affirmation(s). If you can only come up with one affirmation at this time, that is more than acceptable. Perhaps you can return later in your healing process and add more:

This chapter aimed to provide insights into the issue of problematic porn use, the value of having a focused recovery plan, and the importance of building a reliable support system as you navigate your personal journey. The information and exercises were designed to offer tools and understanding to help guide you toward healthier choices if you feel that's the right path for you. It's important to remember that everyone defines healthy sexuality for themselves, and if using porn in a way that doesn't harm or exploit others is part of your life, that's your choice to make. As Will shared in our final sessions, "Porn controlled my life. If I can break free from porn addiction, anyone can!" For those who choose to change their problematic or addictive relationship with porn, healing is possible with commitment, support, and available resources like Twelve-Step groups. Progress might be gradual, but with dedication, you can move forward—one step at a time.

Before moving on to the next chapter, let's take a mindful pause with this affirmation: Like Will, you, too, have the power to create a life free from the grip of compulsive pornography use if your relationship with porn feels unhealthy or out of control. You are a person of immense worth who deserves authentic, connected, and joyful relationships—starting with yourself. Remember, addiction thrives in secrecy and isolation, but there is great strength in reaching out for support.

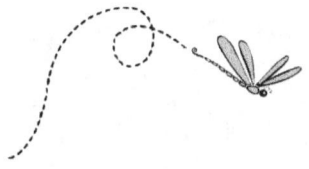

CHAPTER SIX

Betrayal Trauma: From Denial and Deception to Courage and Connection

Wendy Quinton

I learned that courage was not the absence of fear, but the triumph over it...

~ Nelson Mandela

As I greeted Michelle for her first session, it was obvious from the deep creases in her brow that she frowned more often than she smiled. She followed slowly as I led her back to my office and kindly motioned for her to sit in the chair across from mine. As she sank into her seat, I began our time together by inviting Michelle to share what was in her heart.

In a flat voice, she answered, "I recently found out that Ted, my husband, has been viewing pornography constantly and lying to me. I have no idea how to deal with this, and now my whole life feels like a lie. I know that it might not seem like a big deal these days and that everyone watches porn, but this is something I never considered happening in my marriage. It started about four months ago when I walked in on Ted looking at porn depicting scenes of violence toward women on the computer one night. I was so disgusted and hurt that I completely freaked out and started crying and yelling at him, asking him how he could do this to me and our relationship.

"He stayed very calm, looked incredulous, and just shrugged, saying that he must have accidentally clicked on the link while he was looking something else up. He told me that I was being hysterical, that he was offended by my accusation, and that he would never seek out material like that. Then, he shut his laptop and asked what was for dinner. He was so

197 | *The Mindful Way to Wellness Workbook*

nonchalant that I suddenly felt confused and doubted what I had seen. I wanted so much to believe him, and he was so convincing that I accepted what he was telling me. I shook my head as if to rattle it back to reality and common sense and tearfully apologized for accusing him wrongfully.

"A few days went by, but something kept nagging at me, prompting me to check his search history. I talked myself out of it for a time but finally gave in while he was at work one day. I honestly did it just to assure myself that Ted would never purposefully look at that kind of stuff online. I think I went into a state of shock when I saw his search history—it was filled with disturbing pornographic sites, most of which depicted violent rape fantasies, gang assaults, and the degradation of women. As the initial shock began to wear off, I realized that he was sometimes spending several hours a night looking at pornography while I thought he was just reading articles about his favorite sports teams. I could hardly believe my eyes; the Ted I knew and loved would never do this! We had met in church; he was a deacon who taught Sunday school. He didn't smoke and rarely had a drink, and I'd only heard him swear a handful of times. How could it be possible that he was spending excessive amounts of time engaging in this type of behavior and deceiving me?

"As I stood there looking at his computer, my stomach suddenly cramped, and I had to run to the bathroom. I felt so sick. It was as if my body did not want to take in this horrible realization and was actively trying to expel it. When I was finally feeling well enough, I went back to the computer. I wanted to close it, but I also didn't want to touch it. It felt contaminated. I got up the courage to slam it shut and asked God to just shut away the truth I had learned that day and make it go away.

"But of course, it didn't go away, and when Ted came home that night, he could tell something was wrong, especially since I didn't eat dinner with him. He remarked that I looked pale and asked if perhaps I was coming down with something. Unlike last time when I had reacted hysterically, I found myself feeling unusually calm. I simply told him that I had looked at his search history and discovered the type of porn he had been watching for hours each evening.

"When Ted realized that he couldn't talk his way out of this, he reluctantly admitted that I was right and revealed that he had been trying to stop himself for the longest time but couldn't. He said that it was all his dad's fault because his dad bought him a pornographic magazine when he was just twelve and that he was instantly hooked. He told me that he thought things would be better once we were married but that it was difficult for him when I did not want to be intimate. So, he started watching porn online.

"As I listened in disbelief, I felt so many emotions rush through me. I felt anger at Ted for blaming his choices on our sex life. I felt sad for the twelve-year-old boy who had been exposed to porn at a young age by his own father. I was glad that his dad had passed away already, as I'm not sure what I might have said or done with the anger I felt toward him. My thoughts turned inward and, with a sense of confusion, I wondered how I could have missed this. Then came the guilt, the voice in my head taunting me that no wonder he turned to fantasy when I wasn't willing to put aside my discomfort or weariness and have sex whenever he wanted it. This familiar voice was a message that had been ingrained in me from an early age, that a wife should always put her husband first.

With all these emotions swirling around, I only managed to speak in a shaky voice and tell him that I was very hurt but glad all of this was out in the open. I told Ted that I would try to be a better wife and that I really hoped he'd never have to look at porn again. He promised that it wouldn't happen again and apologized. I needed so desperately to believe him that I agreed to put this all behind us. I continued with my busy life caring for our two young children and attending to my husband, our home, our church, and our marriage—like the good wife I had been raised to be.

I tried to ignore the moments of pain that would surface during our times of intimacy when I pictured him leering at other women on the screen or the violent, disturbing images I had witnessed and the husband that I loved and once trusted masturbating to nameless strangers. There were times when we were sexual that it felt like I was leaving my body, just floating away. I would tell myself that it was okay since I was keeping him from having to turn to the internet for satisfaction, which was, once again, a message that I was raised with.

Over the next several months, I occasionally wondered if Ted was still involved with pornography. When I did get my courage up to ask him about something that seemed suspicious, he always had a logical explanation and would angrily accuse me of not trusting him. He locked away his laptop "so the kids wouldn't mess with it," he told me that he had to stay late at the office to "catch up on his work," and he quickly changed the television channel when I came into the room grumbling that "there's nothing on." Sometimes, I felt like I was going crazy as it seemed that there were so many questionable things happening, but I couldn't prove any of them. I chastised myself for not being more trusting, tried harder to ignore any suspicious behavior, and kept being the 'good' wife."

Michelle paused for a moment as tears welled up in her eyes. She reached for a tissue and continued, "But then, a few weeks ago, Ted was running late for work and forgot to shut his laptop. At first, I was able to ignore it, telling myself that I shouldn't be snooping around, but as the day wore on and the kids were down for their naps, I couldn't hold back and checked his history again. And, just like the first time, it was full of hardcore porn sites, even more violent and disturbing than before. His email was filled with memberships to porn and sex worker sites, and the timestamps on the emails aligned with when he said he was working late. All lies, as he had been engaging in all of this from his church office.

"The discovery this time didn't make me feel sick—I felt enraged. That night, as soon as the kids were in bed, I confronted him with what I had found. I expected him to react calmly as he did last time, but instead, he got angry and defensive and told me that he couldn't believe that I didn't trust him and that it was just old stuff from before that was still on his computer. He yelled and asked, 'How are we ever supposed to get past this if you keep snooping around like I'm some kind of criminal?' He stomped out of our bedroom and slept in the den. I didn't know how to respond and just ended up shaking and crying that night—I felt like I was going crazy!

"However, the following day, I read an article on Facebook talking about 'gaslighting.' I'd never heard that word before, but I realized this was what Ted had been doing to me for years. The article suggested finding a therapist to help me figure it out, so that's why I'm here. I feel so confused and angry, and I am mad at myself for being so trusting. What if I was right and Ted had spent hundreds of hours fantasizing about being with other women while the kids and I practically begged him for attention? What if he's still fantasizing about other women when I have tried so hard to be the one to meet all his needs? Why is he turned on by that kind of violence and thinks it is sexy when women are being hurt? And if that turns out to be true, my whole marriage might be a lie. It feels like I have been living with two different men: the one I know and this other guy who was hidden from me! I don't even want to think about that. Maybe I am making too much of all of this, like Ted says. Do I even want to know the truth? I feel like I am losing my mind!"

After hearing Michelle's story, I responded by assuring her that her feelings were completely valid. Though she may feel crazy, she is not. I said, "Michelle, you are not crazy for feeling this way, and it takes tremendous courage to reach out for support. This kind of discovery is what we categorize as betrayal trauma, and when you have been systematically deceived by the person you trusted most in the world, it is incredibly traumatic, hurtful, confusing, and yes, even enraging." Michelle looked at me through tear-filled eyes, and for the first time since entering my office, she took a deep breath. I saw her shoulders relax slightly. I let her know that breathing deeply when we are feeling overwhelmed can be a helpful coping skill and invited her to take another one together with me. We each took in a lung full of air and slowly released it, and for the first time, a small smile peeked through the tears.

Michelle listened intently as I told her that not only had I personally been on a similar journey, but I had also helped many other clients through situations like hers. "I know that trust is very difficult for you right now, and you are so brave to show up here today and allow me into your world. I'm not asking for your complete trust—as I haven't yet earned it—but I am hoping that you can trust me enough to engage in a course of treatment that supports your first healing steps. Might you be willing to do that?" Michelle nodded tentatively and said "yes" in a halting voice, and that was all I needed to begin our work together.

As I explained more about the unique elements of partner betrayal trauma to Michelle, I outlined the next steps and a treatment plan. At the end of the session, I told Michelle that I would be assigning two assessment tools: the Inventory for Partner Attachment, Stress, and Trauma (IPAST) and the Post-Traumatic Stress Index—Revised (PTSI-R). I asked that she complete them before our next meeting. I explained that these were assessment tools developed by the International Institute for Trauma and Addiction Professionals (IITAP), of which I am a member and where I received my training to become a Certified Partner Trauma Therapist (CPTT). I told her that these assessments would help me understand more about her specific symptoms and how her betrayal experiences had affected her.

True to her word, Michelle filled out the assessments, and we went over the results during our next session. I shared with Michelle that many people who have been betrayed by a romantic partner experience symptoms of post-traumatic stress disorder (PTSD), depression, and anxiety (Lonergan, Brunet, Rivest-Beauregard, & Groleau, 2021). She responded that the depression and anxiety made sense, as she felt like she had experienced these since the disclosure of Ted's porn use, but that she was surprised to hear about PTSD and expressed interest in learning more about the studies that have shown that betrayal trauma plays an important role in post-traumatic stress. (Platt & Freyd, 2015).

Based on her specific assessment results, I went on to share with her that the symptoms of PTSD are divided into four main categories: intrusion, avoidance, negative alterations in cognition and mood, and alterations in arousal and reactivity. Symptoms include flashbacks, nightmares, avoidance of trauma reminders, memory issues, negative beliefs, and hypervigilance (American Psychiatric Association, 2022).

As we continued to review her assessment and discussed each category and symptom of post-traumatic stress, Michelle nodded in agreement, sharing that this was exactly what she was experiencing. During that session, she commented, "Although it is really hard to think about all these symptoms I have, like holding back from people who I'm close to, feeling like I'm emotionally on edge all the time, and having disturbing dreams, there is some comfort in knowing these are normal responses to being betrayed and that I'm not the only one to go through this."

As Michelle and I planned out her treatment goals together, she expressed an affinity for a structured program that she could follow with homework and reading assignments. To support her request, we used the workbook *Facing Heartbreak* (Carnes, Lee, & Rodriguez, 2012). As the weeks unfolded, Michelle learned a great deal as we worked through the book chapter by chapter. She gained validation for her trauma, a deeper understanding of addiction, and practical skills such as self-care, setting boundaries, changing words like "sneaking" or "snooping" to "safety seeking behaviors", and advocating for herself. She also learned to express her emotions, honor her anger, and challenge her long held beliefs around marriage and the role of a wife. As she moved forward, Michelle began to regain her peace and confidence, while allowing for consequences for her husband. With my assistance, she developed a recovery plan with non-negotiable boundaries.

Most importantly, Michelle discovered a hopeful truth that sustained her on her restorative journey. About four months into our work, Michelle shared, "I finally realize and accept that I cannot control what Ted does, but I feel more in control of my own life and future than I ever have before. His compulsions and sexual choices are not my fault, and his choice to lie to me and hide parts of himself from me is certainly not because I am not sexual enough or due to the frequency or infrequency of our intimacy.

"I now see that the way I viewed our relationship was based on a lot of pressured, guilt-mongering messages that I have been told my entire life. Being a loving, supportive, and faithful wife does not mean that I deserve to be lied to, bullied, gaslit, manipulated, or made to minimize myself or my hopes and dreams. That is not what God wants for me, that is not what I want for myself, and that is not what I want to model for my precious children. I deserve to have a partner and husband who I can trust and respect—a man who lifts me up, not tears me down." I smiled in reply, noticing Michelle's newly found confidence and determination, and shared that I was celebrating her growth and insights along with her as she continued to heal.

Michelle and I met together weekly for the first year, and after she joined a women's therapy group for betrayed partners, we met bi-weekly for another year. During this time, Michelle worked consistently on her personal growth and healing, maintaining boundaries in her marriage while her husband attempted to rebuild their connection. Michelle shared that after her discovery, Ted seemed as though he was willing to change and started to attend a Twelve-Step group for people with problematic porn use, sometimes referred to as a porn addiction. However, he was reluctant to go to personal counseling or marriage counseling, and eventually, he discontinued attending his Twelve-Step meetings.

During this time, Michelle also found out that Ted had not told her the whole story in his initial disclosure to her, and more of the truth gradually came to light. She learned that he had also spent time at strip clubs and sexual massage parlors, and with this information, another layer of trauma was addressed in our work together.

Although each new piece of information about Ted's behaviors cut deeply and painfully into her soul, Michelle continued to courageously commit to her own process of healing. The straw that broke the proverbial camel's back was learning that her husband was squandering their children's college savings to fund his out-of-control sexual behavior with prostitutes. This was a turning point, and Michelle ultimately chose to leave the marriage and divorce Ted. While this was not a decision she came to lightly, several months post-divorce, Michelle shared that she was living a more peaceful and fulfilling life than she could have imagined.

In a recent check-in session, she shared, "Wendy, the woman who first stepped into your office is not the same woman sitting here today. I feel like I'm blossoming into the person God always intended me to be. I loved being a wife, but my husband was not the person he appeared to be. I cherish being a mother, and that brings me the most joy. Perhaps one day, I'll be a wife again, but I will never again enter a relationship where I am treated like a second-class citizen—where guilt, shame, deception, and emotional abuse are used to control me and keep me in the dark. Never again. My life is incredibly busy and, honestly, exhausting at times as I juggle work and single motherhood, something I never expected. Yet, I'm proud of myself. I'm more focused than ever on building an authentic, fulfilling, and happy life for me and my kiddos."

Like many people healing from betrayal trauma and the impact of gaslighting, the steps to healing had not been easy for Michelle. Yet, I was gratified to witness this woman who had been so shattered and filled with hurt and confusion reclaim and rebuild her dignity, focus on her well-being, and commit to creating a life that centered around safety and support for herself and her children. As a therapist, this is why I do the work I do—I am forever grateful and honored to walk this road with the clients I support.

A word from Wendy

As a licensed clinical social worker who specializes in partner betrayal trauma, many of the clients I work with begin therapy in an emotionally fragile state. They are often traumatized, angry, lonely, confused, conflicted, and sometimes even guilt-ridden if gaslighting has been part of their traumatic experiences. The solid foundation of their lives, which, for some partners or spouses like Michelle, sometimes includes marriage, family, and faith, has been shaken, and they are not sure where to land. They find it difficult to reach out to others for support as they may have been isolated by an abusive partner, are dealing with financial issues, or are too ashamed to tell others the truth about the state of their relationship. Some are in denial, hoping that if they ignore the problems, they will just go away. In my experience, the majority of betrayed partners question their reality.

When I begin working with clients like Michelle, both of us have important roles in the therapy process. Theirs is to tell their story—their whole story—and mine is to provide a safe, compassionate, non-judgmental space for them and to validate the truth of their experiences and emotions. I have learned that responsibly disclosing that I, too, have experienced the agony of betrayal often helps clients feel more comfortable sharing their stories with me. The people I support appreciate that I understand firsthand the emotions they are grappling with.

Though I do not share specific details—since my focus is on the client's pain and progress—I sometimes disclose, when appropriate and supportive, that after discovering my first husband was a sex addict, I had to completely rebuild my life. This included resigning from the Mission Board after 18 years, choosing a new career, and returning to college at forty five years of age. Being able to share a very small part of my own story of healing gives clients a living example of hope. My own experience led me toward a path of healing, which ultimately led me into my profession as a licensed therapist specializing in sex addiction and betrayal trauma. Each step along my journey helped me make meaning out of the anguish of my own betrayal trauma. My clients share again and again that being heard and supported by a fellow human, a therapist, who understands their struggles allows them to experience a glimmer of hope that empowers them to begin rebuilding a solid foundation for themselves.

An important part of treatment involves psychoeducation, which is exploring areas of trauma relevant to the client's distress, helping them understand its roots, and learning strategies to overcome the pain. With clients such as Michelle who have experienced the trauma of being betrayed by their partners, issues such as gaslighting, boundary setting, and developing self-trust in decision-making are important to examine. Let's look at those topics in detail.

Gaslighting

Gaslighting is a term derived from an old film called *Gaslight* (*Cukor*, 1944), in which a husband tries to convince his wife that she is insane, using the secretive lighting and dimming of the gas lamps in their home. Gaslighting is a type of manipulation that occurs when someone tries to make their partner doubt themselves, causing them to question their memory, perception, and even their sanity. This is done through constant denial, misleading information, contradictions, and lies, all aimed at making the partner feel confused and unsure of their own beliefs (Bates, 2020, p.15). In many ways, this is a form of emotional terrorism. The dynamics of gaslighting in relationships can be characterized by four distinct behavioral patterns: love bombing, isolating the victim, the perpetrator's unpredictability, and cold-shouldering (Klein, Li, & Wood, 2023).

The first step in this type of abusive relationship is sometimes love bombing, which Mari explores in depth in Chapter One of this workbook. Love bombing is when one partner overwhelms the other with numerous gifts, compliments, early declarations of love, and promises of a beautiful future together, which leaves the receiving partner feeling flattered, off balance, and not in control (Beri, 2024). This form of manipulation also involves ignoring set boundaries. Love bombing is used by the offender to instill a sense of indebtedness in the victim, leaving them confused about their partner's true character and the nature of their relationship. Perpetrators often use this to gradually distance victims from friends and family, which starts the process of isolation.

Though love bombing is not always a part of the gaslighting, Michelle confirmed that Ted had showered her with gifts, promises, and romance in their whirlwind eight-month courtship, but once married, this had disappeared as he wanted her home most of the time, only running household or child-related errands, and only socializing at church under his watchful eye. When she stepped outside of his demands, he often shamed her or treated her coldly, using silence as violence.

When an offender is working to isolate the victim, they want their target to doubt their own reality and not be around others who might reflect a different point of view or offer support. This behavior often escalates during the time that the partner attends treatment, and Michelle experienced this as she became increasingly assertive with her boundaries and with her husband. Ted tried to get her to stop attending therapy sessions and criticized her for spending time with friends, accusing her of being disloyal to him.

He attempted to shame her for not being a "good Christian woman" and did his best to manipulate her with statements and scriptures meant to induce guilt about his belief that she was neglecting her family and ruining his reputation. When those tactics failed, Ted began criticizing me as her therapist, attempting to cast doubt on the trust we had built in our clinical relationship. Fortunately, Michelle was aware that this was another attempt to control and manipulate her, and she continued to rely on her support system, her recovery tools, and her faith.

Just as love bombing leaves the pursued partner feeling off balance, the unpredictable behavior of the pursuing partner creates further disequilibrium in the relationship. The experience of going from being overwhelmed by affection to having their reality questioned constantly leaves the victim in a state of instability and feeling uncertain about the relationship and their role in it (Tager-Shafrir, Szepsenwol, Dvir, & Zamir, 2024). When the manipulated spouse or partner begins to question the status quo, the manipulator will often punish the partner in various ways, including what is called "cold-shouldering."

Cold-shouldering, in the context of gaslighting, is when someone purposely ignores or emotionally distances themselves from another person to control or dominate them, as Ted did with Michelle. This behavior is a form of emotional abuse that makes the victim feel lonely, unimportant, and unsure of their self-worth, making them more dependent on the victimizer for validation and reassurance. This is especially challenging and frightening for a partner who is financially dependent on their significant other.

Safety-Seeking Behavior

As we learned from Michelle's story, gaslighting may involve common practices by the offender, including lying ("I must have clicked on the link by mistake..."), words that don't match actions ("...promised that he would never do it again...") and projection ("You keep snooping..."). To clarify, what is commonly referred to as "snooping" is known in the realm of betrayal trauma therapy as a form of "safety-seeking behavior." When a partner engages in dishonest behavior or continues to withhold the truth, it can escalate into emotional abuse, often coupled with gaslighting. This manipulation leaves the betrayed partner feeling confused, destabilized, and questioning their own sense of reality. In their desperation to regain a sense of control and validation, they may resort to searching for evidence—checking phones, emails, or social media—to confirm their suspicions and ease the overwhelming sense that they are "going crazy."

These safety-seeking behaviors aren't driven by a desire to invade privacy or cause harm; rather, they stem from the deep psychological need to restore personal safety and emotional equilibrium in the midst of ongoing deception. For many, this becomes a survival mechanism when faced with repeated lies and emotional manipulation. It allows the betrayed partner to reaffirm their perception of reality, even though it can create further trauma for them, straining an already unstable relationship. However, in the context of healing, these behaviors often signal a breakdown in trust and communication, underscoring the need for honesty, transparency, and therapeutic intervention to address the underlying trauma and rebuild safety within the relationship.

The most devastating effect of gaslighting is that it results in a loss of the sense of self (Klein, Li, & Wood, 2023). Over the years, Michelle had been systematically deceived, gradually losing her self-confidence and becoming a shadow of her former self. She began to doubt her own intuition, allowing Ted's distorted reality to overshadow her own. However, as Michelle learned more about gaslighting and its profound impact on her, she started to reclaim her sense of self. Through this awareness, she rediscovered her inner strength and began to rebuild the confidence that had once been eroded.

Boundary Setting

When betrayal occurs in a relationship, the wounded partner's sense of security is damaged. To establish safety, the concept of boundaries must be learned and practiced. Boundaries in relationships are the clear "lines" that define where one begins and ends as an individual, highlighting one's differences from others and helping establish personal limits. They serve as a guide for how one interacts with others while maintaining their own sense of identity and well-being (Cloud & Townsend, 2017, p. 31).

For example, some parents of young children may opt to have a fence around their backyard. This barrier not only keeps out potentially dangerous things (cars, strangers, stray animals) but also keeps the children in, away from the dangers that exist outside the fence.

Personal boundaries are like fences—they are healthy limits we set for ourselves that help us to protect ourselves emotionally, physically, and mentally. These parameters assist us in discerning the unique parts of ourselves: our identity, thoughts, feelings, and experiences. When implemented correctly, they can protect us from being harmed by others who may try to devalue, control, or manipulate us.

A common misunderstanding of boundaries is that they are used to make another person change their behavior. However, healthy boundaries focus on what I have control over and how I will change my behavior to keep myself safe. For example, if I do not feel safe when my partner raises their voice, instead of telling them, "You can't do that," I would say, "If you continue to raise your voice, I will choose to walk away and only continue the conversation when you are calm."

At first, Michelle was afraid that setting boundaries meant that she was being aggressive. Ted had often accused her of being mean or aggressive when she advocated for herself, which was another example of his gaslighting behavior. Michelle learned the difference between aggressive (expressing your opinion in a way that is disrespectful and disregards the rights of others) and assertive communication (expressing your viewpoint in a clear, direct, and respectful manner). The more she practiced this type of healthy communication, the more comfortable she became using her voice.

After years of extreme effort to keep things calm by denying her reality and ignoring the pain she felt, Michelle was hesitant to rock the boat by standing firm. However, with practice, she developed a tolerance that allowed her to stay with the uncomfortable feelings that arose when Ted was upset with her boundaries and the actions she took when he violated them. She learned that true peace arrived when she became comfortable with setting and maintaining her boundaries, which created safety for herself and her children and allowed her husband to experience the consequences of his actions when her boundaries were crossed.

There are numerous types of boundaries that assist in developing healthy relationships, such as emotional, physical, and material. Michelle was eventually able to create healthy boundaries in all these areas of her relationship. Her emotional boundaries included choosing to leave a conversation when Ted tried to avoid the issue that she brought to him by demeaning her or criticizing her behavior. She practiced healthy physical boundaries when she refrained from sexual intimacy with Ted when she discovered he had acted out with a prostitute. She created a material boundary by opening her own checking account so that Ted could no longer use her wages or the children's college tuition to pay for strip clubs and sexual massages.

Eventually, she came to understand that speaking her truth and honoring her voice by setting healthy boundaries was assertive behavior, not aggressive. As Michelle began to feel more comfortable with this approach to her relationship, she naturally developed greater self-trust and confidence.

Additionally, she realized that her instincts were usually spot-on, that she could rely on herself to follow through with consequences for breached boundaries, and that living in truth was more rewarding than living in the false comfort of denial. When Michelle was tempted to doubt herself, she made sure to check in with her support system to be assured of the truth and her strength and be reminded that both are essential for the healing process.

To successfully implement these boundaries, Michelle learned to decide what she needed and what she was willing to do to meet these needs in a healthy way. She began to communicate clearly and ask for help from her support system when she felt too fragile, exhausted, or overwhelmed to enforce her boundaries with Ted.

It is important to note that Michelle's story is not every betrayed partner's story. Each partner has their unique experiences and pain points. Some betrayed partners choose to leave the marriage or relationship immediately upon discovery. Others are naturally assertive, able to set boundaries, and confidently allow for consequences. However, for Michelle and many other partners, they must learn and practice these new ways of communication and self-advocacy.

Self-Trust and Decision-Making

A further skill that Michelle developed during her course of treatment is how to make wise decisions. Due to the complex trauma that resulted from Ted's gaslighting behavior, she had lost nearly all confidence in herself and found it hard to make even simple decisions. To help her gain strength in this area, she started with small choices, like what she wanted for breakfast or what music she enjoyed, and moved on to bigger ones, like how to spend her free time or what she liked to do for fun. Eventually, as she continued to grow and heal, she confronted the decision of whether to stay in her marriage or not.

The decision to stay in a relationship or marriage after betrayal is one of the most difficult choices many of my clients face. Understanding the foundations of healthy decision-making can help navigate this challenge. In my clinical experience, when the partner who betrayed is committed to seeking help, healing their own wounds, and addressing the damage they've caused while consistently being transparent throughout their recovery, trust can slowly be rebuilt, one step at a time.

For some, however, the original marriage feels irreparably broken, and they no longer wish to restore it. Instead, they may be open to creating a new kind of relationship with the same partner—provided their spouse or partner remains committed to recovery and shows tangible signs of change through both words and actions. On the other hand, when the betraying partner refuses to engage in healing or continues to exhibit gaslighting, deception, or other harmful behaviors, it becomes much harder for the wounded partner to consider staying.

Another part of Michelle's journey that allowed her to learn to make wise decisions was to begin to engage in mindfulness-based strategies. Mindfulness is the practice of being fully aware of what you are thinking, feeling, and sensing in your body and the environment around you in the present moment without judgement. The goal is to simply notice these thoughts and feelings without labeling them as good or bad or trying to change them. Key elements of mindfulness are acceptance, self compassion, learning to just observe, and remaining calm and balanced.

Michelle incorporated mindfulness into her routine by starting each day with a few minutes dedicated to herself. She began with deep breathing exercises, followed by a progressive relaxation technique to ease tension throughout her body. Afterward, she spent some time sitting quietly, allowing her mind to settle and calm any anxious thoughts. In the evenings, Michelle found it especially beneficial to journal before bed. She would start by listing at least three things she was grateful for, then note any personal growth she observed during the day. She also reflected on the emotions connected to this growth and where she felt them in her body. These mindful practices bookended her day, helping her stay focused and balanced. For a more in-depth look at other mindfulness based strategies, please refer to Chapter Two of this workbook.

Michelle found that journaling was an effective tool to assist in her decision-making process. She would make a note of a decision that needed to be made, write all the solutions she could think of, and add a pro and con list for each solution. While she was doing this, she paid careful attention to how her body felt while exploring each option. She found that this brought clarity and consistency to her choices, and she learned to listen to and trust her inner voice.

Eye Movement Desensitization and Reprocessing

Part of Michelle's treatment plan included eye movement desensitization and reprocessing (EMDR). EMDR is an evidenced-based trauma therapy that helps clients promote healing of issues such as anxiety, depression, post-traumatic stress disorder (PTSD), and addictive behaviors, and it has been used in therapy for the past thirty years. In an article that summarized the evidence for its effectiveness, it was concluded that for PTSD, EMDR therapy can be a first-choice treatment because there is enough scientific evidence showing it works effectively (de Jongh et al., 2019. P 266). EMDR mimics the body's natural way of processing memories, which happens during the rapid eye movement (REM) stage of sleep.

When we experience trauma, the memories of that trauma can sometimes get "stuck" in the brain, like a too-large folder gets stuck in a filing cabinet. Each time you try to open that drawer, the file sticks out and causes difficulties until you take the time to break it down and clear it out so that it fits in a smaller folder that is the correct size for the drawer. EMDR allows clients to process their traumatic memories, and while doing so, the brain can break those traumatic memories down into manageable parts and file them away into long-term memory so that the painful memory and body sensations are no longer front and center, impacting the client's daily life.

EMDR focuses on three time periods: past, present, and future. Michelle became aware of the experiences in her past that contributed to the pain she experienced in her present relationship and to project where she would like to go in the future. Using a facet of EMDR therapy called the "future template," Michelle was able to explore the outcome of various decisions she could make. A "future template" allowed her to imagine an upcoming situation in the safety of the counseling space and mentally review a positive response. It also afforded her the opportunity to process any triggers and practice new coping skills that might be helpful.

For Michelle, the decision to become more autonomous in her relationship, which would afford her the ability to make better decisions for herself in the future, was one that provoked fear early on in her healing work. She knew that she wanted to open her own bank account and credit card so that she could build her credit history and have funds available should she choose to leave her marriage. However, the thought of walking into the bank and opening an account brought an anxious feeling to her body. Ted had always told her she wasn't smart enough to handle the finances, and unfortunately, she had believed him.

This was one of the first situations we used to create a future template. While doing a technique called bilateral tapping, she was able to picture herself walking into the bank and speaking to the account manager. She envisioned herself breathing deeply, calming her body, and speaking the words she had practiced. Once she could picture herself navigating this stressful situation successfully in an EMDR session, her confidence increased that she could do this in real life. She practiced this scenario a few times at home, and after a pep talk from her best friend, Michelle went to the bank and opened her own account and credit card.

Although this may seem like a simple task to some, those who carry trauma in their bodies often need more than talk therapy to access healing. Supportive, experiential practices can help quiet the mind, regulate the nervous system, and gently shift long-held patterns of pain and self-protection. In the following section, we'll explore breath work, guided imagery, and expressive art experiences—powerful tools that invite deeper awareness, emotional release, and the possibility of transformation from the inside out.

Mindfulness Healing Part I:
Preparation, Assessment, and Script
for Guided Imagery Exercise

Important Safety Tips for Therapists, Facilitators, and Healing Individuals

Environment Consideration and Tips: It can be helpful to "set the stage" prior to a guided imagery exercise. For example, consider the lighting—is it too bright or too low? Another helpful step is putting phones on silent. Also, think about outside distractions, such as barking dogs, traffic, and other interruptions. If possible, minimize outside noises the best that you can. Some individuals like having a blanket or pillow to hold, or you may enjoy diffusing essential oils to support deeper relaxation if there are no allergy concerns. While mindfulness-based guided imagery is not hypnosis, it can be helpful to prepare your environment prior to beginning the guided imagery exercise.

Voice Prosody: An additional gentle reminder is to be aware of your voice prosody. Prosody refers to the rhythm and melody of the voice, including intonation, stress, and pauses. Speaking in a softer tone and slower cadence than your normal speaking voice is useful in supporting the guided imagery practice. If you typically speak more rapidly or loudly, it will take some practice to slow down and modulate your voice.

Diversity Considerations: Consider the client's culture, age, race, physical differences (such as hearing loss), gender and orientation, and other unique experiences that may invite a softer or different speaking tone or pace or require that the client keep their eyes open if they prefer. If you are bi-lingual and you and your client speak the same languages, ask your client what language they prefer. If your client prefers to go by a nickname, a title such as Dr., Mr., or Mrs., or a specific pronoun, honor their request.

Pace Yourself: Remind yourself to take your time as you walk through this process. There is no need to rush. If you are the person facilitating this exercise, slow down for a relaxed, calming pace. Additionally, it is wise for the facilitator to first practice the exercise with themselves prior to practicing with another person or client.

Safety Reminder: Safety is the number one consideration with any therapeutic approach or healing intervention. As you lead your clients through the following guided imagery exercise, please instruct your clients to alert you if they are experiencing any of the following responses. NOTE: If you are an individual doing this work solo, you will also want to consider the following:

- Traumatic memories that are creating a high level of distress
- Feelings of intense fear or panic
- Disturbing or intrusive thoughts
- Suicidal or homicidal thoughts
- Dissociation (if there is an awareness of the dissociative states)
- Other crisis concerns (list on the line): _____

_____

It is also important to ask the client to alert you if they experience any of the following symptoms. Likewise, if someone is doing this work solo, they should pay compassionate and close attention to their process and monitor for distressing or physical symptoms such as:

- A racing heart
- Tightness in the chest
- Shortness of breath
- Nausea or Intestinal distress
- Feeling faint or dizziness

- Body pain
- Feeling as if you are floating outside of your body
- Other somatic concerns (list on the line): _____

Note for Therapist or Facilitator: Before moving into the guided imagery, please have your client begin with the assessment below. If you are not a trained mental health professional and your client is in crisis and exhibiting or discussing symptoms that are out of your scope of practice or experience, please refer your client to an appropriate mental health or medical professional. *If your client is experiencing an immediate life-threatening emergency, please call 911 or the appropriate emergency number if located outside of the United States.*

Note to Solo Reader: *If you are doing this work on your own and believe you are in crisis or may be at risk to yourself, please stop and seek emergency support immediately by calling 911 or your local emergency number.*

Pre-Guided Imagery Assessment Scale

On a scale from 1 to 10, (with 1 = very low, and 10 = very high), please take a mindful moment to assess the following. Circle the number that most accurately applies to you:

Feeling	Assessment (1-10)									
▫ Anxiety	1	2	3	4	5	6	7	8	9	10
▫ Anger	1	2	3	4	5	6	7	8	9	10
▫ Shame	1	2	3	4	5	6	7	8	9	10
▫ Sadness	1	2	3	4	5	6	7	8	9	10
▫ Fear	1	2	3	4	5	6	7	8	9	10
▫ Numbness	1	2	3	4	5	6	7	8	9	10
▫ Confusion	1	2	3	4	5	6	7	8	9	10
▫ Curiosity	1	2	3	4	5	6	7	8	9	10
▫ Hopefulness	1	2	3	4	5	6	7	8	9	10
▫ Calm	1	2	3	4	5	6	7	8	9	10
▫ Joyful	1	2	3	4	5	6	7	8	9	10
▫ Other:	1	2	3	4	5	6	7	8	9	10

Mindfulness Healing Part II:
Breath and Somatic Preparation and Prompts

This exercise involves tuning into your breath and body and is followed by the guided imagery exercise. It's important to note that this may not be suitable for everyone. It's recommended that the following be adapted to the specific needs and comfort levels of the individual(s) involved.

Physical Space and Comfort: Have your client settle into a comfortable sitting or lying down position, with their feet on the floor or cross-legged if that is the preference. If your client—or you if you are doing this solo—has a yoga mat or a couch and prefers to lie down, that is fine. Whatever position will help the client feel comfortable is perfectly acceptable.

Prompt 1: Let's pause while you take a few moments to get comfortable.

Prompt 2: When you are ready, you are welcome to close your eyes if that feels comfortable for you. Or, if you prefer to leave your eyes open, that is just fine. Whatever allows you to feel most secure is more than acceptable. If your eyes remain open, feel free to rest your gaze on a calming point—near the floor if you're sitting or on the ceiling if you're lying down.

Prompt 3: We will now move forward into the grounded breathing exercise. This will take approximately two to three minutes.

> **Grounded Breath Exercise**

Now that you are in a comfortable position, before we begin the guided imagery, let's move through the grounded breathwork.

1. We will start with the 4-2-7 breath. Start by breathing in deeply through the nose to the count of four, hold for two, and then exhale slowly and intentionally through the mouth to the count of seven. Let's do this three times at your own pace. **Note to Facilitator: Count to 20 silently.**

2. Now, let's return to easy, relaxed, deep breathing. Take a long breath in through the nose and let out a long exhale out through the mouth. Continue with this breath. **Note to Facilitator: Count to 20 silently.**

3. As you are noticing the gentle rhythm of deep breathing, I would like you to imagine extending compassion to yourself with each intake breath. **Note to Facilitator: Count to 20 silently.**

Somatic Relaxation Exercise

Now that we have finished with our grounded breaths, please feel free to breathe normally with relaxed, regular breaths. Let's now move into relaxing the body in preparation for guided imagery:

1. Notice that your feet are feeling heavier and more relaxed.

2. Notice that your hands are gently resting at your sides, on your belly, or on your thighs.

3. Feel your jaw relax and your tongue move away from the roof of your mouth.

4. Allow your shoulders to relax down from your ear lobes and your elbows to gently relax down from your shoulders.

5. Bit by bit, the tension moves out of your body as you breathe in and relax and breathe out and relax. Breathe in compassion, hope, and healing, and breathe out stress, judgment, and anger. **Note to Facilitator: Count to 20 silently.**

As we complete our breath work, we will now move on to the guided imagery preparation and exercise section. You can return to your breath work exercises at any point during the guided imagery. The guided imagery exercise will take approximately 10 minutes. You may continue to stay in your comfortable position or shift to a different comfortable position. You may also continue with your eyes closed if that is your preference. At any point, you are welcome to ask for a time out if needed.

Let's move forward.

Mindfulness Healing Part III:
Guided Imagery Exercise
The Bridge: Part A

Note to Therapist or Facilitator: If you notice that the client is highly activated during the guided imagery, perhaps demonstrating rapid or shallow breathing, sobbing, or shaking, please have the client pause as you attend to the individual. This can be done by gently stating that you would like to pause the exercise for a moment, then quietly asking the person by name if they would like a break, support with deep breath work, or to step out of the guided imagery entirely if it has become too overwhelming.

Note to the Reader: If you are doing this solo without the support of a mental health professional, again, please be gentle with yourself. If you have a trusted person to lead you through this, you may want to consider this option, or perhaps you can read this into a recording device and then play it back and follow the prompts. If you become overwhelmed or feel as if you are in a crisis state, please stop and reach out for help if need be. Safety comes first, always.

Note: If you are a person with a disability and are unable to walk, please imagine yourself moving through this guided imagery in whatever manner feels best for you. That could be in a wheelchair, with a cane, with pet assistance, or even flying or floating if you prefer. Your own imagination will be honored and valued.

Purpose of the bridge exercise: This guided imagery exercise is designed to help you explore a pathway from the challenges of your current reality to a future filled with safety, hope, and possibility.

Instructions: This guided imagery exercise will take approximately 8 minutes if ending after the first part of the meditation, 10 minutes if you are ending after the second part of the meditation, or approximately 12 minutes if you are doing the full guided imagery exercise. You will be guided by your mental health professional or trusted facilitator, or you may guide yourself, if you prefer, through each step of the exercise slowly. Recording this script on a device or phone may be helpful if you are doing this on your own. Though questions may be asked of you or you may be given prompts, there is no expectation of a verbal response. You may respond if you would like to do so, or you may quietly respond inside of yourself, which many people prefer. Through this visualization journey, you will be guided to explore what you may need to move toward the future you imagine for yourself and find the courage to do so, practicing gratitude for the journey.

First Step Prompt: Close your eyes, take a deep breath, and allow yourself to sink into a comfortable position. When you are ready, imagine yourself heading out for a walk to clear your head of some of the difficulties you are facing in life. As you walk along, you see that several yards ahead, the road seems to end at a cliff. You remain safe and steady on the road and think that you may like to get a closer look. You step ahead slowly, knowing that you will keep yourself safe by only going as close to the edge as feels comfortable for you. You do not rush, and your feet are secure. You walk toward the edge, and with your feet planted firmly on the road, you feel curiosity and decide to get just close enough to peer over the edge while remaining at a safe distance. You are in no danger of falling.

As you stand at the end of the road, you take a look around, and all you can see are the challenges you are facing in your life. It may be the stinging pain from your partner's betrayal, the distress you feel being stuck in a dead-end job, or an overwhelming "to-do" list. Continue to breathe and carefully select one hardship to focus on so you do not become overwhelmed. Allow yourself a moment to feel this difficulty in your body. You are not alone. You are safe. *Note to Facilitator: Count to 20 silently.*

Next Prompt Step: Now, looking away from your challenge, let your internal gaze look across the deep chasm and begin to notice that you can see the other side. As your eyes adjust to the distance, you observe that it is a beautifully lit place filled with wonderful things. As you look more closely, you see exactly what you've always wanted for yourself...it might be a healthy relationship, working at a job you love that brings a great sense of satisfaction, or having everything crossed off that "to-do" list. Take a deep breath, focus on whatever it is that your heart desires, and allow yourself to feel the longing to be on the other side of the chasm. *Note to Facilitator: Count to 20 silently.*

Next Prompt Step: Eventually, you turn your gaze from the far side of the chasm and look at the space around you. As you take this in, you notice a bridge nearby. A sense of hope begins to rise within you, as this could be a way to reach the other side. You approach the bridge with curiosity, noticing that while it appears narrow and shrouded in mist, it's still a path forward. The fog makes it difficult to see the full length of the bridge, and this uncertainty brings up some hesitation. But take a slow, deep breath and allow yourself to reflect on what might help you feel ready to take that first step. Maybe you imagine a light to guide your way, a map to offer direction or even the comforting presence of someone holding your hand. Visualize whatever you need to feel safe and supported, knowing that you can take your time. The bridge will not let you down. You are safe. Picture it clearly. *Note to Facilitator: Count to 20 silently.*

Next Prompt Step: Now imagine that everything you need to assist you arrives at just the right time. Perhaps it's a light to illuminate the dark bridge, a map that gives you a clear sense of where you need to go, or a safe hand to lead you across at your own pace. Now that you have all you need, imagine yourself taking that first step onto the bridge and then another. Now pause and take a moment to notice how solid and well-built the bridge is, how helpful the bright light is, how assuring it is to have a map that gives you direction, and how comforting it is to have a hand to hold. *Note to Facilitator: Count to 20 silently.*

Next Prompt Step: Now that you are safely on the bridge, allow your eyes to drift back to the cliff that you left. You notice that although it is dark, it is also familiar. You know exactly what to expect on the cliff behind you, but you've never walked across the bridge. Perhaps fear of the unknown begins to surface, or maybe another emotion arises. Notice that now, but you remind yourself that you are safe, you are supported, and you can take this journey one small step at a time. No one is rushing you. You can take this journey at your own pace. You just keep breathing in and out as you turn your focus again to the longing in your heart to reach the brightness of the other side. You feel your courage return as you remember that you're not alone. Take a moment to acknowledge the help and support you have: the light, the map, and the gentle hand. Continue to breathe and relax into the courage you feel. *Note to Facilitator: Count to 20 silently.*

Note to Facilitator:

- This guided imagery can be ended at this point and continued at a future time, depending on where the client is in their healing journey.

- If you are continuing on, skip over the next two prompts.

- If you are ending here, continue with the following two prompts.

Next Prompt Step: Know that you have the strength and resilience to work through the fear of heading into an unknown future. Please remember that you are not alone in this journey of healing; you are supported. No matter the challenges that come your way, remember that you are worthy of a life filled with love, authenticity, respect, joy, and fulfillment. Take a moment now to give yourself an affirmation. Self-affirmations may take you out of your comfort zone, but do your best to stay present with yourself, even in the discomfort. *Note to Facilitator: Count to 20 silently.*

Transitioning to Awareness

Final Prompt Step: When you're ready, if your eyes are closed, notice the light in front of your eyelids. Gently blink your eyes open and bring your awareness back to the present moment.

Note: If you are continuing from above, Part A, start here:

The Bridge: Part B

Next Prompt Step: Now that you have accessed your inner courage, imagine yourself taking one step at a time toward the other side. As you look ahead, the fog starts to lift, and you can feel the warmth of the sun comfortably shining down on your skin. You continue walking, one step at a time, until you reach the other side. As you arrive at the other side, you pause and rest in the gentle light, and you sense an aliveness in the air. What used to appear unknown and unfamiliar no longer brings a feeling of fear, and you feel supported and open to possibility. Take a deep breath and enjoy the relief that comes from knowing that you made it to the other side. *Note to Facilitator: Count to 20 silently.*

Next Prompt Step: From your new vantage point on the other side of the bridge, you see how far you've come. In the distance, you can still see the cliff where you started. It remains covered in a gray cloud, and for a moment, you take a deep breath and allow your body to remember feeling the heaviness of being in that dark place. Then, as you breathe out, you exhale that heaviness, allowing it to fade, and on your next inhale, you feel again the relief of being on the other side, standing in the sun. *Note to Facilitator: Count to 20 silently.*

Note to Facilitator:

- This guided imagery can be ended at this point and continued at a future time, depending on where the client is in their healing journey.

- If you are continuing on, skip over the next two prompts.

- If you are ending here, continue with the following two prompts.

Next Prompt Step: Know that you have the strength and resilience to work through the fear you have of heading into an unknown future. Please remember that you are not alone in this journey of healing; you are supported. No matter the challenges that come your way, remember that you are worthy of a life filled with love, authenticity, respect, joy, and fulfillment. Take a moment now to give yourself an affirmation. Self-affirmations may take you out of your comfort zone, but do your best to stay present with yourself, even in the discomfort. *Note to Facilitator: Count to 20 silently.*

Transitioning to Awareness

Final Prompt Step: When you're ready, if your eyes are closed, notice the light in front of your eyelids. Gently blink, open your eyes, and bring your awareness back to the present moment.

Note: If you are continuing from above, Part B, start here:

The Bridge: Part C

Next Prompt Step: As you continue to stand on the warm, bright side of the bridge, allow your mind to go to a place of gratitude and focus on all the things you are thankful for on this journey. Think about each element that supported you on your crossing: the light, the map, and the hand, or whatever elements or people that come to mind. **Note to Facilitator: Count to 20 silently.**

Next Prompt Step: Take a moment to thank yourself for finding the courage to step onto the bridge and venture to the other side. Continue in a mind state of gratitude as you breathe in the calm, cool air and feel the warmth of the sun on your skin. You are safe. You are not alone. *Note to Facilitator: Count to 20 silently.*

Next Prompt Step: Know that you have the strength and resilience to work through the fear of heading into an unknown future. Please remember you are not alone in this journey of healing; you are supported. No matter the challenges that come your way, remember that you are worthy of a life filled with love, authenticity, respect, joy, and fulfillment. Take a moment now to give yourself an affirmation. Self-affirmations may take you out of your comfort zone, but do your best to stay present with yourself, even in the discomfort. *Note to Facilitator: Count to 20 silently.*

Transitioning to Awareness

Final Prompt Step: When you're ready, if your eyes are closed, notice the light in front of your eyelids. Gently blink, open your eyes, and bring your awareness back to the present moment.

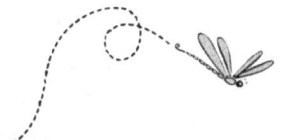

Mindfulness Healing Part IV:
Processing of Guided Imagery
Sharing Your Experience

Purpose for Processing: After the conclusion of the guided imagery, the therapist or facilitator will lead an open and respectful discussion about what you experienced during the guided imagery. The aim is to allow for a compassionate and honest conversation as you highlight important aspects of the guided imagery exercise and what the experience was like.

Note: If you are doing this solo without a therapist or facilitator, please pace yourself and notice your energy. You may journal your responses to the questions below if you are doing this work on your own.

Important Considerations for the Facilitator: It is not the role of the therapist or facilitator to interpret, minimize, or re-direct. Rather, it is important for the facilitator to skillfully hold a safe space for the client to share their experience, including the more difficult aspects. This is a time for the facilitator to honor the pain, as well as highlight and affirm the positive insights the client may have had. Remind the client that participating in a therapy exercise like this is a signal of hope and aids in the possibility of recovery and healing.

Processing Questions

1.   What did you notice in the guided imagery?

2.   What challenges did you experience?

3.   What joys or insights did you experience?

4.   Did you have a breakthrough you'd like to share?

5.   Do you have any concerns that you'd like to share?

6.   What are you feeling in your body currently?

7.   Did you notice any self-growth with insight and compassion toward yourself?

8.   Did you notice any triggers or areas of concern?

Post-Guided Imagery Assessment Scale

Now that you have completed the breath work and somatic exercises, the guided imagery exercise, and the process work, on a scale from 1 to 10 (with 1 = very low, and 10 = very high), let's take a mindful moment to assess the following:

Feeling	Assessment (1-10)									
▫ Anxiety	1	2	3	4	5	6	7	8	9	10
▫ Anger	1	2	3	4	5	6	7	8	9	10
▫ Shame	1	2	3	4	5	6	7	8	9	10
▫ Sadness	1	2	3	4	5	6	7	8	9	10
▫ Fear	1	2	3	4	5	6	7	8	9	10
▫ Numbness	1	2	3	4	5	6	7	8	9	10
▫ Confusion	1	2	3	4	5	6	7	8	9	10
▫ Curiosity	1	2	3	4	5	6	7	8	9	10
▫ Hopefulness	1	2	3	4	5	6	7	8	9	10
▫ Calm	1	2	3	4	5	6	7	8	9	10
▫ Joyful	1	2	3	4	5	6	7	8	9	10
▫ Other:	1	2	3	4	5	6	7	8	9	10

Note to Facilitator or Reader: Engaging in somatic movement, if you are able to do so, such as gentle stretching, walking, rhythmic body movements, or dancing to music, following guided imagery is vital for healing trauma as it allows individuals to release stored tension, process emotions, and reconnect with their bodies, facilitating a holistic approach to healing. Please take 3-5 minutes to move your body in a way that feels good for you. Yoga poses, stretching, dance, bouncing gently, rhythmically swaying, or a short walk are all excellent ways to honor yourself.

Important Reminder: If you, as the facilitator, are not a licensed therapist or trained mental health professional and your client is in crisis and exhibiting or discussing symptoms that are out of your scope of practice or experience, please refer to an appropriate mental health or medical professional. *If your client is experiencing an immediate life-threatening emergency, please call 911 or the appropriate emergency number if located outside of the United States. If you are doing this solo without support and are in a state of emergency, reach out to 911 immediately.*

Mindfulness Healing Part V:

Art Exercise I—The Cliff

Purpose Statement: The purpose of the Cliff Art Exercise is to assist clients in identifying self-limiting mind stories, accessing their inner courage, becoming aware of the support needed to make constructive changes, and feeling hope throughout their entire being. A "mind story" in mindfulness based therapy is a narrative we create—often unconsciously—to explain our experiences, emotions, or identity. These stories can keep us stuck in unhelpful patterns, but by noticing them with awareness and curiosity, we can begin to respond with greater clarity and choice.

Art Exercise Instructions: Gather art supplies such as paper, colored pencils, stickers, or other dry materials. Please be mindful if you choose to use supplies like markers or paints, as these can sometimes bleed through to the next page. You may want to place a blank sheet of paper underneath your work to protect the following pages.

1. Begin by finding a quiet and comfortable space where you can focus without distractions.

2. Take a few moments to center yourself through deep breathing, visualization, or grounding exercises. Allow yourself to become present in the moment, acknowledging any thoughts or emotions that arise.

3. Once you feel grounded, use your art supplies and color the picture of the bridge between two cliffs we have provided on the next page.

4. When you've finished coloring, take a pen. Thinking back to your guided imagery, label the fog in the picture with what painful circumstances darkened your life (betrayal, feeling trapped, financial worries, etc.) Feel free to list additional challenges to the cliff on the left-hand side of the drawing.

5. As you work on your art, pay attention to any emotions or sensations that arise. Allow yourself to explore them openly and without negative self-talk. Remember that there are no right or wrong ways to express yourself through art.

6. Next, label the bridge with what helped you to cross it, or what you will need to help you cross it in the future (for example, the light may have been your higher power, the map may have been a support group, the hand may have been a close friend, etc.).

7. Now, label the sunshine on the other side with what you were grateful for as you traveled, (courage, support, etc.) and the things you hope to experience on the other side of your pain (freedom, deeper relationships, peace, etc.).

8. Once you have completed your art exercise, take a step back and observe your creation. Reflect on the journey it represents, recognizing the challenges you have faced and the progress you have made.

9. Finally, think about strategies that will support your path toward healing.

10. Take a moment to appreciate yourself for engaging in this healing art exercise and for the courage you have shown. Allow yourself to feel a sense of pride and accomplishment as you continue your journey of recovery.

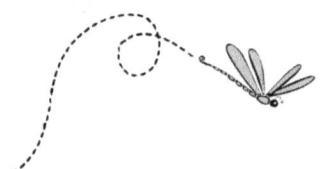

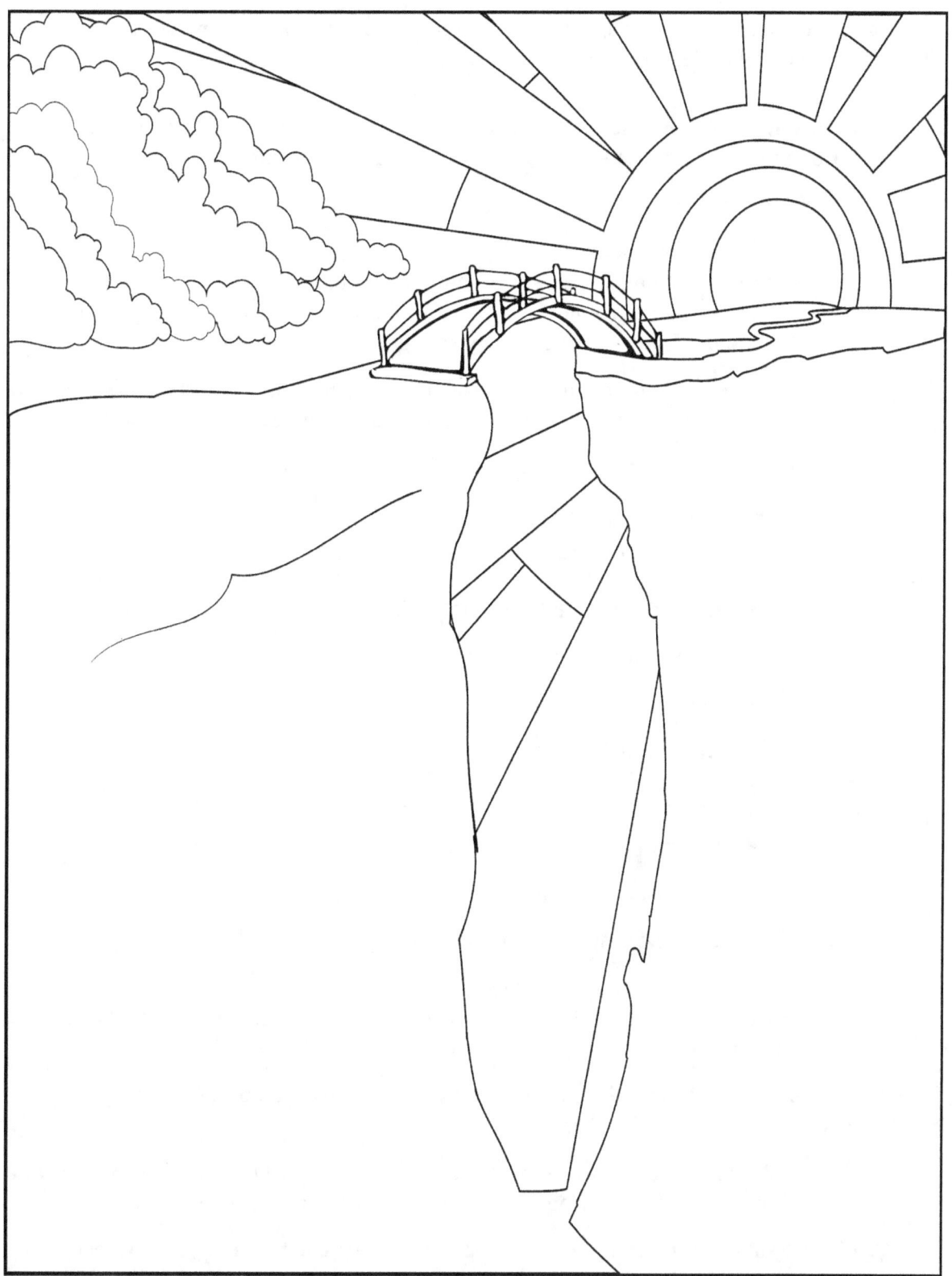

Purpose Statement: The purpose of this healing art exercise is to allow clients to focus on a positive word that describes their journey and access their creativity by completing an acrostic poem.

Art Exercise Instructions: Please locate a pen or a pencil. You may want to place a blank sheet of paper underneath your work to protect the following pages.

1. Begin by finding a quiet and comfortable space where you can focus without distractions.

2. Take a few moments to center yourself through deep breathing, visualization, or grounding exercises. Allow yourself to become present in the moment, acknowledging any thoughts or emotions that arise.

3. Once you feel grounded, read through the example provided that uses the word 'courageous' and fill in the lines with words appropriate to your experience.

   Here is an example using the word **COURAGEOUS**:

   - **C**limbing up, I see

   - **O**n the other side, I am

   - **U**nsure what the future holds, but

   - **R**emembering that I am not

   - **A**ccepting that I

   - **G**ain the support I need through

   - **E**verything I had hoped for is

   - **O**bserving I notice

   - **U**nderstanding that I

   - **S**upport that I can put in place

4. Once you have completed the example, take a step back and observe your creation. Reflect on the journey it represents, recognizing the challenges you have faced and the progress you have made.

Now it's your chance to create your own acrostic poem inspired by the "courageous" example above.

1. Take a moment to pause, reflect and choose a word that best describes your journey across the bridge (examples of words: strength, hope, etc.).

2. Using your writing tool, write that word vertically on a page—with each letter on a new line.

3. Next, starting with the first letter, think of a phrase that describes a part of

your journey and write it beside the letter. Let this be a time of creativity and self-discovery. Be gentle with yourself, trust the process, and see what unfolds.

4. Continue filling in the rest of the lines with phrases to create your own poem.

5. Once you have completed your poem, take a step back and observe your creation. Reflect on the journey it represents, recognizing the challenges you have faced and the progress you have made.

6. Finally, take time to reflect on strategies that can support your path toward healing. Consider what helps you feel grounded, safe, and connected—whether that's engaging in calming rituals, reaching out to a trusted support system, journaling your thoughts, creating art, moving your body, or simply making space for stillness. Healing is not a linear journey, and there is no one-size-fits-all approach. What matters most is finding practices that resonate with you and support your unique process. Give yourself permission to explore, to rest, and to not have all the answers. Every small step you take is an act of courage and self-compassion.

My Acrostic Poem

_____

_____

_____

_____

_____

_____

_____

_____

_____

_____

Mindful Reflection Moment

Now that you have completed your breath work, guided imagery, art, poem, and journal exercises, and before we bring this chapter to a close, please take some mindful time to reflect. You are welcome to answer the following questions in the space below, or write in a journal or notebook of your choice. You may do this with your therapist, or if you are working through this book solo, you can do this on your own.

1. What are you noticing after this chapter?

2.   What awareness and insight have surfaced?

3.   What is the information you have learned?

Write or share your reflections here, or if you prefer, record them in your own journal or notebook to continue processing. As always, please be gentle with yourself:

_____

_____

_____

_____

_____

Final Step: Self-Affirmation Exercise

Instructions: Before moving on to the next chapter, can you give yourself the gift of self-affirmation? It can be difficult for people who have had traumatic experiences, healing from complex betrayal trauma, gaslighting, emotional abuse, spiritual or religious abuse, or struggling with anxiety, depression, or other challenges to affirm themselves. As a support to this step of your healing, affirmation ideas might include statements such as: "I can access supportive connections," "I breathe in courage and breathe out fear," and "My boundaries and voice are important." Please take the space below to honor your own self-affirmation(s). If you can only come up with one affirmation at this time, that is more than acceptable. Perhaps you can return later in your healing process and add more:

In this chapter, my hope was to deepen your understanding of betrayal trauma, gaslighting, and PTSD while introducing the concepts of healing through boundary setting, strengthening self-trust, accessing inner courage, and challenging self-limiting beliefs. You were encouraged to envision your path toward a hopeful future and to mindfully reflect on the support systems you will need to guide you on that journey. Take a moment to reflect on all that you have learned and the courage and strength you are practicing.

As you move ahead, I would like to offer an affirmation to you: You are a person with an innate capacity for a life filled with meaning and purpose, deserving of peace beyond betrayal, trauma, and fear. Within you lies the strength to create a life that aligns with your deepest hopes and dreams, surrounded by people who honor your dreams, respect your gifts and talents, and support your authentic self.

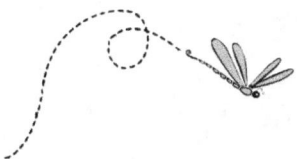

Out of the Minefield:
Overcoming Maternal Trauma Mindfully

Mari A. Lee

I was conditioned to believe that any boundary I wanted was a betrayal of her, so I stayed silent. Cooperative. Mom didn't get better. But I will.

~ Jennette McCurdy

As Suzanne entered the office for her initial therapy session, her posture reflected decades of disappointment and emotional exhaustion. At 43 years old, she had sought support from three previous therapists over the last dozen years. As we sat down for her session, I noticed that her expression was a mixture of resignation and skepticism.

"It's good to meet you, Suzanne. Please make yourself comfortable, and let me know how I can be of support," I said with a welcoming gesture. Placing her sunglasses carefully into her professional-looking purse and taking a quick sip of coffee from her travel cup, Suzanne's voice carried the weight of frustration and sadness. "I'm not sure if you can help me, Mari," she admitted, her words tinged with a hint of uncertainty and vulnerability. "I've been through therapy several times before, but I still feel so lost. I'm consumed by this anger towards my mother, and I can't shake the feelings that are dragging me down. I don't know if I'll ever find peace or if I'll ever feel whole again."

Her words hung in the air, a palpable manifestation of the pain and turmoil she wanted to heal. Extending compassion, I invited Suzanne to share more about her relationship with her mother. As she began recounting her story, it was clear that her journey had been hindered by unresolved and traumatic maternal dynamics. Though her expression remained stoic, behind her eyes lay a reservoir of unshed tears, a testament to the depths of her sadness and a sincere longing to heal from her painful past.

As our work unfolded, I learned that Suzanne's mother had died unexpectedly three months prior at only 61 due to an undiagnosed cardiac issue. She shared that her mother's death was what prompted her to begin this new chapter of therapy. As Suzanne and I slowly but steadily built the trust and rapport that is the necessary foundation of a therapist-client relationship, her past emerged. It was a story fraught with neglect, abandonment, and every form of abuse, not only with her mother but with foster mothers as well.

During the second session, Suzanne began painting the picture of her biological mother, Laney, a colorful but clearly troubled woman. She shared that her mother was first arrested for selling marijuana before it was legal to do so. "Mom was always a rebel. She lived with the wind in her hair and her middle finger in the air. She was a modern-day hippie but kind of classy as well. She was a delicate, innocent-looking beauty who turned heads everywhere, and she used that to her advantage. She was smart as a whip, but had very little common sense. My mother was slim and kept her figure for her entire life, but despite her small stature, she was a force to be reckoned with. She did not let anyone get away with anything; Mom would call a person out without the slightest fear!" Suzanne stated emphatically with a hint of pride in her voice.

As the session unfolded, Suzanne went on to share that she was only eight years old when her young mother went to jail for shoplifting food at a convenience store and having drugs in her car: "This wasn't the first time that mom had been arrested and wasn't the first time child protective services were called, but it was the first time I was placed in foster care, where I was stuck for the next three years. I had no idea what was happening when all of this went down; I just remember my mom in handcuffs, cursing, thrashing around, and screaming for me while a big police officer pushed her into the back of the police car. I was terrified, sobbing, and begging for my mom while a female police officer held me by my arms. Next thing I knew I was at the police station waiting for a social worker to arrive.

"I did not know what a 'social worker' was at that time; it was confusing that this older lady was leading me into her car, and then back to my apartment. As I stood shaking and crying in my tiny bedroom, she curtly instructed me to quiet down while she rifled through my little dresser, grabbing a few items of clothing. When she slammed the door behind us, I pleaded with her to let me go back inside for my favorite stuffed animal, a fuzzy orange cat I had named Cinnamon. I will never forget her response: 'Young lady, that is enough! I am trying to help you. Quiet down and try to show a little gratitude!' as she marched me to her car.

"I recall being on a freeway for what felt like forever, but it was probably only an hour. I counted the telephone poles until they were going by too fast. I knew I was being driven somewhere far away from my mom, our apartment, my friends, my school, and my beloved teacher. I remember picking at a thread on my shorts and using my sleeve to wipe my nose, wondering who was going to water the African violets in the kitchen window that Mom loved so much. Who was going to cuddle with Cinnamon at night? Where would I live?

"When I ventured to ask the social worker what was happening with my mom, she squinted at me in the rearview mirror, a serious look wrinkling her already wrinkly forehead, and flatly said, "Your mother is going to jail. She did something very wrong, little girl. You are going to live with a new family where you will be safe." Trying to wrap my young mind around this felt impossible, so I just leaned my head against the window and looked at the clouds, something I did a lot whenever I was scared," Suzanne said quietly, seemingly drifting away.

With empathy, I leaned in to support Suzanne, helping her stay present and engaged as she recounted the memories that weighed heavily on her. I shared that I work from a mindfulness-based approach, incorporating talk therapy, breath work, somatic body-focused techniques, guided imagery, and eye movement desensitization and reprocessing (EMDR) therapy. Gently, I asked if she would be willing to join me in our first mindfulness exercise: "Suzanne, I appreciate the trust you've shown in sharing this. Before we proceed, can we take a brief mindful pause? I'd like to give you a moment to express how you're feeling in your body right now."

As if waking from a dream, she refocused her gaze and took a thoughtful moment to reflect. Suzanne placed her hand over her stomach. "When I revisit that memory, I feel it right here, in my stomach. It's not exactly pain—more like an ache, a sense of uneasiness, as if someone's poking my belly—an ache from the inside."

Encouraging her to breathe into the sensation, I inquired, "Is there anything you'd like to do with this ache you're experiencing?"

After a pause, she expressed a desire to stand and stretch, Suzanne hesitated. "I feel a bit silly doing it alone. Would you stand and stretch with me, Mari?"

Agreeing without hesitation, we rose together, arms gently lifting, bodies stretching, and then swaying side to side in unison. As we settled back into our seats, Suzanne appeared noticeably more grounded.

When I asked Suzanne what that was like to stand with me and stretch, she candidly shared, "At first, I was irritated when you interrupted me," she confessed, her voice softened by vulnerability, "however, as we stretched and moved—it's strange, I felt like I was back in the car with my younger self, holding her hand and reassuring her that everything would be okay. Is that weird?"

Moved by her words, I reassured her, "Suzanne, that doesn't sound strange or weird. It sounds incredibly courageous. It appears that the younger part of you has been waiting for this moment for a long time. Today, you've reunited with her, offering the nurturing she needed. This is sometimes what healing trauma feels like." A gentle smile spread across my face as I noticed a spark of curiosity and hope in Suzanne's eyes.

● ● ● ● ●

Our first handful of sessions were focused on building trust as she shared different memories during her early years. About six weeks into our work, I noticed that Suzanne seemed subdued and distant. When I asked her about this, she sat quietly for a few moments, twisting a tissue in her hands, and then expressed her need for ample room and space to share her story at her own pace. "My last therapist seemed frustrated with me after a few months as if I needed to heal faster. My therapist before that told me that unless I forgave my mom, I would never get better. I haven't experienced any of this with you—so far, you have been patient and compassionate. But I think I am worried that will change. I don't want to feel rushed, Mari. It's important for me to finally open up about all aspects of my life, especially now that my mother has passed away.

"I realize I held back in the past, sanitizing the abuse and keeping myself small during therapy sessions or feeling ashamed to fully express myself. It's like I felt obligated to protect Mom while she was alive and even in therapy. Even though I appreciated their support and compassion, I wanted to please my previous therapists. I don't want to repeat that pattern with you."

Affirming her needs, I nodded and reassured her, "I am grateful you shared this with me, and we'll move ahead at your pace. I'm glad to know that you received support from your previous therapists, and thank you for also sharing what did not work for you. Now, in this current chapter, I am here to listen to every part of your journey at every age and stage. I respect your timing. This process is solely about you. You don't need to worry about taking care of me during our time together. If we see the pattern repeating, we will notice it together and make a gentle shift. Does that sound like a good plan?" With a sigh of relief, she replied, "Yes, that sounds like a really good plan."

Over the next few weeks, Suzanne dove into the difficult years in the foster care system as a young child, "The first couple that fostered me was the exact opposite of Mom. Religious, solemn, and very abusive. There wasn't a day where my hair wasn't pulled, my face wasn't slapped, or I went to bed hungry with instructions to read my Bible. I was an energetic kid, used to speaking my mind, but I quickly learned to keep quiet, do as I was told, and never ask questions during the year I lived in that dark, oppressive house.

"The next family was nicer, but the dad was a truck driver who was gone most of the time, and the foster mom was overwhelmed. Even though I was just a little kid, I was used as a housecleaner. I stood on a stool and washed dishes until my arms ached, did laundry and folded clothes every night until I was nodding off in front of the washer, and made the beds each morning, which was harder than it might sound. I was also responsible for making breakfast, usually cereal and toast, for the younger foster kids. Let me tell you, I developed some impressive little arm muscles! I had no time for homework and fell behind in school. I was pretty much ignored outside of my chores and babysitting duties. Honestly, I have no idea if they even knew my name during the months I lived with them, but I was so withdrawn by then that it did not matter.

The third family was horrific. They fought all the time, and I was molested by the foster father and older foster brother. I remember my birthday came and went without anyone saying anything. I recall falling asleep on the cot they had given me; it was the night of my birthday. I can still remember feeling tears running out of my eyes, down my chin, and vowing to myself that I would never let anyone see me cry again." With that, Suzanne raised her chin, squaring off her shoulders as if daring me to extend empathy her way.

By now, Suzanne was familiar with our mindful check-ins. I gently began, "Thank you for your trust in sharing with me. That memory holds so much pain, and I want to acknowledge the incredible strength it took to survive that time—and the courage it takes to speak it aloud today."

I paused and softened my tone. "Can we take a breath together—just gently, in and out—and take a moment to notice what's happening in your body right now? When you remember those silent tears on your birthday... where do you feel that in your body? Is there a sensation—tightness, heaviness, or maybe numbness—that shows up as you recall that moment?"

She was quiet, breathing.

"You spoke of the tears rolling down your face and the vow you made never to cry again. That was such a powerful act of self-protection. I see it in the way you lifted your chin just now, how your shoulders squared—it's as if your body still remembers how to armor up, preparing just in case someone offers something you've learned not to trust."

I waited, letting the silence hold us. "And yet, here you are. You're allowing this story to be witnessed. I'm here with you. You don't have to carry this alone right now. If it feels okay, let's stay with your body just a little longer—gently noticing what's there. The sensations, the edges of the emotion. You don't need to change anything or fix anything. Just presence and breath."

Suzanne leaned into the rhythm of my voice. Her shoulders softened. Her pressed lips relaxed. And then the tears came. As she wiped her nose, she looked up slowly and said quietly, "I think my inner child needed this time today, Mari."

· · · · ·

As Suzanne and I stepped into the next chapter of her counseling work, I introduced her to a therapeutic approach called eye movement desensitization and reprocessing (EDMR). EMDR is like a structured roadmap with eight stages designed to guide individuals through the process of dealing with traumatic experiences. Rather than just revisiting the painful event itself, EMDR focuses on the emotions and symptoms that stem from it. The aim of EMDR therapy is to help individuals process these distressing memories, lessening their impact on daily life. By doing so, it opens space for developing healthier ways of coping.

In addition to explaining how EMDR works and guiding Suzanne through each step, I also provided her with resources and techniques to use outside of therapy sessions. This included reflection exercises, relaxation techniques, and journaling prompts tailored to her needs. It was important for Suzanne to feel supported not only during our sessions but also to have tools in her everyday life that she practiced.

During our EMDR sessions, Suzanne and I worked together to confront the past while also building resilience for the future. As Suzanne progressed through EMDR therapy, she noticed subtle shifts in her emotional landscape. The overwhelming feelings of anger, fear, guilt, and anxiety started to lose their grip, making way for a sense of empowerment and clarity. Together, we celebrated each small victory along the way, recognizing the courage it took for Suzanne to target and confront her past traumatic experiences.

Through EMDR and mindfulness-based trauma therapy, Suzanne not only found relief from the burden of her past but also gained valuable insights into herself. As she continued to integrate these newfound coping skills into her life, she was better able to understand and heal the former hurtful memories. Suzanne aptly described the process as "finally unplugging a drain and all of the dirt and debris is finally able to flow through and allow me to feel free."

Over the next several months, Suzanne and I delved deeper. She eventually discussed the challenges she faced upon reuniting with her mother after spending years in the foster care system. She described how she had changed during her time with the foster families she had lived with—becoming withdrawn, quieter, angrier, and more confused, harboring deep-seated mistrust. Suzanne also reflected on her mother's own struggles, understanding that Laney had likely endured extreme hardships during her time in prison. However, instead of seeking counseling or having open conversations about their shared experiences, Suzanne's mother chose to approach their reunion with a façade of toxic resilience.

She recounted her mother's mantra and nickname for her: "Suzy Q, remember what doesn't kill us makes us stronger!" Her mother, with a nod to their Finnish and Norwegian heritage, often invoked their Viking lineage, urging Suzanne to keep her chin up, metaphorically wield her shield and sword, bury her emotions, and face life's challenges head-on. When Suzanne would attempt to share her painful feelings, her mother would often interrupt her: "Quit being such a sensitive, whining baby! Never let them see you cry; never let them see you sweat, Suzy Q!" Then, to the backdrop music of Blondie, Led Zeppelin, or Fleetwood Mac, Suzanne's mother would grab her hand and twirl her around, dancing and singing with perfect pitch, creating fleeting moments of confusing joy and connection amidst the chaos. Suzanne recalled feeling dazzled by her beautiful mother, watching her long fingernails snapping with the music, her hair floating around them, the sound of her silver earrings tinkling, and her long skirt swishing around their bare feet.

Yet, for Suzanne, these moments were tinged with a sense of deep longing. She yearned for her mother's vulnerability, honesty, acceptance, and unconditional love. Instead, she learned that her mother's affection was contingent upon Suzanne embodying a similar mask of strength and resilience, of being her mother's strong, dependable confidant and protector. Despite the outward appearance of love and camaraderie, Suzanne grappled with the weight of her mother's conditional affection, always desiring a deeper, more authentic connection. "It felt like my mom's love could disappear at any moment depending on her mood or if I did not respond in the exact right way. Her affection was like the incense she burned, just a tiny stream of smoke disappearing and then reappearing over and over again."

Suzanne wisely recounted, "Whenever my mother would make that statement about what doesn't kill us makes us stronger, I would think to myself that what we have both been through almost did kill us and didn't make me stronger at all! It made me withdrawn, depressed, anxious, mistrusting, and angry, and it made mom abusive, addicted, and out of control. All the feelings and traumatic experiences that Mom repressed eventually did kill her way too young."

With a catch in her voice, we paused to notice where she was holding this in her body. Breathing into that part of herself, mindfully engaging with me, Suzanne shared, "I lived with mom for another five years until I moved out at seventeen and started living with an older guy I met at the mall. During those years with mom, our life was a revolving door of her boyfriends—moving from one fleabag apartment to a rich guy's mansion, then back to a condo in the valley when they broke up. We'd eventually get kicked out for not paying the rent, live in our car for a while, end up at another man's house by the beach, and eventually land in some rundown duplex in Los Angeles. I honestly can't keep up with how many different schools I attended and the different zip codes we lived in during those years. I felt like Mom was trying to outrun her demons, but they always caught up with us."

When I asked Suzanne what those demons were, Suzanne shrugged, wearily stating, "Booze, pot, pills, cocaine, abusive men, pie-in-the-sky dreams, and her eventual rage and disappointment that would always be directed at me. She would keep me up at all hours of the night, railing about how she could have been somebody great if she did not have a kid weighing her down. I learned to stay small and keep my eyes open and my head down during that time. I learned I was a burden who needed to apologize for my very existence, and I learned never to trust or rely on anyone."

When I asked her what emotion was most present during this part of her session and where she was feeling this, Suzanne expressed with some surprise that even though her voice sounded sad, she felt enraged and that the rage felt "buried deep in my hands and arms." She also noticed that she felt a desire to draw. As I handed her a piece of paper and colored pencils, Suzanne began drawing circles and swirls while she shared further details from this time in her life.

Around this pivotal point in Suzanne's therapy journey, I introduced walk-and-talk therapy. As a therapist, I believe in harnessing the healing power of nature, so we chose to stroll through a serene, tree-lined neighborhood near my office. Its wide side streets and secluded sidewalks provided us with a private and peaceful sanctuary. Suzanne quickly discovered the profound therapeutic benefits of moving her body in nature during her sessions. With each rhythmic step, she allowed her thoughts and emotions to flow freely. The simple act of walking in nature enabled her to better process her memories with greater ease and clarity.

One of the remarkable aspects of walk-and-talk therapy is its ability to engage both the body and mind in the healing process. As Suzanne navigated the winding paths, stopping now and then to notice a particular tree, flower, or bird, she found herself connecting more deeply with her surroundings and, in turn, with herself. The physical movement allowed for deeper presence, introspection, and self-reflection.

Moreover, research (Cooley, S. J. 2020; Robertson, R. 2012) has shown that exposure to nature during therapy sessions and in one's personal life can have profound effects on the nervous system, promoting relaxation and reducing symptoms of stress and anxiety. The gentle rhythm of walking in nature can help regulate the autonomic nervous system, leading to a state of calmness and equilibrium. For Suzanne, this meant that the therapeutic benefits extended beyond our sessions, contributing to her overall sense of well-being and resilience.

As we continued our walk-and-talk therapy sessions, Suzanne experienced transformative benefits. The combination of nature's soothing presence and our therapeutic dialogue provided her with a safe place and pace to heal. With each step taken during our walk-talk sessions, she found herself moving closer to reclaiming her sense of agency and inner peace that she had been seeking for many years.

• • • • •

Suzanne and I worked together for nearly three years and then scheduled periodic check-in sessions for another two years. At the end of one of our last walk-talk sessions, we sat together on the grass under an oak tree that she was often drawn to. After a few moments, she shared, "When I think back to who I was five years ago, I have a lot of compassion for that younger me. I was so broken and consumed by guilt, sadness, and anger when I met you that it seemed impossible to ever move forward.

"Today, I can honestly say that I love myself—every part of me. Even the parts that once felt unfamiliar, frightening, or filled with shame. The parts I buried, ignored, or tried to hide—they all had something to teach me. Each one played a role in my healing. Embracing all of who I am, including the parts I once rejected, has been the most powerful practice of becoming whole. I also understand that this ongoing process of forgiving my mom is understanding her wounds as well. I still struggle with forgiving some of the worst parts of her, but I have learned to give myself permission to take it one step, one moment, and one memory at a time as I move forward."

I will always remember Suzanne closing her eyes, leaning back against that old, crooked oak that had become a friend to us both. As she moved her face toward the sky with a smile and deep sigh, she quietly murmured, "I finally feel safe in my body and in my life. I now understand that I can be my own best mother, and I can nurture myself, grieve the mom I always wanted, and feel compassion for the mother my mom tried to be. All of this can be true at the same time. I will be OK now, Mari. I truly feel free."

A message from Mari

When I first started my clinical practice, I never could have imagined the sheer number of individuals I would meet who are carrying the weight of maternal wounds and trauma inflicted by mothers, stepmothers, foster mothers, mothers-in-law, or maternal figures such as aunts, godmothers, nannies, babysitters, coaches, mentors, or supervisors. As we move through the following pages, it is important to acknowledge that addressing maternal wounding can be a sensitive and complex topic, often laden with emotional triggers and challenging memories. This is particularly true for those who have been conditioned never to criticize their mother, and for those individuals who have only experienced healthy maternal relationships, or those who are loving, nurturing mothers themselves and find it hard to imagine causing harm to their own children.

Lately, I've noticed a recurring theme on social media and other platforms where people are often shamed for speaking openly about their experiences with maternal trauma. Comments like, "Stop blaming your mother; she did the best she could—just forgive her and move on," are commonly echoed in response. While it's true that mothers often play central and influential roles in early development for many people and shouldn't carry the blame for every instance of trauma, this perspective can overlook the valid and complex experiences of those who have suffered maternal abuse.

Trauma is layered, arising from various influences, including societal pressures, environmental factors, and unique personal histories. For some, however, maternal abuse is a very real source of deep-seated pain that has significant impacts on emotional well-being, relational dynamics, and even physical health. Acknowledging this allows us to approach maternal trauma with a more compassionate and nuanced understanding.

Holding space for this concept isn't about casting blame, but rather validating individual experiences. Many who have experienced maternal abuse face the dual burden of working through their trauma while being told their feelings are invalid or disrespectful. It's crucial to create space for those impacted by maternal trauma to process and heal without judgment or shame. Only by listening openly to these experiences can we support resilience, self-compassion, and growth in those who have endured such challenges. Emphasizing healing over blame cultivates an environment where recovery is possible and people feel supported in finding the strength to rebuild their self-worth with compassion and understanding.

For individuals who have had only positive maternal experiences, even acknowledging the existence of maternal wounding may evoke feelings of defensiveness or discomfort. It can challenge their perception of their own upbringing and the relationships they hold dear. Similarly, for mothers who strive to provide love and support to their children, the idea of causing harm to one's child can be deeply unsettling and difficult to reconcile. However, it's crucial to approach discussions about maternal wounding with empathy, openness, and a willingness to listen. Validating the experiences of those who have been wounded by their maternal figures does not invalidate the experiences of those who have had positive relationships with their mothers. Instead, it fosters a deeper understanding of the complexities of the human experience and the impact of early relationships on individual well-being.

By creating a safe and supportive space for dialogue, we can encourage healing and growth for all individuals affected by maternal wounding, whether as survivors or as mothers themselves. It's through these thorny conversations and uncomfortable discussions that we can begin to unravel the layers of maternal wounding and pave the way for healing and reconciliation—if reconciliation is desired.

Suffice to say, maternal wounding is a complex and sometimes overlooked aspect that can affect individuals throughout their lives. Whether it stems from biological mothers, foster mothers, adoptive mothers, mothers-in-laws, stepmothers, maternal mother figures, as explored with Suzanne, the impact of maternal wounds can be profound and long-lasting. Thus, it's essential to recognize the symptoms of maternal wounding to better understand its impact and address them effectively.

Maternal Wounding Symptoms

Symptoms of maternal wounding can manifest in various ways, impacting individuals' self-esteem, relationships, and overall mental and physical health. While there are many symptoms of this type of trauma, the most common include:

- Depression

- Hopelessness

- Self-loathing

- Emotional numbness

- Feelings of inadequacy

- Overcompensating in relationships

- Isolating and avoiding connection

- Extreme self-reliance

- Attachment disorders

- Anger issues

- Addiction

- Anxiety

- Eating disorders

- Co-dependence

- Love addiction

- Workaholism

- Low self-esteem

- Poor boundaries

- Difficulty forming healthy relationships with others

- Acute trust issues

- Feelings of shame

- Fear of abandonment

- Over-giving

- A constant need for validation

- Hyper-independence

- Frequent migraines

- Intestinal issues

- Insomnia

- Body aches

- Sleep disorders

Individuals might find themselves engaging in self-sabotaging behaviors or having trouble expressing their emotions effectively. In severe cases, maternal wounding can lead to suicidal thoughts or self-harming behaviors such as cutting. With many people, unresolved maternal trauma can significantly affect daily functioning and connecting with others in a healthy way. Still, others struggle with addictions—attempting to soothe what is hurting them emotionally (Kong, J. 2018).

Types of Maternal Wounding

The spectrum of maternal wounding encompasses a wide array of experiences. Experiences span from emotional neglect to various forms of abuse, including physical, sexual, financial, and verbal mistreatment. I have outlined these forms of abuse below.

Neglect: This type of abuse can manifest as a profound absence of affection, attention, emotional support, or meeting physical needs from the mother or maternal figure, leaving the child overlooked, unloved, and emotionally and physically deprived. It can also include a maternal figure or mother ignoring violations to the child from others, such as being bullied by a sibling or physical or sexual abuse. This lack of nurturing and safety can sow seeds of painful insecurity, mistrust, and self-doubt, hindering the development of healthy self-esteem and emotional resilience. As Suzanne shared earlier in this chapter, she was never allowed to be vulnerable with her mother. Feelings of fear, confusion, or anger were not allowed to be expressed within their relationship, which left Suzanne struggling to sort through the trauma all alone.

Physical Abuse: The impact of physical abuse on individuals cannot be overstated. This form of abuse can inflict deep and lasting emotional wounds, leaving survivors grappling with profound rage and shame, sometimes for decades. Maternal physical abuse involves the deliberate infliction of bodily harm or injury by the mother or mothering figure, creating a sense of betrayal, humiliation, and fear within that little person. It is not unusual for adult survivors to make excuses for their mothers, such as, "She was overwhelmed," "She did the best she could," or "It was only an occasional beating, spanking, or slap." The scars of physical abuse extend beyond the visible bruises and helplessness, penetrating deep into the psyche and eroding the individual's sense of safety and trust.

Verbal Abuse: This type of abuse inflicts wounds that are invisible yet equally devastating to physical abuse. It encompasses a spectrum of harmful behaviors, including belittling, name-calling, bullying, demeaning, or threatening language that chips away at the child's sense of value and dignity. The words of the maternal figure can become like daggers, piercing the soul and leaving behind emotional scars that can take years to heal. Survivors of verbal abuse may internalize the negative messages they receive, leading to feelings of self-loathing and despair.

Sexual Abuse: This form of abuse is a violation of the most intimate aspect of a person's being. It encompasses any form of unwanted sexual contact or exploitation perpetrated by the maternal figure or when the mother knowingly turns a blind eye to the sexual abuse of the child. Sexual abuse causes immense psychological and emotional distress, and survivors of sexual abuse often struggle with feelings of shame, guilt, rage, self-sabotage, addiction, health issues, and self-blame, as well as difficulties in forming healthy relationships and trusting others. Some survivors of sexual abuse understandably distrust people, while others may attach too quickly. Some survivors have difficulty maintaining good boundaries or honoring their own boundaries. Others struggle to maintain a long-term romantic relationship or stay faithful in monogamous relationships, while other survivors may stay in an unhealthy or abusive relationship. Some survivors struggle with out-of-control sexual behaviors, while others may be sexually anorexic. Sexual anorexia, also referred to as sexual aversion disorder, is characterized by an avoidance of sexual activity. It often involves a deep aversion to sexual intimacy, driven by emotional, psychological, or trauma-based factors. It's not just a lack of interest in sex but rather a strong desire to stay away from sexual activity. This can be caused by emotional pain as well as a fear of being vulnerable with another person.

Inconsistent Parenting: This mothering style adds another layer of complexity as the individual grapples with unpredictable responses and behavior from their maternal figure. This inconsistency can create confusion and instability in the person's sense of self, making it difficult to develop a coherent and secure identity. It can also contribute to feelings of anxiety, insecurity, and distrust in relationships as the child struggles to anticipate and navigate the maternal figure's reactions. This childhood hypervigilance to become accepted and loved often extends to other relationships as the person navigates adulthood. For example, Suzanne shared about her difficulty in forming meaningful connections in romantic relationships, feeling constantly on edge and fearing abandonment. To cope, she adopted a chameleon-like approach, molding herself to match her partner's interests and hobbies instead of embracing her own passions.

Financial abuse: This is another insidious form of maternal wounding that can undermine a young person's sense of safety and security in the world. This may involve withholding financial support or essential resources such as food, clothing, or shelter, leaving the child vulnerable and deprived of basic necessities. Financial abuse can also manifest in controlling or exploitative behaviors that limit the individual's autonomy and independence, further exacerbating feelings of powerlessness and dependency. Suzanne's mother fluctuated between showering Suzanne with money when she was with a wealthy man, withholding money for education when Suzanne displeased her, and demanding that Suzanne financially support her when Suzanne became financially independent.

The aftermath of maternal abuse is often marked by profound feelings of emptiness—as if one is constantly scanning the horizon to find something or someone to fill the hole in the soul. As outlined earlier, survivors may struggle with numerous emotional and psychological challenges, including anxiety, depression, post-traumatic stress disorder (PTSD), disordered sex, disordered eating, or substance abuse. As discussed, the trauma of maternal abuse can also impact the individual's ability to trust others and form healthy relationships, leading to a cycle of isolation and loneliness.

It is essential to approach survivors of maternal abuse with compassion, empathy, and understanding. Healing from this type of complex trauma is a multifaceted and deeply personal journey that requires patience, support, validation, and time. By providing survivors with a safe and supportive environment in which to process their experiences, eventually, they can reclaim their sense of self-worth, heal their shattered trust, and forge a path toward healing and wholeness.

As you can see, maternal wounding encompasses a complex tapestry of experiences that can profoundly shape individuals' emotional landscapes, attachment styles, and relational patterns. Through therapy or other mental health support, these hurting people can begin to untangle the knots of maternal wounding.

Attachment Styles

Attachment styles are pivotal in understanding how maternal wounding influences individuals' relationship dynamics. Secure attachment, characterized by a strong and nurturing bond with the maternal figure, lays the foundation for feelings of safety, trust, and emotional security in relationships. However, maternal abuse can often give rise to insecure attachment styles, which in turn shape how individuals interact with others. (Muller, R. T. 2000). Let's explore this next.

1. **Anxious-Preoccupied Attachment Style:** This style may develop when individuals experience inconsistent caregiving or emotional neglect from their maternal figure. This can lead to a heightened need for reassurance and validation in relationships, as well as an underlying fear of abandonment. As a result, individuals with this attachment style may exhibit behaviors such as seeking constant closeness and attention from others and experiencing heightened anxiety when separated from their loved ones.

2. **Dismissive-Avoidant Attachment Style:** This style may arise from experiences of emotional unavailability or rejection from the maternal figure. Individuals with this attachment style tend to downplay the importance of emotional intimacy and may avoid forming deep connections with others as a means of self-protection. They may appear aloof or detached in relationships, preferring to maintain emotional distance to avoid vulnerability and potential hurt.

3. **Fearful-Avoidant Attachment Style:** Also known as disorganized attachment, this style often stems from experiences of trauma or abuse from the maternal figure. Individuals with this attachment style may oscillate between a desire for closeness and a fear of intimacy, leading to conflicting behaviors in relationships. They may crave connection but struggle to trust others, fearing that they will be hurt or rejected once again.

Additionally, functional freezing, though not an attachment style, is a trauma response and another aspect of maternal wounding where individuals may experience a state of emotional paralysis in response to past trauma. This freezing response serves as a protective mechanism, allowing the individual to cope with overwhelming emotions or threats to their safety. However, functional freezing can hinder emotional processing and prevent the individual from fully engaging in their present experiences.

These disordered attachment styles can create significant challenges in forming and maintaining healthy relationships, both romantic and non-romantic, perpetuating a cycle of emotional distress and relational difficulties. However, with self-awareness and therapeutic and other supportive interventions, individuals can begin to recognize and address the underlying wounds that contribute to their attachment patterns. Recognizing the signs of maternal wounding, understanding its various types, and exploring attachment styles and functional freezing are essential steps in moving forward, leading to a more fulfilling life. With support and specific interventions, many people like Suzanne eventually experience freedom, peace, and a sense of safety.

The Unique Maternal Trauma of Foster Children and Adoptees

One segment of overlooked individuals who experience the most profound maternal wounding are foster care children, orphaned children, adopted children, and stepchildren. As someone who has traversed the complex path of healing from maternal wounds, I intimately understand the profound impact this specific anguish can have on every aspect of a person's life. While this narrative isn't centered specifically on my own experiences, certain aspects resonate deeply with me, particularly Suzanne's time in foster care. My own background involves being in foster care for several years, followed by an adoption into a household fraught with abuse, especially from my adoptive mother, who made it abundantly clear, day in and day out, that my biological sister and I were a nuisance and unworthy of love and nurturing.

My adoptive parents, both older and highly educated, wielded punishments with alarming severity, creating a daily atmosphere of terror. I was a shy and compassionate child by nature who had withdrawn further into myself because of my years in foster care. The reunion with my biological sister when we were young, followed by our adoption into a new household, initially sparked a glimmer of hope for a stable home and family where my younger sister and I would finally be safe. Yet, within a few days, it became evident that we had merely exchanged one form of torment for another—a perpetual nightmare that persisted until I mustered the courage to leave that hell house at the age of sixteen.

At that moment, my resolve crystallized: Foster care had been horrific and harrowing, but the cruelty of this couple surpassed it. Families, in my young mind, were dysfunctional and dangerous, and adults were not to be trusted. I believed my best chance lay in fashioning my own path, free from abusive authority.

So, after months of planning, one afternoon, while my adoptive parents were still at work, I hastily packed what little belongings I had—a pillowcase stuffed with a few items of clothing, a cherished photo of my sister and me, my favorite book, *The Lion, The Witch, and The Wardrobe*, (Lewis, C. S. 1950), the money I had saved from babysitting, and my skateboard. With my sister's blessing, I embarked on a journey with no clear destination, a story woven with many highs and lows best saved for another time. My sister left shortly after, escaping as well. I never glanced back after the day I left, nor did I speak to my adopted parents again until I was in my early twenties. Even then, encounters were rare in the years that followed.

Considering the widespread impact of maternal trauma, it's surprising that so few books address this vital topic in depth. Even more striking is the scarcity of literature specifically exploring the unique experiences and profound wounds often faced by children in foster care and adoptees. For many, the absence of a biological mother or the experience of separation can create complex layers of maternal trauma, often amplifying feelings of loss and displacement. Yet, foster care survivors and adoptees, who endure some of the deepest maternal wounds, are frequently overlooked in this conversation.

While disappointing, this oversight is not entirely unexpected, as foster care and adoption narratives are often sidelined. Bringing more focus to these stories would not only validate the experiences of adoptees and foster children but also deepen our collective understanding of maternal trauma. Expanding literature on this subject could provide critical support for those who seek to heal from these specific wounds and inspire a greater sense of inclusion for voices that too often go unheard.

For example, our experiences as foster children and adoptees are often disregarded in various aspects of life. Medical forms requesting biological family medical history leave us at a loss, forcing us to simply state, "I was adopted," or provide uncertain responses. We feel excluded from family tree projects in school, deprived of the knowledge of our generational roots and stories. Therapists may unwittingly ask a former foster care or adopted client to complete a genogram. A genogram is a visual representation of a type of family tree that includes detailed information about relationships, patterns of behavior, and medical history across multiple generations. We lack tangible connections to our biological lineage—no references to having grandmother's smile or father's eyes. Personally, I didn't discover my ethnicity until my mid-30s, never knowing how to answer when someone asked about my race or background.

As adults, we former fosters without family members sometimes find ourselves alone on the holidays, embarrassed to request an invitation from friends who haven't considered how we spend the holidays if that is not their lived experience. Even as older adults, if we do not go on to marry, have children, or partner with a person who has children, holidays can indeed be a lonely time. Some of us, like myself, have never seen photos of our infancy or toddlerhood. If we were adopted as older children, which in foster care terms means any child over 12 months, our names might be changed upon adoption, adding another layer of identity confusion. In my case, my birth name was Carmel Renton until my adoption was finalized, a name I lived with for the first several years of my life. Afterward, my adoptive parents changed my name, along with my sister's name, to names of their preference—clearly not confusing at all!

The earliest photo I have is from the adoption agency, taken with my sister. To this day, I've never seen a picture of myself younger than four years old. I entered the system at age two and a half, devoid of memories of my biological parents. It wasn't until years later, well into adulthood, that my sister and I engaged in amateur sleuthing when we finally discovered our biological parents' names and learned of a full biological brother who was adopted out of a different county three years after we left the system. His name on the paperwork we uncovered simply reads "Baby Boy Blank." Decades of research and many dead ends led us to this information, yet by then, our biological parents had passed away. The fate of my biological brother remains a mystery to this day.

This narrative underscores the complexities and challenges faced by foster care survivors and some (not all) adoptees, individuals often overlooked in discussions of maternal wounds and familial identity. For those adopted children who were abused or rejected by their adoptive mothers, we have a special thirst for maternal healing and connection, what I call "the-hole-in-the-soul" syndrome. We—who have experienced being given up by, or taken from, our biological mothers, either as infants, toddlers, or older children or adolescents—have a cellular longing for the sustenance of the original mothering bond, even if that bond was only for a small amount of time in utero.

For those of us who were taken from our biological mothers and did not have a happily-ever-after adoption story, the wound is doubly destructive. Just when it seems the yearning our little hearts have desired will finally be fulfilled with an adoptive mother, a nurturing mom who will provide us with safety and love, instead of receiving the comfort we have craved for so long, sometimes for years, we are met with cruelty, criticism, or chronic neglect. It is deeply disappointing, confusing—and at times, infuriating—that we are so often left out of the maternal wound discussions.

Humans are designed for secure attachment. For those of us with unpredictable and unsafe adopted mothers or maternal figures, many of us did our best to stay safe as little ones. We did this by finding ways of adapting to the dangerous mothering minefield as we navigated the abuse through childhood into adulthood. Some of the navigation tools included making ourselves small and invisible, stuck in a chronic state of the limbic freeze response, as we sought to hide from and lessen the pain of cruel mothering. We often learned to perform in perfectionistic ways, being the "straight-A" student who eventually morphs into the workaholic to reduce rejection and ridicule. Some adults who were in foster care or adopted by abusive mothers ambulate through multiple "love" relationships or broken marriages, always in flight and looking for love and acceptance in all the wrong places with all the wrong people. For some former foster care women or men, coping with their unique maternal wound means plastering on a good girl or good boy mask or taking on too much heavy lifting in our relationships and friendships, which may be a fawn or appease trauma response. Other wounded daughters and sons learned to explode or implode when faced with even the gentlest criticism. Their early, unhealed pain is triggered, and a fight response of self-protection erupts. These people often report feelings of chronic sadness, rage, or anxiety, always scanning their environments and waiting for the proverbial other shoe to drop.

Disassociation, or tuning out and turning inward, is another coping mechanism for abused adopted or fosters; it was our safe turtle shell as frightened children. Coping is a way of trying to stay safe in an unsafe system. Abused, abandoned, or adopted children find ways of staying safe through disappearing—into books, art, nature, sports, fantasy, toys, sleeping, alcohol, marijuana, masturbation, people pleasing, rebelling, TV, video games, jobs, studying, porn, excessive exercise, sex, social media, and food—anything to numb the prison of chronic fear they feel trapped in.

In clinical terminology, we refer to this as "maladaptive coping mechanisms." Maladaptive coping mechanisms are unhealthy ways people handle stress or emotions. While they might provide temporary relief, they often lead to bigger problems. For example, using alcohol to numb feelings, avoiding issues, or reacting with anger may seem helpful in the moment but usually make things worse. When it comes to abused or neglected children, I believe they are doing their best to survive in unsafe environments. While their behaviors may be considered maladaptive, these are their ways of adapting to a violent system, trying to stay safe the only way they know how.

Without compassionate support in healing this original attachment and abuse trauma, over time, the coping mechanisms that helped us stay *safe enough* as children in these unsafe family systems no longer work as adults. Unknown and unhealed maladaptive coping mechanisms eventually fossilize into defense mechanisms in adolescence and adulthood. Defense mechanisms no longer keep us distant and numb; rather, they keep us stuck in fear, scarcity, people-pleasing, self-sabotage, mistrust, rage, confusion, isolation, addictions, and shame. We circle the drain, acting out patterns and behaviors that are confusing and detrimental with an implicit sense that something is wrong with us, but we have no idea how to change these destructive patterns. We have no explicit understanding or healthy models of how to grow healthy connections and trust with ourselves and others, especially when it comes to connecting with women in authority.

In abusive foster care and adoption stories, betrayal becomes fused with love, sometimes referred to as a "traumatic bonding," as explored in Chapter One. Hurting young people who then become hurting adults have few words to illustrate this unspoken trauma because, like Suzanne and her mother, our words were not welcomed, heard, or understood. Instead, our expressions and shared experiences were ridiculed or slapped literally and figuratively away. Sadly, the experiences of foster children and abused adoptees continue to be ignored—in our books, movies, articles, or clinical research on attachment.

We foster care kids and abused adoptees learn that silence is our friend, and instead of speaking out and up, we swallow our unnamed pain and stumble through life with a hole in the soul, our sense of self shredded, and our "danger antenna" bent and twisted so that it becomes incredibly difficult to detect the difference between safety and danger in personal relationships. Prior to healing, we have very little, if any, understanding of what makes for a healthy romantic relationship, let alone knowing what a healthy platonic friendship is or how to advocate for ourselves with authority figures, like a supervisor or someone else in a position of power.

Connecting with others, such as colleagues, in-laws, or other acquaintances, is sometimes overwhelming due to second-guessing that person's motives. It is not unusual for those of us who have been betrayed by our mother or mother figures to enter into transactional friendships and relationships—those "friends" that are only in our lives because we provide something for them, pay them for something, or purchase from them. This could be a hairstylist you are chummy with, but only during the service, or a personal trainer who is a friend as long as you are working out with them. Maybe it is a "bestie" who is happy to be a part of your life as long as you are footing the bill, or the neighbor you know because you pay them to watch your pets. Perhaps it is the fair-weather friend who loves hanging out at your fun gatherings but is nowhere to be found when you need someone to lean on. Or the person you are dating who is "all in" as long as your time, effort, attention, and love are focused on them, but they disappear the moment you are dealing with a health issue or turn to them for comfort or support.

Additionally, betrayal bonding is as familiar as the sun in the sky to those of us with this unique wound. Genuine, compassionate, reciprocal relationships feel rare, uncertain, scary, transient, or dependent on us doing all the nurturing and supporting of the marriage, love relationship, or friendship.

The Soundtrack of the Abused Adopted Daughter

This type of pain is carried forward, sometimes for decades, held up by an internal soundtrack that runs in the background: "I don't belong, I am defective, I am not enough, I am broken, I am not worth loving just for me." The body has cellular memory even if we do not or cannot remember traumatic experiences from our past.

These negative core belief messages can be activated by social media posts, especially around Mother's Day. Though we are happy for our friends and colleagues as they post loving words and photos about their moms, there is a melancholy tug that occurs for many who have not had or do not have this experience. No matter where you go during the month of May in the United States, Mother's Day cards seem to line up to mock motherless women. Restaurants, commercials, and advertisements let you know what you are missing each year. We who carry this maternal wounding sometimes feel a deep sense of grief and longing when overhearing snippets of laughter between moms and their beloved girls on a TV show or movie. We may then dissociate for the rest of the episode or film, lost in a world of our own. I wrote the following prose a few years ago highlighting the experience of the motherless on Mother's Day. My hope is that this helps you, the reader, feel seen, heard, and supported if what I am describing resonates with you.

Musings for the Motherless

By Mari A. Lee

Come over; don't be alone today. We can sit in the garden, drink ginger tea, or something fizzy, like champagne. The popping bubbles can represent the hard-won freedom from a physically or sexually abusive or emotionally wounding relationship with a woman you called "Mom."

Or the mom you never knew.

Or both.

Sitting in nature, a jasmine-scented breeze against our skin, a hummingbird zips by, busy, nosing into the nasturtiums who nod in appreciation. The yard kitty, a sweet stray I call Alice, longing to be loved and nurtured, will curl around our ankles, attentive to the healing conversation, laughter, and maybe tears.

When the sun sets and we've had enough talking, we can skinny dip in the stream, floating, hair streaming on the surface, or lay on the damp grass and make angels, green stains on white cotton dresses, moonlight parenting the wounded little girls we once were.

I will make us grilled cheese, and in PJs, we will sleepily discuss our favorite movie scenes that we have studied over the years, rewinding, rewinding again...mothers and daughters sharing sweet moments, arms around each other's shoulders: "Mom, you are my very best friend!" "Oh honey, I couldn't ask for a better daughter!" Or gazing at the social media posts, a foreign smorgasbord we are hungry for, dishes of joy-filled moments, smiles, and hugs between women who share...

Blood

Secrets

Memories

Inside jokes

Facial features

Snippets of conversations overheard on that annual Sunday in May: "My grandma's lemon cookie recipe," "You have your mom's brown eyes," "Let's go shopping tomorrow," and "Thank you for brunch!" The "remember when..." and "I need a hug" moments are all layered like a favorite birthday cake made each year for the lucky ones while we match holders keep the flame alive outside of the window as we watch.

Those of us in our not-so-hidden society who are motherless or childless "by choice" know there was no other choice. The secret word to enter our club was always "escape." We choose safety over insanity. We chose self-care over cruelty. We chose boundaries over betrayal. We chose moxie over manipulation. This felt like less of a choice and more like spiritual CPR.

Run, run away, run quickly! This was the background music of our childhoods.

No child chooses this willingly. The choice is a raft haphazardly set off to sea, the hammered planks of our hearts tied together with the last shreds of dignity. Waves of uncertainty looming in the distance, the sun overhead listening in to our desperation—

"Did you bring water?"

"Oh, shit! Was I supposed to?"

"Damn, what about a compass?"

"Yikes, I didn't know!"

"Snacks?"

"Nope, but I have cigs and books!"

"Oh, and I have a stuffed animal!"

"Well, we can't eat that, dummy!"

"Sorry, we had to flee quickly..."

"I hope they make it to a shore, but they really shouldn't cuss so much," the people say, shielding their eyes, watching us float away, *tsk tsking* as they turn back to their safe sanctuaries and dinner tables.

We do. We make it to a different shore.

Barely.

Sunburned, half-drowned, skinny as fuck.

Over the years, we pick through the piles of confusing scraps left for the motherless. We do our best to build a little life: Maybe this person? Maybe this class? Maybe this job? Maybe this partner? Maybe this friend? Maybe this path? Maybe this house? Followed by the "how-do-I" years: How do I learn to drive? How do I apply for a driver's license? How do I open a checking account? How do I fill out a job application? How do I get birth control? How do I cook eggs? How do I register for college?

The searching, sorting, finding, wondering, worrying, falling, rising, falling, rising, repeating, relearning.

Endless.

Early in this new adventure (which doesn't feel like an adventure), there are judgments and jabs from the observers. Sometimes envious, sometimes incredulous: "Why would she do THAT?" "Why doesn't she do THIS?" "What does she see in HIM?" "Who does she think she IS?"

At night, curled up on someone's couch, Paul speaks words of wisdom to our frightened and shamed souls, *Let it be, let it be*. And I do. And I don't. And I continue my journey, directionless but determined. The couch surfing continues as I ramble on for another year or so, celebrating 18 with no one knowing except the seagulls crying "Happy Birthday" in their sad circles. Learning to surf, the sea lifting me up, bringing buoyancy to my inner mermaid, another girl with no legs under her, the tide moving me toward the bigger waves of a life yet to be lived. Of loves yet to be broken.

As the years float or hurtle me along, I learned the meaning of *sisu*: "sustained will, perseverance and determination in the face of adversity." I learned about my Finnish and Viking roots. We motherless learn, and we unlearn. Rare and remote healers enter our journey, some better than others, and we soak in that temporary nurturance all the way to our marrow. Over time, as the healing wounds turn to wrinkles, the words I now receive from well-meaning strangers have changed, "You are remarkable!" "What a resiliency rebel you are!" "I want to have your life!" or "You're fierce and brave!"

Am I? Is that what I am meant to be?

OK then, let me try putting *that* mask on; maybe this one will finally fit. I look in the mirror, carefully putting the brave girl mask in place. Growling softly, I say, "*Grrrr*, I am fierce!" flexing an arm muscle while my kitty Stanley looks on with a dubious expression. "*Grrrr, grrrr*, kitten head!" I respond with a chuckle.

This mask is interesting; it fits. Sort of. But it is itchy, too. And heavy after a while.

I gently place the "brave girl mask" in the redwood chest. Not Grandma's chest. Not Mom's chest. It is a chest from a dumpster dive at sixteen. A prized possession likely abandoned by a well-mothered beloved girl who had too much. My treasured chest has aged with scars from the decades I've dragged it along. I lift the etched lid, and the other masks gaze up, their eyes empty. In the corner is the people-pleaser mask with a genteel grin. Next to that is the sexy girl mask with the smeared lip gloss and mascara trails. The good Christian girl mask with the lips sewn shut. The angry mask with a grimace of pain. The smart girl mask with the wise eyes. The reliable woman mask with the chubby face.

My brave, fierce girl mask finds its place among the others. Closing the redwood lid, the scent of ancient trees filling me, I look up, chin raised, eyes closed, arms stretching above my head, feet grounded into my little home near the sea, mermaids singing. Arching my back, back over the years, back and back, I breathe in deeply, the breath of God, the breath of possibility, the breath of release, the breath of grief, the breath of gratitude, and I whisper to myself, to my heart...

"Happy Mother's Day, Mari, I love you."

●　●　●　●　●

We abused adoptees or former fostered adults are confronted with our status in nearly every walk of life, from well-meaning therapists asking for family of origin information on intake forms or passwords asking for your maternal grandmother's name. There are questions from interested acquaintances regarding our race, ethnicity, or jokes about orphans, discussions in our friend groups that center around family traditions and happy memories, and conversations that may assume all our mothering stories are the same. And, of course, lest we forget, the endless comments about how lucky we were to be adopted. For the fortunate ones, this is true; for others, not so much.

This secondary trauma, along with books, articles, blogs, and stories that never seem to include the foster or adopted stories, can leave one feeling frustrated, devalued, and unseen. We hesitate to advocate for ourselves to be included for fear of being labeled as pushy or an angry freak with an attachment disorder or being judged for being a person with mental health issues. While mental health challenges and anxious or disorganized attachment are often a consequence of this kind of trauma, assumptive judgments and assigning labels to foster care kids and abused adoptees are incredibly unhelpful and damaging.

Never underestimate the resourcefulness and resilience of any woman—or any person. Whether you're a therapist or not, it's important not to minimize the strength, wisdom, and hard-earned growth that someone has discovered and cultivated through their wounds and their healing process. Every journey holds gifts, and every person carries power shaped by their lived experience. Instead, it is our work as a society, as authors and educators, and certainly, as therapists, one person at a time, to change this toxic mindset and approach each adoptee and former foster person with non-assumptive, inclusive, and compassionate understanding. When we make room for *all* maternal trauma stories at the table, we help abused adoptees or fostered people heal the wounded child within.

These constant reminders of what we never had, of who we never were, or the assumptions of who we never can be are the splinters in the heart that are often too painful to dig out for many women and men. Until consequences become too overwhelming, these people, my younger self included, often suffer alone. Until I began my therapy journey over 30 years ago, I had hobbled along, patching myself together the best I could. Focusing on goals, overachieving, workaholism, and staying busy—along with being depressed and distracted, people-pleasing, and overcompensating in all my relationships—were the rusty tools I relied on until I healed and reclaimed my authentic self. It was a self

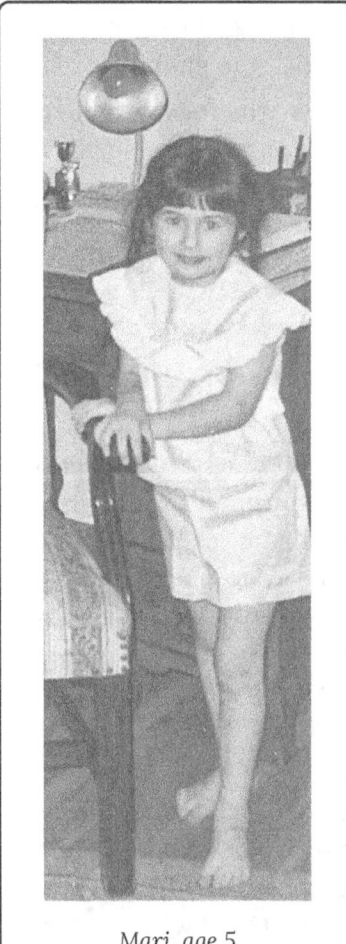

Mari, age 5

buried beneath years of abuse, years of hyper-independence, years of muffling my voice, years of rage, and far too many years of allowing others to trample my boundaries or project their insecurities and then act on them. By healing and integrating the trauma that wrapped around every part of my being, I was then able to understand my value and worth and show up for that inner hurting little girl.

There are women and men who seek me out in my practice who have been dealing with the maternal hole in the soul and their unresolved trauma for decades. They have been soothing their abused and wounded parts in ways that further ravage their self-worth. When it is just too difficult to bear, they finally seek out safe support. Yet, sadly for others, they never find their way to healing.

The Pain of Criticism and Neglect

When the wounds inflicted by our mothers, whether biological, foster, or adopted, remain unhealed, individuals often seek nurturance from other women. This yearning for maternal care and support stems from the deep-seated need that every human being has for validation, attachment, and affection. Criticism and neglect, whether real or perceived, can be particularly painful for those who have experienced abuse or maternal absence. These wounds cut deep into the psyche, leaving lasting scars that impact self-esteem and emotional well-being.

It is not unusual for these people to be on guard for unkind words from others, especially those they may admire or respect. It is also typical for people with maternal wounding to feel incredibly hurt if a friend treats them unkindly or demonstrates a lack of care. Remember, the internal script whispers they are not worth loving, so consistency and predictability in their friendships and relationships are vitally important. In my work as a therapist, I remind these courageous individuals that expressing relational needs does not make them annoying, needy, or "too much"; rather, I help that person understand that their relational needs are just as important as anyone else's needs.

The amygdala, located in the medial temporal lobe near the hippocampus, is central to processing emotions, particularly those related to fear and trauma. In individuals who have experienced maternal abuse or neglect, the amygdala can become hypersensitive, remaining in a state of heightened alert as it scans for perceived threats or potential rejection. This constant arousal often leads to hypervigilance, where neutral or ambiguous situations may be interpreted as dangerous. Such hyperactivity in the amygdala can shape recurring, maladaptive thought patterns, often creating "mind stories" that reinforce feelings of fear and distrust, as explored further in Chapter Two (Ahmed-Leitao, F. 2016).

This hypersensitivity underscores the connection between early trauma and the brain's emotional response systems, influencing both cognitive and emotional experiences in lasting ways. Furthermore, the hippocampus, which is closely linked to memory formation and emotional regulation, may also be affected by maternal wounds. Chronic stress, high cortisol levels, and unresolved trauma can impair the functioning of the hippocampus, leading to difficulties in processing and integrating emotional experiences and memories. This can result in heightened reactivity and difficulties in regulating emotions, making it challenging to navigate interpersonal relationships and cope with stressors effectively (Jedd, K. 2015).

For motherless individuals who have never received nurturing behaviors and the loving language they deserve, off-handed remarks or judgments in adulthood can feel like intentional acts of cruelty. These seemingly innocuous comments can trigger deep-seated feelings of rejection and abandonment, exacerbating existing wounds and reinforcing negative beliefs about oneself.

For women especially, there is an ancient longing for compassionate affirmation and authentic praise from other women with gentle and mothering spirits. Words and actions carry an extra burden and weight for a woman who already feels a deep maternal rejection. This is why hurtful words, unkind lecturing, or neglectful behaviors from friends, colleagues, siblings, and intimate partners or spouses further underscore her sense of uncertainty, rejection, lack of belonging, and unsafety. It is not unusual for the women I work with to name their primary "love language" as words of affirmation or quality time—they have an understandable thirst for affirming kind words and regular time with loving and safe others but are equally ready to be rejected and forgotten at any moment.

Self-loathing is another struggle for some motherless people. It is the internal voice that often reminds them that *their* choices are the *stupidest* choices. That *their* secrets are the *worst* secrets. *Their* ideas are the *worst* ideas. *Their* lies are the *worst* lies. That *they* are the *most* loathsome, and should they let anyone get too close, surely that person would be overwhelmed and repulsed by their thoughts, feelings, choices, needs, struggles, or humanity. In essence, the person with the mother wound is just too much of a burden, and if this person is a woman, she has learned that she needs to reduce herself and be infinitely agreeable and endlessly giving for others to feel good around her and love her.

As you have learned in this chapter, maternal wounds leave a profound imprint on the brain and nervous system, shaping how individuals perceive and interact with the world around them. Healing from these wounds requires compassion, insight, and a willingness to gently confront and address the underlying pain and trauma. Helping these hurting people understand that knowing, naming, and maintaining boundaries is a good thing, and boundaries do not mean abandonment. By leaning into opportunities for healing and growth, individuals with maternal trauma can begin to reclaim their authentic selves and shape healthier relationships with themselves and others.

What If God Was One of Us?

To the faith-based adopted person who was rejected by both the bio mother and the adopted mother, even God (or Goddess, if you prefer) feels like an angry parent in the sky, holding a scorecard of rights and wrongs, ready to burn down that hurting person in an instant with a bolt of lightning. Maddeningly, spiritual shaming is ever present in some faith-based communities, and this shame significantly impacts people with adoption and maternal wounds who are searching for a home to belong to and a community that will finally embrace them. These vulnerable men and women are especially susceptible to pulpit pressure to look, act, and live a "certain way" in order to be loved and accepted by God and others in their church or spiritual family.

I remember going through a challenging period in my early thirties, navigating an unhealthy relationship while working through my own attachment issues, which I was actively addressing in therapy. A long-time Christian female friend who was a few years older expressed her extreme disappointment in me by making statements such as, "Christians don't need therapy," "You are at risk of losing your salvation because of your relationship choices," and eventually, "I won't break bread with sinners," and "Your prayers are worthless if you are living in sin." These statements were like barbed whips striking at my implicit core wounds.

For those who have experienced something similar, the judgments are crystal clear: If you do not step in line, if you struggle or stumble, if you are labeled a sinner who is not worthy to break bread with, or if you are judged to be a person of little faith, you will be cast away, and the casting away process can feel unbearable. Not only is the motherless person not worthy of the love of her earthly mother but her Godly "parent" hates her as well, and she is not worthy of her church family. This, of course, is the exact opposite of what many spiritual teachings espouse, including the Bible.

For those maternal wounded women who have had abortions, affairs, or struggled with addictions, this is typically met with ridicule and rejection in faith-based communities, and harsh criticism is doled out instead of compassion. For abused and abandoned adopted children or motherless foster care girls, understanding how the reproductive system works can be a mystery. Learning about one's body, how to find a gynecologist at a young age, or even knowing how to find birth control can all feel incredibly daunting, frightening, and unknown.

For the foster care adolescent or abused adoptee who finds herself seeking love and belonging through sex, or is the victim of a rape, the unexpected pregnancy can feel horrifying. For some traumatized young women, abortion is a way of avoiding passing potential pain on to the child as the wounded teen or young woman does not feel equipped to parent and, in many cases, can barely take care of herself. The unhealed terror and trauma of her own early abandonment and abuse can sometimes fuel the abandonment of the pregnancy. That haunting choice then regurgitates an acidic message, "You are not worthy of being loved. You are not worthy of being a mother. You will wound your child as your mother wounded you. You are a sinner, and God hates you."

I realize that the topic of abortion, especially in 2024 when I am writing this chapter, is extremely polarizing. I share this not to trigger or politicize but rather to discuss what some adoptees and young women in foster care go through as a result of their own abuse. The intrusive thoughts of terror may include a belief that should they carry to term, once birthed, their child will eventually be taken away, placed into foster care to be molested, tortured, and abandoned, or placed into an abusive adopted situation if that was her experience. This feels like a nightmarish repetition for these young girls and women.

Other women with maternal wounding desire to have many children. I've lost count of the times I have heard from clients and other maternally wounded women say, "I want as many children as possible to create the family I never had," "I never want to be alone in my life again, eating canned turkey soup on Thanksgiving," or "I want to start my own holiday traditions by creating a family that I never had." It is not hard to understand this mind story, and one should never judge women who desire this path in life.

Unfortunately, some traumatized women who go on to have child after child may unwittingly recreate the unwanted dynamics from their own unhealed childhood trauma, passing along the generational baton. For women who have not had access to education, live in poverty, or struggle paycheck to paycheck, their own children may suffer from neglect. Or if abuse or addiction is prevalent, they may end up in the foster care system. To be clear, this is not the story of all foster care or adopted abused women, but it is the story of far too many—unhealed epigenetic trauma being passed along despite a dream of belonging held deeply within that young woman's wounded heart.

Epigenetic trauma refers to the theory that traumatic experiences can leave a lasting impact on gene expression and the transmission of genetic information from one generation to the next. While one's DNA sequence remains unchanged throughout one's lifetime, the way our genes are expressed can be influenced by environmental factors, including stress, trauma, abuse, neglect, and other external stimuli. Epigenetic changes can occur through various mechanisms, such as DNA methylation and histone modification, which can alter the structure of DNA and affect gene activity. These changes can potentially be passed down to future generations, impacting the physical and mental health of offspring. Epigenetic trauma suggests that the effects of trauma are not limited to the individual who experiences it but can reverberate across generations, highlighting the importance of addressing trauma and promoting healing on both individual and societal levels (Chan, J. C., 2018). Scientists are learning that trauma can leave lasting marks on how our genes function—sometimes even affecting children and grandchildren. It's not just what we live through, but what we carry.

The good news is that ongoing research (Yehuda, R. 2018) suggests that epigenetic changes—those influencing how our genes are expressed—are often shaped by our environment and can even be reversible. This means although some of these changes might be passed on, they can still be altered as environments shift.

Understanding how our genes respond to environmental factors, like stress, abuse, or nutrition, remains a key area of study. The idea of "epigenetic flexibility" suggests that if harmful environmental influences are removed or if we develop new ways of managing these influences, our gene expression can adjust accordingly. This flexibility is what allows humans to adapt and overcome challenges, forming the basis of resilience. I invite you to please take a moment to absorb this important and hopeful information.

Controlling the Chaos

The experience of being separated from one's family at birth or during early childhood, enduring a tumultuous journey through foster care systems, and ultimately landing in abusive adoptive homes with mothers who are verbally, emotionally, physically, or sexually abusive is an unfortunate reality for some. While not everyone shares this harrowing story, it is a sobering truth that happens not infrequently.

However, these more challenging stories go unheard amid the tales of happy adoptions and triumphant life transformations that capture headlines. For those who have faced such trauma, the core beliefs of being unlovable, unworthy, and unwanted can permeate every aspect of their lives, breeding uncertainty and insecurity. This uncertainty becomes a constant companion, casting a shadow of doubt and fear over even the simplest of daily decisions. For many wounded individuals, especially motherless women, this state of uncertainty is not just unsettling—it is unbearable.

I share with therapy clients in my practice that it makes sense that abused and traumatized people desire to control outcomes. For women, this coping mechanism is often misunderstood, and they are labeled as "nagging," "bossy," "stuck up," "bragging," "aloof," "bitchy," "angry," "competitive," "controlling," "too direct," "standoffish," "a force to be reckoned with," and "a ball buster." Yet for women with maternal attachment wounds, these ways of managing life, responsibilities, and relationships are often all they have available until they begin to heal and gain compassionate insight into the ways they have been hurt and frightened.

In patriarchal societies, the transmission of the mother wound from one generation to the next can often occur seamlessly, perpetuating cycles of internalized oppression among women. Mothers who have internalized societal norms that position women as inferior may unintentionally pass on these beliefs to their daughters, maintaining a legacy of disempowerment. These norms can also be reflected in certain spiritual systems as well.

Daughters, including fosters and adoptees, raised in such environments often find themselves grappling with a profound dilemma. On one hand, they may feel pressure to conform to their mother's beliefs or even to their culture to maintain a sense of familial harmony and approval. This may involve suppressing their own beliefs and aspirations in favor of adhering to traditional gender roles and cultural expectations.

On the other hand, daughters may recognize the need to challenge these ingrained beliefs and strive for personal empowerment. They may feel a deep-seated desire to break free from the constraints of patriarchal or cultural norms and carve out their own paths independent of societal expectations. This inner conflict can create a sense of internal tension and confusion for daughters as they navigate the complex dynamics of maternal loyalty at all costs versus authentic personal autonomy. These young girls and women may wrestle with feelings of guilt or inadequacy for deviating from their mother's or maternal figures' beliefs while simultaneously yearning for the freedom to pursue their own aspirations.

Ultimately, breaking free from the cycle of the mother wound in patriarchal societies or certain cultural restrictions requires another layer of courage and support for these women. This may involve challenging inherited beliefs, advocating for gender equality, and forging their own paths toward fulfillment and liberation. By recognizing and addressing the impact of patriarchal or cultural norms on mother-daughter relationships, women can begin to unravel the tangled web of internalized oppression and pave the way for generations of empowered women to come.

Helping women who have been negatively labeled understand that their need to control outcomes stems from post-traumatic stress—rooted in complex trauma and reinforced by abusive experiences—offers emotional relief. As they gain insight, recognize their reactions, and cultivate self-awareness, they begin to heal. Over time, their relationship with themselves and others transforms as they enhance self-regulation and agency while reducing feelings of confusion and shame. As described by author, clinician, and researcher, Brené Brown, healing becomes evident when reasonable, clear, and consistent boundaries are set, self-care is prioritized, and the urge to constantly hustle for one's worth diminishes.

Hope or Fantasy—The Double-Edged Sword

Many of the courageous people I work with who suffer from maternal wounding hope that one day their mom will change for the better, acknowledge the harm they have done, and finally show up as a healthy mother. As a child or teen, this hope feels like a life raft as we attempt to keep one nostril above a vicious, unpredictable sea, our eyes always on the horizon, searching for the nurturing we have always wanted. While some mothers may do the work of healing themselves and then healing the relationship with their adult child, sadly, some abusive mothers will not change. They do not heal. They do not mend the holes they have torn into their child's heart.

For adoptees or foster children who were abandoned as infants or toddlers, then rejected as children, teens, and adult daughters and sons, this may eventually manifest as a rejection of self-care, a rejection of self-control, a rejection of self-trust, or a rejection of optimism, a mind state that follows them into adulthood. Instead of moving confidently toward goals and meaningful relationships, a deep mistrust of people may take root because this person has had experiences that have taught them that trusting people equals pain. They have "grown up" far too early, and having had their dreams diminished in childhood, they are reluctant to go down what feels like a dead end again and again. Experience has taught these hurting women and men that trust is equivalent to being taken advantage of, so they keep their antenna ever ready for rejection and abuse.

When it comes to adult female adoptees or former foster daughters, many of these women hold tightly to their tattered hope, believing in a love that was never realized with their mothers. Like the crumbling yellow pages of an old book, these wounded daughters pray that the next emotionally cruel or unavailable partner will somehow rewrite their earlier story, not understanding that they can be the author of each chapter of their life as they heal and grow.

I recall a time when I was about 18 years of age and a boyfriend's mother scolded me for "wasting my God-given intellect" by not attending college and instead going to cosmetology school. She chastened me, stating, "I don't know your parents, but I understand they are both intelligent, highly educated people. I am sure they would be ashamed of you for choosing to be a hair stylist instead of obtaining a bachelor's degree!" I recall how my face burned with confusion and shame, wondering how one goes about obtaining a college degree, not knowing the first thing about college registration. I relied on public transportation during that time in my life and lived with roommates and rescued cats. I barely had two nickels to rub together, and all my internal resources were given over to surviving since moving out on my own at 16 years of age. I did not have any available support, nor did I have the first notion about my worth or "intellect." All I knew was that, once again, an adult was reflecting that I was doing something wrong, letting someone down, and screwing up my life.

I had been so proud of navigating the path to trade school, and the wind was taken out of my wings and replaced by self-doubt. On the outside, I am sure I looked defiant and unmoved, but my insides were fragile and frightened. Ironically, about five years later, now a successful hair stylist living in a cute little beach cottage while working in a salon that catered to wealthy women, this lecturing woman ended up in my chair, appearing older than her years, divorced, and estranged from her daughter.

As I politely styled her hair, she said to me with more than a little bitterness, "What I wouldn't give to be you. Free as a bird, young, beautiful, talented, and successful. You have it all! I remember being so jealous of you and my daughter when you were teenagers. I hated that you were always together and having fun while I was stuck at home with a bunch of kids and a husband who was cheating on me and ogling you while I felt fat and ugly. I grew up with a mother who slapped me, yelled at me every day, and made me feel worthless. Instead of going to college, I married the first loser who got me pregnant so I could escape. I thought if I had my own family, I'd feel happy. But I just turned into my mother, and now my girls won't speak to me."

I nodded empathetically, uncertain exactly how to respond to this woman who seemed both lost and angry with me. I wanted to tell her that I understood her pain more than she might understand but was fearful of incurring more of her rage and projection. It was yet another experience of my younger self swallowing my words and truth in an effort to stay safe.

Very sadly, I learned years later that this woman, who clearly had her own unhealed maternal wounds and went on to wound her own daughters (and me), died from cancer when she was in her late 50s. Her life was cut short. I don't know if she ever resolved her trauma or reconnected with her daughters, but her story serves as a haunting reminder that maternal wounding goes far beyond emotional and mental health consequences, as it also impacts the physical health of many women with mother wounds.

ACEs Study

As explored in another chapter of this workbook, the groundbreaking Adverse Childhood Experiences (ACEs) study examined the profound impact of traumatic experiences during childhood on long-term health and well-being. Over the course of this study, researchers investigated ten different types of adverse experiences, including abuse, neglect, and household dysfunction. The study involved over 17,000 participants and found a striking correlation between the number of ACEs an individual experienced during childhood and their risk for a range of health problems later in life (Felitti, V. J. et al. 1998).

Published in 1998, the ACEs study revealed that individuals who had encountered a higher number of adverse experiences during childhood were more likely to face physical conditions such as heart disease and diabetes, as well as mental health disorders like depression and substance abuse. This research shed light on the profound and lasting impact of childhood trauma on adult health outcomes.

The findings of the ACEs study emphasized the critical importance of early intervention and trauma-informed care in mitigating the negative effects of childhood trauma and promoting resilience. By providing support and resources that recognize and address the impact of trauma, individuals who have experienced adverse childhood experiences can be better equipped to overcome challenges and lead healthier, more fulfilling lives. If you would like to learn more or take the ACEs quiz, please refer to the resource section of this book.

A Message for Mothers, Daughters, and Adults With Maternal Wounding

As we delve deeper into this topic, it has become clear that maternal wounding is far from a one-size-fits-all experience; rather, it is as unique as the person who carries it. Healing from the pain of maternal wounding is an intricate journey, requiring us to unravel and untangle many layers that have been woven around this deep-seated hurt. We don't need to compare whose story is worse—your pain is your pain, and mine is my own. Making gentle space for each other's stories without minimization or criticism is what helps each of us further heal and feel connected.

Beyond a personal mother-daughter/son relationship lies a complex web of experiences and influences, including the traumas of foster care, difficult adoption journeys, childhood abuse, and neglect, as well as societal expectations, ethnic considerations, and cultural norms about motherhood. Woven into this web are spiritual beliefs, personal convictions about what it means to mother and even genetic influences that affect our understanding of being nurtured and how we relate to our own mothers or maternal figures. Together, these factors shape our view of motherhood in powerful, multifaceted ways.

Drawing from my personal journey of healing and in my professional work as a therapist supporting others on similar paths, my sincere hope is that this exploration leads to a profound integration of trauma—an opportunity to reclaim authenticity, awaken one's voice, practice intentional presence, and establish healthy boundaries. Mothers and daughters alike are burdened by the unrealistic expectation of effortlessly juggling multiple roles and responsibilities. This includes the pressure to embody the image of the ever-present, emotionally resilient superwoman who's capable of meeting every demand while sacrificing their own needs and desires. This unattainable standard perpetuates feelings of shame, resentment, exhaustion, and inadequacy, further complicating healing and growth.

Navigating through these societal pressures, mind states and stories, and specific internalized beliefs is a vital aspect of healing the mother wound. It requires individuals to challenge ingrained notions of maternal perfectionism and redefine motherhood in a way that honors their unique experiences, strengths, and vulnerabilities. By reclaiming agency over their narratives and embracing the complexities of maternal identity, individuals can begin to cultivate a sense of empowerment, authenticity, and self-compassion.

For women in particular, I aspire for them to rediscover the essence of their core self and reclaim their sovereignty, standing firmly in their womanhood, whatever womanhood means to that individual, while nurturing and reclaiming the parts of themselves that may have been fractured and scattered.

On the upcoming pages, you'll discover a series of practices tailored specifically for people who are healing from traumatic maternal relationships. First, you'll engage in a breath work exercise aimed at grounding you and fostering a sense of presence within yourself. This foundational practice serves as a cornerstone for the subsequent healing processes.

Following the breath work, you'll embark on a guided imagery journey designed to gently lead you through a nurturing and healing experience. This exercise aims to provide solace and comfort as you gently navigate the complexities of your emotions and memories.

Lastly, you'll be invited to engage in an art reflection exercise, offering you a compassionate opportunity to reconnect with and nurture your inner child. Through the avenue of creative expression, you'll delve into realms of self-compassion and deeper understanding.

As you move ahead, I encourage you to work with a trusted person who can be a journey companion, such as a therapist, coach, friend, or a safe mentor.

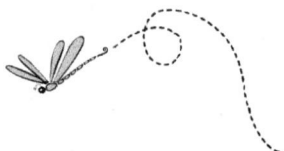

Mindfulness Healing Part I:
Pre-Guided Imagery Preparation and Assessments

Important Safety Tips for Therapists, Facilitators, and Healing Individuals

Environment Consideration and Tips: It can be helpful to "set the stage" prior to a guided imagery exercise. For example, consider the lighting—is it too bright or too low? Another helpful step is putting phones on silent. Also, think about outside distractions, such as barking dogs, traffic, and other interruptions. If possible, minimize outside noises the best that you can. Finally, some individuals like having a blanket or pillow to hold, or you may enjoy diffusing essential oils to support deeper relaxation if there are no allergy concerns. While mindfulness-based guided imagery is not hypnosis, it can be helpful to prepare your environment prior to beginning the guided imagery exercise.

Voice Prosody: An additional gentle reminder is to be aware of your voice prosody if you are leading the guided imagery. Prosody refers to the rhythm and melody of the voice, including intonation, stress, and pauses. Speaking in a softer tone and slower cadence than your normal speaking voice is useful in supporting the guided imagery practice.

Diversity Considerations: Consider the client's culture, age, physical differences (such as hearing loss), gender and orientation, and other unique experiences that may invite a softer or different speaking tone or pace or require that the client keep their eyes open if they prefer. If you are bi-lingual and you and your client speak the same language, ask your client what language they prefer. Ask your client how they wish to be addressed: by name, a nickname, or their preferred pronoun.

Pace Yourself: Remind yourself to take your time as you walk through this process. There is no need to rush. If you are the person facilitating this exercise, slow down and modulate your voice for a relaxed, calming pace. Additionally, it is wise to first practice the exercise with yourself prior to practicing with another person.

Safety Reminder: Safety is the number one consideration with any therapeutic approach or healing intervention. As you lead your client through the following guided imagery exercise, please instruct your client to alert you if they are experiencing any of the following trauma responses. If you are a healing individual doing this work solo, you will also want to consider the following:

- Traumatic memories that are creating a high level of distress
- Feelings of intense fear or panic
- Disturbing or intrusive thoughts
- Suicidal or homicidal thoughts
- Dissociation (if they have developed an awareness of their dissociative states)
- Other crisis concerns (list on the line): _____
  _____

It is also important to ask the client to alert you to the below symptoms or for the person doing this work solo to pay attention if you are experiencing distressing or physical symptoms such as:

- A racing heart
- Tightness in the chest
- Shortness of breath
- Nausea or Intestinal distress
- Feeling faint or dizzy
- Pain in an area of their body
- Feeling as if they are floating outside of their body
- Other somatic concerns (list on the line): _____
  _____

Note for Therapist or Facilitator: Before moving into the guided imagery, please have your client begin with the assessment below. If you are not a licensed therapist and your client is in crisis and exhibiting or discussing symptoms that are out of your scope of practice or experience, please refer your client to an appropriate mental health or medical professional. *If your client is experiencing an immediate life-threatening emergency, please call 911 or the appropriate emergency number if located outside of the United States.*

Note to Solo Reader: *If you are doing this work on your own and believe you are in crisis or may be at risk to yourself, please stop and seek emergency support immediately by calling 911 or your local emergency number.*

Pre-Guided Imagery Assessment Scale

On a scale from 1 to 10 (with 1 = very low, and 10 = very high), please take a mindful moment to assess the following. Circle the number that most accurately applies to you:

Feeling	Assessment (1-10)									
▫ Anxiety	1	2	3	4	5	6	7	8	9	10
▫ Anger	1	2	3	4	5	6	7	8	9	10
▫ Shame	1	2	3	4	5	6	7	8	9	10
▫ Sadness	1	2	3	4	5	6	7	8	9	10
▫ Fear	1	2	3	4	5	6	7	8	9	10
▫ Numbness	1	2	3	4	5	6	7	8	9	10
▫ Confusion	1	2	3	4	5	6	7	8	9	10
▫ Curiosity	1	2	3	4	5	6	7	8	9	10
▫ Hopefulness	1	2	3	4	5	6	7	8	9	10
▫ Calm	1	2	3	4	5	6	7	8	9	10
▫ Joyful	1	2	3	4	5	6	7	8	9	10
▫ Other:	1	2	3	4	5	6	7	8	9	10

Assessment Notes: _____

_____

_____

Mindfulness Healing Part II:

Breath and Somatic Preparation and Prompts

This exercise involves tuning into your breath and body and is followed by the guided imagery exercise and then a final art activity. It's important to note that this may not be suitable for everyone. It's recommended to adapt the following to the specific needs and comfort levels of the individual involved.

Physical Space and Comfort: Find a comfortable sitting or lying down position, with your feet on the floor or cross-legged if that is your preference. If you have a yoga mat or a couch and you or your client prefers to lie down, that is fine. Whatever position will help the person feel relaxed is best.

Prompt 1: Let's pause while you take a few moments to get comfortable.

Prompt 2: When you are ready, you are welcome to close your eyes if that feels comfortable for you. Or if you prefer to leave your eyes open, that is just fine. Whatever allows you to feel most secure is more than acceptable. If your eyes remain open, feel free to rest your gaze on a calming point—near the floor if you're sitting or on the ceiling if you're lying down.

Prompt 3: We will now move forward into the grounded breathing exercise. This will take approximately two minutes.

Grounded Breath Exercise

Prompt: Now that you are in a comfortable position, before we begin the guided imagery, let's move through a minute of grounding breathwork.

1. We will start with the 4-2-7 breath. Start by breathing in deeply through the nose to the count of four, hold for two, and then exhale slowly and intentionally through the mouth to the count of seven. Let's do this three times at your own pace.

2. Now, let's return to easy, relaxed, deep breathing. Take a long breath in through the nose and let out a long exhale out through the mouth. Continue with this breath. **Note to Facilitator: Count to 20 silently.**

3. As you are noticing the gentle rhythm of deep breathing, I would like you to imagine extending compassion to yourself with each intake breath. Then imagine that you are letting go of self-judgment, fear, doubt, shame, or any other emotion you would like to lessen on the release breath. **Note to Facilitator: Count to 20 silently.**

Somatic Relaxation Exercise

Now that we have finished with our grounded breaths, feel free to breathe normally with relaxed, regular breaths. Let's now move into relaxing the body in preparation for guided imagery through the following steps:

1. Notice that your feet are feeling heavier and more relaxed.

2.	Notice that your hands are gently resting at your sides, on your belly, or on your thighs.

3.	Feel your jaw relax and your tongue move away from the roof of your mouth.

4.	Allow your shoulders to relax down from your ear lobes and your elbows to gently relax down from your shoulders.

5.	Bit by bit, the tension moves out of your body as you breathe in and relax and breathe out and relax. Breathe in compassion, hope, and healing, and breathe out stress, judgment, and anger. **Note to Facilitator: Count to 20 silently.**

As we complete this, we will now move into the guided imagery exercise. You can return to your breath work exercises at any point during the guided imagery. The guided imagery exercise will take a few minutes. You may continue to stay in your comfortable position or shift to a different comfortable position. You may also continue with your eyes closed if that is your preference. At any point, you can ask for a time out if needed.

Let's move forward.

Mindfulness Healing Part III:
Guided Imagery
Steps Forward in Healing Maternal Wounds

Note to Therapist or Facilitator: If you notice your client is highly activated during the guided imagery, perhaps demonstrating rapid breathing, shallow breathing, sobbing, or shaking, please have your client pause as you attend to them. This can be done by gently stating that you would like to pause the exercise for a moment, then quietly asking the person by name if they would like a break, support with deep breath work, or to step out of the guided imagery entirely if it has become too overwhelming for them.

Purpose Statement: This guided imagery exercise is designed to assist you in gently and skillfully navigating your next steps forward out of the dark shadows of painful maternal trauma, helping you envision a path forward toward a life characterized by healing and fulfillment. This exercise serves as a tool for reclaiming agency over your boundaries and decisions, increasing self-nurturance, and helping you heal from past painful memories you experienced with your mother or a maternal caregiver. The guided imagery is an empowering support as you learn step-by-step to cultivate a life aligned with your deepest hopes, values, and aspirations free from maternal abuse, criticism, shame, and anger. You deserve to be supported and at peace.

Instructions: This guided imagery exercise will last approximately 15 minutes or so, allowing ample time for each step to unfold gently and respectfully. You are encouraged to move through the exercise at your own pace; there is no rush and no specific expectations other than to honor and support your own process. While prompts or questions may be presented, there is no requirement for verbal responses; you may choose to respond internally if you prefer.

Note: If you are a person with a disability and are unable to walk, please imagine yourself moving through this guided imagery in whatever manner feels best for you. That could be in a wheelchair, with a cane, with pet assistance, or even flying or floating if you prefer. Your own imagination will be honored and valued.

Throughout this visualization journey, you will be guided with care, one step at a time. Memories may surface along the way, but remember, you are not alone. The intention is to help you cultivate the inner strength and clarity needed to lessen the impact of these painful memories. As you visualize yourself navigating out of the shadows, envision emerging on the other side, feeling more healed and whole with a renewed sense of freedom, confidence, and peace.

If you need to take a break, you are welcome to request this at any point.

First Step Prompt: Close your eyes, take a deep breath, and allow yourself to sink into a comfortable position. Imagine yourself standing inside a safe, dark cave; though it is dark, you are safe and not alone. This cave represents the pain and wounds of your relationship with your mother or a maternal figure. You notice that the air inside of the cave feels cold and damp, but you also notice that there is an inviting and gentle light in the distance illuminating the entrance of the cave. Again, you are safe. You are not alone. **Note to Facilitator: Count to 20 silently.**

Next Prompt Step: As you take a step forward, you notice that there are ss emerging from the darkness. Each stone represents a part of your journey toward healing. Notice there are several stepping stones; each stone is wide, secure, solid, and evenly balanced. If you are feeling a challenging emotion as you observe these stones, take a deep breath, acknowledge the emotion, and give yourself permission to notice the emotion without allowing the emotion to overwhelm you. You are safe, you are supported, and you are not alone on this journey. **Note to Facilitator: Count to 20 silently.**

Next Prompt Step: Now, imagine yourself stepping or moving onto the first stone. Feel how solid it is; you have plenty of room to move on this secure stone. As you move onto this first stepping stone, you realize that this stone represents acknowledgment. You deserve to acknowledge the pain and hurt you've experienced in your relationship with your mother or a maternal figure. Your experiences may have been minimized or excused in the past, but together, we are validating that what you endured was wrong and painful. You deserve to have that acknowledged. Allow yourself to feel whatever emotions arise, knowing that it's okay to feel them fully. Notice where the feelings are located in your body, and place your hand there as a comfort if you would like to do so. You are safe, and your experiences and feelings are valid and important. **Note to Facilitator: Count to 20 silently.**

Next Prompt Step: Before we move to the next stone, I invite you to silently ask yourself what you are noticing about this first stone of acknowledgment. What do you need to have acknowledged right now? You can take deep breaths, holding space for any feelings that arise. You are safe and grounded. **Note to Facilitator: Count to 20 silently.**

Next Prompt Step: As you continue to move forward, you reach the next stone, which symbolizes compassion. This stone is also solid and steady, able to fully support you with ease. The compassion stepping stone reminds you to offer yourself compassion and understanding as you navigate through your pain. It also invites you to receive compassionate understanding from safe and supportive people in your life who love you and want to see you heal and be free from the maternal mothering wounds you did not deserve. Let's take a moment on this stone, feeling the compassion and kindness rise around you, reminding you that you are worthy of love and healing. **Note to Facilitator: Count to 20 silently.**

Next Prompt Step: With each stone, you move closer to the entrance of the cave, feeling more liberated and hopeful. The next stone you move to represents boundaries. Take a moment to feel this solid and safe stone supporting you. As you reflect on the boundaries you need to establish to protect yourself and your well-being, can you make gentle room for any emotions that may be surfacing? All emotions are OK to experience, even the more challenging ones. Take a few deep and comforting breaths as you stay on this boundary stone. Then, when you are ready, begin to visualize yourself setting boundaries with your mother or a maternal figure. If they are no longer living, imagine your earlier self who is now setting boundaries with your mother when she was living, or imagine yourself setting boundaries with a person who may currently challenge your boundaries. This may feel difficult, and that is OK. Do your best to imagine sharing your boundaries calmly and with courage and conviction. **Note to Facilitator: Count to 20 silently.**

Next Prompt Step: As you move closer to the cave entrance, you are starting to feel a light breeze on your face. Notice this as you move ahead onto the next solid stone, which represents acceptance. Allow yourself to consider the reality of your relationship with your mother or the maternal figure, living or deceased, without resistance. As emotions rise to the surface, you can observe these feelings without being absorbed into them. Observe, don't absorb. A gentle reminder accompanies this step of this guided journey: Acceptance does not equate to condoning or approving of the past actions of your mother or maternal person. Instead, it signifies an authentic acknowledgment and understanding of the reality of your lived experiences. Accepting the truth of what has transpired without allowing it to define your worth or dictate your future is an important step. Acceptance empowers you to release the burden of resentment and anger, when you are ready, one small step at a time, respecting your pace and allowing space for healing and growth. It's a courageous act of self-compassion, recognizing that while you cannot change the past, you hold the power to shape your present and future with resilience and grace. You get to decide how much or little acceptance of your past you are ready for; your pace is honored. As you stay on this stepping stone, can you start to feel the weight of the pain begin to lift from your shoulders just a little bit? You are moving closer to freedom and healing, and no one is rushing you forward. **Note to Facilitator: Count to 20 silently.**

Next Prompt Step: The final safe stone you move onto represents freedom. Notice this important stone supporting you. This stone is secure, safe, and solid. Remind yourself of how far you've come. Remember, you are not alone on this journey. Allow yourself to reach out for support when needed and continue to nurture yourself with compassion and self-care. You are deserving of healing and wholeness. Take a few moments to breathe this in with slow, deep breaths, in and out, feeling yourself grounded and centered. You can practice feeling free from the burden of pain you did not deserve and no longer need to carry. It may feel different, and that's OK. Freedom is something we practice over time. **Note to Facilitator: Count to 20 silently.**

Next Prompt Step: With a sense of clarity and resolve, move forward at your own pace out of the cave, leaving behind the darkness and pain of the past. Feel the warmth of the sunlight on your skin as you emerge into the open. Take a moment to bask in the light, feeling a sense of freedom and renewal wash over you. Breathe in the sweet, clean air deeply. Remind yourself that you have the strength and resilience to continue your journey toward healing, one step at a time. You are not alone any longer; you are loved and cared for. You are safe. **Note to Facilitator: Count to 20 silently.**

Final Prompt Step: When you're ready, slowly begin to bring your awareness back to the present moment. Wiggle your fingers and toes, if you are able to do so, allowing yourself to fully return to the here and now. Take a deep breath, and if your eyes are closed, notice the light in front of your eyelids. As you exhale, gently open your eyes.

Note to Facilitator or Reader: Engaging in somatic movement, if you are able to do so, such as gentle stretching, walking, rhythmic body movements, or dancing to music, following guided imagery is vital for healing trauma as it allows individuals to release stored tension, process emotions, and reconnect with their bodies, facilitating a holistic approach to healing. Please take 10 minutes minimally to move your body in a way that feels good for you. Yoga, dance, rhythmically swaying, or a short walk are all excellent ways to honor yourself.

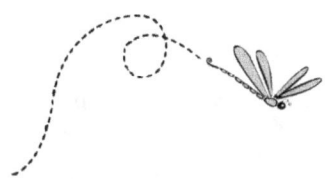

Mindfulness Healing Part IV:

Processing of Guided Imagery
Sharing Your Experience

Purpose for Processing: After the conclusion of the guided imagery, the therapist or facilitator will lead an open and compassionate discussion about what you experienced during the guided imagery. The aim is to allow you to highlight important aspects of the guided imagery and what your experience was like. The facilitator should not judge or correct; instead, extending curiosity and compassion is the goal.

Note: If you are doing this solo without a therapist or facilitator, please pace yourself and notice your energy. Journaling is a beautiful way to mindfully reflect your experience.

Important Considerations for the Facilitator: It is not the role of the therapist or facilitator to interpret, minimize, or re-direct. Rather, it is important for the facilitator to hold a safe space for the client to share their experience and hear the more difficult aspects they may have experienced. This is a time for the facilitator to honor the pain, as well as highlight and emphasize the positive aspects that the client may have experienced during the guided imagery session. Affirm the painful aspects and emotions as well. Remind the client that participating in a mindfulness-based exercise like this is a signal of hope and aids in the possibility of healing and growth.

Note: If you are doing this without a therapist or a facilitator, this is the time to practice self-compassion and being present with yourself.

Processing Questions:

1. What did you notice in the guided imagery?

2. What challenges did you experience?

3. What joys did you experience?

4. Did you have a breakthrough or insight you'd like to share?

5. Do you have any concerns that you'd like to share?

6. What are you feeling in your body currently?

7. Did you notice any self-growth with insight and compassion toward yourself?

8. Did you notice any areas of concern?

Post-Guided Imagery Assessment Scale

Now that you have completed the breath work and somatic exercises, the guided imagery exercise, and the process work, on a scale from 1 to 10 (with 1 = very low, and 10 = very high), let's take a mindful moment to assess the following:

Feeling	Assessment (1-10)									
□ Anxiety	1	2	3	4	5	6	7	8	9	10
□ Anger	1	2	3	4	5	6	7	8	9	10
□ Shame	1	2	3	4	5	6	7	8	9	10
□ Sadness	1	2	3	4	5	6	7	8	9	10
□ Fear	1	2	3	4	5	6	7	8	9	10
□ Numbness	1	2	3	4	5	6	7	8	9	10
□ Confusion	1	2	3	4	5	6	7	8	9	10
□ Curiosity	1	2	3	4	5	6	7	8	9	10
□ Hopefulness	1	2	3	4	5	6	7	8	9	10
□ Calm	1	2	3	4	5	6	7	8	9	10
□ Joyful	1	2	3	4	5	6	7	8	9	10
□ Other:	1	2	3	4	5	6	7	8	9	10

Important Reminder: If you are not a licensed therapist and your client is in crisis and exhibiting or discussing symptoms that are out of your scope of practice or experience, please refer to an appropriate mental health or medical professional. *If your client is experiencing an immediate life-threatening emergency, please call 911 or the appropriate emergency number if located outside of the United States. If you are doing this solo and are in a state of emergency, reach out to 911 immediately.*

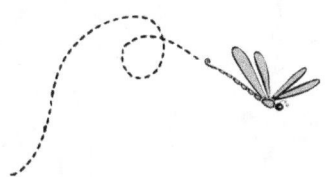

Mindfulness Healing Part V:

Art Exercise—Stepping Stones Forward

Purpose Statement: The following art exercise is designed to help you process and navigate through the journey of healing from the trauma of an abusive relationship with your mother or maternal figure. By illustrating your journey as moving out of a dark cave on a path of secure stepping stones, you will explore and reflect on each stone as you move toward healing while journaling your thoughts and feelings along the way.

Gentle Reminder: Completing this maternal trauma healing art exercise may bring up challenging memories and emotions. Please be gentle with yourself and practice self-care during and afterward. If you feel overwhelmed or need additional support, don't hesitate to reach out to a trusted friend, family member, or mental health professional. Remember, healing is a journey, and you are deserving of love, compassion, and support every step of the way.

Art Exercise Instructions: Gather art supplies such as paper, colored pencils, stickers, or other dry materials. Please be mindful if you choose to use supplies like markers or paints, as these can sometimes bleed through to the next page. You may want to place a blank sheet of paper underneath your work to protect the following pages.

Set aside a quiet moment in your day to complete this exercise at your own pace. You're welcome to use the heart path illustration provided on the next page and color it in, add meaningful words, or name each stone in a way that feels right to you, one at a time. You may also choose to create your own path using real stones, painting words or symbols onto each one. However you choose to engage with this activity, your personal process is honored.

Mindful Reflection Moment

Now that you have completed your guided imagery and art journal exercises, please take some mindful time to reflect on what you have learned. What awareness and insight have surfaced for you from this chapter? Take a moment to write down or share your reflections below. As always, be gentle with yourself:

_____

_____

_____

_____

_____

_____

_____

Instructions: Can you give yourself the gift of self-affirmation? It can be difficult for people who have experienced mother wounds, maternal trauma, abuse, abandonment, criticism, and rejection to affirm themselves. As a support to this step of your healing, affirmation ideas might include statements such as: "I did not and do not deserve any of the abuse from my mother/maternal figure," "I am lovable and valuable and do not need to pay for love or friendship," "My voice and lived experiences matter," and "I am learning to mother myself with compassion and kindness."

In the winged heart on the following page, be present with yourself, take a deep, nurturing breath, and honor your own self-affirmation(s). If you can only come up with one affirmation at this time, that is more than acceptable. If this is too difficult for now, try to think of an affirmation or two for your younger self:

As we close this chapter, I hope what you have learned has deepened your understanding of maternal wounding and its impact, from enmeshment and neglect to various types of abuse and trauma. We explored attachment styles, the unique trauma experiences of foster and adopted children, and maladaptive coping mechanisms that may develop in response.

This chapter also provided a brief look at EMDR and discussed the role of the amygdala, hippocampus, and internalized scripts from trauma. Additionally, we reviewed the ACEs study, epigenetics, and the influence of cultural and patriarchal conformity, including faith-based trauma. Each of these topics invites further exploration as you continue on your journey.

Before you move forward, I want to honor your courage with these affirmations. Take a moment to breathe and let these words settle gently within you: You are significant and deserving of love, care, and healing, even if those meant to nurture you were unable or unwilling to do so. Validating your maternal wounds does not make you ungrateful, weak or unworthy. While your true self is not defined by old wounds or the weight of today's challenges, you have every right to heal, grieve, and grow in your own way and in your own time. You are not invisible or unworthy; your presence matters.

Trust in your journey, and know that this chapter found you precisely when you needed it. You deserve peace, joy, and wholeness. Embrace your capacity for healing and growth step by step, and know you can create a life that feels true and fulfilling. You are a valuable person worthy of love, nurturing, and compassion.

Mari, age 59. Coronado Island.

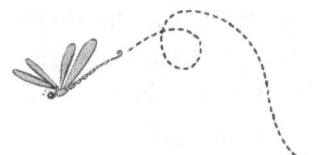

CHAPTER EIGHT

Counterweight Bonding: From Guilt and Exhaustion to Growth and Empowerment

Wendy Quinton

I have come to believe that caring for myself is not self-indulgent.
Caring for myself is an act of survival.

~ Audre Lorde

"I'm such a bad mother!"—those were the words that struck my soul during my first session with Holly. When she walked into my office, she appeared poised and polished, every hair perfectly in place, exuding the confidence of a successful businesswoman. As I prepared for her session, reviewing her intake forms, I had learned she was in her mid-40s, had a degree in business, and had been married once. Holly was also the mother of two children, Brock and Bethany, and had gone through a divorce about two years prior. Yet, despite her outward composure, her words revealed a deep struggle that lay beneath the surface.

From a casual glance, Holly appeared to be the kind of woman who had it all together. Her clothes were well tailored, her makeup was carefully applied, and her outer demeanor seemed confident. As our session started and she accepted my invitation to tell me more about herself, Holly began expanding on her accomplishments, hobbies, and interests, and I found myself wondering, "How does she do it all?" Along with a recent promotion at her job, she was on the board of the local food pantry, helped fund-raise for her city's fire department, and even volunteered, along with her teenage children, at the local animal shelter.

Once Holly finished speaking, I let her know that I appreciated all that she had shared with me about her life and her profession. I continued, "It's good to learn more about those aspects, and if you are ready, I would also like to know what brings you to therapy. From what you alluded to on your intake forms, it seems that there are some challenges you are currently dealing with, and I'd like to know more about them so that I can help."

Holly answered briefly, "Well, in a nutshell, even though I'm doing well at my job, I seem to be failing at all the other parts of my life, especially my relationships. To be concise, my husband divorced me, my son is struggling, and I don't feel like I even know my daughter anymore." I thanked Holly for her summary and added that it seemed as though this was a very painful time in her life and I was glad she had reached out for help. I invited her to share some further background information with me so I could get a clearer understanding of what led up to the divorce, what her son was struggling with, and more about her relationship with her daughter.

Holly agreed and responded, "Sure. Ron and I met at college, fell in love, and had a comfortable life together as we both had good jobs. Like I said, we have two kids, Brock and Bethany, and my life became very busy with all their activities, as well as working full time. I guess Ron and I didn't have much time to connect, and we just seemed to grow apart. Ron did not get involved in as many activities as I did, and when I did stay home on an occasional free night, I noticed that he was drinking more than in the past. He used to have a beer after work or when he was finished mowing the lawn, but it had become three or four most nights. Ron became increasingly withdrawn, not even wanting to participate in the children's activities very often. I just picked up the slack, and the kids and I went on with our lives.

"However, he was soon drinking enough to get drunk, and he was an angry drunk! Sometimes, when he finally came to bed at night, he would yell at me for ignoring him, turning his kids against him, and caring more about my job than I did about being a wife. At first, I was able to brush it off because he was drunk, and Ron didn't seem to remember what he said in the morning. I thought it was a phase. But then it seemed that anytime we had a disagreement, he would tell me that I should spend more time at home with him so things would be better. I begged Ron to stop drinking countless times and told him that if he got some help, then things would improve between us. Ron would just laugh and claim that he didn't have a problem; my absence was the problem."

Holly sighed as she continued with her account. "Ron's constant badgering wore me down, so I stopped going to most of the kids' activities, cut back on my hours at work, and really tried to focus most of my attention and love on him, hoping that it would solve the problem. And, for a time, it really seemed to be working. Ron seemed content with my presence and was more pleasant as he stopped drinking so much. At that time, I remember thinking how good it felt to be the reason that my husband stopped drinking, which was something my mom was never able to accomplish with my father's drinking. I was even able to push down the guilt I felt at not being as available and supportive of the kids because I believed that Ron needed me the most so that he could stay sober."

Holly furthered her story by adding, "Things went on like this for a while, but then one day, I found empty beer cans in the garbage and confronted Ron, demanding to know if he had started drinking again. He denied it and said that they were old cans he had found when cleaning out the garage, and I believed him—or at least I wanted to believe him." Holly looked off into the distance and mused, "I think I wanted so badly for Ron to be sober that I foolishly believed anything he told me." She sat in silence with a far-away look on her face, and I could tell that she was no longer present in the moment.

When I notice this happening with a client, it is an indication to me that they have detached from the here and now, and in order for them to come back into a conscious awareness of the present moment, I would need to help them. Employing mindful techniques to bring the prefrontal cortex back online can be effective since it is responsible for executive functions like decision-making and emotional regulation.

I explained this to Holly, adding that focusing on our five senses can help us reorient ourselves to the present. Continuing, I asked her to look around the room and name five things she could see, four things she could touch, three things she could hear, two things she could smell, and one thing she could taste. At first, Holly looked at me quizzically, but she was a good sport and completed the exercise. When she finished naming all the things, I asked her how she felt. "Well, she said, I was skeptical at first, but I really do feel more present, focused, and calm. I will remember this exercise and practice it when I find my mind wandering at work."

Now that Holly was back in her body and in the present moment, I asked her to pick up her story where she left off. She continued, "One night, I woke up, and Ron wasn't in bed yet. I went looking for him and found him passed out in the living room with empty beer cans shoved under the couch. I mentioned it to him the next day, and he became angry and even threw his shoe across the room hard enough that it dented the wall. He yelled at me for the first time while he was sober and told me that if I would just leave him alone, he wouldn't have to drink so much.

"I was dumbfounded! He had told me before that it was my absence that made him want to drink, and now he claimed that my presence was a hindrance to his sobriety. At this point, I had enough, and I snapped. I yelled at him and asked him what in the world he wanted from me. I accused him of being so unhappy with himself that he was taking it out on me and that I was tired of it. I told him that I had tried to do everything I could to make him stop drinking and go back to being the man that I married but that I was at the end of my rope and didn't know how much longer I could hold on."

Anger edged Holly's eyes as she told me that the words Ron uttered next felt like a dagger to her heart. She continued, "Ron replied calmly with a smirk, saying that what he really wanted from me was a divorce. I was shocked! His calmness and smirk infuriated me all the more, and I barely remember the words I continued to shoot at him. The years of pent-up frustration came pouring out, and I said some very hurtful things", at this point Holly stared at the floor with regret.

Leaning forward, I responded with compassion, "Thank you for sharing that. Given what you've been through, it makes complete sense that anger would come up, and what you are describing is called reactive anger. Reactive anger is a quick, intense response to feeling unsafe, disrespected, or invalidated—often rooted in past experiences where your boundaries were violated, you experienced abuse, or your voice wasn't heard. It's your nervous system trying to protect you, especially when you've been harmed. This kind of anger, while challenging and confusing, isn't a flaw—it's a signal.

Holly nodded in relief, "That makes a lot of sense Wendy! I never thought of it like that before. At the time, I wanted to hurt him as much as he had hurt me. However, looking back, I realize that what I truly wanted was for him to open up and share what was really happening so we could work on fixing it together."

She paused for a moment, then stated in a flat voice, "But that never happened. Ron was unwilling to discuss any problems, and he packed his things and moved to his own apartment shortly afterward." Holly shrugged as she reported, "The divorce was amicable. I think Ron was glad to be free to live his own life again, and the kids seemed to adjust well enough to his absence, as they were already used to it. I think I was just numb at that point, so I threw myself back into being completely involved in the children's activities and made sure I was available for the late-night discussions my kids and I used to enjoy.

At first, they stayed with their dad on most weekends. But when Ron remarried about a year ago and the kids got more involved with activities and friends, it was easier for them to stay with me. Now they only see their dad for special occasions. It seemed to me like the kids were doing fine, but lately, I've been having trouble with my oldest, Brock, who is almost eighteen. A few months ago, I fell asleep on the couch after a long day and woke up when Brock came home after being dropped off from a study session with his friends. He usually slips in without disturbing me, but he was very clumsy that night, and when I got off the couch to hug him goodnight, I distinctly caught the smell of alcohol. I asked him if he had been drinking, and he denied it. Remembering Ron's constant accusations of my nagging, I decided to let it go. I simply chalked it up to teenage experimentation."

Holly sighed and added, "I had almost forgotten about that incident when, a few weeks later, I got a call at work from Brock's school telling me that he was absent that day. In fact, they informed me that there were several unexcused absences recently. This caught me completely off guard, so I immediately called him. He didn't answer. I finished up my day's work quickly and went home in the midafternoon, only to find Brock passed out on his bed and the smell of alcohol filling the room. I looked around and found several empty beer cans under the bed, so I shook him awake, planning to confront him. When I was finally able to rouse Brock, he was very angry. He yelled at me for entering his room without asking, ranting about having no privacy and that he couldn't believe I would snoop through his things. I was shocked into silence as he never talked to me like this before. I quickly exited the room, telling him that we'd talk again when he had sobered up.

"The next day, Brock apologized, telling me that school had been stressful lately and that he would never do it again. Knowing that he had seen what I went through with his dad, I optimistically believed he would straighten himself out. At first, I really tried to do my best to let him live his own life and not nag him about his schoolwork, cleaning up his room, or even his drinking. I just kept hoping that he'd grow out of it or that he wouldn't continue to rebel if I didn't confront him. I realize that I come across as a woman who doesn't put up with any nonsense, but that is my work persona. When it comes to being married and raising children on my own, clearly, I have a lot to learn."

Emotion returned to Holly's voice when she continued, "But Brock did not grow out of it. In fact, things only got worse! When I just couldn't take it anymore, I found myself reverting back to my old behavior, nagging him and trying to control him like I did with Ron. I took

Brock's car keys from him, threatened to ground him, pleaded with him—anything I could think of. But no matter what I say or do, he is still drinking. Except now, he's just getting sneakier about it. I'm at a loss as to what I can do to make him stop. I'm so afraid that he's not going to graduate and that his life will be ruined before he even gets started."

Holly looked at me with pain-filled eyes and added, "Brock is my son, and I am responsible for him. I must take care of him! I had a friend tell me that I need to stop enabling him and that if he continues to drink at home, I should kick him out of the house. But I can't do that! He's my son, and besides, it's probably because of the divorce that he drinks. I can't believe I'm such a horrible mother that my son is turning into an alcoholic." Holly pleaded with me, "Just tell me what to do to make him stop drinking, and I'll do it!"

I sat quietly for a moment and took a deep breath as I processed all that Holly had shared with me. "Holly, thank you so much for sharing your story with me," I said gently. "It takes a great deal of courage to be vulnerable with someone you've just met, and I can see how deeply you love your son and how desperate you are to help him."

Her eyes welled with tears, and for a moment, we sat in silence together. I could feel the weight of what she carried—the heartbreak, the helplessness, the fierce protective instinct of a mother trying to make sense of something overwhelming. There was no need to rush or fix anything in that moment; what mattered most was being present with her in it.

I noted that time was almost up in our first session, so I gently explained to Holly that she had shared some very painful experiences, and that her body was likely in an activated state because of it. I let her know that before she left, I'd like to help her return to a calmer, more grounded place. She nodded in agreement, and we transitioned into a brief mindfulness exercise. We practiced breathing deeply—in through the nose and out through the mouth—allowing each breath to settle her nervous system. We continued until I noticed the tension begin to soften from her shoulders, her breath growing slower and more steady.

Once her body calmed, I asked her if I could leave her with some important words that she could ponder over the coming week. She nodded, and I continued, "I sure wish I had a magic wand that I could wave and relieve all your worries. But the truth is, you can't control the actions of another person, no matter how much you want to, even those of your son. I know that if there was anything in your power that could make Brock stop drinking, you would have already done it. I know that is a very hard truth to wrap your head around. But along with that truth, I will make you a promise that if you can shift your focus back to yourself and keep showing up for yourself, eventually, you will find great relief and peace in knowing that you are only responsible for yourself and you cannot control or change another person, even your seventeen-year-old son."

Holly met my gaze, shook her head in disbelief, and replied, "If I can't do something to help and change Brock, it just feels hopeless." I responded compassionately, "I know it feels that way right now, and all I ask is that you allow me to hold on to this hope for you until you can hold it for yourself. I've been on this same journey for years, and I'm speaking from experience. Will you allow me to hold your hope for the time being?" She thought for a moment and finally answered, "Yes, I've tried everything else, so I can try that."

This agreement marked the beginning of Holly's healing process, one that I was honored to support her through. Her road to recovery was anything but straightforward, filled with challenges and unexpected turns. At first, it was difficult for Holly to shift her focus away from what she wanted to change in other people and concentrate on her own feelings and behavior. However, as we continued to meet, she was able to take a step back from trying to control the chaos, check in with herself, and talk about how life was affecting her.

Using a chart of basic emotions that hangs in my office, Holly became skilled at identifying the exact emotions she was experiencing. It took a little longer for her to pinpoint where in her body she felt those emotions and describe the sensations, but with time, she embraced this practice as well. I knew she had fully internalized this skill during a session when she recounted a recent argument with Brock. He had accused her of "making him drink" because she had tolerated his father's drinking for so long. As Holly shared this with me, she instinctively clutched her stomach, took a deep breath, and said, "I feel so guilty, and it feels like my stomach is being squeezed in a vice."

Because Holly reported that she often feels guilty, we took time to understand what guilt is and how it differs from shame. I explained that guilt says, "I did something wrong," and shame says, "I am wrong." Behaviors that make us feel guilty are ones that we can make amends for, whereas shame is an overarching feeling that we will never be good enough or can never be forgiven.

In continuing our discussion about guilt, Holly shared that she felt remorseful for numerous things: staying too long in a harmful marriage, exposing the kids to their father's alcoholism, being too involved in other things like her work and marriage to give Brock and Bethany the attention they needed, and for not having the power to keep her marriage intact. She also felt guilty for focusing too much on Brock's needs and not spending enough time with Bethany. We discussed the importance of looking at each area that brought feelings of guilt and deciphering whether the guilt she felt was appropriate or not.

For guilt to be appropriate, it must be caused by a behavior that we recognize as going against our own values. Once the guilt is recognized, it can be alleviated through making amends and self-forgiveness. For example, Holly looked at the guilt she felt when thinking that she was ignoring her daughter. She realized that she had spent a great deal of time focusing on Brock's problematic behaviors and just assumed that Bethany was okay without taking the time to check in with her. Holly was aware enough to know that parents cannot always treat their children exactly equally, as they all have different needs at different times in their lives, but she could make a concerted effort to spend more time with her daughter.

At the same time, as we were working on the concept of guilt in our sessions, I suggested to her that she might find it helpful to meet with others who are facing situations like hers. I explained to her that there is a Twelve-Step support group called Codependents Anonymous (CODA). I clarified that while some people connect to the term codependency, others feel like the word insinuates blame and partial responsibility for the behaviors of their spouse, partner, child, or others. I shared that I like to use the term "counterweight bonding" instead of codependency, as it signifies that although the relationship is off balance, it can be restored. I further explained that in the physical world, counterweights are commonly used in various mechanical systems to balance the weight of an object, helping to stabilize the system and maintain equilibrium.

I shared an example of the counterweight bonding principle using the elevator system. The elevator car and the counterweight are connected by a system of pulleys and ropes so that when the car moves up, the counterweight moves down, and vice versa. When it is properly balanced, the counterweight helps to share the load rather than the car bearing the full weight of the load. The counterweight helps reduce the amount of energy needed to force the elevator to move and since the motor is not working as hard the life of the system is extended. As well, the counterweight helps reduce the likelihood of sudden drops and allows it to maintain equilibrium.

Problems arise when the counterweight is off-balance, causing several issues:

- The load is not balanced and unmatched to the weight of the elevator car, so it uses more energy, may overheat, and eventually, the mechanism will fail.

- If the counterweight is not balanced properly, it takes more energy to move the car, increasing with the weight of the elevator.

- The movement of the elevator becomes unstable when the balance is off, and it may take more time to start, stop, and experience jerks and uneven motion. This again causes increased wear and tear on the system's parts.

- Increased wear and tear on the whole system is caused by unequal balance, which leads to frequent breakdowns and an earlier need for replacement.

- If the system is significantly unbalanced, the elevator car could become stuck between floors or even experience brake failure, making the system unsafe.

- With enough vibration caused by an off-balanced counterweight, the soundness of the entire structure puts the elevator services at risk and could cause severe damage over time.

Once Holly was clear about how counterweight balances function in elevators, we had a discussion about how to relate the analogy to her life and the "system" in which she lives with her son, Brock. I reiterated that for the structures of her life to be stable and for her to maintain personal equanimity, the load within their relationship needs to be properly balanced. She and Brock are connected by a system, not of ropes and pulleys, but of life, family, experiences, and responsibilities, and if Holly continues to carry an unequal share of the load, the consequences could be severe. As we looked at each of the problems that can arise with an off-balance counterweight in an elevator, Holly was able to see the dangers of continuing the uneven relationship she has with Brock.

- Holly readily observed that the load of responsibility within her and Brock's relationship is unbalanced and that she is bearing the entire weight of Brock's problematic alcohol use. Just like the elevator, she could see that she would eventually "overheat" and fail, as evidenced by their numerous heated discussions and her resultant exhaustion.

- Holly easily related to the concept of increased energy usage in an unbalanced elevator system, as she constantly feels overwhelmed, and trying to keep Brock balanced is exhausting her limited supply of energy.

- Holly was able to grin briefly when she remembered that an unbalanced counterweight results in jerky movement, as she reported that she often felt like she was being jerked back and forth as she related to Brock. She completely understood the concept of the elevator taking more time to stop and start as she racked her brain to find new approaches to control Brock's drinking. She would have hope and renewed energy as she tried each one, but eventually, her efforts failed, and it took longer and longer for her to try again.

- There was again a brief smile as we looked at the next danger of an off-kilter pulley system, and she reported that she, too, had frequent breakdowns and so much wear and tear on her emotional system that she feels much older than her actual age.

- Holly shared that she often felt like her life was "stuck between floors," and she did not know if she had the strength to move on or the knowledge of how to get back on track in her relationship with Brock and herself. She feels as though she is very close to brake failure in that she will be unable to stop his life or her own from spiraling downward toward a crash.

- As she came to see that an unbalanced counterweight in an elevator would eventually damage the whole structure, Holly shared that not only was her relationship with Brock suffering, but her relationship with her daughter, her performance at work, and many other aspects of her life, including sleeping and eating schedules, were being harmed by her lack of equanimity.

Now that Holly had discovered how her uneven relationship with Brock was damaging to her and those around her, we discussed the "bonding" element of the counterweight system. Even though many partners, parents, friends, and family of those who struggle with addiction are aware of the injury it is afflicting on them, they have difficulty determining how to make lasting changes within the relationship.

Just like the ropes and pulleys of an elevator system can become entwined and unsafe, the bonds between people can become tangled and cause harm. It is one thing to realize that the system is unbalanced and quite another thing to learn how to redistribute the weight to even the load and get unstuck. Just as elevator systems need regular maintenance and inspections, our relationships need regular care and correction. I shared with Holly that before we delve into the process of repairing her unbalanced bonds, I would like to give her further examples of counterweight bonding.

The second analogy I used with Holly is one that I have heard within the recovery community, this one focusing on the process of donating blood. I asked Holly if she knew how much blood is typically taken during a donation, and, as she is a regular donor, her answer was "just under a pint." I then asked her to imagine what would happen if she told the technician that one pint was not nearly enough and that to truly help someone, she needed to donate three pints—the average amount needed for a transfusion. After thinking for a moment, Holly said the technician would probably warn her that taking that much would compromise her health. I agreed and reminded her that the body needs time to recover and replenish blood cells and plasma after a donation before it is safe to donate again. She readily acknowledged that if she gave more than a pint, it could be dangerous to her health, and she, herself, might require a transfusion.

I asked her if she was able to apply this analogy to the concept of counterweight bonding in her life. She thought for a moment and replied, "If I give too much of myself, my time, energy, and attention to Brock or others, I will deplete my own supply. If I give too much of myself away, it will endanger my own health." She sighed deeply when she finished, speaking as though this new realization of counterweight bonding was resting fully on her shoulders.

I spoke gently to Holly and shared that I may be wrong but that it appeared to me that learning about this issue was causing her to feel weighed down. I asked her to take a moment to observe what was happening in her body and to put it into words if she could. She sat in silence for a few moments and replied, "Yes, seeing how unbalanced my relationships are and knowing that I am endangering my health to try to control other's well-being feels like a heavy burden on my shoulders."

I nodded and asked Holly to take some deep breaths and sit with that heavy feeling for a moment longer. Then, I asked what she would like to do with that load. She easily replied that she would like to give it back to whoever it really belonged to or simply put it down, but she was unsure of how to do that. She remarked that she had been carrying this load for so long that she feared that letting go of it would be too unfamiliar or difficult. "I'm not sure who I would be if I wasn't carrying others weight around," she noted.

"Holly," I replied, "this is where I can share my experience, strength, and hope with you." I can assure you it's possible to learn to give a reasonable amount of your time and energy to others while ensuring that you replenish and balance yourself through mindfulness, support systems, and self-care. You can become healthy, stable, and able to support others in an equanimous way." Holly agreed that living the life that I described to her is her ultimate goal and that she would like to begin working on ways to achieve this result. Given this, during our subsequent therapy sessions, that is what we focused on.

I began by outlining the principles of mindfulness, including mind states and mind stories, along with mindfulness practices as outlined in Chapter Two, and Holly learned quickly. She especially enjoyed the yoga class she began to attend, reporting that moving and balancing her body relaxed her muscles and cleared her mind. Her favorite pose was "Mountain Pose," as it reminded her to pay attention to her body's alignment, bringing a sense of calm and stability and helping her set an intention to remain balanced in her relationships.

Holly also began to attend a local Codependents Anonymous (CODA) group and reported that she learned a lot from her exposure to the principles of healthy relationships. She appreciated that her fellow group members offered her the support and encouragement she needed for the tough decisions and conversations that were part of her healing path. During this time, she alternated her CODA meetings with Al-Anon meetings, a special Twelve-Step group for those affected by another's alcoholism, as well.

One principle that Holly learned early in the Twelve-Step program is that she did not cause her son's disordered drinking. She was not able to control it, nor was she able to cure it. In the past, she believed that as Brock's mother, it was her job to get him through anything and that she should have a kind of supernatural ability to do so. Once she realized that she wasn't powerful enough to make him want to choose to stop drinking, Holly was finally able to accept the truth that though she loved her son deeply, she did not cause him to be dependent on alcohol.

Another tool that helped Holly work through her guilt and shame was eye movement desensitization and reprocessing (EMDR). For further information on EMDR, please see Chapter Six. While processing her memories, Holly was able to get to the root of her guilt, which was the mind story she had cultivated through her lived experiences that if she was lovable enough, helpful enough, or wise enough, then those around her would have loved her enough to stop their problematic alcohol use. She realized that she carried this core belief of not being enough all the way from her childhood into her adult relationships.

She also noticed that it showed up in the workplace, where she realized that she was constantly striving to do more so she could be viewed by her boss and coworkers as good enough. During our sessions together, Holly was able to accept that she is inherently enough simply because she is a human being. She also came to understand that trying to control others was a maladaptive coping skill that kept her safe as a child but one that is unnecessary now that she is an adult.

Another emotion that Holly wrestled with is fear, and the confident outer mask that she often wore masked this fear. Her fear was triggered at the start of our work as she began to realize that the best way to care for herself and for Brock was to learn how to set and maintain healthy boundaries. This involved allowing Brock to experience the natural consequences of his own actions rather than swooping in to arrange all the outcomes for him. She had numerous fears when she began this process: fear that he would hate her and choose to live with his father, fear that he would become further entrenched in alcohol dependence, fear that he would blame her for his behavior forever, fear of legal issues, fear that he would accidentally harm himself while intoxicated, and fear that Brock's actions reflected poorly on her parenting skills and that others would judge her as incompetent.

To assist Holly in discovering the root of her fears, we used the Digging for Gold exercise developed by author Todd Pressman in his book *Deconstructing Anxiety* (Pressman, 2019). Pressman explains that to help clients uncover thoughts, feelings, and the causes behind their behaviors, we can ask three main questions. In the same way that a miner digs and sifts through layers of dirt to find gold, asking these questions helps clients get to the valuable insights that are buried beneath the surface of their thoughts and emotions.

Completing this exercise has many benefits, such as:

- **Self-Awareness:** As clients explore and understand the mind stories that motivate their behavior, they will discover more about themselves.

- **Identify Root Causes:** Becoming aware of the mind states that underlie a client's mind stories will allow them to understand and address issues such as relational difficulties, unhealthy coping skills, and harmful thought patterns.

- **Challenging Unhelpful Mind States:** By becoming attuned to emotions through these questions and mindfulness, clients will be more skilled in identifying triggers, which will allow them to maintain regulation and equanimity.

- **Core Values:** Uncovering the "gold" of self-awareness through reflecting on these questions can allow clients to make decisions based on their ideals and principles.

- **Enable Change:** The Digging for Gold exercise can clarify what mind states are driving a client's mind stories, and with this insight, they will be able to develop new strategies to adopt healthy coping skills, leading to behavior that is in line with their core values.

The Digging for Gold exercise, modified to include mindfulness language, involves asking guided questions like the following. Reminder: Think of your mind state as the projector and your mind story as the movie it plays. A mind state is your current emotional or mental condition—like judging, curious, fearful, calm, or angry—that colors how you see the world. The mind story is the narrative your mind creates in that state, often shaped by past experiences or fears. When you become mindful of both, you can pause the movie, adjust the projector, and see things more clearly.

1. What is the underlying fear that is driving this behavior or emotion? What is the mind state that influenced you to act this way?

2. What past experiences may have led to or influenced your current state? What are the mind stories that resulted from the mind state identified in the first question and the resulting patterns and triggers?

3. How does this belief serve you, and what might happen if you let go of it? As you reflect, consider if this behavior is beneficial or if it is holding you back or causing you to suffer.

Holly was able to use this exercise, gradually peeling back layers of thoughts and emotions to reveal deeper truths. It was around this time that she decided she was ready to set a boundary with Brock. She determined that she would no longer be responsible for waking Brock up for school in the morning since it only caused her to start her day feeling anxious and gave Brock an opportunity to be disrespectful to her. She wanted to be able to set this boundary but reported she was too afraid to do so.

Using the questions from the "Digging for Gold" tool, I asked Holly, "'Why is it upsetting to you to give Brock the responsibility to get himself up for school?" She quickly replied that she was afraid that he would be late for school every day. I continued with the next question, inquiring, "What are you afraid will happen next?" Holly answered easily, "That he'll fail his classes, and he won't graduate from high school." When I asked the final question, "What are you afraid that you will miss or lose?" Holly took more time to think, and at first, her answer was that Brock would never have a successful life.

I gently pointed out that she was answering for Brock and not herself, so she paused to reconsider her answer a while longer. Finally, Holly revealed that her fear is that she would lose her esteemed position in the community if people found out that her son did not graduate from high school, and she would be disgraced in front of her ex-husband, Ron, because she did not parent well. After reflecting on her answer, she became aware that what she really feared was her own perceived shame—a feeling that was very uncomfortable for her.

After reviewing what we had previously discussed about shame, Holly realized that the possible consequences of setting a boundary triggered her core fear of being judged as not good enough. She was able to remind herself of her inherent worth and that she was not responsible for other's perceptions of her. Once she recognized this, she was able to refocus on the purpose of the boundary (to let Brock know she would no longer be waking him up for school so she could relieve the stress between them), and it became easier for her to implement it. An added benefit was that she was able to be curious about how this boundary might help Brock (perhaps he would realize that he is responsible for his own choices and consequences), and rather than living in fear of what might happen next

(Brock failing his classes), and the fear of what she might lose (her reputation), she was able to release some of the fear that she had felt trapped in.

As Holly first began to discontinue absorbing the costs of her son's decisions and allow Brock to face natural consequences, their relationship became more strained. Brock was angry that his mom wasn't picking up the pieces of the messes he made, and he tried very hard to manipulate her so that she would give in to his demands. However, as Holly stuck to her boundaries, and with the support of her sponsor and friends, Brock began to see that alcohol was making his life unmanageable. At the same time, Brock's basketball coach and a few of his fellow teammates staged an intervention for him, which they did with empathy and a focus on support, and it proved to be very helpful.

In Brock's structured intervention, the coach first talked to him in private, expressing his concern for the behaviors he had noticed, like Brock arriving late or not at all to practice and that his overall stats were dropping. He assured Brock that he was coming from a place of care and truly wanted to help. After this initial conversation, Brock's teammates also took the opportunity to express their concerns, letting Brock know how his increased drinking was affecting them and the team. They let him know that they were available to him for whatever support he may need.

The coach then explained to Brock that in order to maintain the team's standards, he would be required to attend all practices and fully participate, or they would have to bench him for the remainder of the season to provide a healthy environment for everyone. The coach quickly followed up that boundary by suggesting that Brock might benefit from attending a recovery group for teens and provided him with the details. Brock's best friend on the team offered to accompany him, which gave Brock the courage he needed to begin attending the group. This compassionate and supportive intervention that focused on Brock's well-being was the catalyst he needed to make positive changes in his life.

Holly's healing journey continues to be a work in progress, and her growth has been evident from that first session until now. She remains an active member of the Al-Anon Twelve-Step group, and as part of doing her step work, she came to Step 9 and made amends to her daughter. Step 9 of the Twelve Steps from Alcoholics Anonymous and other 12-Step programs is:

> "Made direct amends to such people wherever possible,
> except when to do so would injure them or others."

She owned the unintentional harm that had been done to Bethany, letting her daughter know that she now understood that by focusing so heavily on trying to control and cure her ex husband Ron, and her son Brock, she overlooked her daughter's needs, and she apologized to her. Holly and Bethany now plan weekly outings and are enjoying a closer relationship.

Although Holly's ex-husband, Ron, has not yet agreed to attend family counseling, he is making efforts to be more present in the children's lives. Holly knows that recovery is a day-by-day process, and although she doesn't know what the future holds, she can now trust herself, with the help of her support system, to take care of herself and set a healthy example for her children.

The term "codependency" has understandably received pushback from some betrayed partners, individuals, and even therapists. For them, this term feels stigmatizing, as if they are being labeled or held accountable for their partner's choices. Others, however, find that it aptly describes the dynamics of their relationship. While I respect each client's preferred language, I have created an alternative term that I find more accurate and less potentially charged: "counterweight bonding."

Counterweight Bonding

This describes a relationship dynamic where one person compensates for perceived or actual deficiencies in the other by taking on the greater share of the responsibility and emotional labor in the partnership. This can lead to an uneven relationship, where one person carries a disproportionate amount of the load (Wilkens & Foote, 2019).

Some examples of counterweight bonding occurring in relationships:

- When one person takes on the position of deciphering and managing the emotional climate, this person is ultra-aware of even slight changes in the other's mood that would indicate that it is becoming negative and modifies their own behavior to mitigate any adverse effects that may occur. This behavior can arise not just in marriages but also in sibling relationships, between parents and children, or even between friends.

- When a roommate assumes all household responsibilities, believing they must do so to maintain harmony or avoid conflict.

- When a parent seeks to keep their child from experiencing the natural consequences of their unwise actions and suffers themselves because of it.

- When one partner continuously nags and scolds the other and spends so much time trying to change the other's behavior that they are blind to their own shortcomings.

Counterweight bonding often involves a silent agreement that one person will "carry the load" while the other is free of responsibility. The stress of being in a relationship marked by counterweight bonding often leads to burnout, frustration, and resentment and can happen across many different types of relationships. Especially for those whose relationships involve a significant other with an addiction, counterweight bonding can have serious mental, physical, and emotional consequences (Blanc et al., 2022).

When the relationship system is unstable and out of balance, the load needs to be redistributed to restore its equilibrium. In relationships, this involves accepting the reality that we do not have control over another person's choices, actions, or recovery. This can be a hard truth to learn and one that I have personally struggled with over the years. Learning that my son had an addiction brought so much pain to my heart that I thought I might not survive. At first, I managed by trying to help him in any way I could—physically, financially, and emotionally. I stopped taking proper care of myself and threw all my energy into trying to heal him. This was especially hard as I was recently divorced and my son lived in another city, but I gave it my all.

Not surprisingly, the relationship became unstable, and I realized that if I did not make changes to my behaviors, I could become financially destitute. I had to accept that my efforts were not bringing about the recovery I wanted for him. With the help of my amazing support system, including therapists, Twelve-Step group members, friends, and therapy group members, I was able to redistribute the weight in the relationship and focus on simply balancing my own load. I am happy to report that my son is sober as of this writing, and our relationship has resumed its rightful balance, with my place in his life being to simply listen, love, and pray.

Emotions

In my work with clients, I have found that people will go to extreme lengths to avoid experiencing painful emotions. Some clients turn to substances such as drugs or alcohol to numb emotional pain. Others may push themselves to the brink of death, debt, or severe illness in an effort to please those they care about, all to avoid the pain of disappointing them.

Helping clients recognize, accept, and feel all their emotions is an integral part of the therapeutic process. The concept of basic emotions was developed by Psychologist Paul Ekman and later enhanced by others such as Psychologist Robert Plutchik and author Pia Mellody (Ekman, 1992). These include:

ANGER	FEAR	PAIN	JOY
Resentment	Apprehension	Sad	Hopeful
Irritation	Overwhelmed	Lonely	Elated
Frustration	Threatened	Hurt	Happy
	Scared	Pity	Excitement

LOVE	SHAME	GUILT	PASSION
Affection	Embarrassment	Regretful	Enthusiasm
Tenderness	Humble	Contrite	Desire
Compassion	Exposed	Remorseful	Zest
Warmth			

Meditation

Once clients become aware of their emotions, learning to tolerate them, rather than judge or escape them, is mastered through the practice of mindfulness, further described in Chapter Two, and meditation can be an excellent place to start. One of the ways we can introduce meditation to our clients is through the RAIN method, outlined by Tara Brach (Brach, 2020). In this approach to meditation, Brach encourages her students to:

> **R**ecognize what is going on: Identify and acknowledge any emotions, thoughts, or physical sensations that are present without judgment.

> **A**llow the experience to be there, just as it is: Create space for emotions without resistance.

> **I**nvestigate with interest and care: Be curious about what you are feeling, gently exploring what needs, beliefs, or fears that are influencing your current mind state.

> **N**urture with self-compassion: Bring a sense of kindness and care to yourself, including affirmations, self-compassionate thoughts, or imagining what you would say to a dear friend in a similar situation.

The RAIN method helps individuals process challenging emotions and experiences in a mindful way, reducing reactivity and fostering self-compassion. By going through these steps, individuals can gain insight into their habitual patterns and cultivate a deeper sense of peace and acceptance.

Dialectical Behavioral Therapy

Along with mindful meditation, learning to tolerate distressing emotions can also be acquired through the practice of Dialectical Behavior Therapy (DBT). It was originally developed by Dr. Marsha M. Linehan as a treatment for borderline personality disorder (Linehan, 1993). Since its inception, it has been adapted for other mental health conditions. There are four modules included in this teaching: Mindfulness, Distress Tolerance, Emotional Regulation, and Interpersonal Effectiveness.

Mindfulness: As it relates to DBT, mindfulness includes a concept called Radical Acceptance, which means that instead of resisting what is happening in our lives, we accept the current situation for what it is. This does not mean that we necessarily approve or feel comfortable with it, nor is meant for us to tolerate abuse. Instead, we refuse to expend precious energy by reacting in anger. Instead of judging the situation or denying how we feel about it, we accept reality. It involves staying in the present moment, not looking back with so much regret that we get stuck in the past, and not focusing so much on the future that we are paralyzed. Once we acknowledge what is happening in the here and now, we can use our energy to be curious about how we can change the situation, if needed, in the future.

Distress Tolerance: This involves practicing important coping skills needed to withstand difficult emotions without resorting to self-harming behaviors. These skills can include self-soothing, participating in healthy activities, and thinking about the outcome of actions before they are taken. Self-soothing involves practicing behaviors that relax the body and the mind. These can include listening to calming music, practicing a safe-place visualization described in detail in the guided imagery section below, or taking a warm shower.

Options for healthy activities may incorporate taking a walk in nature, coloring mandalas, guided imagery, breath work, or reading poetry. Thinking before acting could involve making a pro-con list, creating a list of core values and comparing it to optional responses, and writing out several powerful self-affirmations.

Another valuable exercise is to create two lists of what you do and don't have control over and then explore where you may demonstrate an internal versus an external locus of control:

List One: The Things We Have Control Over

In life, there are certain things we can directly influence. These include our thoughts, actions, responses, and attitudes. We have the ability to set personal boundaries, make decisions, manage our emotions, and choose how we interact with others. By taking responsibility for these aspects of ourselves, we empower our lives and shape our experiences. Focusing on what we can control helps us build resilience, stay grounded, and create positive change within our own lives, no matter the circumstances.

Internal Locus of Control: An internal locus of control supports "list one." This refers to the mindset that one's choices and behaviors directly influence the course of their life. Individuals who hold this perspective often have a strong sense of self-confidence and feel empowered to shape their own circumstances through their actions and decisions. For those who have experienced a great deal of traumatic experiences, mental or physical health challenges, abuse, poverty, or other experiences that have impacted their well-being, forming an internal locus of control can be difficult but not impossible with the appropriate level of self-compassion, support, and healing.

List Two: The Things We Do Not Have Control Over

On the other hand, many aspects of life remain entirely outside our control. We cannot change other people's thoughts, feelings, or behaviors, nor can we cure their addictions or manage their anger. We also can't dictate external events, outcomes, or the functioning of larger societal systems. Realizing how little we truly control can feel surprising—even unsettling at times.

Yet in that realization lies a quiet kind of freedom. When we accept what is beyond our reach, we can let go of unnecessary frustration and worry. By shifting our focus to what is within our control—our choices, responses, values, and boundaries—we create space for greater clarity, inner peace, and personal empowerment.

To be clear, this acceptance doesn't mean we stop advocating for causes that matter to us or give up on meaningful action. It simply means we recognize that while we can show up wholeheartedly, we cannot control outcomes or other people. And that understanding can be both grounding and liberating.

External Locus of Control: Having an external locus of control means believing that forces outside of oneself, such as luck, fate, or the actions of others, determine life's outcomes. For those with this mindset, it can feel as though they have little influence over their own circumstances, leading to feelings of resentment, anger, shame, low self worth, helplessness or frustration. This perspective can be particularly challenging, as it may cause individuals to feel like they are simply reacting to life rather than actively shaping it, making it harder to find motivation or take initiative.

Emotional Regulation: This skill can be acquired by learning how to notice, identify, feel, and appropriately express feelings. By practicing how to understand emotions and pausing to respond (rather than reacting), emotional health can be attained.

Interpersonal Effectiveness: This is a further skill needed to develop and maintain healthy relationships. It involves assertiveness training, models of effective communication, and learning how to maintain a relationship throughout conflict. It allows people to ask for what they want and set healthy boundaries.

Original Wound Theory

Author Judith Beck discussed the theory of an original wound by explaining that when painful things happen to people at a young age, they begin to form basic ideas about themselves and their world (Beck, 2020, p. 30). These core beliefs become so ingrained that they rarely talk about them or question them; they are accepted as truth.

For example, say a child is made to figure out a math equation or learn a new software program while the class looks on. Even though they can solve the problem when calm or with support, due to the fear of being the center of attention, they freeze. The teacher scolds them publicly, commenting that if they can't solve even this easy problem, they will probably always struggle with arithmetic or technology. Because that embarrassing moment becomes locked in the child's memory, they come to believe that they are poor at math or technology, and their grades going forward prove this out.

Other core beliefs that people develop from original wounds are: "I'm not enough," "I must manage others' emotions to feel safe," "I'm clumsy," or even "I'm unlovable." By helping clients heal the trauma that caused their original wound, discover the core beliefs they developed from it, and assist them in challenging and reframing their beliefs about themselves, they can be free to discover who they really are and what they can accomplish.

Generational Trauma

In Holly's story above, you can see that a portion of the trauma she experienced was generational. Generational trauma denotes the psychological effects of trauma that are passed down from one generation to the next. This trauma can be likened to emotional scars that are inherited from your ancestors, which affect you even if you didn't go through the original traumatic event yourself.

Holly witnessed the way her mother interacted with her father regarding his drinking, and she, in turn, related to her son in much the same way. Children living with parents who are experiencing post-traumatic stress can be adversely affected by exposure to this intergenerational trauma. It can happen after horrific events such as genocide, war, slavery, or systemic oppression. Experiencing these events can change the way survivors parent their children, and their offspring can be diagnosed with anxiety, depression, and PTSD even though they did not actually experience these traumatic events firsthand.

Research suggests that parents can pass on the effects of trauma to their children both during pregnancy and even before conception. This occurs through epigenetic mechanisms, which do not change the DNA sequence itself but can influence how genes are expressed—potentially impacting stress responses and emotional regulation in the child (Yehuda, 2018).

As part of the therapeutic process, it's important to help our clients understand that some aspects of their mental health challenges may be inherited. This knowledge can be freeing—it reminds clients that they are not to blame for their struggles, and it can help reduce the shame or stigma that often surrounds seeking help.

At the same time, it offers hope. While we may not be able to change what we've inherited, we can change how we respond to it. Clients can begin to understand that their healing work doesn't end with them—it creates a ripple effect. The effort they put into self-awareness, emotional regulation, and healthier patterns can positively influence their children and future generations. In this way, healing becomes an act of courage, legacy, and love.

Genetic Predisposition to Addiction

Not only can trauma be generational, but the predisposition to addiction can be passed on genetically as well (Koob & Volkow, 2016). There has long been an argument as to whether susceptibility to addiction is caused by nature or nurture, and the most recent evidence is that a person's genetic makeup can account for up to 60% of the variation responsible for a person to develop an addiction.

Educating clients with a family history of addiction about the genetic component of addiction can be a powerful and compassionate part of the healing process. It can help ease the guilt or shame they may carry for developing an addiction themselves, reinforcing that this struggle is not simply a matter of willpower or moral failure.

This understanding also becomes valuable information they can thoughtfully share with their children—not as a prediction or a sentence, but as a gentle warning paired with wisdom. It offers their children awareness, not fear—an invitation to be mindful of their own choices and to understand the risks, while also emphasizing that genetics are only one part of a much larger picture. Empowering clients with this knowledge can help break cycles and encourage healthier patterns for the next generation.

Support System Development

It is well-documented that having a strong social support system can help limit stress and its negative effects by providing physical assistance, emotional support, helpful information, feedback about how we are perceived in the world, and opportunities for socialization (Harandi, Taghinasab, & Nayeri, 2017). Encouraging our clients to develop a strong support system is a valuable part of the healing journey. By creating a safe place where they can learn to trust us, we offer what may be the first supportive relationship in their lives. Once they learn to open up to us, we can assist them in identifying other people and communities who may offer similar safe relationships.

By modeling a healthy relationship, including honesty, integrity, and the ability to talk through difficulties, those we assist will be able to recognize safe people and places for themselves.

Some options include:

- Counseling groups

- Twelve-Step groups

- Faith communities

- Spaces in which people enjoy shared hobbies

- Support groups

- Exercise classes

- Community drop-in centers

Those who struggle with social anxiety can often become comfortable with online groups first, and once their confidence grows, they may be willing to try in-person meetings. Knowing what is available for socialization in our own community can be valuable in assisting our clients in developing a supportive system.

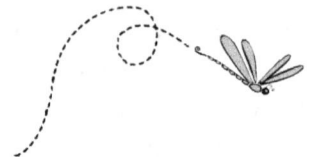

Mindfulness Healing Part I:

Preparation, Assessment, and Script
for Guided Imagery Exercise

Important Safety Tips for Therapists, Facilitators and Healing Individuals

Environment Consideration and Tips: It can be helpful to "set the stage" prior to a guided imagery exercise. For example, consider the lighting—is it too bright or too low? Another helpful step is putting phones on silent. Also, think about outside distractions, such as barking dogs, traffic, and other interruptions. If possible, minimize outside noises the best that you can. Some individuals like having a blanket or pillow to hold, or you may enjoy diffusing essential oils to support deeper relaxation if there are no allergy concerns. While mindfulness-based guided imagery is not hypnosis, it can be helpful to prepare your environment prior to beginning the guided imagery exercise.

Voice Prosody: An additional gentle reminder is to be aware of your voice prosody. Prosody refers to the rhythm and melody of the voice, including intonation, stress, and pauses. Speaking in a softer tone and slower cadence than your normal speaking voice is useful in supporting the guided imagery practice. If you typically speak more rapidly or loudly, it will take some practice to slow down and modulate your voice.

Diversity Considerations: Consider the client's culture, age, race, physical differences (such as hearing loss), gender and orientation, and other unique experiences that may invite a softer or different speaking tone or pace or require that the client keep their eyes open if they prefer. If you are bi-lingual and you and your client speak the same languages, ask your client what language they prefer. If your client prefers to go by a nickname, a title such as Dr., Mr., or Mrs., or a specific pronoun, honor their request.

Pace Yourself: Remind yourself to take your time as you walk through this process. There is no need to rush. If you are the person facilitating this exercise, slow down for a relaxed, calming pace. Additionally, it is wise for the facilitator to first practice the exercise with themselves prior to practicing with another person or client.

Safety Reminder: Safety is the number one consideration with any therapeutic approach or healing intervention. As you lead your clients through the following guided imagery exercise, please instruct your clients to alert you if they are experiencing any of the following responses. **NOTE:** If you are an individual doing this work solo, you will also want to consider the following:

- Traumatic memories that are creating a high level of distress

- Feelings of intense fear or panic

- Disturbing or intrusive thoughts

- Suicidal or homicidal thoughts

- Dissociation (if there is an awareness of the dissociative states)

- Other crisis concerns (list on the line): _____

_____

It is also important to ask the client to alert you if they experience any of the following symptoms. Likewise, if someone is doing this work solo, they should pay compassionate and close attention to their process and monitor for distressing or physical symptoms such as:

- A racing heart

- Tightness in the chest

- Shortness of breath

- Nausea or Intestinal distress

- Feeling faint or dizzy

- Body pain

- Feeling as if you are floating outside of your body

- Other somatic concerns (list on the line): _____

_____

Note for Therapist or Facilitator: Before moving into the guided imagery, please have your client begin with the assessment below. If you are not a trained mental health professional and your client is in crisis and exhibiting or discussing symptoms that are out of your scope of practice or experience, please refer to an appropriate mental health or medical professional. *If your client is experiencing an immediate life-threatening emergency, please call 911 or the appropriate emergency number if located outside of the United States.*

Note to Solo Reader: If you are doing this work on your own and believe you are in crisis or may be at risk to yourself, please stop and seek emergency support immediately by calling 911 or your local emergency number.

Pre-Guided Imagery Assessment Scale

On a scale from 1 to 10 (with 1 = very low, and 10 = very high), please take a mindful moment to assess the following. Circle the number that most accurately applies to you:

Feeling	Assessment (1-10)									
□ Anxiety	1	2	3	4	5	6	7	8	9	10
□ Anger	1	2	3	4	5	6	7	8	9	10
□ Shame	1	2	3	4	5	6	7	8	9	10
□ Sadness	1	2	3	4	5	6	7	8	9	10
□ Fear	1	2	3	4	5	6	7	8	9	10
□ Numbness	1	2	3	4	5	6	7	8	9	10
□ Confusion	1	2	3	4	5	6	7	8	9	10
□ Curiosity	1	2	3	4	5	6	7	8	9	10
□ Hopefulness	1	2	3	4	5	6	7	8	9	10
□ Calm	1	2	3	4	5	6	7	8	9	10
□ Joyful	1	2	3	4	5	6	7	8	9	10
□ Other:	1	2	3	4	5	6	7	8	9	10

Assessment Notes: _____

_____

_____

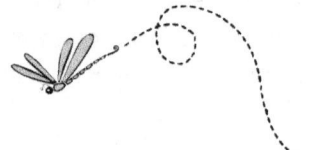

Mindfulness Healing Part II:
Breath and Somatic Preparation & Prompts

This exercise involves tuning into your breath and body and is followed by the guided imagery exercise. It's important to note that this may not be suitable for everyone. It's recommended that the following be adapted to the specific needs and comfort levels of the individual(s) involved.

Physical Space and Comfort: Have your client settle into a comfortable sitting or lying down position, with their feet on the floor or cross-legged if that is their preference. If your client, or you if you are doing this solo, has a yoga mat or a couch and prefers to lie down, that is fine. Whatever position will help the client feel comfortable is perfectly acceptable.

Prompt 1: Let's pause while you take a few moments to get comfortable.

Prompt 2: When you are ready, you are welcome to close your eyes if that feels comfortable for you. Or, if you prefer to leave your eyes open, that is just fine. Whatever allows you to feel most secure is more than acceptable. If your eyes remain open, feel free to rest your gaze on a calming point—near the floor if you're sitting or on the ceiling if you're lying down.

Prompt 3: We will now move forward into the grounded breathing exercise. This will take approximately two to three minutes.

Grounded Breath Exercise

Now that you are in a comfortable position, before we begin the guided imagery, let's move through the grounded breath work.

1. We will start with the 4-2-7 breath. Start by breathing in deeply through the nose to the count of four, hold for two, and then exhale slowly and intentionally through the mouth to the count of seven. Let's do this three times at your own pace. **Note to Facilitator: Count to 20 silently.**

2. Now, let's return to easy, relaxed, deep breathing. Take in a long breath in through the nose and let out a long exhale out through the mouth. Continue with this breath. **Note to Facilitator: Count to 20 silently.**

3. As you are noticing the gentle rhythm of deep breathing, I would like you to imagine extending compassion to yourself with each intake breath. **Note to Facilitator: Count to 20 silently.**

Somatic Relaxation Exercise

Now that we have finished with our grounded breaths, please feel free to breathe normally with relaxed, regular breaths. Let's now move into relaxing the body in preparation for guided imagery:

1. Notice that your feet are feeling heavier and more relaxed.

2. Notice that your hands are gently resting at your sides, on your belly, or on your thighs.

3. Feel your jaw relax and your tongue move away from the roof of your mouth.

4. Allow your shoulders to relax down from your ear lobes and your elbows to gently relax down from your shoulders.

5. Bit by bit, the tension moves out of your body as you breathe in and relax and breathe out and relax. Breathe in compassion, hope, and healing, and breathe out stress, judgment, and anger.

As we complete our breath work, we will now move on to the guided imagery preparation and exercise section. You can return to your breath work exercises at any point during the guided imagery. The guided imagery exercise will take approximately 10 minutes. You may continue to stay in your comfortable position or shift to a different comfortable position. You may also continue with your eyes closed if that is your preference. At any point, you are welcome to ask for a time out if needed.

Let's move forward.

Mindfulness Healing Part III:
Guided Imagery Exercise
Finding a Safe Place

Note to Therapist or Facilitator: If you notice that the client is highly activated during the guided imagery, perhaps demonstrating rapid or shallow breathing, sobbing, or shaking, please have the client pause as you attend to the individual. This can be done by gently stating that you would like to pause the exercise for a moment, then quietly asking the person by name if they would like a break, support with deep breath work, or to step out of the guided imagery entirely if it has become too overwhelming.

Note to the Reader: If you are doing this solo without the support of a mental health professional, again, please be gentle with yourself. If you have a trusted person to lead you through this, you may want to consider this option, or perhaps you can read this into a recording device and then play it back and follow the prompts. If you become overwhelmed or feel as if you are in a crisis state, please stop and reach out for help if need be. Safety comes first, always.

Purpose of the Safe Place: This guided imagery exercise is designed to help you develop the ability to use your mind to relax and calm your body.

Instructions: This guided imagery exercise will take approximately 15 minutes, depending on the amount of interaction you have with the client and how quickly you can take notes. You will be guided by your mental health professional or trusted facilitator, or you may guide yourself if you prefer, through each step of the exercise slowly. If you use this solo, you may want to consider recording this on a device and playing it back for yourself. Though questions may be asked of you or you may be given prompts, there is no expectation of a verbal response. You may respond if you would like to do so, or you may quietly respond inside of yourself, which many people prefer. Through this visualization journey, you will be guided to explore a real or imagined place where you feel safe and secure.

Note to Facilitator: When taking notes through this guided imagery exercise, please be mindful of the sounds that a keyboard makes. We have found that quietly writing in a notebook or clipboard is less distracting for the client.

First Step Prompt: Close your eyes, take a deep breath, and allow yourself to sink into a comfortable position. When you are ready, picture a safe and peaceful place where you feel completely calm and safe. It can be a place where you've been before or a place you've always wanted to visit. This can also be a real place or one that you make up in your imagination. It's a place that does not trigger any stressful feelings or fear, and it is free of annoyances. You might imagine the beach, the mountains, or a midnight walk in the snow. It may even be your home or another place that feels like home to you. It can be any place that evokes peace and calm. Take a moment to imagine your safe place. *Note to Facilitator: Count to 20 silently.*

Next Prompt Step: Once you have your safe place created in your mind, please take a moment and tell me about it. *Note to Facilitator: Allow the client to describe their safe place while you listen and take brief notes.*

Next Prompt Step: Continue to notice more about your safe place.

- What does it look like?
- What does it smell like?
- What sounds do you hear?
- What is the weather and the temperature?
- Is there anything else you notice about your space?

    Note to Facilitator: Allow the client time to answer and continue taking brief notes.

Next Prompt Step: Now, if you were to describe this place in a word or two, what would you call it? It should be a word or words that automatically bring this safe place to your mind whenever you hear it. Once you have decided on a word or phrase, let me know what it is. *Note to Facilitator: Count to 20 silently or until the client has told you their word and write it down.*

Next Prompt Step: As you breathe deeply, listen as I read back to you what you've described. *Note to Facilitator: In a slow, gentle voice, tell the client, "Now we are going to go to _____ [the name for their safe place]," and then read back the description the client gave you. Count to 20 silently.*

Next Prompt Step: *Note to Facilitator: In a slow, gentle voice, ask the client the following questions:*

- Were you able to imagine being in your safe place while I described it to you?
- Is there anything else you noticed about your safe place that you'd like to add?
- Does the name _____ [client's name for their safe place] still describe it well?

- Are there any changes you'd like to make?

  Note to Facilitator: Allow the client time to answer and make any changes given.

Next Prompt Step: You are doing so well with this. Now, we are going to practice using your image of a safe place to help calm your body when it is tense or anxious. First, think about a recent situation that was just a little bit stressful for you. On a scale of 1 to 10, with 1 being the least stressful situation imaginable and 10 being the most stressful situation imaginable, choose something that is about a 2 or 3. **Note to Facilitator: Count to 20 silently.**

Next Prompt Step: Now, please describe the stressful situation to me. *Note to Facilitator: Allow the client time to answer and continue taking brief notes. If the client struggles with this, give them some examples, like waiting in a long line, someone cutting you off in traffic, or getting the wrong order at a coffee shop, a loved one snapping at them, a misunderstanding with a work mate. Allow them time to think until they answer and continue taking brief notes.*

Next Prompt Step: Now, as I read back to you the stressful situation that you described, I want you to imagine that it is happening right now. As you imagine it, focus on the emotion you feel and the physical response in your body. **Note to Facilitator: Read back to the client the description of the stressful situation. When you are finished, ask the client:**

- Can you feel the stress in your body?

- What are you feeling?

- Where do you feel it?

- Is it about a 2 or 3 on the annoyance scale, or is it lower or higher?

  Note to Facilitator: Allow the client time to answer and continue taking brief notes.

Next Prompt Step: Holding that image of the stressful situation in your mind and concentrating on the emotions and sensations of stress in your body, I want you to take a deep, calming breath into the area of your body where you feel the stress, and then exhale. Let's do that now. Now, I want you to go to _____ [the client's name for their safe place]. *Note to Facilitator: Read back the description that the client gave you, then pause for them to enjoy their safe place. After about 20 seconds, ask the client:*

- Were you able to go to your safe place?

- What happened in your body when you imagined being in your safe place?

- How does your body feel now?

  Note to Facilitator: Allow them time to answer.

Next Prompt Step: Next, we're going to practice this exercise again, but this time, I want you to think about a situation that was a bit more stressful. On a scale of 1 to 10, with 1 being the least stressful situation imaginable and 10 being the most stressful situation imaginable, choose something that is about a 5-6 on the stress scale. **Note to Facilitator: Count to 20 silently.**

Next Prompt Step: Now, please describe the stressful situation. **Note to Facilitator: Allow the client time to answer and continue taking brief notes. If the client struggles with this, give them some examples, such as your child being late for curfew, getting a flat tire on *your way to work, or failing an important test. Allow them time to think until they answer and continue taking brief notes.*

Next Prompt Step: I will now read back to you the stressful situation that you described, and I want you to imagine that it is happening right now. Remember, you are safe; you are supported. As you hold this memory, focus on the emotion you feel and the physical response in your body. **Note to Facilitator: Read back to the client the description of the stressful situation. When you are finished, ask the client:**

- Can you feel the stress in your body?

- What are you feeling?

- Where do you feel it?

- Is it about a 5 on the annoyance scale, or is it higher or lower?

   Note to Facilitator: Allow the client time to answer.

Next Prompt Step: Holding that image of the stressful situation in your mind and concentrating on the emotions and sensations of stress in your body, I want you to take a deep, calming breath into the area of your body holding the stress, and then exhale. Now I want you to go to _____ [the client's name for their safe place]. **Note to Facilitator: Read back the description that the client gave you, then pause and allow them to enjoy their safe place. After 20 seconds, ask the client:**

- Were you able to go to your safe place?

- What happened in your body when you imagined being in your safe place?

- How does your body feel now?

   Note to Facilitator: Allow them time to answer.

Next Prompt Step: As we come to the end of this guided imagery exercise, I invite you to go to your safe place one more time with the understanding that you can return to your safe space at any point in the future. This time, I will not describe it to you; I will simply allow you to enjoy being in this peaceful, calm place again. **Note to Facilitator: Count to 20 silently.**

Next Prompt Step: Know that you have the strength and resilience to work through stressful situations mindfully, using your safe place guided imagery exercise. Please remember that you are not alone in this journey of healing; you are supported. No matter the challenges that come your way, remember that you are worthy of a life filled with love, authenticity, respect, joy, and fulfillment. Take a moment now to give yourself an affirmation. Self-affirmations may take you out of your comfort zone, but do your best to stay present with yourself, even in the discomfort. Let's take a moment to breathe in slowly and deeply, and exhale. **Note to Facilitator: Count to 20 silently.**

Transitioning to Awareness

Final Prompt Step: When you're ready, if your eyes are closed, notice the light in front of your eyelids. Gently blink, open your eyes, and bring your awareness back to the present moment. **Note to Facilitator: Once the client has opened their eyes, gently explain to them that they can use this exercise anytime (except when driving or other times when closing**

their eyes would be unsafe) they feel stressed. Encourage them to practice it at home until just thinking of the name of their safe place will allow their bodies to relax.

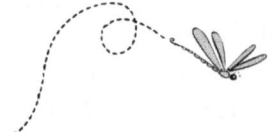

Mindfulness Healing Part IV:
Processing of Guided Imagery
Sharing Your Experience

Purpose for Processing: After the conclusion of the guided imagery, the therapist or facilitator will lead an open and respectful discussion about what you experienced during the guided imagery. The aim is to allow for a compassionate and honest conversation as you highlight important aspects of the guided imagery exercise and what the experience was like.

Note: If you are doing this solo without a therapist or facilitator, please pace yourself and notice your energy. You may journal your responses to the questions below if you are doing this work on your own.

Important Considerations for the Facilitator: It is not the role of the therapist or facilitator to interpret, minimize, or re-direct. Rather, it is important for the facilitator to skillfully hold a safe space for the client to share their experience, including the more difficult aspects. This is a time for the facilitator to honor the pain, as well as highlight and affirm the positive insights the client may have had. Remind the client that participating in a therapy exercise like this is a signal of hope and aids in the possibility of recovery and healing.

Processing Questions

1. What did you notice in the guided imagery?

2. What challenges did you experience?

3. What joys or other emotions did you experience?

4. Did you have a breakthrough you'd like to share?

5. Do you have any concerns that you'd like to share?

6. What are you feeling in your body currently?

7. Did you notice any self-growth with insight and compassion toward yourself?

8. Did you notice any triggers or areas of concern?

Now that you have completed the breathwork and somatic exercises, the guided imagery exercise, and the process work, on a scale from 1 to 10 (with 1 = very low, and 10 = very high), let's take a mindful moment to assess the following:

Feeling	Assessment (1-10)									
▫ Anxiety	1	2	3	4	5	6	7	8	9	10
▫ Anger	1	2	3	4	5	6	7	8	9	10
▫ Shame	1	2	3	4	5	6	7	8	9	10
▫ Sadness	1	2	3	4	5	6	7	8	9	10
▫ Fear	1	2	3	4	5	6	7	8	9	10
▫ Numbness	1	2	3	4	5	6	7	8	9	10
▫ Confusion	1	2	3	4	5	6	7	8	9	10
▫ Curiosity	1	2	3	4	5	6	7	8	9	10
▫ Hopefulness	1	2	3	4	5	6	7	8	9	10
▫ Calm	1	2	3	4	5	6	7	8	9	10
▫ Joyful	1	2	3	4	5	6	7	8	9	10
▫ Other:	1	2	3	4	5	6	7	8	9	10

Note to Facilitator or Reader: Engaging in somatic movement, if you are able to do so, such as gentle stretching, walking, rhythmic body movements, or dancing to music, following guided imagery is vital for healing trauma as it allows individuals to release stored tension, process emotions, and reconnect with their bodies, facilitating a holistic approach to healing. Please take 3-5 minutes to move your body in a way that feels good for you. Yoga poses, stretching, dance, bouncing gently, rhythmically swaying, or a short walk are all excellent ways to honor yourself.

Important Reminder: If you, as the facilitator, are not a licensed therapist or trained mental health professional and your client is in crisis and exhibiting or discussing symptoms that are out of your scope of practice or experience, please refer to an appropriate mental health or medical professional. *If your client is experiencing an immediate life-threatening emergency, please call 911 or the appropriate emergency number if located outside of the United States. If you are doing this solo without support and are in a state of emergency, reach out to 911 immediately.*

Mindfulness Healing Part V:

Purpose Statement: The purpose of this My Safe Place art exercise is to create a visual representation of the safe place you envisioned, allowing yourself to fully immerse yourself in its calming details and atmosphere.

Art Exercise Instructions: Gather art supplies such as paper, colored pencils, stickers, or other dry materials. Please be mindful if you choose to use supplies like markers or paints, as these can sometimes bleed through to the next page. You may want to place a blank sheet of paper underneath your work to protect the following pages.

1. Begin by finding a quiet and comfortable space where you can focus without distractions.

2. Take a few moments to center yourself through deep breathing, visualization, or grounding exercises. Allow yourself to become present in the moment, acknowledging any thoughts or emotions that arise.

3. Once you feel grounded, think back to the guided imagery and remember the image of the safe place you imagined.

4. In the rectangle provided on the next page, use your art supplies to begin drawing or painting a likeness of the safe place you imagined, adding as much detail as you can.

5. As you work on your art, pay attention to any emotions or sensations that arise. Allow yourself to explore them openly and without negative self-talk. Remember that there are no right or wrong ways to express yourself through art.

6. Next, label your drawing with the word or phrase that you chose to use to describe your safe place, or you are welcome to choose a new word if you prefer. You can also add words to the picture that describe what emotions you feel and the sensations that are in your body when you imagine yourself in this place.

7. Once you have completed your art exercise, take a step back and observe your creation. Reflect on the journey it represents, recognizing the challenges you have faced and the progress you have made.

8. Finally, think about strategies that will support your path toward healing.

9. Take a moment to appreciate yourself for engaging in this healing art exercise and for the courage you have shown. Allow yourself to feel a sense of pride and accomplishment as you continue your journey of recovery.

My Safe Place

Mindfulness Healing Part V:

Art Exercise II—God or Higher Power Box

Purpose Statement: The goal of this healing art exercise is to create a physical box where you can mindfully place your worries, offering a way to release them—whether by entrusting them to God, a higher power, or simply setting them aside to bring relief from overthinking.

Note: We recognize that each reader may have their own understanding of what a higher power means, and we deeply respect all faiths, belief systems, and those who may not believe in a higher power or God. A higher power can also take the form of a personal journey, sobriety, nature, or a guiding philosophy. We honor all perspectives in this process.

Art Exercise Instructions: Gather the art supplies you'll need to create a small box. You can use a pre-made wooden box with a lid or slot—often found at craft stores—or repurpose something you already have at home. Options include an empty tissue box, a small shipping box (with labels removed), a shoe box, or any other container that feels right to you. Alternatively, you can construct your own box using cardboard and glue or tape. You may also want to collect materials to decorate your box in a way that feels personal and meaningful—such as paint, markers, wrapping paper, stickers, fabric, or any other creative touches. Lastly, have a blank sheet of paper, a pair of scissors, and a pen or pencil ready for the next step of the activity.

1. Begin by finding a quiet and comfortable space where you can focus without distractions.

2. Take a few moments to center yourself through deep breathing, visualization, or grounding exercises. Allow yourself to become present in the moment, acknowledging any thoughts or emotions that arise.

3. Once you feel grounded, take the materials you have chosen and create a box with a lid or slit on the top.

4. Using your art supplies, decorate your box however you like.

5. Take the blank piece of paper and begin by folding the paper enough times to produce the number of slips needed—one for each of your worries. Then, carefully cut along the folds to create individual slips of paper. Take a moment to think about anything that is worrying you or causing you stress. It may be a lack of finances, the need for a job, relationship worries, or difficulties with changing an unhealthy habit in your life. Write each worry or fear on a separate slip of paper.

6. Take each slip, one at a time, and place it in the box. If you are a person of faith, you can use this to turn your worries over to God or your higher power. If not, you can use it as a way to release your worries and fear, setting them aside in your box. Your worries are in the box and out of sight; this will signal to your brain that the worry is out of your hands and into the hands of God, your higher power, or the Universe.

7. As you work on your art, pay attention to any emotions or sensations that arise. Allow yourself to explore them openly and without negative self-talk. Remember that there are no right or wrong ways to express yourself through art, just as there are no right or wrong emotions.

8. Once you have completed your art exercise, take a step back and observe your creation. Reflect on the journey it represents, recognizing the challenges you have faced and the progress you have made.

9. Finally, think about strategies that will support your path toward healing. Remember that you can add worries to your box whenever you need to, and if you find yourself worrying about that same problem again, remind yourself that it is already in the box. Occasionally, you may wish to open the box and review the worries in it. Most likely, you will be amazed at how many problems have been resolved over time.

10. Take a moment to appreciate yourself for engaging in this healing art exercise and for the courage you have shown. Allow yourself to feel a sense of pride and accomplishment as you continue your journey of recovery.

Mindful Reflection Moment

Now that you have completed your breath work, guided imagery, assessment reflection, and art journal exercise, as we bring this chapter to a close, please take some mindful time to process. You are welcome to answer the following questions in the space below, or write in a journal or notebook of your choice. You may do this with your therapist or facilitator, or if you are working through this book solo, you can do this on your own.

1. What are you noticing after this chapter?

2. What awareness and insight have surfaced?

3. What is the information you have learned?

Write or share your reflections here if you would like to do so. As always, please be gentle with yourself:

_____

_____

_____

_____

_____

Final Step: Self-Affirmation Exercise

Instructions: Before moving on to the next chapter, can you give yourself the gift of self-affirmation? It can be difficult for people who have experienced trauma, are grieving, coping with addiction, experiencing family difficulties, healing from complex trauma, or struggling with anxiety, depression, or other challenges to affirm themselves.

As a support to this step of your healing, affirmation ideas might include statements such as: "I am grounded, centered, and connected to my inner calm," "I am aware of my thoughts and feelings without judgment," "I release what I cannot control and focus on what I can." In the winged heart below, you are invited to list your own self-affirmation(s). If you can only come up with one affirmation at this time, that is more than acceptable. Perhaps you can return later in your healing process and add more:

The aim of this chapter was to introduce the concept of "counterweight bonding" as an alternative term for codependency, to better understand emotions and internal versus external locus of control, and explore addiction in the context of generational trauma and genetic predisposition. Additionally, healthy coping skills were highlighted, including somatic emotional awareness, mindfulness, Dialectical Behavior Therapy (DBT), building support systems, and meditation. My hope is that by engaging with the Safe Place and the God or Higher Power Box exercises, you can significantly improve your distress tolerance, experience calmness, and restore equanimity during times of fear, overwhelm, and stress.

As you complete this chapter, I would like to offer you an affirmation before moving on: You are fully deserving of a life free from the grip of counterweight bonding. Prioritizing your own mental, emotional, and physical well-being is not an act of selfishness but an act of reclaiming your space in the world. Trust yourself as you begin to set healthy boundaries, understanding that each step you take is moving you toward a more balanced, fulfilling, and authentic life. You have the strength to untangle from what no longer serves you and build something new—something entirely yours.

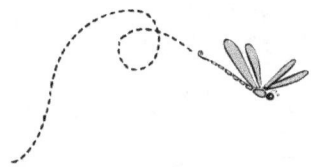

CHAPTER NINE
A Compassionate Path to Inner Peace: Healing From Love Addiction

Mari A. Lee

Romantic love is one of the most addictive substances on earth.

~ Helen Fisher

I had been working with Angela, a 38-year-old woman with a history of unhealthy relationships, for almost six months. Angela grew up amidst the vibrant, bustling streets of Los Angeles with dreams of acceptance and love. Her youthful beauty caught the eye of photographers and casting directors alike by the time she was a shy and slender redhead of only 16 years old. At this tender age, Angela found herself thrust into a whirlwind of flashing lights and fleeting adoration, which felt both overwhelming and exhilarating. She had been long starved for love, acceptance, and nurturance in her childhood, and this unexpected early fame initially filled a deep hole of abandonment and loneliness, which left her yearning for more.

Yet, as the years passed and the lines of age began to appear, she found herself confronting a harsh reality that her youth had been marked by people who had taken advantage of her age and naivety. With no one to protect her, she had been sexually abused several times, pressured to agree to nude photographs, secretly filmed without her consent, and taken advantage of sexually, emotionally, and financially, with many broken promises and harmful relationships along the way.

As my work progressed with Angela, I learned that she had grown up in a single-parent home and was the youngest of three children, unintentionally neglected by her mother, who was a waitress and a hospital worker taking on extra shifts to provide for her children. Angela's father refused financial support or to spend time with her or her siblings. "My mom was exhausted and overwhelmed and worked her tail off, usually 14 hours a day. I don't think I ever saw her in anything but her waitress or hospital uniform, sweatpants, or pajamas. She was juggling so much, and although I know she loved me, at the time, I felt so lost and alone in the world.

My dad was non-existent, an alcoholic, and a loser. I saw him less than a dozen times before my eighteenth birthday, and only when he needed money. My gorgeous and popular sister was six years older than me and did not want me tagging along. I barely knew her; however, I watched her get showered with love and attention from one boyfriend after the next and yearned for that as well. My brother was four years older than me; he was—and is—a handsome and funny guy. He was sweet to me but was always out with friends, being the life of the party. I wanted so much to have a circle of friends like my big brother or to be popular and adored like my sister. However, I usually felt like an unloved Cinderella, just sitting alone in my room or playing by myself in the park, trying to find love and belonging in all the wrong places." My heart went out to Angela as her eyes welled up with tears as she reflected on her younger self and the loneliness she had endured.

As therapy advanced, it was clear that beneath the veneer of carefully coiffed hair and makeup, Angela grappled with deep insecurity. Like many adolescents, she went through the awkward stage of puberty feeling as if she did not fit in, "I was teased for being the tallest in my class and called 'BOB,' which I later found out meant 'bag of bones.' I wore the goofiest glasses until I could afford contacts—I felt like the ultimate ugly duckling during that time."

Angela shared that beginning around age twelve, she would sometimes develop an unhealthy fixation on the opposite sex, starting with boys at her school, or her brother's friends: "It wasn't just a crush; it felt much bigger than that. I found myself completely consumed when I was in this state. I wasn't obsessing over every boy, nor just the cute or popular ones. The ones who drew me in like a magnet were often those who seemed unattainable, maybe even a bit shy like me, and who gave me attention.

If a certain guy looked at me with some interest or was nice to me—especially the ones who were shy, quiet, or a little out of reach—it felt like my whole world tilted toward him. One smile, one soft moment of kindness, and I was gone. It didn't matter if he barely knew I existed; I would weave entire love stories in my mind, where he saw me, needed me, loved me in ways no one ever had. I wrote his name over and over in my journal like a spell. I watched him from across rooms, checked his social media like it might give me answers, found reasons to be nearby, hoping he'd notice. He didn't even have to say much—the mystery was enough. I wasn't just chasing him, that kind of obvious behavior was never really me. I was chasing the feeling that maybe, if someone like him could love me, I could finally be okay. I could be enough."

In one of our early sessions, Angela courageously shared a traumatic memory having to do with a handyman in her apartment building who had molested her over several months when she was just thirteen years old, "He was in his mid-thirties but seemed so fun and young to me. He played cool music, drove a Volkswagen Bug—my favorite car at the time—

surfed, was always tan and muscular, called me "sexy baby," gave me rides to school, and looked at me like I was the most precious person in the world. He brought me little gifts like my favorite candy, CDs of music, or lip gloss. One time, he gave me a silver and turquoise bracelet with a heart charm, which was the most beautiful thing I had ever received. When he put it on my wrist, he promised we would be together forever and made me promise not to tell anyone, saying that we were star-crossed lovers destined to be together.

He would look me in the eye, hold my face, softly kiss my lips, and tell me I was his truest love. I was just a kid, putty in his hands, and I thought I was in love with this older man. At the start, he would only hold my hand or kiss me, and then, over the next few weeks, that moved to intimate touching and then, finally, sex. I started my period during this time, and he was the one who bought me my first tampons and showed me how to use them, telling me I was finally an adult. I would find excuses to ditch my classes when I knew it was his day to be at the building working on things. I had no idea he was married with a child until later when everything blew up and became public. I thought he was my dream guy, the one who would rescue me and make everything better. I finally felt like I mattered. I was so naive and lonely; he was my whole world," Angela quietly stated.

When Angela's brother discovered this abuse of his little sister, a violent fight broke out between the men, property was damaged, the police were called, and the abusive handyman was arrested. Though the molestation ended, Angela shared feeling abandoned, betrayed, and brokenhearted: "I felt like the only person who ever really loved me was being ripped away. On one hand, I knew what we had been doing was wrong, but on the other hand, I felt addicted to his attention and promises. I think I cried every day for the next three months. I had no one to talk to about this, and, at one point, I seriously considered running away from home and begging him to go with me."

Unfortunately, Angela experienced further trauma during the interrogation and court proceedings, which were frightening and confusing. This, along with her mother's constant scolding, greatly impacted Angela on every level of her being. "My mom resented having to take me to court and lose time at work, which impacted her financially. I hardly saw her as it was, but after this, she distanced herself even more. I felt so guilty, like I was a dirty disappointment who was better off dead.

My sister and brother were no help; they were disgusted and let me know that I had ruined my reputation and that everyone was talking about me and our family. My brother, whom I adored, seemed embarrassed to be around me after this." Tears traced down her neck as she recalled this heartbreaking chapter. I handed Angela a tissue, and together, we took in a deep breath while she picked up a foam ball from my mindfulness basket and gently squeezed it.

To compound her distress, she endured additional wounds from the betrayed wife of the offender. Understandably hurt and angry, this young wife, only 21 years old herself, began appearing at Angela's apartment building soon after the arrest. She spread false accusations to neighbors, claiming Angela had seduced her husband, and hurled insults at Angela upon her return home from school each day. "I would hide behind the trash dumpster in the alley, waiting until it was safe for me to sneak up the backstairs with shaking legs," Angela recalled.

When this information eventually made it to the ears of her schoolmates, tragically, Angela then endured relentless bullying from her peers who called her cruel names that left her feeling ashamed and hopeless: "They called me a slut, a whore, a liar, a homewrecker, and a husband stealer. I was slapped, pushed, pinched, grabbed, spit on, and laughed at. Even though I was only thirteen years old when he started grooming me, everyone acted as if I was the abuser. I had no idea I was being groomed; I honestly don't think I ever heard the word "grooming" until the police arrested him and I was forced to testify in court. I truly thought I was all those awful things his wife and my classmates called me for so long, and maybe I still think I am those things," Angela said softly, her head ducking down in shame. It was clear that even though much time had passed, the pain of her early years remained open and raw, festering beneath the surface like a wound that refused to heal.

Angela's journey through her early experiences of sexuality and what she believed to be love was cruelly marred by abuse and molestation at the hands of a manipulative sexual offender. This profound trauma, compounded by neglect and early abandonment, entrenched her in a pattern of confusion and codependency. Over time, her emotional scars manifested as limerence—an insatiable longing for those who could never truly reciprocate her affections. Time and again, she found herself irresistibly drawn to men who mirrored her deepest insecurities and fears. These were men who were unhealthy, deceptive, abandoning, or abusive. She became trapped in a relentless cycle of yearning and rejection, a cycle that seemed to define her existence.

As she moved through adolescence into adulthood, Angela shared that each relationship she entered only deepened her wounds as she clung to the hope that, *this time*, it would be different. She sought validation and love from those who were incapable of providing it, believing that if she could win their affection, it would heal her own sense of worthlessness. Instead, these relationships perpetuated her pain, reinforcing the belief that she was unworthy of genuine love and respect. Angela's desperation for connection led her to ignore red flags and endure mistreatment, hoping that her loyalty and love would eventually be reciprocated. However, each time she was met with abandonment or abuse, her self-esteem took another blow. The cycle continued as a self-fulfilling prophecy of rejection and despair, leaving her feeling more isolated and unlovable with each failed attempt at love.

It is important to clarify that her journey was not just about the men she chose but also about the deep-seated wounds from her past that dictated her choices. Though she looked successful and confident on the outside, breaking free from this pattern required immense strength and self-awareness, as she had to confront the painful memories, distorted beliefs, and maladaptive coping mechanisms that had shaped her understanding of love, attachment, and self-worth. Only by addressing the roots of her trauma could Angela hope to rediscover her authentic self, redefine her relationships, and find a path to healing and genuine love.

As our work continued, Angela shared that marriage had been both a sanctuary and a prison for her, a cycle of fleeting highs and devastating lows. Twice she had walked down the aisle, only to find herself ensnared in the suffocating embrace of disillusionment and heartache. She reflected, "I always seem to pick men who l obsess over, doing all I can to gain their attention and devotion. Or I fall for men who love-bomb me at the start, only to reveal their true selves later—controlling, mean, arrogant jerks. And then there are the guys who love me at first but eventually say they feel smothered and leave." Additionally, the absence of children was a point of grief for Angela and served as a silent testament to the tumultuous nature of her relationships, a stark reminder of the emptiness and loneliness that she had been trying to fill since childhood.

Angela disclosed that regulating her emotions had always been difficult for her, especially as she matured through her teen years into early adulthood. "Some days were easier than others," she explained, "If I was in a relationship and it was going well, I felt on top of the world. However, if I was alone, the relationship was coming to an end, or we were not getting along, I felt so much fear. Sometimes, I could regulate my emotions, and other times, I would lash out or end up in a sobbing heap.

"I wondered if I was bipolar after a boyfriend I adored called me crazy, so I made an appointment with a psychiatrist to see what was going on with me. After the evaluation, the doctor stated that what I was dealing with more closely resembled complex post-traumatic stress disorder than bipolar disorder and recommended therapy. When I shared this news with my boyfriend, certain that he would have compassion and want to help me heal, he just shrugged and broke up with me anyway," she confided with a weary sigh.

Amid the chaos and abuse of her past and the unquenchable obsession with finding her self-worth in men, I was encouraged to see that Angela clung to a flicker of hope—an emerging desire for healing and liberation from the love addiction that bound her. In quiet moments of introspection during our sessions, Angela dared to envision a life untethered from the shackles of her past, a future where she could reclaim her sense of value and find solace and safety in honoring her truest self.

• • • • •

As the months went by, Angela's therapy journey was often challenging and required a great deal of gentleness and patience. Her counseling included weekly sessions, trauma and grief reduction work, mindfulness-based exercises, and eye movement desensitization and reprocessing (EMDR), a psychotherapy approach designed to help people heal from distressing life experiences, particularly trauma (see resource section for information on EMDR).

Another key focus of Angela's therapy was the exploration and healing of her parental wounds, particularly the deep impact of her biological father's abandonment. This wound had left Angela with a longing to be protected, parented, and shielded by a father figure in her romantic relationships. Midway through our work, Angela reflected, "I realize now that I was seeking the qualities I needed from a father in emotionally unavailable—and sometimes even cruel—men. It all makes so much sense to me now, but before this understanding, I was searching for the fatherly love my inner child longed for."

What Angela was beginning to understand is consistent with what clinicians increasingly recognize: love addiction is not merely about romantic obsession—it is an attachment disorder rooted in early relational trauma. When secure attachment is disrupted by abandonment, neglect, or inconsistent caregiving, the child's developing nervous system learns to survive through hypervigilance, people-pleasing, or clinging to emotionally unavailable or abusive figures. These adaptive strategies often solidify into adulthood, manifesting as compulsive relationship patterns where the person unconsciously recreates the emotional landscape of their earliest attachments. Rather than forming secure, reciprocal bonds, individuals with love addiction are often drawn to relationships marked by intensity, unpredictability, and emotional starvation. They confuse emotional activation—such as longing, tension, or fear of loss—for connection, mistaking the highs and lows of relational chaos for love itself. Research by Griffin, Lewis, and Mitchell (2018) supports this, noting that individuals with fearful attachment styles and heightened separation anxiety are at significantly higher risk for love-addictive behaviors. In essence, love addiction is not about weakness—it is about survival strategies that once protected a vulnerable child, now seeking healing through relational repair.

I reassured Angela that as her insight continued to grow and she healed the wound of her father's abandonment, she would discover the gift within that wound—the ability to make healthier choices, not just for her adult self but also for the inner child who had been calling out for her care. While her father may have abandoned her as a child, she was now showing up for that younger part of herself, the part that had been waiting for her all along.

In addition to meeting with me, she began connecting with other women in her support group, where she received consistent encouragement. As her courage, strength, and insight grew, so did her self-discovery and self-compassion. With newfound determination and hard-won resilience, Angela began to make sense of her past, confronting the ghosts that had haunted her.

That spring, during an especially meaningful session, Angela shared that she had always wanted to help others, especially children. When I asked if she had a particular passion as a child, Angela shared, "I always wanted to be the nurse during playtime. I was alone so much as a child, but I would nurse my dolls or the pets in the neighborhood. Helping others has always been important to me. I never wanted to be a model or actress; I just fell into that role. Maybe one day I will figure it out." I nodded in agreement and reflected that I felt certain that whatever she set her mind to, she could make it happen in her life.

Slowly and steadily, I witnessed Angela's incredible resolve to heal. Although the future sometimes seemed fraught with challenges and uncertainty, about a year or so into our work, Angela shared that she now faced each day with a renewed sense of purpose. With each step toward healing, she embraced the inherent imperfections of her humanity, practiced self-compassion—especially for her inner child and other neglected parts—and found strength in vulnerability. In a breakthrough session, Angela shared a poignant journal entry with me:

> *Therapy is not for the faint of heart—that's for sure! It's been really hard at times, but I am learning that healing does not mean that there is never any pain. I think for me that part of my healing has come from the courage to confront my difficult past and even the painful choices I have made without self-judgment. Mari reminds me all the time that embracing and accepting myself, all of my parts, instead of only looking for a man to accept and embrace me, is super important to my growth. Most days, I remind myself that I am allowed to finally experience the goodness of who I am with open arms and an open heart for myself and my inner child. I now know that I no longer need to prove my value to anyone else, obsess over a man, or abandon myself or my boundaries for what I thought was love. For the first time in my life, I am starting to believe that I deserve to show up for myself, to take my time getting to know a man before I give him my heart, my trust, my respect, or my body. Eye opener!!! I am growing stronger each day in trusting myself to make good choices. Plus, I finally have tools to help me manage*

my triggers—hurray! I now understand that I am enough, even if I am alone or if I feel lonely, and I am finally understanding the difference between loneliness and solitude. I am valuable enough, even if a man or any person is not telling me this. I am smart enough, talented enough, kind enough, pretty enough, and lovable enough. I am enough, and I don't need to chase after anyone ever again or fall into obsession to feel worthy, accepted, and loved.

• • • • •

A few years after our work together concluded, I checked my office mail and discovered that I had received a lovely holiday card from Angela. The card featured a photo of her, her husband, and their twin girls, along with a heartfelt letter catching me up on her life. As I sat at my desk wrapping up my day, I learned that after leaving therapy, Angela had pursued her passion for helping others by enrolling in nursing school. She eventually found her calling in the neonatal intensive care unit, where she cared for infants and supported new mothers. It was during her medical program that she met her husband, also a nurse.

In her letter, Angela shared how she had built a stable and fulfilling life—not perfect, as she humbly noted, but she felt very healthy, happy, content, and safe. She expressed pride in how she had relied on her therapy tools throughout her courtship and long engagement, ultimately finding an exceptional partner in her husband, choosing a fulfilling relationship over the endless search for the perfect soulmate. Reading her update filled my heart with warmth, and I remember driving home that night with a smile, reflecting on the remarkable courage she had shown and the profound, positive changes she was now enjoying, thanks to her commitment to growth and healing. These are the moments we, as therapists and mental health professionals, hold dear—reminders of the enduring impact of our work and the incredible resilience of the clients we have the privilege to support.

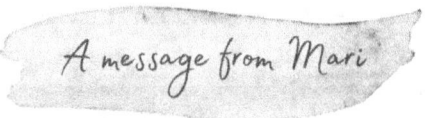

A message from Mari

The Impact of Social Language

The term "soulmate" is deeply embedded in the fabric of many cultures, often introduced through the fairytales and movies that shape our childhoods. This reflects a widely held belief in the existence of one magical and ideal partner who can bring complete fulfillment to one's life. The notion that true happiness hinges on finding this perfect match is reinforced across various forms of media, particularly in music, where countless songs romanticize love at any cost, celebrate the thrill of "falling" in love, or even portray love as an all-consuming, addictive force.

In my own journey in healing from love addiction, I recall a friend in my early twenties sharing a song that was then at the top of the charts, "Addicted to Love," by Robert Palmer. After we listened to the song, she looked at me and said with a laugh, "Those lyrics sum up your love life, Mari—you even look like one of the dancers!" This was back in 1985, and I was still a few years from starting therapy and my healing process. At that time, I laughed along with my friend, but I recall feeling a sense of unease, confusion, and shame.

If you are not familiar with the song "Addicted to Love," I suggest that you find a video that includes the lyrics as it encapsulates the experience of many individuals who struggle with love addiction. The lyrics vividly portray the intense, compulsive nature of a person who struggles with attachment disorders and intimacy issues, mirroring the sentiments of my own and countless recovering love addicts I have worked with over the years, individuals who are diverse in race, age, and orientation. The song, like many others, underscores the pervasive cultural narrative that equates the "perfect" romantic partner as the only path to fulfillment and completeness.

In literature, film, and other forms of storytelling, the pursuit of a flawless "soulmate" is often depicted as the end goal. Think about the stories from your own childhood where beloved characters embark on epic quests, endure great trials, and overcome significant obstacles, all in the name of finding that one flawless person who will finally make them whole and happy. These narratives, while captivating, can set unrealistic expectations and place immense pressure on individuals to find their "other half," or, in the words of Tom Cruise's character in the movie *Jerry Maguire*, to find the person who will say, "You complete me." While I embrace various aspects of healthy romance and realistic ideas of love, it is the love that unattainable fantasies are made of that is the ultimate pot of gold at the end of the rainbow for love addicts. What these movies, TV shows like *The Bachelor* and romance novels fail to mention is that the pot of gold in finding the "perfect" mate and locating a flawless love match is a myth.

This notion can inadvertently overshadow the significance of various other relationships and sources of fulfillment. While romantic partnerships are undeniably significant, friendships, family bonds, spirituality, creativity, personal achievements, and self-love play equally crucial roles in fostering a fulfilling life. When the emphasis on romantic love becomes too obsessive or pronounced, individuals may inadvertently neglect or undervalue these other vital aspects of their lives.

For those struggling with love addiction, these unrealistic messages can be particularly harmful. Love addicts are generally vulnerable, well-meaning people and are easy targets for predators, abusers, or grifters. People who struggle in this way often enter relationships with an idealized vision of romance, and given the unresolved trauma and feelings of low self-worth, they often seek validation and self-worth through their partners.

To be clear, many love addicts can appear quite confident and successful on the outside, but the inner turmoil is hidden behind a mask of illusion. Some may not consider themselves to be a person who struggles with value and self-worth, yet the mates they are drawn to often reveal deeper, sometimes implicit areas of pain. They may believe that finding the "perfect" partner will solve their problems and heal their emotional wounds—after all, isn't that what all the stories, songs, and movies promise? Or they share that they feel as if they have known their romantic interest in another life or across many lifetimes. Still, others are waiting for their knight in shining armor to gallop up and save them. However, as Angela discovered, this often leads to a cycle of dependency, overreliance, despair, and emotional turmoil, as no partner can ever truly fulfill such unrealistic expectations.

Pathological Affection Dependency

Love addiction can often begin just like any other romantic relationship, full of excitement and strong feelings. However, what sets it apart is the overwhelming focus on the romantic partner, often accompanied by a desperate need to please them—people who experience this often confuse intensity for true intimacy. As time goes on, this behavior can escalate into an unhealthy obsession where the love-addicted person starts to rationalize and overlook their partner's problematic behavior. Healthy boundaries blur, and the person may begin to withdraw from friends and give up activities they once enjoyed in an effort to maintain the relationship at any cost.

In my clinical work, I have identified three main stages of love addiction, what I call P.A.D., which is an acronym for *Pathological Affection Dependency©*. Let's explore more on the stages of P.A.D. as it relates to love addiction.

The P.A.D. Stages of Love Addiction

1. **Infatuation Stage:** Much like Angela's struggle, the love-addicted person focuses on their partner with an intensity that goes beyond the norm. Their world begins to revolve around this person, and they feel a powerful urge to gain their approval and affection at any cost. During the COVID-19 outbreak and months of sheltering in place, I noticed an increase in P.A.D., particularly among those who were isolated, unemployed, or living alone. These individuals were especially susceptible to attaching very quickly or developing an intense connection with a love interest in a short period of time. This doesn't necessarily mean they are "love addicts," but it is worth noting that a traumatic crisis like a worldwide pandemic can impact how human beings connect and what they are willing to tolerate or overlook in a new relationship.

   When it comes to love addiction, what might start as a desire to please their new partner soon morphs into something more consuming. They may clear their calendar and refuse to make plans with friends or family members in case they miss out on time with the person on whom they are romantically fixated. Early into the relationship, they begin to overlook red flags, excusing behaviors they might normally question, or keep secrets in an effort to protect their love interest. They adamantly dismiss the concerns of friends and family and will respond defensively or "ghost" the person questioning their relationship. As their fixation deepens, they refuse to vet their new person, or they may start to pull away from loved ones, deceive family members, neglect hobbies, and let their own needs slide, all in the name of maintaining the relationship.

   People who struggle with love addiction often tell themselves a story about their relationship that becomes their complete truth, even if reality does not support this. This internal messaging might sound like, "He has a busy schedule, and this is why he can never spend important holidays with me," or "I haven't met her friends or family even though we have been together for a year because she is a private person," or "I never know when we will be able to see each other or where he is at any given time because his job is very important and secretive and he cannot share his location," or "She hasn't made time to meet my friends because her schedule is so unpredictable that even a thirty-minute coffee date is out of the question." If their self-talk is questioned by important and trusted people in their life, such as a sibling, best friend, parent, or therapist, they will usually withdraw, become enraged, or simply vanish. They are in the throes of idealization, which often blocks their ability to exercise personal insight.

2. **Escalation Stage:** In the escalation stage of P.A.D., the dynamics of the relationship take a more concerning turn. The love-addicted person works harder to ignore or explain away the growing cracks or incongruencies in the relationship. For example, they may accept bare minimum efforts, never challenging their romantic interest. Sadly, their life becomes smaller and smaller—no planned vacations, no social gatherings, no consistent holiday events, no shared time with friends, and no outings like dinner dates, plays, movies, dances, weddings, or other activities that healthy, committed couples typically enjoy.

    If their romantic interest works all the time, the love addict will begin to work all the time or stay busy all the time. They will mirror their partner's interests and tastes at the expense of their own interests and tastes. If their romantic interest doesn't like something, such as watching TV or a certain style of clothing or food, the love-addicted person will soon fall into line. Should they be asked to be the secret keeper for their significant other, they will bear the symptoms of those secrets at this stage. Symptoms like anxiety, guilt, confusion, doubt, and even self-blame start to take hold, eroding their self-worth and sense of security.

    The unhappiness or anxiety they may experience during this stage is usually managed by blaming others for their discomfort: a boss, a coworker, a neighbor, or a concerned friend. Desperation to keep the relationship intact leads to increasing compromises—compromises that often chip away at their own values and boundaries. What they never thought they would tolerate, such as isolation, deception, chronic excuses, broken plans, keeping secrets from their loved ones, infidelity, addiction, or abuse, is now tolerated and their new normal.

    At this stage, the earliest seeds of anger, frustration, and disappointment begin to quietly take root. Despite their best efforts, the individual finds themselves trying—often in vain—to support their partner by offering an unhealthy level of understanding, overcompensating for problems, and making repeated excuses for hurtful behavior. Over time, as their own needs remain unmet or are only inconsistently acknowledged, feelings of resentment begin to grow. In an attempt to regain control or restore connection, they may resort to criticism, manipulation, or blame—strategies aimed at changing their partner rather than confronting the painful truth of the dynamic.

    These difficult emotions are often misdirected, projected onto concerned friends or family members rather than being linked to the unfulfilling relationship itself. As a result, loved ones may begin to pull away, particularly if their attempts to stay connected are consistently met with defensiveness or distance. If deception is part of the relationship, the love-addicted partner may begin to gaslight themselves—questioning their own instincts, minimizing red flags, and internalizing the blame for the cognitive dissonance they feel.

During this P.A.D. stage, the stress of maintaining the relationship might push the love-addicted individual toward unhealthy coping mechanisms, like out-of-control shopping, eating disorders, isolation, obsessive routines, intense amounts of excuse-making, hyper-busy schedules to occupy themselves, chronic defensiveness, or addictive behaviors. Self-messaging at this stage often includes the following: "Things will change. They are doing the best they can. No one understands our unique relationship. Their schedule will free up. We are the only people who really understand one another. Eventually, I will meet their family and friends, and they will meet my friends. Someday, we will have the holidays together. One day, he or she will get it together, and then our relationship will be wonderful. I need him or her for support. I can't imagine life without them. We were always meant to be. This is my one true love; we will get through the hard times. It is us against the world."

3. **Despair Stage:** By the time the relationship reaches the P.A.D. despair stage, it has often become a source of unhappiness, loneliness, or toxicity. It may take months, years, or, sadly, even decades to reach this point. During this stage, the love-addicted person starts to put the clues together. Usually, something is revealed or discovered, and they can no longer live in denial. To be clear, a betrayed partner of a sexually compulsive person is not necessarily a love addict; that is a different type of complex trauma discussed in another chapter of this workbook. However, love addicts at this stage do experience betrayal, and begin to feel stuck, knowing the relationship is harmful or deeply unfulfilling, yet they are terrified of leaving.

Terror is an emotion that is often experienced by the clients I work with when they begin to consider leaving the love-addicted relationship. They have often been in a state of denial for so long that what is real and what is not real is confusing. I describe this as being in a jail cell with the door wide open and the key in hand, yet feeling as if leaving is impossible. This is an element of trauma bonding that is explored in depth in Chapter One. The fear of being alone or abandoned keeps them trapped, even as their self-esteem continues to erode, even if the doubts they have been harboring become impossible to ignore.

If a love-addicted or trauma-bonded person is financially or physically dependent on their spouse or partner, facing a custody threat, or feeling that this is their last chance at love—especially as an older adult—it becomes even harder to break free. Years of gaslighting or deception only make the process more difficult. Additionally, some people in this stage feel shame knowing that the concerns their loved ones shared were valid—they are now worried about appearing foolish or ignorant to important people in their lives if they leave the relationship or share their disillusionment. They may also lack the support of friends or family by this stage, not knowing who to talk to because they have allowed their important friendships to erode.

The internal messaging usually sounds like, "I've invested so much—my time, trust, love, support, energy, even my financial resources. How can I ever rebuild my life?" or "I've burned all of my bridges with my loved ones, they will never forgive me," or "I am too old, too tired, too scared, too poor, too [fill in the blank] to start over with someone new or on my own," or "My children will suffer if I leave," or "I will be financially destitute." Though the concerns are to be held with compassion, by this stage, their lives are not in balance and they do not live an authentic existence. In worst cases, they may be dealing with health issues, chronic pain, digestive issues, or sleep disorders. An increase in anxiety or depression is typically present as well.

At this point, their sense of self-worth is almost entirely tied to the relationship, feeling as if that person is their only source of support, occasional excitement, and connection, or the only one who can provide them with comfort periodically—the breadcrumb effect. This creates a vicious cycle of emotional pain and dependency. The need to escape this inner turmoil often drives them further into destructive behaviors, or they may isolate or push people away, making it even harder to break free.

As you've come to understand through these Pathological Affection Dependency (P.A.D.) stages, individuals who struggle with love addiction need a great deal of support and compassion. They aren't "crazy," "pitiful," "stupid," or excessively "needy," and they certainly aren't like the "bunny boiler" stereotype from the movie *Fatal Attraction*. Instead, they are hurting people who need help to heal and learn how to build healthy, balanced, and connected relationships. Unfortunately, some love addicts have been exploited by individuals with predatory or manipulative tendencies, liars who are drawn to their deep desire for love and belonging. Rather than offering the love and acceptance these individuals seek, these predators exploit their vulnerabilities. Those prone to love addiction are often trying to heal long-standing emotional wounds with people who are neither capable, interested in long-term relationships, nor healthy enough to engage in a truly supportive relationship.

What Is Love Addiction?

The late Pia Mellody was a respected author and educator in the fields of addictions and relationships. Her popular book, *Facing Love Addiction*, was written for those who felt compulsively drawn into toxic, obsessive, or painful relationships. Mellody defines love addiction as "an unhealthy relationship which involves obsessive time, attention, and value given to another person." I would also include in this definition ongoing fantasies about the person of interest, social media stalking, regularly daydreaming about the person, and defending the person against real or perceived criticisms at any cost. Having your spouse or romantic partner's back is a good thing—until it is not.

A distinction that is important to note is that love addiction should not be confused with polyamory. Polyamory is a relationship style where individuals engage in multiple consensual, romantic, or sexual relationships simultaneously with the full knowledge and consent of everyone involved. Unlike traditional monogamous relationships, where partners agree to be exclusive to each other, polyamory embraces the idea that people can love more than one person at a time. Communication, honesty, and mutual respect are key elements in maintaining healthy polyamorous relationships, so all parties are aware of and agree to the arrangement.

"Love addiction" is a term some experts use to describe a behavioral addiction centered around romantic love. While current research suggests that attachment issues and emotional dysregulation are significant factors in this condition, more studies are needed to fully understand the connection. A notable 2022 study led by Alice Salani and her team delved into the potential link between love addiction, attachment issues and styles (from both childhood and adulthood), and emotional dysregulation. The study compared two groups of women: 155 in a clinical group and 189 in a control group. The findings revealed that the women in the clinical group exhibited much higher levels of emotional dysregulation and alexithymia. They also reported more experiences of parental control, had more preoccupied attachment styles, and received lower levels of parental care.

A 2022 study (Salani, A.) found several connections among these factors and suggested that love addiction might be influenced by negative attachment experiences throughout life, with emotional dysregulation and alexithymia playing key roles. Alexithymia is a condition where people have difficulty identifying and expressing their emotions. This can make it hard for them to understand their own feelings or share them with others, leading to challenges in emotional awareness and in building healthy attachments.

As discussed in other chapters of this book, early childhood trauma can significantly impact attachment styles, making it difficult for individuals to form healthy romantic connections in their adult lives. Experiences such as neglect, abuse, sexual molestation, sexual abuse experiences like Angela survived, or abandonment during formative years can disrupt the development of secure attachment bonds, leading to insecure, avoidant, or anxious attachment styles that persist into adulthood. Additionally, undiagnosed anxiety disorders or other mental health challenges may also contribute to love addiction. Angela experienced all of this in her family of origin and would often share feelings of haunting loneliness and a craving for belonging as some of her first remembered emotional needs.

People with anxious attachment styles may develop an intense fear of abandonment, constantly seeking reassurance and validation from their partners. This can result in what is sometimes referred to as "controlling," "needy," or "clingy" behaviors as they struggle to feel secure in their relationships. Conversely, those with avoidant attachment often become emotionally distant and self-reliant, fearing intimacy and vulnerability. They might find it hard to trust others and avoid forming deep connections to protect themselves from potential pain, especially if they have been hurt by a father, parental figure, or spouse or have been previously betrayed in love. These avoidant women and men may be attracted to partners who flow in and out of their lives, easily believing and even embracing the excuses that are given on why their new love interest is not more consistently present.

For women like Angela who struggle with what we will refer to as love addiction, as that is the term Angela herself most closely identified with and preferred using, these attachment issues can be particularly challenging. Love addiction, as stated earlier, involves an obsessive preoccupation with romantic relationships. As you are learning, this preoccupation is driven by an underlying need to fill emotional voids created by early trauma. For example, women with love addiction may repeatedly seek out relationships to soothe their pain, loneliness, or longing, hoping to find the love and validation they lacked in childhood. Sadly, the very patterns of attachment formed in response to their early trauma can undermine their efforts to connect. Anxious attachment can lead to a cycle of desperation, obsession, limerence, and ultimately fear and disappointment as these women may pursue or stay with partners who are unable or unwilling to meet their emotional needs. This often results in tumultuous relationships characterized by high levels of conflict and instability.

If you're unfamiliar with the term "limerence," let me explain further. In my clinical experience, it is almost always present in individuals facing these challenges. Limerence is more consuming than a crush or a passing romantic interest in someone. Rather, it is a deeply intense, almost obsessive feeling that goes beyond mere infatuation—as if the mind becomes completely focused on this person, and they can't stop thinking about them. These individuals might find themselves daydreaming about being with their romantic obsession to distraction, constantly analyzing every little interaction, plotting how to run into this person "accidentally," and feeling an incredible rush of excitement when they are around or crushing disappointment if they are not. They may even experience anxiety whenever they think about this person.

For love addicts, this can feel all-consuming, almost as if they are on an emotional rollercoaster, and it can sometimes make it hard to concentrate on anything else, including self-care, goals, career or academic responsibilities, family or parenting obligations, friendships, and hobbies. For some, the romantic person of interest becomes their daily obsession. For others, it doesn't matter if that person is already married or in a monogamous relationship. The movie *Fatal Attraction* and the shows *Presumed Innocent* and *Baby Reindeer* touch on the more troubling and dangerous aspects of romantic obsession that go much further than a mere crush. While not every person who experiences limerence or love addiction will obsess to this degree, for some—especially if there is a comorbid diagnosis—it can create dangerous consequences and even legal issues for that person.

With some anxiously attached people, they may connect with an opportunist who seeks to take advantage of their vulnerabilities. For example, the love-addicted person may inadvertently find that they are slowly being groomed for the role of caretaker for a partner who exhibited red flag behaviors that they previously overlooked. Once aware, they are unsure of how to leave the relationship. I have coined this aspect of love addiction with the term F.F.O.O.G. This is an acronym for "Fantasy, Fear, Obsession, Obligation, Guilt." As the fog (or F.F.O.O.G.) begins to clear over time, the hurting individual ultimately wonders how they ended up financially supporting this person, becoming their sole caregiver, or became trapped in a relationship that seems nearly impossible to leave.

In Chapter One on trauma bonding, I explore this aspect in depth. In my work with anxiously attached, love-addicted clients who may be trauma-bonded to their significant other, I remind them that "Caretaking is different than caregiving." Extending healthy levels of care to important people in one's life is natural. However, healthy adults do not need a caretaker. Caretaking is for infants, small children, people with severe mental health or physical challenges, those who are ill or recovering from surgery, or elderly individuals who need high levels of support. There is a great deal of trauma reduction work necessary to help these clients give themselves permission to step out of the fog of an anxiously attached or trauma-bonded relationship and walk into the light.

In an especially challenging session with Angela about mid-way through her therapy journey, I explained that "limerence is a powerful experience, yet it's important to recognize that it's often more about the fantasy or the idea of the person rather than who they really are. It's common in the early stages of romantic attraction, but when it becomes all-consuming, it can get in the way of having a healthy relationship with yourself and others." I assured Angela that we would continue to work on understanding her intense feelings while finding ways for her to manage them so they did not continue to overtake her life.

While Angela had an anxious attachment style, it is important to note that individuals with avoidant attachment styles may also find themselves gravitating toward partners who exhibit low levels of effort, inconsistency in presence, or tendencies toward deception and manipulation. This inclination toward less invested partners may arise from a subconscious preference for what feels familiar or easier to handle rather than seeking out deeper connections that require vulnerability, an investment of time, and an ongoing daily commitment. In some cases, individuals with avoidant attachment may inadvertently push away partners, even as they yearn for closeness, leading to a persistent sense of isolation and unmet longing that is perplexing for both them and their partners.

Transactional Relationships

Another aspect that impacts individuals grappling with love addiction is that they often find themselves ensnared in transactional relationships, where they perceive a constant need to pay for affection or companionship. We explore this in depth in the maternal wounding chapter of this workbook. This phenomenon extends beyond mere material exchanges; it encompasses emotional, psychological, and even spiritual transactions, where love-addicted individuals feel compelled to offer something of value in exchange for love. This could be money, or it could be providing support, running errands, providing encouragement, consistently being the one to extend a listening ear, being the person who always makes the plans, or doing nearly all of the emotional heavy lifting in the relationship.

In these kinds of transactional dynamics, a person may find themselves caught in a painful cycle of giving without receiving much in return. The act of giving—whether it's time, money, attention, or affection—can become a way to secure or maintain the love and connection they long for. This might look like showering a partner or friend with gifts, feeling like they have to pay for meals or outings just to be included, offering money they can't afford to give, constantly seeking approval through acts of service, picking up the tab for a group dinner, exchanging sex for companionship, or regularly ignoring their own needs in hopes of feeling valued and wanted.

As Angela experienced all too often during her early years as a model and actress, these patterns can leave someone vulnerable to being taken for granted—or worse, exploited—by people who don't have their best interests at heart. This doesn't mean Angela was to blame. Rather, it reflects the deeper trauma that shaped her understanding of love, worth, and connection.

For some, the belief that love must be earned or purchased stems from childhood experiences where affection was conditional upon meeting certain expectations or standards set by caregivers. Others may have internalized societal messages equating love with material wealth, beauty, or status, leading them to believe that they must constantly prove their worth through tangible offerings.

Transactional relationships, however, rarely fulfill the genuine emotional needs of those involved, especially for the wounded love addict whose core schema message is often, "I am not enough," "I am not worthy of love," or "I am not worthy of someone investing in me." Instead, they find themselves in a cycle of dependency and dissatisfaction, where authentic connection is overshadowed by the exchange of commodities or continued acts of never-ending support. Over time, the wounded individual may find themself increasingly resentful, disillusioned, and drained, as the superficial nature of these relationships fails to quench their deeper longing for authentic, mutually reciprocated love and acceptance. Bottom line: No one likes to feel as if they must pay for love.

For the love addict, breaking free from the grip of transactional relationships is one of the more difficult aspects of their healing and requires courage, insight, and support. This healing entails challenging the ingrained beliefs about love and worthiness and practicing mindfulness-based strategies in building what the esteemed psychiatrist Dr. Daniel Siegel calls the "window of tolerance." Siegel's concept of the window of tolerance refers to the range of emotional and physiological arousal levels within which a person can function effectively and manage stress. When someone is within their window of tolerance, they can think clearly, respond to challenges with resilience, develop personal insight, regulate emotions, and maintain a sense of well-being and equanimity. By recognizing and addressing the underlying insecurities and pain points driving their transactional behavior, individuals can begin to forge connections based on mutual respect, trust, and genuine affection rather than the exchange of goods or services.

Emophilia vs. Love Addiction

Love addiction and emophilia are both complex relational patterns, but they differ in how individuals engage with and seek relationships. Love addiction often involves an intense craving for connection and affirmation from another person, sometimes to the point where a person feels incomplete or lost without a partner. As we have explored in this chapter with Angela, this dependency can drive individuals to form attachments quickly, stay in unhealthy relationships, or idealize partners, often overlooking red flags. Love addicts may also experience cycles of emotional highs and lows, heavily influenced by their partner's attention or withdrawal, which can create a pattern of emotional turbulence.

Emophilia, on the other hand, is characterized by an individual's tendency to "fall in love" very quickly and intensely with new people. Unlike love addiction, which involves a hyper focus on one partner, emophilia drives a person to seek rapid attachment and novelty in relationships, often leading to frequent changes in partners. Emophiles may mistake initial infatuation for true love, leading to impulsive decisions in pursuit of that intense feeling. Once in the relationship, if they perceive something negative about their new love, they are on the hunt again, believing the grass is always greener. Conversely, love addiction may tie individuals to a single partner through dependency and trauma bonding; emophilia propels individuals into serial romantic entanglements, each driven by an idealized image of love and excitement. (Jones, 2024)

Novelty is the key for emophilia—the thrill of new romantic connections rather than a need for a lasting relationship. Individuals with high emophilia are drawn to the exhilarating feelings that come with new love, often pursuing it impulsively. This thrill-seeking behavior triggers their brain's reward centers, reinforcing the cycle of falling quickly and deeply, sometimes without sufficient discernment. This impulsivity can make these individuals more susceptible to toxic or unsuitable relationships, as the drive for excitement can overshadow careful evaluation of the partner's compatibility or intentions.

Rather than a steady desire for closeness, emophiles are driven by a craving for the intense highs of early romance. The chase and excitement of a fresh relationship become almost a pursuit in themselves, leading them to dive headfirst into new connections. This pattern may keep them from establishing deeper, stable bonds, as the allure of "new love" takes precedence over emotional intimacy, which typically develops over time.

Love Addiction and Manipulation

Another crucial aspect of love addiction is the tendency for individuals, particularly women with a trauma history, to overlook warning signs when entering romantic relationships. They may fail to recognize subtle or overt red flags, especially if they dismiss the importance of introducing their new partner to trusted people in their life due to fear of criticism or judgment. In doing so, they run the risk of isolating themselves or concealing information that loved ones would question.

They may withdraw from meaningful friendships or familial connections in a desperate attempt to shield their new love interest from the vetting process. Vetting in relationships simply means introducing a new romantic partner to trusted people and inviting them to appropriately weigh in with their non-invasive, compassionate feedback and gentle observations. Notice that I include the words "invite," "trusted," "non-invasive," and "compassionate." Vetting is not an invitation for loved ones to judge, control, or cross boundaries; rather, it is an opportunity for people who know you well to provide feedback that may help you gain insight into your new love interest.

Far too often, if a love-addicted individual's partner exhibits deceptive, manipulative, or abusive behavior and a friend or family member points this out, no matter how gently or kindly, the feedback is often resisted for fear of losing the relationship. Instead, they may find themselves fiercely defending the relationship when friends or family express concern. This defense may escalate to severing ties with cherished friends or distancing themselves from supportive family members. This misguided loyalty to their new partner can exacerbate feelings of anger toward those who are concerned as they withdraw from their social circle. This leads to further isolation and estrangement from their support networks, leaving them vulnerable to further manipulation and possible harm.

Clearly, not all love-addicted individuals end up in relationships with dishonest or manipulative partners. However, certain warning signs should not be ignored. For instance, if a new partner avoids meeting close friends or family members after many months or even years have passed, or if the love addicted individual has limited knowledge of their new love interest's social circle or whereabouts, it may warrant concern. Recurring situations where the love addict is often alone, uncertain whether their partner will join them for holidays, or given dubious explanations—such as demanding work schedules that don't match their partner's profession or far-fetched excuses like being trapped in another country without any way to communicate—should raise alarm bells. These patterns of behavior may indicate underlying issues that require further scrutiny and consideration.

As an aside, if you have a loved one—perhaps an adult child, sibling, or close friend—whom you believe is being manipulated and deceived by a new romantic partner, and they refuse to consider your concerns despite your compassionate efforts, it's important to remind yourself that they are an adult capable of making their own choices, no matter how difficult that may be to accept. Even if it is as plain as the sky above you that this person is not a healthy match, if your loved one has adamantly refused to accept your feedback time and again, respect their boundaries and let the wheel of time turn. Unless your loved one's life is in danger, the best you can do is hold space, hoping they will eventually see the truth, step out of the fog, and break free from the closed system they've created.

Healthy relationships thrive on fundamental principles such as mutual respect, trust, and transparent communication. Unlike closed systems, healthy relationships welcome the involvement of others and do not foster isolation or secrecy. They prioritize all aspects of life rather than neglecting certain areas for the sake of the relationship. Additionally, healthy relationships do not promote fear-based ideologies or extreme ideals that are manipulative, cult-like, or implausible.

Love addicts are often drawn to people who seem uniquely special, mysterious, or exciting. They can easily become immersed in a fantasy world, susceptible to grooming and manipulation, particularly if they are facing pre-existing challenges such as grief, loneliness, stress, job loss, illness, financial strain, recent breakups, single parenting, caring for an elderly parent, boredom, or the effects of a global pandemic or some other calamity. If you are presently reading this section and find yourself relating to what I am sharing yet resisting this information, I understand. Many years ago, as an intelligent young woman in the corporate business world, appearing confident and successful, I would have been deeply offended if someone had made these suggestions during the height of my love addiction.

By investing in strong connections with a diverse network of individuals and prioritizing self-love and personal growth, people healing from love addiction can cultivate resilience and independence, safeguarding themselves against the pitfalls of unhealthy relationships. Early in our work together, Angela rejected some of this as well, stating, "I don't want to turn into a paranoid person afraid of love and questioning every man who crosses my path!" My response was, "For love addicts in recovery, it's about practicing new skills, not marinating in paranoia." Recognizing the value of all types of relationships and sources of fulfillment allows individuals to lead balanced, fulfilling lives enriched by an array of connections and experiences.

In therapy, a significant part of recovery for love addicts involves challenging these deeply ingrained cultural narratives that support a perfect twin flame or fantasy soul mate—to understand the difference between healthy intimacy versus obsessive, isolating intensity. An essential part of recovery is practicing a more balanced and realistic understanding of attachment styles, love, and relationships. This includes recognizing that while romantic love can be a beautiful and enriching part of life, it is not the sole source of happiness or self-worth, and it never requires that we reduce ourselves or withdraw from important relationships.

By engaging in therapy, attending support groups, and practicing mindfulness-based activities and exercises, such as those outlined at the conclusion of this chapter, as well as staying connected to loving and trusted family and friends, recovering love addicts can move forward into a more positive relationship with themselves. Through these practices, they reduce anxiety, fantasy-based thinking, and abandonment trauma and, instead, cultivate self-compassion, self-acceptance, and emotional resilience. This newfound self-awareness leads them to recognize their intrinsic worth as complete and valuable individuals, irrespective of their relationship status.

As healing progresses, something powerful begins to happen—people start trusting themselves in ways they never have before. They become more aware of red flags and feel less vulnerable to manipulation or emotional harm from unhealthy partners. For example, instead of making excuses for someone who cancels plans repeatedly or crosses a boundary, they might speak up or even walk away, honoring their own worth instead of clinging to the hope that things will magically change.

They also notice that the panic or fear of being abandoned—what once felt overwhelming—starts to soften. That deep, aching terror of being left or unloved eases as they begin to nurture the parts of themselves that were ignored or silenced for years. This kind of self-reconnection gives them the courage to say things like, "This doesn't feel right to me," or "I need space to think about what I want," without crumbling under guilt or anxiety.

With this deeper sense of self, they stop building relationships based on fantasy or the illusion of a perfect partner. Instead, they begin choosing connections based on mutual respect, emotional safety, and shared values. They feel less need to hide their relationship or guard it from the people who care about them. Gone are the days of obsessing over the "mystery man" or woman while friends and family watch with growing concern. Now, they invite others in, seeking support and perspective—not secrecy.

For healing love addicts, privacy is a healthy boundary—an intentional choice about what to share, when, and with whom. Secrecy, however, hides behavior out of fear, shame, or control. Where privacy creates space for self-respect, secrecy often deepens the cycle of isolation, disconnection, obsession, and self-abandonment.

This kind of healing work doesn't just change how they relate to others—it brings a stronger sense of balance, grounding, and peace. Relationships begin to feel more stable, more real, and far more fulfilling.

As Angela learned through her personal journey, the notions of the perfect soulmate that would ultimately save her advanced unrealistic expectations and behaviors. These concepts often perpetuate the belief that love must be enigmatic, extraordinary, and unparalleled. By confronting this in our work together and cultivating a more nuanced perception of love and self-value, Angela developed healthier, more gratifying relationships and ultimately created a much more fulfilling life for herself.

As you have learned in this chapter, early childhood trauma can deeply affect attachment styles, making it difficult to form healthy connections. For those struggling with love addiction, these challenges can be particularly pronounced, often leading to a cycle of obsession and unhealthy relationships. Healing involves understanding and addressing the impact of early trauma, developing self-awareness, and fostering secure, healthy attachments. The next part of this chapter will allow you, the reader, to explore some of these concepts through guided imagery, art, and self-reflection.

Mindfulness Healing Part I:
Preparation, Assessment, and Script
for Guided Imagery Exercise

Important Safety Tips for Therapists, Facilitators, and Healing Individuals

Environment Consideration and Tips: It can be helpful to "set the stage" prior to a guided imagery exercise. For example, consider the lighting—is it too bright or too low? Another helpful step is putting phones on silent. Also, think about outside distractions, such as barking dogs, traffic, and other interruptions. If possible, minimize outside noises the best that you can. Some individuals like having a blanket or pillow to hold, or you may enjoy diffusing essential oils to support deeper relaxation if there are no allergy concerns. While mindfulness-based guided imagery is not hypnosis, it can be helpful to prepare your environment prior to beginning the guided imagery exercise.

Voice Prosody: An additional gentle reminder is to be aware of your voice prosody. Prosody refers to the rhythm and melody of the voice, including intonation, stress, and pauses. Speaking in a softer tone and slower cadence than your normal speaking voice is useful in supporting the guided imagery practice. If you typically speak more rapidly or loudly, it will take some practice to slow down and modulate your voice.

Diversity Considerations: Consider the client's culture, age, race, physical differences (such as hearing loss), gender and orientation, and other unique experiences that may invite a softer or different speaking tone or pace or require that the client keep their eyes open if they prefer. If you are bilingual and you and your client speak the same languages, ask your client what language they prefer. If your client prefers to go by a nickname, a title such as Dr., Mr., or Mrs., or a specific pronoun, honor their request.

Pace Yourself: Remind yourself to take your time as you walk through this process. There is no need to rush. If you are the person facilitating this exercise, slow down for a relaxed, calming pace. Additionally, it is wise for the facilitator to first practice the exercise with themselves prior to practicing with another person or client.

Safety Reminder: Safety is the number one consideration with any therapeutic approach or healing intervention. As you lead your clients through the following guided imagery exercise, please instruct your clients to alert you if they are experiencing any of the following responses. NOTE: If you are an individual doing this work solo, you will also want to consider the following:

- Traumatic memories that are creating a high level of distress

- Feelings of intense fear or panic

- Disturbing or intrusive thoughts

- Suicidal or homicidal thoughts

- Dissociation (if there is an awareness of the dissociative states)

- Other crisis concerns (list on the line): _____
_____

It is also important to ask the client to alert you if they experience any of the following symptoms. Likewise, if someone is doing this work solo, they should pay compassionate and close attention to their process and monitor for distressing or physical symptoms such as:

- A racing heart
- Tightness in the chest
- Shortness of breath
- Nausea or Intestinal distress
- Feeling faint or dizzy
- Body pain
- Feeling as if you are floating outside of your body

- Other somatic concerns (list on the line): _____
_____

Note for Therapist or Facilitator: Before moving into the guided imagery, please have your client begin with the assessment below. If you are not a trained mental health professional and your client is in crisis and exhibiting or discussing symptoms that are out of your scope of practice or experience, please refer your client to an appropriate mental health or medical professional. *If your client is experiencing an immediate life-threatening emergency, please call 911 or the appropriate emergency number if located outside of the United States.*

Note to Solo Reader: *If you are doing this work on your own and believe you are in crisis or may be at risk to yourself, please stop and seek emergency support immediately by calling 911 or your local emergency number.*

Pre-Guided Imagery Assessment Scale

On a scale from 1 to 10 (with 1 = very low, and 10 = very high), please take a mindful moment to assess the following. Circle the number that most accurately applies to you:

Feeling	Assessment (1-10)									
▢ Anxiety	1	2	3	4	5	6	7	8	9	10
▢ Anger	1	2	3	4	5	6	7	8	9	10
▢ Shame	1	2	3	4	5	6	7	8	9	10
▢ Sadness	1	2	3	4	5	6	7	8	9	10
▢ Fear	1	2	3	4	5	6	7	8	9	10
▢ Numbness	1	2	3	4	5	6	7	8	9	10
▢ Confusion	1	2	3	4	5	6	7	8	9	10
▢ Curiosity	1	2	3	4	5	6	7	8	9	10
▢ Hopefulness	1	2	3	4	5	6	7	8	9	10
▢ Calm	1	2	3	4	5	6	7	8	9	10
▢ Joyful	1	2	3	4	5	6	7	8	9	10
▢ Other:	1	2	3	4	5	6	7	8	9	10

Assessment Notes: _____

_____

_____

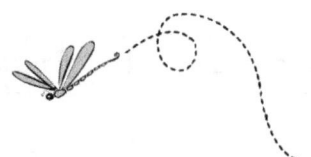

Mindfulness Healing Part II:
Breath and Somatic Preparation & Prompts

This exercise involves tuning into your breath and body and is followed by the guided imagery exercise. It's important to note that this may not be suitable for everyone. It's recommended that the following be adapted to the specific needs and comfort levels of the individual(s) involved.

Physical Space and Comfort: Have your client settle into a comfortable sitting or lying down position, with their feet on the floor or cross-legged if that is the preference. If your client—or you if you are doing this solo—has a yoga mat or a couch and prefers to lie down, that is fine. Whatever position will help the client feel comfortable is perfectly acceptable.

Prompt 1: Let's pause while you take a few moments to get comfortable.

Prompt 2: When you are ready, you are welcome to close your eyes if that feels comfortable for you. Or, if you prefer to leave your eyes open, that is just fine. Whatever allows you to feel most secure is more than acceptable. If your eyes remain open, feel free to rest your gaze on a calming point—near the floor if you're sitting or on the ceiling if you're lying down.

Prompt 3: We will now move forward into the grounded breathing exercise. This will take approximately two to three minutes.

Grounded Breath Exercise

Now that you are in a comfortable position, before we begin the guided imagery, let's move through the grounded breath work.

1. We will start with the 4-2-7 breath. Start by breathing in deeply through the nose to the count of four, hold for two, and then exhale slowly and intentionally through the mouth to the count of seven. Let's do this three times at your own pace. *Note to Facilitator: Count to 20 silently.*

2. Now, let's return to easy, relaxed, deep breathing. Take in a long breath in through the nose and a long exhale out through the mouth. Continue with this breath. *Note to Facilitator: Count to 20 silently.*

3. As you are noticing the gentle rhythm of deep breathing, I would like you to imagine extending compassion to yourself with each intake breath. *Note to Facilitator: Count to 20 silently.*

Somatic Relaxation Exercise

Now that we have finished with our grounded breaths, please feel free to breathe normally with relaxed, regular breaths. Let's now move into relaxing the body in preparation for guided imagery:

1. Notice that your feet are feeling heavier and more relaxed.

2. Notice that your hands are gently resting at your sides, on your belly, or on your thighs.

3.   Feel your jaw relax and your tongue move away from the roof of your mouth.

4.   Allow your shoulders to relax down from your ear lobes and your elbows to gently relax down from your shoulders.

5.   Bit by bit, the tension moves out of your body as you breathe in and relax and breathe out and relax. Breathe in compassion, hope, and healing, and breathe out stress, judgment, and anger. **Note to Facilitator: Count to 20 silently.**

As we complete our breath work, we will now move on to the guided imagery preparation and exercise section. You can return to your breath work exercises at any point during the guided imagery. The guided imagery exercise will take approximately 10 minutes. You may continue to stay in your comfortable position or shift to a different comfortable position. You may also continue with your eyes closed if that is your preference. At any point, you are welcome to ask for a time out if needed.

Let's move forward.

Mindfulness Healing Part III
Guided Imagery: The Stairway

Note to Therapist or Facilitator: If you notice that the client is highly activated during the guided imagery, perhaps demonstrating rapid or shallow breathing, sobbing, or shaking, please have the client pause as you attend to the individual. This can be done by gently stating that you would like to pause the exercise for a moment, then quietly asking the person by name if they would like a break, support with deep breath work, or to step out of the guided imagery entirely if it has become too overwhelming.

Note to the Reader: If you are doing this solo without the support of a mental health professional, again, please be gentle with yourself. If you have a trusted person to lead you through this, you may want to consider this option, or perhaps you can read this into a recording device and then play back and follow the prompts. If you become overwhelmed or feel as if you are in a crisis state, please stop and reach out for help if need be. Safety first, always.

Note: If you are a person with a disability and are unable to walk, please imagine yourself moving through this guided imagery in whatever manner feels best for you. That could be in a wheelchair, with a cane, with pet assistance, or even flying or floating if you prefer. Your own imagination will be honored and valued.

Purpose of the Stairway Guided Imagery: This guided imagery exercise is designed to help you practice mindful and compassionate presence with yourself. As you move through the exercise, the aim is to help you envision safe supports in your life and a feeling of moving up, cultivate a sense of self-agency, and change internal negative messages.

Instructions: This guided imagery exercise will take approximately 10 minutes. You will be guided by your mental health professional or trusted facilitator (or you may guide yourself if you prefer) through each step of the exercise slowly. If you do not have a therapist, sponsor, mentor, coach, or trusted friend or family member to facilitate this, you can always read the guided imagery script below aloud to yourself while recording this on your smartphone or device and then play the recording back to yourself. Though questions may be asked of you by the therapist or facilitator, or you may be given prompts if you are doing this with someone, there is no expectation of a verbal response. You may respond if you would like to do so, or you may quietly respond inside of yourself, which many people prefer. Through this visualization journey, you will be guided to explore your internal world, strengths, and resiliency in a new way.

First Step Prompt: Close your eyes, take a deep breath, and allow yourself to sink into a comfortable position. When you are ready, picture a stairway. The stairway is a safe place, and it can be a familiar stairway or one you are imagining for the first time now. It can be an outdoor or indoor stairway—whatever you prefer is fine as long as it is safe. **Note to Facilitator: Count to 20 silently.**

Next Prompt Step: Now, imagine that you are at the bottom of the stairway, calm and secure, but you would like to invite someone on this journey with you. This could be a compassionate support who is alive, someone who has passed, your higher power, a friend, a family member, or even a pet. Take a moment to invite them to join you at the bottom of the stairway, and let them know this will be a safe journey. **Note to Facilitator: Count to 20 silently.**

Next Prompt Step: Now that you have invited your supportive journey companion, begin to slowly move up the stairway in a way that is best for you or them—one step at a time or with assistance if needed. Notice the feeling of moving up the stairway. What are you noticing? What sounds, sights, and smells? Is there a rail? Is there carpeting or art? Notice this now as you continue up the stairway. If you need to stop and take a breath, you can do that as well. **Note to Facilitator: Count to 20 silently.**

Next Prompt Step: As you breathe deeply and move off the stairway onto a safe and secure landing, you will notice a door with a lock in front of you. Notice the door, reminding yourself that you are safe and the door is not frightening; there are no surprises waiting to hurt or harm you. What shape is the door? What type of lock and handle is on the door? Take a moment to observe this. **Note to Facilitator: Count to 20 silently.**

Next Prompt Step: Your safe companion will hand you the key to the door. What does the key look like? Is it attached to anything? Can you feel the weight of this in your hand? Does it have a certain color or shape? Notice that now. **Note to Facilitator: Count to 20 silently.**

Next Prompt Step: It is time to unlock the door and step into the room; remember, this is a very gentle and safe journey. If you need to take a deep breath, you can do that now. Your journey companion can go in with you, or you can request that they wait just outside of the door for you. **Note to Facilitator: Count to 20 silently.**

Next Prompt Step: As you unlock the door and step into the room, you realize with a sense of happiness that this room is a room designed exactly how you would like it to be designed. It can be an inside room or an outside space, whatever you prefer. Notice if there is furniture, a fireplace, a piano, or something else you like. Is it daylight, sunrise, sunset, or evening? If the room is an inside room, what do the views out of the windows look like? Are the windows open? Is it breezy, rainy, or sunny? What is the temperature in the room? Is there music or other sounds? Take a moment to get to know this room. **Note to Facilitator: Count to 20 silently.**

Next Prompt Step: You now notice a small container in your room. This interests you, and you do not feel any fear, only anticipation. Perhaps the container is a box, a jar, a drawer, a bowl, or some other type of container. Take a moment and imagine this now. Look at the details of your container before you open it. What are you noticing? **Note to Facilitator: Count to 20 silently.**

Next Prompt Step: Now, open your container. Inside, you will see a small piece of paper with a short and compassionate message just for you. What color and texture is the paper? As you unfold or unfurl the paper, you read the message. This message could be from your inner child, a part of yourself, a friend, a family member, or a loved one who is alive or has passed. It could be from your higher power, a mentor, or even someone you respect or admire that you've never met. Take a moment to gaze at this healing message that has been waiting just for you. What does the loving message say? How do you feel when you read this? What sensations do you feel in your body? Take a moment to stay with this experience **Note to Facilitator: Count to 20 silently.**

Next Prompt Step: As you place your message into your special container for safe keeping and close the lid, you can be reassured that this message will always be here waiting for you at any time. Before moving toward the door, take another look around your beautiful, peace-filled room. Are you noticing anything new and supportive at this time? **Note to Facilitator: Count to 20 silently.**

Next Prompt Step: You are now feeling ready to say goodbye to your room for now, knowing you can confidently return to this space whenever you would like to do so. As you move back outside of the door, you turn to lock your special room, taking away a more solid feeling of your own self-worth, dignity, and courage. You are welcome to keep the key, or you may give it to your safe companion to hold for you, whatever you prefer. **Note to Facilitator: Count to 20 silently.**

Next Prompt Step: It is now time to move back down the stairway, either one step at a time at the pace that is best for you or with assistance if you prefer. As you move off the last step of your safe stairway, you turn to your companion, thank them for their support, and say farewell for now, knowing you can invite them back at another time if you choose to do so. **Note to Facilitator: Count to 20 silently.**

Next Prompt Step: Before we come back to the present, know that you have the strength and resilience to work through the challenges that you have been facing. Those challenges may be due to relationship struggles with yourself or someone else. Or perhaps they involve fear, abandonment, love addiction, anxiety, or other difficulties. Please remember that you are not alone in this journey of healing. You are supported. No matter the challenges that come your way, remember that you are worthy of a life and relationships filled with love, authenticity, respect, joy, and fulfillment. Take a moment now to give yourself an affirmation. Self-affirmations may take you out of your comfort zone, but do your best to stay present with yourself, even in the discomfort. **Note to Facilitator: Count to 20 silently.**

Transitioning to Awareness

Final Prompt Step: When you're ready, if your eyes are closed, notice the light in front of your eyelids. Gently blink, open your eyes, and bring your awareness back to the present moment.

Note to Facilitator or Reader: Engaging in somatic movement, if you are able to do so, such as gentle stretching, walking, rhythmic body movements, or dancing to music, following guided imagery is vital for healing trauma as it allows individuals to release stored tension, process emotions, and reconnect with their bodies, facilitating a holistic approach to healing. Please take 3-5 minutes to move your body in a way that feels good for you. Yoga poses, stretching, dance, bouncing gently, rhythmically swaying, or a short walk are all excellent ways to honor yourself.

Mindfulness Healing Part IV:
Processing of Guided Imagery
Sharing Your Experience

Purpose for Processing: After the conclusion of the guided imagery, the therapist or facilitator will lead an open and respectful discussion about what you experienced during the guided imagery. The aim is to allow for a compassionate and honest conversation as you highlight important aspects of the guided imagery exercise and what the experience was like.

Note: If you are doing this solo without a therapist or facilitator, please pace yourself and notice your energy. You may use a journal of your choice to answer the process questions listed below and write about your experience.

Important Considerations for the Facilitator: It is not the role of the therapist or facilitator to interpret, minimize, or re-direct during the client's process of discussing their guided imagery experience. Rather, it is important for the facilitator to skillfully hold a safe space for the client to share their experience, including the more difficult aspects. This is a time for the therapist or facilitator to honor the pain, as well as highlight and affirm the positive insights the client may have had. Remind the client that participating in a mindfulness-based exercise like this is a signal of hope and aids in the possibility of recovery and healing.

Processing Questions

1. What did you notice in the guided imagery?

2. What challenges did you experience?

3. What joys or other emotions did you experience?

4. Did you have a breakthrough you'd like to share?

5. Do you have any concerns that you'd like to share?

6.   What are you feeling in your body currently?

7.   Did you notice any self-growth with insight and compassion toward yourself?

8.   Did you notice any triggers or areas of concern?

Message in a Bottle Mindful Moment

Before we move on to the post-assessment, let's take a moment for you to either write the message that was in your container during the guided imagery on the paper in the bottle illustration, or you can create a different message or even a drawing if you prefer. You can also add other drawings inside or outside of the bottle if you would like to do so. Imagine that this message in a bottle will find you exactly when needed:

Helpful Tip: If you would like to take a photo of this image to keep on your phone so that this message is handy, we encourage you to do that when you have completed your drawing.

Post-Guided Imagery Assessment Scale

Now that you have completed the breath work and somatic exercises, the guided imagery exercise, the message in the bottle, and the process work, on a scale from 1 to 10 (with 1 = very low, and 10 = very high), let's take a mindful moment to assess the following:

Feeling	Assessment (1-10)									
▫ Anxiety	1	2	3	4	5	6	7	8	9	10
▫ Anger	1	2	3	4	5	6	7	8	9	10
▫ Shame	1	2	3	4	5	6	7	8	9	10
▫ Sadness	1	2	3	4	5	6	7	8	9	10
▫ Fear	1	2	3	4	5	6	7	8	9	10
▫ Numbness	1	2	3	4	5	6	7	8	9	10
▫ Confusion	1	2	3	4	5	6	7	8	9	10
▫ Curiosity	1	2	3	4	5	6	7	8	9	10
▫ Hopefulness	1	2	3	4	5	6	7	8	9	10
▫ Calm	1	2	3	4	5	6	7	8	9	10
▫ Joyful	1	2	3	4	5	6	7	8	9	10
▫ Other:	1	2	3	4	5	6	7	8	9	10

Next: Take a moment to compare your pre-assessment scale to your post-assessment scale and assess changes, if any, that have occurred. List out what you believe may have contributed to these changes:

_____

_____

_____

_____

_____

Important Reminder: If you, as the facilitator, are not a licensed therapist or trained mental health professional and your client is in crisis and exhibiting or discussing symptoms that are out of your scope of practice or experience, please refer your client to an appropriate mental health or medical professional. *If your client is experiencing an immediate life-threatening emergency, please call 911 or the appropriate emergency number if located outside of the United States. If you are doing this solo without support and are in a state of emergency, reach out to 911 or an emergency team in your area immediately.*

Mindfulness Healing Part V:

Purpose Statement: The purpose of this healing art exercise is to guide you in exploring the idea that while healthy romantic love can be a beautiful and enriching experience, it is not the sole source of your worth or happiness. Through this exercise, you will learn to embrace the power within yourself, recognizing that you are fully capable of being your own "champion in shining armor." You are whole and complete as you are, regardless of whether or not you are in an intimate relationship. This practice encourages you to cultivate self-love, self-compassion, and a deeper understanding that your value comes from within and that you are enough just as you are. By engaging in this creative process, you will begin to see yourself as the hero of your own journey who's capable of thriving and flourishing on your own terms.

Art Exercise Instructions: Gather art supplies such as paper, colored pencils, stickers, or other dry materials. Please be mindful if you choose to use supplies like markers or paints, as these can sometimes bleed through to the next page. You may want to place a blank sheet of paper underneath your work to protect the following pages.

1. Begin by finding a quiet and comfortable space where you can focus without distractions.

2. Take a few moments to center yourself through deep breathing, visualization, or grounding exercises. Allow yourself to become present in the moment, acknowledging any thoughts or emotions that arise.

3. Once you feel grounded, imagine that the champion in shining armor has just galloped up beside you. As they hop down off the horse and lift the front of the helmet, you notice that it is *your* face smiling back at you—you are the champion! Think of the armor as your boundaries that protect you— a healthy shield that you control.

4. Using your art supplies, begin to draw the face inside of the helmet on the next page; it can be your exact face, you at a certain age, a part of you, or even something that represents you. Your creativity is honored here.

5. As you work on your art, pay attention to any emotions or sensations that arise. Allow yourself to explore them openly and without negative self-talk. Remember that there are no right or wrong ways to express yourself through art.

6. Once you have completed your art exercise, take a step back and observe your creation. Reflect on the journey it represents, recognizing the challenges you have faced and the progress you have made.

7. Finally, think about strategies that will support your path toward healing.

8. Take a moment to appreciate yourself for engaging in this healing art exercise and for the courage you have shown. Allow yourself to feel a sense of pride and accomplishment as you continue your journey of recovery.

Mindful Reflection Moment

Now that you have completed your breath work, guided imagery, assessment reflection, and art journal exercises, as we bring this chapter to a close, please take some mindful time to process. You are welcome to answer the following questions in the space below, or write in a journal or notebook of your choice. You may do this with your therapist or facilitator, or if you are working through this book solo, you can do this on your own.

1. What are you noticing after this chapter?

2. What awareness and insight have surfaced?

3. What is the information you have learned?

Write or share your reflections here if you would like to do so. As always, please be gentle with yourself:

_____

_____

_____

_____

_____

_____

Final Step: Self-Affirmation Exercise

Instructions: Before moving on to the next chapter, can you give yourself the gift of self-affirmation? Affirming oneself can be difficult for those who have experienced wounding in intimate relationships, suffered betrayal or abuse, or are dealing with love addiction, healing from complex trauma, or struggling with anxiety or depression.

As a support to this step of your healing, affirmation ideas might include statements such as: "I am whole, complete, and worthy of love, regardless of my relationship status," "I have the strength within me to be my own champion and create the life I desire," and "My value is not defined by others; I am enough exactly as I am." Please take a mindful moment in the winged heart below to honor your own self-affirmation(s). If you can only come up with one affirmation at this time, that is more than acceptable. Perhaps you can return later in your healing process and add more:

As we conclude this chapter, let's reflect on some of the complex dynamics discussed. We explored the deep impact of sexual molestation on attachment styles and self-perception, which can often lead individuals to form relationships built on insecure attachments. In cases of love addiction and limerence, for example, the drive for external validation can create an emotional dependency that feels all-consuming, sometimes resulting in idealization of a partner, isolation from others, and transactional relationship patterns that ultimately limit genuine connection. While love addiction is an emerging area of study with limited research, we considered its patterns through the lens of attachment theory.

In discussing transactional relationships, we examined how unmet emotional needs can lead to viewing relationships as exchanges, where self-worth becomes tied to what we give or receive rather than mutual care. Similarly, idealization can serve as a defense mechanism, helping individuals feel secure but often at the expense of seeing their partner clearly, sometimes leading to emotional isolation. Ultimately, whether we're dealing with patterns of love addiction, transactional dynamics, or insecure attachment, each topic underscores the importance of cultivating self-awareness, boundaries, and the courage to prioritize healthy connections that are rooted in respect and authenticity.

Before moving forward, I'd like to offer a gentle affirmation: You are a whole and unique person, valuable just as you are. Your worth is inherent and doesn't depend on anyone else's validation—you are enough, just as you are. Know that you deserve joy, peace, and fulfillment simply because you exist. Take a moment to acknowledge all the work you've done in this chapter. You are healing, growing, and moving forward in ways that honor your journey.

As you carry these thoughts with you, I'd like to share a quote that has held deep meaning for me on my own path, and I hope it brings you comfort, too:

You are the sky. Everything else is just the weather.

~ Pema Chödrön

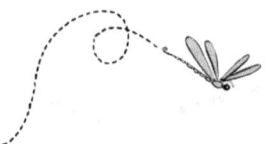

CHAPTER TEN

Showing Up: From Scared and Suppressed to Safe and Seen

Wendy Quinton

The greatest wound a child can receive is the rejection of (their) authentic self.

~ John Bradshaw

"Gabriela?" I questioned as I faced the lone woman in my waiting room. She nodded her head in agreement, and I commented further, "I am glad to meet you, and what a beautiful name you have." She murmured a quiet "Thank you." I continued, "Do your friends call you Gabriela, or have they shortened your name?" She replied, "They call me Gabby—but whatever you want is fine." "Well, I would like to call you whatever you like best!" I exclaimed, and she looked up, seemingly surprised. She replied tentatively, "I like Gabby better—only my parents still call me Gabriela—but if you forget, that's okay. I'll answer to anything." "Okay, Gabby, it is," I replied, making a mental note to explore her reluctance to state her preference.

Once we had finished covering the usual formalities, I invited Gabby to share what had led her to seek therapy. "Well," she stuttered as she shrugged and looked down, "I should tell you that it wasn't my idea. I'm sure you're a great therapist and all, but this is something I never thought I'd do. As a Latina raised in the Catholic church, I've been taught that the only help you need is from the church, God, or your family. So, it feels weird to be sitting here with a stranger, getting ready to talk about my life. But my partner said that if I don't start 'showing up' in our relationship, she is going to break up with me." Gabby's voice faded as she quietly added, "I honestly don't even know what showing up means."

I assured Gabby that she had already started showing up by coming to therapy and that I would be glad to help her explore the idea further. I invited her to start by telling me a little more about herself. She thought for a moment and said, "There isn't much to tell. I'm twenty-six years old, and I was born in the Dominican Republic but lived most of my life here in the States. I work in a law office, and I have a girlfriend. Her name is Ashley—oh, so I guess you now know that I'm a lesbian," she added with a nervous laugh. She sat in silence and looked uncomfortable as she glanced around the room.

"Thank you, Gabby," I responded. "Is it okay if I repeat back to you what I've heard you say so far?" She nodded her consent, and I gave her a summary of the details about her life that she had revealed to me. She listened closely and seemed shocked—perhaps that she had revealed so much to a stranger or that I had actually listened to her.

"And, Gabby, please correct me if I'm wrong, but you seemed to struggle when you told me about your girlfriend, so I'm guessing that you are not usually very open about being gay? Is that something you'd like to talk about? I think it might be an important piece to look at as we explore what it can mean to 'show up.' Is this an uncomfortable topic for you?"

She briefly met my eyes and nodded her head. After fiddling with the tissue in her hands for a moment, she began, "Well, I was raised as a strict Catholic—baptized as an infant, first communion at eight, and confirmed in the church when I turned fourteen. My dad was very strict and cold, and he could be really mean to my mom. But she just did whatever he said and made sure that my siblings and I did, too. I was raised to believe that we had to look like the perfect family wherever we went, regardless of the way we were treated at home. Mom measured everything by 'what will people think,' and even though she seemed very unhappy with her life, she dressed up and attended mass each Sunday and made sure we did as well. She always smiled in the presence of others, and I learned to behave just like her. I assumed that's how every family functioned." Gabby's voice was tight, and with the stress her body was clearly holding, she continued to wring the tissue between her clenched fists.

I nodded encouragingly, inviting Gabby to take a deep breath and continue when she was ready. Gabby seemed grateful for the pause, took a shaky breath, and shared, "I learned early in life that putting on a good front for others meant hiding my feelings because I was punished for outwardly showing anger or unhappiness. So, I got pretty good at burying my emotions and continued to hide my attraction to women. I knew that our church taught that being gay was a sin, and I tried hard to ignore what I felt and kept it a secret.

"I struggled with guilt every time I went to church because experience taught me that I couldn't measure up to what they told me God required, and, as the years went on, I became more and more withdrawn. I felt like a fraud but continued to paste on a smile whenever I was around other people, just like I was taught."

Gabby stopped talking as a tear slid down her cheek, but she quickly shook her head, wiped it away, and continued her story. "As I got older, it got harder to deny my sexuality, and I finally built up the courage to mention to my mom that I wondered if I was gay, just to see what she would say. Immediately, her face turned red, and she yelled, 'You're not gay! You know that homosexuality is against the teachings of the church, and I don't want to ever hear you talk about this again! You will find a nice Catholic boy and have lots of babies—do you understand me?' I instantly felt my head nodding in agreement as I was trained to do, knowing that I couldn't bear it if my mom was disappointed in me. I pushed down all the pain and continued to keep all my feelings inside of me.

"After I graduated from high school and went away to college, I finally thought that I could be myself, and I began my first relationship with a girl. But I didn't tell anyone in my family. We dated casually for a while, but since I wasn't publicly 'out' yet, she felt like I was ashamed of her and broke up with me. I had some other brief relationships, but nothing serious, and I was beginning to think that I would never find someone who would be worth the risk of my family's rejection."

Gabby continued, with a small smile brightening up her face, "But then, about a year ago, I met Ashley. She is everything that I'm not—outgoing, confident, open about her sexuality... She even talks about her feelings all of the time. We often laugh about how 'opposites attract.' Eventually, Ashley wanted to meet my family, and I had to confess to her that we couldn't visit them because my family disapproved of same-sex relationships. I remember mumbling quietly that I hadn't yet told them that I was dating a woman.

Ashley was shocked and wanted to know how I coped with this and why I had never been honest with her about my relationship with my family. I told her that I was afraid of my dad becoming violent if he found out that I was gay and that my mom would probably disown me. I shared my fear that my siblings would have to choose sides and risk my parents' wrath if they continued to communicate with me. I knew that I couldn't change any of this, so I kept pretending that I got along well with my family. I didn't tell her the truth because I didn't see the point—it is what it is."

By this stage in her story, Gabby's smile had faded, and the pain was back in her eyes. Her voice got quieter as she continued, "That's when I saw a side of Ashley that I hadn't before. She was so hurt and upset. She told me then how hard it was becoming for her to be with me because she never knows what I am feeling. She was hoping that I would change as we got to know each other better, but she shared that she feels like our relationship is going nowhere. She felt that hiding my true relationship with my family from her was a betrayal of her trust, and that's when she gave me the ultimatum: Either I learn to start showing up, or she will leave." Gabby hurriedly brushed aside another tear and pleaded, "I really love her—can you help me?"

I took a deep breath, invited Gabby to do so as well, and then let her know that I could feel how painful this situation was for her and that I would be honored to work with her to find a solution.

I continued by sharing with Gabby that I recognized an emerging pattern in the way that she dealt with painful emotions: denying and suppressing them in an effort to not consciously feel them. As we went through that first therapy session together, I explained to Gabby that the way we learn to cope with difficulties as children often becomes ingrained patterns in our lives and that while these patterns keep us safe while we are young, they eventually impede our growth as adults.

To illustrate this concept, I invited Gabby to join me in a brief exercise if she was willing. Gabby nodded curiously, and I asked her to take another deep breath with me, center herself, and then think about a time in her early life when she felt frightened and to share it with me if she could. Picking at her nail polish, she was quiet for a long time and then spoke in a soft voice, telling me that one of her earliest memories was being lost in a store and feeling scared. Her mom eventually found her, but instead of trying to comfort her sobbing little girl, her mother berated her for crying and making her look like a bad mom to the other shoppers. Gabby shared that her mom continued to rant, and it was only when she was finally able to choke back the tears and apologize to her mom that her mother stopped her tirade.

After Gabby finished sharing this memory, I asked her to locate the feeling of fear in her body, breathe deeply while continuing to experience it, and then gently release the tension with each exhale. I paid attention to Gabby's breathing as well as the way she held her body, and as her breathing became gentler, her shoulders relaxed, and the tension on her face softened, I knew that she was ready to move on.

Next, I asked her to think about what she may have learned from this experience of being lost and then scolded by her mother. After a few minutes of silent thought, she reported that she became aware that she held many memories of similar experiences as a child, and she learned that it was unacceptable to express negative emotions and that looking good on the outside was all that mattered. Gabby then looked at me with hopeful eyes and said, "Somehow, I've made it this far in my life by not allowing myself to feel much of anything, and I don't know how to do it differently... but I want to learn."

I assured Gabby that the bravery she exhibited by showing up for herself, coming to therapy, and asking for help would get her through the work that we would do together and that I would be with her step-by-step. I let her know that if she put in the work, over time she would learn how to feel and express her emotions, set boundaries with her family, and, most of all, learn to accept all of herself.

Gabby sat for a moment contemplating and, with a shaky but determined voice, replied, "I'm really scared, but I think I'm ready." I smiled and pointed out that she had already taken the first step by sharing with me how she honestly felt. I noted that when she returned my gaze, she was sitting up just a little straighter in her chair, and there was a faint glimmer of hope behind her solemn expression.

That hope grew stronger as we worked together over the next 18 months, during which Gabby learned many things about herself and her emotions. At first, she was fearful that if she allowed herself to feel the true depth of her emotions, they would swallow her up and that she would be rejected by others if she expressed them openly. Gradually, Gabby began to understand and practice mindfulness, which included identifying her emotions, not judging them as good or bad, and giving herself permission to feel and express them honestly. When describing mindfulness-based therapy to Gabby, I explained, "It's about becoming fully present in the moment, learning to observe your thoughts and emotions without judgment, and cultivating a sense of awareness that helps you respond to life's challenges with greater clarity and calm, rather than reacting out of habit or stress." I explore this concept further in Chapter Two of this workbook.

Eventually, Gabby began attending a therapy group, and with the help of the other women in the group, she was able to practice expressing her emotions in a safe place with supportive others. The group gave her honest feedback, and she learned that being authentic drew her closer to others. During one group meeting, Gabby agreed to participate in a psychodrama, a concept further explored in Chapter Twelve, in which she acted out the role of her younger self, remembering what it was like to be that little girl who had been stifled and wounded. This practice, referred to as "inner child" work, is a helpful part of treatment that involves reconnecting with and caring for our younger selves. This process means giving ourselves the love and nurturing we needed as children but may not have received. It includes recognizing that we all have a younger part inside us, often shaped by past traumas, which can influence how we act as adults. It is further explored in the "Word from Wendy" in this chapter.

During the psychodrama, one group member took on the role of Gabby's mother, and another played the part of Gabby as a young child. Gabby gave them the lines to speak so that they could act out the interaction that occurred between them when Gabby got lost and her mother got angry. During the role-play, when her mother began to yell at her, the group leader asked Gabby to take on the role of a mediator, someone who would stand up for and protect little Gabby.

At first, Gabby was not even sure how to do this, so various group members were invited to step in and make suggestions about what they thought young Gabby needed to navigate this painful interaction. An older woman in the group walked up to the person playing the role of Gabby's mother and stepped in front of her, effectively shielding young Gabby from her mother, and spoke in a calm, stern voice, telling Gabby's mother that Gabby did not deserve to be yelled at and to please lower her voice and communicate appropriately. Another group member came and held little Gabby's hand, whispering to her that her mom was not capable of handling her own emotions in a mature way, that she was just taking out her own frustration on little Gabby, and that she did not have to accept her mother's words as the truth.

Once Gabby heard these suggested responses, she took her place beside the member playing little Gabby and spoke these words to her: "Little Gabby, I can see how frightened you are when your mom yells at you, and I need to tell you that I know that you didn't get lost on purpose and that it is perfectly fine to have such big emotions because you were really scared. I wish that you had a good enough mom who was able to see your pain rather than focusing on her own shame. You deserved to be hugged and comforted until you became calm again, and you do not have anything to apologize for. You are loved and accepted and perfect just the way you are."

There was not a dry eye in the room as the group members witnessed adult Gabby stand up for her younger self and comfort her the way she should have been comforted as a child. When the psychodrama ended and Gabby was asked to reflect on what the experience had meant for her, she shared that for the first time, she could clearly see that she was acting appropriately for a young child and that the onus should have been on her mother to work through her emotions. Her mom should never have demanded that little Gabby shrink and stifle her true self in an attempt to calm and please her mother.

Through the experience of using psychodrama to become reacquainted with her inner child, Gabby was able to access the wounded child inside her who wanted so much to be seen and accepted. As her healing progressed, Gabby learned to nurture that tender part of herself.

Another significant moment of growth came a few weeks later when Gabby invited Ashley to a conjoint therapy session. Together, we practiced healthy communication skills in a supportive environment. This experience allowed them to engage in safe, honest conversations that not only strengthened their trust, but also deepened their emotional connection. It also inspired them to seek couple's therapy to further learn and develop their communication skills.

With Ashley's support and growing confidence in their relationship, Gabby recently found the courage to tell her family that she is a lesbian and in a relationship with a girlfriend who she loves. She let them know that if they were willing, she would love to have them meet Ashley. Her parents have not yet responded to her, but her sister responded with love and support and set a lunch date. Gabby is still hopeful that her parents will one day accept all of who she is, and in the meantime, she is committed to being real—with herself and others.

As I conclude this chapter and reflect on Gabby's courage, I am once again filled with a deep sense of joy. Witnessing her transformation and the congruence she has brought into her life has been incredibly rewarding. Though she still experiences moments of fear and pain when the urge to withdraw surfaces, Gabby remains steadfast in mindfully processing her emotions. She is now living an authentic life, one she has worked hard to create and embrace.

A word from Wendy

In full transparency, my own personal journey to discovering who I am and creating a life in which I feel safe to be my authentic self did not begin until I was in my mid-forties, and it was a difficult but rewarding process. This is partly why working with clients like Gabby brings me immense joy. Helping them discover and express their true selves is one of the most fulfilling and rewarding experiences of my life.

Those of us who have grown up in a family where we were not accepted or understood have learned to survive by hiding who we are—sometimes even from ourselves. We discovered that asking for things or "being a bother" brought anger or punishment from our caretakers, or worse yet, we were simply ignored. We became experts at swallowing our emotions and striving to be exactly who our caretakers wanted us to be. This pattern can continue into our marriages and adult friendships. For Gabby, it was pretending that she was not attracted to females. For others, it may be pretending that they love sports and joining teams because they know that it will make Dad proud, or making a career choice based solely on what their parents deem as an acceptable line of work. We stifle our own wants and needs to meet the expectations of others.

The first step toward authenticity for those who are not comfortable acknowledging and feeling their emotions is to understand a core concept of mindfulness: That a feeling is just a feeling, which is explored further in Chapter Two. Although certain emotions are painful, feelings will not *usually* kill us. I add the word *usually* with asterisks because experiencing emotions can be extremely difficult for people who are struggling with untreated mental illness, clinical depression, and other acute challenges. Additionally, for those who numb their feelings with addictive substances and behaviors, fatalities can occur.

Unconditional Self-Worth

As a clinician, it is my job to provide clients with a safe place in which they can explore their feelings, and I serve my clients best by listening and accepting all their emotions as valid. As clients experience validation, this can elevate their self-worth and give them the ability to accept the truth that they are precious—simply because they are human. Understanding and accepting their valuable humanity can, in turn, increase self-compassion, which will decrease negative self-talk and allow them to understand that they deserve to have and express their feelings, needs, and wants (Faustino, Vasco, Silva, & Marques, 2020).

Healthy Communication

People who grew up without experiencing unconditional love often feel that they are not good enough and that they do not deserve to have or express emotions and needs. Often, when they have worked up the courage to ask for what they need, they have been called disrespectful, demanding and aggressive. Therefore, learning the difference between aggressive and assertive is important, and healthy, assertive communication is a skill that most clients who have stifled their emotions will need to learn.

I have found that teaching a structured approach to communication, such as Gottman's Imago Communication Method (Gottman & Gottman, 2015), can assist clients in learning how to share their needs and boundaries. I use an adaptation of this method and teach the following skills:

- Using "I" Statements

    - Example: Instead of saying, "You are so inconsiderate," say, "I feel hurt when you make decisions without asking for my input."

- Omitting the Use of "Never" or "Always"

    - Example: Instead of saying, "You never take the garbage out," say, "I was upset because I counted on you to take the garbage out, and you did not follow through."

- Active Listening

    - Example: Instead of looking at your phone and nodding occasionally, maintain eye contact and interact with words, not just sounds.

Scripted Conversations

Note: This technique may feel awkward at first, but as you practice with this format—it will become more natural over time. You might be surprised by how much you gain from these interactions. Below is a simplified example to illustrate the approach.

1. The speaker starts with a statement: *I tried to do the budget last night, and I found a lot of errors. I felt confused and scared. We need to figure out a better way to keep track of our money.*

2. The listener repeats and asks if they understood correctly: *I heard you say that you're angry with me because I forgot to enter a few expenditures in the checkbook. Is that right?*

3. If not, the speaker repeats what they said: *Thank you, I will clarify; I did not say that I was angry or that it was only you. I have forgotten as well. I said that I was confused and scared and that I would like us to work together to find a better solution.*

4. The listener repeats again and asks if they understood correctly: *Okay—I'm sorry for being defensive* (if the listener was defensive). *I heard you say that you feel confused and scared and that you'd like us to figure this out together...Is that correct? Is there more?*

5. Continue this process until the speaker feels fully heard.

At times, even when using structured communication, either the listener or speaker can become overwhelmed with the conversation and need to take a break. It is useful to agree upon a code word or a signal before either party becomes flooded with emotion.

Using a word or a respectful gesture or signal can create safety in conversations. I have clients choose a word or gesture that they can use to temporarily halt the conversation if either person feels unsafe (either with their own emotions or due to the emotions of the other). This word or gesture should be non-triggering. A harmless word like "pickle" or the universal "time out" hand signal are two examples.

Some couples also like to use a color system where the hearer and speaker can check in with each other periodically during the conversation, and they report their level of ability to continue the conversation using colors. Green can represent feeling safe and energized, yellow denotes that the conversation may need to slow down, and red signifies that the conversation needs to stop for an agreed-upon period of time, such as 20-30 minutes, and be resumed later.

Self-Care

As the client is learning who they are, how to express themselves, and how to live an open and vulnerable life, the importance of self-care must also be acknowledged. Unseen children can grow up to be adults who do not know how to nourish and replenish themselves and may need help to learn how to care for themselves in a healthy way.

Self-care encompasses activities that foster physical, emotional, social, spiritual, and mental health. Examples can include the following:

- **Physical:** Exercise, movement, mindful eating, sufficient sleep, and addressing concerns with a healthcare professional.

- **Emotional:** Practicing mindful meditation, developing a supportive social network, and participating in activities that bring joy and meaningfulness to life.

- **Social:** Spending time with loved ones, participating in community activities, joining organizations such as Twelve-Step groups, and taking care of a pet.

- **Spiritual:** Practicing gratitude, involvement with a community that aligns with your beliefs, spending time in nature, connecting with a higher power and practicing meaningful rituals,

- **Mental:** Managing stress (through meditation, working with a therapist, and journaling), keeping the mind stimulated (through games, reading, learning new skills), finding creative outlets (painting, crafting, music), and maintaining an organized living space.

Sometimes, the best way to decide what appropriate self-care in a situation might be is to ask yourself, "If my friend was struggling with [insert current stressor], what would I want to do for them?" Once you have the answer, do that thing for yourself.

Inner Child Work

In addition to self-validation and self-care, inner child work is also an effective part of treatment (Smith, 2017). Inner child work involves reparenting our younger selves and is the process of giving yourself the loving, unconditional nurturing that you deserved as a child but did not receive from your caretakers (Bradshaw, 1988). Inner child work includes acknowledging that there is a young part in all of us, the child that was wounded by various traumas, and that this younger self is often present and "running the show" in our adult lives (Wong, 2023).

When guiding a client through inner child work, I encourage them to stay curious and explore whether their current reactions to stressors and relationship issues mirror how they responded to similar situations in childhood. Once clients recognize the resemblance, they can gently acknowledge that their unhealed inner child is still present, influencing their responses to adult situations as if they were still a child, navigating the world on their own.

Understanding this concept can allow them to be gracious and understanding with themselves, and as they learn to give their inner child what was lacking, such as kindness, compassion, and guidance, the adult part of themselves can be present to handle the pressures of life (Hestbech, 2018).

A key part of managing life's pressures is maintaining healthy relationships with others. When a client describes a recent argument with a loved one, I often ask them to pause and reflect on how old they felt during the conflict. Their responses can range from feeling like a scared child to a confused pre-teen or a rebellious teenager. Once they make this connection, we explore how a healthy, compassionate adult might have handled the situation differently. Together, we develop shame-free strategies for future conversations so that when their inner child is triggered, they can figuratively place that part of themselves in a safe space and engage only from their adult self.

John Bradshaw, a renowned counselor and teacher, emphasizes the importance of revisiting key stages of childhood development—including infancy, toddlerhood, preschool, school age, and adolescence—in his book *Homecoming: Reclaiming and Championing Your Inner Child* (Bradshaw, 1990). He advocates for directing self-compassion toward these parts of ourselves as we work through inner child healing.

As Gabby became familiar with doing this work, she found that reparenting her inner child through these various stages was helpful and healing. To enhance this process, she brought in pictures of herself at these stages to a recent therapy session and went through them chronologically. As she looked at herself at each stage, she discovered what she would have liked to hear from her caretakers or how she would have liked to be able to think about herself at that age. When she mindfully gazed at herself as an infant, she was able to vocalize, "I welcome you with joy and acceptance." Next, looking at her toddler self, she was now able to appreciate the twinkle in her eye, the way she had learned to say "no," and discovering that she was a separate entity from her parents. She imagined her parents telling her that making mistakes is the way that we learn and that she did not need to pretend to be perfect to be loved.

The next picture showed Gabby in a frilly dress, surrounded by her preschool cohorts, looking uncomfortable. She remembered that she hated wearing dresses and playing with dolls and felt guilty when her parents told her to "act like a lady." She cried when telling her younger self that she is perfect the way she is. Gabby also reminded her younger self that trying to fit into the mold that others had forced her into did not mean she was flawed; it meant that she was beautifully unique. She pictured her parents telling her that she was free to dress and play in the way she wanted.

In another session, we looked at Gabby's school picture from her first day of sixth grade. She stated that although she was smiling in the picture, she could still feel the churning in her stomach that came from knowing that she had to get good grades or she would be punished. She was able to take a deep breath and visualize that moment with me as I safely supported her while she comforted her school-aged self. She vocalized that she loved her younger self unconditionally, not based on achievements. She then imagined coming home with a "C" on her report card and her dad asking if he could do anything to help her with that subject. She further imagined her mother letting her know that she saw the effort Gabby put into her schoolwork, and loved Gabby no matter what grade she got.

An especially poignant session occurred when Gabby and I looked at a photo of her as a senior in high school. Tears began to flow easily now as she remembered the pain of having to hide her same-sex attraction. As we breathed together through this traumatic memory, Gabby shared the horrific feelings that she experienced: shame, confusion, and feeling sinful in her very core. By now, Gabby could easily practice self-soothing by squeezing a pillow from my therapy couch or a stress ball from the bowl. During this particular session, Gabby spent a long time soothing this teenage part of herself. She allowed herself to be present with her inner teenager, letting her know that she would eventually come to accept herself and find a loving relationship. Gabby also allowed herself to think about the possibility of her parents finally accepting all of her and how wonderful that would feel.

After getting in touch with herself at various stages of development and offering herself the kindness, acceptance, and compassion she needed, Gabby was encouraged to go a step further and write a letter to her younger self. I will include part of that letter (with her permission) as an example. A gentle reminder: All names and recognizable details have been changed to protect confidentiality and privacy:

Dear Little Gabby,

I want you to know that I see you, and I love you. I know growing up was hard, that you often felt alone and like you didn't belong. I see how much effort you put into becoming what others wanted, and I understand how that caused you to lose sight of who you truly are. But let me remind you—you are not wrong, unworthy, or strange. Your feelings matter, and they are real.

Little Gabby, I ask for your forgiveness for the times I stifled your natural joy and curiosity. You deserve to be celebrated exactly as you are. I'm so sorry that you felt guilty for your anger, forced to hide it away as if it didn't belong. You should have had every one of your emotions recognized and accepted.

Know this: You never have to feel alone or afraid to express your thoughts and feelings because I am here for you, always. I understand that it's hard to love yourself when others struggle to show their love, but I love you deeply—and I always will.

With all my love,
Grown-Up Gabby

Mindfulness Healing Part I:
Preparation, Assessment, and Script
for Guided Imagery Exercise

Important Safety Tips for Therapists, Facilitators, and Healing Individuals

Environment Consideration and Tips: It can be helpful to "set the stage" prior to a guided imagery exercise. For example, consider the lighting—is it too bright or too low? Another helpful step is putting phones on silent. Also, think about outside distractions, such as barking dogs, traffic, and other interruptions. If possible, minimize outside noises the best that you can. Some individuals like having a blanket or pillow to hold, or you may enjoy diffusing essential oils to support deeper relaxation if there are no allergy concerns. While mindfulness-based guided imagery is not hypnosis, it can be helpful to prepare your environment prior to beginning the guided imagery exercise.

Voice Prosody: An additional gentle reminder is to be aware of your voice prosody. Prosody refers to the rhythm and melody of the voice, including intonation, stress, and pauses. Speaking in a softer tone and slower cadence than your normal speaking voice is useful in supporting the guided imagery practice. If you typically speak more rapidly or loudly, it will take some practice to slow down and modulate your voice.

Diversity Considerations: Consider the client's culture, age, race, physical differences (such as hearing loss), gender and orientation, and other unique experiences that may invite a softer or different speaking tone or pace or require that the client keep their eyes open if they prefer. If you are bilingual and you and your client speak the same languages, ask your client what language they prefer. If your client prefers to go by a nickname, a title such as Dr., Mr., or Mrs., or a specific pronoun, honor their request.

Pace Yourself: Remind yourself to take your time as you walk through this process. There is no need to rush. If you are the person facilitating this exercise, slow down for a relaxed, calming pace. Additionally, it is wise for the facilitator to first practice the exercise with themselves prior to practicing with another person or client.

Safety Reminder: Safety is the number one consideration with any therapeutic approach or healing intervention. As you lead your clients through the following guided imagery exercise, please instruct your clients to alert you if they are experiencing any of the following responses. **NOTE:** If you are an individual doing this work solo, you will also want to consider the following:

- Traumatic memories that are creating a high level of distress

- Feelings of intense fear or panic

- Disturbing or intrusive thoughts

- Suicidal or homicidal thoughts

- Dissociation (if there is an awareness of the dissociative states)

- Other crisis concerns (list on the line): _____
_____

It is also important to ask the client to alert you if they experience any of the following symptoms. Likewise, if someone is doing this work solo, they should pay compassionate and close attention to their process and monitor for distressing or physical symptoms such as:

- A racing heart
- Tightness in the chest
- Shortness of breath
- Nausea or intestinal distress
- Feeling faint or dizzy
- Body pain
- Feeling as if you are floating outside of your body

- Other somatic concerns (list on the line): _____
_____

Note for Therapist or Facilitator: Before moving into the guided imagery, please have your client begin with the assessment below. If you are not a trained mental health professional and your client is in crisis and exhibiting or discussing symptoms that are out of your scope of practice or experience, please refer to an appropriate mental health or medical professional. *If your client is experiencing an immediate life-threatening emergency, please call 911 or the appropriate emergency number if located outside of the United States.*

Note to Solo Reader: *If you are doing this work on your own and believe you are in crisis or may be at risk to yourself, please stop and seek emergency support immediately by calling 911 or your local emergency number.*

On a scale from 1 to 10 (with 1 = very low, and 10 = very high), please take a mindful moment to assess the following. Circle the number that most accurately applies to you:

Feeling	Assessment (1-10)									
▫ Anxiety	1	2	3	4	5	6	7	8	9	10
▫ Anger	1	2	3	4	5	6	7	8	9	10
▫ Shame	1	2	3	4	5	6	7	8	9	10
▫ Sadness	1	2	3	4	5	6	7	8	9	10
▫ Fear	1	2	3	4	5	6	7	8	9	10
▫ Numbness	1	2	3	4	5	6	7	8	9	10
▫ Confusion	1	2	3	4	5	6	7	8	9	10
▫ Curiosity	1	2	3	4	5	6	7	8	9	10
▫ Hopefulness	1	2	3	4	5	6	7	8	9	10
▫ Calm	1	2	3	4	5	6	7	8	9	10
▫ Joyful	1	2	3	4	5	6	7	8	9	10
▫ Other:	1	2	3	4	5	6	7	8	9	10

Assessment Notes: _____

_____

_____

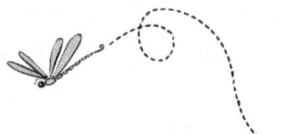

Mindfulness Healing Part II:

Breath and Somatic Preparation and Prompts

This exercise involves tuning into your breath and body and is followed by the guided imagery exercise. It's important to note that this may not be suitable for everyone. It's recommended that the following be adapted to the specific needs and comfort levels of the individual(s) involved.

Physical Space and Comfort: Have your client settle into a comfortable sitting or lying down position, with their feet on the floor or cross-legged if that is the preference. If your client—or you if you are doing this solo—has a yoga mat or a couch and prefers to lay down, that is fine. Whatever position will help the client feel comfortable is perfectly acceptable.

Prompt 1: Let's pause while you take a few moments to get comfortable.

Prompt 2: When you are ready, you are welcome to close your eyes if that feels comfortable for you. Or, if you prefer to leave your eyes open, that is just fine. Whatever allows you to feel most secure is more than acceptable. If your eyes remain open, feel free to rest your gaze on a calming point—near the floor if you're sitting or on the ceiling if you're lying down.

Prompt 3: We will now move forward into the grounded breathing exercise. This will take approximately two to three minutes.

Grounded Breath Exercise

Now that you are in a comfortable position, before we begin the guided imagery, let's move through the grounded breath work.

1. We will start with the 4-2-7 breath. Start by breathing in deeply through the nose to the count of four, hold for two, and then exhale slowly and intentionally through the mouth to the count of seven. Let's do this three times at your own pace. **Note to Facilitator: Count to 20 silently.**

2. Now, let's return to easy, relaxed, deep breathing. Take in a long breath in through the nose and a long exhale out through the mouth. Continue with this breath. **Note to Facilitator: Count to 20 silently.**

3. As you are noticing the gentle rhythm of deep breathing, I would like you to imagine extending compassion to yourself with each intake breath. **Note to Facilitator: Count to 20 silently.**

Somatic Relaxation Exercise

Now that we have finished with our grounded breaths, please feel free to breathe normally with relaxed, regular breaths. Let's now move into relaxing the body in preparation for guided imagery:

1. Notice that your feet are feeling heavier and more relaxed.

2. Notice that your hands are gently resting at your sides, on your belly, or on your thighs.

3. Feel your jaw relax and your tongue move away from the roof of your mouth.

4. Allow your shoulders to relax down from your ear lobes and your elbows to gently relax down from your shoulders.

5.   Bit by bit, the tension moves out of your body as you breathe in and relax and breathe out and relax. Breathe in compassion, hope, and healing, and breathe out stress, judgment, and anger. *Note to Facilitator: Count to 20 silently.*

As we complete our breath work, we will now move on to the guided imagery preparation and exercise section. You can return to your breath work exercises at any point during the guided imagery. The guided imagery exercise will take approximately 10 minutes. You may continue to stay in your comfortable position or shift to a different comfortable position. You may also continue with your eyes closed if that is your preference. At any point, you are welcome to ask for a time out if needed.

Let's move forward.

Mindfulness Healing Part III:
Guided Imagery Exercise
Permission to Feel: A Reparative Experience

Note to Therapist or Facilitator: If you notice that the client is highly activated during the guided imagery, perhaps demonstrating rapid or shallow breathing, sobbing, or shaking, please have the client pause as you attend to the individual. This can be done by gently stating that you would like to pause the exercise for a moment, then quietly asking the person by name if they would like a break, support with deep breath work, or to step out of the guided imagery entirely if it has become too overwhelming.

Note to the Reader: If you are doing this solo without the support of a mental health professional, again, please be gentle with yourself. If you have a trusted person to lead you through this, you may want to consider this option, or perhaps you can read this into a recording device and then play back and follow the prompts. If you become overwhelmed or feel as if you are in a crisis state, please stop and reach out for help if need be. Safety first, always.

Purpose of the Permission to Feel Guided Imagery: This exercise is designed to help you reconnect with your inner child, allowing them to feel seen, heard, and understood. By attuning to this younger part of yourself, you can validate their emotions, provide comfort, and cultivate a sense of safety. This feeling of safety will bring peace to your adult life, encouraging you to express your thoughts and feelings more openly, and fully embrace your authentic self.

Instructions: This guided imagery exercise will take approximately 10 minutes. You will be guided by your mental health professional or trusted facilitator (or you may guide yourself if you prefer) through each step of the exercise slowly, recording the prompts to play back to yourself can be helpful if you are doing this solo. Though questions may be asked of you or you may be given prompts, there is no expectation of a verbal response.

You may respond if you would like to do so, or you may quietly respond inside of yourself, which many people prefer. Through this visualization journey, you will be guided to explore feelings that you had as a child. If you would like to include a blanket in this guided imagery, feel free to do so.

First Step Prompt: Close your eyes, take a deep breath, and allow yourself to sink into a comfortable position. When you are ready, picture a warm, cozy blanket covering you from your toes all the way up to your shoulders or covering as much of you as is comfortable. As you imagine the blanket's warmth and weight, know that your blanket is your safe haven, a protection and comfort to help you tolerate any activating or challenging emotions or fears that arise. *Note to Facilitator: Count to 20 silently.*

Next Prompt Step: If you would like to imagine a safe person sitting with you, a current or past pet, or even a toy that brought you comfort as a child, take a moment to visualize that now. *Note to Facilitator: Count to 20 silently.*

Next Prompt Step: With the assurance that you are safe and supported, gently bring to mind a childhood memory that stirred an emotional response. This memory should not be part of any ongoing or severe trauma but rather something that left a strong impression at the time. It could be a moment when you, like Gabby, felt lost and scared as a child, or perhaps a time when you did poorly on a test and experienced embarrassment in front of your classmates. Maybe you felt lonely when a close friend moved away. Take a moment to recall a memory like this—one that lingers with a feeling in your body. *Note to Facilitator: Count to 20 silently.*

Next Prompt Step: Knowing that you are safe in this moment, as you think about the emotional situation you were in as a child, can you be curious as you reflect on this memory? How old were you? Where were you? What were you wearing? What was the weather like that day? What did you hear? Were there any distinct smells? If you feel too overwhelmed at any time, you can request a time out, use your breath work, or end the guided imagery. *Note to Facilitator: Count to 20 silently.*

Next Prompt Step: Continue focusing on the memory, and turn your attention to the emotions that you felt: Were you feeling sad...mad...scared...lonely...or some other emotion? How did you express that emotion? As you picture yourself as a child, are you crying, yelling, stomping, quiet, looking around confused, or something else? What is your body doing? Is it shaking, rocking, hiding, or something else? Allow yourself to identify and feel that emotion and locate it in your body, honoring the way you felt at that age. Remember that if the emotion feels too intense, you can return to the safe, warm feeling of the blanket covering you. If the emotion feels intolerable, let me know that you need to choose a less intense memory, or we can stop if you prefer. You are safe. You control this. *Note to Facilitator: Count to 20 silently.*

Next Prompt Step: As you feel these emotions in your body, you begin to notice something new. You hear a soft sound and realize that someone safe and compassionate is approaching. At first, you may feel a bit startled, but that fear quickly melts away as you hear the gentle swish of their clothing as they come closer. A sense of calm washes over you with their presence. As you look up, your eyes meet theirs—a beaming smile and compassionate gaze await you. This person feels deeply familiar, warm, and completely safe. *Note to Facilitator: Count to 20 silently.*

Next Prompt Step: This compassionate person asks what they can do to help. Perhaps you ask them for a hug, so they hold out their arms and envelop you in the best and safest hug you've ever had. Or perhaps you prefer not to be held, and instead, you need comforting words. They whisper softly that it's okay to feel the big emotion you have and assure you that they are here to keep you safe through it. They tell you all the things that your heart needs to hear, like "You are loved," "You are safe," "You are allowed to feel exactly as you do," "I'm here for you," and "Let me know what you need." As you continue to breathe, spend some time relaxing in their presence, listening to this loving voice tell you whatever your young self needs to hear. **Note to Facilitator: Count to 20 silently.**

Next Prompt Step: As you spend time in their presence, listening to the soothing voice, you feel your strong emotion gradually melt away. Whatever you are feeling begins to fade. Perhaps your fear vanishes. Perhaps your embarrassment turns to courage. Perhaps your loneliness is replaced with acceptance and love. **Note to Facilitator: Count to 20 silently.**

Next Prompt Step: Now, focus again on your body. You realize how much calmer you feel and how your inner child, the younger you who experienced that emotional situation as a child, feels grounded and secure. The soothing presence assures you that you are perfect as you are and that you can safely express your emotions and ask for what you need without fear. **Note to Facilitator: Count to 20 silently.**

Next Prompt Step: Once you are feeling completely calm, you look again at the face of this loving presence and realize that this compassionate being is you—your adult self. As you become aware of this, you feel completely at ease, knowing that whenever your inner child needs comfort, the warm, accepting presence you need will be right there—because it is you. You remind yourself that you have all that you need to show up for your inner child. **Note to Facilitator: Count to 20 silently.**

Next Prompt Step: As you breathe deeply, you gently come back to the present moment. When you are ready, visualize yourself slowly removing the blanket from your body. If you'd like to act that out, you are welcome to do so. Feel the softness of the blanket as you remove it first from your shoulders, then your torso, your stomach, legs, and finally, your feet. Continue breathing gently in and out as you do this, knowing that you can return to this place of comfort and safety whenever you need to. **Note to Facilitator: Count to 20 silently.**

Next Prompt Step: As you sit in peace, remind yourself that you have the strength and resilience to work through emotional childhood memories and feel the feelings you hid back then. Please remember that you are not alone in this journey of healing. You are safe, and you are supported. No matter the challenges that come your way, remember that you are worthy of a life filled with love, authenticity, respect, joy, and fulfillment. Take a moment now to give yourself an affirmation. Self-affirmations may take you out of your comfort zone, but do your best to stay present with yourself, even in the discomfort. **Note to Facilitator: Count to 20 silently.**

Transitioning to Awareness

Final Prompt Step: When you're ready, if your eyes are closed, notice the light in front of your eyelids. Gently blink, open your eyes, and bring your awareness back to the present moment.

Mindfulness Healing Part IV:
Processing of Guided Imagery
Sharing Your Experience

Purpose for Processing: After the conclusion of the guided imagery, the therapist or facilitator will lead an open and respectful discussion about what you experienced during the guided imagery. The aim is to allow for a compassionate and honest conversation as you highlight important aspects of the guided imagery exercise and what the experience was like.

Note: If you are doing this solo without a therapist or facilitator, pace yourself and notice your energy. You may journal your responses to the questions below if you are doing this work on your own.

Important Considerations for the Facilitator: It is not the role of the therapist or facilitator to interpret, minimize, or re-direct. Rather, it is important for the facilitator to skillfully hold a safe space for the client to share their experience, including the more difficult aspects. This is a time for the facilitator to honor the pain, as well as highlight and affirm the positive insights the client may have had. Remind the client that participating in a therapy exercise like this is a signal of hope and aids in the possibility of recovery and healing.

Processing Questions

1. What did you notice in the guided imagery?

2. What challenges did you experience?

3. What joys or other emotions did you experience?

4. What did you notice from your inner child perspective?

5. What did you notice from your comforting adult perspective?

6. Did you have a breakthrough you'd like to share?

7. Do you have any concerns that you'd like to share?

8. What are you feeling in your body currently?

9. Did you notice any self-growth with insight and compassion toward yourself?

10. Did you notice any triggers or areas of concern?

Now that you have completed the breath work and somatic exercises, the guided imagery exercise, and the process work, on a scale from 1 to 10 (with 1 = very low, and 10 = very high), let's take a mindful moment to assess the following:

Feeling	Assessment (1-10)									
□ Anxiety	1	2	3	4	5	6	7	8	9	10
□ Anger	1	2	3	4	5	6	7	8	9	10
□ Shame	1	2	3	4	5	6	7	8	9	10
□ Sadness	1	2	3	4	5	6	7	8	9	10
□ Fear	1	2	3	4	5	6	7	8	9	10
□ Numbness	1	2	3	4	5	6	7	8	9	10
□ Confusion	1	2	3	4	5	6	7	8	9	10
□ Curiosity	1	2	3	4	5	6	7	8	9	10
□ Hopefulness	1	2	3	4	5	6	7	8	9	10
□ Calm	1	2	3	4	5	6	7	8	9	10
□ Joyful	1	2	3	4	5	6	7	8	9	10
□ Other:	1	2	3	4	5	6	7	8	9	10

Note to Facilitator or Reader: Engaging in somatic movement, if you are able to do so, such as gentle stretching, walking, rhythmic body movements, or dancing to music, following guided imagery is vital for healing trauma as it allows individuals to release stored tension, process emotions, and reconnect with their bodies, facilitating a holistic approach to healing. Please take 3-5 minutes to move your body in a way that feels good for you. Yoga poses, stretching, dance, bouncing gently, rhythmically swaying, or a short walk are all excellent ways to honor yourself.

Important Reminder: If you, as the facilitator, are not a licensed therapist or trained mental health professional and your client is in crisis and exhibiting or discussing symptoms that are out of your scope of practice or experience, please refer to an appropriate mental health or medical professional. *If your client is experiencing an immediate life-threatening emergency, please call 911 or the appropriate emergency number if located outside of the United States. If you are doing this solo without support and are in a state of emergency, reach out to 911 immediately.*

Mindfulness Healing Part V:

Art Exercise I—Revisiting an Emotion

Purpose Statement: The purpose of this healing art exercise is to mindfully create a tangible representation of a childhood emotion you once had to suppress or manage in isolation. This process allows you to gently explore and give voice to feelings that were once left unspoken.

Art Exercise Instructions: Gather art supplies such as paper, colored pencils, stickers, or other dry materials. Please be mindful if you choose to use supplies like markers or paints, as these can sometimes bleed through to the next page. You may want to place a blank sheet of paper underneath your work to protect the following pages.

1. Begin by finding a quiet and comfortable space where you can focus without distractions.

2. Take a few moments to center yourself through deep breathing, visualization, or grounding exercises. Allow yourself to become present in the moment, acknowledging any thoughts or emotions that arise.

3. Once you feel grounded, gently bring to mind the emotion you experienced as a child during the guided meditation. Where did you notice it in your body? Allow yourself to reconnect with that feeling in this moment. Simply observe the sensation without judgment or expectation. If you feel overwhelmed, you may pause and come back to this when ready.

4. With that emotion in mind and locating the sensation in your body, answer the following questions to prepare for the activity:

    • How big does that emotion feel?

    • Does it have a color?

    • Does it have texture?

    • Is it hot or cold or a different temperature?

    • Is it heavy or light or a different weight?

    • What shape is it?

5. Take a deep breath and allow the image and sensation to move from your body to the space provided on the next page. Use your art supplies to draw or paint the emotion as it felt in your mind and body.

6. As you work on your art, pay attention to any emotions or sensations that arise. Allow yourself to explore them openly and without negative self-talk. Remember that there are no right or wrong ways to express yourself through art, just as there are no right or wrong emotions.

7. Once you have completed your art exercise, take a step back and observe your creation. Reflect on the journey it represents, recognizing the challenges you have faced and the progress you have made.

8. Finally, think about strategies that will support your path toward healing.

9. Take a moment to appreciate yourself for engaging in this healing art exercise and for the courage you have shown. Allow yourself and your inner child to feel a sense of pride and accomplishment as you continue your journey of recovery.

Mindfulness Healing Part V:

Art Exercise II—Letter to Inner Child

Purpose Statement: The purpose of this healing art exercise is to write a letter to your inner child. It can assist you in healing unresolved childhood wounds, cultivating self-compassion, enhancing self-awareness, fostering emotional release, and strengthening the inner connection.

Exercise Instructions: Gather a writing instrument, such as a pen or pencil, or you may use a device if you prefer. You are also welcome to use the lined area provided after the instructions to write your letter.

1. Begin by finding a quiet and comfortable space where you can focus without distractions.

2. Take a few moments to center yourself through deep breathing, visualization, or grounding exercises. Allow yourself to become present in the moment, acknowledging any thoughts or emotions that arise.

3. Once you feel grounded, think back to the emotional childhood memory that you focused on in the guided imagery exercise. Remember the comforting words that your calm adult self spoke to your inner child.

4. Begin to write a letter to your inner child, expressing understanding, empathy, acceptance, and love—everything that your inner child needed to hear during that particular emotional experience.

5. As you work on your letter, pay attention to any emotions or sensations that arise. Allow yourself to explore them openly and without negative self-talk. Remember that there are no right or wrong ways to express yourself.

6. Once you have completed your letter to your inner child, take a step back and read your letter out loud to your inner child. Honor any emotions that surface. Reflect on the journey this letter represents, recognizing the challenges you have faced and the progress you have made.

7. Finally, think about strategies that will support your path toward healing.

8. Take a moment to appreciate yourself for engaging in this healing exercise and for the courage you have shown. Allow yourself to feel a sense of pride and accomplishment as you continue your journey of recovery.

Note: You are welcome to use the lines provided on the next page, or if you prefer, you can type your letter in a document or write it on your own on a separate piece of paper or in your journal.

Letter to My Inner Child

_____
_____
_____
_____
_____
_____
_____
_____
_____
_____
_____
_____
_____
_____
_____
_____
_____
_____
_____
_____
_____
_____
_____
_____
_____

Mindful Reflection Moment

Now that you have completed your breath work, guided imagery, and art and inner child letter exercises, please take some mindful time to reflect before we bring this chapter to a close. You are welcome to answer the following questions in the space below, or write in a journal or notebook of your choice. You may do this with your therapist or support person. If you are working through this book solo, you are welcome to do this on your own.

1. What are you noticing after moving through this chapter?

2. What awareness and insights have surfaced?

3.   What have you learned?

Write or share your reflections here or in your own journal or notebook if you prefer if you would like to process further. As always, please be gentle with yourself:

_____

_____

_____

_____

_____

_____

Final Step: Self-Affirmation Exercise

Instructions: Before moving on to the next chapter, can you give yourself the gift of self-affirmation? Affirming oneself can be difficult for those who have experienced trauma, felt abandoned or unloved as a child, or are navigating grief, addiction, complex trauma, anxiety, depression, or other challenges.

As a support to this step of your healing, affirmation ideas might include statements such as: "My emotions are valid," "I am able to comfort and support my inner child," and "It is safe to express my deepest authentic self in this moment." Please use the winged heart below to honor your own self-affirmation(s). If you can only come up with one affirmation at this time, that is more than acceptable. Perhaps you can return later in your healing process and add more:

In this chapter, you learned about key coping skills such as embracing your self-worth, identifying and honoring your emotions, supporting your authentic self, outlining ways to practice mindful self-care, exploring tools and a script to foster healthy communication, and mindfully outlining how to provide your inner child with loving nurturance. Through the chapter's exercises, my sincere hope is that you will have given yourself the gift of presence as you honor your memories and your emotions and engage in meaningful communication with your younger self. As you move forward on your life path, may your growth and healing continue to flourish.

As you complete this chapter, I would like to offer an affirmation to you before moving on: You are no longer silenced, and your voice matters. What you endured was not your fault, and your emotions are valid. You deserve to be heard, seen, and valued for exactly who you are. As you continue to heal, remember that it's your time to express yourself fully and freely. You are worthy of love, peace, and understanding.

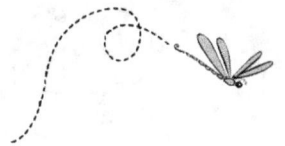

CHAPTER ELEVEN

The Storm of Anger: Reclaiming Your Calm

Mari A. Lee

Between stimulus and response, there is a space. In that space is our power to choose our response. In our response lies our growth and our freedom.

~ Viktor Frankl

It was a rare, rainy Wednesday in Southern California when Michael arrived for his first therapy session. The expression on his face matched the unexpected weather conditions, and it was clear that this man was struggling with an internal storm. When scheduling his first session, Michael shared that he was a military veteran injured in active duty many years ago, returning from his service in a wheelchair. Shaking the raindrops from his jacket, he moved down the hallway and into my office. As he positioned himself across from me, Michael's shoulders slumped with a heavy sigh.

"Tell me what brings you to therapy today, and how can I help?" I asked as I handed him a paper towel to dry his face. "Mari, I never thought I would be in a situation like this. I lost my temper with my wife last week and punched a hole in the wall, something I often do, but this time, she kicked me out, saying that I had turned into my angry father and that she has had it! Our twentieth wedding anniversary is coming up this summer, and I am afraid I have finally lost her." With this admission, Michael dropped his head into his hands, quietly stating, "I don't know how to manage my emotions. I feel like such a loser. I am so ashamed, and I don't deserve her love."

As we moved through his first therapy hour, I felt a depth of compassion for this struggling human being, as well as empathy for his hurting wife. Slowly and painstakingly, Michael shared his story, a journey that began with his biological mother dying while giving birth to him and his grief-stricken father blaming him for this traumatic loss. "Dad was a hard worker, a mechanic who had his own shop and ran a tight ship at home. I'd sit at the dinner table every night, looking at the grease under his nails and wondering when those fingers would once again turn into fists directed at me.

"It seemed like anything I did or said, just my very existence, could set him off. I was never allowed to ask any questions about my mom, and the very few times I did, he would shoot me the most threatening look imaginable and tell me to shut my mouth. Anytime I heard his truck pull up in the gravel driveway, my sister and I would jump up from whatever we were doing if it wasn't chores or homework. Watching a cartoon, playing with toys, or just reading a comic book were some of the worst things we could do according to dear old Dad. I guess I inherited his short fuse, and my sister inherited his drinking problem." Michael's voice trailed away as he recounted these childhood experiences.

Toward the end of his second session, my clinical optimism surfaced as I witnessed Michael's sincere desire to learn ways of understanding and managing his anger. Our work would focus on restoring trust and respect for himself and healing the hurt he had inflicted on his wife, his children, and his marriage. I explained that his treatment plan would include weekly therapy, group therapy, healing childhood trauma, EMDR, domestic violence education, anger reduction and management, and practicing and applying mindfulness-based tools.

As I went over this, it was clear that Michael was anxious about the arduous journey ahead. With wide eyes, he exclaimed, "Wow, you don't mess around, Mari! Do I have to do all this stuff?" I looked him steadily in his eyes, responding, "Michael, I am not going to sugarcoat this. What you are about to embark on is not going to be easy, but change is possible. It will require digging deep and accepting that there will be some days or weeks where you feel on top of the world and other days or weeks where you want to throw in the towel. I won't work harder than you, but I will meet you in this work with solid clinical support and accountability. If, however, you are looking for a bobblehead therapist you can bully, or you show up in this process in a halfhearted way, then I am not the therapist for you." Michael responded with a chuckle and nod of his head, "I have clearly met my match with you, Mari. If I don't do this now, I never will. My life is a mess, and I know I need help. So let's do this!"

Opening my office door to escort him out, I noticed the first glimmer of hope in his eyes as Michael reiterated that he was finally ready to learn, build insight, and grow, "Mari, I know this is going to be a hard process. I'm a tough nut to crack, and I am obviously filled with anger and pride, but I am up for the challenge—I can't keep hurting the people I love."

⁙ ⁙ ⁙ ⁙ ⁙

As our work together unfolded, I found Michael to be one of the most focused and engaging individuals I had ever worked with at that point in my practice. Without fail, he arrived at his sessions on time and usually 15 minutes early. One of the first mindfulness-based tools I taught Michael was the power of being present with his emotions as we waded through his childhood traumatic experiences. When I initially discussed the importance of mindfulness-based healing, he scoffed, "Mari, I have no interest in talking about poor little me and my childhood. I'm not into all of that 'woo woo' head-shrinker stuff. I'm no therapist, but I don't want to live in the past."

My gentle response was, "Michael, you don't have to live in the past, but your past lives in you and will continue to inform your emotions, behaviors, and words until you take a season to understand and heal those hurting parts. It's your choice, but understand that if you are working with me, then part of our work will be revisiting your past from time to time." With some grumbles that sounded more like growls, he reluctantly agreed to give it a go, and with this, a first baby step of trust was born. This began a three-year counseling trek for Michael, a man with a childhood filled with various abuses, abandonments, and attachment issues and many of the existing traumas that numerous veterans deal with.

About three months into our work, a significant breakthrough happened when Michael shared an event from his teen years that he believed created one of the first roots of his internal rage, "I was only sixteen years old but very tall for my age and very strong from being in sports and weightlifting. One Saturday morning, I abruptly woke up to my dad pulling me out of bed, punching and kicking me for accidentally chipping a tile in the kitchen during a household chore he had assigned to me. Though I was an athlete who appeared tough on the outside, I was sort of a shy, gentle kid who loved nature, dogs, basically all animals, and anything Star Wars. That morning, something broke in me—I remember pushing my dad against the wall with superhuman strength, and then I saw red and sort of blacked out. It wasn't until my sister was screaming and crying my name, trying to pull me off Dad, that I realized I had beaten him nearly unconscious. I stumbled back, horrified, looking at the blood on his shirt.

"When I drove him to the emergency room to get stitches, Dad muttered that we were to tell them that he had fallen down the stairs. My sister and I were scared to death. I was in a state of shock, I think, so we silently nodded and went along with the lie. From that day forward, it was as if a beast of anger was born inside of me. Anytime anyone tried to mess with me or my sister, including my father, they would meet my rage. If anyone picked on a friend at school or bullied someone in my presence, that would awaken my internal beast. I used my rage to control the situation, and I liked the feeling of power.

"As I got older, it was as if I shapeshifted and became the controlling bully. This was apparent during my time in the military but also encouraged. Later, when my sweet wife and kids frustrated me, talked back to me, or did something I did not like, they would meet my wrath. I never laid a hand on my wife or my children, but my threatening looks, yelling, fist pounding, punching walls, breaking things, and cursing did the same damage in many ways.

"I guess that is what I thought a real man was supposed to be like—threatening, strong, stoic, emotionless, angry, and tough. After I lost the use of my legs, I felt like half a person in every way and took out my rage on people around me instead of dealing with everything I had been through." With that, Michael began to weep, tears that had been held at bay for decades, trapped in a cage of assumptions that real men don't cry, grieve, or feel much of anything at all. This memory, along with Michael's courage to stay present with his emotions and recognize that men experience the same emotions as everyone else, opened the door to deeper healing.

Over time, through our individual sessions and his time in my men's therapy group, along with connecting with other veterans through volunteer work, Michael slowly moved from shame, rage, and pain to an integrated, mindfully present man of integrity and joy. He was a person who eventually rebuilt love, trust, and respect with his wife, children, and friends as he demonstrated healing through consistency, transparency, and dedication.

Toward the end of our three years together, Michael shared the following letter to his younger self in one of the last men's support group sessions he attended, a testament to his insight and courage:

Dear 16-year-old Michael,

You were a great kid! You were smart, funny, curious, hardworking, fair-minded, sensitive, and kind. Even though Dad tried to beat these qualities into the ground, you were clever enough to understand how to protect our God-given personality traits until I was ready to heal. You were so brave, watching me make a mess of my life but never giving up on the potential you knew I could achieve. You've been waiting a long time for me to show up for myself, for us. I am sorry it took me so long to figure it out and come back to my authentic self, but here I am. I am ready for you to take a well-deserved break now, to be the boy you were meant to be, to have fun, to enjoy play, to rest, and to have healthy relationships with everyone around you. I won't let us down any longer; you don't have to be afraid of my anger or worry about me any longer. I have the tools, the support, and most of all, the trust in myself that I can be the man I was always meant to be: smart, funny, curious, hardworking, fair-minded, sensitive, and kind.

A message from Mari

As a therapist specializing in addiction, betrayal, anger, anxiety, and complex trauma, I have had the honor of working with countless individuals whose stories resonate with the struggles that Michael has faced. Through my experience, I've observed that beneath the surface of anger often lies a deep reservoir of pain, a protective mechanism shielding the vulnerable, hurting parts of a person's psyche. The rage that manifests is frequently a mask, concealing the underlying wounds that have yet to be fully integrated and healed.

It is important to state that violence, in any form, is never acceptable. While anger may appear to be the "front seat driver" for those overwhelmed by nervous system dysregulation, it is essential to recognize that these outbursts are often driven by non-integrated trauma, what I call the back seat drivers. This unresolved trauma, combined with a flood of overwhelming emotions, such as confusion, humiliation, frustration, fear, and betrayal, can create the perfect storm for abusive anger. In these moments, the person is not just reacting to the present situation; often, past traumatic experiences inform their current rage. These previous traumatic experiences impacted their sense of safety, and control was compromised.

It's crucial to understand that anger itself is not inherently destructive. Rather, it is the way in which anger is expressed—through words and actions—that can inflict harm on both the person experiencing the anger and certainly those around them. Once the initial wave of anger subsides, individuals dealing with anger issues are sometimes left with feelings of shame, guilt, and self-loathing, which can perpetuate the cycle of rage and regret.

When working with clients who struggle with uncontrolled anger, my first step is to guide them in understanding the functioning of their sympathetic and parasympathetic nervous systems. This foundational psychoeducation, combined with mindfulness-based interventions, empowers clients to regulate their emotional responses and communicate more effectively. By adopting an integrated, trauma-informed approach, we can create a space for clients to become more present and aware as they navigate a new relationship with their anger.

As we collaborate to develop a comprehensive toolkit of resources and mindfulness-based strategies—some of which are detailed within other chapters of this workbook—the clients I support begin to gain a profound understanding of how former traumatic situations influence their mood regulation and communication. Over time, they learn to effectively manage their triggers and regulate intense emotions like rage through mindfulness practices and other therapeutic techniques. This process not only boosts their confidence but also leads to more meaningful and successful outcomes and relationships in their lives (Wright, S., Day, 2009).

Helping clients understand the "storm" of their emotions from the inside out can be a truly transformative part of the healing process. In clinical terms, this approach is often referred to as "bottom-up" processing—a trauma-informed method that begins with the body's responses before shifting into cognitive or "top-down" work.

Why does this matter? Because the body remembers what the mind can't always process—trauma can live in our muscles, breath, and nervous system for years or decades even. Clients may experience intense emotional reactions, physical tension, dissociation, or panic, even when their logical minds know they're safe. Bottom-up approaches—like breathwork, somatic awareness, grounding, and guided imagery—help regulate the nervous system and restore a sense of safety before engaging in more traditional cognitive work.

Once the body begins to feel more settled, top-down tools like reframing thoughts, insight-building, and narrative processing can be integrated more effectively. This dual approach—honoring both the emotional and cognitive layers of trauma—leads to more comprehensive and lasting healing. As clients learn to attune to their internal cues and regulate their responses, they're not just managing symptoms—they're reclaiming a sense of control, connection, and inner safety.

When I begin working with clients who struggle with mood regulation and rage responses, I like to start by helping them understand the different branches of their nervous system. This knowledge is not only crucial for their healing but also sparks a sense of curiosity and empowerment. Clients often find it fascinating to learn about these parts of themselves and the science that drives their emotional experiences. With that in mind, let's dive a little deeper into this topic.

The Autonomic Nervous System (ANS)

The autonomic nervous system, or ANS, is the part of our nervous system that handles all the involuntary actions in our body—things like heart rate, blood pressure, digestion, and even some aspects of our emotional responses. It operates largely outside of our conscious control, and it's divided into two main branches: the sympathetic nervous system (SNS) and the parasympathetic nervous system (PSNS).

These two branches play a significant role in how we respond to stress, manage our emotions, and navigate through challenging situations. Understanding how they work can give us valuable insights into why we react the way we do, especially when we feel threatened or overwhelmed.

Sympathetic Nervous System (SNS)

The sympathetic nervous system is our body's natural alarm system. It's responsible for the "fight, flight, freeze, or appease" responses that kick in when we perceive danger. When the SNS is activated, a cascade of physiological changes occurs. For instance, the pituitary gland releases a hormone called adrenocorticotropic (ACTH), which in turn increases cortisol levels in the body. This stress hormone prepares us to respond quickly to threats by increasing our heart rate, sharpening our focus, and directing energy to the muscles needed to either fight, run away, freeze in place, or appease the perceived threat.

The "fight" response might manifest as anger or aggression, while "flight" could make someone want to escape or avoid the situation entirely. The "freeze" response often leaves a person feeling paralyzed, unable to take any action. The "appease" or "fawn" response, which is less commonly discussed but just as important, can involve people-pleasing behaviors, excessive apologizing, or even flattering someone in an attempt to defuse the perceived danger. The fawn response is a learned adaptation to perceived or real danger in relationships. When fight or flight aren't possible—especially in cases of childhood neglect, emotional abuse, or inconsistent caregiving—fawning becomes the way the body and mind try to maintain connection and avoid harm. It is the nervous system's way of saying, "*If I can just stay agreeable and invisible, maybe I'll be safe.*"

For individuals who have experienced complex trauma or post-traumatic stress disorder (PTSD), these responses can become overactive. Their nervous system is like a car that's constantly revving its engine, always ready to react to the slightest trigger. This hyper-vigilance can make it incredibly challenging to regulate emotions and can lead to chronic states of anxiety, anger, or fear.

Parasympathetic Nervous System (PSNS)

On the other hand, we have the parasympathetic nervous system, which is often referred to as the "rest and digest" system. The PSNS helps to calm the body down after the threat has passed. It slows the heart rate, reduces blood pressure, and promotes relaxation. Essentially, it brings the body back to a state of balance after the SNS has done its job.

For many people with trauma, however, the transition from a state of heightened arousal (SNS activation) to a state of calm (PSNS activation) doesn't happen as smoothly as it should. Their bodies can get stuck in that heightened state, making it difficult for them to relax, even when they're no longer in danger. This chronic state of tension can contribute to a range of emotional and physical health issues, including anxiety, depression, digestive problems, and even chronic pain.

For example, some of the rest and digest PSNS actions include:

- Crying
- Sexual arousal
- Digesting food
- Salivating
- Slowing heart rate
- Slowing breathing rate

As you can see, the PSNS is a parallel peer of the SNS, but each is equally important to our survival and mortality. As mentioned, when the parasympathetic nervous system (PSNS) is engaged, it works to calm the body by slowing down the heart rate, easing our breathing, and lowering blood pressure. It also stimulates digestion, helping our body shift into a state of rest and restoration. This relaxed state is crucial for recovery, as it allows our body to heal and rejuvenate. The more frequently we can access and sustain this state of calm, the better our overall health and well-being become.

Bringing It All Together

As we explore these systems, I help my clients understand how their sympathetic and parasympathetic nervous systems are working together—or sometimes against each other—in their daily lives. By learning about these processes, clients begin to recognize the signs of nervous system activation in their own bodies. This awareness is the first step toward gaining control over their responses rather than being controlled by them.

For example, a client might start to notice that their heart rate increases, their jaw tightens, or their muscles tense up when they feel anger rising. With this knowledge, they can begin to use mindfulness-based strategies to engage their parasympathetic nervous system, helping them calm down before their anger escalates into a rageful outburst.

This is not to be confused with reactive anger. Reactive anger, as explored in Chapter One, is a momentary, protective response to an ongoing pattern of feeling threatened, hurt, or emotionally abused—often rooted in a real-time trigger or threat. Ongoing anger issues, by contrast, reflect a persistent pattern of irritability, resentment, or explosive reactions that may stem from unresolved trauma, unmet needs, or difficulty regulating emotions.

Over time, this understanding of the nervous system not only helps clients manage their emotions more effectively but also builds their confidence. They start to see that they have the power to influence their own emotional states rather than being at the mercy of them. This shift from reactive to proactive emotional regulation is a key part of the healing process and leads to greater resilience and well-being.

By the end of our work together, clients with anger issues typically have a much clearer picture of how their body, brain, and mind are interconnected. One of the most important distinctions I help clients explore is the difference between the brain and the mind—two words that are often used interchangeably, but actually refer to very different things.

The brain is a physical organ. It's made up of neurons, chemicals, and structures like the amygdala, hippocampus, and prefrontal cortex. These parts work together to regulate our emotions, reactions, memories, and executive functions. The brain can be seen and studied through scans; it is a sense organ that responds to trauma, stress, and healing in observable, measurable ways. It runs the machinery of our thoughts, feelings, and behaviors. Think of the brain as the train, and the mind as the conductor.

The mind, on the other hand, is more abstract. It's the seat of our consciousness—our beliefs, self-talk, inner narratives, and interpretations of the world around us. The mind creates meaning out of what the brain and body are experiencing. It holds our identities, our stories, and our sense of self. While the brain processes incoming signals, the mind, like a conductor, decides what those signals mean based on past experience, emotion, and perception.

One of my favorite ways to help clients understand the connection between the brain, the body, and the mind is by comparing it to the relationship between a musical instrument, the musician, and the music itself. Your brain is like a finely tuned instrument—full of intricate wiring, structures, and systems. Your body is like the musician—bringing energy, breath, and movement to the instrument. And your mind is the music—the intangible, living experience that flows from the two working together. While you can see and touch the instrument and the musician, you cannot hold the music itself. You can only experience it. In the same way, the mind is not something we can touch or measure directly, but it is very real—shaped by the brain's biological systems and expressed through the body's lived experience.

In therapy, especially when working with clients with PTSD who are experiencing anger or other strong emotions, it's essential to engage both. We might work with the brain through somatic awareness, mindfulness practices, and regulating the nervous system, while also working with the mind by challenging unhelpful thought patterns, reframing narratives, and increasing self-awareness. When clients begin to understand how these systems work together—how a bodily sensation can spark a thought, or how a belief can trigger a physiological response—they're empowered to interrupt the cycle, regulate more effectively, and respond rather than react. This mind-body-brain integration then becomes the foundation for long-lasting emotional healing and self-trust.

Eventually clients come to understand that emotions are not just something that happens to them but rather a complex interplay of physiological and psychological processes that they can learn to navigate and manage. This insight is not just empowering; it's transformative! This allows them to move forward with a greater sense of control, peace, and confidence in their lives.

The Impact of Complex Trauma

People with complex trauma or post-traumatic stress disorder often share that their traumatic experiences fall into the following categories:

- Emotional abuse
- Physical abuse
- Sexual abuse or assault
- Neglect
- Abandonment
- Violence
- Domestic violence
- Unexpected accidents
- Health issues (including no access to medical support)
- Housing insecurities or issues
- The death of a loved one or caregiver
- Bullying
- Teasing
- Molestation
- Poverty
- Physical injuries
- Brain injuries
- Chronic hunger

- Military active duty
- Other types of complex trauma

Often, these vulnerable and hurting people have not had the opportunity or support to heal. As such, they deal with sympathetic nervous system "knee-jerk" responses to real or perceived threats, which may include:

> **Terror:** Freezing, shutting down, bargaining, shaking, crying
>
> **Rage:** Yelling, punching, breaking things, driving fast, holding one's breath
>
> **Confusion:** Stuttering, misunderstanding, dissociating
>
> **Shame:** Crying, blaming, projecting, stonewalling, isolating
>
> **Fawning:** Profusely apologizing, accepting blame, acceding to demands
>
> **Defensiveness:** Projecting, denying, sarcasm, using cruel humor, lying

However, an even deeper layer of this conversation involves the vagus nerve, a critical component of the parasympathetic nervous system.

The Vagus Nerve

One essential nerve worth getting acquainted with is the vagus nerve, pronounced like the city of Las Vegas. While the phrase "What happens in Vegas, stays in Vegas" might be famous, the opposite is true for the vagus nerve—it's all about communication!

The vagus nerve, often referred to as the "wandering nerve" due to its extensive reach throughout the body, is the tenth and longest of the cranial nerves and is a vital component of the parasympathetic nervous system. This powerful nerve extends from the brainstem through the neck and chest, branching out to various organs, including the heart, lungs, and digestive system. Its primary role is to help regulate essential bodily functions such as heart rate, digestion, and respiratory rate, all of which contribute to our overall sense of calm and well-being.

The vagus nerve acts as a communication highway between the brain and the body, sending signals that either promote relaxation or prepare us to respond to stress. When activated, it helps to slow down the heart rate, deepen breathing, and stimulate digestion, guiding the body into a state of rest and recovery. This process is crucial for counteracting the effects of stress and for maintaining balance in our nervous system. In essence, the vagus nerve is a key player in helping us move from a state of heightened arousal and reactivity into a place of calm, safety, and healing.

One of the most important functions of the vagus nerve is that it acts as a sensor *and* as a motor nerve as well—this means that it is constantly sending important messages from your body to your brain! When you hear the phrase, "Trust your gut," you can thank the vagus nerve for helping you do this—it is a bit like an internal phone tree system. The vagus nerve retrieves various messages from the body by communicating with the ganglia nerves. Think of the ganglia nerves as little groups of nerve bodies that hang out together but are also extensions of the PSNS nerves. These ganglia "friend groups" are located within or near the organs in the body and work together with the vagus nerve to send message signals where they need to go.

When a person has unresolved, non-integrated trauma, they are usually in a consistent state of sympathetic nervous system hyperarousal; every glance, every word, every expression, every interaction, the tone or prosody of someone's voice, and every social or professional event can feel like a tiger is on their tail! When one has spent years in this chronic state of high stress, implicitly and explicitly scanning for real or imagined threats, stress hormones, such as adrenaline and cortisol, are simmering through the body and bloodstream. When high cortisol levels are present, the body begins to break down over time, resulting in physical and mental health problems, which can include:

Chronic pain	Rapid heartbeat
Gut inflammation	Anxiety
Autoimmune disorders	Depression
Difficulty regulating moods	Sleep Issues
Intestinal issues (such as acid reflux)	Increased Anger

As you can see, learning about one's nervous system is vitally important, especially for clients like Michael, who struggle with PTSD, mood regulation and rage. Current research indicates (Steenbergen, L., 2021) that the vagus nerve is a key player in supporting safety and survival, as well as calming and balancing the overall nervous system.

Vagus Nerve Health

Clients also enjoy learning they can support better vagus nerve health by practicing vagus nerve toning. Like other parts of the body, the vagus nerve needs support to stay healthy. By naturally strengthening and calmly stimulating your vagus nerve, a person is more likely to improve stress and reduce high cortisol levels (Vanderhasselt, M. A., 2022). Toning the vagus nerve can be achieved through a variety of accessible practices that stimulate its function, promoting relaxation and overall well-being. Here are some effective and simple ways to tone the vagus nerve:

Deep Breathing: Slow, deep breathing, especially diaphragmatic breathing, stimulates the vagus nerve. This type of breathing increases oxygen exchange, lowers heart rate, and promotes a state of calm. Here is an exercise to practice right now if you are open to doing so:

Diaphragmatic Breathing: The Umbrella Metaphor

Imagine your breath as an umbrella opening and closing. When you take a shallow breath into your chest, it's like opening just the very tip of the umbrella—it barely expands, and it doesn't offer much coverage or support. These quick, surface-level breaths often happen when we're anxious, stressed, or in "survival mode."

But when you breathe deeply into your belly, it's like opening the entire "umbrella" from the center outward. The ribs expand, the belly rises, and the breath fills all the way down to the diaphragm. This full expansion creates a sense of grounding, calm, and safety—just like a fully open umbrella shelters you from the storm.

How to Practice (with the Umbrella in Mind):

1. Sit or lie comfortably, placing one hand on your belly and one on your chest.

2. Inhale slowly through your nose, imagining your breath opening your body like an umbrella—starting at your belly and gently expanding upward.

3. Exhale slowly through your mouth, picturing the umbrella softly folding inward, drawing your breath back down.

4. Repeat for several cycles, letting each breath open and close the umbrella in a calm, steady rhythm.

With practice, diaphragmatic breathing can become your go-to tool for calming the nervous system—your own inner umbrella of support, always available to carry with you, rain or shine.

Cold Exposure: Brief exposure to cold, such as splashing cold water on your face, taking a cold shower, or even immersing your face in cold water, can activate the vagus nerve and reduce the "fight or flight" response.

Humming and Singing: The vagus nerve is connected to the vocal cords, so activities like humming, singing, or chanting can help stimulate it. This is particularly effective because these activities create vibrations that resonate in the vagus nerve.

Gargling: Gargling with water can stimulate the vagus nerve by activating the muscles in the back of the throat. This can be an easy daily practice that contributes to vagal tone.

Yoga and Meditation: Practices that involve mindful movement and deep relaxation, such as yoga and meditation, help tone the vagus nerve by reducing stress and enhancing the body's relaxation response.

Socializing and Laughter: Positive social interactions and laughter can stimulate the vagus nerve, as they help promote a sense of safety and connection, which activates the parasympathetic nervous system.

Massage: Many of us love a relaxing massage. Neck and foot massages, particularly those that target the carotid sinus (located near the vagus nerve in the neck), can help stimulate the nerve and enhance its function.

Microbiome Support: Ongoing research (Gershon, M. D., & Margolis, K. G., 2021) suggests that maintaining a healthy gut microbiome with the help of probiotics and healthy food choices may positively affect the vagus nerve, as the gut and brain are closely connected through this nerve. I recommend an excellent documentary on Netflix called *Hack Your Gut* for more information about improving microbiomes. Incorporating these practices into daily life can gradually improve vagal tone, contributing to better emotional regulation, reduced stress, and overall improved health.

There are numerous benefits as a result of vagus nerve toning, sometimes referred to as noninvasive vagus nerve stimulation (VNS) (De Smet, 2021). Among these benefits are:

- Reduced depression

- Reduced anxiety

- Increased emotional regulation

- Reduced blood pressure
- Reduced inflammation
- Improved sleep
- Lowered heart rate

Now that you understand how important a healthy vagus nerve is to one's mental, emotional, and physical health, let's explore a few additional ways that a person can support their vagus nerve.

Exercise: Most of us understand the benefits of exercise. When we move our bodies, this lowers our sympathetic nervous system activity while controlling the parasympathetic response. This creates a beautiful balance between the cardiovascular system and respiratory system—a win-win!

Nature: As we have learned, the vagus nerve wanders through our bodies, and, just like this miraculous tenth cranial nerve, when we take time to wander through nature, we give a gift to our nervous system. A moderate hike through the forest, exploring tide pools at the beach, watching the sunset in the desert, going to a local park to run around with a child or pet, or enjoying our own backyard is beneficial to health and well-being. Take time each day to go out and smell the roses—your vagus nerve will thank you!

Yoga: It is worth repeating that the benefits of yoga are countless, especially for clients who are dealing with mood regulation, addictions, trauma, and anger. Michael, the client who came to see me to better regulate his emotions and reduce his rage, was somewhat reluctant to try yoga: "Isn't that for skinny, flexible, young people?" With some encouraging reassurance and a release from his doctor, Michael began attending gentle adaptive yoga classes for beginners.

After moving through his initial anxiety at trying something so completely out of his comfort zone, Michael shared, "Why did I wait so long to do this? I can't believe that I look forward to going to yoga class. I feel so relaxed and focused afterward; it's almost like a secret superpower!" By lowering stress levels, Michael was able to assist in his own healing through yoga practice.

Sounds Baths: Another gentle practice that may support your nervous system is participating in a sound bath. If this is new to you, a sound bath is different from a bathtub bath, it involves being surrounded by soothing tones created by instruments like singing bowls, gongs, or chimes. These calming vibrations invite your body and mind to slow down, soften, and settle into a state of rest. While sound baths are not a medical treatment, early research and clinical observations suggest that sound-based practices can activate the body's relaxation response, helping to regulate heart rate, breath, and tension—key functions of the vagus nerve. Some studies have explored how auditory stimulation, including low-frequency sounds, may engage the auricular branch of the vagus nerve (the part connected to the ear), promoting calm and reducing stress (Lehrer et al., 2020; Kraus et al., 2007). Whether you attend a live sound bath or listen to recorded sound healing at home, this can be a nurturing option to explore as part of your nervous system care routine.

Meditation: The American Heart Association has touted the benefits of meditation practices in lowering blood pressure and heart rate for the last few decades. Beyond our Western medical research on meditation, Tibetan Buddhist monks have understood and enjoyed the benefits of practicing daily meditation for centuries. Dr. Zoran Josipovic, a research scientist and adjunct professor at New York University, has been scanning the brains of monks while they meditate for many years. Dr. Josipovic's research indicates that individuals who practice meditation often experience a more tranquil and enjoyable life. According to Dr. Josipovic, "Meditation research, particularly in the last ten years or so, has shown to be very promising because it points to an ability of the brain to change and optimize in a way we didn't know previously was possible" (Danzico, 2011).

Although I am not trained to scan my clients' brains, my nearly two decades as a psychotherapist incorporating mindfulness-based practices and meditation into treatment have yielded remarkable results. Mindfulness and meditation are crucial elements in the therapeutic process, offering significant benefits to clients by fostering greater self-awareness, emotional regulation, and overall well-being. As healing professionals, cultivating our own mindfulness and meditation practices is equally important. It not only enhances our ability to support clients but also contributes to our personal and professional growth.

While entire books have been written about the nervous system and the vagus nerve (see the resource section), my goal with this brief overview is to inspire you to take proactive steps in caring for your nervous system. You can start with these essential practices, what I call the "12 Steps Toward Peace," that I have each client follow.

12 Steps Toward Peace

Consistently practicing the following steps is an excellent way to support emotional regulation, as well as optimal physical and mental health. Start slowly, be gentle with yourself, and remember that perfect doesn't exist.

Step 1: Reduce Inflammation Through a Balanced Diet and Regular Exercise

While I am not a dietician, it is common knowledge that adopting a balanced diet rich in anti-inflammatory foods like fruits, vegetables, whole grains, and omega-3 fatty acids can significantly lower inflammation in the body. Combined with regular exercise, this approach not only enhances overall health but also improves mood regulation and energy levels, contributing to both physical and emotional well-being.

Step 2: Limit Inflammatory Substances Such as Sugar and Alcohol

Research indicates (Ma, X. 2022) that reducing the intake of sugar and alcohol is crucial for minimizing inflammation, as both substances can trigger inflammatory responses in the body. By cutting back on these, you allow your body to function more optimally, reducing the risk of chronic diseases and improving your mental clarity and emotional stability.

Step 3: Heal Trauma With the Guidance of a Trauma-Trained Therapist

Working with a trauma-trained mental health professional can help you process and integrate past traumas, leading to a more balanced emotional state. Through tailored therapeutic techniques, you can address unresolved issues, reduce their impact on your daily life, and foster resilience and self-compassion.

Step 4: Manage Stress Effectively Through Various Stress-Reduction Techniques

Learning and practicing stress-reduction techniques, such as deep breathing, yoga, or time management, can greatly improve your ability to handle life's challenges. These methods help you maintain a calmer mind, lower stress hormones, and prevent stress from escalating into more serious mental or physical health issues.

Step 5: Aim for at Least Seven Hours of Sleep Each Night

Prioritizing a full night's sleep of at least seven hours is essential for your body and mind to recover, repair, and rejuvenate. Adequate sleep enhances cognitive function, emotional regulation, and immune response, laying a strong foundation for overall health and well-being. If seven hours is not possible, then aim for at least six hours.

Step 6: Develop Healthy Boundaries and Communication in Your Relationships

Establishing and maintaining healthy boundaries is key to nurturing respectful and fulfilling relationships. Learning effective communication skills allows you to express your needs clearly and assertively, reducing the likelihood of misunderstandings and conflicts while enhancing trust and connection.

Step 7: Incorporate Meditation in Your Daily Routine

Regular meditation practice can help clear your mind, reduce stress, and increase your capacity for mindfulness and self-awareness. By setting aside time each day for meditation, you can cultivate inner peace, improve focus, and better manage your emotional responses.

Step 8: Practice Guided Imagery to Foster Emotional Balance

Engaging in mindfulness practices, such as guided imagery, allows you to connect with your emotions in a non-judgmental way, fostering greater emotional balance and resilience. These techniques help you stay present, manage stress more effectively, and respond to life's challenges with a calm and centered mindset (Skottnik, L., 2019).

Step 9: Take Care of Your Vagus Nerve

Supporting the health of your vagus nerve is vital for regulating the body's stress response and maintaining a state of relaxation. Activities like deep breathing, laughter, and singing can stimulate the vagus nerve, enhancing its tone and contributing to better physical and mental health.

Step 10: Enjoy Time in Nature

This could involve activities like taking a walk, watering your garden barefoot, sitting in a park, or relaxing in your backyard. If outdoor space is limited, consider volunteering at a community garden. Even nurturing a window garden or houseplants that allow you to connect with nature offer health benefits! Brief daily exposure to natural surroundings can lower stress levels, enhance mood, and promote a sense of well-being.

Step 11: Spend Time With Animals or Pets

Interacting with animals can be incredibly soothing and grounding, offering a sense of companionship and unconditional acceptance. Whether it's playing with a pet or simply observing wildlife, this connection with animals can help reduce stress and foster a sense of calm and well-being.

Step 12: Engage in Art or Volunteering

Participating in creative activities like drawing, painting, or crafting allows for self-expression and emotional release, which can be therapeutic. Similarly, volunteering provides a sense of purpose and connection to others, enhancing overall health by contributing to a greater cause.

· · · · ·

Now that you have a better understanding of the nervous system and its crucial role in mood regulation, mental health, and overall well-being, let's explore how guided imagery exercises and mindfulness-based activities can further support your healing, integration, and personal growth.

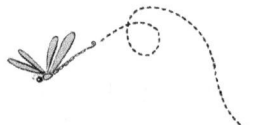

Mindfulness Healing Part I:

Preparation, Assessment, and Script
for Guided Imagery Exercise

Important Safety Tips for Therapists, Facilitators, and Healing Individuals

Environment Consideration and Tips: It can be helpful to "set the stage" prior to a guided imagery exercise. For example, consider the lighting—is it too bright or too low? Another helpful step is putting phones on silent. Also, think about outside distractions, such as barking dogs, traffic, and other interruptions. If possible, minimize outside noises the best that you can. Some individuals like having a blanket or pillow to hold, or you may enjoy diffusing essential oils to support deeper relaxation if there are no allergy concerns. While mindfulness-based guided imagery is not hypnosis, it can be helpful to prepare your environment prior to beginning the guided imagery exercise.

Voice Prosody: An additional gentle reminder is to be aware of your voice prosody. Prosody refers to the rhythm and melody of the voice, including intonation, stress, and pauses. Speaking in a softer tone and slower cadence than your normal speaking voice is useful in supporting the guided imagery practice. If you typically speak more rapidly or loudly, it will take some practice to slow down and modulate your voice.

Diversity Considerations: Consider the client's culture, age, race, physical differences (such as hearing loss), gender and orientation, and other unique experiences that may invite a softer or different speaking tone or pace or require that the client keep their eyes open if they prefer. If you are bilingual and you and your client speak the same languages, ask your client what language they prefer. If your client prefers to go by a nickname, a title such as Dr., Mr., or Mrs., or a specific pronoun, honor their request.

Pace Yourself: Remind yourself to take your time as you walk through this process. There is no need to rush. If you are the person facilitating this exercise, slow down for a relaxed, calming pace. Additionally, it is wise for the facilitator to first practice the exercise with yourself prior to practicing with another person or client.

Safety Reminder: Safety is the number one consideration with any therapeutic approach or healing intervention. As you lead your client through the following guided imagery exercise, please instruct your client to alert you if they are experiencing any of the following responses. NOTE: If you are an individual doing this work solo, you will also want to consider the following:

- Traumatic memories that are creating a high level of distress

- Feelings of intense fear or panic

- Disturbing or intrusive thoughts

- Suicidal or homicidal thoughts

- Dissociation (if there is an awareness of the dissociative states)

- Other crisis concerns (list on the line): _____

_____

It is also important to ask the client to alert you if they experience any of the following symptoms. Likewise, if someone is doing this work solo, they should pay compassionate and close attention to their process and monitor for distressing or physical symptoms such as:

- A racing heart

- Tightness in the chest

- Shortness of breath

- Nausea or intestinal distress

- Feeling faint or dizzy

- Body pain

- Feeling as if you are floating outside of your body

- Other somatic concerns (list on the line): _____

_____

Note for Therapist or Facilitator: Before moving into the guided imagery, please have your client begin with the assessment below. If you are not a trained mental health professional, and your client is in crisis and exhibiting or discussing symptoms that are out of your scope of practice or experience, please refer your client to an appropriate mental health or medical professional. *If your client is experiencing an immediate life-threatening emergency, please call 911 or the appropriate emergency number if located outside of the United States.*

Note to Solo Reader: *If you are doing this work on your own and believe you are in crisis or may be at risk to yourself, please stop and seek emergency support immediately by calling 911 or your local emergency number.*

> ## Pre-Guided Imagery Assessment Scale

On a scale from 1 to 10 (with 1 = very low, and 10 = very high), please take a mindful moment to assess the following. Circle the number that most accurately applies to you:

Feeling	Assessment (1-10)									
▫ Anxiety	1	2	3	4	5	6	7	8	9	10
▫ Anger	1	2	3	4	5	6	7	8	9	10
▫ Shame	1	2	3	4	5	6	7	8	9	10
▫ Sadness	1	2	3	4	5	6	7	8	9	10
▫ Fear	1	2	3	4	5	6	7	8	9	10
▫ Numbness	1	2	3	4	5	6	7	8	9	10
▫ Confusion	1	2	3	4	5	6	7	8	9	10
▫ Curiosity	1	2	3	4	5	6	7	8	9	10
▫ Hopefulness	1	2	3	4	5	6	7	8	9	10
▫ Calm	1	2	3	4	5	6	7	8	9	10
▫ Joyful	1	2	3	4	5	6	7	8	9	10
▫ Other:	1	2	3	4	5	6	7	8	9	10

Assessment Notes: _____

_____

_____

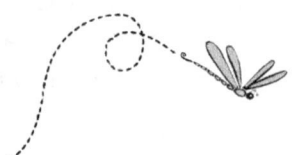

Mindfulness Healing Part II:

Breath and Somatic Preparation & Prompts

This exercise involves tuning into your breath and body and is followed by the guided imagery exercise. It's important to note that this may not be suitable for everyone. It's recommended that the following be adapted to the specific needs and comfort levels of the individual(s) involved.

Physical Space and Comfort: Have your client settle into a comfortable sitting or lying down position, with their feet on the floor or cross-legged if that is the preference. If your client—or you if you are doing this solo—has a yoga mat or a couch and prefers to lay down, that is fine. Whatever position will help the person feel comfortable is perfectly acceptable.

Prompt 1: Let's pause while you take a few moments to get comfortable.

Prompt 2: When you are ready, you are welcome to close your eyes if that feels comfortable for you. Or, if you prefer to leave your eyes open, that is just fine. Whatever allows you to feel most secure is more than acceptable. If your eyes remain open, feel free to rest your gaze on a calming point—near the floor if you're sitting or on the ceiling if you're lying down.

Prompt 3: We will now move forward into the grounded breathing exercise. This will take approximately two to three minutes.

Grounded Breath Exercise

Prompt: Now that you are in a comfortable position, before we begin the guided imagery, let's move through the grounded breathwork.

1. We will start with the 4-2-7 breath. Start by breathing in deeply through the nose to the count of four, hold for two, and then exhale slowly and intentionally through the mouth to the count of seven. Let's do this three times at your own pace. **Note to Facilitator: Count to 20 silently.**

2. Now, let's return to easy, relaxed, deep breathing. Take in a long breath in through the nose and a long exhale out through the mouth. Continue with this breath. **Note to Facilitator: Count to 20 silently.**

3. As you notice the gentle rhythm of deep breathing, I would like you to imagine extending compassion to yourself with each intake breath. **Note to Facilitator: Count to 20 silently.**

Somatic Relaxation Exercise

Now that we have finished with our grounding breaths, please feel free to breathe normally with relaxed, regular breaths. Let's now move into relaxing the body in preparation for the guided imagery:

1. Notice that your feet are feeling heavier and more relaxed.

2.   Notice that your hands are gently resting at your sides, on your belly, or on your thighs.

3.   Feel your jaw relax and your tongue move away from the roof of your mouth.

4.   Allow your shoulders to relax down from your ear lobes, and your elbows to gently relax down from your shoulders.

5.   Bit by bit, the tension moves out of your body as you breathe in and relax and breathe out and relax. Breathe in compassion, hope, and healing, and breathe out stress, judgment, and anger. **Note to Facilitator: Count to 20 silently.**

6.   As we complete our relaxation body work, we will now move into guided imagery. You can return to your breath work at any point during the guided imagery. The guided imagery exercise will take approximately 10 minutes or so. You may continue to stay in your comfortable position or shift to a different comfortable position. You may also continue with your eyes closed if that is your preference, or leave your eyes open. At any point, you are welcome to ask for a time out if needed.

Let's move forward.

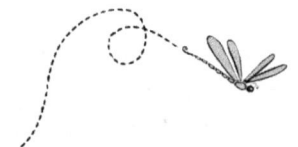

Mindfulness Healing Part III:
Lighthouse Guided Imagery Script

Note to Therapist or Facilitator: If you notice that the client is highly activated during the guided imagery, perhaps demonstrating rapid or shallow breathing, sobbing, or shaking, have the client pause as you attend to the individual. This can be done by gently stating that you would like to pause the exercise for a moment, then quietly asking the person by name if they would like a break, support with deep breath work, or to step out of the guided imagery entirely if it has become too overwhelming.

Note to the Reader: If you are doing this solo without the support of a mental health professional, again, please be gentle with yourself. If you have a trusted person to lead you through this, you may want to consider this option, or perhaps you can read this into a recording device and then play back and follow the prompts. If you become overwhelmed or feel as if you are in a crisis state, please stop and reach out for help if need be. Safety first, always.

Note: If you are a person with a disability and are unable to walk, please imagine yourself moving through this guided imagery in whatever manner feels best for you. That could be in a wheelchair, with a cane, with pet assistance, or even flying or floating if you prefer. Your own imagination will be honored and valued.

Purpose of the Lighthouse Exercise: The primary goal of this guided imagery exercise is to help you reduce tension, enhance relaxation, regulate anger, and cultivate self-compassion, insight, peace, and calm. This exercise is particularly beneficial for individuals who struggle with anger, as it provides a structured approach to recognizing emotional triggers, interrupting the trauma response, and making more mindful decisions when expressing emotions. By focusing on the imagery of a lighthouse, you can develop greater emotional awareness and control.

Instructions: This guided imagery exercise will take approximately 10 minutes. You will be gently guided through each step, with ample time to absorb the experience. While you may be prompted with questions or suggestions, there is no obligation to respond aloud. You are welcome to answer internally or remain silent, whatever feels most comfortable to you.

First Step Prompt: Close your eyes, take a deep breath, and allow yourself to sink into a comfortable position. When you are ready, imagine you are in a boat. It can be any boat of your choosing: large or small, a sailboat, a rowboat, or a larger boat—whatever boat you choose. As you envision your boat, imagine that you are on the ocean—whatever ocean you choose. You are not lost at sea; you are safe, and you can still see the shoreline in the distance. *Note to Facilitator: Count to 20 silently.*

Next Prompt Step: You are enjoying this time in your boat, feeling the gentle rocking back and forth. As you gaze up at the sky, you notice that it is getting darker and stormier. The wind is starting to whip up, and the waves are growing larger. However, you are safe. You are secure. You are only noticing this change in weather. You are observing without absorbing. If challenging emotions surface, notice them without judgment. *Note to Facilitator: Count to 20 silently.*

Next Prompt Step: As the storm grows, you are confident in knowing how to keep yourself and your boat safe and steady. You know just how to tie off the ropes, bring in the sails, or tend to the motor. You move with intention and focus; you are feeling in control and calm. You feel grounded in managing your boat in this storm. You remind yourself that you are safe and prepared. *Note to Facilitator: Count to 20 silently.*

Next Prompt Step: As the storm breaks full force and rain whips across the deck, notice the lightning crackling across the sky, the water from the sea misting into your face, and the saltiness on your lips. You are safe, you are secure. Feel yourself at the wheel, standing secure, confidently steering your boat to a safe harbor near the shoreline. You are managing this challenge with confidence. *Note to Facilitator: Count to 20 silently.*

Next Prompt Step: Breathing normally and deeply, you are fully in control of your boat. It is up to you to move your boat to calmer water—bit by bit, wave by wave, breath by breath. Very soon, you notice a lighthouse in the distance guiding you into the safe and calm boat harbor. You are safe and secure. *Note to Facilitator: Count to 20 silently.*

Next Prompt Step: As you focus on the lighthouse, which helps you navigate to safety, you find yourself breathing in calmness and breathing out any challenging emotions such as fear, frustration, or tension. Continue to breathe normally and deeply while focusing on the welcoming lighthouse in the distance. *Note to Facilitator: Count to 20 silently.*

Next Prompt Step: As you steer your boat into the sheltered slip of the harbor, the storm is behind you now. You drop anchor and breathe in a confident sigh of relief and pride. Yes, you felt the intensity of the storm, but you were able to observe and stay in control versus absorbing the storminess and getting lost in your emotions. **Note to Facilitator: Count to 20 silently.**

Next Prompt Step: Now that your boat is secured and safe, you move off of the boat onto the dry dock, watching the sun break through the once-cloudy sky. The cool breeze moves across your face. You feel the gentle warmth of the sun, and you hear the seagulls and lapping of the tide. A sense of peace and accomplishment fills your being as you move back into your session here. **Note to Facilitator: Count to 20 silently.**

Next Prompt Step: Before we move out of the guided imagery, know that you have the strength and resilience to learn to manage your stormy emotions or anger triggers, and increase self-regulation when you are feeling triggered. Please remember that you are not alone in this journey of healing. You are supported. No matter the challenges that come your way, remember that you are worthy of a life filled with love, authenticity, respect, joy, and fulfillment. Take a moment now to give yourself an affirmation. Self-affirmations may take you out of your comfort zone, but do your best to stay present with yourself, even in the discomfort. **Note to Facilitator: Count to 20 silently.**

Transitioning to Awareness

Final Prompt Step: When you're ready, if your eyes are closed, notice the light in front of your eyelids. Gently blink, open your eyes, and bring your awareness back to the present moment.

Note to Facilitator or Reader: Engaging in somatic movement, if you are able to do so, such as gentle stretching, walking, rhythmic body movements, or dancing to music, following guided imagery is vital for healing trauma as it allows individuals to release stored tension, process emotions, and reconnect with their bodies, facilitating a holistic approach to healing. Please take 3-5 minutes to move your body in a way that feels good for you. Yoga poses, stretching, dance, bouncing gently, rhythmically swaying, or a short walk are all excellent ways to honor yourself.

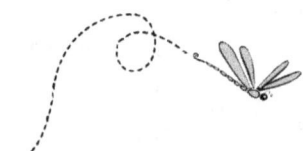

Mindfulness Healing Part IV:
Processing of Guided Imagery
Sharing Your Experience

Purpose for Processing: After the conclusion of the guided imagery, the therapist or facilitator will lead an open and respectful discussion about what you experienced during the guided imagery. The aim is to allow for a compassionate and honest conversation as you highlight important aspects of the guided imagery exercise and what the experience was like.

Note: If you are doing this solo without a therapist or facilitator, please pace yourself and notice your energy. You may use a journal of your choice to answer the process questions listed below and write about your experience.

Important Considerations for the Facilitator: It is not the role of the therapist or facilitator to interpret, minimize, or re-direct during the client's process of discussing their guided imagery experience. Rather, it is important for the facilitator to skillfully hold a safe space for the client to share their experience, including the more difficult aspects. This is a time for the therapist or facilitator to honor the pain, as well as highlight and affirm the positive insights the client may have had. Remind the client that participating in a mindfulness-based exercise like this is a signal of hope and aids in the possibility of recovery and healing.

Processing Questions:

Feel free to write your answers in the space below each question, or use a notebook or journal if you prefer.

1. What did you notice in the guided imagery?

2. What challenges did you experience?

3. What joys or other emotions did you experience?

4. Did you have a breakthrough you'd like to share?

5. Do you have any concerns that you'd like to share?

6. What are you feeling in your body currently?

7. Did you notice any self-growth with insight and compassion toward yourself?

8. Did you notice any triggers or areas of concern?

> *Post-Guided Imagery Assessment Scale*

Now that you have completed the breath work and somatic exercises, the guided imagery exercise, as well as the process work, on a scale from 1 to 10 (with 1 = very low, and 10 = very high), let's take a mindful moment on the next page to assess the following:

Feeling	Assessment (1-10)									
▫ Anxiety	1	2	3	4	5	6	7	8	9	10
▫ Anger	1	2	3	4	5	6	7	8	9	10
▫ Shame	1	2	3	4	5	6	7	8	9	10
▫ Sadness	1	2	3	4	5	6	7	8	9	10
▫ Fear	1	2	3	4	5	6	7	8	9	10
▫ Numbness	1	2	3	4	5	6	7	8	9	10
▫ Confusion	1	2	3	4	5	6	7	8	9	10
▫ Curiosity	1	2	3	4	5	6	7	8	9	10
▫ Hopefulness	1	2	3	4	5	6	7	8	9	10
▫ Calm	1	2	3	4	5	6	7	8	9	10
▫ Joyful	1	2	3	4	5	6	7	8	9	10
▫ Other:	1	2	3	4	5	6	7	8	9	10

Next: Take a moment to compare your pre-assessment scale to your post-assessment scale and assess changes, if any, that have occurred. List out what you believe may have contributed to these changes:

_____

_____

_____

_____

_____

Important Reminder: If you, as the facilitator, are not a licensed therapist or trained mental health professional and your client is in crisis and exhibiting or discussing symptoms that are out of your scope of practice or experience, please refer your client to an appropriate mental health or medical professional. *If your client is experiencing an immediate life-threatening emergency, please call 911 or the appropriate emergency number if located outside of the United States. If you are doing this solo without support and are in a state of emergency, reach out to 911 or an emergency team in your area immediately.*

Mindfulness Healing Part V:

Understanding the Storm

Purpose Statement: The storm artwork will give you an opportunity to identify the current life "storms" you are dealing with.

Art Exercise Instructions:

A) The lightning bolt represents something that is happening that is out of your control or a current or past traumatic event. Write that by or on the bolt.

B) The cloud is a place to share about the internal struggle you are dealing with but don't often reveal to those around you.

C) The raindrops represent the various emotions that you are dealing with, including those feelings such as anger, sadness, fear, or shame, that are especially difficult to experience or regulate. This may manifest as the internal struggle bursts out of you like an out-of-control thunderstorm.

Exercise Reflection:

When you reflect on your current challenges as outlined on the cloud art and what you have learned about the nervous system and vagus nerve, what step(s) can you take to support yourself?

Step 1: _____

Step 2: _____

Step 3: _____

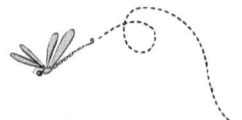

Mindfulness Healing Part V:

Navigating the Storm

Art Exercise II—The Lighthouse

Purpose Statement: The following lighthouse illustration will help you create a visual grounding tool to assist you in your mindfulness practice. If you are an individual who is vision-impaired, this can be done by seeking assistance from a person who can help you with this exercise.

Art Exercise Instructions: Gather art supplies such as paper, colored pencils, stickers, or other dry materials. Please be mindful if you choose to use supplies like markers or paints, as these can sometimes bleed through to the next page. You may want to place a blank sheet of paper underneath your work to protect the following pages.

First steps:

1. Begin by finding a quiet and comfortable space where you can focus without distractions.

2. Take a few moments to center yourself through deep breathing, visualization, or grounding exercises. Allow yourself to become present in the moment, acknowledging any thoughts or emotions that arise.

3. Once you feel grounded, using your art supplies:

   Within the Dome: List your healing goals or hopes or the future.

   Within the Beams of Light: List the people, pets, places, practices, or higher power that guide and support you.

   Within the Structure of the Lighthouse: On the lines, write activities or areas of your life that help you feel grounded, balanced, and solid.

   Optional Use: Place this somewhere visible—on your mirror, refrigerator, or bulletin board—as a daily supportive reminder of your growth and intentions.

Once you have completed your art exercise, take a deep breath, sit back, give yourself the gift of being present, and observe your creation. Reflect on the journey it represents, recognizing the challenges you have faced and the progress you have made. Think about strategies that will support your path toward healing.

Take a moment to appreciate yourself for engaging in this healing art exercise and for the courage you have shown. Allow yourself to feel a sense of pride and accomplishment as you continue your journey of recovery. If you have a higher power, enjoy reflecting with gratitude.

Mindful Reflection Moment

Now that you have completed your breath work, guided imagery, assessment reflection, and art exercise, as we bring this chapter to a close, please take some mindful time to process.

You are welcome to answer the following questions in the space below, or write in a journal or notebook of your choice. You may do this with your therapist or facilitator, or if you are working through this book solo, you can do this on your own.

1. What are you noticing after completing this chapter?

2. What awareness and insight have surfaced?

3. What is the information you have learned?

Write or share your reflections here if you would like to do so. As always, please be gentle with yourself:

_____

_____

_____

_____

_____

Final Step: Self-Affirmation Exercise

Instructions: Before moving on to the next chapter, can you give yourself the gift of self-affirmation? Affirming oneself can be difficult for those who have experienced post traumatic stress disorder, are struggling to understand and regulate challenging emotions like anger, are healing from complex trauma, or struggling with anxiety, depression, or other challenges.

As a support to this step of your healing, affirmation ideas might include statements such as: "I am learning that I can regulate my anger," "I am willing to practice the tools I have learned," and "I am worthy of a life that is peace-filled." Please use the space in the winged heart below to honor your own self-affirmation(s). If you can only come up with one affirmation at this time, that is more than acceptable. Perhaps you can return later in your healing process and add more:

The goal of this chapter was to introduce you to practical tools for calming and regulating your system when emotions begin to escalate. You've learned how to take a nervous system "timeout" using breath work, explored ways to tone the vagus nerve, and practiced activities that support emotional regulation. You were also encouraged to work with the "12 Steps to Peace" and use guided imagery as a means of shifting your mental and emotional state.

These strategies are designed to help you interrupt the "storm" of anger and rage, creating space for more mindful, grounded responses during stressful moments. With consistent practice, these tools can do more than just help you manage anger—they can support a deeper sense of peace, emotional control, increase better health, and support self-compassion as you continue on your healing path.

As you complete this chapter, I want to offer you an affirmation: You deserve to create a life grounded in peace and purpose, free from the weight of unresolved rage. The journey to healing trauma-driven anger involves equipping yourself with mindfulness-based tools that can truly enhance your everyday experiences. These tools can open the door to relationships built on mutual respect and trust. By embracing these practices, you are nurturing a life that feels more balanced and fulfilling, where you can trust yourself to navigate both the large and small storms that inevitably come your way.

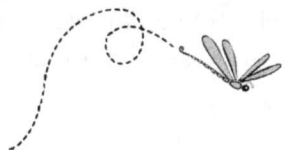

CHAPTER TWELVE

Spiritual Bypassing: From Silence and Shame to Self-Compassion and Serenity

Wendy Quinton

*All emotions are gifts. They are a part of the human experience,
and they help us to understand the world and ourselves.*

~ Deepak Chopra

As I ushered Natasha into my counseling office, I offered a welcoming smile and could feel the uncertainty in her return glance. As we settled into our chairs, I explained that this was a safe space and that if she was ready, she could begin to tell me about herself, and let me know how I could best support her.

As she adjusted in her chair and placed her keys inside her purse, I took that moment to respectfully observe her appearance, noting that she seemed to be in her early 30s and of average height and build. Her clothing and makeup suggested she had put thought into preparing for our session, and I also noticed she might be of mixed heritage. These types of details help me gain insight into clients I am honored to support even before we begin our conversation.

After a brief hesitation, Natasha began, "Wendy, you were recommended to me by a friend who knows what I've been dealing with, but I must admit that I was hesitant to make an appointment with you." Swallowing nervously, she proceeded, "I was worried because your website stated that among the types of therapy you provide, you offer 'faith-based counseling,' and I'm not sure that's what I need or even want right now. However, I also read that you are comfortable working with those who are exploring their spirituality and those who identify as atheist or agnostic. As of today, I'm not sure which category I fit into."

Natasha seemed at a loss for what to say next, and wanting to put her at ease, I interjected, "Thank you for sharing. How about we don't worry about categories? I find that it's rare for any of us to fit neatly into just one of them anyway." She seemed slightly relieved but still unsure of how to proceed, so I continued gently, "Natasha, I can see the pain in your eyes. Can you tell me what brought you here today?"

She looked down for a moment, then appeared to gather courage as she looked up and returned my gaze. As Natasha launched into her story, the words began flowing out of her like a dam that had finally been breached. "I grew up in a large city a couple of hours from here, and I'm the daughter of a mixed-race marriage as my dad is black and my mom is white. I had a good childhood that basically revolved around our involvement in an evangelical church. We attended Sunday school, church, youth group—all the things. I grew up knowing that God loved me and believed that if I followed what the Bible says the best I could, my life would be happy and fulfilling. I even married a guy, Jalen, who I met in our youth group and dreamed of having a large family, as I had been taught that being a wife and a mother was a woman's highest calling."

Natasha continued, "However, that dream hasn't come true yet. We've been married for seven years, and two years into our marriage, we started trying to get pregnant, never thinking that it would be a problem. When it didn't happen right away, we started praying about it. People kept asking us when we were going to have a baby, and it was so painful to just smile and answer, 'In God's time,' but I was starting to doubt that God was even listening to my prayers. When a year passed, and I still hadn't conceived, we made an appointment at a fertility clinic and decided to look into other methods. This was not an easy decision, but we started with IUI (intrauterine insemination). When that didn't work, we started trying IVF (In vitro fertilization). We've made so many trips to the clinic I can't even count them; my stomach looks like a black and blue pincushion from all the injections. On top of this, our bank account is slowly draining away, and every month when my cycle comes, I feel like a piece of me dies."

Natasha's voice faltered as she proceeded with her story. "I know that Jalen is hurting, too, and he and I have chosen to keep this part of our journey private—we have only shared it with our parents and a few close friends. So, every Sunday, I put on a brave face, knowing that I will have to face the well-meaning people who tease us about 'getting to work on building our family,' and offer meaningless platitudes. We regularly hear that 'God's timing is perfect' and that 'all things work together for good to those who love God.' Lately, I almost choke on the lyrics of the songs we sing in church that talk about God's goodness and the way He answers prayers, knowing that I don't totally believe the words anymore.

"It's even hard to interact with my in-laws because they just kept trying to give us 'helpful' advice, telling us to 'spend more time in prayer,' 'have more faith,' or 'let go and let God.' We even lost one set of close friends that we had confided in because they didn't agree with us seeking medical intervention for something that was, to them, only in God's hands. They told us that we must be harboring some secret sin, or else God would have blessed us with a baby already. With all these messages swirling around in my head, I started to doubt myself, thinking that maybe it was my fault. Was there something else I could do to help with the process? Was God punishing me for some misdeed I committed in my youth? Was my faith too small to make a difference?

"And then, a few months ago, during all that confusion, we got the amazing news that the most recent implantation had been successful, and I was finally pregnant after so many years. We were beyond thrilled, as were our parents and our closest friends. Finally, our prayers were answered, and my dream life was becoming a reality!"

Natasha suddenly stopped talking and became quiet as tears began to stream down her face. My heart ached for her as I anticipated what she would tell me next. When she was able, she spoke in a small, broken voice, "When we went for our three-month ultrasound, they couldn't detect any movement, and the baby's heart wasn't beating. At that moment, I felt like my heart stopped, too, and would never beat again. I had thought that the pain of getting my monthly cycle was devastating, but it was nothing compared to this agony. The next few weeks were all a blur. I didn't want to see or talk to anyone. Most days, I barely got out of bed.

"The people who knew what I had experienced tried to be helpful, but their words cut deeper than ever. They told me, 'At least you know you can get pregnant—you should be happy about that.' 'First pregnancies often don't take; you'll have another.' 'God must have known that you weren't ready yet, or he would have kept the baby healthy.' 'Just try again.' 'You have to stop feeling sorry for yourself and trust God.' 'Depression is a sin.' But as painful as those words were, the words that I spoke to myself during the sleepless nights were even worse: 'If I had really been trusting God, this wouldn't have happened.' 'God must be very angry with me to allow this to happen.' 'I probably didn't eat well enough or exercise enough.' 'Maybe our friends were right, and God didn't want us to use medical intervention.'

Natasha took an exhausted breath after recounting the painful words, wiped tears from her eyes, and resumed her story. "Jalen has been so supportive through this whole journey, but seeing his heart break too felt unbearable. I started to think that perhaps he would be better off with someone who could make him the father he always wanted to be. Those were dark days."

Then, as if getting a second wind, Natasha's voice became louder, and she stated, "And then, the anger came. I started to really question my faith and my understanding of God. I mean, what kind of a cruel God would give us this hope just to take it away? If God is in charge, why was this allowed to happen? I have so many questions and no place to ask them. When I was brave enough to share with a few close friends that I was struggling with feeling angry at God, they were so quick to offer the usual spiritual clichés—words that I used to believe but sound so hollow now." Natasha's next words bordered on desperation as she spat out, "They all say that they are praying for me and that if I just stay strong, I'll understand God's purpose someday. But I don't need some meaningless platitudes—I need help to get through today!"

As Natasha finished speaking, I could see that her distress was physical—her chest was heaving, her legs bounced, and her fists were tightly clenched. Most often, when a client is this agitated, I would respond by inviting them to relax their bodies using deep breathing, but instinctively, I knew that asking Natasha to move into a calmer state would add me to the list of people who found her strong emotions unacceptable. Instead, I matched her energy and let her know that what she was experiencing caused me to feel very sad and very angry as well.

I stated, "Natasha, as you share the ways that others have responded to you, your anger is understandable. In fact, I feel my own anger well up in my body in response, starting in my stomach, then moving to my limbs, and finally into my throat." I invited her to take a moment, tune into her own body, and let me know what she was feeling. She quickly acknowledged that she could feel the anger in her body, too, especially in her neck and hands. I asked what she usually does when her body is feeling strong emotions, and she thought for a moment and answered, "Nothing really; I just ignore it and hope that it goes away." She inquired of me, "Why? Is there something that I could do?"

I responded that when I feel anger in my body like this, I like to do something physical to get it out. She appeared confused, so I explained. "Anger causes many things to happen in the body: Our brain assesses the threat, hormones get released into our systems, our heart rate goes up, our muscles tense, and our liver even releases glucose" (Yadav, Yadav, & Sapkota, 2017). All these somatic responses can potentially have damaging long-term effects if we don't find a healthy way to express them." I then encouraged her to take a moment to feel her anger and see if there was anything that her body felt like doing. As she sat, she began to rock back and forth, and then her hand clasped her neck as she let out a guttural moan. I gently nodded as she continued, and her groan gradually subsided and body stilled. After having her take a few deep breaths, I asked her to check in and see how her body felt now, and she replied in a surprised tone, "A little better." Natasha added that she found it strange because she had been taught that expressing volatile emotions was wrong, and she had been afraid to do so in the past.

I assured her that she was brave for trying this exercise during our first session! I also added, "Natasha, I do not have all the answers to your questions, but I can offer you a safe place to explore your doubts, emotions, and your future if you'd like..." She nodded quickly, and I continued, "I especially want to commend you for not bypassing these understandable and very challenging emotions, given everything that you've been through." She thanked me for allowing her to feel so safe. I asked her to practice noticing and validating her emotions over the next week, locating those emotions in her body, and then moving her body in a way that supported her. She agreed to this, and we set up her next appointment before she left my office.

During our next session, I explained to Natasha that what she had shared with me about the way that her friends, family, and church community were communicating with her is called "spiritual bypassing" or "toxic positivity."

Noticing her curious gaze, I moved into a psychoeducational approach and explained that spiritual bypassing involves labeling certain emotions as negative and suppressing them while using "spiritual" concepts and language to present oneself as constantly positive. I went on to share with Natasha that when people use happy, optimistic language to describe all situations, it is called toxic positivity. In both cases, reality is suppressed, glossed over, or overgeneralized, and a cheerful demeanor is presented.

"Natasha, think of spiritual bypassing this way—it is like putting a bandage on a deep and serious puncture wound and calling it healed. It's the act of using spiritual beliefs or practices as a way to sidestep uncomfortable emotions or unresolved pain, creating an illusion of peace without addressing the underlying issues. Instead of doing the difficult inner work, some people may hide behind positive affirmations, meditation, or religious doctrines, hoping that by focusing only on the light, the shadows will disappear. But true healing requires turning toward those shadows, not avoiding them." Nataha's eager nod let me know this information resonated with her.

To make this personal to her experiences, I asked Natasha the following questions:

- Do you often feel guilty about what you feel?

- Do you find yourself pushing aside the things that upset you by saying, "It is what it is"?

- Do you feel that you need to hide or cover up your true feelings to yourself and others?

- Have you ever been shamed by others when you expressed your frustration?

- Do you find yourself quoting or responding to scriptures in a way that feels shaming or fear-inducing?

She answered all these questions affirmatively and conveyed that she was beginning to understand these concepts, "Wendy, I feel as if a light is going on inside of me! This validates exactly what I have been experiencing my entire life!" Her homework for the following week was to pay attention to the words of friends, family, and social media and write down anything she believed was toxic positivity or spiritual bypassing. Natasha eagerly agreed to do this, saying with some humor, "Let me tell you, I will probably fill an entire notebook before our next session!" I smiled in return and encouraged her to take it one step at a time without judging herself or others. "See what you record, Natasha. Remember to observe but not absorb as you move through this next step."

During our third session, as anticipated, Natasha arrived with an extensive list, remarking on how surprised she was by the sheer number of statements she had heard and noted. Before we examined her list, I encouraged her to take several deep breaths to soothe her nervous system and prepare for the potentially triggering material we were about to explore. Once she was centered, I asked her to read each statement aloud, pausing afterward to identify the emotion it evoked and to locate where she felt it in her body. Her first example was spoken by a close friend who said to her, "Everything happens for a reason; maybe you're meant to learn a deeper spiritual lesson from this experience." Natasha reported that these words brought up anger and that she felt it in the pit of her stomach, like a flame. I then invited her to take a deep breath in and exhale, releasing the emotion from her body as she did, creating space to address the next statement. As we continued through her list Natasha was surprised at the array of emotions she felt and how they manifested in her body.

Following that therapy session, Natasha's homework for the upcoming week was to observe her own thoughts and inner dialogue, noting any instances she identified as spiritual bypassing or toxic positivity. When she brought her list to the next session, we followed the same format to process her list as we did with her previous one. An example of her own spiritual bypassing that she had written in her journal was the thought that "I shouldn't feel sad or disappointed because this is obviously part of a higher plan, and I need to just accept it and stay positive." She reported that reading these words out loud brought up a sorrowful feeling that made her heart feel heavy. As before, once she had identified the emotion and what it felt like in her body, she took a deep breath in and released the sadness with her exhale. After completing this exercise on her entire list, she commented that she had been unaware until now of how many times she ignored or invalidated her own emotions.

Once Natasha became aware of her own inclination to pretend to be constantly positive or use spirituality to avoid her emotions (Patel, Sharma, & Kumar, 2020), I explained that the exercise in identifying her emotions and where she felt them in her body is part of a concept called "mindfulness." When I asked if she was familiar with the term or its concepts, I could sense a tenseness in Natasha's face and body. She explained that she was very hesitant to practice mindfulness, sharing that she feared it was in opposition to her faith, "What if I disappoint God? Is this against my faith?"

In my experience working with some clients, including Evangelical Christians, they may fear mindfulness because they perceive it as conflicting with their beliefs. Mindfulness practices, often rooted in Buddhist traditions, are sometimes seen by faith-based clients as spiritual or meditative techniques that draw attention away from a personal relationship with God. For those who prioritize prayer and scripture-based meditation, mindfulness might feel like a secular or even "new age" practice that encourages self-reliance or detachment, which could be viewed as contradictory to Christian teachings on dependence on God. Because mindfulness encourages non-judgmental awareness and self-exploration, some Christian clients may see this as focusing too much on the self rather than seeking divine guidance. There's also concern among some that mindfulness could inadvertently open the door to non-Christian influences or philosophies, which some might fear leads to spiritual confusion or away from biblical teachings.

Acknowledging Natasha's concerns, I reassured her that, in contrast to the understandable fears she expressed, once they better understand the practice, many Christians do embrace mindfulness, interpreting it as a way to deepen their faith, increase present awareness, and foster a more conscious relationship with God. I then gave her a worksheet, and together, we went over the list below as a way of alleviating her fears, "Natasha, thank you for sharing your concerns. I want to reassure you that mindfulness is not a sin. It is important to understand that mindfulness can be practiced in a way that aligns with a person's faith, your faith. Let's go over the following information and see if this helps you feel safer."

1. **Mindfulness is about awareness, not worship:** Mindfulness is simply the practice of being fully present in the moment, noticing thoughts, feelings, and sensations without judgment. It does not involve worshiping other gods or engaging in practices contrary to Christian beliefs. It's about observing one's thoughts rather than embracing any specific religious doctrine.

2. **Mindfulness can enhance faith:** For many Christians and other people of faith, mindfulness can complement one's spiritual practices by helping the person to be more present during prayer, scripture reading, and connecting with God. By quieting the mind and focusing on the present moment, mindfulness can lead to a deeper awareness of God's presence in everyday life.

3. **Biblical support for mindfulness-like practices:** The Bible encourages reflection and being mindful in different forms. Scriptures like Psalm 46:10, "Be still, and know that I am God," or Philippians 4:8, "focusing on whatever is true, noble, right, and pure," highlight the value of stillness and reflection and focusing on the good. These are core elements of mindfulness as well.

4. **It's about self-awareness, not self-centeredness**: Some Christians fear that mindfulness is too focused on the self. However, mindfulness doesn't encourage self-centeredness but instead fosters self-awareness, helping individuals to be more thoughtful, present, patient, compassionate, and loving—qualities that align with Christianity and other spiritual teachings.

5. **Mindfulness is a tool, not a belief system**: Mindfulness is not a religion or spiritual belief system but rather a tool to manage stress, improve mental health, and be more present in daily life. It's like any other practice, such as breathing exercises or journaling, that can help deepen one's emotional and spiritual well-being.

As Natasha followed along, she was relieved to understand mindfulness as a practice and was especially keen to learn ways that could help her identify and accept her emotions. As a therapist working with people of faith—regardless of their religion or spiritual beliefs—I've found that framing mindfulness as a tool to enhance focus, reduce stress, and cultivate intentionality helps ease concerns. By demonstrating that mindfulness can deepen rather than conflict with Christian faith (or any faith), clients become more open to seeing it as a valuable, faith-compatible practice.

As we moved forward in this part of her healing work, Natasha began to learn the following practices:

- **Mindful Breathing**: Mindful breathing is the practice of focusing your attention on your breath, observing each inhale and exhale without judgment. It helps calm the mind, reduce stress, and bring you into the present moment. Simply notice the rhythm of your breathing, allowing distractions to pass without attachment, and bring awareness back to your breath each time your mind wanders.

- **Body Scan Meditation**: Body scan meditation is a practice where you bring focused awareness to different parts of your body, from head to toe, noticing sensations without judgment to cultivate a deeper connection between mind and body.

- **Noticing and Labeling Emotions**: Noticing and labeling emotions involves consciously identifying and naming your feelings in the moment without judgement, a process that helps to create a pause between the emotion and your reaction, allowing for greater emotional clarity and regulation.

- **Allowing Yourself to Feel Emotion Without Judgment**: Feeling emotion without judgment means embracing feelings just as they are, giving them space to exist without labeling them as good or bad and opening a path to genuine self-compassion and healing.

- **Locating the Emotion in Your Body**: Locating the emotion in the body involves tuning into the physical sensations that accompany feelings, uncovering where tension, warmth, or tightness resides, and gaining deeper insight into emotional states.

- **Breathing Into the Sensation of the Emotion in Your Body**: Breathing into the sensation of the emotion in the body is focusing the breath on the specific area where the emotion is felt, allowing each inhale to gently expand around the sensation and each exhale to soften its intensity, promoting relaxation and presence.

- **Gently Exploring the Source of Emotions**: Gently exploring the source of the emotion involves approaching the feeling with curiosity, allowing insights to surface naturally about its origin without forcing answers or passing judgment.

- **Gaining Discernment on the Message the Emotion Is Carrying**: Gaining discernment on the message the emotion is carrying means tuning into the emotion's underlying signals, interpreting what it reveals about unmet needs or boundaries, and using this insight to guide thoughtful action.

- **Communicating Emotions With Awareness**: Communicating emotions with awareness involves expressing feelings clearly and mindfully, choosing words that reflect the inner experience while fostering understanding and connection with others.

- **Mindful Journaling**: Mindful journaling is the practice of writing with full presence, capturing thoughts and emotions as they arise, without judgment, to deepen self-awareness and foster emotional balance.

- **Practicing Self-Compassion Through Meditation**: Practicing self-compassion through meditation involves directing kindness and understanding inward, using focused attention to nurture a gentle, non-critical relationship with oneself during moments of struggle.

By regularly practicing these mindfulness techniques, Natasha became attuned to her emotional states, developed a deeper understanding of them, and was able to express them in a healthy and mindful way. During a session later in her treatment, she shared, "In the past I have never felt free to be my true self in my home or church community, but now I am beginning to experience a new sense of peace, and I think it's because I don't have to suppress all the emotions I thought were unacceptable." She shared that her mood, and her body, were beginning to feel lighter and that gradually she was becoming more of her authentic self.

During another session, I introduced Natasha to the concept of "role-playing" (Jiang, Alizadeh, & Cui, 2023). In this instance, she switched between playing the roles of both her and God. In the role of Natasha, she asked God some of the hard questions that were so confusing to her. Once she asked a question, she would switch roles to play the part of God. Although she was initially hesitant to speak for God, after we discussed that the point of the exercise was to find out what she really believed, she was eager to participate. She asked numerous questions and really dug deep to answer as she thought God would answer. From this she learned that she still did believe that God was real and that He did love all parts of her. Afterward, she reported that an added effect of this experience was an increased ability to be honest with God and, in turn, with other people.

It's important to note that Natasha referred to God as "He," while others may have different ways of identifying or understanding God, and that it's our job, as therapists, to support clients' personal beliefs, not to judge or impose our own beliefs on them.

• • • • •

After a few months of individual work, I suggested to Natasha that she may want to join a diverse women's therapy group, and she agreed. Through interacting with the others in the group, she was exposed to various belief systems and life experiences, which were enlightening to her. As Natasha watched other group members do their healing work, it helped her develop her own voice of truth based on her personal beliefs, her deepening faith, and her experiences. During group therapy sessions, she took the opportunity to use her authentic voice, no longer influenced by external opinions, societal pressures, and superficial beliefs, allowing her to connect more deeply with her true self and others around her.

Natasha found that one of the most effective therapy modalities used in the women's group was psychodrama. Psychodrama involves acting out a part of your life (past or future) as if it were happening in the present, thus gaining valuable insight into your behaviors and getting to practice new behaviors.

Natasha described her first experience participating in a psychodrama during a recent therapy session. "I was nervous at first, but once we got started, I almost forgot that I was the center of attention. I wanted to practice using my voice, so I told each group member a phrase that I had heard recently that expressed either spiritual bypassing or toxic positivity. I gave one member the saying, 'You should be grateful for what you have.' To the others, I gave, 'Others have it worse than you,' 'You're too blessed to be stressed,' 'Let go and let God,' 'Think happy thoughts!' and 'Don't think about it, just move on.' 'Pray more and have more faith.'"

Natasha continued, "Then, one at a time, each member repeated their sentence to me and paused so that I could form a reply. At first, it was hard because it felt like my brain froze, and then, even after I thought of a response, it felt like my words were stuck in my throat. But as I practiced breathing deeply and relaxing my body, my rebuttals began to flow. To the first group member, I was able to say, 'I am grateful for all I have, and I also feel sad that my prayer has not been answered. I can feel grateful and sad at the same time.' To the next, I stated, 'Yes, I know that others have it worse than I do, but suffering is not a contest, and my pain is real to me and to God.' To the third member, I replied, 'Yes, I am blessed in my life, but those blessings don't take away the stress I feel when going through a hard time. And by paying attention to my stress, I can do something about it like pray, go for a walk, or talk with a friend.'

"To the next group member, I responded, 'Honoring my God-given feelings and fears is not a bad thing. I can feel what I feel, and trust that God can also help me as I help myself.' To the next person, I responded, 'I do have some happy thoughts, but I also have thoughts that are sad, fearful, or even angry. God already knows all my thoughts, so I don't need to hide them. My true friends also want to know my honest thoughts, so I don't want to pretend with them either.' The next group member's statement was difficult to reply to as 'not thinking and just moving on' is how I had lived most of my life. It took some time but I was eventually able to say, 'The difficult times that I go through are too important to just forget them because they can teach me so much. I want to go through each minute of my day mindfully, experiencing all that my life brings, and once I've processed reality, I can then form a wise plan of action. I want to be intentional and congruent with everything I do.' Finally, to the last group member I responded, 'My prayer life and my faith are some of the most important parts of my life. When I hear you tell me to 'pray more', it feels assumptive and shaming, and I would like you to please consider this when speaking with me in the future.' The words gradually came to me, and I was able to say them in a calm, clear voice."

After sharing her experience with me, Natasha added, "It felt so good to take the time to think through my responses, have a safe place to share them, and to hear myself saying the words. Since participating in that psychodrama, it's been easier to speak up to those in my life who offer toxic positivity or spiritual bypassing as a solution and to speak the truth in love. It has brought me peace and freedom."

Along with attending the women's group, Natasha was also pleased to find a virtual support group for women with fertility challenges. This group was immensely helpful for her, as she no longer felt so alone and had another safe space to express all her emotions with women who shared her struggles.

As we approached our first year of working together, an important piece of Natasha's counseling experience was exploring the "what ifs" in her life. To get to the most important question that she needed to ask herself, we first explored her fears. Her infertility journey had brought up many insecurities, and she was readily able to list them: "What if I miscarry again? Will I survive?" "What if this heartbreak comes between my husband and me?" "Who will remember me if I don't have offspring?" "Is there a reason for my existence if I don't experience a live birth of my own?"

From these various fears, Natasha was able to discern that the main question she needed to ask herself was, "Can I live a meaningful life without becoming a mother?" At first, she did not want to entertain this question as she found it so painful. Gradually, she was able to use her mindful coping skills and allow herself to sit with the discomfort of imagining a life without children of her own. As she did, she took time to honestly examine her values, self-worth, and purpose in the world. She concluded that by remaining authentic, honoring her emotions, and staying true to her own voice, she would continue to be a congruent, loving presence for herself and others, and that would be living her best life.

Natasha continues to do well and attends bi-monthly counseling sessions. At a recent appointment, she was happy to announce that she would be speaking at the next women's meeting at her church and sharing about her healing journey. She was both nervous and excited to share what she had learned about toxic positivity and spiritual bypassing and hoped that others would find it as helpful as she did. "I even plan on teaching a couple of the mindfulness tools I've learned—wish me luck!"

An especially poignant moment came when Natasha shared an excerpt from her planned presentation in a session. She read, "What I would really like each of you to take away with you today after listening to my story is this: Being shamed or feeling guilty for having real emotions is not how we're meant to live. We are made up of many parts, and we can learn from all of them. We don't need to put on happy faces when we're struggling, and we don't need to use spiritual bypassing with each other. We also don't need to lie to ourselves anymore, and we can have an honest relationship with God. We can learn new ways to talk to ourselves when we're struggling and gently say: 'All my emotions are okay. I am loved for exactly who I am and not because I'm perfect. Stumbling is a part of life, and I don't need to be or feel any certain way.'

"As we all acknowledge our acceptance from God, we can then accept all parts of ourselves, and, in turn, we can accept each other, too. As the quote attributed to the 13th-century Persian poet Jalaluddin Rumi states: 'The wound is the place where the Light enters you.' A scripture that aligns with this is found in 2 Corinthians 4:7 (NIV): 'But we have this treasure in jars of clay to show that this all-surpassing power is from God and not from us.' This verse suggests that, despite our fragility and brokenness, God's power and light are made evident through us. Let's be honest about our woundedness, allow the Light to enter us, and then we can be fully a part of this inclusive, loving community of people where we can all grow in grace."

As I listened to Natasha's speech, tears came to my eyes as I remembered the nervous, confused, hurting woman who entered my office that first time, and I was in awe of the honest, courageous, wise woman she had become through her diligence, insight, and compassion toward herself.

A word from Wendy

Spiritual Bypassing

Spiritual bypassing is a term created by psychologist John Welwood in 1984. It describes the concept of dodging painful psychological issues using spiritual practices and beliefs (Picciotto & Fox, 2018). Instead of mindfully facing our inner wounds and underdeveloped coping skills, we avoid facing them by pretending (sometimes unknowingly) that these "earthly" issues don't bother us as we have risen above them. We use bypassing to avoid staying present with the messiness of our humanity and instead skip over the pain to convince ourselves and others that we are at peace. This can be harmful to oneself and can be devastating when we judge others and try to force these views onto them. Instead of inspiring their faith, whatever that faith may be, it will invalidate others' emotions, often leaving them feeling judged, angry, hurt, and wanting to withdraw in shame.

To further understand spiritual bypassing, we can see that it is the opposite of mindfulness, which was discussed in depth in Chapter Two (Fox, Cashwell, & Picciotto, 2017). Instead of seeing, understanding, and accepting all human emotions, people within faith communities sometimes divide emotions into categories of "good" and "bad" or "spiritual" and "unspiritual." As a result, they seek to deny the "bad" emotions and focus solely on the "good" emotions. Therefore, feeling anger, fear, sadness, or frustration is unacceptable. It is sometimes expected within these groups to feel or pretend to feel joy and peace all the time, no matter how difficult the situation. The confusing part of this is that deep down, we know that we aren't always experiencing these types of feelings, and consequently, we feel wrong and guilty for having real, complex human emotions. Instead of mindfully staying present with our current circumstances, some use spiritual bypassing to escape the reality of problems and the feelings that go along with them.

Mindfulness also encourages us to pay attention to our bodies and where we feel our emotions. However, when someone is using spiritual bypassing, they rationalize their feelings so that they do not have to experience the distress that comes with feeling painful emotions. The emphasis on thinking rather than feeling can also lead to a disconnect with the body and a lack of presence and self-care.

Mindfulness encourages us to recognize and accept our emotions and thoughts as natural parts of our human experience, even when they differ from what others think. It helps us stay open and aware of ourselves, allowing us to express our feelings without worrying about being judged. This approach promotes honest communication and stronger connections because it means being true to ourselves rather than changing to fit what others expect.

In contrast, spiritual bypassing often sees conflict and confrontation as "ungodly" or bad, suggesting that real spirituality means avoiding difficult emotions or conversations. This way of thinking can lead to hiding our true feelings and choosing a fake sense of peace over being honest. People who use spiritual bypassing might avoid direct communication, pull away from relationships, or use passive-aggressive behavior to show their displeasure. This avoidance leaves problems unresolved and prevents real connection and growth in relationships.

Mindfulness practices encourage us not to become too attached to any one thing, even to our own identities as we see them. When we are mindful, we see all parts of ourselves and accept them as they are in the here and now, even though we may be working toward changing habits and behaviors that do not serve us well. Those who practice spiritual bypassing, no matter what their worldview or spirituality may be, use their spiritual identity to defend themselves against feeling inadequate or weak, thinking that if they identify as a faith-based person, then nothing else matters. Unfortunately, we often witness this in the political arena, where a candidate may engage in reprehensible behavior, yet their actions are overlooked if they profess to be a person of faith. This occurs across all political parties. Similarly, it happens within faith communities and among their leaders. Instead of openly acknowledging their struggles and seeking help or attending counseling to heal, some hide behind scripture, religion, or legalism as a means of avoiding accountability and personal growth.

Toxic Positivity

Toxic positivity is a term that has surfaced organically and has been adopted by the mental health field (Salopek & Eastin, 2024). It describes the concept of invalidating the true human experience by focusing solely on happy thoughts and portraying these optimistic attitudes in every circumstance. This concept only allows space for enforced positively and disavows all other emotions. It is similar to spiritual bypassing, but it applies to those who don't necessarily subscribe to a higher power.

Similar to spiritual bypassing, people who are toxically positive judge their emotions as good and bad, and the positive thoughts and emotions are valued highly, and the negative thoughts and emotions are disregarded. To maintain this optimistic attitude requires stifling emotions that are deemed unacceptable. Researcher and author Brené Brown shares, "We think that denying our emotions makes us stronger and more resilient, but the research shows that it actually makes us less resilient" (Wyatt, 2024).

Toxic positivity fosters an inauthentic life where meaningful self-reflection and genuine connection with others become difficult. Those who engage in toxic positivity often judge others for experiencing real emotions like anger, sadness, or disappointment, viewing them as weak or lacking faith. This judgment stems from their own inability to confront and be vulnerable in these emotional areas, which they suppress in themselves.

Believing that having a positive attitude is the only correct way to navigate life can have damaging effects on both the holder of this belief and those around them (Tran & Rimes, 2017). No one can experience positive circumstances all the time, and when something tragic happens, the toxically positive person will experience emotions that they deem negative, and this can lead to guilt, shame, or anxiety. The person will judge themselves as a failure, which will bring increased negative emotions as they struggle to remain positive—at least outwardly.

Living with the contradiction of feeling negatively but trying to remain relentlessly positive can lead to deep psychological problems, such as depression and shame (Lukin, 2020). Also, this dichotomy can lead to serious medical issues as true emotions are pushed down and remain unaddressed in the body. In a recent study, researchers observed that those who believed that feeling and communicating certain emotions was wrong experienced numerous health problems, such as digestive issues like irritable bowel syndrome, depression, eating disorders, and chronic fatigue syndrome (Quintero, 2021).

Toxic positivity and spiritual bypassing can be passed down generationally as some parents pressure their children to always present a positive attitude. This can be a parent's way of coping with their own inability to be present with the range of emotions their children experience. If caregivers cannot bear to feel angry or hurt, they will not be able to handle their children's emotions, and thus, they will avoid them or discourage their expression. Children who grow up in an environment where emotions are judged as either acceptable or unacceptable can be negatively impacted. They will learn early on to hide away their objectionable emotions to be loved by their caregivers and deny the reality of their feelings (Sinclair, Hart, & Lomas, 2020).

Toxic positivity is also in opposition to mindfulness in the same way as spiritual bypassing is rival to mindfulness. A toxically positive person will tell someone struggling with a health issue to just be happy that something worse hasn't happened to them, whereas mindfulness allows us to look honestly at our circumstances, grieve our losses, practice gratitude, and do the same for others. As Tich Nat Hahn often said, "Deep compassionate listening is the kind of listening that can help relieve the suffering of another person. You listen with only one purpose: to help them to empty their heart."

Toxic positivity requires that only positive emotions be expressed, whereas mindfulness recognizes that we can experience two or more emotions at the same time, and they are all valid. For example, we can feel overwhelmingly sad that our elderly parents have passed on and relieved that we no longer must care for them. We can love someone and be very angry with them simultaneously. We can feel proud of the professional invitation to speak at a conference and experience the fear of public speaking at the same time. All emotions are acceptable.

Those who are toxically positive tend to speak on behalf of the Universe, God, or a higher power, making broad declarations of right, wrong, and justice. Mindfulness realizes that everyone's experience is unique and that we can only answer for ourselves. As we learn to accept and understand that all emotions are part of the human experience, we practice what is called equanimity, which allows us to respond to ourselves and others with congruence and empathy.

As I look back on my own life, I can see numerous times when I used spiritual bypassing and toxic positivity to cope with life's circumstances. As a missionary, I was required to write a monthly prayer letter to update family and friends and those who supported us financially and in prayer. When I sat down to write the letter, I would reflect on the previous month. Most often, there were numerous instances of difficult times (sickness, tribal violence, long hours of language and culture study, and missing home and family). However, I felt that I needed to present a positive picture of what life was like on the mission field so that others would want to join us in service and continue to send us financial support. So, I pushed aside thoughts of the dark times and scoured my memory for anything positive that I could convey.

My letters were full of thanking God for his blessings, reports of new cultural concepts learned, and hopes for the future. While those things were true, I feel that I did a disservice to myself and others by not sharing a realistic view of what life is like in a developing country. I often wondered how many people read my letters and felt guilt or shame that their lives weren't as abounding in positivity as mine appeared. This question was answered whenever we came back to North America to give a report to our supporting communities, as almost everyone we met stated, "I could never do what you do." It has taken me years to learn that I, in all my messy humanity, am acceptable just as I am and to be able to offer this gracious acceptance to others, as well.

Psychodrama

As mentioned above in Natasha's story, an important part of her treatment involved psychodrama (López-González, Morales-Landazábal, & Topa, 2021). It was first created by Jacob Moreno in 1921, inspired by improvisational theater. This is a form of therapy that uses guided drama and role-playing and involves acting out a part of your life (past or future) as if it were happening in the present, often with the help of a therapist and other group members.

As Natasha experienced, psychodrama has numerous positive outcomes, including increasing social skills, uncovering hidden emotions, allowing clients to practice a variety of outcomes to problematic situations, and providing closure to painful circumstances that were not able to be experienced in the past. Moving forward into the next sections of this chapter, I invite you to welcome your most authentic—and perhaps hidden—parts into the following guided imagery and exercises.

Mindfulness Healing Part I:

Preparation, Assessment, and Script
for Guided Imagery Exercise

Important Safety Tips for Therapists, Facilitators, and Healing Individuals

Environment Consideration and Tips: It can be helpful to "set the stage" prior to a guided imagery exercise. For example, consider the lighting—is it too bright or too low? Another helpful step is putting phones on silent. Also, think about outside distractions, such as barking dogs, traffic, and other interruptions. If possible, minimize outside noises the best that you can. Finally, some individuals like having a blanket or pillow to hold, or you may enjoy diffusing essential oils to support deeper relaxation if there are no allergy concerns. While mindfulness-based guided imagery is not hypnosis, it can be helpful to prepare your environment prior to beginning the guided imagery exercise.

Voice Prosody: An additional gentle reminder is to be aware of your voice prosody. Prosody refers to the rhythm and melody of the voice, including intonation, stress, and pauses. Speaking in a softer tone and slower cadence than your normal speaking voice is useful in supporting the guided imagery practice. If you typically speak more rapidly or loudly, it will take some practice to slow down and modulate your voice.

Diversity Considerations: Consider the client's culture, spirituality, age, race, physical differences (such as hearing loss), gender and orientation, and other unique experiences that may invite a softer or different speaking tone or pace or require that the client keep their eyes open if they prefer. If you are bilingual and you and your client speak the same languages, ask your client what language they prefer. If your client prefers to go by a nickname, a title such as Dr., Mr., or Mrs., or a specific pronoun, honor their request.

Pace Yourself: Remind yourself to take your time as you walk through this process. There is no need to rush. If you are the person facilitating this exercise, slow down for a relaxed, calming pace. Additionally, it is wise for the facilitator to first practice the exercise with yourself prior to practicing with another person.

Safety Reminder: Safety is the number one consideration with any therapeutic approach or healing intervention. As you lead your clients through the following guided imagery exercise, please instruct your clients to alert you if they are experiencing any of the following trauma responses. If you are an individual doing this work solo, you will also want to consider the following:

- Traumatic memories that are creating a high level of distress
- Feelings of intense fear or panic
- Disturbing or intrusive thoughts
- Suicidal or homicidal thoughts
- Dissociation (if there is an awareness of the dissociative states)
- Other crisis concerns (list on the line): _____
_____

It is also important to ask the client to alert you if they experience any of the following symptoms. Likewise, if someone is doing this work solo, they should pay compassionate and close attention to their process and monitor for distressing or physical symptoms such as:

- A racing heart
- Tightness in the chest
- Shortness of breath
- Nausea or Intestinal distress
- Feeling faint or dizziness

- Body pain
- Feeling as if you are floating outside of your body
- Other somatic concerns (list on the line): _____

Note for Therapist or Facilitator: Before moving into the guided imagery, please have your client begin with the assessment below. If you are not a trained mental health professional and your client is in crisis and exhibiting or discussing symptoms that are out of your scope of practice or experience, please refer to an appropriate mental health or medical professional. *If your client is experiencing an immediate life-threatening emergency, please call 911 or the appropriate emergency number if located outside of the United States.*

Note to Solo Reader: *If you are doing this work on your own and believe you are in crisis or may be at risk to yourself, please stop and seek emergency support immediately by calling 911 or your local emergency number.*

Pre-Guided Imagery Assessment Scale

On a scale from 1 to 10 (with 1 = very low, and 10 = very high), please take a mindful moment to assess the following. Circle the number that most accurately applies to you:

Feeling	Assessment (1-10)									
▫ Anxiety	1	2	3	4	5	6	7	8	9	10
▫ Anger	1	2	3	4	5	6	7	8	9	10
▫ Shame	1	2	3	4	5	6	7	8	9	10
▫ Sadness	1	2	3	4	5	6	7	8	9	10
▫ Fear	1	2	3	4	5	6	7	8	9	10
▫ Numbness	1	2	3	4	5	6	7	8	9	10
▫ Confusion	1	2	3	4	5	6	7	8	9	10
▫ Curiosity	1	2	3	4	5	6	7	8	9	10
▫ Hopefulness	1	2	3	4	5	6	7	8	9	10
▫ Calm	1	2	3	4	5	6	7	8	9	10
▫ Joyful	1	2	3	4	5	6	7	8	9	10
▫ Other:	1	2	3	4	5	6	7	8	9	10

Mindfulness Healing Part II:
Breath and Somatic Preparation & Prompts

This exercise involves tuning into your breath and body and is followed by the guided imagery exercise. It's important to note that this may not be suitable for everyone. It's recommended that the following be adapted to the specific needs and comfort levels of the individual(s) involved.

Physical Space and Comfort: Have your client settle into a comfortable sitting or lying down position, with their feet on the floor or cross-legged if that is the preference. If your client—or you if you are doing this solo—has a yoga mat or a couch and prefers to lay down, that is fine. Whatever position will help the client feel comfortable is perfectly acceptable.

Prompt 1: Let's pause while you take a few moments to get comfortable.

Prompt 2: When you are ready, you are welcome to close your eyes if that feels comfortable for you. Or, if you prefer to leave your eyes open, that is just fine. Whatever allows you to feel most secure is more than acceptable. If your eyes remain open, feel free to rest your gaze on a calming point—near the floor if you're sitting or on the ceiling if you're lying down.

Prompt 3: We will now move forward into the grounded breathing exercise. This will take approximately two to three minutes.

> ### *Grounded Breath Exercise*

Now that you are in a comfortable position, before we begin the guided imagery, let's move through the grounded breath work.

1. We will start with the 4-2-7 breath. Start by breathing in deeply through the nose to the count of four, hold for two, and then exhale slowly and intentionally through the mouth to the count of seven. Let's do this three times at your own pace. ***Note to Facilitator: Count to 20 silently.***

2. Now, let's return to easy, relaxed, deep breathing. Take a long breath in through the nose and a long exhale out through the mouth. Continue with this breath. ***Note to Facilitator: Count to 20 silently.***

3. As you are noticing the gentle rhythm of deep breathing, I would like you to imagine extending compassion to yourself with each intake breath. ***Note to Facilitator: Count to 20 silently.***

Now that we have finished with our grounding breaths, please feel free to breathe normally with relaxed, regular breaths. Let's now move into relaxing the body in preparation for guided imagery:

1. Notice that your feet are feeling heavier and more relaxed.

2. Notice that your hands are gently resting at your sides, on your belly, or on your thighs.

3. Feel your jaw relax and your tongue move away from the roof of your mouth.

4. Allow your shoulders to relax down from your ear lobes, and your elbows to gently relax down from your shoulders.

5. Bit by bit the tension moves out of your body as you breathe in and relax and breathe out and relax. Breathe in compassion, hope, and healing, and breathe out stress, judgment, and anger. **Note to Facilitator: *Count to 20 silently.***

As we complete our breath work, we will now move on to the guided imagery preparation and exercise section. You can return to your breath work exercises at any point during the guided imagery. The guided imagery exercise will take approximately 10 minutes. You may continue to stay in your comfortable position or shift to a different comfortable position. You may also continue with your eyes closed if that is your preference. At any point, you are welcome to ask for a time out if needed.

Let's move forward.

Mindfulness Healing Part III:

Guided Imagery Exercise
Safe Bubble Self-Regulation

Note to Therapist or Facilitator: If you notice that the client is highly activated during the guided imagery, perhaps demonstrating rapid or shallow breathing, sobbing, or shaking, please have the client pause as you attend to the individual. This can be done by gently stating that you would like to pause the exercise for a moment, then quietly asking the person by name if they would like a break, support with deep breathwork, or to step out of the guided imagery entirely if it has become too overwhelming.

Note to the Reader: If you are doing this solo without the support of a mental health professional, again, please be gentle with yourself. If you have a trusted person to lead you through this, you may want to consider this option, or perhaps you can read this into a recording device and then play back and follow the prompts. If you become overwhelmed or feel as if you are in a crisis state, please stop and reach out for help if need be. Safety first, always.

Purpose of the Safe Bubble Self-Regulation Exercise: This guided imagery exercise is designed to help you gain the ability to create a barrier that shields you from the toxic, judgmental, or dismissive words of others, allowing you a few moments of presence to self-regulate, breathe, and honor your thoughts and feelings.

Instructions: This guided imagery exercise will take approximately 10 minutes. You will be guided by your mental health professional or trusted facilitator, or you may guide yourself if you prefer, through each step of the exercise slowly. If you are doing this independently, you are welcome to record the following prompts to place back to yourself if that is helpful. Though questions may be asked of you or you may be given prompts, there is no expectation of a verbal response. You may respond if you would like to do so, or you may quietly respond inside of yourself, which many people prefer. Through this visualization journey, you will be guided to explore how to place a barricade between you and the words of those who use spiritual bypassing or toxic positivity, allowing you the space to connect with *and* express your true emotions.

First Step Prompt: Close your eyes, take a deep breath, and allow yourself to sink into a comfortable position. When you are ready, think back to a time when someone spoke to you in a way that felt like toxic positivity or spiritual bypassing. Perhaps you shared with them a health concern or a distressing situation, and they simply replied, "It could be worse," or "You should be grateful for what you do have." Take a moment to remember those words. **Note to Facilitator: *Count to 20 silently.***

Next Prompt Step: As you imagine hearing these words again, picture the words pushing against you, and feel the weight of the words trying to force you to restrain your true emotions. Remember, though, that you are choosing to remain mindful and that you want to feel all your feelings. Now, imagine that you look beside you and see a large bubble—big enough for you to stand up in. You gently step inside the bubble and as soon as you do you feel calm and peaceful. **Note to Facilitator: *Count to 20 silently.***

Next Prompt Step: Take a moment to observe the peaceful and safe bubble. What does it look like? What color is it, and what is the temperature like inside it? Take a moment to enjoy this peaceful space, breathing in and out slowly. **Note to Facilitator: *Count to 20 silently.***

Next Prompt Step: As you relax inside your bubble, you begin to notice something remarkable—only the words you choose to let in can enter your space. You listen carefully to the words others speak, deciding whether to welcome them inside where they can take root or leave them outside, allowing them to drift away. Words that are toxically positive or spiritually bypassing, even those spoken with good intentions, simply bounce off the bubble and dissolve, fading into nothingness. **Note to Facilitator: *Count to 20 silently.***

Next Prompt Step: Now, take a moment to enjoy the space around you, noticing that it is no longer infiltrated with anything repressive. Notice what words and emotions you are inviting into your safe bubble. **Note to Facilitator: *Count to 20 silently.***

Next Prompt Step: As you attend to your self-care and regulate, you feel confident in stepping outside of your bubble now. You are now free to feel and express all your emotions, set boundaries, and offer responses, knowing all that you are feeling, thinking, and saying is important and valid. Even if others disagree, you can honor their perspective, but you do not need to agree or accept their words as your own. Simply breathe and enjoy the vast space that is yours to think and grow. **Note to Facilitator: *Count to 20 silently.***

Next Prompt Step: Take this moment to remind yourself that anytime you feel like the words of toxic positivity or spiritual bypassing are crowding in on you, you can settle yourself, imagine yourself stepping into your safe bubble for a few minutes, breathe deeply in and out, experience peace and calm, and create spaciousness between you and the oppressive messages. You will be free to experience and express your own truth. **Note to Facilitator: Count to 20 silently.**

Next Prompt Step: Know that you have the strength and resilience to put a helpful barrier between your heart and harmful messages. Please remember that you are not alone in this journey of healing; you are supported. No matter the challenges that come your way, remember that your feelings and experiences matter. Take a moment now to give yourself an affirmation. Self-affirmations may take you out of your comfort zone, but do your best to stay present with yourself, even in the discomfort. **Note to Facilitator: Count to 20 silently.**

Transitioning to Awareness

Final Prompt Step: When you're ready, if your eyes are closed, notice the light in front of your eyelids. Gently blink, open your eyes, and bring your awareness back to the present moment.

Mindfulness Healing Part IV:
Processing of Guided Imagery
Sharing Your Experience

Purpose for Processing: After the conclusion of the guided imagery, the therapist or facilitator will lead an open and respectful discussion about what you experienced during the guided imagery. The aim is to allow for a compassionate and honest conversation as you highlight important aspects of the guided imagery exercise and what the experience was like.

Note: If you are doing this solo without a therapist or facilitator, please pace yourself and notice your energy. You may journal your responses to the questions below if you are doing this work on your own.

Important Considerations for the Facilitator: It is not the role of the therapist or facilitator to interpret, minimize, or re-direct. Rather, it is important for the facilitator to skillfully hold a safe space for the client to share their experience, including the more difficult aspects. This is a time for the facilitator to honor the pain, as well as highlight and affirm the positive insights the client may have had. Remind the client that participating in a therapy exercise like this is a signal of hope and aids in the possibility of recovery and healing.

Processing Questions

1. What did you notice in the guided imagery?

2. What challenges did you experience?

3.   What joys did you experience?

4.   Did you have a breakthrough you'd like to share?

5.   Do you have any concerns that you'd like to share?

6.   What are you feeling in your body currently?

7.   Did you notice any self-growth with insight and compassion toward yourself?

8.   Did you notice any triggers or areas of concern?

Post-Guided Imagery Assessment Scale

Now that you have completed the breath work and somatic exercises, the guided imagery exercise, and the process work, on a scale from 1 to 10, (with 1 = very low, and 10 = very high), let's take a mindful moment to assess the following:

Feeling	Assessment (1-10)									
▫ Anxiety	1	2	3	4	5	6	7	8	9	10
▫ Anger	1	2	3	4	5	6	7	8	9	10
▫ Shame	1	2	3	4	5	6	7	8	9	10
▫ Sadness	1	2	3	4	5	6	7	8	9	10
▫ Fear	1	2	3	4	5	6	7	8	9	10
▫ Numbness	1	2	3	4	5	6	7	8	9	10
▫ Confusion	1	2	3	4	5	6	7	8	9	10
▫ Curiosity	1	2	3	4	5	6	7	8	9	10
▫ Hopefulness	1	2	3	4	5	6	7	8	9	10
▫ Calm	1	2	3	4	5	6	7	8	9	10
▫ Joyful	1	2	3	4	5	6	7	8	9	10
▫ Other:	1	2	3	4	5	6	7	8	9	10

Note to Facilitator or Reader: Engaging in somatic movement, if you are able to do so, such as gentle stretching, walking, rhythmic body movements, or dancing to music, following guided imagery is vital for healing trauma as it allows individuals to release stored tension, process emotions, and reconnect with their bodies, facilitating a holistic approach to healing. Please take 3-5 minutes to move your body in a way that feels good for you. Yoga poses, stretching, dance, bouncing gently, rhythmically swaying, or a short walk are all excellent ways to honor yourself.

Important Reminder: If you, as the facilitator, are not a licensed therapist or trained mental health professional and your client is in crisis and exhibiting or discussing symptoms that are out of your scope of practice or experience, please refer to an appropriate mental health or medical professional. *If your client is experiencing an immediate life-threatening emergency, please call 911 or the appropriate emergency number if located outside of the United States. If you are doing this solo without support and are in a state of emergency, reach out to 911 immediately.*

Mindfulness Healing Part V:

Art Exercise I—Toxic Messages

Purpose Statement: The purpose of this art exercise is to mindfully reflect on and explore any messages of toxic positivity or spiritual bypassing you have received.

Art Exercise Instructions: Gather art supplies such as paper, colored pencils, stickers, or other dry materials. Please be mindful if you choose to use supplies like markers or paints, as these can sometimes bleed through to the next page. You may want to place a blank sheet of paper underneath your work to protect the following pages.

1.   Begin by finding a quiet and comfortable space where you can focus without distractions.

2.   Take a few moments to center yourself through deep breathing, visualization, or grounding exercises. Allow yourself to become present in the moment, acknowledging any thoughts or emotions that arise. If this exercise feels overwhelming, it's okay to take a break. Be gentle with yourself—your emotional well-being matters most.

3.   Once you feel grounded, recall any toxically positive or spiritual bypassing statements that you have heard from your family, friends, faith community, and society. They may be words of judgment that you were told God was saying to you, unhelpful advice, or words meant to shame you for expressing authentic emotions.

4.   Choose the most hurtful of these messages, and using your pen or pencil, write them in the boxes provided in the picture on the next page.

5. As you work on your art, pay attention to any emotions or sensations that arise. Allow yourself to explore them openly and without negative self-talk. Remember that there are no right or wrong ways to express yourself through art, just as there are no right or wrong emotions.

6. Once you have completed your art exercise, take a step back and observe your creation. Reflect on the journey it represents, recognizing the challenges you have faced and the progress you have made.

7. Finally, think about strategies that will support your path toward healing.

8. Take a moment to appreciate yourself for engaging in this healing art exercise and for the courage you have shown. Allow yourself to feel a sense of pride and accomplishment as you continue your journey of recovery.

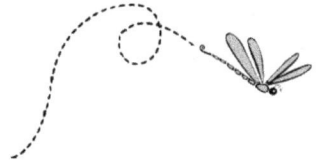

Mindfulness Healing Part V:

Art Exercise II—Affirming Messages

Purpose Statement: The purpose of this healing art exercise is to create healthy, affirming statements that counter the toxic words of others.

Art Exercise Instructions: Gather art supplies such as paper, colored pencils, stickers, or other dry materials. Please be mindful if you choose to use supplies like markers or paints, as these can sometimes bleed through to the next page. You may want to place a blank sheet of paper underneath your work to protect the following pages.

1. Begin by finding a quiet and comfortable space where you can focus without distractions.

2. Take a few moments to center yourself through deep breathing, visualization, or grounding exercises. Allow yourself to become present in the moment, acknowledging any thoughts or emotions that arise.

3. Once you feel grounded, think of the truthful messages you would like to use in response to the toxically positive, spiritually bypassing, or negative messages that you filled in on the previous illustration, and then add those more compassionate and healthy messages to the hearts surrounding the superwoman illustration on the following page.

4. As you work on your art, pay attention to any emotions or sensations that arise. Allow yourself to explore them openly and without negative self-talk. Remember there are no right or wrong ways to express yourself through art.

5. Take a moment to review the two pictures, scared woman and superwoman, paying attention to the words you wrote and the faces of the women pictured. First, read aloud the harmful messages and notice how your body feels when you say them. Next, read aloud—in a confident voice—the healing messages you wrote, and pay attention to how your body feels as you do. This may feel foreign at first, and that is OK. You are learning a new way to express yourself and a new way to accept or not accept messages and opinions from others.

6. Once you have completed your art exercise, take a step back and observe your creation. Reflect on the journey it represents, recognizing the challenges you have faced and the progress you have made.

7. Finally, think about strategies that will support your path toward healing. I thought it would be helpful to list a few ideas in the next section.

Strategies to Counter Toxic Positivity

Allow All Emotions to Exist: Give yourself permission to feel anger, sadness, grief, fear—whatever is real for you. These emotions are valid and necessary for healing.

Use Affirmations That Honor Complexity:

- Instead of "just think positive," try:
    - "I am doing the best I can with what I have."
    - "It's okay to not be okay right now."

Surround Yourself with Emotionally Honest People: Seek out relationships where vulnerability is welcomed and feelings are not dismissed or minimized.

Practice Self-Compassion Instead of Toxic Optimism: Talk to yourself like you would a friend, "This is hard. I'm allowed to feel this way."

Challenge "Shoulds" and Emotional Expectations: Watch out for thoughts like "I should be over this" or "I should be grateful." Healing has no deadline or perfect emotion.

Strategies to Counter Spiritual Bypassing

- **Integrate, Don't Escape**: Spiritual tools (meditation, prayer, rituals) should support you in facing pain—not bypassing it. Use them to ground and process, not to avoid.

- **Stay Grounded in Your Humanity**: You can be both spiritual and human—allow space for suffering, shadow work, and imperfection.

- **Name What's Real Before Seeking Transcendence**: Acknowledge what hurts. You can't transform what you won't touch.

- **Work with a Trauma-Informed Therapist or Spiritual Mentor**: Healing is relational. Having a guide who honors your emotional experience and doesn't dismiss it with spiritual clichés is essential.

- **Use Mindfulness to Be Present, Not to Dismiss**: Mindfulness is about observing what "is", not pretending things are fine. Sit with your truth, even if it's uncomfortable.

Take a moment to appreciate yourself for engaging in this healing art exercise and for the courage you have shown. Allow yourself to feel a sense of pride and accomplishment as you continue your journey of recovery.

Mindful Reflection Moment

Now that you have completed your breath work, guided imagery, and art and journal exercises, please take some mindful time to reflect before we bring this chapter to a close. You are welcome to answer the following questions in the space below, or write in a journal or notebook of your choice. You may do this with your therapist, or if you are working through this book solo, you can do this on your own.

1. What are you noticing after this chapter?

2. What awareness and insight have surfaced?

3. What is the information you have learned?

In the space below or in your own journal or notebook, write or share your reflections if you would like to process further. As always, please be gentle with yourself.

_____

_____

_____

_____

_____

Final Step: Self-Affirmation Exercise

Instructions: Before moving on to the next chapter, can you give yourself the gift of self-affirmation? Affirming oneself can be difficult for those who have experienced trauma, been the target of toxic positivity, or faced spiritual bypassing—whether within themselves or from others. It can also be challenging for those navigating grief, addiction, betrayal, anxiety, depression, or other struggles. As a support to this step of your healing, affirmation ideas might include statements such as: "All my feelings are normal and acceptable," "I choose to let go of toxic messages from others," and "I give myself permission to struggle and be authentic." Please use the winged heart below to honor your own self-affirmation(s). If you can only come up with one affirmation at this time, that is more than acceptable. Perhaps you can return later in your healing process and add more:

In this chapter, my goal was to introduce the concepts of spiritual bypassing, toxic positivity, encouraging you to mindfully reflect on how they may have affected you. We also explored the therapeutic practice of psychodrama. Through mindful exercises like breath work, somatic visualization and the safe bubble guided imagery, you were able to reflect on the harmful messages you've heard and internalized and contemplate how you might respond to these messages in the future. By developing healthy rebuttals to these toxic beliefs, my hope is that you now feel more empowered to embrace all of your emotions as valid and deserving of acceptance.

As you complete this chapter, I'd like to offer a gentle affirmation before you move on: It's okay to feel exactly what you're feeling; every emotion is valid. You don't need to mask your experience behind constant positivity or spiritual phrases to prove your strength or faith. True healing comes from honoring your full range of emotions, even the uncomfortable ones. You deserve the space to be authentic, vulnerable, and fully human. Remember, you are appreciated simply for being yourself, and everyone—regardless of gender, orientation, spirituality, ability, or age—deserves respect and love. No one has the right to shame you for your journey.

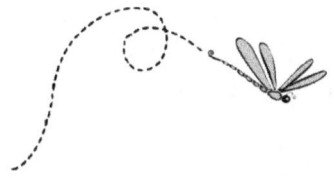

Final Message from the Authors

Be a lamp, or a lifeboat, or a ladder. Help someone's soul heal.
Walk out of your house like a shepherd.

~ Rumi

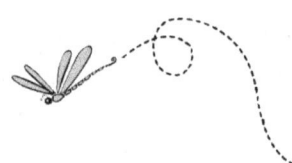

As we come to the close of this mindfulness workbook, we want to take a moment to thank you—from the heart—for allowing us to be part of your healing journey. It's been our deep honor to walk alongside you as you explored your inner world with courage, curiosity, and compassion.

Our hope is that the stories, insights, educational information, mindfulness based exercises, guided imagery, and creative activities offered throughout these pages have served as gentle companions, helping you take meaningful steps toward healing and deeper self-acceptance.

Please hold onto this reminder: healing is not a destination—it's a lifelong, evolving process. Each of us is a beautiful work in progress. You are worthy of every single step you take toward wholeness. Even the smallest moments—waking up, making your bed, taking a breath, being kind to yourself, sharing space with a loved one or a pet—these are not insignificant. These are the quiet triumphs of healing. They matter deeply.

There's no need to rush or compare your path to anyone else's. Honor your pace. Trust your timing. And know that within you is the strength to live a life grounded in authenticity, connection, and meaning.

Thank you for your trust. It has truly been our privilege to support you through this process and through these pages. May the work you've done here continue to unfold in ways that nourish and sustain you. Practice self compassion, and keep going—you're doing beautifully.

With warmth and respect,
Mari & Wendy

About the Authors

Mari A. Lee, MA, LMFT, CSAT-S, CPTT-S, MBATT-CS

Mari is a Licensed Marriage and Family Therapist, a Certified Sex Addiction Therapist and Supervisor (CSAT-S), a Certified Partners Trauma Therapist and Supervisor (CPTT-S), a Certified Mindfulness Based Addiction and Trauma Therapist and Consulting Supervisor, (MBATT-CS), and is trained in Gottman's Couples Therapy, and EMDR. She is the founder of Growth Counseling Services, located in Southern California. Since 2007, Mari has helped individuals and couples heal from sexual compulsivity, pornography addiction, and betrayal trauma. Her other specializations include anxiety disorders and depression.

Additionally, Mari is a member of the faculty and ethics board with the International Institute of Trauma and Addiction Professionals (IITAP), and she is a senior faculty member and ethics member with The Mindfulness Academy of Addiction and Trauma Training (TMAATT). She provides instructional classes and workshops for therapists around the world.

Mari is also a national speaker on the topics of addiction, betrayal trauma, women's issues, and mindfulness, and is a trusted supervisor and business coach with over 32 years of experience in supporting professionals.

In addition to her clinical work, Mari has authored and co-authored several books, including *Facing Heartbreak: Steps to Recovery for Partners of Sex Addicts, Healing from Betrayal, The Creative Clinician, Fisci the Fire Safety Fox and Friends,* and she is a contributing author to *Behavioral Addictions: Criteria, Evidence and Treatment.* Her next book, *The Gift in the Wound,* will be out soon.

For business coaching inquiries, you can connect with Mari at mari@thecounselorscoach.com. If you would like to invite Mari to speak at your conference or event, please visit **www.TheCounselorsCoach.com**. To learn more about Mari's clinical work, feel free to reach out at **mari@growthcounselingservices.com** or visit her counseling website at **www.GrowthCounselingServices.com**.

Mari A. Lee

About Wendy Quinton, LCSW, CAADC, CPTT, MBATT

Wendy is a Licensed Clinical Social Worker, and a Certified Advanced Alcohol and Drug Counselor. She is the sole proprietor of Wendy Quinton, LCSW, located in Central Pennsylvania, and provides outpatient and telehealth therapy.

Beginning in 2014, Wendy has worked with individuals, couples, and groups to help guide their recovery from various substance use disorders, betrayal trauma, narcissistic abuse, depression, and anxiety.

In addition to her clinical work, Wendy also holds a Certified Partner Trauma Therapist certification from the International Institute of Trauma and Addiction Professionals. She is a member of the ethics committee at The Mindfulness Academy of Addiction and Trauma Training and supervises addiction counselors who support those involved with the Department of Justice.

Previous to her clinical experience, Wendy earned an associate's degree in Biblical Studies and Cultural Ministries, and spent thirteen years serving as a missionary in Papua New Guinea. While there, she also served as a Consultant on the Language and Culture Acquisition Committee.

Additionally, Wendy has worked as the Director of Youth Ministries and Christian Education at a local church. Wendy is married and has two children and two stepchildren.

You may contact Wendy at: **wendyquintonlcsw@gmail.com**. To learn more about Wendy's clinical work: **www.WendyQuintonlcsw.com**.

Wendy Quinton

Glossary

Given the comprehensive nature of this workbook, we recognize that it wasn't feasible to include every term and definition as outlined within the main chapters. However, we want to ensure you have as many resources as possible to navigate this material. To support your understanding and enhance your experience, we've carefully compiled a glossary of key terms and definitions.

This section is designed to serve as a helpful reference, allowing you to quickly access explanations and deepen your comprehension of the concepts discussed throughout the workbook. We hope this resource will be a valuable companion as you continue your journey of learning, healing, and growth.

· · · · ·

Addiction: Addiction is a chronic condition characterized by the compulsive need to engage in a behavior or use a substance despite harmful consequences. It involves a loss of control over the activity, leading to physical, emotional, or social problems, and is often accompanied by cravings and withdrawal symptoms when the behavior or substance is reduced or stopped.

Adverse Childhood Experiences Questionnaire: A survey designed to investigate the correlation between traumatic childhood events that occurred before the age of 18 and long-term negative health effects.

Assessment (Screening) Tools: Standardized and researched tools designed to quickly and efficiently determine whether a person is experiencing mental health symptoms that warrant further evaluation or intervention.

Attachment Styles: Attachment styles refer to the patterns of emotional bonding and relationship behaviors developed in early childhood based on the responsiveness and consistency of caregivers. These styles—secure, anxious, avoidant, and disorganized—shape how individuals perceive intimacy, trust, and connection in adult relationships. Secure attachment fosters healthy interdependence, while insecure styles may lead to fear of abandonment, emotional withdrawal, or conflicting desires for closeness and distance. Understanding one's attachment style can offer insight into relational patterns and guide the healing of early emotional wounds.

Autonomic Nervous System (ANS): A part of the nervous system that regulates automatic bodily functions such as heart rate, breathing, digestion, and stress responses. It is divided into the sympathetic system, which activates the body's "fight, flight, or freeze" response, and the parasympathetic system, which promotes relaxation, healing, and restoration.

Betrayal Trauma: This occurs when someone experiences profound emotional or psychological harm from a trusted person, such as a partner, parent, or authority figure. This type of trauma results from a violation of trust, such as infidelity, abuse, or deceit, which shatters the victim's sense of safety and security in the relationship. Betrayal trauma can lead to intense feelings of confusion, fear, anger, and grief, as well as long-lasting impacts on emotional well-being, self-esteem, and the ability to trust others in future relationships.

Body Scan: A method of bringing focused attention to different parts of the body, gradually and intentionally relaxing them, and identifying where emotions are held. This practice increases awareness of physical sensations, tension, or discomfort, helping to deepen the mind-body connection.

Boundary: A clear limit that a person sets to protect their physical, emotional, and mental health ensuring they can remain autonomous and enjoy healthy relationships.

Brain: The brain is a physical sense organ made up of neurons, chemicals, and structures like the amygdala, hippocampus, and prefrontal cortex. It regulates emotions, memory, executive function, and physical responses. The brain can be seen through imaging and physically responds to trauma, stress, and healing.

Brain Spotting: Brainspotting is a therapeutic technique that uses specific eye positions to access and release trauma-related memories and emotions. By connecting with areas in the brain where trauma is stored, it promotes mindful processing of distress, supporting healing for trauma, anxiety, and physical pain.

CATI: The Compassionate Attachment Theory Interview (CATI) is an instrument created by therapist Mari A. Lee. It is used to assist the client in processing and integrating non-integrated attachment trauma, aiding the client and therapist in being present with whatever thoughts and feelings arise without judgment or resistance.

Cognitive Behavioral Therapy: A type of talk therapy that teaches that the way we think about a situation affects how we feel and act and that by changing our thoughts, we can change our behaviors.

Cold Shouldering: Purposely ignoring or emotionally distancing from another person to control or dominate them.

Complex Trauma: This refers to repeated or prolonged exposure to traumatic events, typically during childhood or adolescence, that involve interpersonal harm or betrayal, such as abuse, neglect, or chronic emotional neglect. Unlike a single traumatic event, complex trauma impacts multiple areas of a person's emotional, psychological, and relational development, often affecting their sense of safety, identity, and ability to trust others. The long-term effects of complex trauma can include difficulties with emotional regulation, self-esteem, relationships, and a heightened sensitivity to stress or triggers.

Counterweight Bonding: A relationship dynamic term coined by therapist Wendy Quinton, where one person compensates for perceived or actual deficiencies in the other by taking on the greater share of the responsibility and emotional labor in the partnership.

CPTT: Certified Partner Trauma Therapist is a certification earned from the International Institute for Trauma and Addiction Professionals and awarded to licensed mental health therapists.

CSAT: Certified Sex Addiction Therapist is a certification earned from the International Institute for Trauma and Addiction Professionals and awarded to licensed mental health therapists.

Cultural Competency: The ability to interact effectively with people from diverse cultural backgrounds. It involves being aware of one's own worldview, recognizing and respecting cultural differences, and adapting communication and behaviors to work effectively in cross-cultural situations.

Deep Breathing: The practice of taking long, slow breaths while paying attention to the rhythm and sensations of the inhalation and exhalation.

Dialectical Behavioral Therapy (DBT): A formulated therapy that helps people manage their emotions, cope with stress, and improve their relationships, including teachings regarding mindfulness, distress tolerance, emotional regulation, and interpersonal effectiveness.

Diversity Sensitivity: Refers to acknowledging and respecting the differences in clients' backgrounds, identities, and experiences, including race, gender, sexuality, culture, religion, and socioeconomic status. It involves creating an inclusive, culturally sensitive space where all clients feel understood and valued.

Domestic Violence: Domestic violence is a pattern of abusive behavior in a relationship where one partner seeks to control or dominate the other through physical, emotional, psychological, sexual, or financial abuse. It can occur in any type of relationship and often escalates over time, impacting the victim's safety, well-being, and autonomy.

Dual Process Model of Grief: Identifies two types of stressors that individuals who are grieving must navigate following a loss: loss-oriented and restoration-oriented stressors.

Ego States: The concept of ego states was developed by psychiatrist Eric Berne, the founder of Transactional Analysis (TA), in the 1950s. Berne proposed that a person's personality is made up of three distinct ego states: Parent, Adult, and Child, and these ego states interact dynamically in everyday life, shaping how we communicate and relate to others.

Emophilia: A tendency to fall in love quickly and intensely, driven by a craving for novelty and rapid emotional attachment. Unlike love addiction, which centers on fixation with one partner, emophilia often leads to serial romantic relationships. Emophiles may mistake infatuation for true love, make impulsive decisions, and move on quickly when flaws appear, always chasing the next intense connection.

Epigenetics: The study of how our behaviors and environment can cause changes in the way our genes work without altering the DNA sequence itself and how these changes can be passed down to future generations.

Equanimity: A state of mental serenity and composure, even amid life's hardships.

Eye Movement Desensitization and Reprocessing (EMDR): An evidence-based trauma therapy that allows clients to process their traumatic memories, enabling the brain to break them down into manageable parts and file them away into long-term memory so that the painful memory and body sensations are no longer front and center in the client's life.

F.F.O.O.G. (Fantasy, Fear, Obsession, Obligation, Guilt): A term created by Therapist Mari A. Lee, LMFT, CSAT-S, describing the emotional fog that can trap love-addicted individuals in unhealthy relationships. F.F.O.O.G. reflects how fantasy, fear, obsession, obligation, and guilt can cloud judgment until awareness clears the path to healing.

Formal Disclosure: This is a structured, multi-stage process facilitated in a therapeutic location, where one partner, often in cases of infidelity or addiction, reveals hidden behaviors to the betrayed partner in a safe, controlled environment. Guided by a therapist or trained mental health professional, this approach aims to promote transparency, rebuild trust, and foster healing within the relationship while acknowledging that outcomes cannot be guaranteed and either partner in the relationship may choose to leave the relationship.

Gaslighting: A type of manipulation that occurs when the perpetrator attempts to make the victim doubt their reality, causing them to question their memory, perception, and even their sanity.

Generalized Anxiety Disorder 7-Item Scale (GAD-7): A self-report test used to rate the frequency and severity of anxiety symptoms, readministered frequently to monitor how symptoms may change over time.

Generational Trauma: Generational trauma denotes the psychological effects of trauma that are passed down from one generation to the next, like emotional scars that are inherited from your ancestors, even without a person experiencing the original traumatic event themselves.

Genetic Predisposition: The tendency to inherit certain traits or health issues (such as addiction) from your relatives due to your genes.

Gottman's Imago Communication Method: A structured approach to communication that teaches the skills necessary to share needs and boundaries in a safe manner.

Guided Imagery: This is a therapeutic technique that involves using mental visualization to create calming, positive, or healing images in the mind, often guided by a therapist or audio prompts. In the context of healing and therapy, guided imagery helps individuals tap into their imagination to reduce stress, manage pain, and process emotions.

Hypersexual Disorder: This is a behavioral condition characterized by compulsive and uncontrollable sexual thoughts, urges, or behaviors that interfere with a person's ability to function in daily life. This is sometimes referred to as "sexual addiction" in layman's terms.

IITAP: International Institute for Trauma and Addiction Professionals.

IPAST: Inventory for Partner Attachment, Stress, and Trauma is an assessment tool developed by the International Institute for Trauma and Addiction Professionals.

Inner Child Work: The process of reparenting our younger selves, giving oneself the loving, unconditional nurturing that you deserved as a child but did not receive from caretakers.

Intimacy: This is characterized as a deep emotional, physical, or psychological connection between individuals, characterized by trust, vulnerability, and closeness. This connection may or may not include sexual activity.

LGBTQIA+: This is an acronym that stands for Lesbian, Gay, Bisexual, Transgender, Queer or Questioning, Intersex, and Asexual or Ally. It represents a diverse community of individuals with different sexual orientations, gender identities, and expressions. The term is inclusive of a broad spectrum of identities, acknowledging the varied and unique experiences of each group within the acronym. The "+" sign stands for all of the other identities not encompassed in the short acronym.

Limbic System: The limbic system is a complex group of brain structures responsible for regulating emotions, memory, and motivation. It plays a key role in processing feelings like fear, pleasure, and anger and is involved in forming long-term memories. Key components of the limbic system include the amygdala, hippocampus, and hypothalamus, which work together to influence emotional responses and survival instincts.

Limerence: An intense emotional and mental state characterized by obsessive infatuation and romantic desire for another person, often accompanied by an overwhelming need for reciprocation.

Locus of Control: The conviction of the extent to which a person can control the things that affect them and can be classified as internal or external. An internal locus of control is the belief that a person's choices and actions control the outcome of life situations. An external locus of control is the belief that outside circumstances or forces control life's outcomes and that people have limited influence over what happens to them.

Love Addiction: This is a compulsive pattern of seeking out intense romantic relationships to fill unmet emotional needs, often at the expense of one's well-being. Those struggling with love addiction may become overly dependent on their partner for validation, leading to unhealthy and obsessive behaviors. This can result in a cycle of intense highs and lows.

Love Bombing: Love bombing is a manipulative tactic where someone showers another person with excessive attention, flattery, and affection in a short period of time, often to gain control or influence over them. It can be part of a cycle of emotional abuse, where the intense affection is followed by manipulation or withdrawal.

Maladaptive Coping Mechanism: A maladaptive coping mechanism is a behavioral or psychological response to stress or emotional pain that may provide temporary relief but ultimately worsens the problem or creates new issues. These coping strategies, such as avoidance, substance abuse, or self-isolation, are often unhealthy and prevent effective resolution or healing.

Maternal Wounding: Refers to emotional or psychological harm caused by an unhealthy, abusive, or dysfunctional relationship with one's mother or primary female maternal figure or figures.

MBATT: This is an acronym for a Mindfulness-Based Addiction and Trauma Therapist. The certification is awarded to licensed mental health therapists through The Mindfulness Academy for Addiction and Trauma Training (TMAATT).

MBRC: This is an acronym for a Mindfulness-Based Recovery Coach. The certification is awarded to specific mental health professionals through The Mindfulness Academy for Addiction and Trauma Training (TMAATT).

Meditation: Meditation is a practice where you focus your mind and calm your thoughts, often by using techniques like deep breathing, mindfulness, or repeating a mantra, to achieve relaxation and mental clarity. Over time, regular meditation can promote greater self-awareness, reduce anxiety, and foster a deeper connection to the present moment.

Mind: The mind is the abstract seat of consciousness, where beliefs, emotions, self-talk, and personal narratives are formed. It assigns meaning to experiences, shaping identity and perception, and guides how we interpret the signals received from the brain and body.

Mind States: A programmed pattern of thinking that has become deeply rooted over time; the way a person perceives the world that involves the awareness that the mind can become fixed in conditions such as focused, scattered, calm, agitated, judgmental, reactive, aversive, etc.

Mind Stories: Internal dialogues created by our core beliefs about what happened to us and that influence how we perceive reality.

Mindful Eating: The practice of bringing focus and intention to the experience of eating by becoming aware of the sensations of hunger and fullness and savoring the food, paying special attention to the smell, look, textures, and flavors of the food, as well as the emotions experienced before, during, and after eating.

Mindful Walking: The practice of bringing focus and attention to the movement of the body while walking, giving attention to the feeling of the ground under the feet, the way that the legs move, and the sound of the breath.

Mindfulness: The quality of being aware of the present moment with curious, open-minded, non-judging, non-striving, and accepting attitudes without being preoccupied by thoughts of the future or the past.

Mother Enmeshed Male (M.E.M.): A term coined by Dr. Kenneth Adams, a M.E.M. refers to a man whose emotional boundaries with his mother are blurred or overly intertwined, often resulting in an unhealthy and dependent relationship dynamic.

Motivational Interviewing: An approach to counseling and healthcare intervention that assists clients in understanding and resolving their ambivalence to change and allows them to access the motivation for behavioral change, especially as it relates to addiction.

Multiple Addiction Interaction: Multiple addiction interaction refers to the phenomenon where an individual struggles with more than one addiction simultaneously or sequentially, such as substance abuse, gambling, sex addiction, or food addiction. These addictions often influence and reinforce one another, making recovery more complex as each addiction can trigger or intensify the others, creating a cycle that is harder to break.

Original Wound Theory: A theory developed by Judith Beck that proposes traumatic events experienced at a young age can cause people to form basic ideas about themselves and their world, and the resulting mind states are often harmful to their sense of self.

Parasympathetic Nervous System: The branch of the autonomic nervous system responsible for calming the body after stress. It supports relaxation, digestion, healing, and a return to a balanced, restful state often called "rest and digest."

Pathological Affection Dependency (P.A.D.): A clinical model created by Therapist Mari A. Lee, LMFT, CSAT-S, describing the three-stage progression of love addiction. P.A.D. explains how intense emotional dependence on a romantic partner can lead to idealization, blurred boundaries, and emotional pain. Those struggling with P.A.D. often seek validation through relationships, mistaking intensity for true intimacy. Healing involves rebuilding self-trust, setting healthy boundaries, and finding self-worth from within.

Polyvagal Theory: Polyvagal theory, developed by Dr. Stephen Porges, explains how our autonomic nervous system regulates responses to stress and safety through three key states: the parasympathetic (calm and connected), sympathetic (fight or flight), and a shutdown or freeze response. The theory emphasizes the role of the vagus nerve in influencing emotional regulation, social connection, and how we respond to perceived threats, helping us understand how our nervous system supports both survival and well-being.

Primary Gains: In therapy, primary gains refer to the internal psychological benefits a person derives from maintaining a symptom or behavior, often unconsciously. These gains typically involve the reduction of emotional distress or anxiety by avoiding or diverting attention from a deeper, underlying issue.

Problematic Pornography Use: Sometimes referred to as pornography addiction, it refers to excessive or compulsive engagement with pornography that negatively impacts a person's relationships, emotional well-being, or daily responsibilities. It involves difficulty controlling the behavior despite recognizing its harmful effects.

Projection: This refers to a psychological defense mechanism where an individual unconsciously attributes their own unwanted thoughts, feelings, or behaviors onto someone else. Instead of recognizing these aspects within themselves, they project them outward, often blaming or accusing others of possessing those same traits or emotions.

Psychodrama: Created by Jacob Moreno and inspired by improvisational theater, it is a form of therapy that uses guided drama and role-playing and involves acting out a part of your life (past or future) as if it were happening in the present, often with the help of a therapist and other group members.

PTSI-R Post-Traumatic Stress Index-Revised: This is an assessment tool developed by the International Institute for Trauma and Addiction Professionals.

PTSD: Post-traumatic stress disorder is a clinical diagnosis; the symptoms are divided into four main categories: intrusion, avoidance, negative alterations in cognition and mood, and alterations in arousal and reactivity.

Reactive Abuse: Reactive abuse happens when someone, after enduring ongoing emotional, psychological, or physical abuse, responds in a way that appears or is aggressive or intense. This reaction might involve yelling, profanity, striking back, or heated words, often because the person feels pushed to their limit. Abusers may intentionally provoke this kind of response for weeks, months, or years and then use it to paint the victim as the aggressor, flipping roles to appear as if they are the ones being harmed.

Safety-Seeking Behaviors: These are behaviors exhibited in an attempt to avoid or reduce physical or emotional harm where real or perceived threats exist. Behaviors can include constantly monitoring a partner's phone, email, texts, social media, location, and actions, seeking excessive reassurance, interrogating, ultimatums, and avoiding certain situations that cause fear and distress.

Secondary Losses: Additional losses that come as a result of a primary loss, such as loss of companionship, financial stability, or identity, which can significantly impact a person's ability to heal and adapt to the loss.

Secondary Gains: Refers to the external, often unintended, benefits that a person receives from maintaining a symptom or behavior. Unlike primary gains, which are internal psychological benefits, secondary gains involve advantages such as increased attention, support, or avoidance of responsibilities that come as a consequence of the symptom.

Self-Care: A concept that encompasses activities that foster physical, emotional, social, spiritual, and mental health.

Sex Addiction: See hypersexual disorder as defined above.

Spiritual bypassing: A term that describes the concept of dodging painful psychological issues using spiritual practices, beliefs and platitudes.

SDI 4.0: The Sexual Dependency Inventory (SDI) 4.0 is an assessment tool provided by the International Institute of Trauma and Addiction Professionals (IITAP). It helps clinicians evaluate problematic sexual behaviors. This assessment is designed for use in cases of sex addiction and related issues, offering crucial insights for treatment planning. Clinicians certified through IITAP's CSAT program typically administer the SDI 4.0 as part of their comprehensive evaluation.

Stages of Grief: The various emotional phases that individuals often experience after a significant loss, including anger and acceptance.

Sympathetic Nervous System: The branch of the autonomic nervous system responsible for mobilizing the body's resources during perceived threat or stress. Activation of the sympathetic nervous system triggers physiological changes such as increased heart rate, elevated blood pressure, pupil dilation, and the release of stress hormones, preparing the body for a "fight, flight, freeze or fawn" response.

Tapping: Tapping therapy, commonly referred to as the Emotional Freedom Technique (EFT), is a therapeutic approach that uses gentle tapping on specific acupressure points on the body. This technique aims to support emotional regulation, reduce stress, and alleviate anxiety by addressing both the physical and emotional aspects of distress.

Toxic Positivity: A term that describes the concept of invalidating the true human experience by focusing solely on happy thoughts and portraying these optimistic attitudes in every circumstance.

Trauma Blocking: This is a coping mechanism where individuals unconsciously or intentionally suppress or avoid traumatic memories and associated emotions. This can manifest through behaviors like an excessive amount of time spent on social media, gaming, excessive work, substance use, or other distractions that prevent confronting painful memories. Trauma blocking temporarily shields the person from emotional distress but may hinder long-term healing and emotional processing.

Trauma Bonding: This is a psychological phenomenon where a person forms a strong emotional attachment to an abusive person through cycles of abuse and intermittent positive reinforcement. This bond, fueled by intense emotions, leads the person to depend on the abuser for emotional validation, mistaking fear and control for love. As a result, they find it difficult to leave the relationship, as the bond distorts their perception of reality and self-worth. It is important to note that many forms of abuse can create a trauma bond, such as emotional abuse, verbal abuse, financial abuse, sexual abuse, spiritual abuse, verbal abuse, and threats of abandonment.

Twelve-Step Groups: Peer-led organizations that support recovery from addiction, compulsive behaviors, or other challenges. There are Twelve-Step groups that support families and loved ones of people with addiction as well.

Unconditional Self-Worth: Understanding and accepting the truth that everyone has intrinsic value simply because they exist.

Vagus Nerve: The vagus nerve is the 10th and longest cranial nerve in the body, extending from the brainstem down to the abdomen. It plays a crucial role in regulating various involuntary bodily functions, including heart rate, digestion, and respiratory rate. It is a key component of the parasympathetic nervous system, helping to calm the body after stress and promoting relaxation and recovery.

Vagal Toning: Vagus nerve toning, or natural vagal stimulation, refers to practices that stimulate and strengthen the vagus nerve, which plays a key role in regulating the body's parasympathetic nervous system. This helps promote relaxation, reduce stress, and improve emotional regulation. Techniques such as deep breathing, cold exposure, humming, and meditation are common ways to naturally tone the vagus nerve, enhancing the body's ability to calm itself and recover from stress.

Window of Tolerance: Dr. Daniel Siegel's concept of the window of tolerance refers to the range of emotional and physiological arousal levels within which a person can function effectively and manage stress.

Worden's Four Tasks of Mourning: Conceptualizes four tasks that must be completed to cope with loss, including accepting the reality of the loss, processing the pain of grief, adjusting to a world without the deceased, and finding an enduring connection with the deceased while moving forward with life.

Bibliography

Research Articles on Mindfulness, Guided Imagery, Vagus Nerve

Chiesa, A., & Serretti, A. (2014). Are mindfulness-based interventions effective for substance use disorders? A systematic review of the evidence. *Substance Use & Misuse, 49*(5), 492-512.

Greenbaum, H. K., & Benedetto, T. M. (2019). *Guided Imagery and Progressive Muscle Relaxation in Group Psychotherapy.* The George Washington University.

Hackmann, A., Bennett-Levy, J., & Holmes, E. A. (2011). *Oxford guide to imagery in cognitive therapy.* Oxford University Press.

Khanna, S., & Greeson, J. M. (2013). A narrative review of yoga and mindfulness as complementary therapies for addiction. *Complementary Therapies in Medicine, 21*(3), 244-252.

Kiley, K. A., Sehgal, A. R., Neth, S., Dolata, J., Pike, E., Spilsbury, J. C., & Albert, J. M. (2018). The effectiveness of guided imagery in treating compassion fatigue and anxiety of mental health workers. *Social Work Research, 42*(1), 33-43.

Kimbrough, E., Magyari, T., Langenberg, P., Chesney, M., & Berman, B. (2010). Mindfulness intervention for child abuse survivors. *Journal of Clinical Psychology, 66*(1), 17-33.

Mellenthin, C. (2021). Guided imagery. In H. G. Kaduson & C. E. Schaefer (Eds.), *Play therapy with children: Modalities for change* (pp. 125–139). American Psychological Association.

Michalak, J., Crane, C., Germer, C. K., Gold, E., Heidenreich, T., Mander, J., ... & Segal, Z. V. (2019). Principles for a responsible integration of mindfulness in individual therapy. *Mindfulness, 10*, 799-811.

Nasiri, S., Akbari, H., Tagharrobi, L., & Tabatabaee, A. S. (2018). The effect of progressive muscle relaxation and guided imagery on stress, anxiety, and depression of pregnant women referred to health centers. *Journal of Education and Health Promotion, 7*(1), 41.

Özü, Ö. (2010). Guided imagery as a psychotherapeutic mind-body intervention in health psychology: A brief review of efficacy research. *Europe's Journal of Psychology, 6*(4), 227-237.

Sackeim, H. A., Dibué, M., Bunker, M. T., & Rush, A. J. (2020). The long and winding road of vagus nerve stimulation: challenges in developing an intervention for difficult-to-treat mood disorders. *Neuropsychiatric Disease and Treatment*, 3081-3093.

Sancho, M., De Gracia, M., Rodriguez, R. C., Mallorquí-Bagué, N., Sánchez-González, J., Trujols, J., ... & Menchón, J. M. (2018). Mindfulness-based interventions for the treatment of substance and behavioral addictions: A systematic review. *Frontiers in Psychiatry, 9*, 95.

Utay, J., & Miller, M. (2006). Guided imagery as an effective therapeutic technique: A brief review of its history and efficacy research. *Journal of Instructional Psychology, 33*(1), 40-43.

Research Articles for Chapter One: Trauma Bonding and Intimate Partner Abuse

Barrios, Y. V., Gelaye, B., Zhong, Q., Nicolaidis, C., Rondon, M. B., Garcia, P. J., ... & Williams, M. A. (2015). Association of childhood physical and sexual abuse with intimate partner violence, poor general health and depressive symptoms among pregnant women. *PloS one, 10*(1), e0116609.

Beri, R. (2024). A study on love bombing, narcissism and emotional abuse among young adults in relationship and situationship. *International Journal of Interdisciplinary Approaches in Psychology, 2*(6), 22-46.

Black, M. C. (2011). Intimate partner violence and adverse health consequences: Implications for clinicians. *American Journal of Lifestyle Medicine, 5*(5), 428-439.

Cacioppo, J. T., & Cacioppo, S. (2014). Social relationships and health: The toxic effects of perceived social isolation. *Social and personality psychology compass*, 8(2), 58-72.

Campbell, W. K., & Miller, J. D. (2011). *The Handbook of Narcissism and Narcissistic Personality Disorder: Theoretical Approaches, Empirical Findings, and Treatments.* Wiley.

Carnes, P. J. (2018, August). *Betrayal bond, revised: Breaking free of exploitive relationships.* Hci.

Charuvastra, A., & Cloitre, M. (2008). Social bonds and posttraumatic stress disorder. *Annu. Rev. Psychol.*, 59(1), 301-328.

Dutton, D. G., & Painter, S. (1993). Emotional attachments in abusive relationships: A test of traumatic bonding theory. *Violence and Victims*, 8(2), 105.

Farrell C, Doolin K, O' Leary N, Jairaj C, Roddy D, Tozzi L, Morris D, Harkin A, Frodl T, Nemoda Z, Szyf M, Booij L, O'Keane V. (2018). DNA methylation differences at the glucocorticoid receptor gene in depression are related to functional alterations in hypothalamic-pituitary-adrenal axis activity and to early life emotional abuse. *Psychiatry Res.* 2018 Jul;265:341-348. doi: 10.1016/j.psychres.2018.04.064. Epub 2018 May 8. PMID: 29793048.

Ferrari, G., Agnew-Davies, R., Bailey, J., Howard, L., Howarth, E., Peters, T. J., ... & Feder, G. S. (2016). Domestic violence and mental health: A cross-sectional survey of women seeking help from domestic violence support services. *Global Health Action*, 9(1), 29890.

Foster, J. A., & Neufeld, K. A. M. (2013). Gut–brain axis: How the microbiome influences anxiety and depression. *Trends in Neurosciences*, 36(5), 305-312.

Kost, K. (2019). *Fostering creativity for healing: A literature review on the use of art therapy and mindfulness with traumatized adults.*

Mohajeri, M. H., La Fata, G., Steinert, R. E., & Weber, P. (2018). Relationship between the gut microbiome and brain function. *Nutrition Reviews*, 76(7), 481-496.

Orzeck, T. L., Rokach, A., & Chin, J. (2010). The effects of traumatic and abusive relationships. *Journal of Loss and Trauma*, 15(3), 167-192.

Park, C., Rosenblat, J. D., Brietzke, E., Pan, Z., Lee, Y., Cao, B., ... & McIntyre, R. S. (2019). Stress, epigenetics and depression: A systematic review. *Neuroscience & Biobehavioral Reviews*, 102, 139-152.

Patton, S. C., Szabo, Y. Z., & Newton, T. L. (2022). Mental and physical health changes following an abusive intimate relationship: A systematic review of longitudinal studies. *Trauma, Violence, & Abuse*, 23(4), 1079-1092.

Peirce, J. M., & Alviña, K. (2019). The role of inflammation and the gut microbiome in depression and anxiety. *Journal of Neuroscience Research*, 97(10), 1223-1241.

Pepping, C. A., & Halford, W. K. (2016). Mindfulness and couple relationships. *Mindfulness and Buddhist-Derived Approaches in Mental Health and Addiction*, 391-411.

Radtke, K. M., Ruf, M., Gunter, H. M., Dohrmann, K., Schauer, M., Meyer, A., & Elbert, T. (2011). Transgenerational impact of intimate partner violence on methylation in the promoter of the glucocorticoid receptor. *Translational Psychiatry*, 1(7), e21-e21.

Rakovec-Felser, Z. (2014). Domestic violence and abuse in intimate relationships from a public health perspective. *Health Psychology Research*, 2(3).

Strutzenberg, C. (2016). *Love-bombing: A narcissistic approach to relationship formation.*

Turecki G, Meaney MJ. (2016). Effects of the social environment and stress on glucocorticoid receptor gene methylation: A Systematic Review. *Biol Psychiatry.* 2016 Jan 15;79(2):87-96. doi: 10.1016/j.biopsych.2014.11.022. Epub 2014 Dec 13. PMID: 25687413; PMCID: PMC4466091.

Winter, F., Steffan, A., Warth, M., Ditzen, B., & Aguilar-Raab, C. (2021). Mindfulness-based couple interventions: a systematic literature review. *Family Process*, 60(3), 694-711.

Zurbriggen, E. L., Gobin, R. L., & Kaehler, L. A. (2012). Trauma, attachment, and intimate relationships. *Journal of Trauma & Dissociation*, 13(2), 127-133.

Research Articles for Chapter Two: Mindfulness (States & Stories), Motivational Interviewing, and Screening Tools

Creswell, J. D., Pacilio, L. E., Lindsay, E. K., & Brown, K. W. (2016). Mindfulness training and physical health: Mechanisms and outcomes. *Biological Psychiatry*, 80(1), 33-40.

Ford, D., Cosper, C., & Bordey, C. (2017). *Transforming the addictive mind: The first month of mindfulness-based addiction therapy (MBAT)*. Sano Press.

Gotink, R. A., Chu, P., Busschbach, J. J., Benson, H., Fricchione, G. L., & Hunink, M. M. (2018). Standardized mindfulness-based interventions in healthcare: An overview of systematic reviews and meta-analyses of RCTs. *Mindfulness*, 9(6), 1675-1695.

Hölzel, B. K., Carmody, J., Vangel, M., Congleton, C., Yerramsetti, S. M., Gard, T., & Lazar, S. W. (2011). Mindfulness practice leads to increases in regional brain gray matter density. *Frontiers in Psychology*, 3, 57.

Jordan, P., Shedden-Mora, M. C., & Löwe, B. (2017). Psychometric analysis of the Generalized Anxiety Disorder scale (GAD-7) in primary care using modern item response theory. *PLoS One*, 12(8), e0182162.

Kabat-Zinn, J. (1982). An outpatient program in behavioral medicine for chronic pain patients based on the practice of mindfulness meditation: Theoretical considerations and preliminary results. *General Hospital Psychiatry*, 4(1), 33–47.

Kabat-Zinn, J. (2013). *Full catastrophe living: Using the wisdom of your body and mind to face stress, pain, and illness*. Bantam Books.

Lefcourt, H. M. (2014). *Locus of control: Current trends in theory and research*. Psychology Press.

Laudet, A. B., Savage, R., & Mahmood, D. (2023). Revisiting 12-step approaches: An evidence-based perspective. *IntechOpen*. https://doi.org/10.5772/intechopen.93678

Löwe, B., Decker, O., Müller, S., Brähler, E., Schellberg, D., Herzog, W., & Herzberg, P. Y. (2008). Validation and standardization of the Generalized Anxiety Disorder Screener (GAD-7) in the general population. *Medical Care*, 46(3), 266-274.

Lomas, T., Edginton, T., Cartwright, T., & Ridge, D. (2015). Cultivating equanimity through mindfulness meditation: A mixed methods enquiry into the development of decentering capabilities in men. *International Journal of Wellbeing*, 5(3), 88-106. https://doi.org/10.5502/ijw.v5i3.7

Luberto, C. M., Hall, D. L., Park, E. R., Haramati, A., & Cotton, S. (2019). A perspective on the similarities and differences between mindfulness and relaxation. *Mindfulness*, 10(4), 823-833.

Marks, J. S. (1998). Relationship of childhood abuse and household dysfunction to many of the leading causes of death in adults: The Adverse Childhood Experiences (ACE) Study. *American Journal of Preventive Medicine*, 14(4), 245-258.

Miller, W. R., & Rollnick, S. (2013). *Motivational interviewing: Helping people change (3rd ed.)*. Guilford Press.

Narcotics Anonymous. (n.d.). *Narcotics Anonymous*. https://m.na.org/

Nhat Hanh, T. (1998). *The heart of the Buddha's teaching: Transforming suffering into peace, joy, and liberation*. Broadway Books.

O'Reilly, G. A., Cook, L., Spruijt-Metz, D., & Black, D. S. (2014). Mindfulness-based interventions for obesity-related eating behaviours: A literature review. *Obesity Reviews*, 15(6), 453-461.

Petruccelli, K., Davis, J., & Berman, T. (2019). Adverse childhood experiences and associated health outcomes: A systematic review and meta-analysis. *Child Abuse & Neglect*, 97, 104127.

Rahman, H., & Kodikal, R. (2020). Understanding transactional analysis of managers: An empirical study in India. *Problems and Perspectives in Management*, 18(1), 141-152.

Shahoud, R., et al. (2023). The effect of slow-paced breathing on cardiovascular and emotion functions: A meta-analysis and systematic review. *Mindfulness*.

Sharma, A., Rushton, K., Lin, I., Wadden, D., Lucas, K., Miner, A., Nguyen, T., & Althoff, T. (2023). Cognitive reframing of negative thoughts through human-language model interaction. In A. Rogers, J. Boyd-Graber, & N. Okazaki (Eds.), Proceedings of the 61st Annual Meeting of the Association for Computational Linguistics (pp. 9977-10000). *Association for Computational Linguistics*.

Sleicher, D., Maron, D. D., Shihab, H. M., Ranasinghe, P. D., Linn, S., Saha, S., Bass, E. B., & Haythornthwaite, J. A. (2014). Meditation programs for psychological stress and well-being: A systematic review and meta-analysis. JAMA *Internal Medicine*, 174(3), 357-368.

Strauss, C., Bibby-Jones, A., Jones, F., Hayward, M., Chadwick, P., Whittington, A., Davies, L., McGregor, A., Otahal, P., & Crane, C. (2023). Clinical effectiveness and cost-effectiveness of supported mindfulness-based cognitive therapy self-help compared with supported cognitive behavioral therapy self-help for adults experiencing depression: The Low-Intensity Guided Help Through Mindfulness (LIGHTMind) randomized clinical trial. JAMA Psychiatry, 80(5), 415-424.

Tolle, E. (1997). *The power of now: A guide to spiritual enlightenment*. New World Library.

Weber, J. (2021). A systematic literature review of equanimity in mindfulness-based interventions. *Pastoral Psychology*, 70(2), 151–165.

White, W., Galanter, M., Humphreys, K., & Kelly, J. (2020). "We do recover": Scientific studies on Narcotics Anonymous. *Cochrane Database of Systematic Reviews*, 3, CD012880.

Research Articles for Chapter Three: Infidelity, Betrayal Trauma, and Formal Disclosure with Couples

Atkinson, B. J. (2013). Mindfulness training and the cultivation of secure, satisfying couple relationships. *Couple and Family Psychology: Research and Practice*, 2(2), 73.

Schneider, J. P., & Corley, M. D. (2012). *Surviving disclosure: A partner's guide for healing the betrayal of intimate trust*. Recovery Resource Press.

Barnes, S., Brown, K. W., Krusemark, E., Campbell, W. K., & Rogge, R. D. (2007). The role of mindfulness in romantic relationship satisfaction and responses to relationship stress. *Journal of Marital and Family Therapy*, 33(4), 482-500.

Brewer, G., Hunt, D., James, G., & Abell, L. (2015). Dark Triad traits, infidelity and romantic revenge. *Personality and Individual Differences*, 83, 122-127.

Carnes, P. J. (2018). *Betrayal bond, revised: breaking free of exploitive relationships*. Hci.

Carnes, S., & Lee, M. A. (2014) *Staggered disclosure as a trauma to the partner. Criteria, Evidence, and Treatment*, 270

Corley, M. D., Schneider, J. P., & Hook, J. N. (2012). Partner reactions to disclosure of relapse by self-identified sexual addicts. *Sexual Addiction & Compulsivity*, 19(4), 265–283. https://doi.org/10.1080/10720162.2012.712022.

Courtois, C. A. (2004). Complex trauma, complex reactions: Assessment and treatment. *Psychotherapy: Theory, Research, Practice, and Training, 41*, 412-425.

Fife, S. T., Gossner, J. D., Theobald, A., Allen, E., Rivero, A., & Koehl, H. (2023). Couple healing from infidelity: A grounded theory study. *Journal of Social and Personal Relationships, 40*(12), 3882-3905.

Ford, J. D., & Russo, E. (2006). A trauma-focused, present-centered, emotional self-regulation approach to integrated treatment for post-traumatic stress and addiction: *Trauma Adaptive Recovery Group Education and Therapy (TARGET). American Journal of Psychotherapy, 60*, 335-355

Gambrel, L. E., & Keeling, M. L. (2010). Relational aspects of mindfulness: Implications for the practice of marriage and family therapy. *Contemporary Family Therapy, 32*, 412-426.

Gottman, J. M., & Gottman, J. S. (2015). Gottman couple therapy. In A. S. Gurman, J. L. Lebow, & D. K. Snyder (Eds.), *Clinical Handbook of Couple Therapy* (pp. 129-157). The Guilford Press.

Heintzelman, Ashley & Murdock, Nancy & Krycak, Romana & Seay, Larissa. (2014). Recovery From Infidelity: Differentiation of Self, Trauma, Forgiveness, and Posttraumatic Growth Among Couples in Continuing Relationships. *Couple and Family Psychology: Research and Practice, 3.* 13. 10.1037/cfp0000016.

Hudson, R. (2021). *Exploring the impact of sexual addiction and compulsive sexual behaviour on couples' relationships.*

Jones, S.M., Hansen, W. (2015). The Impact of Mindfulness on Supportive Communication Skills: Three Exploratory Studies. *Mindfulness, 6,* 1115-1128

Kozlowski, A. (2013). Mindful mating: exploring the connection between mindfulness and relationship satisfaction. *Sexual and Relationship Therapy, 28*(1-2), 92-104.

Laaser, D.W., Putney, H.L., Bundick, M.J., Delmonico, D.L., & Griffin, E.J. (2017). Posttraumatic growth in relationally betrayed women. *Journal of Marital and Family Therapy, 43* 3, 435-447.

Laltrello, N. (2019). Clinical guidelines for working with the spouse in a marriage impacted by sex addiction: A relational understanding and approach. In *Clinical Management of Sex Addiction* (pp. 88-100). Routledge.

O'Kelly, M., & Collard, J. (2012). Using mindfulness with couples: Theory and practice. In *Cognitive and Rational-Emotive Behavior Therapy With Couples: Theory and Practice* (pp. 17-31). New York, NY: Springer New York.

Sescousse, G., Caldú, X., Segura, B., & Dreher, J.-C. (2013). Processing of primary and secondary rewards: A quantitative meta-analysis and review of human functional neuroimaging studies. *Neuroscience & Biobehavioral Reviews, 37*(4), 681-696.

Shapiro, F. (2001). Eye movement desensitization and reprocessing: Basic principles, protocols, and procedures. *New York: Guilford Press.*

Steffens, B. A., & Rennie, R. L. (2006). The traumatic nature of disclosure for wives of sexual addicts. *Sexual Addiction & Compulsivity, 13*(2-3), 247-267.

Warach, B., & Josephs, L. (2021). The aftershocks of infidelity: a review of infidelity-based attachment trauma. *Sexual and Relationship Therapy, 36*(1), 68-90.

Research Articles for Chapter Four: Grief, Bereavement Stress, and Mourning

Beck, J. S., & Fleming, S. (2021). A brief history of Aaron T. Beck, MD, and cognitive behavior therapy. *Clinical Psychology in Europe, 3*(2), Article e4821.

Carnes, S. (Ed.). (2009). *Mending a shattered heart: A guide for partners of sex addicts.* Gentle Path Press.

Devine, M. (2017). *It's OK that you're not OK: Meeting grief and loss in a culture that doesn't understand.* Sounds True.

Eisma, M. C., de Lang, T. A., & Stroebe, M. S. (2021). Restoration-oriented stressors of bereavement. *Anxiety, Stress, & Coping, 35*(3), 339–353.

Gottman, J., & Gottman, J. (2017). The natural principles of love. *Journal of Family Theory & Review, 9*(1), 7-26.

Huey, S. J., Jr., Park, A. L., Galán, C. A., & Wang, C. X. (2023). Culturally responsive cognitive behavioral therapy for ethnically diverse populations. *Annual Review of Clinical Psychology, 19*, 51-78.

Kessler, D. (2019). *Finding meaning: The sixth stage of grief.* Simon and Schuster.

Komischke-Konnerup, K. B., O'Connor, M., Hoijtink, H., & Boelen, P. A. (2023). Cognitive-behavioral therapy for complicated grief reactions: Treatment protocol and preliminary findings from a naturalistic setting. *Cognitive and Behavioral Practice.*

Kübler-Ross, E. (1969). *On death and dying.* Macmillan.

Kübler-Ross, E., & Kessler, D. (2005). *On grief and grieving: Finding the meaning of grief through the five stages of loss.* Scribner.

Rando, T. A. (2018). Grief and mourning: Accommodating to loss. In *Dying* (pp. 211-241). Taylor & Francis.

Schneider, J. P., Weiss, R., & Samenow, C. (2012). Is it really cheating? Understanding the emotional reactions and clinical treatment of spouses and partners affected by cybersex infidelity. *Sexual Addiction & Compulsivity, 19*(1-2), 123-139.

Stroebe, M., Schut, H., & Boerner, K. (2017). Cautioning health-care professionals: Bereaved persons are misguided through the stages of grief. *OMEGA—Journal of Death and Dying, 74*(4), 455-473.

Worden, J. W. (2009). *Grief counseling and grief therapy* (5th ed.). Springer Publishing Company.

Zhai, Y., & Du, X. (2020). Loss and grief amidst COVID-19: A path to adaptation and resilience. *Brain, Behavior, and Immunity, 87*, 80-81.

Research Articles for Chapter Five: Problematic Porn Use (PPU) and Childhood Trauma

Addictive online behaviors: Block, J. J. (2008). Issues for DSM-V: Internet addiction [Editorial]. *American Journal of Psychiatry, 165*, 306.

Bittoni, C., & Kiesner, J. (2023). *When the brain turns on with sexual desire: fMRI findings, issues, and future directions.* Sexual Medicine Reviews, 11(4), 296–311.

Bőthe, B., Nagy, L., Koós, M., Demetrovics, Z., Potenza, M. N., & Kraus, S. W. (2020). Problematic pornography use across countries, genders, and sexual orientations: Insights from the International Sex Survey and comparison of different assessment tools. *Journal of Behavioral Addictions, 9*(2), 297-307.

Carnes, P. J., Murray, R. E., & Charpentier, L. (2005). Bargains with chaos: Sex addicts and addiction interaction disorder. *Sexual Addiction & Compulsivity, 12*, 79-120.

Clancy EM, Howard D, Chong S, Klettke B. (2021). Dream it, do it? Associations between pornography use, risky sexual behaviour, sexual preoccupation and sexting behaviours among young Australian adults. *Sexes, 2*(4):433-444.

Fraumeni-McBride, J. (2019). Addiction and mindfulness; pornography addiction and mindfulness-based therapy ACT. *Sexual Addiction & Compulsivity, 26*(1-2), 42-53.

Goodman, A. (2008). Neurobiology of addiction: An integrative review. *Biochemical Pharmacology, 75*(1), 266-322.

Griffiths, M. D. (1996). Behavioural addictions: An issue for everybody? *Journal of Workplace Learning*, 8(3), 19-25.

Henry, B., Bridges, C. W., & Shaw, S. L. (2025). The correlation of adverse childhood experiences and pornography consumption among males. Journal of Counseling Sexology & Sexual Wellness: Research, Practice, and Education, 6(1).

Kivisto, K. L., Welsh, D. P., Darling, N., & Culpepper, C. L. (2015). Family enmeshment, adolescent emotional dysregulation, and the moderating role of gender. *Journal of Family Psychology*, 29(4), 604-613.

Kuss, D. J., Griffiths, M. D., Karila, L. & Billieux, J. (2014a). Internet addiction: A systematic review of epidemiological research for the last decade. *Current Pharmaceutical Design*, 20, 4026-4052.

Kuss, D. J., & Griffiths, M. D. (2015). Internet addiction in psychotherapy. *London: Palgrave.*

Lehmiller, J. J., & Gormezano, M. E. (2023). *Sexual fantasy research: A contemporary review.* The Journal of Sex Research.

Lloyd, C., Wong, S. R., & Petchkovsky, L. (2007). Art and recovery in mental health: A qualitative investigation. *British Journal of Occupational Therapy*, 70(5), 207-214.

Love T, Laier C, Brand M, Hatch L, Hajela R. (2015). Neuroscience of Internet Pornography Addiction: A Review and Update. *Behavioral Sciences*, 5(3):388-433.

Pareek, S., Jain, G., & Gupta, R. K. (2023). Efficacy of mindfulness meditation as a therapeutic tool in problematic pornography consumption. *Sexual Health & Compulsivity*, 30(4), 365-379.

Park BY, Wilson G, Berger J, Christman M, Reina B, Bishop F, Klam WP, Doan AP. (2016). Is internet pornography causing sexual dysfunctions? A Review with Clinical Reports. *Behavioral Sciences*, 6(3):17.

Pontes, H. M., Kuss, D. J. & Griffiths, M. D. (2015). The clinical psychology of Internet addiction: A review of its conceptualization, prevalence, neuronal processes, and implications for treatment. *Neuroscience and Neuroec.*

Schneider, J. P., & Irons, R. R. (2001). Assessment and treatment of addictive sexual disorders: Dependency relapse. *Substance Use and Misuse*, 36, 1795-1820.

Schindler, A., & Bröning, S. (2015). A review on attachment and adolescent substance abuse: Empirical evidence and implications for prevention and treatment. *Substance Abuse*, 36(3), 304-313.

Sniewski, L. (2020). Change through stillness: Qualitative explorations of heterosexual men as they utilise meditation as an intervention for self-perceived problematic pornography use (Doctoral dissertation, Auckland University of Technology).

Sniewski, L., Krägeloh, C., Farvid, P., & Carter, P. (2022). Meditation as an intervention for men with self-perceived problematic pornography use: A series of single case studies. *Current Psychology*, 1-12.

Research Articles for Chapter Six: Betrayal, Exploitive Relationships, and Betrayal Trauma

American Psychiatric Association. (2022). *Diagnostic and statistical manual of mental disorders* (5th ed., text rev.). Arlington, VA: American Psychiatric Publishing.

Bates, E. A. (2020). "Walking on eggshells": A qualitative examination of men's experiences of intimate partner violence. *Psychology of Men & Masculinities*, 21(1), 13-24.

Beri, R. (2024). A study on love bombing, narcissism and emotional abuse among young adults in relationship and situationship. *International Journal of Interdisciplinary Approaches in Psychology*, 2(6), 22-46.

Carnes, P. J. (2018). *Betrayal bond, revised: Breaking free of exploitive relationships.* Hci.

Carnes, S., Lee, M. A., & Rodriguez, A. (2012). *Facing heartbreak: Steps to recovery for partners of sex addicts.* Gentle Path Press.

Clancy EM, Howard D, Chong S, Klettke B. (2021) Dream it, do it? Associations between pornography use, risky sexual behaviour, sexual preoccupation and sexting behaviours among young Australian adults. *Sexes,* 2(4):433-444.

Cloud, H., & Townsend, J. (2017). *Boundaries: When to say yes, how to say no to take control of your life* (Updated and expanded ed.). Zondervan.

de Jongh, A., Amann, B. L., Hofmann, A., Farrell, D., & Lee, C. W. (2019). The status of EMDR therapy in the treatment of posttraumatic stress disorder 30 years after its introduction. *Journal of EMDR Practice and Research,* 13(4), 261-269.

Klein, W., Li, S., & Wood, S. (2023). A qualitative analysis of gaslighting in romantic relationships. *Personal Relationships,* 30(4), 1316–1340.

Lonergan, M., Brunet, A., Rivest-Beauregard, M., & Groleau, D. (2021). Is romantic partner betrayal a form of traumatic experience? A qualitative study. *Stress and Health,* 37(1), 19-31.

Platt, M. G., & Freyd, J. J. (2015). Betray my trust, shame on me: Shame, dissociation, fear, and betrayal trauma. *Psychological Trauma: Theory, Research, Practice, and Policy,* 7(4), 398.

Tager-Shafrir, T., Szepsenwol, O., Dvir, M., & Zamir, O. (2024). The gaslighting relationship exposure inventory: Reliability and validity in two cultures. *Journal of Social and Personal Relationships.*

Research Articles for Chapter Seven: Maternal Wounding, Childhood Abuse, Foster Children Trauma and Adoptee Trauma

Ahmed-Leitao, F., Spies, G., van den Heuvel, L., & Seedat, S. (2016). Hippocampal and amygdala volumes in adults with posttraumatic stress disorder secondary to childhood abuse or maltreatment: a systematic review. *Psychiatry Research: Neuroimaging,* 256, 33-43.

Anderson, C. L., & Alexander, P. C. (2014). The effects of abuse on children's development: An attachment perspective. In *Handbook for the Treatment of Abused and Neglected Children* (pp. 3-23). Routledge.

Aral, N., Gürsoy, F., & Dizman, H. (2006). A comparison of depression in children with and without mothers. *Psychological Reports,* 99(2), 619-629.

Bartholet, E. (2000). *Nobody's children: Abuse and neglect, foster drift, and the adoption alternative.* Beacon Press.

Beyerlein, B. A., & Bloch, E. (2014). Need for trauma-informed care within the foster care system. *Child Welfare,* 93(3), 7-22.

Bowers, M. E., & Yehuda, R. (2016). Intergenerational transmission of stress in humans. *Neuropsychopharmacology,* 41(1), 232-244.

Brodzinsky, D., Gunnar, M., & Palacios, J. (2022). Adoption and trauma: Risks, recovery, and the lived experience of adoption. *Child Abuse & Neglect,* 130, 105309.

Chan, J. C., Nugent, B. M., & Bale, T. L. (2018). Parental advisory: Maternal and paternal stress can impact offspring neurodevelopment. *Biological Psychiatry,* 83(10), 886-894.

Cooley, S. J., Jones, C. R., Kurtz, A., & Robertson, N. (2020). "Into the Wild": A meta-synthesis of talking therapy in natural outdoor spaces. *Clinical Psychology Review,* 77, 101841.

Earley, M. D., Chesney, M. A., Frye, J., Greene, P. A., Berman, B., & Kimbrough, E. (2014). Mindfulness intervention for child abuse survivors: A 2.5-year follow-up. *Journal of Clinical Psychology,* 70(10), 933-941.

Ensink, K., Fonagy, P., Normandin, L., Rozenberg, A., Marquez, C., Godbout, N., & Borelli, J. L. (2021). Post-traumatic stress disorder in sexually abused children: secure attachment as a protective factor. *Frontiers in Psychology*, 12, 646680.

Fagan, M. (2011). Relational trauma and its impact on late-adopted children. *Journal of Child Psychotherapy*, 37(2), 129-146.

Felitti, V. J., Anda, R. F., Nordenberg, D., Williamson, D. F., Spitz, A. M., Edwards, V., Koss, M. P., & Marks, J. S. (1998). Relationship of childhood abuse and household dysfunction to many of the leading causes of death in adults: The Adverse Childhood Experiences (ACE) Study. *American Journal of Preventive Medicine*, 14(4), 245-258. https://doi.org/10.1016/S0749-3797(98)00017-8

Forkey, H., & Szilagyi, M. (2014). Foster care and healing from complex childhood trauma. *Pediatric Clinics*, 61(5), 1059-1072.

Greeson, J. K., Briggs, E. C., Kisiel, C. L., Layne, C. M., Ake, G. S., Ko, S. J., ... & Fairbank, J. A. (2011). Complex trauma and mental health in children and adolescents placed in foster care. *Child Welfare*, 90(6), 91-108

Harris, P. (2014). Meeting the adoption support needs of adopted adults who have been abused in their adoptive family: lessons from historical placements. *Adoption & Fostering*, 38(1), 49-59.

Hughes, M., & Cossar, J. (2016). The relationship between maternal childhood emotional abuse/neglect and parenting outcomes: A systematic review. *Child Abuse Review*, 25(1), 31-45.

Jedd, K., Hunt, R. H., Cicchetti, D., Hunt, E., Cowell, R. A., Rogosch, F. A., ... & Thomas, K. M. (2015). Long-term consequences of childhood maltreatment: Altered amygdala functional connectivity. *Development and Psychopathology*, 27(4pt2), 1577-1589.

Joss, D., & Teicher, M. H. (2021). Clinical effects of mindfulness-based interventions for adults with a history of childhood maltreatment: a scoping review. *Current Treatment options in Psychiatry*, 8, 31-46.

Kimbrough, E., Magyari, T., Langenberg, P., Chesney, M., & Berman, B. (2010). Mindfulness intervention for child abuse survivors. *Journal of Clinical Psychology*, 66(1), 17-33.

Kong, J. (2018). Childhood maltreatment and psychological well-being in later life: The mediating effect of contemporary relationships with the abusive parent. *The Journals of Gerontology: Series B*, 73(5), e39-e48.

Kundakovic, M., Champagne, F. (2015). Early-life experience, epigenetics, and the developing brain. *Neuropsychopharmacol*, 40, 141-153.

Lewis, N. V., Gregory, A., Feder, G. S., Angill-Williams, A., Bates, S., Glynn, J., ... & Malpass, A. (2023). Trauma-specific mindfulness-based cognitive therapy for women with post-traumatic stress disorder and a history of domestic abuse: intervention refinement and a randomized feasibility trial (coMforT study). *Pilot and Feasibility Studies*, 9(1), 112.

McSherry, D., & McAnee, G. (2022). Exploring the relationship between adoption and psychological trauma for children who are adopted from care: A longitudinal case study perspective. *Child Abuse & Neglect*, 130, 105623.

Muller, R. T., Sicoli, L. A., & Lemieux, K. E. (2000). Relationship between attachment style and posttraumatic stress symptomatology among adults who report the experience of childhood abuse. *Journal of Traumatic Stress: Official Publication of The International Society for Traumatic Stress Studies*, 13(2), 321-332.

Ortiz, R., & Sibinga, E. M. (2017). The role of mindfulness in reducing the adverse effects of childhood stress and trauma. *Children*, 4(3), 16.

Papovich, C. (2020). Trauma & children in foster care: A comprehensive overview. *Forensic Scholars Today*, 5(4), 1-5.

Riebschleger, J., Day, A., & Damashek, A. (2015). Foster care youth share stories of trauma before, during, and after placement: Youth voices for building trauma-informed systems of care. *Journal of Aggression, Maltreatment & Trauma*, 24(4), 339-360.

Robertson, R., Robertson, A., Jepson, R., & Maxwell, M. (2012). Walking for depression or depressive symptoms: a systematic review and meta-analysis. *Mental Health and Physical Activity*, 5(1), 66-75.

Varghese, A. M. (2023). Mother Wound, Creative Collaboration and Relational Healing: Examining Graphic Vignettes from Are You My Mother?. *Graphic Medicine Review*, 3(1).

Yehuda, R., Daskalakis, N. P., Bierer, L. M., Bader, H. N., Klengel, T., Holsboer, F., & Binder, E. B. (2015). Intergenerational transmission of trauma effects: Putative role of epigenetic mechanisms. *World Psychiatry*, 14(3), 243-257.

Yehuda, R., & Lehrner, A. (2018). Intergenerational transmission of trauma effects: putative role of epigenetic mechanisms. *World Psychiatry*, 17(3), 243-257.

Research Articles for Chapter Eight: Counterweight Bonding

Beck, J. S. (2020). *Cognitive behavior therapy: Basics and beyond* (3rd ed.). Guilford Publications.

Blanc, V., Brady, J. L., Hadden, B. W., & Riehl, D. J. (2022). Codependency in romantic relationships: A systematic review. *Journal of Clinical Psychology*, 78(5), 884-899. https://doi.org/10.1002/jclp.23247

Brach, T. (2020). *Guided meditation – The practice of RAIN*. https://www.tarabrach.com/wp-content/uploads/pdf/TaraBrach_RAIN_A-Practice-of-Radical-Compassion-HR.pdf

Ekman, P. (1992). An argument for basic emotions. *Cognition and Emotion*, 6(3-4), 169-200.

Harandi, T. F., Taghinasab, M. M., & Nayeri, T. D. (2017). The correlation of social support with mental health: A meta-analysis. *Electronic Physician*, 9(9), 5212-5222.

Koob, G. F., & Volkow, N. D. (2016). Neurobiology of addiction: A neurocircuitry analysis. *The Lancet Psychiatry*, 3(8), 760-773.

Linehan, M. M. (1993). *Cognitive-behavioral treatment of borderline personality disorder*. New York: Guilford Press.

Pressman, T. (2019). *Deconstructing anxiety: The journey from fear to fulfillment*. Rowman & Littlefield.

Pressman, T. (2021, May 21). 3 questions that will reveal your core fear. *Psychology Today*.

Wilkens, C., & Foote, J. (2019). "Bad parents," "codependents," and other stigmatizing myths about substance use disorder in the family. In J. Avery & J. Avery (Eds.), *The Stigma of Addiction* (pp. 25-40). Springer, Cham.

Yehuda, R. (2018). Intergenerational transmission of trauma effects: Putative role of epigenetic mechanisms. *World Psychiatry*, 17(3), 243-257.

Research Articles for Chapter Nine: Love Addiction and Compulsive Sexuality

Blycker, G. R., & Potenza, M. N. (2018). A mindful model of sexual health: A review and implications of the model for the treatment of individuals with compulsive sexual behavior disorder. *Journal of Behavioral Addictions*, 7(4), 917-929.

Burkett, J. P., & Young, L. J. (2012). The behavioral, anatomical and pharmacological parallels between social attachment, love and addiction. *Psychopharmacology*, 224, 1-26.

Chandiramani, K. (2017). A role for mindfulness meditation in treating sexual addiction. In *Routledge International Handbook of Sexual Addiction*
(pp. 260-267). Routledge.

Dhuffar, M. K., & Griffiths, M. D. (2015). Understanding conceptualisations of female sex addiction and recovery using interpretative phenomenological analysis. *Psychol. Res*, 5, 585-603.

Fisher, H. E., Xu, X., Aron, A., & Brown, L. L. (2016). Intense, passionate, romantic love: a natural addiction? How the fields that investigate romance and substance abuse can inform each other. *Frontiers in Psychology*, 7, 190300.

Griffin, M., Lewis, C. A., & Mitchell, D. (2018). Risk factors for love addiction in a sample of young adult students. *Addictive Behaviors Reports*, 7, 32–38.

Jones, D. N., & Curtis, S. R. (2017). Emophilia, sociosexuality, and anxious attachment: Approach and inhibition differences. *Personality and Individual Differences*, 106, 325-328.

Jones, D. N. (2024). Emophilia: An overlooked (but not forgotten) construct in relationships and individual differences. *Personality and Individual Differences*, 221, 112551.

Lorenzo Borrello, Paolo Antonelli, Gioele Salvatori & Davide Dèttore. (2023) The relationship between love addiction and sex addiction and the influence of social support: An exploratory empirical research. *Sexual Health & Compulsivity*
30:2, 176-196.

Rogier, G., Di Marzio, F., Presicci, C., Cavalli, R. G., & Velotti, P. (2024). Love addiction and sexual satisfaction within the attachment perspective: an empirical contribution. *Psychology & Sexuality*, 1-16.

Salani, A., Antonelli, P., Salvatori, G., Gritti, M. C., Bisciglia, R., Mascherini, F., & Dèttore, D. (2022). Love Addiction, Emotional Dysregulation and Attachment Bonds: A Quantitative Study of 344 Females. *Sexual Health & Compulsivity*,
29(3-4), 127-148.

Simpson, J. A. (1990). Influence of attachment styles on romantic relationships. *Journal of Personality and Social Psychology*, 59(5), 971–980.

Slavin, M. N., Scoglio, A. A., Blycker, G. R., Potenza, M. N., & Kraus, S. W. (2020). Child sexual abuse and compulsive sexual behavior: A systematic literature review. *Current Addiction Reports*, 7, 76-88.

Sussman, S. (2010). Love Addiction: Definition, Etiology, Treatment. *Sexual Addiction & Compulsivity*, 17(1), 31-45.

Van Gordon, W., Shonin, E., & Griffiths, M. D. (2016). Meditation awareness training for the treatment of sex addiction: A case study. *Journal of Behavioral Addictions*, 5(2), 363-372.

Van Lith, T., Schofield, M. J., & Fenner, P. (2013). Identifying the evidence-base for art-based practices and their potential benefit for mental health recovery: A critical review. *Disability and rehabilitation*, 35(16), 1309-1323.

Research Articles for Chapter Ten: Inner Child and Self-Care

Bradshaw, J. (1988). *Healing the shame that binds you*. HCI.

Bradshaw, J. (1990). *Homecoming: Reclaiming and championing your inner child*. Bantam.

Edalat, A., Farsinezhad, M., Bokharaei, M., & Judy, F. (2022). A pilot study to evaluate the efficacy of self-attachment to treat chronic anxiety and/or depression in Iranian women. *International Journal of Environmental Research and Public Health*, 19(11), 6376.

Eller, L. S., Lev, E. L., Yuan, C., & Watkins, A. V. (2016). Describing self-care self-efficacy: Definition, measurement, outcomes, and implications. *International Journal of Nursing Knowledge, 29*(1), 38-48.

Faustino, B., Vasco, A. B., Silva, A. N., & Marques, T. (2020). Relationships between emotional schemas, mindfulness, self-compassion, and unconditional self-acceptance on the regulation of psychological needs. Research in *Psychotherapy: Psychopathology, Process and Outcome, 23*(2), Article 442.

Gottman, J. M., & Gottman, J. S. (2015). *The seven principles for making marriage work.* Harmony.

Hestbech, A. M. (2018). Reclaiming the inner child in cognitive-behavioral therapy: The complementary model of the personality. *Psychotherapy, 55*(2), 123-131.

Smith, J. (2017). Working with the inner child. In *Psychotherapy* (123-140). Springer, Cham.

Wong, M. F. Y. (2023). Inner child self-reflection & why it is important. *Journal of Early Years Research, 3*(2), 15-22.

Research Articles for Chapter Eleven: Post-Traumatic Stress Disorder, Anger and Mood Regulation

Ackerman CJ, Turkoski B. Using guided imagery to reduce pain and anxiety. *Home Healthc Nurse.* 2000 Sep;18(8):524-30; quiz 531.

Borders, A., Earleywine, M., & Jajodia, A. (2010). Could mindfulness decrease anger, hostility, and aggression by decreasing rumination?. *Aggressive Behavior: Official Journal of the International Society for Research on Aggression, 36*(1), 28-44.

Clancy, J. A., Mary, D. A., Witte, K. K., Greenwood, J. P., Deuchars, S. A., & Deuchars, J. (2014). Non-invasive vagus nerve stimulation in healthy humans reduces sympathetic nerve activity. *Brain Stimulation, 7*(6), 871-87

Danzico, M. (2011, April 24). Brains of Buddhist monks scanned in meditation study. BBC *News.* https://www.bbc.com/news/world-us-canada-12661646

De Smet, S., Baeken, C., Seminck, N., Tilleman, J., Carrette, E., Vonck, K., & Vanderhasselt, M. A. (2021). Non-invasive vagal nerve stimulation enhances cognitive emotion regulation. *Behaviour Research and Therapy, 145*, 103933.

Galland, L. (2014). The gut microbiome and the brain. *Journal of Medicinal Food, 17*(12), 1261-1272.

Gershon, M. D., & Margolis, K. G. (2021). The gut, its microbiome, and the brain: connections and communications. *The Journal of Clinical Investigation, 131*(18).

Kenny BJ, Bordoni B. (2022). *Neuroanatomy, Cranial Nerve 10 (Vagus Nerve).* 2021 Nov 14. In: StatPearls [Internet]. Treasure Island (FL): StatPearls Publishing; 2022 Jan–. PMID: 30725856.

Khusid, M. A., & Vythilingam, M. (2016). The emerging role of mindfulness meditation as an effective self-management strategy, part 1: Clinical implications for depression, post-traumatic stress disorder, and anxiety. *Military Medicine, 181*(9), 961-968.

Krau SD. *The Multiple Uses of Guided Imagery.* Nurs Clin North Am. 2020 Dec;55(4):467-474. doi: 10.1016/j.cnur.2020.06.013. Epub 2020 Oct 14. PMID: 33131625.

Ma, X., Nan, F., Liang, H., Shu, P., Fan, X., Song, X., ... & Zhang, D. (2022). Excessive intake of sugar: An accomplice of inflammation. *Frontiers in Immunology, 13*, 988481.

Ooi SL, Giovino M, Pak SC. Transcendental meditation for lowering blood pressure: An overview of systematic reviews and meta-analyses. *Complement Ther Med.* 2017 Oct;34:26-34.

Remmers, C., Topolinski, S., & Koole, S. L. (2016). Why being mindful may have more benefits than you realize: Mindfulness improves both explicit and implicit mood regulation. *Mindfulness, 7*, 829-837.

Roemer, L., Williston, S. K., & Rollins, L. G. (2015). Mindfulness and emotion regulation. *Current Opinion in Psychology, 3*, 52-57.

Siciliano RE, Anderson AS, Compas BE. (2022). Autonomic nervous system correlates of posttraumatic stress symptoms in youth: Meta-analysis and qualitative review. *Clin Psychol Rev.* 2022 Mar;92:102125. doi: 10.1016/j.cpr.2022.102125. Epub 2022 Jan 18. PMID: 35078039; PMCID: PMC8858870.

Siegel, J.P. (2013), Breaking the links in intergenerational violence: An emotional regulation perspective. *Fam. Proc.*, 52: 163-178.

Skottnik, L., & Linden, D. E. (2019). Mental imagery and brain regulation—New links between psychotherapy and neuroscience. *Frontiers in Psychiatry, 10*, 779.

Steenbergen, L., Maraver, M. J., Actis-Grosso, R., Ricciardelli, P., & Colzato, L. S. (2021). Recognizing emotions in bodies: Vagus nerve stimulation enhances recognition of anger while impairing sadness. *Cognitive, Affective, & Behavioral Neuroscience, 21*, 1246-1261.

Vanderhasselt, M. A., & Ottaviani, C. (2022). Combining top-down and bottom-up interventions targeting the vagus nerve to increase resilience. *Neuroscience & Biobehavioral Reviews, 132*, 725-729.

Van Lith, T., Fenner, P., & Schofield, M. (2011). The lived experience of art making as a companion to the mental health recovery process. *Disability and Rehabilitation, 33*(8), 652-660.

Wright, S., Day, A., & Howells, K. (2009). Mindfulness and the treatment of anger problems. *Aggression and Violent Behavior, 14*(5), 396-401.

Yuan H, Silberstein SD. (2016). *Vagus Nerve and Vagus Nerve Stimulation, a Comprehensive Review: Part I.* Headache. 2016 Jan;56(1):71-8. doi: 10.1111/head.12647. Epub 2015 Sep 14. PMID: 26364692.

Yuen, A. W., & Sander, J. W. (2017). Can natural ways to stimulate the vagus nerve improve seizure control?. *Epilepsy & Behavior, 67*, 105-110.

Zitron, L., & Gao, Y. (2017). The effects of mindfulness based interventions on physiological regulation. In *Weaving complementary knowledge systems and mindfulness to educate a literate citizenry for sustainable and healthy lives* (pp. 387-400). Brill.

Research Articles for Chapter Twelve: Spiritual Bypassing and Toxic Positivity

Fox, J., Cashwell, C. S., & Picciotto, G. (2017). The opiate of the masses: Measuring spiritual bypass and its relationship to spirituality, religion, mindfulness, psychological distress, and personality. *Spirituality in Clinical Practice, 4*(4), 274–287.

Jiang, L., Alizadeh, F., & Cui, W. (2023). Effectiveness of drama-based intervention in improving mental health and well-being: A systematic review and meta-analysis during the COVID-19 pandemic and post-pandemic period. *Healthcare, 11*(6), 839.

López-González, M. A., Morales-Landazábal, P., & Topa, G. (2021). Psychodrama group therapy for social issues: A systematic review of controlled clinical trials. *International Journal of Environmental Research and Public Health, 18*(9), 4442.

Lukin, K. (2020). Toxic positivity: The harmful effects of saying "everything happens for a reason". *Psychology Today.* https://www.psychologytoday.com

Patel, A., Sharma, P. S. V. N., & Kumar, P. (2020). Application of mindfulness-based psychological interventions in infertility. *Journal of Human Reproductive Sciences, 13*(1), 3-21.

Picciotto, G., & Fox, J. (2018). Exploring experts' perspectives on spiritual bypass: A conventional content analysis. *Pastoral Psychology, 67*(1), 65-84.

Quintero, N. (2021). The dark side of positive vibes: How toxic positivity can harm mental health. *Verywell Mind.*

Ran, L., Wang, W., Ai, M., Kong, Y., Chen, J., & Kuang, L. (2021). Psychological resilience, depression, anxiety, and somatization symptoms in college students in China: A cross-sectional study. *International Journal of Environmental Research and Public Health, 18(9),* 4442.

Salopek, A. H., & Eastin, M. S. (2024). Toxic positivity intentions: An image management approach to upward social comparison and false self-presentation. *Journal of Computer-Mediated Communication, 29(3),* Article zmae003.

Sinclair, E., Hart, R., & Lomas, T. (2020). Can positivity be counterproductive when suffering domestic abuse? A narrative review. *International Journal of Wellbeing, 10(1),* 101-119.

Tran, L., & Rimes, K. A. (2017). Unhealthy perfectionism, negative beliefs about emotions, emotional suppression, and depression in students: A mediational analysis. *Personality and Individual Differences, 110,* 144-147.

Wyatt, Z. (n.d.). *The Dark Side of #PositiveVibes: Understanding Toxic Positivity in Modern Culture. Psychiatry.*

Yadav, P. K., Yadav, R. L., & Sapkota, N. K. (2017). Anger; its impact on the human body. *Innovare Journal of Health Sciences, 4(5),* 3-5.

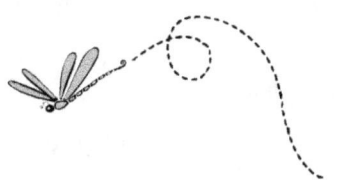

Resources

To further support your healing, we've compiled a list of resources you may find helpful. While not exhaustive, we hope these selections offer meaningful guidance. Please note that we do not specifically endorse any of the individuals, organizations, or materials listed. They are provided for informational purposes only. If you don't see a particular book or author here, please know it was not an intentional exclusion.

Books

Adams, K. M., Meyer, M. E., & Vande Garde, C. L. (2023). *When he's married to mom: how to help mother-enmeshed men open their hearts to true love and commitment.* Touchstone.

Adams, K. M. (2011). *Silently seduced: When parents make their children partners.* Health Communications, Incorporated.

Adams, K. M., Meyer, M. E., & Vande Garde, C. L. (2023). *A light in the dark: The hidden legacy of adult children of sex addicts.* Health Communications, Inc.

Anderson, K. (2018). *Difficult mothers, adult daughters: A guide for separation, liberation & inspiration.* Mango Press.

Arshad, Z. (2022): *Stronger together: A couple's guide to navigating your relationship after baby.* ebookIt.

Bercaw, B, & Bercaw, G. (2010). *The couple's guide to intimacy.* California Center for Healing.

Black, C., & Tripodi, C. (2012). *Intimate treason: Healing the trauma for partners confronting sex addiction.* Central Recovery Press.

Boole, W. (2019). *You got this: Healing through divorce.*

Bradshaw, J. (1992). *Homecoming: Reclaiming and championing your inner child.* Bantam Books.

Bresler, D. E., & Rossman, M. L. (2003). *Guided imagery for self-healing.* Healing Arts Press.

Brooks, D. (2023). *How to know a person: The art of seeing others deeply and being deeply seen.* Random House.

Brown, B. (2015). *Rising strong.* Spiegel & Grau.

Brown, K. (2022). *Navigating grief and loss: 25 Buddhist practices to keep your heart open to yourself and others.* Prometheus Books.

Carnes, P., Adams, K (Ed.). (2019). *Clinical management of sex addiction.* Routledge.

Carnes, P. (2015). *Facing the shadow: Starting sexual and relationship recovery* (3rd ed.). Gentle Path Press.

Carnes, P. (2019). *The betrayal bond: Breaking free of exploitive relationships.* Health Communications Inc.

Carnes, S. (2020). *Courageous love: A couples guide to conquering betrayal.* Gentle Path Press.

Carnes, S. (Ed.). (2011). *Mending a shattered heart: A guide for partners of sex addicts.* Gentle Path Press.

Carnes, S., Lee, M. A., & Rodriguez, A. D. (2012). *Facing heartbreak: Steps to recovery for partners of sex addicts.* Gentle Path Press.

Cedarleaf, G. (2019). *A guide for writing and recording guided imagery meditations: 70 healing scripts included: For yourself, your clients, patients, and students.*

Chödrön, P. (1997). *When things fall apart: Heart advice for difficult times.* Shambhala Publications.

Clarke, M. (2022). *Healing your wounded inner child: A CBT workbook to overcome past trauma, face abandonment and regain emotional stability.* Independently published.

Cloud, H., & Townsend, J. (1999). *Boundaries in marriage.* Zondervan.

Corley, D., & Schneider, J. (2012). *Disclosing secrets: An addict's guide for when, to whom, and how much to reveal.* Createspace.

Davenport, L. (2016). *The healing power of guided imagery: How to use your imagination for health and wellness.* Celestial Arts.

Davies, J. B. (1992). *The myth of addiction: An application of the psychological theory of attribution to illicit drug use.* Harwood Academic Publishers.

De Becker, G. (1997). *The gift of fear: And other survival signals that protect us from violence.* Little, Brown and Company.

Farris, M. (2019). *Taming your anger workbook.*

Fisher, H. (2005). *Why we love: The nature and chemistry of romantic love.* Holt Paperbacks

Ferree, M. (2010). *No stones: women redeemed from sexual addiction,* (2nd ed.). IVP.

Ford, D. (2019). *Awakening from the sexually addicted mind: A compassionate guide to recovery.* Sano Press.

Ford, D., Cosper, C., Bordey, C. (2017). *Transforming the addictive mind: the first month of mindfulness-based addiction and trauma therapy.* Sano Press.

Forward, S., & Frazier-Glynn, D. (2014). *Mothers who can't love: A healing guide for daughters.* Harper Paperbacks.

Gibson, L. (2015). *Adult children of emotionally immature parents: How to heal from distant, rejecting, or self-involved parents.* New Harbinger Publications

Goodman, W. (2024). *Toxic positivity: Keeping it real in a world obsessed with being happy.* TarcherPerigee.

Gottman, J, & Gottman, J, (2024), *Fight right: How successful couples turn conflict into connection.* Harmony.

Gunaratana, H. (2002). *Mindfulness in plain English.* Wisdom Publications.

Hooper, K., Resnick, M., & Diep, H. (2021). *All the love: Healing your heart and finding meaning after pregnancy loss.* Turner Publishing Company.

Hutcherson, W, & Williams, C. (2021). *Seen: Despair and anxiety in kids and teenagers and the power of connection.* Parent Cue.

James, J. W., & Friedman, R. (2017). *The grief recovery handbook: The action program for moving beyond death, divorce, and other losses including health, career, and faith.* William Morrow Paperbacks.

Johnson-Young, J. (2018). *Someone I love just died: what happens now?* CreateSpace.

Johnson-Young, J. (2018). *Your own path through grief: A workbook for your journey to recovery.* CreateSpace.

Juergensen-Sheets, C., & Katz, A. J. (2019). *Help her heal: An empathy workbook for sex addicts to help their partners heal.* Sano Press.

Juergensen-Sheets, C. (2021). *Help them heal: An empathy workbook for sex addicts to help their partners heal.* Sano Press.

Juergensen-Sheets, C. (2025). *Helping couples heal from infidelity and find love again.* Sano Press.

Juergensen-Sheets, C., & Turo-Shields, C. (2020). *Transformations: A woman's journey of self discovery.* Sano Press.

Juergensen-Sheets, C., & Turo-Shields, C. (2020). *Unleashing your power: Moving through the trauma of partner betrayal.* Sano Press.

Katehakis, A. (2016). *Sex addiction as affect dysregulation: A neurobiologically informed holistic treatment.* W. W. Norton & Company.

Katehakis, A, Bliss, T., et al. (2014). *Mirror of intimacy: Daily reflections on emotional anderotic intelligence.* CreateSpace Independent Publishing.

Keffer, S. (2018). *Intimate deception: Healing the wounds of sexual betrayal.* Revell.

Kessler, D. (2020). *Finding meaning: The sixth stage of grief.* Scribner.

Kübler-Ross, E., & Kessler, D. A. (2005). *On grief & grieving: Finding the meaning of grief through the five stages of loss.* Scribner.

Lee, M. A. (2018). *Healing betrayal.* Archieboys Publications, Inc.

Lerner, H. (2014). *The dance of anger: A woman's guide to changing the patterns of intimate relationships.* Harper Paperbacks.

Levine, A., & Heller, R. (2012). *Attached: The new science of adult attachment and how it can help you find—and keep—love.* TarcherPerigee.

Levine, P. A. (1997). *Waking the tiger: Healing trauma.* North Atlantic Books.

Litton, K. L. (2024). *I do it for her: A memoir of recovery and redemption from sex, love, and substances.* Sano Press.

Maltz, W., & Maltz, L. (2008). *The porn trap.* Harper Collins.

Martin, S. (2024). *Cutting ties with your parents: A workbook to help adult children make peace with their decision, heal emotional wounds, and move forward with their lives.* New Harbinger Publications

Martin, S. (2021). *The better boundaries workbook.* New Harbinger Publications

Martin, S. (2019). *The cbt workbook for perfectionism: evidence-based skills to help you let go of self-criticism, build self-esteem, and find balance.* New Harbinger Publications

Masters, R. A. (2010). *Spiritual bypassing: When spirituality disconnects us from what really matters.* North Atlantic Books.

Maté, G. (2003). *When the body says no: Exploring the stress-disease connection.* Wiley.

Maté, G. (2010). *In the realm of hungry ghosts: Close encounters with addiction.* North Atlantic Books.

Maté, G. (2022). *The myth of normal: Trauma, illness, and healing in a toxic culture.* Avery.

McCurdy, J. (2022). *I'm glad my mom died.* Simon & Schuster.

McDaniel, K. (2021). *Mother hunger.* Hay House.

Mellody, P. (2003). *Facing love addiction: Giving yourself the power to change the way you love.* Harper One.

Naparstek, B. (1994). *Staying well with guided imagery.* Warner Books.

Neff, K. (2015). *Self-compassion: The proven power of being kind to yourself.* William Morrow.

Norwood, R. (2024). *Women who love too much: When you keep wishing and hoping he'll change.* TarcherPerigee.

O'Brien, C. (2020) *Happy with baby: Essential relationship advice when partners become parents.* Higher Shelf Publishing Company

Parnell, L. (2013). *Attachment-focused EMDR: Healing relational trauma (1st ed.).* W. W. Norton & Company.

Peabody, S. (2005) *Addiction to Love: Overcoming obsession and dependency in relationships.* Clarkson Potter/Ten Speed; 3rd edition

Porges, S. (2011). *The polyvagal theory: neurophysiological foundations of emotions, attachment, communication, and self-regulation.* Norton & Co.

Real, T. (1997). *I don't want to talk about it: Overcoming the secret legacy of male depression.* Scribner.

Real, T. (2008). *The new rules of marriage: What you need to know to make love work.* Ballantine Books.

Rosenberg, S. (2017), *Accessing the healing power of the vagus nerve: Self-help exercises for anxiety, depression, trauma, and autism.* North Atlantic Books.

Rosenberg, K. P., & Feder, L. C. (Eds.). (2014). *Behavioral addictions: Criteria, evidence, and treatment.* Elsevier Academic Press.

Salas, M. (2020). *Bridging the sex addiction divide: Mindful considerations for vulnerable clients.* Sano Press.

Samuels, H. (2021). *Love addiction workbook: Evidence-based tools to support recovery and help you build healthy long-term relationships.* Callisto.

Schneider, J. (2015). *Back from betrayal: Recovering from the trauma of infidelity.* Recovery Resources Press; 4th edition.

Schwartz, R., & Sweezy, M. (2019). *Internal family systems therapy,* (2nd ed.). The Guilford Press.

Shapiro, F. (2001). *Eye movement desensitization and reprocessing (EMDR): Basic principles, protocols, and procedures* (2nd ed.). Guilford Press.

Shapiro, F. (2013). *Getting past your past: Take control of your life with self-help techniques from EMDR therapy.* Rodale Books.

Shoshanna, B. (2005). *The anger diet: Thirty days to stress free living.* Andrews McMeel Publishing, LLC.

Siegel, D. J. (2010). *The mindful therapist: A clinician's guide to mindsight and neural integration* (Illustrated ed.). W. W. Norton & Company.

Siegel, D. J. (2020). *The developing mind: How relationships and the brain interact to shape who we are* (3rd ed.). Guilford Press.

Siegel, D. J., & Bryson, T. P. (2011). *The whole-brain child: 12 revolutionary strategies to nurture your child's developing mind.* Delacorte Press.

Siegel, D. J., & Bryson, T. P. (2020). *The power of showing up: How parental presence shapes who our kids become and how their brains get wired.* Ballantine Books.

Skinner, K. (2023). *Rebuild your relationship after sexual betrayal: A couples guide to healing.* Kskinner Corp.

Smith, C. B. (2023). *Anxious grief: A clinician's guide to supporting grieving clients experiencing anxiety, panic, and fear.* PESI Publishing Inc.

Sprout, S. (2015), *Naked in public: A memoir of recovery from sex addiction and other temporary insanities.* Recontext Media.

Tatkin, S. (2012). *Wired for love: How understanding your partner's brain and attachment style can help you defuse conflict and build a secure relationship.* New Harbinger Publications.

Tatkin, S. (2023). *In each other's care: A guide to the most common relationship conflicts and how to work through them.* Sounds True.

Tucker, R. (2022). *Vagus nerve: How to relieve anxiety, reduce chronic inflammation, and prevent illness by stimulating vagal tone to restore balance.* Rhys Tucker.

Van der Kolk, B. (2014). *The body keeps the score: Brain, mind, and body in the healing of trauma.* Viking.

Webster, B. (2021). *Discovering the inner mother: A Guide to healing the mother wound and claiming your personal power.* William Morrow.

· · · · ·

A Note About the Resources Below: While the links provided aren't clickable in this format, we've included them so you can still explore the information by typing the web address directly into your browser. We've chosen to share these resources because we believe they may offer helpful insights along your journey. That said, this list isn't exhaustive, and no author or organization was intentionally left out. Please know that we are not formally endorsing any of the websites or materials listed—they are simply offered for your consideration. We encourage you to decide what feels right and useful for you. All links were current at the time this workbook was published.

Forms and Assessments

Formal Disclosure Materials Packet for Therapists
Website for documents: www.thecounselorscoach.com
Toolbox page: https://www.thecounselorscoach.com/formal-disclosure-documents-csat-therapists

ACES Study (Adverse Childhood Experiences)
https://www.acesaware.org/wp-content/uploads/2022/07/
ACE-Questionnaire-for-Adults-Identified-English-rev.7.26.22.pdf

GAD-7
Screening tool for anxiety severity
https://www.hiv.uw.edu/page/mental-health-screening/gad-7

PHQ-9: Depression Screening Tool
Brief self-assessment for symptoms of depression
https://www.mdcalc.com/phq-9-patient-health-questionnaire-9

The Relationship Attachment Style Test (by Diane Poole Heller)
https://dianepooleheller.com/attachment-test

The PCL-5: PTSD Checklist for DSM-5
Screens for symptoms of Post-Traumatic Stress Disorder
https://www.ptsd.va.gov/professional/assessment/adult-sr/ptsd-checklist.asp

Videos

1. **Brené Brown**—*The Power of Vulnerability*
https://www.ted.com/talks/brene_brown_the_power_of_vulnerability

2. **Kristin Neff**—*The Space Between Self-Esteem and Self-Compassion*
https://www.youtube.com/watch?v=IvtZBUSplr4

3. **Paula Hall**—*A Mind Map on Sex and Porn Addiction*
https://www.youtube.com/watch?v=1BHAREf9zmU

4. **Philip Zimbardo**—*The Demise of Guys*
https://www.ted.com/talks/philip_zimbardo_the_demise_of_guys

5. **Stan Tatkin**—*Relationships Are Hard, Until They're Not*
https://www.youtube.com/watch?v=2xKXLPuju8U

6. **Gabor Maté**—*The Power of Addiction and The Addiction of Power*
https://www.youtube.com/watch?v=66cYcSak6nE

7. **Susan David**—*The Gift and Power of Emotional Courage*
https://www.ted.com/talks/susan_david_the_gift_and_power_of_
emotional_courage

8. **Terry Real**—*What Men Need to Know About Love (TEDx Talk)*
https://www.youtube.com/watch?v=bvCSp8pnnO4

9. **Anjali Nayar (director)**—*Hack Your Health: The Secrets of Your Gut Documentary*
https://www.netflix.com/title/81436688

Inpatient Treatment

The Meadows
Address: 1655 N Tegner St, Wickenburg, AZ 85390
Phone: (928) 668-4999
Website: themeadows.com

Pine Grove Behavioral Health & Addiction Services
Address: 2255 Broadway Dr, Hattiesburg, MS 39402
Phone: (601) 288-2273
Website: pinegrovetreatment.com

Keystone Treatment Center
Address: 1010 E 2nd St, Canton, SD 57013
Phone: (605) 987-2751
Website: keystonetreatment.com

The Ranch
Address: 6107 Pinewood Rd, Nunnelly, TN 37137
Phone: (888) 645-5297
Website: recoveryranch.com

Sierra Tucson
Address: 39580 S Lago Del Oro Pkwy, Tucson, AZ 85739
Phone: (855) 844-5591
Website: sierratucson.com

Begin Again Institute
14-Day Sex Addiction or Betrayal Trauma Intensives
Address: 3601 N. Stagecoach Road, Ste. 202. Longmont, CO 80503
Phone: (720) 702-4608
Website: beginagaininstitute.com

Domestic Violence & Sexual Abuse Resources

National Domestic Violence Hotline (U.S.): www.thehotline.org
Phone: 1-800-799-7233

RAINN (Rape, Abuse, & Incest National Network): www.rainn.org
Phone: 1-800-656-4673

Safe Horizon: www.safehorizon.org
Phone: 1-800-621-4673

VictimConnect Resource Center: www.victimconnect.org
Phone: 1-855-484-2846

Women's Law (Legal Information and Support): www.womenslaw.org

1in6: 1in6.org
Support for men who have experienced sexual abuse or assault, which often overlaps with DV experiences.

Professional Training

The Mindfulness Academy for Addiction and Trauma Training (TMAATT):
https://www.tmaatt.com

International Institute for Trauma and Addiction Professionals (IITAP):
https://iitap.com

The Association of Partners of Sex Addicts Trauma Specialists (APSATS):
https://www.apsats.org

Eye Movement Desensitization and Reprocessing (EMDR) International Association:
https://www.emdria.org

Internal Family Systems (IFS) Institute: https://ifs-institute.com

The Gottman Institute: https://www.gottman.com

Low-Cost Therapy / Crisis Support / Mental Health Information

The resources listed below are for informational purposes only and do not imply endorsement. These organizations were active at the time of printing, but availability, quality of support, and services may change. Please use your discretion when seeking support.

Center For Interactive Mental Health Solutions
Free online therapy 8-week session CBT for Depression
https://cimhs.com

Crisis Counselor Volunteer
Text HOME to 741741
Website: https://www.crisistextline.org

TherapyAid
Free & Low Cost Short-term Therapy for United States
Healthcare Professionals and First Responders
https://www.therapyaid.org

Foothill Family (California)
https://www.foothillfamily.org/contact

Mental Health America (MHA)
Free screening tools, resources, and information about mental health conditions
https://www.mhanational.org

NAMI (National Alliance on Mental Illness)
Education, support groups, and resources for
individuals and families affected by mental illness
1-800-950-NAMI (6264)
https://www.nami.org

Open Path Collective
Affordable therapy for individuals, couples, and families
https://www.openpathcollective.org

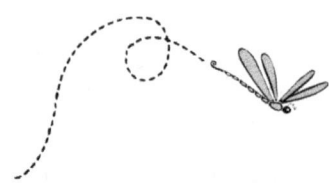

NOTES

NOTES

www.ingramcontent.com/pod-product-compliance
Lightning Source LLC
Chambersburg PA
CBHW080943120626
46546CB00010B/2826